LEONARD LEWISOHN

ESOTERIC TRADITIONS IN ISLAMIC THOUGHT

An Anthology of Texts on Esoteric Knowledge and Gnosis in Islam

ONEWORLD ACADEMIC

Oneworld Academic

An imprint of Oneworld Publications Ltd

Published by Oneworld Academic in 2024

A CIP record for this title is available from the British Library

ISBN 978-0-86154-864-4
eISBN 978-0-86154-865-1

Typeset by Geethik Technologies
Printed and bound in Great Britain by Clays Ltd, Elcograf S.p.A.

Oneworld Publications Ltd
10 Bloomsbury Street
London WC1B 3SR
England

Praise for *Esoteric Traditions in Islamic Thought*

'Professor Lewisohn gives us so much with this splendid collection of beautiful, perspicacious translations, many focusing on the distinctive tradition of Islamic gnosis. This volume will stimulate much-needed research, even as it reminds us of our great loss a few years ago with the author's premature death. There is no one of his generation who has contributed more to the study of Sufism and mysticism in Islam through writing, teaching, lecturing, editing, organising conferences and emulating the beautiful, compelling tradition of which he writes, so it seems, without effort. This book shows an ever-expanding mastery of the mystical verve of Islamic thought and thus highlights the great debt owed, by a frequently unwitting world, to generations of Muslim thinkers for their dedication, devotion and humanity, for this priceless gift of the mindful heart.'

Todd Lawson, Emeritus Associate Professor,
University of Toronto

'A joy to read, a nourishment for the heart and mind, and for the specialist and non-specialist alike. The study of esotericism and what is called *erfan* in Iran desperately needed just this sourcebook, not least because many readers on Sufism and esotericism often neglect works from a Shīʿite provenance. It also demonstrates that esotericism often transcends Sunni and Shīʿite confessional particularity. There was no better person than Lenny Lewisohn to put it together, a specialist and insider to the Sufi and esoteric traditions who is sorely missed in the field. This publication is a wonderful legacy, as well as a reminder of what we have lost.'

Sajjad H. Rizvi, Professor of Islamic Intellectual History,
University of Exeter

'A remarkable collection of beautifully and clearly translated texts from the Islamic esoteric tradition, rendered with sensitivity and fluidity of expression from the original Arabic and Persian. In this work, published posthumously, Lewisohn demonstrates his nearly unparalleled mastery of Islamic esotericism and its literary expressions in both languages. The extensive introduction to the collection that he provides, as well as the helpful introductions to the selected authors and translated texts, allows the reader to appreciate the richness and diversity of this tradition, as well as the shared concepts, ideas and terminology – particularly as related to epistemology and various forms of spiritual knowing – that give a certain unity to this tradition across both time and geographic space. The twelve Muslim authors whose works were selected for the volume represent well-known pillars of the Islamic esoteric tradition and seem to have been carefully chosen to demonstrate the range of this tradition, not only across time and space, but also with respect to differing religious affiliations (Shīʿite and Sunni) and different primary classifications as theologians and mystics. Bringing together in translation so many penetrating discussions about this essential topic from such a wide array of writers allows the reader to see the through lines, the genealogy and the discursive development of the conception of knowledge in the Islamic esoteric tradition and reveals the profound influence of earlier authors upon those writing in later centuries. The collection of excerpts, together with the author's framing and introduction, validates his key argument that the Muslim esoteric tradition lies at the heart of all the Islamic religious sciences and should be rigorously studied as such. This volume will serve as a compelling introduction to any future study in this vein.'

Maria M. Dakake, Associate Professor of Religious Studies, George Mason University

CONTENTS

ACKNOWLEDGEMENTS ix

INTRODUCTION 1

Esoteric Traditions in Islam 1
The Authors and Translated Texts 17
Esoteric Knowledge and Gnosis (*ma'rifat*) 28
Hermeneutics and the Language of Symbolism in Islamic Esotericism 46

I. THE SCIENCE OF SYMBOLIC ALLUSIONS: SELECTIONS FROM ABŪ IBRĀHĪM ISMĀʿĪL B. MUḤAMMAD MUSTAMLĪ BUKHĀRĪ'S (D. 434/1042–43) *SHARḤ TAʿARRUF LI-MADHHAB AL-TAṢAWWUF* 55

II. ON THE TRUE MEANING OF ESOTERIC KNOWLEDGE: ABŪ ḤĀMID AL-GHAZĀLĪ'S (D. 505/1111) *AL-RISĀLAT AL-LADUNĪ* 79

III. ESOTERIC PSYCHOLOGY AND KNOWLEDGE OF THE HEART: SELECTIONS FROM RASHĪD AL-DĪN MAYBUDĪ'S (D. 520/1126) *KASHF AL-ASRĀR WA ʿUDDAT AL-ABRĀR* 151

IV. TYPOLOGIES OF GNOSIS AND KNOWLEDGE: RASHĪD AL-DĪN MAYBUDĪ'S COMMENTARY ON QUR'ĀN V:98 IN HIS *KASHF AL-ASRĀR* 164

V. GNOSIS AND THE *VIA NEGATIVA*: ʿAYN AL-QUḌĀT HAMADHĀNĪ (EXECUTED 526/1132) ON GNOSIS 174

VI. THE INITIATIC SCIENCE OF UNVEILING: SELECTIONS FROM IBN ʿARABĪ'S (D. 638/1240) *AL-FUTŪḤĀT AL-MAKKĪYYA* 193

VII. THE TYPOLOGY OF KNOWLEDGE IN SUFISM: SELECTIONS FROM ʿIZZ AL-DĪN MAḤMŪD KĀSHĀNĪ'S (D. 735/1334) *MIṢBĀḤ AL-HIDĀYA WA MIFTĀḤ AL-KIFĀYA* 229

VIII. EPISTEMOLOGICAL DELIBERATIONS ON GNOSIS AND VISIONARY UNVEILING: A CHAPTER FROM SAYYID ḤAYDAR ĀMULĪ'S (D. AFTER 787/1385) *KITĀB NAṢṢ AL-NUṢŪṢ* (*FĪ SHARḤ FUṢŪṢ AL-ḤIKAM*) 251

IX. THE SEVEN STAGES OF THE SPIRITUAL HIERARCHY: ṢĀ'ĪN AL-DĪN TURKAH IṢFAHĀNĪ'S (D. 830/1427) *RISĀLA YI SHAQQ AL-QAMAR VA SĀʿAT* 273

X. VISIONARY UNVEILING AND THE ESOTERIC SCIENCES: SELECTIONS FROM MULLĀ ṢADR'S (D. 1045/1636) *MAFĀTĪḤ AL-GHAYB* 326

XI. ESOTERIC AND EXOTERIC PATHS OF KNOWLEDGE IN ISLAM: SELECTIONS FROM ʿABD AL-RAZZĀQ LĀHĪJĪ'S (D. 1072/1661–2) *GAWHAR-I MURĀD* 361

XII. THE REALITY OF VISIONARY UNVEILING: SELECTIONS FROM SABZIWĀRĪ'S (D. 1289/1873) CORRESPONDENCE 401

SELECTED BIBLIOGRAPHY 414

INDEX OF QUR'ĀNIC REFERENCES 425

GENERAL INDEX 427

Dedicated to Dr. Farhad Daftary and Lenny's friends and colleagues at the Department of Academic Research and Publications of the Ismaili Institute.

ACKNOWLEDGEMENTS

Not to acknowledge any favour is a sign of ignorance.
The knowledge of the Truth and cognizance
of God is but to give each man his due.
Shabistarī, *Garden of Mystery*

This book is being published posthumously. Dr. Lewisohn worked on it on and off for close to fifteen years and completed it just a few months before he passed away on 6 August 2018.

Many are the friends, mentors and esteemed colleagues, absent and present, who have assisted the author in compiling and translating this anthology. I know that if Dr. Lewisohn were here, he would thank each of you; I would like to thank you on his behalf.

First of all, I would like to thank all Dr. Lewisohn's colleagues at the Department of Academic Research and Publications of the Institute of Ismaili Studies, London, who have all always been very supportive of all the author's endeavours over the years. In particular I would like to thank Dr. Farhad Daftary, the emeritus head of the Department of Academic Research and Publications of the Institute, with whom Dr. Lewisohn worked closely from 1989 through 2005.

Dr. Daftary initially proposed creating an anthology of esoteric traditions in Islam; that initial proposal eventually resulted in the current volume. Thanks go to Kutub Kassam from the Institute, who also worked closely with Dr. Lewisohn. Thanks also to Professor Hermann Landolt and Professor Seyyed Hossein Nasr, who were instrumental in planning the schema and scope of the anthology and recommending which texts to include. Dr. Landolt and Professor Clifford Edmund Bosworth provided illuminating comments on the arcanum and more mysterious and technical aspects of the Persian and Arabic texts. I would like to acknowledge the kindness of Dr. Lewisohn's friends and colleagues: Dr. Reza Shah-Kazemi, Mr. Terry Graham, Mr. Muhammad Reza Juzi, Dr. Muhammad Isa Waley and Dr. Mohammed Rustom, who read early versions of various chapters, kindly offering interesting insights into their meanings and suggesting additional references to consider. A special thanks to Robert Darr, who helped decipher some of the references to numerical symbolism, and to Dr. Rahim Gholami, who provided valuable comments on alternative manuscripts.

I am especially grateful to Dr. Reza Tabandeh, who meticulously went over the manuscript, making sure everything was in its right place, checking *ḥadīth* references and compiling the bibliography for the anthology.

If I have forgotten anyone, and for any flaws in the presentation of the anthology that remain, the fault is mine and I apologize.

Jane Lewisohn
Eydon, July 2024

INTRODUCTION

ESOTERIC TRADITIONS IN ISLAM

The birth and genesis of Islamic civilization in the first four centuries C.E. was shaped by many sources and currents of ideas. Some of these were indigenous, coming out of the collective encounter of the Muslims with the event of the Qur'ān and the charisma of the Prophet; whereas others emerged from the complex, pluralistic, cultural milieu that arose from the Arab military conquests of the first century. Consequently, two diverse currents of esoteric thought emerged within the promiscuous religious topography of the early Islamic Near East.

The first, being largely non-Islamic in inspiration, was fed from multiple source-springs in Late Antiquity[1] including native Near Eastern and Semitic 'paganism' (such as the Sabaeans of Harrān, who survived for several centuries under Islam) and, especially, Christian doctrines of Gnosis[2] (featuring the second-century Christian Gnostics Valentinus and Basilides amongst its most important thinkers, as the seminal studies of

1 See Robert Hoyland, "Early Islam as a Late Antique Religion," in S.F. Johnson (ed.), *The Oxford Handbook of Late Antiquity* (Oxford: Oxford University Press 2012), pp. 1053–77.

2 Alessandro Bausani reminds us: "what the Qur'an and Islam brought to seventh-century Persia was not as alien as would have been the case for, say, China or India. Persia in some ways had after all long been 'Gnosticized' and 'Semitized', and the reader should not forget that Semitic Aramaic was the court and international language [of Sassanian Iran]." – *Religion in Iran*, trans. [from Italian] J.M. Marchesi (New York: Bibliotheca Persica 2000), p. 114.

Hans Jonas and G.R.S. Mead teach us).[3] They also include Alexandrian

---

3 The literature on the Christian Gnostic schools is far too vast to even summarize here. Some of the better known specialist works include: Walter Scott, *Hermetica: The Ancient Greek and Latin Writings which Contain Religious or Philosophic Teachings Ascribed to Hermes Trismegistus* (Boston: Shambhala 1993); Hans Jonas, *The Gnostic Religion* (Boston: Beacon Press 1958); G.R.S. Mead, *Thrice Greatest Hermes: Studies in Hellenistic Theosophy and Gnosis* (York Beach, Maine: Samuel Weiser 2001); R.M. Wilson, *The Gnostic Problem* (London: Mowbray 1958); R.M. Grant, *Gnosticism: An Anthology* (London: Collins 1976); James M. Robinson (ed.), *The Nag Hammadi Library in English* (Leiden: Brill 1977); Simone Pétrement, *A Separate God: The Christian Origins of Gnosticism*, trans. [from French] by Carol Harrison (London: Darton, Longman and Todd 1991); Yuri Stoyanov, *The Other God: Dualist Religions from Antiquity to the Cathar Heresy* (New Haven: Yale University Press 2000); Dylan M. Burns, *Apocalypse of the Alien God: Platonism and the Exile of Sethian Gnosticism* (Philadelphia: University of Pennsylvania Press 2014); and Roelof van den Broek and Wouter J. Hanegraff (eds.), *Gnosis and Hermeticism: From Antiquity to Modern Times* (Albany: SUNY Press 1998). General works written for non-specialist audiences that analyse the cosmopolitan influence of gnostic doctrines on both Eastern and Western thought, include: Elaine Pagels, *The Gnostic Gospels* (London: Weidenfeld and Nicolson 1979); Bruno Borchert, *Mysticism: Its History and Challenge* (Maine: Samuel Weiser 1994); Tobia Churton, *Gnostic Philosophy: From Ancient Persia to Modern Times* (Rochester, Vermont: Inner Traditions 2005). The latter work contains an excellent chapter (5) on Sufism and Gnosis. Mark Sedgwick's article on "Neo-Sufism," in Wouter J. Hanegraff (ed.), *Dictionary of Gnosis and Western Esotericism* (Leiden: Brill 2005), II, pp. 846–49 provides a good synopsis of the impact of Western mystical and gnostic doctrines on Sufi teachers in the Western world during the twentieth century – also treated in depth in the same author's *Against the Modern World: Traditionalism and the Secret Intellectual History of the Twentieth Century* (Oxford: Oxford University Press 2004). A dearth of comparative studies on the relationship between the Western (Christian, Jewish, Gnostic ...) gnostic theosophy of Late Antiquity and later Islamic Sufism and other gnostic doctrines exists at present. Micheal G. Morony's *Iraq After the Muslim Conquest* (Princeton: Princeton University Press 1984), chap. 13: "Pagans and Gnostics" provides an introductory overview of the topic. Also cf. Steven Wasserstrom, "The Moving Finger Writes: Mughīra b. Saʿīd: Islamic Gnosis and the Myths of its Rejection," *History of Religions* XXV (1985), pp. 1–29; Peter Kingsley, "From Empedocles to the Sufis: 'The Pythagorean Leaven'," in *idem.*, *Ancient Philosophy,*

Gnosticism (found in the Hermetic Corpus), Gnostic-Manichaeism,[4] Mandeanism,[5] Mithraism,[6] Taoism,[7] as well as traditional Christian mystical theology (whether from the Persian Nestorian, Chaldeo-Persian,[8] Byzantine Orthodox, or Monophysite denominations), Jewish theosophical speculations,[9] as well as Zoroastrian,[10] Hindu and

---

Mystery, and Magic: Empedocles and Pythagorean Tradition (Oxford: Clarendon Press 1995), pp. 371–91.

4 See Hans-Joachim Klimkeit, *Gnosis on the Silk Road: Gnostic Texts from Central Asia* (San Francisco: HarperSanFransico 1993), featuring translations of key texts of Central Asian Manichaean gnosis and theology; see also Bausani, *Religion in Iran*, chaps 2–3; Richard Foltz, *Religions of the Silk Road: Overland Trade and Cultural Exchange from Antiquity to the Fifteenth Century* (New York: St Martin's Griffin 1999), chap. 4.

5 Richard Foltz, *Religions of Iran: From Prehistory to the Present* (London: Oneworld 2013), chap. 9.

6 See Jacque Duchesne-Guillemin, *Symbols and Values in Zoroastrianism: Their Survival and Renewal* (New York: 1966) pp. 157–62.

7 See J.C. Coyajee, "The Sraosha Yasht: its Place in the History of Mysticism," in *idem.*, *Cults and Legends of Ancient Iran* (Bombay: 1940), pp. 161–83, for the influence of some Taoist doctrines on Sufi ideas.

8 Wilson, *The Gnostic Problem*, p. 206.

9 Paul Fenton, "Judaism and Sufism," in S.H. Nasr and Oliver Leaman (eds.), *History of Islamic Philosophy* (London: Routledge 1996), vol. I, pp. 755–68; 'Obadyāh b. Abraham b. Moses Maimonides, *The Treatise of the Pool* (*Al-Maqāla al-Ḥawḍīyya*), trans. Paul Fenton (London: Octagon Press 1981), introduction, pp. 1–24; Diana Lobel, *A Sufi-Jewish Dialogue: Philosophy and Mysticism in Baḥya Ibn Paqūda's* Duties of the Heart (Philadelphia: University of Pennsylvania Press 2007); Josef Meri, *The Cult of Saints Among Muslims and Jews in Medieval Syria* (Oxford: Oxford University Press 2002), chap. 1; Yafiah Katherine Randall, *Sufism and Jewish-Muslim Relations: The Derekh Avraham Order in Israel* (London: Routledge 2016), chap. 3.

10 I. Goldziher, "The Influence of Parsism on Islam," in C.P. Tiele (ed.), *The Religion of Iranian Peoples* (Bombay: Parsi Publishing Co. 1912), pp. 163–86; A.M. Taher Rezwi, "Parallel Thoughts in Islam and Zoroastrianism," in *Dinshah Irani Memorial Volume: Papers on Zoroastrian and Iranian Subjects* (Bombay: 1943), pp. 153–72; Bausani, *Religion in Iran*, chap. 3: "The Problem of Iranian Islam;" A.S. Melikian-Chirvani, "The Wine-Bull and the Magian Master," in Philippe Gignoux (ed.), *Recurrent Patterns in Iranian Religions: From Mazdaism to Sufism* (Paris: Association

even Central Asian Buddhist[11] and Taoist[12] mystical doctrines and writings.[13]

The second, more directly Islamic, current of esotericism appears in the theories of Muslim neo-Platonism (as, for instance, in the *Rasā'īl* of the Ikhwān al-Ṣafā), the (largely Sunni) Sufis and various esoteric Shī'ite doctrines,[14] both Twelver Shī'ite and Ismā'īlī.[15] In fact, it was this universal

---

pour l'Avancement des Études Iraniennes 1992), pp. 101–42; S. Shaked, "Some Iranian Themes in Islamic Literature," in *Recurrent Patterns in Iranian Religions*, pp. 143–58.

11 Assadullah Souren Melikian-Chirvani, "L'Évocation Littéraire du Bouddhisme dan l'Iran Musulman," *Le Monde Iranien et l'Islam* I (1971), pp. 1–72; Pio Filippani-Ronconi, "The Soteriological Cosmology of Central-Asian Ismā'īlism," in S.H. Nasr (ed.), *Ismā'īlī Contributions to Islamic Culture* (Tehran: Imperial Academy of Philosophy 1977), pp. 99–120.

12 See J.C. Coyajee, *Cults and Legends of Ancient Iran and China* (Bombay: 1936), pp. 162–83.

13 As Wilson commented: "Gnosticism is an atmosphere, not a system; it is the general atmosphere of the period [late antiquity of the Hellenistic world] and affects to some extent all the religions and philosophies of the time." *The Gnostic Problem*, p. 261. Historians of Islamic mysticism sometimes stress the influence of Neo-Platonism and Gnosticism on early Sufism; for a good overview of this, see Mircea Eliade, *A History of Religious Ideas*, III: *From Muhammad to the Age of Reforms*, trans. [from French] by Alf Hiltebeitel and Diane Apostolos-Cappadona (Chicago: University of Chicago Press 1985), pp. 122–25. Some Sufis themselves occasionally described their esoteric tradition as having an extra-Islamic as well as a purely Islamic origin, having existed "since the very beginning of creation." – see Ma'ṣūm Muḥammad Ma'ṣūm Shīrāzī, *Ṭarā'iq Al-ḥaqā'iq* (Tehran: Intishārāt-i Sanā'ī 1345 A.Hsh./1966), vol. 1, pp. 152–57.

14 On the development of notions of esoteric knowledge and gnosis in early Ismā'īlism and Sufism, see Ali Humayun Akhtar, *Philosophers, Sufis, and the Three Rival Caliphs: Politics and Authority from Cordoba to Cairo and Baghdad* (Cambridge: Cambridge University Press 2017), chap. 1.

15 One of similarities between early Christian gnosticism and Ismā'īlism that one encounters is that the latter "transforms the literal forms of the Koranic Revelation in the same way that the gnosis of antiquity worked with the given forms of Christianity: it performs a transformation of all these forms, events, and persons into symbols. In so doing, it realizes a transmutation of the soul, its resurrection (*qiyāma*) – and thereby bears the fundamental feature that relates it to other forms of gnosis." – Henry Corbin,

prevalence of esotericism in early Near Eastern religious thought which effected the notorious differences and polemics between Sufi mystics, who interpreted the contents of the Qur'ānic revelation sapientially and intuitively and those *'ulamā'* who relied exclusively on ratiocination and the legalistic doctrines of exoteric faith, thereafter causing the esoteric (*bāṭin*) – exoteric (*ẓāhir*) dichotomy to infiltrate most aspects of Islamic theology.[16]

Although there have been many investigations and interpretations of both the Islamic and non-Islamic sources of esotericism in recent scholarship (authors such as Louis Massignon, Tor Andrea, Fritz Meier, Alessandro Bausani, 'Abd al-Ḥusayn Zarrīnkūb, S.H. Nasr, Shaul Shaked, Annemarie Schimmel, Henry Corbin and Roger Arnaldez may here be mentioned), little recognition has been given of the pervasive formative effect upon Islamic culture of that large and complex reservoir of ideas, attitudes and practices, which is termed the *esoteric tradition*. Yet there are few areas of Islamic intellectual and spiritual life which were not informed, in one way or another, by forms of thought which may be designated as 'esoteric'. The same observation can be made with regard to the study of esotericism in medieval Europe, which had close historical connections with the Islamic traditions, and its contributions to the Renaissance and the rise of the Enlightenment.

In the context of Islamic Studies, 'Esoteric traditions in Islam' is perhaps best described as the mystico-gnostic dimension of theology-cum-theosophy and metaphysics-cum-mysticism better known as *Islamic spirituality* in English, *'Irfān* ('mystical knowledge') in Persian and *ma'rifa* ('gnosis') and *'ilm al-bāṭin* ('esoteric knowledge', 'sapience of the inner psyche') in Arabic. In early Islamic thought, 'esoteric knowledge' or *'ilm al-bāṭin* comprised three basic motifs:

i) Knowledge of ways to train the soul, being a *psychic discipline* attainable by a mystic through his own mental effort.

"From the Gnosis of Antiquity to Ismaili Gnosis," in his *Cyclical Time and Ismaili Gnosis*, trans. Ralph Manheim and James Morris (London: KPI in association with Islamic Publications 1983), p. 154.

16 See Frederick de Jong and Bernd Radtke (eds.), *Islamic Mysticism Contested: Thirteen Centuries of Controversies and Polemics* (Leiden: Brill 1999); Reza Tabandeh and Leonard Lewisohn, *Sufis and Their Opponents in the Persianate World* (Irvine: UCI Jordan Center for Persian Studies 2020).

ii) Knowledge acquired only through *secrecy* and *initiation*, through the private relation between master and disciple. This knowledge could be apprehended subjectively by an adept but not comprehended objectively by the non-adept, for "even if the uninitiated came across a work of esoteric truth, it would not, in principle, be intelligible to him, though he might mouth its words uncomprehendingly." The esoteric knowledge was written in a coded language such that "if a work should fall into improper hands, its more delicate points would not be even half-understood; they have so written that the barriers imposed by nature were further reinforced by art."[17]
iii) An *interior wisdom* or gnostic inference that enables the mystic to interpret the Qur'ān and the Sunna from within himself.[18]

The notion of *'ilm al-bāṭin* from its inception in Islam thus indicated in the first place a kind of understanding obtained through undergoing a difficult interior contemplative discipline; in the second place, a knowledge acquired by means of private initiation rather than conventional education; and thirdly, the acquisition of an interior illumination[19] and understanding of the Qur'ān. In the history of Islam, at least down to the early twentieth century, this sort of knowledge was generally not considered marginal to the mainstream, normative tradition. On the contrary. It must be emphasized that during the Islamic medieval and late classical periods mystical experiences formed, as American historian Marshall Hodgson has pointed out, the "most popular" form of piety, which in turn constituted "a basis for social life."[20]

17 M.G.S. Hodgson, *The Venture of Islam* II (Chicago: University of Chicago Press 1977), II, pp. 195–96.

18 Radtke, "Bāṭen," *EIr* III, p. 860.

19 Underlining the latter motif, Corbin notes that gnosis in Islam is "a *mode* of understanding which is not a simple act of knowing ... It is an esoteric knowledge (*'ilm al-Bāṭin*), a knowledge of the Truth (*'ilm al-Ḥaqīqa*) that, as such, gives rise to a new birth, a metamorphosis, the salvation of the soul." – Corbin, "From the Gnosis of Antiquity to Ismaili Gnosis," p. 153.

20 Hodgson adds, "It can seem paradoxical that the subjective, ineffable, extraordinarily personal experience of Ṣūfism could become a basis for social life and become historically decisive; that the most personal and esoteric form of piety should be the most popular. This is in part due to the effective way in which mystical forms and language can

Belief in the veracity of knowledge acquired through 'visionary unveiling' (*kashf*) and symbolic interpretation of the scripture, for instance, was common to intellectual thought in diverse walks of educated Muslim society; it was endorsed by philosophers, Sufis and theologians alike, regardless of sectarian persuasion.[21] Describing the esoteric style in literature which developed in the medieval Islamic world following the death of Ghazālī (1111), Hodgson notes that "an indirect style" of "mytho-visional" writing, a type of literature aimed at the moral rather than scientific interpretation

---

sanction elements of religious life downgraded by a strongly kerygmatic approach ... If such [mystical] experiences carry authority and are found relevant to the ordinary course of living – the decisive criterion of mysticism from a historical point of view – then their consequences will be unpredictable and may invade any sphere of human activity. Once their validity is accepted, they must determine all of life." Hodgson, *The Venture of Islam* II, pp. 204–5.

21 Cf. W.C. Chittick, "Mysticism Versus Philosophy in Earlier Islamic History: The Al-Ṭūsī, Al-Qūnawī Correspondence," *Religious Studies* 17 (1981), pp. 87–104. Highlighting the similarities between Shī'ite mystical thought, *ḥikmat* philosophy and Sufism, Nikki Keddie, "Symbol and Sincerity in Islam," *Studia Islamica* XVII (1963), pp. 27–63, also points out (p. 27) that "the work which modern scholars have done on notions of esoterism, dissimulation, and pious fabrication in traditional Islamic culture does not seem to have an adequate impact on studies of modern Islamic intellectual history." She further remarks: "The sectarian Shī'a, the philosophers, and the Ṣūfīs are groups which show strong interconnections. In particular, a Neo-Platonic cosmology which sees creation as a process of successive emanations from the unmoving One through planes corresponding to the celestial spheres and ending with the lowest emanation of the multiple and contingent world, and salvation as renascent of these planes to reunion with the One, is common to a part of all three groups ... Neo-Platonism appears first among the philosophically minded, and is found in philosophers like Fārābī, Avicenna, and the Iranian philosophic school of more recent centuries; in Ismā'īlī Shī'a from the 10th century on; in philosophical mystics like Ibn al-'Arabī and Suhrawardī; and particularly after the destruction of the Ismā'īlīs' political power and their consequent merging with the Ṣūfīs, in Ṣūfī theosophy and poetry. There are also other similarities among the three groups. For example, despite the aberrance of their ideas, all are concerned to uphold their orthodoxy ... In addition all three groups manifest a feeling which we may call in modern terms *alienation* from society as it was ... the idea that the real meaning of existence must be outside the everyday plane of the world as it is now is one clue to the centrality of esoterism in all these groups." (pp. 47–49).

of experience, became widespread. Works of this genre attempted "a comprehensive vision of the totality of life; and unlike even the most comprehensive factional novel, do this by way not of imagined example but of direct, if symbolic and mythic, description of the world as a whole, or some sector of it."

> In Modern times, fascinated with the triumphs of our specialized natural sciences and with the subtle psychological observations of our novelists, there has been less call than once there was for such a genre. Hesiod and Genesis appear to many as merely historical curiosities. Writers like Boehme or Swedenborg attract us little and even Dante is commonly read now for merely lyric delight. And we scarcely know what to make of Yeats or Teilhard or Toynbee. But some of the most important works of prose of the Islamic Middle Periods were of a mythic-visional type, which tends to get misread and so miscomprehended and undervalued.[22]

From the eleventh century down to early modern times, such esoteric mythic-visional modes of expression enjoyed great popularity throughout Islamdom. Amongst philosophers, Sufis and Shīʿites in particular, "a certain gradation and concealment of knowledge became normal."[23] Three sorts of lore were thus usually treated as esoteric: the metaphysics and natural sciences of the philosophers, the interpretations of the Qur'ān made by Shīʿites and the personal disciplines, visions and speculations of the Sufis. Such privileged lore was out of reach to the Sharīʿa-minded *ʿulamāʾ*, and "to be protected by being made artificially difficult of access."[24]

To omit this esoteric lore from the purview of Islamic Studies simply because it appears to us today as outlandish or heterodox, and not to say something about beliefs in relation to their living experience furnishes an unbalanced picture of the Islamic intellectual tradition to say the least. The vast body of excluded knowledge known as 'esoteric traditions in Islam' have almost always been excluded from the curriculum of modern university faculties simply because the formal, so-called 'empirical' approach to

22 *The Venture of Islam* II, p. 313.

23 *The Venture of Islam* II, p. 312; also cf. similar observations made by Keddie, "Symbol and Sincerity," pp. 53ff.

24 *The Venture of Islam* II, p. 196.

learning which Academe endorses as 'truth' is uneasy with any type of knowledge which claims to be 'inspired'. Needless to say, it does a great disservice to the cause of the advancement of the field of Islamic Studies to let this canon and corpus at the very centre of the Muslim intellectual tradition remain unexplored, unedited and untranslated. The contemporary discomfort of the academic community with the study of Islamic esotericism can, psychologically speaking, be interpreted as a thinly veiled sign of shame at our ignorance of this vast corpus, indicating how orientalists in particular and Western culture in general have been cut off from the real sources of the perennial wisdom of Islam. It is my hope that this anthology may make some slight contribution toward rectification of this bias.

It is hardly incidental that the same prejudice has prevailed regarding the study of Western esotericism, as Antoine Faivre – former Chair and Professor of "History of Esoteric and Mystical Currents in Modern and Contemporary Europe" at the Sorbonne in Paris – reveals:

> Vast areas of our Western cultural history, obscured a priori by theological or epistemological positions, were deliberately omitted, abandoned to the curiosity of eccentrics or even cranks and to capricious handling, which only increased the distrust of serious, albeit somewhat prejudiced investigators and established thinkers vis-à-vis this peripheral domain. The distrust is so pervasive that many scholars are still wondering what esotericism is or whether it truly merits study.[25]

Professor Faivre highlights the existence of a "confusion" provoked by "an inquisitorial spirit between esotericism and religious marginality." Esoteric currents, he protests, cannot "except by intellectual dishonesty, be defined as by nature marginal to the churches."[26] Yet, due to the unfortunate bias of our modern secular mentality, only the most exoteric mode of rational thinking is presumed to constitute the correct and 'orthodox' type of apprehension and perception, even when it comes to affairs of the spirit and religious experience. Academic prejudice still continues to dictate that "the

---

25 Antoine Faivre, *Access to Western Esotericism*, SUNY Series in Western Esoteric Traditions (Albany: SUNY Press 1994), p. ix.

26 Faivre, *Access to Western Esotericism*, p. 6.

status of esoteric currents cannot be defined except as a function of their relationships to the dominant religions."[27]

From Faivre's remarks it is easy to see why both defining and examining the corpus of esoteric traditions in Islam is also so difficult. First of all, as regards definition, one immediately is made aware that a neat division and separation of the 'esoteric' from other related categories in Islamic thought is impossible, for mystical inspiration interpenetrates the gnostic mode of expression in most types of *'irfān*, just as visionary consciousness infiltrates metaphysical thinking in numerous schools of *falsafa*.[28] An esoteric mode of thought permeates not only the entire body of Muslim Neo-Platonic writings; for example, the works of Shihāb al-Dīn Suhrawardī (d. 587/1191) and the whole Ishrāqī school (the "Platonists of Persia" as Henry Corbin called them), from Seljuk down to Safavid times, but also the writings of the great Persian and Arabic Sufi mystical masters and poets, from Manṣūr al-Ḥallāj (d. 304/922) to Niẓāmī (d. 598/1202), from Ibn Fāriḍ (d. 633/1235) to Rūmī (d. 672/1273), were 'esoteric'. Although much of the doctrines of the texts in this anthology relate to mytho-visional thought and mystical experiences, it should be stressed that such modes of apprehension were, to reiterate Marshall Hodgson's observations cited above, socially well respected and culturally highly popular in medieval Islam.[29] Furthermore, belief in the veracity of knowledge acquired through 'visionary unveiling' (*kashf*) was an assumption common to intellectual thought throughout diverse walks of educated society – shared by philosophers, Sufis and theologians alike during the same period.[30]

A brief examination of the etymology of the word 'esoteric' in the Western spiritual tradition[31] following the researches of Antoine Faivre here, will help us sketch the lineaments and expose the foundations of the study of Islamic esotericism. Faivre points out that 'esotericism' has never

---

27 Faivre, *Access to Western Esotericism*, p. 6.

28 Henry Corbin, *Histoire de la philosophie islamique* (Paris: Gallimard 1964), points out "*on ne pourrait exposer ce qu'il en fut de la hikmat en Islam, sans traiter de la mystique, c'est-à-dire du soufisme sous ses différents aspects, tant ceux de son expérience spirituelle que ceux de sa théosophie spéculative, laquelle a ses racines dans l'ésotérisme shī'ite.*" p. 15.

29 *The Venture of Islam* II, pp. 204–5.

30 Cf. W.C. Chittick, "Mysticism Versus Philosophy," pp. 87–104.

31 See Antoine Faivre, *Access to Western Esotericism.*

been a precise term and from the outset of its study, the term "has begun to overflow its boundaries on all sides."[32] Examining the word, one finds that 'Eso' means 'inside' and 'ter' implies opposition, and that "the adjective appeared long before the noun, which dates only from the beginning of the nineteenth century."[33] The Greek word *esōteros* means 'inner', its etymology referring to an "interiorism" which implies "an entry into the self through a special knowledge or gnosis, in order to attain a form of enlightenment and individual salvation."[34]

Bāṭinīyya, the term that most closely corresponds to our 'esotericists' evokes a similar imprecision in the field of Islamic Studies. The term refers to those who profess to be introspective in their exegesis of the Qur'ān, who claim access to an esoteric sense underlying the literal meaning of the Scripture (it was thus the name given in medieval Islam to the Ismā'īlīyya, for example, to whom the literal scripture was all a cryptic allegory), an epithet applied more or less to anyone else who interpreted the Qur'ān on purely symbolical grounds while rejecting its literal meaning.[35] Although there is no reason to believe that the Greek term *esōteros* ever directly influenced the development of doctrines which came to be associated with its sister-term *bāṭin* in Islam, there is much evidence that considerable intellectual fraternity between the two modes of thought does exist. And even from the doctrinal point of view, some contiguity between *bāṭin* and *esōteros* is not wholly unlikely.[36]

---

32 Faivre, *Access to Western Esotericism*, p. 3.

33 Faivre, *Access to Western Esotericism*, p. 4.

34 A. Faivre, "Esotericism," in *The Encyclopedia of Religion* V, p. 157. This is also the dominant meaning of gnosis among the early Christian Gnostics, whose "use of it differs from the standard usage in that they often employ the word gnosis in an absolute way ... to refer to a revealed knowledge, given to humanity by God and not resulting from the effort of human reason." Simone Pétrement, *A Separate God: The Christian Origins of Gnosticism*, trans. [from French] by Carol Harrison (London: Darton, Longman and Todd 1991), chap. 1 "Salvation by Knowledge," p. 130.

35 Hodgson, "Baṭiniyya," *EI2* II, p. 1098.

36 Thus H. Halm ("Bāṭenīya," *EIr* III, p. 861) underlines that "Christian, Jewish, and Gnostic influences" on the thinking of various early Bāṭinīyya groups "cannot be ruled out but are hard to prove in particular cases." Thus, Henry Corbin notes that "the word *ḥikmah* is identical to the Greek *sophia*, and term *ḥikmat ilāhīyah* corresponds literally to

In fact, many parallelisms between the two terms' conceptualization in Muslim and Christian civilizations do exist. Faivre thus delineates the three basic meanings of Western esotericism as follows:

i) Etymologically considered, the main connotation of 'esotericism' is that of a secret lore through which "we can access understanding of a symbol, myth, or reality only by a personal effort of progressive elucidation through several successive levels, i.e. by a form of hermeneutics."[37]

ii) The actual subject matter of esotericism, its 'knowledge' "concerns the relationships that unite us to God or to the divine world and may also include a knowledge of the mysteries inherent to God himself (in which case it is, strictly speaking, theosophy). To learn these relationships, the individual must enter, or 'descend', into himself by means of an initiatory process, progressing along a path that is hierarchically structured by a series of intermediaries."[38] Other concomitants of esotericism are that the initiate usually must have access to an initiator, a master who can regenerate his consciousness and reconnect him with the sacred realm and vouchsafe to him an experience of the esoteric knowledge which is best described as 'gnosis'.

iii) In a more general sense, it implies "a type of knowledge, emanating from a spiritual center to be attained after transcending the prescribed ways and techniques – quite diverse considering the schools or the currents – that can lead to it. This spiritual locus, this higher level of 'knowledge' would overarch all particular traditions and initiations, which are only so many means of access. It is identical to all who achieve it; experience of its attainment is the proof or guarantee of the 'transcendent unity of religions'. Let us note also that in this context, 'esotericism' means as much the ways that lead to this 'center' as the 'center' itself. Esotericists who speak of esotericism in this second sense tend, just like mystics, to maintain a discourse marked by subjectivity."[39]

---

the Greek *theosophia*." – *Histoire de la philosophie islamique* (Paris: Gallimard 1964), p. 14.

37 Faivre, *Access to Western Esotericism*, p. 5.

38 Faivre, "Esotericism," in *The Encyclopedia of Religion* V, p. 157.

39 Faivre, *Access to Western Esotericism*, p. 5.

All three connotations, interestingly enough, correspond quite closely to the three above-designated meanings of *'ilm al-bāṭin* in Islamic thought, suggesting the probable intellectual contiguity of the terminology of the two fields, and that the identity of *bāṭinīyya* with 'esotericists' and *al-bāṭin* with 'esotericism' is more or less methodologically sound. With this comparative background in mind, it will be somewhat easier to outline the contours of Islamic esotericism.

In his study of the development of early Shī'ism, Mohammad Ali Amir-Moezzi points out that the dominant form of philosophical speculation during the first few centuries of Islamic civilization among the Shī'ites was precisely of an 'esoteric' type, noting that "the original Imamite doctrine, presented through the words of the imams and registered by the first compilers, of which Ibn Bābūye represents the last great name, was clearly of 'heterodox' esoteric and mystical – indeed, even magical and occult – character."[40] In other words, mysticism and esotericism – what Amir-Moezzi calls "esoteric non-rational Imamism"[41] – dominated the first three and half centuries of Shī'ite thought.[42] Discussing "esotericism and rationalization," he underlines that it was only from the time of the Occultation – that is, from the middle of the fourth/tenth century when under the influence of Mu'tazilite rationalism, and to defend itself against it by means of an apologetic theology – that Shī'ism took on a rationalistic character. From the time of the minor occultation onwards occurred what Amir-Moezzi refers to as "a progressive silencing" of the original esoteric mystical theology of early Shī'ism.[43] However, as Farhad Daftary in a number of groundbreaking works has demonstrated, much of this early Shī'ite esoteric tradition survived

40 *The Divine Guide in Early Shi'ism: The Sources of Esotericism in Islam*, trans. [from French] D. Streight (Albany: SUNY Press 1994), p. 18. He adds: "One result of this progressive silencing is that these essentially Imamological traditions, with a quite original metaphysical and mystical (and thus 'heterodox') scope in Islam, take a turn towards rationalization and attempts at rapprochement with 'orthodox' positions, attempts led by al-Mufīd and al-Murtaḍā."

41 *The Divine Guide in Early Shi'ism*, p. 19.

42 He emphasizes this point in his conclusion as well: "Every facet of early Imamism studied throughout the course of this work confirms that early Imamism is an esoteric doctrine." – *The Divine Guide in Early Shi'ism*, p. 126.

43 *The Divine Guide in Early Shi'ism*, p. 19.

within the confines of Ismāʿīlī thought in the form of a theosophical esotericism[44] refined into a creed and consolidated into a religious doctrine, which is the reason why Ismāʿīlism represents, as Henry Corbin pointed out many decades ago, "the most significant recurrence of gnosis in Islam"[45] being "*à l'avant-garde de la métaphysique et de la gnose en Islam.*"[46]

While this very important esoteric – Ismāʿīlī – tradition is present, nurtured within the bosom of Shīʿism, in Islam, if one considers the public expression of both the institutional forms and initiatory rites of most of what constitutes the 'interior life' in Islam, the most visible form of Islamic esotericism occurs in Sufism (*taṣawwuf*) and its Orders (*silsila-yi ṭarīqat*). Yet, while Sufism is indeed "the common element in both Sunnism and Shiism," to cite Henry Corbin once again: "*taṣawwuf* does not constitute the entire mystical spirituality in Islam."[47] Rather, Sufism and Shīʿism, more often than not, historically paralleled and mutually influenced each other, partaking of many of the same key doctrines (sainthood: *wilāyat* and similar notions of an esoteric hierarchy, in particular).[48] Although delineation of the precise historical and doctrinal relationship between the two movements is beyond the scope of this introduction, it is clear theosophists within both movements often shared a common vocabulary of esoteric technical terms with not entirely dissimilar meanings, as many of the texts translated here reveal.

---

44 See especially his *The Ismaʿilis: Their history and doctrine* (Cambridge: Cambridge University Press 1990), pp. 137, where he notes that the "early Ismāʿīlīs soon came to be regarded as the most representative Shīʿī group espousing esotericism and gnosticism in Islam."

45 Henry Corbin, "From the Gnosis of Antiquity to Ismaili Gnosis," in his *Cyclical Time and Ismaili Gnosis*, trans. Ralph Manheim and James Morris (London: KPI in association with Islamic Publications 1983), p. 152. In this context, Corbin stresses that the renaissance in Ismāʿīlī studies during the second half of the twentieth century is as important for the understanding gnosis in Islam as the discovery of the Coptic manuscripts at Nag Hammadi.

46 Henry Corbin, *En Islam iranien: Aspects spirituels et philosophiques* (Paris: Éditions Gallimard 1971), vol. I, p. x.

47 Henry Corbin, *Histoire de la philosophie islamique* (Paris: Gallimard 1964), p. 392.

48 Kamil al-Shaibi, *Sufism and Shiʿism* (Surrey: LAAM 1991), chaps 1–3.

This commonly shared lexicon of technical terms brings us to one of the fundamental premises underlying the compilation of the present anthology: that the category of *the esoteric* (*bāṭin*) itself, comprising the gnosis (*ma'rifat*), the basic interior knowledge or *'ilm al-bāṭin* of any given field of Muslim science, resides within the bosom of nearly *all* Islamic theology, philosophy and gnosis. 'Esotericism', depending on one's methodology, can be approached both through (1) the outsider's academic perspective as a separate field of study within Islamic Studies, or through (2) the insider's perspective advocated by the Muslim gnostics (*'urafā'*) who generally understood the *bāṭin* to constitute the essential 'common ground' of all Islamic fields of knowledge, *falsafah*, whether *ishrāqī* or peripatetic, and *kalām*, as well as all *'irfān*, *ḥikmat* and *taṣawwuf* itself.[49] The following diagram illustrates the two perspectives:

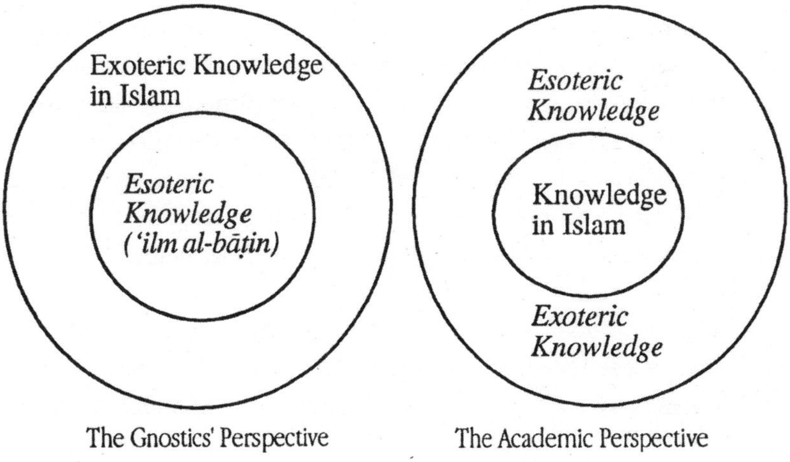

The great Safavid theologian and mystical philosopher Shaykh Bahā' al-Dīn al-'Āmilī (d. 1030–1/1621) probably gave the best synopsis of the 'gnostics' perspective' in Islam that apprehends the ubiquity of the esoteric vision

49 See Russell Tracey McCutcheon, *The Insider/Outsider Problem in the Study of Religion: A Reader* (London: Cassell 1999). For a similar approach to Western esotericism, see Wouter J. Hanegraaff, *New Age Religion and Western Culture: Esotericism in the Mirror of Secular Thought* (Albany: SUNY Press 1998); *idem.*, "Empirical Method in the Study of Esotericism," *Method and Theory in the Study of Religion* 7, no. 2 (1995), pp. 99–129.

shared in common by so many Muslim philosophers, theologians and Sufis, in his celebrated stanza:

> The sages and the men of analytic intellect
> Use postulations of their reason in the quest
> For you; one mad with love, the wandering fool
> Seeks you beyond tradition and religion too,
> And yet, this garden's heady blossom who
> Can scent? For each the tongue of praise is different:
> The dove croons country tunes, the nightingale serenades.[50]

Approached externally as a field of academic study, Islam's esoteric traditions embrace epistemologically various types of gnostic lore defined by a vast lexicon of technical terms. These include not only obvious terms indicating the hidden nature of the field such as 'gnosis' (*ma'rifat*), 'esoteric knowledge' (*'ilm al-bāṭin*), 'occult science' (*'ilm al-ghayb*),[51] 'revelation' (*ilhām*), 'faith born of heart-conviction' (*īmān az taṣdīq*), 'visionary unveiling' (*kashf*), 'mystical unveiling'/'spiritual illumination' (*ishrāq*), 'illuminative theophany' (*tajallī, maẓhar*) and 'esoteric hermeneutical exegesis' (*ta'wīl*) – but many other terms drawn from fields as far apart as Alchemy, Pseudo-Empedoclean and Pythagorean doctrine,[52] Hermetic philosophy, Neo-Platonism and Zoroastrian Mazdaism.[53]

An examination of the historical origins and linguistic development of some of the key esoteric terms in the Qur'ān, *ḥadīth* and other Islamic sources (Sufism in particular) has been already undertaken by a number of scholars

---

50 *Kulliyāt-i ash'ār va āthār-i fārsī-yi Shaykh Bahā'ī*, ed. 'Alī Kātibī (Tehran: Nashr-Chakāma, n.d.), p. 348.

51 For further information about occult sciences, séances with the souls of the dead, and appeals to saintly powers, see Alireza Doostdar, *The Iranian Metaphysicals: Explorations in Science, Islam, and the Uncanny* (Princeton: Princeton University Press 2018).

52 On which, see Peter Kingsley, "From Empedocles to the Sufis: 'The Pythagorean Leaven'," in his *Ancient Philosophy, Mystery and Magic: Empedocles and Pythagorean Tradition* (Oxford: Oxford University Press 1997), pp. 371–91, and his appendix III: "Empedocles and the Ismā'īlīs."

53 On which, see Henry Corbin, *Les motifs zoroastriens dans la philosophie de Sohrawardī (Shaykh-ol-Ishrāq) (ob. 587/1191)* (Tehran: Editions du Courrier 1946).

including Louis Massignon,[54] Henry Corbin,[55] Paul Nwiya,[56] and more recently, by Michael Sells[57] and John Renard.[58] The present anthology serves not only – hopefully – to complement the research works of the foregoing authors, but aspires to something else as well: to present the common ground of esoteric thought and terminology and show the unity of perspective among Muslim spirituals. In this respect, the project of the present anthology dovetails the task enunciated in the prologue and inaugurated by Corbin in his *Spiritual Body and Celestial Earth: From Mazdean Iran to Shīʿite Iran.*[59]

THE AUTHORS AND TRANSLATED TEXTS

Although the texts translated in this anthology are arranged in a chronological order, stretching from the mid-eleventh to the late nineteenth centuries, neither the linear progression of the texts nor what scholars call 'history of ideas' has been my primary concern. Rather, independent of the horizontal line of historical causation, the aim of this anthology, following the

---

54 See his *Essai sur les origines du lexique technique de la mystique musulmane* (Paris: 1992). See also the English translation by Bemjamin Clark: *Essay on the Origins of the Technical Language of Islamic Mysticism* (Indiana: University of Notre Dame Press 1997). This pioneering work is of immense importance, but its scope of reference is restricted largely to the early lexicon of asceticism and Sufism in Arabic.

55 The works of Henry Corbin, in particular his *Histoire de la philosophie islamique* (Paris: Gallimard 1964), analyse the development of 'esoteric thinking' in Islam and outline its philosophical contours, providing a helpful historical framework for the ongoing terminological and textual studies proposed here.

56 See his *Exégèse Coranique et langue mystique* (Beirut: 1970) which goes into more detail and depth than Massignon, especially in his study of Jaʿfar al-Ṣādiq and certain lesser studied Sufi thinkers, although examination of the lexicon of Ismāʿīlī and philosophical speculation is largely omitted.

57 Michael Sells, *Early Islamic Mysticism: Sufi, Qur'an, Miʿraj, Poetic and Theological Writings* (New Jersey: Paulist Press 1996).

58 John Renard in his *Knowledge of God in Classical Sufism: Foundations of Islamic Mystical Theology* (New York: Paulist Press 2004) provides a comprehensive account of some of the various meanings of *maʿrifa* and *ʿilm* in Sufism in his introduction.

59 Trans. N. Pearson (London: I.B. Tauris 1990), p. ix.

phenomenological approach of Henry Corbin, has been to expose the presence of a vertical, *metahistorical* commonality of ideas across sectarian boundaries and philosophical schools.[60]

Although linguistically the anthology is divided into (i) seven selections translated from the Persian, and (ii) four selections translated from the Arabic,[61] the difference between these two tongues is not of real consequence to any of the theological and theosophical arguments adduced therein. I believe the authors' choice of language in the selections was largely of incidental significance, unrelated to either the substantial tenor,

60 Henry Corbin criticizes the hollowness of the historicist approach to esotericism based only on the causality of objects and "the obsessive fantasy of purity of 'sources'" which "then blinds one to any but an artificial unity of disparate elements." Such research "conceives itself entirely as a history of themes, or motifs, as well as of concrete existences of individuals and groups which support them." Such themes are then "converted into abstractions which are totally divorced from the real underlying factors which brought about the Event. These motifs are also endowed with a sort of causality of their own, whose true nature is assumed rather than clearly defined. These morphological units then take turns playing the roles of cause and effect – their forms are determined purely by each other, in an order of succession which is simply that of historical chronology. Never is there any recognition of a need to transcend them, to question them as *phenomena* – in other words, to ask the paramount questions of what is showing itself, to *whom* it is shown, and *who* is making it shown." The main drawback of the purely historicist approach is that it cannot deal with the living philosophical or theosophical dimension of esotericism, writes Corbin, for "this type of historicist knowledge is especially unable to comprehend anything but the *past*. It follows that everything has to be 'explained' by reducing it to the already-seen, the already-known. The notion of something spontaneous and original then appears as vaguely scandalous, since it is inexplicable." – Henry Corbin, "Iranian Studies and Philosophy," in *idem.*, *The Voyage and the Messenger*, trans. J. Rowe (Berkeley: North Atlantic Books 1998), pp. 53–54. He finally posits that "there had to be gnostics in order for gnosticism to come about," noting that "merely adding together different types of worldviews or ways of perceiving, yields only a virtual totality. The mere juxtaposition of them could never be the *explanation* of this virtuality becoming an actualization." – Corbin, "Iranian Studies and Philosophy," p. 56.

61 The eleven texts in this book are organized linguistically are as follows: (i). Persian: Bukhārī, Maybudī, Hamadhānī, 'Izz al-Dīn Maḥmūd Kāshānī, Turkah Iṣfahānī, 'Abd al-Razzāq Lāhījī, Sabziwārī, and (ii) Arabic: Ghazālī, Ibn 'Arabī, Ḥaydar Āmulī, Mullā Ṣadrā.

aesthetic purpose or philosophical content of the subjects discussed, ultimately a matter of personal taste relating to an individual writer's preferred linguistic vehicle of expression. Some of the selections are a melange of Arabic and Persian; others, in Persian being fully lilted with a top-heavy Arabic vocabulary (Maḥmūd Kāshānī, Lāhījī), while a few written in Arabic by authors who were equally good stylists in Persian (Ghazālī, Mullā Ṣadrā). In expressing internal matters of faith, choice of language is thus largely of marginal significance; as the Persian poet Sanā'ī put it:

> If Arabic held the custody of God's Canon Law
> Then Abu Lahab the Damned I declare is moon and sun!
> If Abu Lahab came from the holy land of Yathrib,
> So what? He had no heart for prayer or rites divine.
> Salman came from Iran, but how he careened
> Full tilt on the feet of faith! The Spirit's life
> Lies in reason, in knowledge and sapience;
> The Spirit cares not a whit whether the tongue
> you speak be Persian or Arabic.[62]

The philosophical persuasions and religious affiliations of the authors divide themselves into the following three groupings:

i) *Shī'ite philosopher-mystic (Ḥakīm):* Ḥaydar Āmulī, Mullā Ṣadrā, 'Abd al-Razzāq Lāhījī, Hadī Sabziwārī
ii) *Sunni Sufi:* Bukhārī, Maybudī, 'Ayn al-Quḍāt Hamadhānī, Ibn 'Arabī, 'Izz al-Dīn Maḥmūd Kāshānī
iii) *Sunni Sufi philosopher:* Ghazālī, Ṣā'īn al-Dīn Turkah Iṣfahānī

As is evident from this tripartite division, a third of the selection comprise Shī'ite authors while two-thirds constitute Sunnis. Furthermore, all the authors in the last two categories stand squarely within the Sufi esoteric

---

62 Abū'l-Majdūd ibn Ādam Sanā'ī, *Ḥadīqat al-ḥaqīqa*, ed. Muḥammad Rawshan (Tehran: Intishārāt-i Nigāh 1377 A.Hsh./1998), p. 291. Translation mine. For further discussion of these verses, see Mohammad Ali Amir-Moezzi, "Persian, the Other Sacred Language of Islam: Some Brief Notes," in *Fortresses of the Intellect: Ismaili and other Islamic Studies in Honour of Farhad Daftary*, ed. Omar Ali-de-Unzaga (London: I.B. Tauris and the Institute of Ismaili Studies 2011), pp. 59–75 [p. 74, n. 52].

tradition. But denominations are deceptive if not misleading in the realm of Islamic esotericism. As we shall see, the discourse of *ʿilm al-bāṭin* appears in many of our authors as a kind of language of the Spirit, which literally transports them outside their respective sectarian affiliations. Their statements concerning *kashf, shuhūd, taʾwīl,* etc., are often much better understood as statements of a kind of timeless Islamic *prisca theologia* than as pronouncements of learned doctors and clerics made to curry the favour of church or state, or as epiphenomenal 'intellectual influences' evoked by the constant perusal of texts and tracts of the great masters.

Due to reasons of size and space, the anthology has inevitably been forced to limit the scope of its contents and in the process omitted a large number of good authors and reputable works from its purview. There is no doubt that the founder of the School of Oriental Theosophy or Illuminationism, Shihāb al-Dīn Yaḥyā Suhrawardī (*Shaykh al-ishrāq*, d. 587/1191), deserved to be featured in these pages, insofar as his school is one of the most obvious examples of Islamic esotericism, the ecumenical scope of which has effected a renaissance in Iranian philosophical thought in recent decades.[63] In the modern West, since the monumental edition of his collected Arabic and Persian works by Henry Corbin and S.H. Nasr, the study of Suhrawardī has itself blossomed to form a separate sub-field of studies in Islamic philosophy, featuring many prominent scholars numbering among its chief authorities, including the likes of such as John Walbridge, Hossein Ziai, Hermann Landolt, Mehdi Aminrazavi and Mehdi Hairi Yazdi.[64] Suhrawardī's works include not only *Aurorial Philosophy* (*Ḥikmat*

---

63 Of course, both the Sufi and Ishrāqī traditions, by medium of a number of authors translated in these pages, are indirectly represented (Mullā Ṣadrā, for instance, was strongly influenced by Ishrāqī thought), even if some of their better-known members are absent from this collection.

64 It would be impossible to provide a comprehensive bibliography of works here, but (aside from the well-known works of Corbin and Nasr) some of the important monographs or articles on aspects of his life and thought that have been written over the past few decades include:

- John Walbridge, *The Science of Mystic Lights: Qutb al-Din Shirazi & the Illuminationist Tradition in Islamic Philosophy* (Cambridge: Harvard University Press 1992);
- Suhrawardī, *The Book of Radiance*, trans. Hossein Ziai (Costa Mesa: Mazda 1998);
- Mehdi Aminrazavi, *Suhrawardi and the School of Illumination* (London: Curzon Press 1997);

al-ishrāq),[65] his *opus major*, but also a number of important Arabic and Persian works, a full account of which is already given in a number of well-known sources.[66] Being the most significant Platonic philosopher in medieval Islam, as well as a kind of irregular Sufi mystic, whose writings were highly influential on the intellectual development of the Neo-Platonist thinkers of the School of Isfahan, it was originally planned that at least one selection from the Master of Oriental Wisdom's writings should be featured in this anthology.

Yet, it should be emphasized that this anthology makes no pretensions to be a general history or comprehensive survey of Islamic esotericism. What has been attempted is merely to sketch out the contours of some of the salient currents, ideas and works in this field, research on which is still in its infancy. The range of the selections in this anthology is extremely wide both chronologically and geographically, together covering nearly a millennium, and featuring works from eleven different authors who flourished in Persia, Central Asia and Asia Minor from the early eleventh to the late nineteenth centuries – the first author being Mustamlī Bukhārī (d. 434/1042–43) and the last Hadī Sabziwārī (d. 1289/1873). The

---

- Ian Netton, *Allāh Transcendent: Studies in the Structure and Semiotics of Islamic Philosophy, Theology and Cosmology* (London: Routledge 1989), pp. 256ff;
- Hossein Ziai, "Shihāb al-Dīn Suhrawardī: founder of the Illuminationist school," in S.H. Nasr and Oliver Leaman (eds.), *History of Islamic Philosophy* (London: Routledge 1996), I, pp. 434–64;
- Suhrawardi, *The Philosophical Allegories and Mystical Treatises*, parallel Persian–English text, ed. and trans., W.M. Thackston (Costa Mesa: Mazda 1999).

65 Suhrawardi, *The Philosophy of Illumination: A New Critical Edition of the Text of* Ḥikmat al-ishrāq *with English Translation, Notes, Commentary, and Introduction* by John Walbridge and Hossein Ziai (Provo: Brigham Young University Press 1999); Suhrawardi, *The Philosophical Allegories and Mystical Treatises*, parallel Persian–English text, ed. and trans., W.M. Thackston (Costa Mesa: Mazda 1999).

66 S.H. Nasr, "Shihāb al-Dīn Suhrawardī Maqtūl," in M.M. Sharif (ed.), *A History of Muslim Philosophy* (Delhi: D.K. Publishers repr. 1995), I, pp. 372–99; Hossein Ziai, "Shihāb al-Dīn Suhrawardī: founder of the Illuminationist school," in Oliver Leaman and S.H. Nasr (eds.), *History of Islamic Philosophy* (London: Routledge 1996), pp. 434–64; *idem.*, "The Illuminationist Tradition," in *History of Islamic Philosophy*, pp. 465–96; Aminrazavi, *Suhrawardi and the School of Illumination* (London: Curzon Press 1997).

chronological scope of the collection thus stretches from the late classical period (eleventh-century Khurāsān) down to early modern times (nineteenth-century Qājār Iran).

Contentwise, this volume is primarily devoted to texts on gnosis and esoteric knowledge (*ma'rifa*). Its twelve chapters treat topics such as knowledge (*'ilm*), revelation (*waḥy*), inspiration (*ilhām*), wisdom (*ḥikmat*), visionary disclosure or mystical unveiling (*kashf*), spiritual illumination (*ishrāq*) and illuminative theophany (*tajallī, maẓhar*). Each chapter features an introduction of varying length about the author, his life, works and thought, along with a discussion of his mystical persuasion (*mashrab*), sectarian affiliation (*madhhab*) and philosophical school (*maktab*), followed by an analytical synopsis of the translated text. All the chapters are fully annotated, Qur'ān and *ḥadīth* references being provided, with extensive notes on technical terms, proper names and relevant historical and theological references also furnished. The various texts translated here it is hoped will serve as a small first step in demonstrating that there does exist, in the first place a distinct universe of the *bāṭin* in Islam, and in the second, that there is more unity than divisiveness within this universe.

In this context, it should be emphasized that the *bāṭin* has always constituted the interior 'core' part of the intellectual and spiritual life in Islam.[67] As S.H. Nasr points out, "gnosis has played a more central role in the Islamic tradition than it has in the West."[68] It is due to this centrality of gnosis in Islam that Abū Ḥāmid al-Ghazālī, Islam's most celebrated mystical theologian, made it the key element in his theology, referring to the science of disclosure (*'ilm al-mukāshafa*) as the sole means by which one can "gain knowledge of the meaning of prophecy and the prophet, and of the meaning of revelation (*al-waḥy*)."[69]

---

67 It is high time that we discard the traditional polemical connotation of the term *bāṭinīyya* (=esoteric latitudinarians) propagated by medieval Sunni heresiologists to lambast the Ismā'īlīs (on which, see Hodgson, "Baṭiniyya," *EI2* I, p. 1099).

68 S.H. Nasr, "Theology, Philosophy, and Spirituality," in S.H. Nasr (ed.), *Islamic Spirituality II (Manifestations)* (New York: Crossroad 1991), p. 395.

69 See N.A. Faris, *The Book of Knowledge, Being a Translation with Notes of the Kitāb al-'Ilm of al-Ghazzālī's Iḥyā' 'Ulūm al-Dīn* (Lahore: 1962), p. 47; N. Heer, "Abū Ḥāmid al-Ghazālī's Esoteric Exegesis of the Koran," in Leonard Lewisohn (ed.), *The Heritage of Sufism: Classical Persian Sufism: from its Origins to Rūmī*, I (Oxford: Oneworld 1999), p. 247.

Although probably not adverse to the academic approach found in this anthology, the gnostics themselves of course taught that the esoteric can only be accessed through a variety of contemplative disciplines and spiritual methods: practice of forms of prayer, observance, meditation, etc. In this respect, Ghazālī's statement below typifies the views of all the authors given here:

> Another characteristic of the learned man is that he devotes the greatest part of his attention to esoteric knowledge, the observation (*murāqabah*) of the heart, the path of the hereafter and how to journey thereon, as well as to an abiding faith in finding that path through self-mortification (*mujāhadah*) and observation. For self-mortification leads to contemplation (*mushāhada*) and through the intricate details of the sciences of the heart fountains of wisdom gush forth. Books and formal education are of little help in this field because the wisdom which passes all understanding is achieved only through self-mortification, observation and watching, the active fulfilment of outward and inward duties, coming before God (*julūs*) in solitude (*khalwah*) and bringing the heart before His presence (*ḥudūr*) through pure reflection (*fikr*) and sole devotion to Him. This is the key of illumination (*ilhām*) and the fountainhead of revelation (*kashf*). For while many a student has persisted in his studies but was unable to go beyond the words he had heard, many have confined their attention in their studies to what was important and were active in works, and bent on observation of their hearts; consequently God has blessed them with wisdom which passes all understanding ... And had it not been for the fact that the enlightenment of the heart of him who has a heart with the inner light determines the exoteric knowledge (*ʿilm al-ẓāhir*) the Prophet would not have said, "Consult thy heart whenever they should recommend something to thee and give thee a dispensation [to do it]." ... Many are the subtle meanings of the Qur'ān which dawn upon the hearts of those who have devoted themselves to invocation (*dhikr*) and reflection (*fikr*), but are not found in the books of commentary and remain unknown to the best commentators.[70]

70 N.A. Faris, *The Book of Knowledge, Being a Translation with Notes of the Kitāb al-ʿIlm of al-Ghazzālī's Iḥyā' ʿUlūm al-Dīn* (Lahore: 1962), pp. 189–90.

However, understanding the science of disclosure and viewing things from the "gnostic perspective" described by Ghazālī here (and outlined in the diagram cited a few pages back) has never been accessible to all and sundry. S.H. Nasr underlines that "esotericism is that inward dimension of tradition which addresses the inner man, *ho esö anthröpos* of Saint Paul. It is hidden because of its very nature and accessible to only the few because in this stage of human history only the few remain aware of the inner dimensions of their nature; the rest live on the periphery of the circle of their own existence, oblivious to the Center which is connected by the esoteric dimension of tradition to the circumference or periphery."[71]

In the phenomenological school of comparative religion, the primacy of self-verificatory subject-centricism (that can be viewed as an intellectual reprise to *kashf-i taḥqīqī*, the Sufi notion of self-verification by visionary knowledge) in the study of religion is thus axiomatic.[72] John Baillie, for instance, maintains that religion can only justly be estimated "from within."[73] Therefore, the science of religion is

> ... defective simply because it has tried to be a natural science and has essayed to treat the faith of mankind as so much *dead matter*, to be understood not by introspective insight but by internal inspection and comparison. But the truth is that, regarded from this point of view, the religious experience of mankind is the merest chaos of kaleidoscopic forms; and that only by regarding it from within, and through the glass of experience itself, can either meaning or order be discerned in it.[74]

---

71 S.H. Nasr, *Knowledge and the Sacred* (Albany: SUNY Press 1989), p. 77.

72 I am referring in particular to the Swedish theologian Nathan Söderblom, the German theologians Rudolf Otto and Van der Leeuw, and the Scottish philosopher and theologian John Baillie. Otto thus points out the sense of the Numinous, which is dependent upon what he calls "creature feeling," "is itself a first subjective concomitant." *The Idea of the Holy: An Inquiry into the non-rational factor in the idea of the divine and its relation to the rational*, trans. J. Harvey (Oxford: Oxford University Press 1958), p. 10; also cf. ch. 7. On Van der Leeuw, see Eric Sharpe, *Understanding Religion* (London: Duckworth 1983), pp. 230–31.

73 See E. Sharpe, *Comparative Religion* (Wiltshire: Duckworth, 2nd edn, 1986), p. 169.

74 Baille, *The Interpretation of Religion* (New York: 1956), p. 122.

A musical analogy is often used to illustrate the condition of someone not attuned to the Sacred. Just as the study of music may yield a purely theoretic and mathematical unity of notes to someone who is musically insensitive, such that neither its aesthetic beauty or auditory harmony will be apprehended, likewise, for one who approaches religion from without, 'information' and 'facts' are readily available, religious *meaning* will always remain elusive.[75] Again, S.H. Nasr points out:

> To carry out the study of other religions in depth requires a penetration into the depth of one's own being and an interiorizing and penetrating intelligence which is already imbued with the sacred. Ecumenism if correctly understood must be an esoteric activity if it is to avoid becoming the instrument for simple relativization and further secularizaton.[76]

Today, religious experience is largely understood as a reality pertaining to the social, intellectual or ethical dimensions of faith and, as a consequence, a "narrowing of the frontiers of religion has occurred." "Personal religious experience, particularly that involving 'altered states of consciousness'," as Eric Sharpe observes, "is disdained as a self-indulgent flight from 'reality'. Intellectual reflection is permissible only to the extent that it addresses the ethical question: otherwise it is 'irrelevant'. The social forms of religion are wherever possible reshaped into pressure groups, and where this proves impossible, they are condemned as 'ghettos'. 'God's frozen people', 'the comfortable pew' and the like, and abandoned for more responsive organizations."[77]

The current embarrassment of both the public and the academic community with the study of Islamic esotericism thus reflects the general disdain for the esoteric that has prevailed for over a century now in the West. As R.P. Blackmoor put it, when writing about the poetry of W.B. Yeats in 1936, "Fatalism, Christianity, and magic are none of them disciplines to which many minds can consciously appeal today. The supernatural is simply not part of our mental furniture."[78] So we can see how in today's

---

75 S.H. Nasr, *Knowledge and the Sacred*, p. 284.

76 Nasr, *Knowledge and the Sacred*, p. 282.

77 Sharpe, *Understanding Religion*, pp. 105–6.

78 Cited Kathleen Raine, *W.B. Yeats and the Learning of the Imagination* (Ipswich: Golgonooza Press 1999), p. 1.

Academe certain inherent prejudices derived from our secular, largely laicizated conception of religion tend to unconsciously tarnish any serious empirical investigation of the mystical and occult dimensions of religion and provoke a virtual 'esoteric-phobia' in the student.

The conscientious scholar must therefore avoid all reductionist presuppositions about the main categories of esoteric thinking in Islam (as in 'nothing but' explanations confined to purely socio-political or theological-juridical categories of thought), maintaining a rigorous detachment from all the usual monolithic categories of Islamic Studies; that is, reject as unscientific the intellectually pious but false platitude that juxtaposes a normative Exoteric-cum-'orthodox' to a non-normative Esoteric-cum-'heterodox' Islamic tradition.[79] Similarly, stereotypical neo-Marxist interpretations of mystical experience – as characteristic of men suffering from a state of social alienation – are to be approached sceptically. In short, the serious student must be wary of any *a priori* presumptions which hold that esoteric

79 Likewise, one must be wary of succumbing to modern misinterpretations of Islam that conflates it with its fundamentalist and literalist interpretations popularized by the media. Carl Ernst points this out in regard to the relation of Sufism and fundamentalism in particular, noting: "It has been pointed out that Western journalists are too often content to accept the self-interpretation of Muslim fundamentalists as the sole authentic custodians of tradition. One would never guess from most media reports that fundamentalists usually constitute no more than twenty percent of any Muslim population and that in this respect they are likely to have the same proportion as fundamentalists in Christian, Hindu, or Buddhist societies. Like the spin doctors who attempt to mold public opinion through commentary, fundamentalist spokesmen attempt through their rhetoric of total confrontation to claim representation of Islam. For this effort to succeed, they must discredit and disenfranchise all other claimants to the sources of authority in the Islamic tradition. There is no stronger rival claim on these sources than in Sufism. Modern studies of Muslim fundamentalism rarely point this out, preferring instead to dwell on confrontation with European colonialism and the secular state as the proximate cause of this ideology. By the principal early fundamentalist movement, the Wahhabism that swept Arabia in the nineteenth century, had nothing to do with responses to Europe. While resistance to the Ottoman empire may have been a factor, there was a basic religious struggle going on between Wahhabis and Sufis for the control of central religious symbols. Fundamentalist articulated their goal as the domination of the symbol of Islam." – *The Shambhala Guide to Sufism* (Boston: Shambhala 1997), pp. 212–13.

'rites of initiation', mystical 'unveiling'/'spiritual illumination' (*kashf, ishrāq*), beliefs in an invisible mystical hierarchy (*abdāl, imām, insān al-kāmil, quṭb*, etc.), or illuminative modes of theophany (*tajallī, maẓhar*), etc., are in anyway 'abnormal' or alien to the Muslim religious life.

Here, it is well to point to an important paradox that lies within the motifs of secrecy, initiation and knowledge communicable only by means of code and symbol that typifies esotericism in all the world's major religious traditions.[80] Although the initiated adept lays claim to a novel and original vision that is only subjectively verifiable on the basis of a personally realized intuitional discovery (through *kashf* and *taḥqīq*), at the same time he asserts his experience to be completely in congruence with a previous spiritual 'tradition' and in accordance with the primordial revelation of scripture. His or her esoteric vision is thus 'original' and 'traditional' at once. This is probably what Sufyān al-Thawrī meant when he quipped: "If on some mountaintop somewhere there were a single person of understanding, he would constitute the Muslim Community." That is also why the crass sociology which measures a religion's vibrancy through statistical analysis of numbers of 'believers' and surveys its practices by ethnographical mapping of "performances" of ceremonies, rites and rituals, will remain forever excluded from gaining any insight into this field.[81]

Below, I have provided an extended survey of the two theosophical notions: (i) Hermeneutics and the Language of Symbolism, and (ii) Esoteric Knowledge and Gnosis (*ma'rifat*) that are featured amongst every type and denomination of author translated here; notions which are composed of basically similar common – or perhaps better said, similar uncommon – components. While there was certainly much polarity and opposition in the realm of

---

80 On this issue, see Paul Valliere, "Tradition," in Mircea Eliade (ed.), *The Encyclopedia of Religion* (New York: Simon & Schuster Macmillan 1995), vol. 15, p. 13. For an in-depth study, see Sissela Bok, *Secrets: On the Ethics of Concealment and Revelation* (Oxford: Oxford University Press 1984), in particular chapters 1, 2, 4, 5, 6.

81 "Our religion vulgarly stands on numbers of believers. Whenever the appeal is made – no matter how indirectly – to numbers, proclamation is then and there made, that religion is not. He that finds God in a sweet, enveloping thought to him never counts his company. When I sit in that preserve, who shall dare to come in? When I rest in perfect humility, when I burn with pure love, what can Calvin or Swedenborg say?" – Ralph Waldo Emerson, "The Oversoul," in *Ralph Waldo Emerson: Essays and Lectures* (Cambridge: Cambridge University Press 1983), p. 399.

exoteric religious doctrine and dogmatic theology between these groups, we find more *common ground* than difference in their theosophies, technical mystical terminology, ethical doctrines, their spiritual methods and psychologies. In other words, within the realm of the esoteric or *bāṭin* they constitute a unified community: a *communio sanctorum* in the sphere of *wilāya*: theirs is an ever-continuing school of love, a sacred *temenos*.

ESOTERIC KNOWLEDGE AND GNOSIS (*MAʿRIFAT*)

> The worship of God (*ʿibādat*) is nothing but gnosis (*maʿrifat*) of Him.
>
> Rūzbihān Baqlī (d. 606/1210)[82]

> "What," it well be Questioned, "When the Sun rises, do you not see A round disk of fire somewhat like a Guinea?" O no, no, I see an Innumerable company of the Heavenly host crying "Holy, Holy, Holy Is the Lord God Almighty." I question not my Corporeal or Vegetative Eye any more than I would Question a Window concerning A Sight. I look thro' it and not with it.
>
> William Blake[83]

> For in truth there has been a great destruction of hopes in the West, and there is no telling where this will end. Its most alarming symptom is the pious agnosticism that is paralyzing excellent minds and inspiring them with a panic terror before everything with the suspect aroma of "gnosis."
>
> Henry Corbin[84]

---

82 Rūzbihān Baqlī Shīrāzī, *Sharḥ-i shaṭḥīyyāt*, ed. H. Corbin (Bibliothéque Iranienne 12; Tehran: Departement d'iranologie de l'Institut Franco-iranien 1966), p. 94.

83 "A Vision of the Last Judgment," in *The Complete Writings of William Blake*, ed. G.L. Keynes (Oxford: Oxford University Press 1966), p. 617. Cited by Kathleen Raine, "The Underlying Order: Nature and the Order of the Imagination," in Barry MacDonald (ed.), *Seeing God Everywhere: Essays on Nature and the Sacred* (World Wisdom 2010), chap. 11, p. 174.

84 *Spiritual Body and Celestial Earth: From Mazdean Iran to Shīʿite Iran*, trans. [from French] Nancy Pearson (London: I.B. Tauris 1990), p. viii. Published in French as *Terre céleste et corps de résurrection: de l'Iran mazdéen à l'Iran shīʿite* (Paris: Buchet-Chastel 1960).

> There was a gnosis in Christianity; there has been one, and perhaps there still is, in Islam – and perhaps it may yet provide for an unforeseeable spiritual encounter between Orient and Occident. For gnosis itself, in all its manifold forms and variants, also deserves to be called a *Weltreligion*.
>
> Henry Corbin[85]

We must be grateful for several excellent studies that have explained the significance, place and historical development of *maʿrifa* (gnosis) in Islamic esotericism, thanks to which a thorough study of the history and conceptualization of the term in Muslim mystico-epistemological thought need not detain us here.[86] Furthermore, since *maʿrifa* and its sister terms *ʿilm* and *kashf* comprise central subjects of this anthology, the diverse meanings of these terms (and others related thereto), are exhaustively analysed throughout nearly all its chapters and their introductions, which the reader may access there.

A number of recent scholars (Roger Arnaldez,[87] John Renard,[88]

85 Henry Corbin, "From the Gnosis of Antiquity to Ismaili Gnosis," in *idem.*, *Cyclical Time and Ismaili Gnosis*, trans. Ralph Manheim and James Morris (London: KPI in association with Islamic Publications 1983), p. 193.

86 See Farid Jabre, *La Notion de la* maʿrifa *chez Ghazali* (Beirut: Éditions Les Lettres Orientales 1958); Franz Rosenthal, *Knowledge Triumphant: The Concept of Knowledge in Medieval Islam* (Leiden: Brill 1970), pp. 97–154; Reza Shah-Kazemi, "The Notion and Significance of *Maʿrifa* in Sufism," *Journal of Islamic Studies* XIII/2 (2002), pp. 155–81; John Renard, *Knowledge of God in Classical Sufism: Foundations of Islamic Mystical Theology* (New York: Paulist Press 2004), introduction.

87 R. Arnaldez, "Maʿrifa," *EI2* VI, pp. 568–71 [p. 571].

88 John Renard, *Knowledge of God in Classical Sufism: Foundations of Islamic Mystical Theology* (New York: Paulist Press 2004), p. 11 argues that gnosis appears to him to be an inadequate translation of *maʿrifa*, that the term means "access to the divine presence, perhaps even an invasion or being overcome by the reality of God. It includes both the experiential dimension and knowing in a way that 'gnosis' cannot quite convey. Aquinas's *cognito experimentalis* more closely approximates the meaning of *maʿrifa* as the Sufis developed it." However, Renard's strictures appear hardly apropos since the term gnosis (see below) always does imply a considerable degree of mystical experience as well as knowledge.

William Chittick,[89] Alexander Trieger[90]) have argued that the term 'gnosis'

89 He proposes to translate *maʿrifa* as "recognition," and *ʿārif* as "recognizer," arguing that "the distinction between *ʿilm* and *maʿrifa* coincides more or less with that between 'knowing' and 'recognizing' in English. 'Knowing' is such a basic human experience that it cannot be defined, not least because it is presupposed in every definition. 'Recognizing' is then a specific sort of knowledge, namely recovering in yourself a knowledge that you already know ... There are major problems, however, with using the words *gnosis* and *gnostic* [for *maʿrifa* and *ʿārif*], the least of which is that people associate these words with an ancient Christian heresy. A deeper problem is simply that Arabic *maʿrifa* is an everyday verb and noun, whereas in English *gnosis* is never used in daily conversation ... Another problem can be observed in practically all translations of Sufi texts available in English. In discussions of the recognizers – the 'gnostics' – the verbal form of *maʿrifa* is often used to explain the sort of knowing in question, which is to say that the sense of the passage hinges on using the word *maʿrifa* as a verb. But English has no verb for gnosis, so the specific characteristics of *maʿrifa* get lost in translation." – "Ibn al-ʿArabī: The Doorway to an Intellectual Tradition," *Journal of the Muhyiddin Ibn ʿArabi Society* LIX (2016), pp. 1–15 [p. 3]. However, the problems with these views are manifold, *viz.* (a) traditionally in neither classical nor modern theological discourse have English mystical writers have ever used 'recognizer' and 'recognition' to connote the type of 'esoteric sapience' and 'inspired knowledge' that *maʿrifa* normally refers to; (b) it is a far worse neologism to attempt to use a word for a connotation it doesn't possess, than to use a traditional word (such as gnosis) that has practically a synonymous meaning vis-à-vis the source-language word; (c) to expect native speakers of the English language to recast their usage of common terms such as 'recognizer' and 'recognition' (both of which have purely profane and secular connotations) to mean something as spiritually recondite as *ʿārif* and *maʿrifa* is I believe a kind of philological vandalism. Lastly (d), in another work on Ibn ʿArabī written 25 years earlier, he maintains precisely the opposite view, observing how many Sufis "placed *maʿrifa* at a higher stage than *ʿilm*, and in this context *it would be fair to translate the first as gnosis* and the second as knowledge. Then *maʿrifa* is equivalent to the direct knowledge called unveiling, witnessing and tasting." – *The Sufi Path of Knowledge: Ibn al-ʿArabī's Metaphysics of Imagination* (Albany: SUNY Press 1989), p. 148. Italics mine.

90 Alexander Trieger, *Inspired Knowledge in Islamic Thought: Al-Ghazālī's Theory of Mystical Cognition and its Avicennian Foundation* (London: Routledge 2012), p. 33 argues that since there is only a "soft" distinction between *ʿilm* and *maʿrifa* in Ghazālī's thought these terms are "virtually interchangeable," and therefore translation of the latter term as 'gnosis' is strictly inaccurate. Conceding the truth of this in some of Ghazālī's writings (although it does *not* apply at all to the treatise by Ghazālī translated below), Ghazālī's

should not be used to translate *ma'rifa*, despite the fact that this term is a traditional translation employed by a number of scholars in the field for nearly a century now, including the likes of E. Blochet,[91] R.A. Nicholson,[92] A.J. Arberry,[93] Paul Nywia,[94] Louis Massignon,[95] Titus Burckhardt,[96] Henry Corbin,[97] Carl Ernst[98] and Reza Shah-Kazemi,[99] etc. Accordingly, I

particular conflation of the two terms cannot be generalized to apply to all Islamic spirituality and esotericism, where the two terms are usually quite distinct. The problems with Trieger's own choice of translation of *ma'rifa* ('cognizance') and *al-'ārifūn* (as 'those who cognize') is that (a) these terms fail to connote any sense of mystical sapience or spiritual knowledge conveyed by their Arabic originals (see above note); and (b) when lifted outside the rather homely cardboard binding of his book, citation of his translations will require a battalion of footnotes to make any sense to the common reader.

91 See E. Blochet, whose *Etudes sur le gnosticisme musulman* (Rome 1913), is cited by Henry Corbin ("Iranian Studies and Philosophy," in his *The Voyage and the Messenger*, trans. J. Rowe [Berkeley: North Atlantic Books 1998], p. 43) who notes this work "identifies links between Hermeticism and the Iranian world." These links, which are further elaborated by Corbin in his "From the Gnosis of Antiquity to Ismaili Gnosis," pp. 151–93, are explored in greater detail by Keven van Bladel in *The Arabic Hermes: From Pagan Sage to Prophet of Science* (Oxford: Oxford University Press 2009), chap. 2: "Hermes in Sasanian Iran."

92 See his translation of Hujwīrī's *Kashf al-maḥjūb: The "*Kashf al-maḥjūb:*" The Oldest Persian Treatise on Sufism*, trans. R.A. Nicholson (Gibb Memorial Series, no. 17. 1911), reprinted frequently.

93 See A.J. Arberry's translation of Kalābādhī's *Kitāb al-ta'arruf* as *The Doctrine of the Sufis* (Cambridge: Cambridge University Press 1972), chapters 21–22.

94 P. Nwyia, *Exégèse Coranique et Langage Mystique* (Beirut: 1970), p. 107.

95 L. Massignon, *Essai sur les origines du lexique technique de la mystique musulmane* (Nouvelle édition) (Paris: J. Vrin 1954), pp. 65–66.

96 Titus Burckhardt, *Introduction auz doctrines ésotériques de l'Islam* (Paris: Editions Devry 1996), pp. 42–42 (using the French term '*gnose*').

97 See Corbin's "From the Gnosis of Antiquity to Ismaili Gnosis," p. 183 (rendering gnosis as *'ilm al-bāṭin*).

98 Carl Ernst "The Stages of Love in Early Persian Sufism," in Leonard Lewisohn (ed.) *The Heritage of Sufism*, vol. I: *Classical Persian Sufism from its Origins to Rumi (700–1300)* (Oxford: Oneworld 1999), pp. 436–37.

99 Reza Shah-Kazemi, "The Notion and Significance of *Ma'rifa* in Sufism," *Journal of Islamic Studies* XIII/2 (2002), p. 155, n. 1.

have favoured the latter more commonsense term – which is, incidentally, the majority view. The term 'gnosis' may have been abused, but the context of its proper use is explained *in extenso* by our authors below.

In the present anthology, the term *ma'rifa*, which denotes an experimental spiritual knowledge or esoteric sapience infused into the soul, thus has usually been rendered as *gnosis*, but occasionally also as *gnostic sapience* or *esoteric knowledge* depending on author, text or context; in certain places, it has been translated as *inspired knowledge* or *mystical knowledge* as well. In this respect, Antoine Faivre, taking a cue from Henry Corbin, underlines the contiguity of meaning obtained between the Greek term *gnōsis* and Islamic mystical knowledge or *ma'rifa*:

> The Greek word *gnōsis*, as also the related Sanskrit *jñāna*, means both 'learning' and 'sapiential wisdom', a double meaning that it tends to lose in late Greek thought and patristic Christianity. Its root, which also appears in the word *genesis*, in fact implies both learning and coming into being ... By giving birth to us – or rather rebirth – gnosis unifies and liberates us. To know is to be liberated. It is not enough to know symbols and dogmas in a merely external fashion; one must be engendered by them. Gnosis is thus not mere knowledge; between believing and knowing there is the knowledge of interior vision proper to the *mundus imaginalis*. These various types of knowledge have been clearly distinguished within Islamic gnosis as intellectual knowledge (*'aql*), knowledge of traditional facts that are the object of faith (*naql*), and knowledge through inner vision or intuitive revelation (*kashf*). It is this last that opens up the world of the imaginal.[100]

The doctrine of *kashf* is the fundamental principle of gnosis understood by all authors in this anthology. In Arabic, *kashf* literally means 'rending the veil' and is best translated by the French *dévoilement*,[101] signifies "obtaining consciousness of invisible spiritual conceptions or ideas and matters relating to divine 'truths' by means of interior vision (*shuhūd*) and presential

100 "Esotericism," in *Encyclopedia of Religion*, ed. M. Eliade (New York: Macmillan 1987), vol. 5, pp. 156–63 [pp. 157–58].

101 Farid Jabre, *Essai sur le lexique de Ghazali* (Beirut: L'Université Libanaise 1970), pp. 174–75.

intellectual vision (*ḥuḍūr*);"[102] also connoting "discovery, interior revelation, visionary perception, divination by the active imagination, in a word, all that is described by the word *hierognosis*, whose contact is the esoteric, the hidden, the supersensible, ... [and whose apprehension is by] intuitive perception and theosophical intuition."[103] As shall be seen, Abū Bakr al-Kalābādhī, Abū Ḥāmid al-Ghazālī, 'Ayn al-Quḍāt Hamadhānī,[104] Ibn 'Arabī, 'Izz al-Dīn Maḥmūd Kāshānī, Sayyid Ḥaydar Āmulī, Mullā Ṣadrā, 'Abd al-Razzāq Lāhījī and Hādī Sabziwārī all endorsed similar doctrines of gnosis and visionary unveiling with very little distinction in their mystical theologies. Sabziwārī, the leading philosopher of nineteenth-century Persia, went so far as to even pronounce visionary unveiling (*kashf*) to be the "fundamental principle" of all Islamic *ḥikmat* philosophy.[105]

Professor Faivre in the above quotation is thus entirely correct to interpret *ma'rifa* as the first fruits of intuitive revelation (*kashf*) and to equate this Muslim mystical intuitive vision with Greek *gnōsis*. Abū Bakr al-Kalābādhī, the first author translated in the anthology below, in this sense describes *ma'rifa* as leading to exactly the same sort of 'liberation' that is a

---

102 From the *Definitions* of Jurjānī: Mīr Sayyid Sharīf Jurjānī, *Kitāb al-ta'rīfāt*, ed. Ibrāhīm al-Abyārī (Beirut: 1985), p. 237. Thorough-going studies of this term can be found in Cyrus Ali Zargar, "Kašf o šohud," *EIr* XV, pp. 668–73; L. Gardet, "Kashf," *EI2* IV, pp. 696–68; and J. Nurbakhsh, *Sufi Symbolism* VII, pp. 34–38. As Jane Clark puts it, *kashf* refers "a moment of real insight when our vision penetrates through the veils of ordinary causality and we see for ourselves – witness – the underlying reality." – "Mystical Perception and Beauty: Ibn 'Arabī's Preface to the *Tarjumān al-ashwāq*," *Journal of the Muhyiddin Ibn 'Arabi Society* LV (2014), pp. 33–61 [p. 49]. In the text translated in chapter 11, 'Abd al-Razzāq Lāhījī notes thus: "the meaning of unveiling or visionary disclosure (*kashf*) is precisely this: that one contemplates and perceives things without any veil (*bī-parda*)."

103 Henry Corbin, "Traditional Knowledge and Spiritual Renaissance," trans. [from French] Kathleen Raine, *Temenos Academy Review* I (1998), pp. 29–45 [p. 38].

104 For further information about 'Ayn al-Quḍāt, see Mohammed Rustom, *Inrushes of the Heart: The Sufi Philosophy of 'Ayn al-Quḍāt* (Albany: SUNY Press 2023).

105 He maintained that it was of two types: spiritual and supraformal (*ma'nawī*), or sensory and formal (*ṣūrī*). The former enables the gnostic to grasp himself, God or the affairs of the hereafter through intuitive conjecture (*ḥads*) and meditative reflection (*fikr*), and the latter, apprehended through the ocular, olfactory faculties and the faculty of touch, occurs through an epiphany of various divine Names.

key characteristic of *gnösis* in Greek thought. The mystic, asserts Kalābādhī, must undergo a process of gradual character development by way of spiritual discipline, acquainting himself with the vices of the soul (*'ilm āfāt al-nafs*), knowledge of which then endows him with an understanding "the science of *theosophia* or esoteric sapience (*ḥikmah*)." After this,

> The soul perseveres in adhering to what has been prescribed for it, so that it learns good breeding and manners and becomes schooled in theomorphic ethics (*ādāb Allāh*), reining in its members and guarding its limbs and all its senses, then it becomes easy for a person to amend its character, and reform the soul's exterior so that it is no longer preoccupied with its own affairs, thus shunning and turning away from this world. Thereafter such a person is able to watch over his stray thoughts and purify his innermost consciousness. And this is what constitutes the science of gnosis (*'ilm al-ma'rifat*).[106]

Nearly a century and a half before Kalābādhī, Dhū'l-Nūn al-Miṣrī (d. 246/861): "the man who, more than any other, deserves to be entitled the founder of theosophical Ṣúfism,"[107] and who had advanced the first systematic teaching concerning the mystical states and spiritual stations (*aḥwāl u maqāmāt*), provided some of the first statements about *ma'rifa* in which he distinguished it from academic knowledge or *'ilm*. In the following saying we can see the experiential content of *ma'rifa* reflected:

> The Sufi is one whose conversation expresses the realities of the mystical state he experiences. Unless he *is* actually it, he says nothing; while when he falls silent, his conduct bears witness to his state, attesting to his severance of all attachments.[108]

Perhaps the most famous of early Persian Sufis, his contemporary Bāyazīd (or Abū Yazīd) Bisṭāmī, d. 234/848 or 261/875), was widely famed as the 'King of the Gnostics' (*Sulṭān al-'ārifīn*), renowned for his ecstatic sayings

---

106 The full passage is featured below in chapter one.

107 As R.A. Nicholson adjudicated: "A Historical Enquiry," p. 309.

108 'Aṭṭār, *Tadhkirat al-awliyā'*, p. 150; cited by Nurbakhsh, *Dhū'l-Nūn Miṣrī: Az Mashāhīr-i dānishmandān u ṣūfiyān-i Miṣr* (London: Khānaqāhī Ni'matu'llāhī 1999), p. 189.

and extraordinary spiritual discourses that are unsurpassed in depth and intensity by Sufis of either preceding or succeeding generations.[109] Bāyazīd's notion of esoteric knowledge is inextricably tied to his conception of mystical annihilation or *fanā'*, of which doctrine he is usually considered to be the founder.[110] He was once asked, "When does a man know that he has attained the reality of gnosis (*ḥaqīqat-i maʿrifat*)?" He replied, "Whenever he becomes annihilated under the omniscience of God and becomes eternally subsistent upon the wide expanse of God, without any self or creature. In this wise, he is a perishable being (*fānī*) who is eternal (*bāqī*), an eternal being who is perishable, a dead person who's living, a living person who is dead, a veiled person who is visibly exposed, and a clearly revealed being who is hidden from sight."[111]

In all such cases, *maʿrifa* involves an inspired state of mind;[112] that is, it expresses exactly the kind of sapience that the Sanskrit *jñāna* and the Greek *gnōsis*, as Faivre asserted above, denote. The locus of *maʿrifa*, however, is in the heart, not the brain or head, as Ghazālī states (*maḥall maʿrifat Allāh*, Pers. *maḥall-i maʿrifat-i khudā*).[113] In his *Risālat Ladunīyya*, translated in chapter two below, Ghazālī propounds that "the heart possesses its own organ of vision (*oculus cordis*) just like the body, so that just as the ocular eye beholds outward things, the intellectual eye (*ʿayn al-ʿaql*) perceives inward things, the esoteric spiritual realities (*al-ḥaqā'iq*)." In Sufism, most

109 On whom, see Leonard Lewisohn, "Bayazid Bistami," *The Encyclopædia of Religion*, ed. Lindsay Jones (New York: Macmillan Reference & Thomson Gale 2005), vol. II, pp. 955–57.

110 See R.A. Nicholson, "A Historical Enquiry concerning the Origin and Development of Sufism, with a list of definitions of the terms 'ṣūfī' and 'taṣawwuf', arranged chronologically," *Journal of the Royal Asiatic Society*, Part I, 1906, p. 325.

111 'Aṭṭār, *Tadhkirat al-awliyā'*, ed. R.A. Nicholson, I, pp. 168–69; cf. Nicholson, "A Historical Enquiry," p. 327.

112 This aspect of *maʿrifa* is elaborated by Reza Shah-Kazemi, "The Notion and Significance of *Maʿrifa* in Sufism," *Journal of Islamic Studies* XIII/2 (2002), pp. 155–81 [esp. pp. 155, 159, 162, 164–69].

113 Alexander Trieger, *Inspired Knowledge in Islamic Thought: Al-Ghazālī's Theory of Mystical Cognition and its Avicennian Foundation* (London: Routledge 2012), p. 17.

of whose key terms are of Qur'ānic inspiration and origin, spiritual intelligence is always located in the heart, not the head.[114]

As with the Greek word *gnōsis*, in Sufism, *ma'rifa* from its earliest usage has also been spoken of as comprising esoteric knowledge inspired by a certain state of soul; it is a condition of *being* as much as a species of *knowledge*.[115] According to Ghazālī, gnosis (*ma'rifat*) can only be obtained by means of the Sufi practices of remembrance of God and contemplation (*al-dhikr wa'l-fikr*) and abstaining from all but God Almighty.[116] Sufis thus discriminated between *'ilm-i kasbī* and *'ilm al-ilhām*: acquired and divinely infused knowledge, and asserted the latter to be superior to the former.[117] A succinct summary of the difference between these two types of knowledge, that is, academic ratiocination vs. mystical gnosis, or exoteric vs. esoteric knowledge, occurs in Rūmī's *Mathnawī*:

---

114 The key verses in the Qur'ān concerning the intelligence of the heart are as follows: "They have hearts, but they do not understand with them" (VII:179). "It is not the eyes that are blind, but blind are the hearts within the breasts." (XXII:46). "What, do they not ponder the Qur'ān. Or is it that there are locks on their hearts?" (XLVII:24). "You will not find the company of those who have faith in God and the Last Day loving those who oppose God and his Messenger even though they are their fathers or their sons or their brothers or their tribes. They are those upon whose hearts God has inscribed faith, and has strengthened them with a Spirit from him." (LVIII:22). Pickthall translation. Cited by William Chittick and Sachiko Murata, *The Vision of Islam*, p. 38, where they point out that the term "heart" as used in the Qur'ān "is not primarily the place of emotions. Rather, it is the specific faculty or spiritual organ that separates human beings from nonhuman beings. Usually we refer to it by words such as *intelligence* ... in the Qur'ānic view of things, a rational animal is an animal with a heart. A human being without a functioning heart is an animal, or worse." For further discussion, see Trieger, *Inspired Knowledge*, chap. 1: "Heart, Intelligence, Knowledge"; S.H. Nasr, "Scientia Sacra," in his *Knowledge and the Sacred* (Albany: SUNY Press 1989), pp. 150–51.

115 As Shah-Kazemi writes: "It is the conjunction between perfect knowledge and pure being that defines the ultimate degree of *ma'rifa*." – "The Notion and Significance of *Ma'rifa* in Sufism," p. 155.

116 *Kitāb al-Maḍnūn bi 'alā ghayr ahlihi*, cited by Ghulām Ḥusayn Ibrāhīmī Dīnānī, *Manṭiq u ma'rifat dar naẓar-i Ghazālī* (Tehran: Amīr Kabīr 1375 A.Hsh./1996), p. 193.

117 See Fadlou Shehadi, "Theism, Mysticism and Scientific History," in M. Marmura (ed.) *Islamic Theology and Philosophy: Studies in Honor of George F. Hourani* (Albany: SUNY Press), chap. 17.

> Intelligence (*'aql*) is of two types: the first is academic that you learn when a boy at school. Your mind comes to excel others through books and teachers, reflection and memorization, and by learning fine and novel ideas and sciences, although you are burdened down by the intellectual powers of retention that this requires. In the rotundas and pathways of the Academe, you become known as being a 'walking book' with a record memory. However, one who transcends this becomes a slate of knowledge that is divinely preserved.
>
> This other type of intelligence is a gift of God, a fountain that springs up within the soul. When that water of knowledge spurts from the breast, it never becomes stagnant, old or stale. If its channel becomes closed off, don't grieve, for it continues to gush out of the house every moment.
>
> Academic intelligence is just a drain-pipe that runs from the house into the street, which when the conduit of its water supply is blocked, becomes useless: you must then seek the fountain from within yourself.[118]

As Rūmī explains, left to itself, human academic intelligence can do nothing but acquire, retain, co-ordinate and perfect the second-hand materials with which it has been supplied by the senses and imagination, Rūmī informs us. The privilege of discovery of novel truths and bringing to light (*istikhrāj*) the unknown belongs only to the gnostics (*'urafā'*) who have reached the ultimate source of knowledge through *kashf* and become organs of the Universal Mind, for all sciences, arts and crafts derive ultimately from divine revelation.[119]

The second type of divinely bestowed intelligence, which is a product of visionary unveiling (*kashf*), the inspired sage of Konya calls the "Intellect of the Intellect" or "Supreme Intellect" (*'aql-i 'aql*) or "Universal Intellect" (*'aql-i kull*). This esoteric level of understanding is contrasted with the dry shell of academic reason (*qishr-i 'aql*) that blackens the pages of books but leaves the heart devoid of illumination.[120] Identical with 'particular reason'

---

118 *The Mathnawí of Jalálu'ddín Rúmí*, ed. R.A. Nicholson, 8 vols. (London: E.J.W. Gibb Memorial Trust 1924–40), Bk. IV: 1960–68. The above prose translation is mine.

119 See *Mathnawí* IV: 1292–1300.

120 Much of Rūmī's *Mathnawī* is devoted to explaining how one can transcend one's self-centred, deranged vision based on delusionary estimation (*wahm*) and reach the

(*'aql-i juzwī*) and 'worldly reason' (*'aql-i ma'āsh*), the latter sort of intelligence corresponds to the discursive reason of the natural philosophers. And only by spiritual practice and discipline can the supreme level of the Universal intellect be realized.[121]

In near identical terms, Ibn 'Arabī affirms in one of the texts from the *Futūḥāt* translated below:

> For the Sufis (*al-qawm*), gnosis (*ma'rifat*) is a practical path, a methodical way (of spiritual practice) (*maḥajja*), and thus gnosis involves every kind of knowledge that may be obtained through spiritual practice (*'amal*), god-fearing piety (*taqwā*), and through faring the (Sufi) path of ethical conduct (*sulūk*), since it is been obtained through visionary unveiling experientially verified and personally realized (*kashf muḥaqqiq*), to which no doubts or misgivings penetrate.

Similarly, Ḥaydar Āmulī (782/1380) asserts (in the extract translated below in chapter VIII) that anyone who seeks the knowledge of the divinely infused sciences (*al-'ulūm al-ilāhī al-ladunī*) "must engage in ascetic discipline (*al-riyāḍat*), practise bouts of solitary isolation (*al-khalwat*) and spiritual warfare (*al-mujāhadat*). He should strive to totally focus his attention on God, practise voluntary death (*al-mawt al-irādī*) and aspire to mystical annihilation (*fanā' al-'irfānī*) which will lead him to eternal life (*al-baqā' al-abadī*)."[122]

The earliest Sufi theorists such as Abū Naṣr al-Sarrāj (d. 378/988),[123] Ḥujwīrī (d. 463/1071) and Abū'l-Qāsim al-Qushayrī (d. 465/1074)

---

clear intellectual vision of the Truth underlying religious diversity – obtained only through different types of esoteric sapience and revelatory vision (*waḥy, kashf, ilhām, tajallī*). For a comprehensive discussion of which, see John Renard, *All the King's Falcons: Rumi on Prophets and Revelation* (Albany: SUNY Press 1994), pp. 28–30.

121 See *Mathnawí*, III: 2526–33. On the different degrees of mystical *'ilm* in the *Mathnawī*, see M. Estelami's excellent study: "The Concept of Knowledge in Rūmī's Mathnawī," in Leonard Lewisohn (ed.), *The Heritage of Sufism*, vol. I: *Classical Persian Sufism: from its Origins to Rūmī* (London: Oneworld 1999), pp. 401–8.

122 See my introduction to chapter eight.

123 See Michael Sells, *Early Islamic Mysticism: Sufi, Qur'an, Mi'raj, Poetic and Theological Writings* (New Jersey: Paulist Press 1996), p. 233.

advocated the strict separation of *'ilm* (traditional 'scientific' discursive knowledge) from *ma'rifa*, viewing the former as secular and general to ordinary theologians, and the latter as particular to the Sufis who are adepts in contemplative practices and spiritual vision.[124] We find this same strict division between *'ilm* and *ma'rifa* reiterated by Ḥaydar Āmulī (782/1380) in chapter VIII below.[125]

---

124 "As religious scholars generally use the term, *ma'rifa* is synonymous with *'ilm*, so that every variety of *'ilm* is a form of *ma'rifa*, and all *ma'rifa* belongs to the category of *'ilm*. Therefore, everyone who possesses *'ilm* about God possesses *ma'rifa*, and vice versa. According to the Sufis, however, *ma'rifa* is characteristic of an individual who is intimately familiar with God through His names and attributes, and whose actions towards God are entirely authentic, whose character has been rid of destructive tendencies and faults, who awaits God's pleasure, and whose heart is endlessly held in reserve for God. Such a person enjoys a beautiful closeness to God, and God in turn accommodates Himself to all the individual's spiritual states." – From Qushayrī's *Risāla*, trans. John Renard, *Knowledge of God in Classical Sufism: Foundations of Islamic Mystical Theology* (New York: Paulist Press 2004), p. 287. For the original, see *Al-Risāla al-Qushayrīyya*, ed. Khalīl al-Manṣūr (Beirut: Dār al-Kutub al-'Ilmīyah 1418/1998), *Bāb al-ma'rifat bi'llāh*, p. 342. Hujwīrī likewise explains: "Theologians make no distinction between knowledge (*'ilm*) and gnosis (*ma'rifa*), except that they say that God may be called *'ālim* (knowing) but not *'ārif* (gnostic), inasmuch as the latter epithet lacks Divine blessing. But the Sufi Shaykhs give the name of *ma'rifat* (gnosis) to every knowledge that is allied with (religious) practice and feeling (*ḥāl*), and the knower of which expresses his feeling; and the knower thereof they call *'ārif*. On the other hand, they give the name of *'ilm* to every knowledge that is stripped of spiritual meaning and devoid of religious practice, and the one who has such knowledge they simply call *'ālim*." – Hujwīrī, *Kashf al-maḥjūb*, ed. V.A. Zhukovskii (St. Petersburg 1899; repr. Leningrad 1926), p. 498; R.A. Nicholson (trans.), *The* "Kashf al-maḥjūb*:" The Oldest Persian Treatise on Sufism*, p. 382; also cited by Javad Nurbakhsh, *Sufi Symbolism: The Nurbakhsh Encyclopedia of Sufi Terminology*, trans. Terry Graham (London: KNP 1995), vol. IX, p. 148. For excellent analyses of the historical and philological distinctions between *'ilm* and *ma'rifa* in Sufism, see Shah-Kazemi, "The Notion and Significance of *Ma'rifa* in Sufism," pp. 156–64, and Renard, *Knowledge of God*, pp. 14–20.

125 E.g. his statement: "Gnosis (*al-ma'rifa*) to them (the true Sufis) is something quite different from knowledge (*al-'ilm*), and that gnosis, whether vis-à-vis the Necessary Being or of anything else, is of a higher degree than knowledge." And (later in the same text): "knowledge is more general and common than gnosis, while gnosis is more

However, this terminological distinction is seldom water-tight and for many of the authors in this anthology their difference is negligible, so that they largely categorize the varieties of esoteric knowledge as species of *'ilm*. In chapter four for instance, Rashīd al-Dīn Maybudī (d. 520/1126) explains the difference between three main types of knowledge in Islam as being the academic-homiletic (*'ilm-i ta'līmī*), logical-circumstantial (*'ilm-i istidlālī*), and the divinely infused esoteric (*'ilm-i ladunī*). He then elaborates the ten different branches of Islamic learning as being the science of divine Unity (*'ilm-i tawḥīd*), the science of jurisprudence (*'ilm-i fiqh*), the science of preaching and the academic sermon (*'ilm-i wa'ẓ*), the science of interpretation (of dreams and visions) (*'ilm-i ta'bīr*), the science of medicine (*'ilm-i ṭibb*), the science of astronomy (*'ilm-i nujūm*), the science of scholastic theology (*'ilm-i kalām*), the science of earning a livelihood (*'ilm-i ma'āsh*), the science of philosophy (*'ilm-i ḥikmat*) and the science of divine Reality (*'ilm-i ḥaqīqat*). In none of these passages is the word *ma'rifa* used at all.

Likewise, in chapter VII, we find Izz al-Dīn Maḥmūd Kāshānī (d. 735/1334) elaborating the tripartite division of "esoteric or divinely infused knowledge (*'ilm-i ladunī*)," subdivided into: divine revelation (*waḥy*), inspiration (*ilhām*) and cardiognosy (*firāsa*), in which esoteric knowledge is defined as a species of *'ilm*, not *ma'rifa*; it is *'ilm* that is, so to speak, gnostic and mystical by implication. Yet elsewhere in the same book, Kāshānī speaks of *ma'rifa* as gnosis in a similar language.[126]

---

particular and exclusive than knowledge, although both of them (*al-'ilm* and *al-ma'rifa*) can be designated as (modes of) 'knowledge'."

126 The following passage (from *Bāb-i sivām dar Ma'ārif ... Faḍl-i awwal dart ta'rīf-i ma'rifat*) is typical: "Gnosis (*ma'rifa*) signifies the recognition of universal objects of knowledge in their particularized forms. In the same way that in the science of Grammar, for instance, one recognizes how what action each verbal and phonetic form accomplishes – knowledge of which in summary form is the science of Grammar – ... Likewise, gnosis of God, which relates to and concerns has knowledge of the soul (*ma'rifat-i nafs*), just as the *ḥadīth* relates 'Whosoever knowledge himself knows his Lord,' signifies recognition of the divine Essence and Attributes in the particularized forms of the actions, occurrences, and circumstances, after in a summative manner (*sabīl-i ijmāl*) one has already understood that God Almighty is [alone] the Real Existent Being and the Absolute Agent." – *Miṣbāḥ al-hidāya wa miftāḥ al-kifāya*, ed. Jalāl al-Dīn Humā'ī (Tehran: Intishārāt-i Kitābkhāna-yi Sanā'ī, 2nd edn, n.d.), p. 80. See also Javad

In two out of the four selections translated below from his *Futūḥāt,* we find Ibn 'Arabī utilizing the term *'ilm,* not *ma'rifa,* in fact, to refer to gnosis. In the first (basing himself on Qur'ān LVIII:11), he distinguishes between two ways of acquiring knowledge of God: that obtained by "visionary unveiling (*al-kashf*), the knowledge of which is intuitively self-evident (*'ilm ḍarūrī*)," and "the way of reflection and demonstration by logical methods of reasoning and argumentation (*ṭarīq al-fikr wa'l-istidlāl bi'l-burhān al-'aqlī*)." In the second selection, he describes the three types of sciences – (i) rational science (*'ilm al-'aql*), (ii) the science of mystical states (*'ilm al-aḥwāl*) and (iii) the sciences of mysteries (*'ulūm al-asrār*) – making references to third type of mystical knowledge as *'ilm.* In neither of these passages is there any reference to *ma'rifa* at all.

In the third selection, however, which is devoted to "the Station of Gnosis (*maqām al-ma'rifa*)" and the one endowed with it who is named the "gnostic (*al-'ārif*)," he explicitly devotes himself to expounding the meaning of *ma'rifa.* Yet he refuses to take a stand in this terminological debate, and considers the divergence of views among scholars and mystics on the usage of *'ilm* and *ma'rifa* merely a matter of individual taste. Their differences of opinion on this matter are superficial, "insofar as what they denote as 'knowledge,' we interpret to be 'gnosis,' and what they designate as 'gnosis' we interpret as 'knowledge.' So our disagreement is merely verbal.'

Several of our authors, including Kāshānī and 'Ayn al-Quḍāt Hamadānī, make gnosis conditional upon following a Sufi teacher or the Prophet Muḥammad (or both). Although ultimately, all knowledge – even that derived from the Sufi master or from the Prophet Muḥammad – is self-knowledge, since all knowledge depends, epistemologically speaking, on self-awareness and consciousness,[127] it is incumbent that one recognize the

Nurbakhsh, *Sufi Symbolism: The Nurbakhsh Encyclopedia of Sufi Terminology,* trans. Terry Graham (London: KNP 1995), vol. IX, p. 140, for an alternative translation.

127 Thus, Rumi maintains the guidance of the spiritual master to be ultimately dependent upon the seeker's realization of his own 'universal intellect'. Intelligence is the true spiritual guide, he declares, and the 'spiritual master' (*pīr*) is ultimately that same illuminated intelligence (*pīr, pīr-i 'aql bāshad*) within him. – *Mathnawi* IV: 2163; see the ensuing passage in the *Mathnawi* (IV: 2164–81) where Rūmī discusses the fact that it is the intellect, as Universal Reason, which is real spiritual master, not the white-bearded shaykh, who is solely needed for those imprisoned in the veil of blind conformism, copying religious precedence (*taqlīd*).

role of the spiritual hierarchy in matters of gnosis. 'Ayn al-Quḍāt best expresses this paradox as follows:

> Once a man attains a spiritual station (*maqām*) in which he becomes intoxicated by the wine of gnosis (*sharāb-i maʿrifat*), so that he realizes the farthest degree of intoxication and the ultimate limit of his 'soul' (*khwud*), the soul of Muḥammad (*nafs-i Muḥammad*) is manifested to him, for [as the verse attests], "There has come to you a messenger from amongst yourselves."[128] All the days of his life then become like a garment whose embroidery is the "delight and peace of one who witnesses it." This must needs a fortune above and beyond which no higher fortune exists. Whoever obtains self-knowledge, realizing gnosis of his own soul (*maʿrifat-i nafs-i khwud*) also obtains knowledge and gnosis of Muḥammad's soul. Whosoever gains gnosis of the soul of Muḥammad sets the foot of his aspiration upon gnosis of the Divine Essence (*maʿrifat-i dhāt Allāh*). This is the meaning of (the Prophet's saying) "Whoever has seen me, has seen God,"[129] for whoever does not have self-knowledge or gnosis of himself does not have knowledge of Muḥammad, so how can he ever become a knower, a gnostic of God?[130]

Here, prophetology is the *fons et origo* of epistemology, and gnosis a species of the genus of prophecy. Kāshānī affirms exactly the same idea (using, however, *ʿilm* in lieu of *maʿrifa*) as well: "By knowledge (*ʿilm*) is meant a light derived from the Niche of Prophecy (*mishkāt-i nubuwwat*) that shines within the heart of the faithful devotee, by means of which he finds the way to God, or to a godly deed or to a divine precept." Kāshānī emphasizes the centrality of the Prophet in the acquisition of gnosis in this passage:

> Know that the origin (*maṣdar*) and source (*mansha'*) of all the sciences (*ʿulūm*) is the Divine Presence. Now, the first source-spring

128 Qur'ān IX:128.

129 Furūzānfar, *Aḥādīth-i Mathnawī*, p. 63.

130 The Persian text, which is slightly less formal and polished, literally reads: "Whosoever knows not himself is not a knower of Muḥammad, so how can he be a knower of God?" For further on this question of *maʿrifa* and the Prophet, see my translation of several passages from 'Ayn al-Quḍāt's *Tamhīdāt*, cited by Renard, *Knowledge of God in Classical Sufism*, pp. 52–54.

> from which the pre-eternal divine knowledge showered its grace was the pure heart of Muḥammad, whose pure prophetic soul, by means of a divine purification and purgation, had been purged of the murky blemishes of passional desire and the infirmities of nature ... And from the enlightened heart and pure soul of the Prophet flowed all the grace of the sciences (*'ulūm*), mystical states (*aḥwāl*) and all the ethics (*akhlāq*) and [performance of] meritorious deeds (*a'māl*) into the hearts and souls of the rest of the Muslim community (*ummat*) ... Every scintillation of light not derived from the Lamp of his Prophethood (*nubuwwat*) cannot in reality be called 'knowledge' (*'ilm*), for the sciences (*'ulūm*) of all the learned scholars (*'ulamā'*) are but a drop of water derived from the grace of his knowledge.

Likewise, acquisition of gnosis depends upon keeping the company (*ṣuḥbat*) of a spiritual master (*pīr*, *murshid*). As 'Ayn al-Quḍat relates in an autobiographical passage in his earliest extant composition, it was only due to his encounter with his master Aḥmad Ghazālī that his eye of inner vision itself was opened.[131]

Another important related matter of concern to the mystics in this anthology is the notion of the spiritual hierarchy of adepts that determines their degree of knowledge and gnostic realization. The idea of the esoteric hierarchy of the cosmos, although omnipresent throughout all schools of Islamic esotericism, has not really been the subject of any major study, although a number of good studies of theories of individual figures can be found.[132] The texts by Ṣā'īn al-Dīn Turkah Iṣfahānī (d. 830/1427) and 'Abd al-Razzāq Lāhījī (d. 1072/1661–2) translated in this anthology are largely devoted to delineating the hierarchy of spiritual adepts and the hierarchical classification of modes of gnosis.

Ṣā'īn al-Dīn Turkah proposes a sevenfold classification of adepts who are differentiated by their increasingly refined degrees of esoteric sapience.

---

131 This passage is cited in full in Lewisohn, "In Quest of Annihilation," pp. 291–92. See also Firoozeh Papan-Matin, *Beyond Death: The Mystical Teachings of 'Ayn al-Quḍāt Hamadhānī* (Leiden: Brill 2010), pp. 147–49.

132 On the notion of the esoteric hierarchy in Ibn 'Arabī's writings, for instance, see Michel Chodkiewicz, *Seal of the Saints: Prophethood and Sainthood in the Doctrine of Ibn 'Arabī*, trans. Liadain Sherrard (Cambridge: Islamic Texts Society 1993), pp. 103–15; Todd Lawson, "Friendship, Illumination and the Water of Life," *Journal of the Muhyiddin Ibn 'Arabi Society* LIX (2016), pp. 41–43.

The first three groups are exotericists (*ahl-i ẓāhir*) and the last four esoteric adepts (*ahl-i bāṭin*) belong to four respective schools: (1) Oriental Theosophers or Illuminationists (*ishrāqiyān*), (2) realized adepts in Sufism (*muḥaqqiqān-i ṣūfiyya*), (3) hermeneuts of the Qur'ān (*Ramz-khwānān-i ḥurūf-i Qur'ānī*) and lastly, (4) adepts in Qur'ānic Arithmomancy (*jafr*). Each school specializes in a different type of esoteric knowledge; each possesses a degree of insight and understanding higher than the adept inhabiting the degree immediately inferior.

As has been shown below in the introduction to the selections from 'Abd al-Razzāq Lāhījī's (d. 1072/1661–2) *Gawhar al-murād*, this Persian Shī'ite gnostic was indebted to the conception of the spiritual hierarchy of adepts outlined by Sunni Sufi Judge Ṣā'in al-Dīn Turkah Iṣfahānī. Both Lāhījī and Ṣā'īn al-Dīn Turkah spoke of complementary exoteric and esoteric ways and wayfarers to God; both maintained the two ways are distinguished in their exoteric approaches, as well as their conceptions of the esoteric *via mystica*. For Lāhījī, Sufism was one among the two 'esoteric ways' in the tradition of Islamic *theosophia* (*ḥikmat*), the other being illuminationism (*ishrāq*). The two exoteric ways are Peripatetic Philosophy (*mashshā*) and Scholastic Theology (*kalām*). Pursuit of the esoteric way, states Lāhījī, demands divine revelation, direction and guidance of a prophet, unlike the exoteric way, for the prophet has not been ordained to guide people "on the exoteric path and the way of logical demonstration (*rāh-i ẓāhir u istidlāl*)."

Lastly, almost all works on mystical epistemology in Islam in general, and in this anthology in particular situate gnosis (*ma'rifa*) at the supreme level of the sciences of realization of divine Unity (*tawḥīd*). Qushayrī in his celebrated *Al-Risāla fī 'ilm al-taṣawwuf* thus explains how the three stages of mystical visionary knowledge (*muḥāḍara* → *mukāshafa* → *mushāhada*) culminate in *ma'rifa* as follows:

> First comes presential vision (*muḥāḍara*), then contemplative unveiling (*mukāshafa*), then contemplation itself (*mushāhada*). The first [presential vision] is the presence of the heart (*ḥuḍūr al-qalb*) while it is dependent on the continuation of demonstrations (*tawātur al-burḥān*), and though the heart is still veiled, it is present through the overwhelming presence of the power to divine invocation (*sulṭān al-dhikr*). Then comes contemplative unveiling, which is the presence of the heart with greater clarity ... Then comes contemplation, which is the presence of God without a shadow of doubt. The adept in presential vision is

> restricted [in his contemplation] to the signs of God; the adept in contemplative unveiling experiences spiritual expansion through God's attributes, whereas [the knowledge of] the adept in contemplation is inspired by the divine Essence. The adept in presential vision is directed by his intelligence (*'aql*); the adept in contemplative unveiling experiences proximity to God through his knowledge (*'ilm*); and the adept in contemplation is annihilated in his gnosis (*ma'rifat*).[133]

Ultimately, through gnosis alone that one can find salvation, whether in this world or the Next. 'Ayn al-Quḍāt incites his reader:

> My cherished friend! Edify yourself through gnosis of your self, for gnosis in this world is the seed (which sprouts up into) the *Visio Dei* hereafter. What have you heard? I say: whoever possesses gnosis (*ma'rifat*) today will perceive the divine Vision (*ru'yat*) tomorrow ... Eternal felicity is inextricably tied to human self-knowledge: every person's portion of felicity will be in the same measure as his or her self-knowledge or gnosis of self (*ma'rifat-i khwud*).

The Persian poet Ḥāfiẓ, a poet for whom gnosis held a special place,[134] being famed as "the Tongue of the Invisible (*Lisān al-ghayb*) and the Interpreter of Mysteries (*tarjumān al-asrār*),"[135] expressed this truth in the following verse:

> Seek to gain the jewel of gnostic sapience;
> – Seize that for yourself and carry it away.
> Others shall be heirs of silver, gold and lucre.[136]

---

133 *Al-Risāla al-Qushayrīyya fī 'ilm al-taṣawwuf*, ed. Khalīl al-Manṣūr (Cairo: Maktabat Muḥammad 'Alī Ṣubayḥ 1386/1966), p. 111 (my translation). This passage is also cited by Trieger, *Inspired Knowledge*, p. 43.

134 I have discussed this aspect of the poet in a forthcoming article on "Ḥāfiẓ and Islamic Philosophy in Persia."

135 According to 'Abd al-Raḥmān Jāmī, *Nafaḥāt al-uns min ḥaḍarāt al-quds*, ed. Maḥmūd 'Ābidī (Tehran: Intishārāt-i Iṭilā'āt 1370 A.Hsh/1991), pp. 611–12.

136 *Dīwān-i Khwāja Shams al-Dīn Muḥammad Ḥāfiẓ*, ed. Parvīz Nātil Khānlarī (Tehran: Intishārāt-i Khawārazmī 1359 A.Hsh./1980), ghazal 360: 9.

HERMENEUTICS AND THE LANGUAGE OF SYMBOLISM IN ISLAMIC ESOTERICISM

These are only hints and guesses,
Hints followed by guesses; and the rest
Is prayer, observance, discipline, thought and action.

T.S. Eliot (*The Four Quartets*)

Looking at the first selection of the anthology, one of the most fascinating aspects of Mustamlī Bukhārī's (d. 434/1042–43) commentary is his discussion (see parts V-VI in chapter I below) of the mystical "science of symbolic allusions" (*'ilm al-ishārāt*), traditionally classified amongst the "esoteric sciences" (*'ulūm-i bāṭin*) of the Sufis.[137] Although symbolist discourse is, as Abū Bakr Kalābadhī (d. 380/990, whose text is the subject of Bukhārī's commentary) states, a "specialist science" reserved for the Sufis,[138] the language and literature of anagogy, allegory and symbolism in Islam was far from being their exclusive prerogative or preserve. Philosophers such as Ibn Sīnā (d. 428/1037) and Shihāb al-Dīn Yaḥyā Suhrawardī in fact elaborated important facets of their thought through visionary recitals that utilized allegorical-symbolical tales full of enigmatic ciphers (*ramz*) to convey important philosophical truths.[139] It might be said that the science of symbolic allusions played the same role in mystical hermeneutics (whether of scripture or poetry) in Islam as negative theology played in the Muslim scholastic philosophy (*Kalām*).

Symbolic discourse was also a highly developed feature of classical Persian Sufi erotic poetry,[140] whence 'Aṭṭār of Nishapur (d. c.627/1229) reminds us:

Love's discourse is all symbolic allusion (*ishārat*);
Love's not confined by borrowed tropes.[141]

---

137 Najm al-Dīn Rāzī, *Mirṣād al-'ibād*, ed. Muḥammad Amīn Riyāḥī (Tehran: Intishārāt-i 'Ilmī u farhangī 1374 A.Hsh./ 1995), pp. 481–82.

138 An hour perusing Javad Nurbakhsh's monumental sixteen-volume work: *Sufi Symbolism* (London and New York: KNP 1983–2004) suffices to prove the truth of Kalābadhī's claim.

139 Cf. W.P. Heinrichs, "Ramz," *EI2* VIII, p. 427; Peter Heath, *Allegory and Philosophy in Avicenna* (Philadelphia: 1992).

140 J.T.P. de Bruijn, *Persian Sufi Poetry* (Richmond: Curzon Press 1997), pp. 70–71.

141 *Dīvān-i 'Aṭṭār*, ed. T. Tafaḍḍulī (Tehran: B.T.N.K. 1967), p. 82.

Sufis such as 'Aṭṭār understood that the world invisible could be best beheld "by types, shadows, and metaphors" because, as John Bunyan put it:

> The prophets used much by metaphors
> To set forth truth; yea, who so considers
> Christ, his Apostles too, shall plainly see,
> That truths to this day in such mantles be.
> Am I afraid to say that Holy Writ
> Which for its style and phrase puts down all wit,
> Is everywhere so full of all these things
> (Dark figures, allegories), yet there springs
> From that same book that lustre and those rays
> Of light that turns our darkest nights to days.[142]

It is exactly for this reason that 'Izz al-Dīn Maḥmūd Kāshānī (d. 735/1334), a major selection of whose work is also translated in this anthology, points out that "no one can speak about knowledge of the Spirit (*ma'rifat-i rūḥ*) in mere descriptive expressions (*'ibārat*); it can only be spoken of in a language of allusion (*zabān-i ishārat*), as the adage goes: 'For the free man a single hint suffices (*Al-ḥurr yakfiyihi al-ishārat*).'"[143] All the great Persian poets, and so many of the thinkers featured in this anthology, knew this particular maxim by heart,[144] and used it to express their views on the ineffable realities of metaphysical speculation.[145] Kāshānī's contemporary, the poet Ḥāfiẓ (d. 791/1389) had summed it up in his celebrated verse,

142 R. Sharrock (ed.), *The Pilgrim's Progress* (London: Penguin Books 1987), p. 46.

143 *Miṣbāḥ al-hidāya*, ed. Jalāl al-Dīn Humā'ī (Tehran: Intishārāt-i Kitābkhāna-yi Sanā'ī, 2nd edn, n.d.), p. 94.

144 Cf. Rūmī, *Mathnawī*, ed. R.A. Nicholson, V: 1248; Sa'dī, *Būstān*, in *Kulliyāt-i Sa'dī*, ed. Muḥammad 'Alī Furūghī (Tehran: Amīr Kabīr 1363 A.Hsh./ 1984), p. 243. See also 'Alī Akbar Dihkhudā, *Amthāl va ḥikam* (Tehran: Intishārāt-i Amīr Kabīr 1388 A.Hsh./2009), vol. 2, p. 1086.

145 See, for example, 'Ayn al-Quḍāt Hamadānī, *Nāmahā-yi 'Ayn al-Quḍāt al-Hamadānī*, vol. 2, ed. 'Afīf 'Usayrān and 'Alīnaqī Munzawī (Tehran: Intishārāt-i Zawwār 1362 A.Hsh./1983), p. 274, lines 12–20.

The lesson visionaries inculcate
Consists of just one hint (*ishārat*):
That hint I've said and won't repeat it.[146]

Kāshānī's contrast between symbolist discourse and literalist expression, between the science of subtle mystical intimations and explicit literal statements (*'ibāra*), in Islamic esotericism goes at least as far back to Ja'far al-Ṣādiq (d. 148/765), who taught that there were four levels of interpretation of the Scripture, beginning with literal expressions (*'ibāra*), advancing to symbolic allusions (*ishāra*), to spiritual subtleties (*laṭā'if*) and finally ascending to esoteric truths and realities of the Spirit (*ḥaqā'iq*). In al-Ṣādiq's hermeneutics, as Paul Nwyia comments in his monograph on esoteric Qur'ānic exegesis, "each of these levels of interpretation was accompanied by the revelation of a proportionate interior illumination within the devotee, and out of this encounter between his mystical experience and the text was generated a new language, the mystical language."[147] This was not too different from the theory of the fourfold allegorical senses of the Christian scriptures that had been devised centuries earlier by Church Fathers, who divided their hermeneutics into literal, allegorical, moral and anagogical levels, with the significant difference that in Sufi teaching the expression and understanding of the final, anagogical sense (more or less corresponding to the level of *ishāra*) was viewed as *dependent upon* direct mystical experience (*kashf, shuhūd*).

Furthermore, the Sufi theorists of symbolism, unlike many of the Christian mystical theologians, such as Thomas Aquinas,[148] did not finesse the difference between the esoteric symbolical senses found in sacred scripture and those present in profane poetry. Both scripture and poetry were potentially held to harbour higher meanings; in fact, *Sufi poetry* came to be considered to be an expression of the language of allusion par excellence. Major chapters of treatises on *samā'*, such as the *Bawāriq al-ilmā'* by Aḥmad

146 *Dīwān-i Ḥāfiẓ*, ed. Parwīz Nātil Khanlarī (Tehran: Sahāmī 'ām 1362 A.Hsh./1983; 2nd edn), ghazal 345: 3.

147 *Exégèse Coranique et Langue Mystique* (Beirut: Dar El-Machreq 1970), p. 211.

148 On the Thomist view that secular poetry had only a literal, and not any higher, sense, see Umberto Eco, *The Aesthetics of Thomas Aquinas*, trans. Hugh Bredin (Cambridge: Harvard University Press 1988), pp. 148–65.

b. Muḥammad al-Ṭūsī[149] and even an entire book of *The Revivification of the Sciences of Religion* by Abū Ḥāmid al-Ghazālī[150] came to be composed – elucidating the proper method of listening to and comprehending the hidden mysteries within poetry and becoming attuned to its symbolic correspondences and mystical references. According to certain authors, listening to poetry was considered to be even more conducive to rapture than hearkening to recitation of the Qur'ān, due to the liturgical limitations of its prearranged system of cantillation.[151]

Underlying the philosophy of symbolic allusions propounded by Kalābādhī and Bukhārī was the distinction between three different modes of communion between God and man, respectively designated by the Sufis as inspiration (*ilhām*), symbolic allusion (*ishārat*) and the divine word (*kalām*). The first (*ilhām*) is defined as "God's summons addressed to the heart, through intuited by sapiential 'taste' (*dhawq*), but is not accompanied by conscious discrimination." The second degree (of symbolic allusion) "is a divine address intuited by means of sapiential 'taste' (*dhawq*), apprehended with conscious discrimination, but through a coded symbol (*ramz*) that is indirectly and only implicitly expressed." The knowledge and science of symbolic allusions (*'ilm al-ishārat*) can only be apprehended through the subtle organ of the heart (*'ayn al-qalb*).[152] The ultimate degree, that of the divine word, is a "divine address intuited by means of sapiential 'taste' (*dhawq*), apprehended with conscious discrimination, clearly and directly communicated."[153]

Likewise, (within the second degree) there are two types of symbolic allusion: of God and of man. As Rūzbihān Baqlī (d. 606/1210) – an author central to the Sufi esoteric tradition but omitted from this anthology only

149 See James Robson, *Tracts on Listening to Music* (London: RAS, Oriental Translation Fund, vol. 34 NS, 1938).

150 Abū Ḥāmid al-Ghazālī's *Kitāb ādāb al-samā'y wa'l-wajd*, in his *Iḥyā' 'ulūm al-dīn* (Damascus: n.d.), II, pp. 246ff.

151 Ghazālī, *Iḥyā' 'ulūm al-dīn* II, p. 261. See also my "The Sacred Music of Islam: *Sama'* in the Persian Sufi Tradition," *The British Journal of Ethnomusicology* VI (1997), pp. 1–33.

152 Hence, Ḥakīm al-Tirmidhī states: "The heart, then, is the seat of knowledge of allusion (*'ilm al-ishārah*)." – Kenneth L. Honerkamp (trans.), *Three Early Sufi Texts:* Two texts from the Path of Blame by Abū 'Abd al-Raḥmān al-Sulamī al-Naysabūrī (d. 412/1021) and *A Treatise on the Heart,* attributed to Al-Ḥakīm al-Tirmidhī (d. c.300/912), trans. Nicholas Heer (Louisville: Fons Vitae 2003), p. 27.

153 Rāzī, *Mirṣād al-'ibād*, p. 366.

for lack of space – explained: the first is from the gnostic to the divine Object of Knowledge (*'ārif bi-ma'rūf*) and the second from the divine Object to the gnostic (*ma'rūf bi'ārif*). The former type of allusion is merely delusion, albeit divinely inspired: it is "God's deceit unto the soul (*makr-i Ḥaqq bi-nafs*)." The latter type has its own dangers as well because "when the gnostic becomes preoccupied with these dark communications he will fall into associating others with God (*shirk*) and heresy (*kufr*)."[154] For this reason Bukhārī underlines that "symbolic allusions must be made directly *through* God," that is, there must be no interference from the ego, otherwise one falls into the heresy of anthropomorphism (*tashbīh*). One cannot reach God either through a thought or a symbolic allusion starting *from oneself*: one must start *from God* Who Himself communicates Himself symbolically.[155] Hence, Bukhārī takes care to stress that the "divine locution" addressed to the innermost-heart-consciousness (*sirr*) of the mystic, if understood in its deepest sense, "is not God's own allusion, although its *deeper interior signification* does indeed point to God."

Mustamlī Bukhārī also emphasizes Islamic sciences, particularly the science of social transactions (*'ilm-i mu'āmalāt*) and that knowledge of symbolic allusions depends on having a thorough background in the other science of *theosophia* or esoteric sapience (*'ilm-i ḥikmah*). It is necessary that the mystic be well grounded in different varieties of knowledge (*'ilm*), that the interior consciousness of her heart purified and in ascetic struggle (*ṣidq-i mujāhidat*) she be adept, since whoever "occupies himself with the science of symbolic allusions while not having learned the other sciences, will fall into error and make mistakes." One recalls Ḥāfiẓ's famous quip in this context:

When you hear the words of the heart-specialists,
Don't say they're wrong. As an assessor of words,
You're not a good judge, my dear; that's where the error is.[156]

---

154 Rūzbihān, *Sharḥ-i shaṭḥiyyāt*, ed. Henry Corbin (Tehran: Institut Français d'Iranologie 1981), p. 268.

155 As Hellmut Ritter points out, the Sufis generally avoided all expressions that contained *ishāra ilā'llāh*, that is, explicit allusions to God as being in a certain place. See his *The Ocean of the Soul: Men, the World and God in the Stories of Farīd al-Dīn 'Aṭṭār*, trans. John O'Kane (Leiden: Brill 2003), p. 81.

156 *Dīwān-i Ḥāfiẓ*, ed. Khānlarī, ghazal 26, v. 1. Translated by Robert Bly and Leonard Lewisohn.

And because the science of symbolic allusions is the supreme science, Mustamlī Bukhārī deduces that its knower – "the true Sufi – is one who in reality is the most learned person of his day and age."

In Ibn 'Arabī's theosophy, the ability to decode the esoteric senses of the Scripture and understand the multivalence of its allusions – the *ishāra* which the mystic finds within himself – is what fundamentally sets the exoteric *Sharī'a*-oriented jurist at odds with the Sufi adept. When divine grace vouchsafes to the mystic a revelation of the hierarchy of inner senses within the sacred text, the envy of the exoteric authorities who lack (and thus reject) such knowledge is aroused; consequently, he asserted, "no one is more onerous and troublesome for the Sufis than the exoteric scholars (*'ulamā al-rasūm*)."[157] To protect themselves from such literalists congenitally insensible to all higher allegorical interpretations, the language of the heart, that is, of symbolic allusions, has been established.[158] If a novice enters among the Sufis for the first time, while knowing nothing of these allusions, Ibn 'Arabī explains that he seems automatically to become "attuned" to all the meanings of their technical terms. Those terms and allusions are apprehended spontaneously just as poetry is appreciated by the poetically minded: imbibed through the faculty of heart-savour (*dhawq*). Contrary to all the other sciences that are learned methodically through study and memorization of their technical terms, for the Sufi novice God immediately "opens the eye of his understanding and he takes form his Lord at the beginning of his sapiential spiritual savour, even though he had no news of the terminology they were using ... Then this sincere seeker understands everything they are talking about, as if he had established the technical terms. He shares with them in their conversation and does not find that strange within himself. On the contrary, he finds it all a self-evident knowledge which he is unable to repel. He does not know how he gained it. But the one who comes from the outside, in all the other groups, never finds this unless someone has first acquainted him with the terms."[159]

In the first selection below (chap. I), Bukhārī explains that symbolic allusions are manifestations of affectional states of mystical consciousness known as *aḥwāl*: they represent the adept's attempt at indicating (*ishāra bi*) the ineffable states of his heart, states incomprehensible to anyone who has not experienced them. Hence, Bukhārī informs us, these allusions transcend "literal

157 From the *Futūḥāt*, cited by William Chittick, *The Sufi Path of Knowledge*, p. 246.

158 Chittick, *The Sufi Path of Knowledge*, p. 247.

159 Chittick, *The Sufi Path of Knowledge*, p. 250.

representation, qualification and finite limitation, such that anyone might be able to describe, designate, qualify or determine its meaning according to some limited, literalistic definition." As for the actual content of *ishārāt,* Paul Nwyia's observation[160] that the basic polarity between *ibāra* and *ishāra* is *not* like the opposition of realistic language to symbolical language, but rather more like the opposition of communicable types of expression (explicit literal definitions of an idea, for instance) to incommunicable and ineffable modes of discourse (implicit meanings within bars of music, for instance), clarifies that they belong to the Islamic discourse of apophasis.[161]

Stressing the inspired nature of symbolic allusions, Bukhārī informs us that they are constantly in transit and flux, since they have been generated from flashes of "revelation and ravishing, revealing and stealing," that is, born of instants of contemplative awareness and vision. This is, of course, what poets the world over have held to be true regarding the language of imagination as well. Referring to the same idea, the nineteenth-century 'Transcendentalist' philosopher Ralph Waldo Emerson wrote, "the quality of the imagination is to flow and not to freeze. The poet did not stop at the colour, or the form, but read the meaning; neither may he rest in this meaning ... For all symbols are fluxional; all language is vehicular and transitive and is good, as ferries and horses are, for conveyance, not as farms and houses are, for homestead."[162]

Mystics and poets throughout the world have complained that, in John Donne's words, "Language thou are too narrow"[163] and the sentiment that REALITY is an expanse too constricted for words leads naturally to a symbolist mentality in which polysemy is a basic assumption in all forms of linguistic expression. According to Bukhārī's theory, the secret source and ultimate significance of all vocalized speech is symbolic speech (*ishāra*). All outward thoughts are actually derivative reflections of the esoteric intentions of the conscience and heart; hence: "outer verbal expressions (*'ibārat*) are but the effect of the inner language of symbolic allusion (*ishārat*), just as one's outer physical activity is but the effect of inner thoughts and

---

160 "Ishāra," *EI2* IV, p. 114.

161 On which, see Michael Sells, *Mystical Languages of Unsaying* (Chicago: University of Chicago Press 1994), introduction.

162 "The Poet," in *Ralph Waldo Emerson: Essays and Lectures,* p. 463.

163 From his "Elegie: Death," in *The Complete Poetry and Selected Prose of John Donne,* ed. Charles Coffin (New York: Modern Library 2001), p. 225.

reflections." Words here take on multiple meanings.[164] "Symbolic allusion" is thus not only the natural linguistic expression of the Sufi mystical experience, but the central ontological fact of both language and being.[165]

Ultimately, the only way to approach the language of the heart, upon which Kalābādhī and Bukhārī's theory of *ishārāt* is based, is to recapture the language of analogy whose terms establish relations of an imaginal character, within a transcendent, immaterial hierarchy of being that is considered today by our contemporary rationalist mentality to be a completely fanciful and vacuous delusion.[166] Hence, we need to recreate the universe of reference – the theological spiritual and intellectual contexts of the esotericism upon which such thought is based. In the lexicon of criticism, this is called "the anagogic phase" of literary symbolism. Northrop Fyre's classic analysis of this level of symbolism here merits citation:

> In the anagogic phase, literature imitates the total dream of man, and so imitates the thought of a human mind which is at the circumference and not at the center of its reality ... When we pass into anagogy, nature becomes, not the container, but the thing contained, and the archetypal universal symbols, the city, the garden, the quest, the marriage, are no longer desirable forms that man constructs inside nature, but are

164 The modern French Sufi thinker, René Guénon, in this respect observed, "every expression, every formulation, whatever it may be, is a symbol of the thought that expresses it outwardly. In this sense, language is nothing other than symbolism. There can be no opposition, therefore, between the use of words and the use of figurative symbols; rather, these two modes of expression should be complementary to one another." "Word and Symbol," in Guenon, *Fundamental Symbols: The Universal Language of Sacred Science*, trans. Alvin Moore (Cambridge, UK: Quinta Essentia 1995), p. 13.

165 Guénon's reflections here are also relevant, "If the Word [Logos] is Thought inwardly, and Word outwardly, and if the world is the result of the Divine Word at the beginning of time, then nature in its entirety can be taken as a symbol of supernatural reality. Everything that exists, whatever its mode, having its principle in the Divine Intellect, translates or represents this principle in its own way and according to its own order of existence ... This correspondence is the veritable basis of symbolism and this is why the laws of a lower domain can always be taken to symbolize realities of a higher order." – "Word and Symbol," p. 15.

166 On which, see Kathleen Raine's essay "On the Symbol," in *idem.*, *Defending Ancient Springs* (Cambridge: Golgonooza Press 1985), pp. 105–22.

> themselves the forms of nature. Nature is now inside the mind of an infinite man who builds his cities out of the Milky Way ... The form of literature most deeply influenced by the anagogic phase is the scripture or apocalyptic revelation. The god, whether traditional deity, glorified hero, or apotheosized poet, is the central image that poetry uses in trying to convey the sense of unlimited power in a humanized form.[167]

Thus, when Bukhārī affirms that "symbolic allusions must be made directly *through* God, not acquired and learned (by human means)," he means exactly what Plato in the Ion calls the inspiration of the Muses which come to poets who write directly from the imagination, what great poets such as Shelley and Blake meant when they said that their poems were not written "by labour or study."[168] It is for this reason that poetry became the major vehicle for Sufi ideas in later Islamic thought, for the anagogic mode of understanding as Fyre put it "is to be discovered chiefly in the more uninhibited utterances of the poets themselves."[169]

---

167 Northrop Frye, *Anatomy of Criticism: Four Essays* (Princeton: Princeton University Press 1971, 3rd edn), pp. 119–20. I have discussed Frye's theory of the anagogic phase of literature in my "English Romantics and Persian Sufi Poets: A Wellspring of Inspiration for American Transcendentalists," in Mehdi Aminrazavi (ed.), *Sufism and American Literary Masters* (Albany: SUNY Press 2014), pp. 15–52.

168 Cf. Shelley: "Poets are the Hierophants of an unapprehended inspiration, compelled to serve the power which is seated in the throne of their own soul ... I appeal to the greatest poets of the present day, whether it is not an error to assert that the finest passages of poetry are produced by labour and study." Blake, introducing his poem *Milton*, likewise stated that portions of his poem were written "from immediate dictation, twenty or thirty lines at a time without Premeditation and even against my Will ... all produced without Labour or Study."

169 Frye, *Anatomy of Criticism*, p. 122. Some of the reasons why poetry represents the height of esoteric language of *ishāra* are discussed by Cyrus Ali Zargar, "The Poetics of *Shuhūd:* Ibn al-ʿArabī's 'Intuitive, Enamored Heart' and the Composition of Erotic Poetry," *Journal of the Muhyiddin Ibn ʿArabi Society* XXXV (2013), pp. 13–36.

I

THE SCIENCE OF SYMBOLIC ALLUSIONS

Selections from Abū Ibrāhīm Ismā'īl b. Muḥammad Mustamlī Bukhārī's (d. 434/1042–43) *Sharḥ Ta'arruf li-madhhab al-taṣawwuf*

Chapter one offers the first substantial translation into any European language from the earliest and the first major work on Sufism written in Persian, namely *Sharḥ al-Ta'arruf*,[1] a multi-volume commentary by Abū Ibrāhīm Ismā'īl b. Muḥammad b. 'Abdu'llāh Mustamlī Bukhārī on the *Introduction to the Creed of the Sufis* (*Kitāb al-ta'arruf li-madhhab ahl al-taṣawwuf*) by Abū Bakr b. Abī Isḥaq b. Muḥammad b. Ibrāhīm b. Ya'qūb al-Kalābādhī al-Bukhārī (d. 380/990). As with so many scholars and mystics of his day, very little biographical information on Mustamlī Bukhārī is extant. Like Kalābādhī,[2] of whom he may have been a student, Mustamlī Bukhārī followed the Ḥanafī rite, a juridical school particularly favoured by the Persian Samānids (204/819–395/1005) and actively promoted and

1 Edited by Muḥammad Rawshān (Tehran: Intishārāt-i Asāṭīr 1363 A.H.sh./1984), 5 vols. The original Arabic source that was the object of his commentary was translated into English by A.J. Arberry as *The Doctrine of the Sufis* (Cambridge: Cambridge University Press 1972). An abridged Persian edition of the commentary came out in Tehran in 1970, the *Khulāsa-yi Sharḥ al-Ta'arruf*, ed. Aḥmad 'Alī Rajā'ī. The commentary itself sailed under a number of names in various manuscripts, including *Nūr al-murīdīn wa faḍīḥat al-mudda'īn* and *Kashf al-maḥjūb Sharḥ al-Ta'arruf*.

2 S.H. Nasr, "Sufism," in R.N. Fyre (ed.), *The Cambridge History of Iran: From the Arab Invasion to the Saljugs* (Cambridge: Cambridge University Press 1975), vol. IV, pp. 442–63 (461). On Kalābādhī, see W. Madelung, "Abū Bakr al-Kalābādī," *Encyclopædia Iranica* I, pp. 262–63; Ahmet Karamustafa, *Sufism: The Formative Period* (Edinburgh: Edinburgh University Press 2007), pp. 69–70; Suhaylā Ghaḍanfarī, "Abū Bakr Kalābādhī," *Dānishnāma-yi zabān u adab-i fārsī*, ed. Ismā'īl Sa'ādat (Tehran: Farhangistān-i zabān u adab-i fārsī 1384 A.Hsh./2005), I, pp. 120–21.

patronized by the Seljuks (431/1040–590/1194).[3] Famed for its emphasis on faith over works,[4] the Ḥanafite school was popular amongst many Sufis in Transoxiania.[5] Mustamlī Bukhārī was tolerant, open-minded and a devoted lover of the Persian language and letters. Samʿānī (d. 562/1166), in his famous biographical dictionary of scholars, *Al-Ansāb*, seems to object to Bukhārī's personality for this very open-mindedness:

> He was a jurisprudent and traditionalist who tended towards following the denomination of the scholastic theologians (*mutakallimūn*) in the principles of jurisprudence, but in this book – *Sharḥ al-Taʿarruf* – he has mentioned some heretical innovations of which one should be beware.[6]

Kalābādhī's *Introduction to the Creed of the Sufis* is an important summary of, as well as integration of, Islamic exotericism with Sufism. It bears comparison with "the oldest surviving general account of Sufism"[7] written in Arabic, namely, the *Illumination of Sufism* (*Kitāb al-lumaʿ fī'l-taṣawwuf*) composed by his contemporary fellow-Khurāsānian Sufi master Abū Naṣr Sarrāj al-Ṭūsī (d. 378/988), which influenced Kalābādhī in places.[8] Both Sarrāj al-Ṭūsī and Kalābādhī al-Bukhārī, by means of extensive quotation from earlier Muslim mystics and sages, and through citation of relevant Qur'ānic verses and *ḥadīth*, endeavoured to reconcile the doctrines and *ṭarīqat* of Sufism with the *sharīʿat* of Islam.[9]

In the later Sufi tradition the importance of Kalābādhī's manual is reflected in the oft-quoted Arabic maxim: "If it weren't for the *al-taʿarruf*, Sufism would have all gone to waste." (*law lā al-taʿarruf la-baṭala*

---

3 Martin Nguyen, *Sufi Master and Qur'an Scholar: Abūl-Qāsim al-Qushayrī and the Laṭā'if al-Ishārāt* (Oxford: Oxford University Press in association with the Institute of Ismaili Studies 2012), pp. 39–40.

4 Merlin Swartz, "Hanafite Madhab," *Encyclopædia Iranica* I, pp. 651–53 [p. 652].

5 Karamustafa, *Sufism: The Formative Period*, pp. 96–108.

6 Cited by Muḥammad Rawhan, *Sharḥ al-Taʿarruf* I, introduction, p. 7.

7 A.J. Arberry, *Sufism: An account of the Mystics of Islam* (New York: 1970), p. 67.

8 Ahmet Karamustafa, *Sufism: The Formative Period* (Edinburgh: Edinburgh University Press 2007), p. 69.

9 Muḥammad Rawshān (ed.), *Sharḥ al-Taʿarruf*, introduction, p. 5; ʿAbd al-Ḥusayn Zarrīnkūb, *Justujū-yi dar taṣawwuf-i Īrān* (Tehran: Amīr Kabīr 1357 A.Hsh./1978), p. 69.

al-taṣawwuf).[10] Bukhārī's commentary on Kalābādhī is also important in several ways; on the one hand, it is "one of the richest sources for the study of the history and doctrine of early Sufism,"[11] and on the other, constitutes "the earliest work on Sufism in Persian,"[12] codifying and expanding its doctrines. Yet Mustamlī Bukhārī's *Sharḥ al-Taʿarruf* has received far less attention and study than it deserves from scholars of early Khurāsānian Sufism.[13]

It should be underlined that Bukhārī's vast mystical encyclopaedia (1818 pages of small print, published in four large volumes, with a fifth volume featuring extensive indices) is a far more ancient, far more original and in many respects, a more important work than ʿAlī Hujwīrī's (d. 464/1071–2) *Kashf al-maḥjūb* (Unveiling of Mysteries). The latter work, a systematic manual on Sufi methodology, teachers, doctrines, terminology and mystical theology written in Persian, was heavily influenced by Sarrāj's Arabic *Kitāb al-lumaʿ*. Hujwīrī's work certainly was *not*, as its English translator R.A. Nicholson claimed, "the most ancient and celebrated Persian treatise

10 Zarrīnkūb, *Justujū*, p. 70. For a good account of Kalābādhī's *Taʿarruf* and its place in the Sufi tradition, see also Renard, *Knowledge of God*, pp. 31–33.

11 S.H. Nasr, "Sufism," in R.N. Fyre (ed.), *The Cambridge History of Iran: From the Arab Invasion to the Saljugs* (Cambridge: Cambridge University Press 1975), vol. IV, pp. 442–63 [p. 461].

12 Naṣru'llāh Pūrjavadī, "Fārsī-gū'ī ʿārifān-i nakhustīn," Part 2, *Nashr-i Dānish*, Year 20, No. 1, Spring 1382 A.Hsh./ 2003), p. 12; and Muhammad Rawshan, *Sharḥ al-Taʿarruf*, introduction, p. 3.

13 For instance, it is overlooked by Jacqueline Chabbi, in her "Remarques sur le développement historique des mouvements ascétiques et mystiques au Khurasan," *Studia Islamica* XLVI (1976): 5–72. Paul Nywia, in his article on "Al-Kalābā<u>dh</u>ī" (*EI2* IV, p. 467), does not even mention it, and W. Madelung, in his article on "Abū Bakr Kalābā<u>d</u>ī Bo<u>k</u>ārī Moḥammad b. Abī Esḥāq Ebrāhīm b. Yaʿqub" (*EIr* I, pp. 262–63), cites it but seems unaware of Rawshan's monumental critical edition of this text. Many important scholars in Iran, such as Muḥammad Taqī Bahār in his discussion of early Persian Sufi works (*Sabk-shināsī: Tārīkh-i taṭawwur-i nathr-i fārsī* [Tehran: Chāpkhāna-yi Khwud-kār, n.d.], II, p. 53), seem completely unaware of this work. Even Dhabīḥu'llāh Ṣafā, *Tārīkh-i adabiyāt-i Īrān* (Tehran: Intishārāt-i Firdaws 1373 A.Hsh./1994, 13th edn), II, p. 227, skips over the work as being just a Persian "translation" of Kalābādhī without noting either its content or importance!

on Súfism."[14] Rather, if to any work such a label can be more or less accurately given, it should be Mustamlī Bukhārī's *Sharḥ al-Ta'arruf*.[15]

In the prologue to the *Sharḥ al-Ta'arruf*, Mustamlī Bukhārī explains that he composed his commentary "in order to become worthy of being graced by the blessings of the sages of ore, that I might myself become an advanced adept rather than just a novice – so that none would be able to pick fault with me. Therefore, everything I have said, I have corroborated by reference to either a verse from the Book of God Almighty or else to a report (*khabar*) from God's messenger or citation of a relevant juridical doctrine. I have consecrated this book to expounding the [true orthodox] belief regarding divine Unity (*tawḥīd*), true piety (*diyānāt*), mystical states (*aḥwāl*), spiritual stations (*maqāmāt*), divine realities (*ḥaqā'iq*), contemplative experience (*mushāhadat*), arcane mysteries (*rumūz*), symbolic allusions (*ishārāt*) and to citing the *dicta* and *exempla* of the past Sufi masters, according to the doctrine of [those who follow the] *Sunnat va jamā'at*."[16] Little else than this is known of Bukhārī's mission or motives in composing his work.

The selections translated from this work here, which also include an extract from the text of Kalābādhī's *Kitāb al-ta'arruf*, are devoted to elucidating the meaning of some of the most basic Sufi concepts relating to esoteric knowledge, revealing the basic gist and sense of 'theosophical wisdom' (*ḥikmat*), 'gnosis' (*ma'rifa*), 'visionary unveiling' (*kashf*), 'symbolic

14 *Kashf al-maḥjūb*, trans. R.A. Nicholson, p. xvii.

15 See Jawid Mojaddedi, "Kašf al-Maḥjub of Hojviri," *EIr* XV, pp. 664–66 [p. 664]. As Gerhard Böwering put it: "This is the oldest surviving Ṣūfī treatise in Persian prose ... The value of this voluminous source for the development of Sufism in Transoxiana lies in its copious comments on each Ṣūfī statement quoted in the *Ta'arruf*, and in the fact that it was compiled with apparently no motive other than the instruction of Ṣūfī disciples. From the point of view of the Persian language, the work gives testimony to dialectical forms of tenth-century Persian, with an extraordinary frequent occurrence of Arabic words." "Kalābādhī, Al-," *Encyclopædia of Religion*, ed. M. Eliade, 1st edn, VII, p. 230.

16 *Sharḥ al-Ta'arruf* I, pp. 33–34. This was the epithet that members of the Ḥanbalī school gave themselves and all those whom they deemed to be 'orthodox' Muslims. Despite belonging to the Ḥanafī school, in theology Kalābādhī adhered closely to the creed of Abū Ḥanbal. As Arberry observes, the introduction of the *al-Ta'arruf* "reads like an amplification of the *Fiqh Akbar*," the famous work on Ḥanbalī theological doctrine. *Doctrine of the Sufis*, p. xiv, n. 2.

allusions' (*ishārāt*), 'esoteric knowledge' (*ʿilm al-bāṭin*), etc. One of the most important of these themes: the "science of symbolic allusions (*ʿilm al-ishārāt*), has already been discussed in a separate section on "Hermeneutics and the Language of Symbolism" of the introduction above. Since both the theological doctrines and theosophical subject matter of the passage under commentary will appear out of context unless situated within Kalābādhī's whole chapter, I have retranslated – so as to better introduce the text of the commentary which follows – the Arabic text of a large part of Kalābādhī's chapter 31, from its beginning down to the last line of the section subject to Mustamlī Bukhārī's exegesis.[17] I have already given a summary of the basic motifs and ideas in these passages in my introduction above (see "Hermeneutics and the Language of Symbolism in Islamic Esotericism").

The expression and elaboration of all these concepts in later Sufism over the course the ensuing centuries, whether in prose in mystical *rasāʾil* or in verse in Sufi *dīwāns*, has been heavily indebted to – and in fact often modelled on – Mustamlī Bukhārī's lexicon of terminology. His analytical depth, literary verve and his success in the delicate task of reconciliation of theology with mysticism particularly should be underlined. In this respect, Mustamlī Bukhārī's commentary on Kalābadhī stands shoulder to shoulder in importance with other famous commentaries in Sufi literary history, such as Qayṣarī's commentary on Ibn ʿArabī's *Fuṣūṣ al-ḥikam*, Muḥammad Lāhījī's exegesis on Shabistarī's *Gulshan-i rāz* or Lāhūrī's commentary of the *Dīvān* of Ḥāfiẓ.[18]

---

17 Bukhārī translated Kalābādhī's Arabic text into Persian before commenting on it. My translation of the latter is slightly more literary (and hopefully slightly more faithful) than Arberry's translation given in *The Doctrine of the Sufis* (pp. 74–76) and also differs in respect to rendition of technical Sufi terms. I have followed Bukhārī's text of the book wherever it differs from Arberry's published text of the Arabic. I have mainly relied on the edition prepared by ʿAbd al-Ḥalīm Maḥmūd and ʿAbd al-Baqī Surwar (Cairo: Dār Iḥyāʾ al-Kutub al-ʿArabīyya 1380/1960), pp. 86–89, since it is closer to the text of Bukhārī's gloss than the Arabic text edited by Arberry back in 1935.

18 The section that is translated below represents approximately a ten-page extract from the author's commentary on chapter 31 of Kalābādhī's *Kitāb al-taʿarruf.* In A.J. Arberry's English translation of the *text*, this section covers only *one page* (76), while in Bukhārī's Persian work (pp. 1122–44) the *commentary* on same section comprises *over twenty pages.*

THE *KITĀB AL-TAʿARRUF* OF AL-KALĀBĀDHĪ

Chapter XXXI: The Ṣūfī Sciences of Mystical States[19]

[I.] I say (and from God all succour comes): it should be understood that the sciences of the Sufis are the sciences of mystical states (*aḥwāl*), and these states are fruits produced by[20] spiritual practices or works (*aʿmāl*),[21] and no one is ever bequeathed the patrimony of mystical states unless his works have been right. Now the first step to right conduct is to know the sciences thereof, namely, the legal prescriptions, consisting of the principles of law (*fiqh*) governing prayer, fasting and other religious duties, as well as the science of social transactions (*ʿilm al-muʿāmalāt*), regulating marriage, divorce, commerce and other matters affecting human life which God has laid down and prescribed as indispensable.

These are the sciences which are acquired by learning: and it is a man's first duty to strive to seek after this science and discover its rules, so far as he is able within the limits of the capacity of his nature and understanding, after being thoroughly grounded in theology and the use of the Qur'ān, the Sunna and the consensus of the fathers, to the extent of ascertaining for himself the sound doctrine of the congregation of orthodox Muslims. If God helps him to higher achievement than this, so he can dispel any misgivings that beset him – whether these stem from fleeting thoughts or rational speculations – it is well. But if he turns from evil thoughts by taking refuge in all that he comprehends, and avoids viewpoints and perspectives of those who dispute and contend with him and which keep him far (from God), this will then provide some comfort and space for him, *deo volente*; for he is

19 The Roman numerals within brackets denote particular passages from the text, the commentary upon which by Bukhārī I have selected for translation.

20 *Mawārith* literally means 'legacies', 'patrimonies' or 'heritage' but here this is meant in the wider sense of 'fruit', 'net-result', 'upshot', 'product', etc.

21 Referring to religious exercises. For Ibn 'Arabī, for instance, knowledge without spiritual practice is a purely theoretical knowledge; true knowledge must be united with good works. See William Chittick, *Ibn 'Arabī's Metaphysics of Imagination: The Sufi Path of Knowledge* (Albany: SUNY Press 1989), pp. 151–52. See also Farīd al-Dīn 'Aṭṭār, *The Speech of the Birds, Concerning Migration to the Real, The Manṭiqu'ṭ-Ṭair*, trans. Peter Avery (Cambridge: Islamic Texts Society 1998), pp. 482–83, n. 111.

occupied in the practice of his knowledge, and practises according to what he knows.[22]

It is first of all necessary, then, that he should be acquainted with the vices of the soul (*'ilm āfāt al-nafs*) and, being adept in such knowledge, thoroughly understand how the soul is to be disciplined and how its moral character can be improved and refined; he must know the wiles of the Enemy, apprehend the temptations of the world and how to eschew them. [II.] This is the science of *theosophia* or esoteric sapience (*ḥikmah*). When the soul perseveres in adhering to what has been prescribed for it, so that it learns good breeding and manners and becomes schooled in theomorphic ethics (*ādāb Allāh*), reining in its members and guarding its limbs and all its senses, then it becomes easy for a person to amend its character, and reform the soul's exterior so that it is no longer preoccupied with its own affairs, thus shunning and turning away from this world. Thereafter such a person is able to watch over his stray thoughts and purify his innermost consciousness. [III.] And this is what constitutes the science of gnosis (*'ilm al-ma'rifat*).

[IV.] Beyond this are the sciences of stray thoughts (*'ulūm al-khawāṭir*) and the sciences of visionary contemplation and interior revelations (*'ulūm al-mushāhadāt wa'l-mukāshafat*): [V.] and these sciences are entirely comprised within the science of symbolic allusions (*'ilm al-ishārat*), [VI.] which is the science par excellence of the Sufis, which they acquire once they have mastered all the sciences that we have mentioned. The term "symbolic allusion" is given to this science for this reason: the contemplations enjoyed by the heart and the revelations accorded to the secret transconscious (*asrār*)[23] cannot be expressed in any definite positive terms; they

22 As A.J. Arberry notes here, this is an obvious reference to the *ḥadīth*: "If a man practises according to what he knows, God will bequeath him the knowledge of what he does not know."

23 The term *al-sirr* (pl. *asrār*) literally means 'secret' or 'mystery': the Latin "*arcanum, secretum*". Vullers, *Lexicon Persico-Latinum* (Graz: Akademische Druck – U. Verlagsanstalt 1962, s.v.). In Sufism, *al-sirr* refers to "the innermost part of the heart where divine revelation is experienced" (Schimmel, *Mystical Dimensions of Islam*, p. 192), which is also "the intimate and ineffable centre of consciousness, the point of contact between the individual and his Divine principle." (Burckhardt, *Introduction aux doctrines ésotériques de l'islam* [Paris: Editions Dervy 1996], p. 181.) In his famous *Definitions of Terms* (*al-Ta'rīfāt*, trans. Ḥasan Sayyid 'Arab and Sīmā Nūrbakhsh [Tehran: Farzān 1377 A.Hsh./1998], p. 87) Mīr Sharīf Jurjānī (d. 816/1413) writes that "*al-sirr* is a divine subtlety (*lāṭīfa*) which has been

are learnt through actual experience of the mystical, through its raptures and ecstasies, and are only known to those who have experienced these mystical states and lived in these spiritual stations.

Sa'īd ibn al-Musayyib[24] (d. c.94/713) relates on the authority of Abū Hurayra[25] (d. 59/679) that the Prophet said: "Verily, there is a sort of knowledge, the form of which is esoteric (*maknūn*), and which no one comprehends except those who are adepts in divine gnosis (*ahl ma'rifat Allāh*). When they speak about it, it is criticized by those who are heedless of God." [VII.] The following narrative goes back to 'Abdu'l-Wāḥid ibn Zayd:[26] "I asked al-Ḥasan about the science of esoteric knowledge (*'ilm al-bāṭin*), and he said, 'I asked Ḥudhayfa ibn al-Yamān[27] about the science of esoteric knowledge,

---

deposited in the heart (*qalb*), like the spirit (*rūḥ*) is in the body. The *sirr* is the locus of contemplation of God, just as the Spirit is the locus of Love (*maḥabbat*) and the heart is the locus of gnosis (*ma'rifat*)." For this reason, the term has been translated by the more discerning scholars such as Henry Corbin, as the "superconscious" or "transconsious." Yet Bukhārī doesn't always use the term in this deeper esoteric sense of 'transconscious', but often simply as a synonym for *qalb*, 'heart'. Hence, in the text below a number of different translations are provided of *al-sirr*, ranging from "heart's mystery" to "heart's interior consciousness," to "transconscious mystery of the heart," etc.

24 An important genealogist and expert in Islamic law in Medina belonging to the second generation after the Prophet, who also figures highly among the Sufis (see Hujwīrī, *Kashf al-maḥdjūb*, ed. Zhukovskī [St. Petersburg: 1899; repr. Leningrad: 1926; repr. Tehran: Ṭahūrī 1375 A.Hsh./1996], pp. 105–7; Nicholson's translation, p. 87). He died in 93–4/291–92.

25 One of the most famous companions of the Prophet, who was appointed governor of Baḥrayn under 'Umar's caliphate, passing away in 58/677–78. Although a celebrated narrator of traditions, the accuracy and authority of his statements has been subjected to a devastating critique by Fatima Mernissi, *The Veil and the Male Elite*, trans. Mary Jo Lakeland (New York: Perseus Books 1991), chap. 4.

26 Famous for his piety and doctrine of solitude, an associate of Ḥasan al-Baṣrī (d. 110/728, who is also referred to here), he died in 177/793–94.

27 An early convert to Islam, who later became governor of Madā'īn under 'Umar's and 'Alī's caliphate, he died in 36/656–67. Typical of the veneration accorded by the Sufis for his interest in matters of esoteric knowledge, is the following tale told by 'Aṭṭār in the *Muṣībat-nāma* (ed. N. Viṣāl, Tehran: Zawwār 1349 A.Hsh./1970; p. 57) of Ḥudhayfa's posing the question to 'Alī as to whether there was any type of divine revelation (*waḥy*) in the world besides the Qur'ān today? "There isn't any 'revelation' besides the Qur'ān,

and he said, I asked the Messenger of God about the science of esoteric knowledge, and he said, I asked Gabriel about the science of esoteric knowledge, and He said, It is a secret of My secret: I set it in the heart of My servant, and none of My creatures understands it.'" Abū'l-Ḥasan ibn Abī Dharr quotes the following verses of Al-Shiblī in his book, the *Minhāj al-dīn*:

The science of the Sufis has no bound
 A science high, celestial, divine:
In it the Masters' hearts have plunged profound,
 And men of wit appraise them by that sign.

* * *

As we can see from the above passage, a number of the most essential epistemological notions relating to esoteric knowledge that are found in later Sufism – the sciences of mystical states, theosophia, gnosis, stray thoughts, contemplative unveiling and the science of symbolic allusions, etc. – have been raised here by Kalābādhī in a summary manner. The most important parts of Mustamlī Bukhārī's commentary, elaborating in detail the Sufis' esoteric and gnostic sciences mentioned in the above passage, are translated below.

* * *

SHARḤ AL-TAʿARRUF OF MUSTAMLĪ BUKHĀRĪ

I. The Unity of the Esoteric and Exoteric, and the Letter and Spirit of the Law (*Sharīʿa*)

I say (and from God all succour comes): it should be understood that the sciences of the Sufis are sciences of mystical states (*aḥwāl*), and these states are the fruit produced by spiritual practices or works

---

and yet, God has friends to whom he has given a very sound understanding (*fahm*), by means of which you come to realize that their understanding arises in the same exact manner as divine revelation, so that in respect to His words, they speak truly." Bukhārī's doctrine is quite similar to this (below, VII).

(*aʿmāl*), and no one is ever bequeathed the patrimony of mystical states unless his works have been right.[28]

If it were possible for the subtle or esoteric being (*bāṭin*) of man to be amended and reformed without rectification of the exterior and outward being (*ẓāhir*), then the mission of the divine messengers and their drawing up of sacred laws would have been to no avail, for such messengers would then have come solely bringing along with themselves the command for the subtle or esoteric being to be amended and reformed. However, since their missionary endeavour (*daʿwat*) combined reformation of the subtle being through faith in divine Unity, with imposition of legal obligations upon the outer being to perform the duties stipulated by the Canon Law of Islam (*sharīʿat*), and since people were not excused from fulfilling those legal obligations, such that a fixed penalty and punishment was specified either in this world or the next for anyone who trespassed against the Canon Law, it can thus be established that soundness of the outer being demands soundness of the subtle or esoteric being as well, according to the arguments adduced above.[29]

... Now, this science whose works and acts can be made "right" (as the author states) is the science of the religious law (*sharīʿa*) as well as the science of the principles of jurisprudence (*ʿilm-i uṣūl-i fiqh*) – which consists of [the knowledge of] ritual prayer and fasting and other obligatory acts, and the science of dealings with one's fellow men and women (*ʿilm-i muʿāmalāt*) which involves [knowing the necessary procedures regarding] marriage, divorce and commercial transactions (*mubāyaʿāt*). Now, the reason why the author asserted this to be the case is because some people belonging to a group of libertines (*mubāḥiyyyān*)[30] have attached themselves to this company (the Sufis), asserting that the devotee may reach a station where he may dispense with formal acts of service altogether. The master – may God be content with him – exposes this to be an utter error, pronouncing that in proportion to one's inner being (*bāṭin*) becoming

---

28 *Sharḥ al-Taʿarruf* III, p. 1119: 1–2.

29 *Sharḥ al-Taʿarruf* III, p. 1121: 2–7.

30 Referring to Muslims who adopt a permissive attitude bordering on laxity or indifference (*mubāḥ*) towards certain principles of the Law (cf. J. Schacht, "Ibāḥa," *EI2* III, pp. 660–62). For this doctrine in Sufism, see Hujwīrī, *Kashf* (ed. Zhukovskī), p. 164; trans. R.A. Nicholson, p. 131.

purified, refined, wholesome and brought nigh to God, one's outward social self (*ẓāhir*) will thereby behave with discipline, respect and reverence.

Furthermore, were it possible that something better than the practical devotional activities of the Canon Law of Islam (*muʿāmalat-i Sharīʿat*) was demanded to reform and rectify the inner and subtle being (*bāṭin*) then God Almighty would have decreed it, for He is the Wise (*Ḥakīm*) and it is wrong to attribute any error or aberrancy to Him. Since God Almighty is the Friend of the Faithful (as He himself declares: "God is the Loving Friend of those who have faith" [II:257]), a friend only instructs his friend to do what is meet and right. God also declared in the same verse that, "He will bring them out of darkness into light." That "darkness" pertains both to the subtle, inner being (*bāṭin*), and to the outward being (*ẓāhir*); the darkness of the former consisting in infidelity (*kufr*), error (*ḍalālat*) and heretical innovation (*bidʿat*), and the darkness of the latter lying in irreverence (*bī-ḥurmatī*), moral indiscipline (*bī-adabī*) and deviance. Hence, dispelling the darkness of the subtle inner being makes it sound, while dispelling the darkness of the outer being sets it sound, since the outer follows the suit of the inner, and the exoteric pursues the esoteric. The outer being will be inspired and stimulated to move in exact proportion to the amount of movement and motion found in the subtle, inner being, for the inner being is like a prince and the outer being as his retinue.[31]

II. *Theosophia* or the Science of Esoteric Sapience (*Ḥikmat*)

This science is the science of *theosophia* or esoteric sapience (*ḥikmat*).[32]

The science that we have mentioned is called *theosophia*: "the science of esoteric sapience, or wisdom (*ʿilm-i ḥikmah*)."[33] The wise savants (*ḥakīmān*)

31 *Sharḥ al-Taʿarruf* III, p. 1122: 16–26.

32 *Sharḥ al-Taʿarruf* III, p. 1129: 3.

33 *Ḥikmat*, according to context, can signify 'philosophy' (being thus equivalent to *falsafa*), philosophical mysticism, sagesse, gnostic lore, esoteric sapience, wisdom; the term is identical in meaning, as Henry Corbin (*Temple and Contemplation*, p. 68) with the medieval Latin term *theosophia*. Here, the commentator uses the term in a peculiarly Sufi sense, his definition being more or less equivalent to the following pronouncement delivered by Shāh Niʿmatu'llāh (d. 835/1431) almost four centuries later, "Sufism is to

are those who are accomplished in the knowledge of the lower soul (*'ilm al-nafs*), the world and Satan,[34] so that the soul (*nafs*) might become thereby reformed and made sound, and so be kept safe and secure from Satan, enabling it to abandon and relinquish the world. Hence, those who belong to this company are known to be the "sage" or "wise" (*ḥakīm*). This science is called *ḥikmat* because it pertains to the precepts issued through God's legislating activity or 'decree' (*aḥkām-i amr*), and indeed, all such directives have simply been issued so that one might be able to preserve and protect oneself against the incursions of the lower soul, Satan and the world.[35]

III. The Science of Mystical Gnosis

... And this is what constitutes the science of gnosis (*'ilm al-ma'rifat*).[36]

---

assume the character traits of God (*taṣawwuf takhalluq ast bih akhlāq ilāhīyya*) ... And in Sufism it is required that the Sufi be a sage (*ḥakīm*), because Sufism is all esoteric sapience (*ḥikmat*), for [as the adage goes] "Sufism is all courtesy (*al-taṣawwuf kulluhu adab*). Now, 'assuming the character traits of God' requires that one possess complete gnosis (*ma'rifat-i tāmma*), a superior intellect (*'aql-i rājiḥ*), spiritual presence and stability (*ḥuḍūr wa tamkīn*), so that one is not controlled by passionate desires." *Majmū' al-laṭā'if*, in Dr. Javad Nurbakhsh (ed.), *Risālahā-yi Shāh Ni'matu'llāh Walī* (Tehran: Intishārāt-i Khānaqāh-i Ni'matu'llāhī 1357 A.Hsh./1978), IV, pp. 269–70.

34 The Persian text reads *'ilm-i nafs u dunyā u shayṭān dānand*. These three (soul, world and Satan) personify three aspects of the knowledge of a single reality, for as Rūmī says: "the soul (*nafs*) and world (*dunyā*) have always been one and same thing." Hujwīrī (*Kashf*, ed. V.A. Zhukovskii, p. 262) likewise writes, "Satan cannot find a place to enter the heart and inner being of a devotee until the desire to commit a sin occurs within him. But once the substance of passion appears in his heart, Satan seizes upon it and embellishes it. This is what is called diabolic suggestion or satanic temptation (*waswās*). All temptation thus begins from passion, for (as the adage goes) 'the tempter is the worst of oppressors', and in reference to this the Word of God Almighty attests, where, in reply to Iblīs's threat to 'mislead every one of them' (XV:39), God said: 'Verily, you have no power over my devotees' (XV:42). Therefore, 'Satan' depends upon the real substance of man's lower soul (*nafs*) and passions."

35 *Sharḥ al-Ta'arruf* III, p. 1129: 3–8.

36 *Sharḥ al-Ta'arruf* III, p. 1133: 8.

The science of gnosis is just what we have mentioned before, as being that through which all diverse ideas and significations become synthesized, made into a single sense and significance, all longings and desires becoming transformed into one desire. At that point, the gnostic (*ʿārif*) attains perfection, beholding all creatures as being utterly powerless and weak. He then understands the semblance of the world for what it really is, and so eschews it, knowing God in truth – in His majestic almightiness – to be of imperious might, overpowering force and everlasting and victorious in omnipotence. So he draws near to God and thenceforth becomes a gnostic adept (*ʿārif*), so that no deluding fancies can enter his thought.[37]

This is because one strays into error only when one's consciousness is dispersed in a state of multiplicity (*ḥāl-i kathrat*), whereas when one is focused and concentrated upon oneness no aberrancy can ever afflict, nor blunders overcome one. "One who is concentrated and united in himself makes no mistakes nor does anyone who takes hold of the One ever stray into error."[38] It takes duality for one to be 'wrong' and another 'right': it's 'twoness' that demands that one be 'correct' and the other 'incorrect'. But in unity conflicting qualities are not allowed, for in oneness, these two contradictory qualities dissolve away.[39]

IV. The Sciences of Stray Thoughts, Visionary Contemplation and Interior Revelation

> Beyond this are the sciences of stray thoughts (*ʿulūm al-khawāṭir*) and the sciences of visionary contemplation and interior revelations (*ʿulūm al-mushāhadāt wa'l-mukāshafat*).[40]

---

37 The Persian text here, which reads *ū rā khāṭir-i khaṭṭā nayaftad*, might also be translated as "so that he is not waylaid by aberrant thoughts." Given the context of the previous passage (not translated here), the commentator seems to be referring to the practice of maintaining a pure mind, guarding the soul from the interference of 'stray thoughts' (*khāṭir*) hailing from inferior psychological or demonic planes of consciousness. Most of the previous two pages (1131–32) were devoted to this subject.

38 This sentence, in Arabic, is apparently a maxim.

39 *Sharḥ al-Taʿarruf* III, p. 1133: 7–17.

40 *Sharḥ al-Taʿarruf* III, p. 1133: 18.

The organization of the sciences has been laid down in accordance with the principle cited above. That is to say, in the first place comes the science of divine Unity (*'ilm-i tawḥīd*), which is the principle of all the sciences. Then, the science of the holy Law of Islam (*'ilm-i sharī'at*), which is its derivative corollary, for from its soundness can be inferred [the soundness of] one's inner being (*bāṭin*). Then comes the science of *theosophia* or esoteric sapience (*'ilm-i ḥikmat*), which consists in comprehension and cognisance of the lower soul (*nafs*), and in teaching it strict discipline and refining its moral character, while being on guard against and recognizing the subtle stratagems of the enemy, as well as knowing the wickedness of the world and restraining oneself from it. Then comes the science of gnosis (*'ilm-i ma'rifat*), which involves not only relinquishing and avoiding the world but morally improving and reforming the lower soul, keeping one's senses under strict control, the heart and mind pure, while watching over stray thoughts – as has already been commented upon above.

Hence, it is only after this point that "the sciences of thoughts, the sciences of contemplation and revelations" appear. The reason for this is that as long as one's powers of will are not concentrated, one's conscience (*sirr*) corrupted with vice, and one's thoughts engaged with each and every thing that happens, all that enters one's head or crosses one's eyesight will stay invisible and hidden. Thus, one cannot tell if one's thoughts hail from worldly pride (*ghurūr-i dunyā*), satanic temptation, a scruple of the carnal soul (*hājis-i nafs*), an angelic inspiration, or a divine idea inspired by God (*khāṭir-i Ḥaqq*). But when one's stray thoughts are focused and concentrated and when one guards against everything ungodly, whatever appears to one's thought or one contemplates in one's heart is all God. Now, when one occupies one's heart's interior consciousness (*sirr*) with something, all that one contemplates and sees *becomes that thing*, such that one is not aware of anything else. The tongue is the interpreter of the heart's secret mystery (*sirr*), and it simply expresses in speech here whatever the heart sees. Thus, one who is veiled from the heart's mystery never utters even one single word of truth his entire life long, while one who has unveiled his heart's secret, never speaks a single word *unless* it be truth his whole life long.[41]

---

41 Alternatively, this sentence could be translated as: "Whereas one who is veiled from the interior heart's secret core never says a single word for the sake of God his entire life

Externally, a good example of this is the fact that whoever keeps the company of different types of people always suffers from scattered intentions and inability to focus the will; and since he mixes himself up with various types of people, flitting from this to that and that to this, he commits many mistakes and errors. However, whoever keeps his company down to a single kind of people, makes far fewer errors, which is exactly what the jurisprudents mean by their adage: "Whenever I disputed with a master of a single art, I was vanquished, but whenever I disputed with a master of diverse arts, I vanquished him."

Now a mystery lies hidden here, which is that when one's thoughts are dispersed, whatever you say depends on the point of view that the innermost part of your heart (*sirr*) regards.[42] Therefore, you let flux and variability enter in, allowing yourself to make blunders and errors respecting the object of vision.[43] Since the very object of one's vision is subject to flux and change, the beholder is also afflicted by the same erratic variability in vision; hence, all those who are changeable are bound to commit errors and be careless. But when one's mind is concentrated and thoughts collected, the innermost heart then rests upon the Truth, gazes on God, so neither error nor aberrancy is allowed to affect either one's object of sight or the beholder. Whoever looks crookedly, talks about crooks and crookedness; whoever looks correctly and rightly, discourses of righteousness and uprightness.[44] At that point, if the gaze of the innermost heart rests on something other than God, (at least) the thing will be beheld at the degree of conscious discrimination (*tamyīz*), since whatever falls *below* this degree is sometimes right and other times wrong.

Likewise, when God contemplates the innermost heart and becomes his interior Witness (*chūn shāhid-i sirr ḥaqq bāshad*), the mystic is then subjugated and subdued by God. One who is so subjugated, has no discrimination,

---

long, one who has his heart's secret core unveiled, never utters a word his whole life long unless it be for God's sake." The Persian text conveys both these connotations, I believe.

42 The author is trying to say that sight of any object of vision depends on the viewpoint of the viewer. Cf. Blake: "The eye of the sun when he unfolds it / Depends upon the eye that beholds it."

43 In other words, one allows changeability, error and aberrancy to affect the object of one's sight.

44 This sentence could also be translated as: "Whoever looks at things straight and correct, everything he utters is right and true."

but rather abides in and lives through the descriptive attributes of the One who has overwhelmed him (God), and (having no independent will of his own), is free from all blunders and immune from error. God (*Ḥaqq* = the Truth, Divine Reality) is the Manifestor and Agent of all that becomes manifest through him, and whatever the Truth makes manifest cannot be other than true and real (*ḥaqīqat*).

Not only can this characteristic be found in such a seer (*shāhid*), but in lovers (*ʿushshāq*) and lunatics (*majānīn*) as well. One who is in love is never subject to reproach (*tuhmat*), rather it is only debauchery (*fisq*) that is ever reproached.[45] As long as any vein of discrimination (*tamyīz*)[46] still survives in the lover, the quality of his love is not yet perfect, but when his love reaches perfection, all his qualities become controlled by and subjugated to his innermost secret heart (*sirr*), and his heart in turn becomes subject to Love (*maḥabbat*). Since his innermost secret heart contemplates only the Friend, he hears whatever is spoken to him as if it were coming from the Friend; whatever is shown to him he sees as if coming from the Friend; in fact, whatever he speaks is spoken in converse with the Friend.

Lunacy is of the same nature, in regard to the idea that has driven the person mad: all his replies whenever he speaks, solely concerns the (non) sense of his madness. Since one who is overcome by love and madness is like this, how will be in the state of one overcome by God?[47]

45 This sentence could also be translated as: "Blame and reproach (*tuhmat*) cannot be levelled at anyone truly in love; it is only lewd debauchery (*fisq*) that is ever a subject of reproach."

46 I.e. the true lover is concentrated exclusively on the Beloved, unable to concentrate on or discriminate between anything or anyone else, as Shakespeare has the Duke say in *Twelfth Night* (II:17ff.):

For such as I am, all true lovers are,
Unstaid and skittish in all motions else,
Save in the constant image of the creature
That is belov'd.

47 *Sharḥ al-Taʿarruf* III, pp. 1133:18–1135:8.

V. The Science of Symbolic Allusions (*ʿilm al-ishāra*)[48]

> ... and these sciences are entirely comprised within the science of symbolic allusions (*ʿilm al-ishārat*).[49]

The writer (Kalābādhī) goes on to say that (knowledge of) these sciences of stray thoughts, visionary contemplation and interior revelations are reserved exclusively for those who study the science of symbolic allusions (*ʿilm-i ishārat*). They've designated it by this name since all that is revealed to the mystic transcends literal representation, qualification and finite limitation, such that anyone might be able to describe, designate, qualify[50] or determine its meaning according to some limited, literalistic definition. What then happens is that something becomes palpable to his innermost heart's consciousness (*sirr*), the reality of which has been manifested by God, nothing else. Now, the circumstances of this are such that anything that he says or that falls off his tongue is not *in essence* God's own expression, but rather (you could say that) it is a divine dictum in respect to its *deeper sense* and *inner signification* (*maʿnā*).[51] Likewise, whatever sort of symbolic allusion (*ishārat*) enters his innermost heart's conscience (*sirr*), is not God's own allusion, although its *deeper interior signification* does indeed point to God. Similarly, "God" does not literally "speak" through the tongue of a dream-interpreter, nor through the words of a guidance counsellor. Nonetheless, certain moral qualities of character appearing on the mystic's

48 For an overview of this Sufi science, see the introduction to the anthology.

49 *Sharḥ al-Taʿarruf* III, p. 1133: 9.

50 The printed text here reads *takthīf*, which makes little sense, in all probability being a scribal error for *takyīf*, as I have translated it.

51 The Persian text here (*ʿayn-i ʿibārat-i Ḥaqq nīst; maʿnā ʿibārat-i Ḥaqq ast*) contrasts the symbolic reality of *ishārat* with the literal expression of words (*ʿibārat*), and asserts that if the mystic's tongue is not actually *in essence* (*ʿayn*) identical with God's discourse, but there is *a deeper spiritual sense belonging to an ineffable interior reality* (*maʿnā*) in which all his words are spoken by God. The controversy concerning the verity of the Sufis' 'ecstatic locutions' (*shaṭḥiyyāt*) and the theological dilemmas posed by this experience is the subject of Rūmī's discussion of Bāyazīd's utterance "Subḥānī" in his *Mathnawī*, ed. R.A. Nicholson (London: Luzac & Co. 1925–40), IV: 2112–44. For a good discussion of these doctrines, see Carl Ernst, *Words of Ecstasy in Sufism* (Albany: SUNY Press 1985), pp. 25–45.

outer being, furnish evidence of his interior contemplative discernment and vision, showing from which spiritual degree or station his inner being regards. If, for instance, whilst absorbed in contemplation, his heart's mysterious core (*sirr*) was grounded in the spiritual station of Fear of God (*khawf*), this will be visible quite conspicuously from his external state. The same thing applies to "Hope in God (*rajā'*),"[52] as well as other similar qualities. However, since nothing of this can be comprehended except through an allusive and indirect language, for this reason, they designated this lore as being a "science of symbolic allusions."

Now, it should be understood that outer verbal expressions (*'ibārat*) are but the effect of the inner language of symbolic allusion (*ishārat*), just as one's outer physical activity is but the effect of inner thoughts and reflections. Just as the act of serving a master does not impose any levy, or set limits upon, that master but rather furnishes evidence of his mastership, so the language of symbolic allusion behaves in the same manner. Similarly, just as God's expressions (*'ibārat-i Ḥaqq*) cannot be limited to or confined by purely rational (human) expressions, but rather these expressions demonstrate that their underlying intention was the One Interpreted from them, so stray thoughts act just like this in respect to the heart's transconscious mystery.

If one endeavours to reach the Necessary Being through stray thoughts and allusive esoteric symbols, this is anthropomorphism (*tashbīh*).[53] But if symbolic allusions are not made *through* God, this then is pure theological agnosticism (*ta'ṭīl*).[54] For Divine Unity (*tawḥīd*) to become an actual

---

52 Fear and Hope constitute respectively the first two stations on the Sufi Path according to nearly all the classical masters See Javad Nurbakhsh, *Sufism II: Fear and Hope, Contraction and Expansion, Gathering and Dispersion, Intoxication and Sobriety, Annihilation and Subsistence*, trans. William C. Chittick (London: KNP 1982), pp. 1–40 and also *idem.*, *Ma'ārif Ṣūfiyya* (London: KNP 1983), vol. 2, pp. 7–52.

53 *Tashbīh* literally means to be similar or comparable, but implies likening God to something in His creation. For a good account of anthropomorphism, see John Renard, *Islamic Theology: A Primary Source Reader* (Oakland: University of California Press 2014), pp. 145–46; 199–200.

54 In Islamic theology, *ta'ṭīl* signifies "stripping the concept of God of its contents, as pure *kenôsis*" – Ignaz Goldziher, *Introduction to Islamic Theology and Law*, trans. Andras and Ruth Hamori (Princeton: Princeton University Press 1981), p. 96 – and it is often

reality beyond both anthropomorphism and theological agnosticism, symbolic allusions must be made directly *through* God, and must not be acquired and learned (*bī-taḥṣīl*, i.e. by human means), so that the reality of divine unity (*tawḥīd*) without either anthropomorphism and agnosticism be established. Perhaps it has been called the 'science of symbolic allusions' (*'ilm-i ishārat*) for precisely this: that it consists of stray thoughts (*khaṭirāt*) which are exactly like accidents that do not last more than a moment each.

This is because if the soul's visionary contemplation (*mushāhadat-i nafs*) were to last longer than a moment, the mystic would be overcome and the religious law (*sharīʿa*) would become overturned and revoked. Visionary contemplation involves thus both a revelation and a ravishing (*namūdan u rabūdan*, lit. 'revealing and stealing').[55] When revelation is shown, one is ravished away, and when God reveals Himself, He enravishes and enraptures you so that the revelation itself does not abide. The visionary contemplation known by the heart's transconscious mystery (*mukāshafāt-i sirr*) today is similar to the revelation of oracular vision (*mukāshafāt-i 'ayn*) that will be enjoyed Tomorrow.[56] When the *Visio Dei* becomes manifest, the devotee passes away from all other spiritual realities; when he is made naught before all those realities, the religious law is revoked and suspended, and peace of the innermost heart appears – for the heart has no peace without the Friend.

Hence, it is necessary that the Holy Law (*sharīʿa*) abide and remain, insofar as the law is the ornament of devotional service, since it is hardly fitting for someone who has not been enriched and beautified through devotional service to have his subtle or esoteric being amended and reformed.[57] Since this knowledge consists of a kind of revelation and

described as theological "agnosticism" or "abstractionism." See Henry Corbin, *Histoire de la philosophie islamique* (Paris: Éditions Gallimard 1964), p. 122; 281.

55 That is to say, a revelation of God *to* the devotee, with a simultaneous ravishing of the devotee *from* himself.

56 Interior contemplative experiences which the mystic enjoys on the temporal plane of the world are reflections of the beatific vision of God in the hereafter.

57 In other words, whoever is not beautified by devotional service is undeserving of realizing any true spiritual refinement and unable to obtain a sound moral character.

ravishing, a revealing and a stealing' (*namāyish u rabāyish*), in this sense it has been termed the 'science of symbolic allusions'.[58]

VI. Symbolic Allusions and the Tradition of Islamic Learning

> ... the science of symbolic allusions (*'ilm al-ishārat*), which is the science par excellence of the Sufis, which they acquire once they have mastered all the sciences which we have mentioned.[59]

The author states that the science of symbolic allusions is a type of lore that the Sufis particularly reserve for themselves, that is, they claim that this science is known to themselves alone and nobody else. But this science can only be acquired *after* they have comprehended all the other sciences that we have mentioned, so this statement also implies that unless they *first* acquire those other sciences, they will never be able to reach the science of symbolic allusions. This is because unless one is sincerely devout in one's ascetic struggle (*ṣidq-i mujāhidat*), no purity of heart (*ṣafwat-i sirr*) can be attained, and unless heart's interior consciousness be purified, it cannot be affirmed that symbolic allusions are sound. The reason for this is whoever sees things in darkness is sometimes in the wrong and sometimes in the right, and whoever sees things in light and clarity, sees everything truthfully and properly. Now, no one can be sincerely devout in ascetic struggle without knowledge (*'ilm*), and that is the reason why the Sufis first learn the other sciences.

In this chapter one can find also proof of the fact that *the true Sufi is one who in reality is the most learned person of his day and age*. When he occupies himself with the science of symbolic allusions while not having learned the other sciences, he will fall into error and make mistakes, and blunders in this subject have the most serious consequences than in any other subject matter because the object of knowledge of this science is the Truth (God = *Ḥaqq*), whereas other sciences focus on objects of knowledge other than the Truth-who-is-God Almighty (*Ḥaqq ta'ālā*), so to fall into error in regard to things other than the Truth is far easier than to err regarding the Truth.

58 *Sharḥ al-Ta'arruf* III, pp. 1135: 9–1136: 14.

59 *Sharḥ al-Ta'arruf* III, p. 1137: 15–16.

Another idea (contained in this statement) is that whoever has not correctly learned the science of social transactions (*ʿilm-i muʿāmalāt*) and the science of *theosophia* or esoteric sapience (*ʿilm-i ḥikmah*), is unable to see himself properly. Now how can someone who can't even see himself properly, who is helpless vis-à-vis himself (in matters of self-contemplation), ever be able to behold God?

This science also belongs particularly to the Sufis – according to the description of the type of Sufi that we have given – because the Sufis do not seek (for themselves alone) either any particular knowledge or transaction out of their pursuit of knowledge and transactions.[60] Rather, they seek the deeper interior signification (*maʿnā*) from both these, since the 'symbolic allusion' itself lies in knowing that deeper sense and meaning. Hence, knowing this interior sense is itself the 'symbolic allusion'.[61]

VII. The Heart's Mystery and Esoteric Knowledge

> The following narrative goes back to 'Abdu'l-Wāḥid ibn Zayd: "I asked al-Ḥasan about the science of esoteric knowledge (*ʿilm al-bāṭin*), and he said, 'I asked Ḥudhayfa ibn al-Yamān about the science of esoteric knowledge, and he said, I asked the Messenger of God about the science of esoteric knowledge, and he said, I asked Gabriel about the science of esoteric knowledge, and He said, It is a secret of My secret: I set it in the heart of My servant, and none of My creatures understands it.'"[62]

This narrative is a further proof that the science of symbolic allusions is true (*ʿilm-i ishārat ḥaqq-ast*). This is because the 'science of esoteric knowledge' (*ʿilm-i bāṭin*) is itself the 'science of symbolic allusions' (*ʿilm-i ishārat ast*), whereas 'exoteric knowledge' (*ʿilm-i ẓāhir*) is not called a 'science of symbolic allusions'. However, when a certain word is uttered by the tongue, beneath which there is another meaning that is not explicit or clear, the Arabs say, "I *alluded to* (*ishāra*) to such and such a matter by my words," but

60 That is, the Sufi pursues the interior reality underlying all sciences, religious exercises and social relations.

61 *Sharḥ al-Taʿarruf* III, pp. 1137: 15–1138: 8.

62 *Sharḥ al-Taʿarruf* III, pp. 1140: 28–29; 1141: 1–3.

when the words are clear and plain, they say merely, "I *said* (*qāla*) such and such a thing" and never that, "I *alluded to*." You can comprehend from this therefore that symbolic allusions are esoteric spiritual significations (*maʿnā-yi bāṭin*) hidden within verbal expressions (*ʿibārat*). Since this is the significance of symbolic allusions, and since by this narrative the 'science of esoteric knowledge' is established as sound and orthodox (*durust gardad*), then the 'science of symbolic allusions' is proven to be sound and orthodox as well.

In this narrative another proof as well is found that the 'science of symbolic allusions' arises from *within* the subtle or esoteric being (*bāṭin*) and is not (generated) from literal rational expressions (*ʿibārat*). This is because knowledge is itself a quality belonging the subtle or esoteric being (*bāṭin*) rather than an attribute of the exterior personality (*ẓāhir*). Therefore, anything related by outward literal expressions is a kind of 'esoteric knowledge', and anything that such 'esoteric knowledge' infers from those expressions constitutes an 'esoteric symbolic allusion'.[63]

... In this narrative can also be found proof that the elect (*khawāṣṣ*) are privy to certain esoteric secrets from which commoners (*ʿawāmm*) are excluded. Whosoever is more singularly elect before God is given greater confidentiality in sharing His mysteries. Demonstration of this is found in the Ascension (*miʿrāj*) of Muḥammad (peace be upon him). When God spoke to him about something which was proper for the multitude (*khalq*) to hear, He put Gabriel there as an intermediary, but when God wished to relate to him a mystery (*sirrī*) unacceptable for the masses of the people to apprehend, He dismissed Gabriel from this intermediary position, so that his (the Prophet's) rank might remain a mystery and his words would stay secret as well. Hence, there is a mystery concerning the Prophet's spiritual rank (*maqām*) in what He said, "Until he was the distance of two bows' length or even closer" and there is also a 'mystery' in the discourse (*kalām*) that He uttered next, "So He revealed by inspiration to His servant that which He revealed!"[64] At the rank where the Prophet Muḥammad was numbered among the company of the elect, Gabriel was counted among the company of vulgar commoners. If Gabriel had been worthy of that mystery, he would have been found worthy of reaching that degree. As the

63 *Sharḥ al-Taʿarruf* III, p. 1141: 3–14.

64 Qur'ān LIII:9–10.

adage goes: "Amongst the supremely elect, the elect are numbered among the riffraff."[65]

... And also in this narrative can be found proof that it is God Almighty who has placed this mystery in the devotee's heart. It provides corroboration and evidence as well for the view of the party of those who profess, 'My heart speaks of my Lord to me', for no error can befall that which God has vouchsafed within him. Since all of this has been understood as correct and true, it should be understood that the deeds and labours of the elect are the exact reverse of the efforts and exertions of the masses and common herd. The subtle or esoteric being (*bāṭin*) of the ordinary common man or woman accords with the temper of his or her outward, exterior self (*ẓāhir*); that is, for the vulgar mob, their outward, public, exoteric persona is their master and their inward, private, esoteric self his slave, for their innermost heart (*sirr*) pays all its regard and attention to the lower soul (*nafs*). However, for the elect, the subtle or esoteric being is their master, and their outward, public persona its captive slave, while their lower carnal soul (*nafs*) focuses all its regard and attention upon their innermost transconscious heart (*sirr*).[66] ... Therefore, one can say that the lower soul of the elect has taken on the nature of their secret transconscious heart (*sirr*), and their heart has adopted the divine temperament, the very nature of God (*tabʿ-i Ḥaqq*), such that their lower soul is subjugated to their heart and their heart subjugated to God.[67]

... Another topic that must be fathomed is that it is God Almighty who is the stimulator (*fāʿil*) of this 'mystery' within the devotee's heart. As long as the devotee has not proven himself worthy of guarding this mystery, he will not be entrusted with it. Trustworthiness consists in preservation of courtesy and good manners (*ādāb*). Thus, whoever better preserves the proper manners and etiquette of the holy Law (*sharīʿat*) is the more trustworthy, and will be the one to whom God confides mysteries. The reason for this is that the religious law is the portion meted out to the public exoteric persona, while mysteries are what are allotted to the subtle or esoteric being within.[68]

65 *Sharḥ al-Taʿarruf* III, p. 1141: 26–29 – p. 1142: 1–8.

66 *Sharḥ al-Taʿarruf* III, pp. 1142:25–29 – p. 1143:1–3.

67 *Sharḥ al-Taʿarruf* III, p. 1143: 8–9.

68 Alternately, this sentence may be translated as: "The *sharīʿa* is the lot of the public exoteric persona, while the 'mystery' is the lot of the subtle or esoteric being."

The exoteric dimension is given to all and sundry, but the esoteric side is not the lot of just everyone. So if a person is unable to preserve and protect the exoteric dimension, how can he be considered worthy of protecting and preserving the esoteric?[69]

69 *Sharḥ al-Taʿarruf* III, p. 1143: 25–29 – p. 1144: 1–2.

II

ON THE TRUE MEANING OF ESOTERIC KNOWLEDGE

Abū Ḥāmid al-Ghazālī's (d. 505/1111) *Al-Risālat al-ladunī*

GHAZĀLĪ'S LIFE, WORKS AND LEGACY

Abū Ḥāmid al-Ghazālī's birth in Ṭūs in Khurāsān in 450/1058 took place in the heartland of the Persian Sufi tradition at the best possible historical moment. "Today, the shadow of divine favour has been extended all throughout the province of Khurāsān," announced Ghazālī's contemporary 'Ali b. 'Uthmān Jullābī Hujwīrī (d. between 465/1072 and 469/1076), author of an early systematic Persian manual on Sufi methodology and mystical theology. Adding a touch of personal poetic verisimilitude to the pious hyperbole, Hujwīrī boasts, "... I myself met three hundred people in Khurāsān, each of whom was graced with such theosophical accomplishments (*mashrabī*), such that even a single one of them would have sufficed for the whole world."[1] Ghazālī's advent occurred at the peak of the arch of the development of Islamic mystical tradition in Khurāsān: at the precise cusp where one half of the tangent of the Perso-Arabic mystical tradition projected upwards, the rise of Arabic mystical literature (mostly composed, incidentally, by Persian Sufis) buttressing it up, facing the other half-curve of the arch, soaring outwards supporting the first beginnings of Sufi literature in Persian.

Crowning the two curves of this arch – at this cusp where the two great liturgical languages of Islam: Arabic and Persian, chronologically intersect – one beholds the grand commentary by Abū Ibrāhīm Mustamlī Bukhārī (d. 434/1042–3) on al-Kalābādhī's (d. 380/990) *Introduction to the Creed of the Sufis* (*Kitāb al-ta'arruf li-madhhab ahl al-taṣawwuf*), entitled *Sharḥ*

1 Hujwīrī, *Kashf al-maḥdjūb*, ed. Zhukovskī (Tehran: Ṭahūrī 1375/1996), p. 216. For a good discussion of the Sufi background of Ghazālī's education, see Osman Bakar, *Classification of Knowledge in Islam: A Study in Islamic Philosophies of Science* (Kuala Lumpur: 1992), p. 155ff.

al-Ta'arruf, selections of which have just been featured in chapter one. Although this was "the earliest work on Sufism in Persian,"[2] codifying and expanding its mystical doctrines, yet it has been seriously neglected by modern scholars.[3] One of the two pillars on which this grand arch rested was the Sufi doctrine of rapture[4] and *malāmatī* spirituality of the ecstatic mystic and founder of institutional Sufism, Abū Sa'īd Abī'l-Khayr (d. 440/1049, a decade before Ghazālī), having been the author of the earliest known Persian Sufi poetry. The other pillar of the arch rests on the philosophy of Abū 'Alī Sīnā (Avicenna) (d. 428/1037) – who, being affected by and profoundly influencing by the Sufism of his day, wrote a number of visionary works in Arabic (and the earliest philosophical work in Persian)[5] that provided the speculative premises for the development of the love-mysticism espoused by the later Persian Sufi poets. Significant other figures in the early Sufi tradition, such as Abū'l-Ḥasan Kharaqānī (d. 426/1034) and Abū'l-Muẓẓafar Ardashīr al-'Ibādī (d. 444/1052), who belonged to the generation immediately before Ghazālī's birth, helped fill in the bedrock under the edifice of the Persian Sufi tradition.

So it is on this spiritual bedrock of the Persian Sufi tradition that Ghazālī's theological achievement rests, without which it would have been unthinkable. Nearly all the major founders of Khurāsānī Sufism had flourished during Ghazālī's day and age, having been born either in decades immediately before or after his birth. These included the likes of Abū 'Abd al-Raḥmān al-Sulamī (d. 412/1021), one of the main chroniclers of early Sufism, best known for his Arabic tract, *The Generations of Sufis* (*Ṭabaqāt aṣ-ṣūfiyya*), a compendium of the biographies of Sufis of five earlier generations, "the main source which has shaped our knowledge and ideas on early

2 Naṣru'llāh Pūrjavadī, "Fārsī-gū'ī 'ārifān-i nakhustīn," *Nashr-i Dānish*, Year 20, No. 1 (Spring 1382 A.Hsh./ 2003), p. 12.

3 Edited by Muḥammad Rūshān (Tehran: Chāpkhāna-yi Ṣanūwār 1363 A.H.sh.), 5 vols. (see chapter one of this anthology). The original Arabic source that was the object of his commentary was translated into English by A.J. Arberry as *The Doctrine of the Sufis* (Cambridge 1972). An abridged Persian edition of Mustamlī's commentary came out in Tehran in 1970, the *Khulāsa-yi Sharḥ al-Ta'arruf*, ed. Aḥmad 'Alī Rajā'ī (Tehran: 1970).

4 See Terry Graham, "Abū Sa'īd ibn Abī'l-Khayr and the School of Khurāsān," in Leonard Lewisohn (ed.), *The Heritage of Sufism* I, pp. 116–35.

5 Referring to his *Dānish-nāma 'alā'ī*; on which, see M. Achena, "Avicenna. xi. Persian Works," *EIr* I, p. 99ff.

Sufi history."[6] 'Abdu'llāh Anṣārī (d. 482/1089) of Herat, who translated and adapted Sulamī's book into Persian, was the leading stylist of Persian rhyming prose, and a founder of the Sufi school of thought known as the Religion of Love (*madhhab-i 'ishq*)[7] in classical Persian poetry.[8] Almost as important as Sulamī's *Ṭabaqāt* is the definitive *Treatise* (*Risāla*) on Sufism in Arabic by Abū'l-Qāsim al-Qushayrī (d. 465/1072) of Nishapur, "probably the most widely read summary of early Sufism."[9] All of these sources Ghazālī read and knew, often reproducing them verbatim in his works.

Between these two pillars – Khurāsānī mysticism sustaining one side, Avicennean philosophy buttressing the other – with the two arches of the Persian and Arabic languages and literatures catapulting in the airy vault between them, it can be seen how natural a figure Ghazālī now appears, posed with his monumental compositions in its elegant archway, born in the middle of this most mystical century.[10]

Ghazālī was a student of the Ash'arite theologian Imām al-Ḥaramayn Abu'l-Ma'ālī al-Juwaynī (d. 478/1085), who taught him the principles of the Ash'arite *Kalām*, to which he adhered and for which he acted as an apologist for the rest of his life.[11] While studying with Juwaynī in Nishapur, Ghazālī also sat at the feet of the Sufi master Abū 'Alī Fārmadhī (d. 477/1084–85),

6 Sara Sviri, "Ḥakīm Tirmidhī and the Malāmatī Movement in Early Sufism," in Leonard Lewisohn (ed.), *The Heritage of Sufism: Persian Sufism from its Origins to Rumi* (Oxford: Oneworld 2000), I, pp. 594–95.

7 For further information about "the Religion of Love" (*madhhab-i 'ishq*), see Leonard Lewisohn, *Hafiz and the Religion of Love in Classical Persian Poetry* (London: I.B. Tauris 2010).

8 Leonard Lewisohn, "Preface: Ansari and Early Persian Erotic Spirituality," in Nahid Angha (trans.), *Ansari's* Hundred Fields: *An Early Persian Treatise on the Sufi Way* (London: Archetype 2010), p. 8.

9 A. Schimmel, *Mystical Dimensions of Islam* (Chapel Hill: University of North Carolina 1975), p. 88.

10 For a good overview of Sufism in the life and times of Ghazālī, see Hamid Dabashi, "Historical Conditions of Persian Sufism in the Seljuk Period," in Leonard Lewisohn (ed.) *The Heritage of Sufism* (Oxford: Oneworld 1999), I, pp. 137–74.

11 Massimo Campanini, "Al-Ghazzālī," in S.H. Nasr and O. Leaman (eds.), *History of Islamic Philosophy* (London: Routledge 1996), I, p. 259; M. Marmura, "Ghazālī. vi. Ghazālī and Theology," *Encyclopædia Iranica* X, p. 374.

who was a disciple of Abū Sa'īd b. Abi'l-Khayr.[12] His youth, in fact, had been filled with frequenting Sufi séances in secret, enjoying the dervishes' ecstatic musical *Samā'* concerts,[13] where he was already an adept in the manners and mysteries of the *Khānaqāh* (Sufi assembly lodges).[14] Ghazālī's brother, Aḥmad Ghazālī (d. 520/1126) was one of the major Sufi masters of the period, who himself initiated celebrated Sufis such as 'Ayn al-Quḍāt Hamadhānī (d. 525/1131) and Abū'l-Najīb al-Suhrawardī (d. 563/1168) into the Khurāsānī mystical tradition.[15]

In 1091, aged thirty-four, he was appointed by the Seljuk statesman Niẓām al-Mulk (d. 485/1092) to be the Director of the Niẓāmīyya University in Baghdad, and professor of Shāfi'ite jurisprudence there. He filled this position with considerable success until 1095: he was often consulted by the Caliph, and he also played a key political role in Seljuk politics and possessed substantial prestige as a theologian.[16] He was a loyal courtier, court theologian and supporter of the 'Abbasid rule.[17] Although Ghazālī was a quietist, politically speaking, and avoided controversy whenever possible, being a staunch support of the Abbasid state,[18] in 488/1095, at age

12 Gerhard Böwering, "Ghazālī. i. Biography," *Encyclopædia Iranica* X, p. 358.

13 In defence of which Ghazālī wrote what still remains the most definitive Muslim theological apology, for a study of which see Leonard Lewisohn, "The Sacred Music of Islam: *Sama'* in the Persian Sufi Tradition," *British Journal of Ethnomusicology* VI (1997), pp. 1–33.

14 'Abd al-Ḥusayn Zarīnkūb, *Farār az madrasa* (Tehran: Amīr Kabīr 1364 A.Hsh./1985, 3rd edn), p. 27.

15 "It is because of the latter [Abū'l-Najīb al-Suhrawardī] that the initiatic chains (*selsela*) of the Sohrawardī order and its derivatives such as the Kobrawīya, the Mawlawīya, and the Ne'mat-Allāhīya go back to Aḥmad Ghazālī." Nasrollah Pourjavady, "Ghazālī, Aḥmad," *Encyclopædia Iranica* X, p. 378. On Aḥmad Ghazālī's place in the Sufi tradition, see also J.S. Trimingham, *The Sufi Orders in Islam* (Oxford: Oxford University Press 1971), pp. 29–30.

16 Jean Calmard, "Ghazālī, al- (1058–1111)," *Dictionnaire de l'Islam: religion et civilization, Encyclopædia Universalis* (Paris: Albin Michel 1997), p. 319.

17 Campanini, "Al-Ghazzālī," p. 260.

18 Campanini summarizes Ghazālī's political attitude quite well: "Political quietism is functional to the renaissance of religious sciences. Nobody – and surely not a scholar or a mystic – can look after his or her conscience if the outside world is troubled by wars and injustice. The reform of the heart needs social peace and harmony, even though this

thirty-eight, he had a mysterious spiritual crisis that led to a nervous breakdown, and ultimately to his abandonment of his academic teaching career. It lasted almost six months, during which he vacillated between his worldly and spiritual vocations. Finally, the crisis became so intense that he became physically paralyzed and unable to speak.[19] He secretly left Baghdad, deserting his wife and family, and spent some eleven years in meditation and prayer.

Ghazālī consecrated two works to the Neo-Platonic philosophers, al-Fārābī (d. 339/950) and Avicenna (d. 428/1037)[20] in particular. The first of these works was his *The Objectives of the Philosophers* (*Maqāṣid al-falāsifa*). Written in Arabic, it closely followed Avicenna's Persian work *Dānish-nāma 'alāl'ī*,[21] providing an overall account of the history of Muslim philosophy, and a lucid exposition of the philosophical doctrines that he later means to criticize. The second work, entitled *The Incoherence of the Philosophers* (*Tahāfut al-falāsifa*), was an attack on the metaphysics of the philosophers.[22] Both works were composed shortly before his spiritual breakdown, that is, between 1091 and 1095.

From the point of view of subsequent Islamic philosophy, Ghazālī's most important work is *The Incoherence of the Philosophers*,[23] in which he sets out to prove that the philosophers are unable to prove religious truths from a

---

silence has to be paid for with an autocratic power. The wise person may, however, close the windows of the world to open the door of the soul." – Campanini, "Al-Ghazzālī," p. 260.

19 This crisis is recorded in his autobiographical treatise: *al-Munqidh min al-Dalāl*, ed. Farīd Jabre (Beirut: Librairie Orientale 1969), pp. 18–27; *Deliverance from Error: An Annotated Translation of al-Munqidh min al-Dalāl and other relevant works of al-Ghazālī*, trans. by R.J. McCarthy (Louisville: Fons Vitae, n.d.). Ghazālī's life, crisis, times and legacy has been excellently dramatized in the award-winning film by Ovidio Salazar: *Al-Ghazali: The Alchemist of Happiness* (London: Matmedia Productions 2006), the script of which is largely adapted from his autobiography.

20 For further information about Ibn Sina, see Jules Janssens, *Ibn Sina and his influence on the Arabic and Latin World* (London: Routledge 2018).

21 On which, see Parviz Morewedge (trans.), *The Metaphysica of Avicenna (ibn Sīnā)* (New York: Columbia University Press 1973).

22 Calmard, "Ghazālī, al- (1058–1111)," p. 323. Al-Ghazālī, *The Incoherence of the Philosophers*, trans. Michael Marmura.

23 Al-Ghazālī, *The Incoherence of the Philosophers*, Marmura's introduction, p. xix.

theoretical point of view.[24] In this book, he gives a list of twenty problems in which he endeavours to expose the contradictions of the philosophers' theses. Out of these twenty headings, only on three counts does he reckon the philosophers as infidels:

i) Denial of the Resurrection of the bodies;
ii) Their affirmation of the Eternity of the world;
iii) Their assertion that God knows universals but not particulars (Avicenna's tenet).

"These three subjects were enough," Campanini underlines, "to transform the philosophical message into a potentially corrupting theory."[25] Seventeen other propositions of the philosophers he also condemned as heretical innovations. Michael Marmura, introducing his translation of the book, sums up the impact of the *Tahāfut* on later Islamic theology as follows:

> The *Tahāfut* certainly put Islamic philosophy on the defensive in a way that it had never been before. Paradoxically, however, it also served to make it better known in the Islamic world. It brought to the fore the conflict between philosophy and more traditional Islamic belief. But perhaps more to the point, in order to refute the Islamic philosophers, al-Ghazālī had to explain them. He explained them so clearly and well that he rendered philosophical ideas accessible to nonphilosophers. Inadvertently, so to speak, the *Tahāfut* helped spread philosophical ideas, as it also set a new tradition in *kalām*. After al-Ghazālī, no Islamic theologian worth his salt avoided detailed discussion of the philosophical theories al-Ghazālī had criticized. *Kalām* thereafter became, as it had never been before, thoroughly involved with the theories of the *falāsifa*.
>
> The *Tahāfut* also marks a high point in the history of medieval Arabic thought because of its intellectual calibre. Although its motivation is religious and theological, it makes its case through closely argued criticisms that are ultimately philosophical. A logical critique, largely of the emanative metaphysics, causal theory and psychology of Avicenna (Ibn Sīnā, d. 1037), it is incisive and thorough. It is true

---

24 Campanini, "Al-Ghazzālī," p. 261.

25 Campanini, "Al-Ghazzālī," p. 262.

> that theological criticism of philosophy was not entirely new in medieval Islam: one does encounter before al-Ghazālī *kalām* criticisms of philosophical ideas. But one does not encounter anything like the comprehensive, sustained criticism of the *Tahāfut* – a work entirely devoted to refuting the philosophers. Whatever its failings – some of these shown by the answer Averroes (Ibn Rushd, d. 1198) gave to it in his *Tahāfut al-Tahāfut* (The Incoherence of the Incoherence) – it remains a brilliant, incisive critique.[26]

In the *Tahāfut,* Ghazālī singles out Fārābī and Avicenna for his main criticism,[27] clarifying that he wishes to refute the philosophers' doctrines by particular reference to them,[28] but mostly directing his attacks at Avicenna. He makes clear that his argument with the philosophers is not with their mathematics, astronomical sciences, or logic – matters that he considers to be of neutral relevance to religion – but with their philosophical theories that contravene the theories of religion.[29] Similarly Ghazālī had complained in *Al-Munqidh* that students of logic "draw up a list of conditions to be fulfilled by demonstration, which are known without fail to produce certainty. When, however, they come at length to treat of religious questions, not only are they unable to satisfy these conditions, but they admit an extreme degree of relaxation (of their standards of proof)." Thus, "the student who admires logic and sees its clarity, imagines that the infidel doctrines attributed to the philosophers are supported by similar

26 Al-Ghazālī, *The Incoherence of the Philosophers,* trans. Michael Marmura (Provo: Brigham Young University Press 1997), pp. xv–xvi.

27 Al-Ghazālī, *The Incoherence of the Philosophers,* trans. Michael Marmura, intro., p. xix.

28 Al-Ghazālī, *The Incoherence of the Philosophers,* trans. Michael Marmura, text, p. 5 supra.

29 Al-Ghazālī, *The Incoherence of the Philosophers,* trans. Michael Marmura, intro., p. xxii. Hodgson (*The Venture of Islam* II, p. 182) notes, "While rejecting Falsafah metaphysics, Ghazâlî held, therefore, that Muslims should accept the findings of the Falsafah sciences in their proper sphere – knowledge of nature – contrary to the attitude of many Sharī'ah-minded persons. Moreover, he went on later to apply to the Islamic tradition itself a basic principle of Falsafah, that truth must be ultimately accessible to and verifiable by any individual human consciousness; he did not, however, call the principle 'Falsafah' at that point."

demonstrations, and hastens into unbelief before reaching the theological (or metaphysical) sciences."[30]

Ghazālī was the author of some sixty works – which are certainly by him – and some 300 other works of dubious ascription.[31] His compositions divide into roughly five categories:

i) Legal writings, in which he adheres to the Shafi'ite School of Law, which include compositions on legal applications (*furū' al-fiqh*), on the foundations of Islamic jurisprudence (*uṣūl al-fiqh*). Böwering points out: "Except for Sufism, no other field of the Islamic sciences absorbed so much of Ghazālī's time and energy as that of jurisprudence."[32]
ii) Works on Islamic philosophy: these include his *Maqāṣid al-falāsifa* and the *Tahāfut al-falāsifa*. The latter treatise was translated into Latin in the twelfth century and into Hebrew in the thirteenth and became highly acclaimed.[33] He also wrote two treatises on logic: *Mi'yār al-'ilm* and *Kitāb Miḥikk al-naẓar*, and a treatise on philosophical ethics *Mīzān al-'amal.*
iii) Works on Islamic theology (*'ilm al-kalām*). Ghazālī's innovation in theology was to use "the Aristotelian syllogism and systematically apply it to theological thought."[34] His main work on theology was *Al-Iqtiṣād fi'l-i'tiqād* ('The just mean in belief') written in 488/1095. Here he shows himself to be opposed to a theology based on *taqlīd* and polemics, and in his *Iḥyā'* and the *Munqidh* his opposition turns to outright rejection of theology as certain truth.[35] His polemics against the Ismā'īlīs (such as *Faḍā'ih al-baṭiniyyah wa faḍā'il al-mustaẓhiriyyah* (The Infamies of the Bāṭinites and the Excellencies of the Mustaẓhirites), also belong to this theological works, as well as his *Fayṣal al-tafriqa bayna'l-Islām wa'l-zandaqa* (The arbiter between Islam and heresy).[36]

30 W. Montgomery Watt (trans.), *The Faith and Practice of Al-Ghazālī* (Oxford: Oneworld 1994 repr. of the 1953 edition), p. 36 (95).

31 Böwering, "Ghazālī. i. Biography," *Encyclopædia Iranica* X, p. 359.

32 Böwering, "Ghazālī. i. Biography," *Encyclopædia Iranica* X, p. 360.

33 Böwering, "Ghazālī. i. Biography," *Encyclopædia Iranica* X, p. 360.

34 Böwering, "Ghazālī. i. Biography," *Encyclopædia Iranica* X, p. 360.

35 Böwering, "Ghazālī. i. Biography," *Encyclopædia Iranica* X, p. 360.

36 Translated by R.J. McCarthy, *Deliverance from Error*, pp. 145–74. See also Farouk Mitha, *Al-Ghazālī and the Ismailis: A Debate on Reason and Authority in Medieval Islam* (London: I.B. Tauris in association with the Institute of Ismaili Studies 2001).

iv) Persian works on mystical theology, ethics and politics. In this category are included his *Kīmiyā-yi sa'ādat* (a synopsis of the Iḥyā') that treats religious ethics, and his *Naṣīḥāt al-mulūk*, which belongs to the 'mirror for princes' genre.

v) Arabic Sufi works on mystical theology (that combine theology and philosophy). Among this category are included small Arabic treatises such as his *Mishkat al-anwār*, *Al-Munqidh min al-ḍalāl*, and his *Risālat al-ladunī*. Among this category is also found his *Iḥyā' 'ulūm al-dīn*, half of which is devoted to Sufi themes. This monumental opus is divided into forty books that are arranged in four different volumes:
   1. *'ibādāt* (modes of religious worship);
   2. *ādāt* (social observances);
   3. *muhlikāt* (faults of character: literally 'what leads to perdition');
   4. *munjīyāt* (virtues: literally 'what leads to salvation')

Composed sometime between 1095 and 1106 during his period of concealment, the *Iḥyā 'ulūm al-dīn* belongs to the period of Ghazālī's life after his crisis came to a head in July 1095. It was his most important work in theology, his monumental attempt to revive Islamic faith and piety on the basis of Sufism.[37] Of this work, Ahmad Mahdavi Damghani rightly points out that "Scholars and students of Islamic studies throughout the world would unanimously agree, I think, that if one were to select twenty representative works whose contribution marked an occasion of supreme importance in the development of Islamic culture, the *Iḥyā' 'ulūm al-dīn* would certainly be numbered amongst them."[38]

Pointing to the mystical piety and inspiration underlying this work, which "advocates Sufi spirituality as the fulcrum of Islamic religion,"[39] Campanini places Ghazālī's *Iḥyā'* within a biographical context:

> The long period of concealment witnessed a deep transformation of al-Ghazzālī's speculative interests and even of his *Weltanschauung*.

37 See W. Montgomery Watt, "Ghazālī. iii. The *Eḥyā' 'Olūm al-Dīn*," *Encyclopædia Iranica* X, pp. 363–69; also cf. T.J. Winter, "Appendix II: Translations of the Revival into European Languages," in *Al-Ghazālī on Disciplining the Soul ...*, pp. 225ff.

38 "Persian Contributions to Sufi Literature in Arabic," in Leonard Lewisohn (ed.), *The Heritage of Sufism* I, pp. 41–42.

39 Böwering, "Ghazālī. i. Biography," *Encyclopædia Iranica* X, p. 359.

> He did not attend any more to philosophy and applied himself totally to Sufism and to the renewal of orthodox religion. In the *Munqidh*, the spiritual autobiography composed approximately between 501/1107 and 503/1109, he reveals an almost messianic feeling of being aware that "God Most High has promised to revive His religion at the beginning of each century" ... Al-Ghazzālī had the conviction that he was the person designated to carry out this task for his epoch, and pursued his reforming aim by composing a great work, whose title is significantly *The Revivification of the Sciences of Religion.*[40]

In this regard, it is necessary to recall that Ghazālī had been practically engaged in Sufi disciplines since he was a teenager, having been initiated during his late teens in 467/1058 into the *ṭarīqa* by the Sufi master Yūsuf al-Nassāj;[41] later he submitted to Shaykh Abū 'Alī al-Fārmadhī (d. 477/1084–85) as his spiritual guide in Sufism. Ghazālī was fully committed to the principle of the necessity for a spiritual guide on the Sufi Path.[42] His brother, Aḥmad al-Ghazālī (d. 520/1126) was one of the leading Sufi masters of the day.[43]

Ghazālī's writings, and the *Iḥyā' 'ulūm al-dīn* in particular, had a profound impact on the later Islamic theological tradition. There are several reasons for this. One was the cosmopolitan compendiousness of his compositions. "There is probably no writer in the Ṣūfī tradition," writes Eric Ormsby, "who incorporates within his work so much terminology, method and material derived from other sources as does al-Ghazālī."[44] Two other reasons

40 Campanini, "Al-Ghazzālī," p. 264.

41 Carol Bargeron, "Sufism's Role in Al-Ghazālī's First Crisis of Knowledge," *Medieval Encounters* IX/1 (2003), pp. 36; 49–50.

42 For an excellent overview of Ghazālī's engagement with both theoretical and practical Sufism, see Muhammad Abul Quasem, "Al-Ghazālī's Evaluation of Abū Yazīd Al-Bisṭāmī and his Disapproval of the Mystical Concepts of Union and Fusion," *Asian Studies* III/2 (1993), pp. 143–64 (on Ghazālī's practical Sufism, see esp. pp. 158–64).

43 See Leonard Lewisohn, "Al-Ghazali, Ahmad," in *The Encyclopedia of Philosophy*, 2nd edn, ed. Donald Borchert (New York: Macmillan Reference & Thomson Gale 2006), vol. I, pp. 117–18.

44 Ormsby, "The Taste of Truth," p. 149. As J.W. Morris points out ("Ibn 'Arabī and His Interpreters, Part II," p. 738): "There is still no single study showing how Ghazālī creatively transformed the meaning of elements from other intellectual traditions – Ash'arite

for the immense impact of his works on later Islamic thought were his integration of philosophy into Sufism and his stress on esoteric Sufi hermeneutics, which are discussed in the ensuing section.

GHAZĀLĪ'S ESOTERIC SUFI HERMENEUTICS

In Ghazālī's autobiography, *Al-Munqidh min al-ḍalāl*, written about five years before his death, he explains how he was drawn to investigate the truth claims and methods advanced by four different schools of thought[45]:

i) Theologians (*mutakallimūn*, scholastic theologians who engage in apologetic theology or *Kalām*), proceeding by dialectic and argumentation;
ii) Ismā'īlī authoritarianism (*ta'līm*), applied by authoritarian methods, coupled with the belief in a sinless *imām*;
iii) Philosophy (*falsafa*), depending on reason and demonstration;
iv) Sufism (*taṣawwuf*), the practical path of inner transformation, inspiration and illumination.[46]

Ghazālī examined each of these four schools – the first and third of which represented exoteric, and the second and fourth of which represented esoteric, initiatory positions[47] – and concluded that the Sufi way was the highest and most perfect of them. In chapter three of *Al-Munqidh*, devoted

kalam, Avicennan *falsafa*, and Shiite writings – in light of ... the unifying spiritual (both philosophic and Sufi) perspective and multifaceted rhetorical methods and intentions that tie together his outwardly disparate writings."

45 For an exhaustive study of this classification, see Osman Bakar, *Classification of Knowledge in Islam: A Study in Islamic Philosophies of Science* (Cambridge, U.K.: Islamic Texts Society 1998), chap. 8. This division into four schools is perhaps under the influence of 'Umar Khayyām's *Risālah dar 'ilm kulliyāt-i wujūd*, trans. Mehdi Aminrazavi, *The Wine of Wisdom: The Life, Poetry and Philosophy of Omar Khayyam* (Oxford: Oneworld 2005), pp. 303–10. As Aminrazavi observes (p. 136), both Khayyām and Suhrawardī Maqtūl shared the same fourfold classification of seekers of the truth.

46 Eric Ormsby, "The Taste of Truth: The Structure of Experience in al-Ghazālī's *Al-Munqidh Min Al-Ḍalāl*," *Islamic Studies Presented to Charles J. Adams*, ed. W.B. Hallaq and D.P. Little (Leiden: Brill 1991), p. 137.

47 Hodgson, *The Venture of Islam* II, p. 184.

to the various 'classes of seekers', he accords only two paragraphs to the first category, the theologians, but consecrates a very long section to the philosophers.[48] He also devotes seven pages to the Ismāʿīlīs and the "dangers of their doctrine."[49] Lastly, he dedicates six pages to the Sufi way, which, he

48 See his *al-Munqidh min al-ḍalāl*, ed. Farīd Jabre (Beirut: Librairie Orientale 1969), pp. 18–27; trans. by R.J. McCarthy, *Deliverance from Error: An Annotated Translation of al-Munqidh min al-Dalāl and other relevant works of al-Ghazālī* (Louisville: Fons Vitae, n.d.), pp. 60–70.

49 Jabre, pp. 27–34; McCarthy, pp. 71–77. Hodgson (*op. cit.* II, p. 184ff.) believed that Ghazālī attacked the Ismāʿīlīs not so much because they were a substantial political threat to the Seljuq state that he worked for, but because he found their position on authority, which after all had similarities to that of the Sufis which he endorsed as truth, too persuasive to ignore. However, it is obvious that his anti-Ismāʿīlī stance was also stimulated by the political crisis generated by Ḥasan-i Ṣabbāḥ's Nizārī state in the Alamūt region. His polemic against them, the *Faḍā'ih al-baṭinīyyah wa faḍā'il al-mustaẓhirīyyah* (*The Infamies of the Bāṭinites and the Excellencies of the Mustaẓhirites*), was obviously written not only to defend his position as a Sunni theologian, but also, as Farouk Mitha pointed out, because "Ḥasan's movement had taken on, for the Saljuqs, the proportions of an uncontrollable political menace which insidiously threatened the very fabric of their empire. For al-Ghazālī, this fabric was none other than the Sunni ethos of the empire." *Al-Ghazali and the Ismailis: A Debate on Reason and Authority in Medieval Islam* (London: I.B. Tauris in association with the Institute of Ismaili Studies 2001), p. 23. In fact, the Niẓāmīyya colleges founded by Niẓām al-Mulk, in one of which Ghazālī was a tenured professor, were partly intended to train scholars to counter the religious propaganda of the Fatimids. See Al-Ghazālī, *The Incoherence of the Philosophers*, trans. Michael Marmura (Provo: Brigham Young University Press 1997), introduction, p. xvii. With the benefit of hindsight, it is clear that Ghazālī's attitude towards Ismāʿīlī spirituality in all his works was largely politically motivated by Sunni apologetics, and, intellectually speaking, lacking in nuance. He was loath to acknowledge the presence of any authentic esoteric element or *bāṭin* in Ismāʿīlī hermeneutics (*ta'wīl*), restricting access to that inner dimension solely to Sufi adepts. By excluding any notion of the existence of an initiatic and supra-rational character in the Ismāʿīlī concept of authority (*taʿlīm*), as Osman Bakar points out, he "thus greatly diminished the significance of the Ismāʿīlī methodology as a means of attaining knowledge of the true reality of things." Osman Bakar, *Classification of Knowledge in Islam: A Study in Islamic Philosophies of Science* (Cambridge, U.K.: Islamic Texts Society 1998), p. 194.

concludes, is the supreme and best path.[50] Describing the various 'classes of the Sufis," Ghazālī writes:

> I thus comprehended their fundamental teachings on the intellectual side, and progressed, as far as is possible by study and oral instruction, in the knowledge of mysticism. It became clear to me, however, that what is most distinctive of mysticism is something which cannot be apprehended by study, but only by immediate experience (*dhawq* – literally 'tasting'), by ecstasy and by a moral change. (*Mā lā yumkin al-wuṣūl ilayi bi'l-ta'allum bul bi'l-dhawq wa'l-ḥāl wa tabaddul al-ṣifāt*) ... I apprehended that the Sufis were men who had real experiences, not men of words, (*arbāb al-aḥwāl, lā aṣḥāb al-aqwāl*), and that I had already progressed as far as was possible by way of intellectual apprehension. What remained for me was not to be attained by oral instruction and study but only by immediate experience and walking in the mystic way.[51]

For Ghazālī, Sufism penetrated all aspects of Islamic piety and practice. It was the supreme science.[52] Ghazālī's endorsement of Sufism had a most important unstated implication, which was the intimate relationship between Sufism and prophecy in his thought, as Hodgson points out:

> One must be able to perceive the ultimate truth, in however slight a measure, in the same way the prophets perceived it, in order to verify definitely that they were prophets – just as one must be in some slight measure oneself a physician to judge of physicians. One must know what it is, to have not merely knowledge about the truth but immediate acquaintance with it as prophets had. Otherwise the cumulative experience would still allow only a superior sort of *kalām*, merely probable in its conclusions. A further way to truth was called for, beyond *kalām*, beyond *falsafah*, beyond even an ordinary pursuit of

50 Jabre, pp. 35–40; McCarthy, pp. 77–83.

51 Adapted from M. Watt's translation, *The Faith and Practice of al-Ghazālī* (Oxford: Oneworld, repr. 1994), pp. 56–58; for the Arabic text, see Jabre, *al-Munqidh*, p. 35.

52 Jabre, *al-Munqidh*, p. 39; McCarthy, *Deliverance from Error*, p. 81 (para. 94).

> an authority that would meet the needs that reason disclosed. This lay in the Sûfî experience.[53]

Ghazālī's approach to the prophetic experience and his belief that true Sufis may gain a partial access to this experience is in accord with Avicenna's view of the faculty of intuition and imagination that certain adept Sufis possessed that enabled them to have access to illumination of the Active Intelligence.[54] Ghazālī's gnostic perspective expresses the centrality of esoteric visionary thinking in Islamic epistemology. For Ghazālī, only through the science of disclosure (*'ilm al-mukāshafa*) can one "gain knowledge of the meaning of prophecy and the prophet, and of the meaning of revelation (*al-waḥy*)."[55]

Despite the fact that Ghazālī was deeply steeped both in Peripatetic and Neo-Platonic philosophy,[56] as well as in scholastic theology, perhaps

53 Hodgson, *The Venture of Islam* II, p. 187.

54 Cf. Hodgson, *The Venture of Islam* II, p. 172. For a good discussion of the influence of Avicenna's theory of prophecy upon Ghazālī, see Frank Griffel, "The Introduction of Avicennean Psychology into Muslim Theological Discourse," *Transcendent Philosophy* IV (2002): 359–70.

55 See N.A. Faris, *The Book of Knowledge, Being a Translation with Notes of the Kitāb al-'Ilm of al-Ghazzālī's Iḥyā' 'Ulūm al-Dīn* (Lahore: 1962), p. 47; also N. Heer, "Abū Ḥāmid al-Ghazālī's Esoteric Exegesis of the Qur'ān," in Leonard Lewisohn (ed.), *The Heritage of Sufism*, vol. I: *Classical Persian Sufism: from its Origins to Rūmī* (Oxford: Oneworld 1999), p. 247.

56 As Farid Jabre (*La Notion de la* ma'rifa *chez Ghazali* [Beirut: Éditions Les Lettres Orientales 1958], p. 131) notes: "Ghazālī's work that is related to Sufism is neo-platonic in its inspiration; his *ma'rifa* is the adoption of a Plotinian schema, but in the climate of orthodox Muslim thought." Oliver Leaman (*An Introduction to Classical Islamic Philosophy* [Cambridge: Cambridge University Press 2002, repr. of 1985 ed], p. 26) makes a similar observation in this context: "Although al-Ghazālī's crisis of faith led him to abandon theoretical approaches to Islam that were not mystical, there is obviously a great deal of philosophy in his mysticism." (also cf. Hodgson, *The Venture of Islam* II, p. 182). M. Saeed Sheikh likewise notes, "In spite of his initial denunciation of philosophy, al-Ghazālī could never completely part company with it. His Sufi mysticism was as much influenced by his thorough study of philosophy as by theology; in its final development it was the mysticism of a philosopher and a theologian. There is a marked tone of Hellenic thought in his mystical doctrines and even the tracings of Neo-Platonism, and yet paradoxical though it

because neither theology nor philosophy yielded for him any ultimate certainty,[57] Sufi theories of knowledge took centre-stage in his epistemological thinking. Yet Sufism for him was not "simply an individual path to reach perfection but a whole conception of life including ethics and morality, behaviour and belief, cosmology and metaphysics. In this sense, it is perhaps true that al-Ghazzālī's mysticism is not *only* a lived experience but also a rational construction by which the learned person can *taste* the beatitude of ecstasy without relinquishing the satisfaction of theoretical inquiry."[58]

The technical term 'taste' (*dhawq*) here was the central notion in his concept of knowledge and certitude; it was also the highest characteristic of the Sufis.[59] Ghazālī "considered theoretical certainty as an effect of the highest kind of knowledge, a knowledge which attains its top level by mystical experience and taste (*dhawq*)."[60] For Ghazālī, the intuitive savour and sapience of the heart (*dhawq-i qalbī*) was superior to all other knowledge (*'ilm*).[61] "Sufis profess," Ghazālī informs us in the *Risālat ladunī*, that "the heart possesses its own organ of vision (*oculus cordis*) just like the body, so

may seem they remain circumscribed within the limits of orthodoxy." Chap. XXXI, "Al-Ghazālī. A. Mysticism (Continued)," in M.M. Sharif (ed.), *A History of Muslim Philosophy* (Delhi: D.K. Publications 1995; repr. of the 1961 edition), I, p. 617. For the neo-Platonic substrate of his thought, also see my annotations to the ensuing text.

57 Massimo Campanini, "Al-Ghazzālī," in S.H. Nasr and O. Leaman (eds.), *History of Islamic Philosophy* (London: Routledge 1996), I, pp. 258–59.

58 Campanini, "Al-Ghazzālī," p. 266.

59 Ormsby, "The Taste of Truth: The Structure of Experience in al-Ghazālī's *Al-Munqidh Min Al-Ḍalāl*," *Islamic Studies Presented to Charles J. Adams*, ed. W.B. Hallaq and D.P. Little (Leiden: Brill 1991), p. 142; on *dhawq* in Ghazālī, see also T.J. Winter's translation of the *Iḥyā*'s Book XL: *Al-Ghazālī: Remembrance of Death* (Cambridge: Islamic Texts Society 1995), p. xviii.; Alexander Treiger, *Inspired Knowledge in Islamic Thought: Al-Ghazālī's Theory of Mystical Cognition and its Avicennian Foundation* (London: Routledge 2012), chap. 3.

60 Campanini, "Al-Ghazzālī," p. 259.

61 "Knowledge is above faith, and tasting is above knowledge." Al-Ghazālī, *The Niche of Lights: Mishkat al-anwār*, trans. David Buchman with parallel Arabic text (Provo: Brigham Young University Press 1998), p. 38. Also see Ghulām Ḥusayn Ibrāhīmī Dīnānī's discussion of this and other similar passages in Ghazālī's works in his *Manṭiq u ma'rifat dar naẓar-i Ghazālī* (Tehran: Amīr Kabīr 1375 A.Hsh./1996), p. 189.

that just as the ocular eye beholds outward things, the intellectual eye (*'ayn al-'aql*) perceives inward things, the esoteric spiritual realities (*al-ḥaqā'iq*)." The organ of intuitive gnosis and perception is thus the heart, not sensory eyesight. In his *Exegesis of the Marvels of the Heart*, as 'Abd al-Ḥusayn Zarrīnkūb informs us, Ghazālī elaborated this sophisticated and complicated spiritual cardiology as follows:

> Following the Sufis, Ghazālī held the path of the heart to be nearest of all other paths in the disclosure of Reality (*kashf-i ḥaqīqat*). Sensory and psychological perception are subsumed by cognizance of the heart, compared to which even reason and intelligence (*'aql*) were accounted to be but a small part. The heart, however, was in no way, opposed to reason. According to Ghazālī, the highest degree of intelligence (*'aql*) appertains to the prophet, who is able to acquire gnosis (*ma'rifat*) by means of divine inspiration (*ilhām-i rabānī*) through visionary unveiling (*kashf*) without recourse to any effort to acquire or labour to obtain his knowledge ... In Ghazālī's view, the heart can be rightly compared to a mirror in the acquisition of gnosis (*ma'rifat*); he affirms that the heart holds the same relation to actual metaphysical realities as a mirror does to images of physical things. In the manner that images of physical things are reflected on the surface of a mirror, the [metaphysical] reality of things (*haqīqat-i ashyā'*) also has images reflected on the mirror of the heart.[62]

Just as the clarity of the reflection of objects in the mirror may be occluded by layers of dust and grime upon its surface, the reflection of spiritual realities in the heart's mirror may be darkened by sensual attachments, sensory engagements and egocentric preoccupations.[63] One of the worst impediments to purity and clarity of the heart's looking glass and its realization of certitude is religious fanaticism and the blind imitation (*taqlīd*) of others respecting the principles of religious faith.[64]

---

62 'Abd al-Ḥusayn Zarrīnkūb, *Farār az madrasa: darbāra-yi zindigī va andīsha-yi Abū Ḥāmid Ghazālī* (Tehran: Amīr Kabīr 1364 A.Hsh./1985), p. 200.

63 Carol Bargeron, "Sufism's Role in Al-Ghazālī's First Crisis of Knowledge," pp. 49–50.

64 Zarrīnkūb, *Farār az madrasa*, p. 201. Ghazālī thus pronounces: "How many upright individuals who reflect on the realms of heaven and earth are veiled by varieties of adherence to uncritical assent that congeal in their souls and take deep root in their

The source of true religious knowledge is unveiling (*kashf*), which is "a more veracious alternative to knowledge acquired by sensory or rational means," and since seeing is, after all, believing, to Ghazālī mystical insight came to be considered ultimately "more beneficial than reports or transmissions."[65] He noted that "whoever thinks that the illumination of visionary unveiling depends on strict rational proofs has constricted for himself the vast mercy of God."[66] In this respect, his views anticipate those of Ibn 'Arabī a century later, whose writings on this subject (see the selections on 'unveiling' translated below in this anthology) closely resemble Ghazālī's.[67] Gnosis (*ma'rifat*) is to be obtained by means of the Sufi practices of remembrance of God and contemplation (*al-dhikr wa'l-fikr*) and abstaining from all but God Almighty.[68] Only those Sufis who have enough

---

hearts, so that a veil comes between them and the perception of realities." – From his *Kitāb sharḥ 'ajā'ib al-qal*, cited by John Renard, *The Knowledge of God in Classical Sufism: Foundations of Islamic Mystical Theology* (New York: Paulist Press 2004), p. 303. For an excellent discussion of the place of blind imitation (*taqlīd*) versus the personal experimental verification (*taḥqīq*) of religious doctrine and truth in Ghazālī's works, see Dīnānī, *Manṭiq u ma'rifat*, pp. 68–74.

65 On the knowledge of unveiling (*kashf*) in Ghazālī, see Treiger, *Inspired Knowledge in Islamic Thought*, pp. 42–47; Cyrus Ali Zargar, "Kašf o Šohud," *Encyclopædia Iranica* XV, pp. 670–71.

66 *Al-Munqidh*, ed. Jabre, p. 14.

67 As T.J. Winter observes, "The popularity of Ghazālī's methodologically rigorous harmonization of scripture and mysticism did much to prepare the ground for the success of Ibn 'Arabī's doctrine, the rapid spread of which has been seen as enigmatic. Similarly, his critique of philosophical epistemology whereby he showed that the underlying premises of knowledge are themselves without proof, perhaps facilitated the later emphasis in Islamic civilization on mystical rather than ratiocinative knowledge." – T.J. Winter (trans.), *Al-Ghazālī on Disciplining the Soul: Kitāb Riyāḍat al-nafs & on Breaking the Two Desires: Kitāb Kasr al-shahwatayn*, Bks. 22–23 of *The Revival of the Religious Sciences* (Cambridge: Islamic Texts Society 1995), p. lxxii, no. 1. J.W. Morris also points out that "Ghazālī is certainly the most important 'precursor' of the explicitly metaphysical aspect of Ibn 'Arabī's writings." "Ibn 'Arabī and His Interpreters, Part II: Influences and Interpretations," *JAOS* 106/4 (1986), p. 738.

68 *Kitāb al-Maḍnūn bi 'alā ghayr ahlihi*, cited by Dīnānī, *Manṭiq u ma'rifat*, p. 193.

heart-savour to apprehend the meaning of visionary unveiling (*dhawq-i mukāshafa*) can obtain access to this degree.[69]

Steeped as he was in both Peripatetic and Neo-Platonic philosophy, Ghazālī had his own peculiar understanding of the relationship between philosophy and Sufism. The Sufi mystics and the Peripatetic philosophers differed profoundly in their outlook on both life and God, on knowledge of this world and knowledge of the Creator. The mystics tried to actualize knowledge (*'ilm* or *ma'rifat*) by mystical precepts and practices.[70]

Approaching the dichotomous opposition between rational academic and mystical inspirational knowledge, Ghazālī took the Qur'ān and *kalām*-theology as his starting points, and proceeded onwards and outwards from there. His was therefore not the philosopher's, the rationalist way, which had approached the divine Law with a more open-minded attitude, based on free inquiry. As again Mahdi notes: "Philosophy was thus understood by analogy to the human arts whose practice is demanded by the divine law, but a divine law that left man free to perfect these arts according to his natural light."[71]

As was pointed out above, from the post-Ghazālī period in Islam down to early modern times, esoteric modes of expression enjoyed great popularity. It is this esoteric attitude that Hodgson labels 'Sufi elitism', illustrating this in the following diagram:[72]

---

69 Zarrīnkūb, *Farār az madrasa*, p. 202. For Ghazālī's own theories of the heart, see John Renard's partial translation of Bk. 21 of the *Iḥyā*, the *Kitāb sharḥ 'ajā'ib al-qal*, in his *The Knowledge of God in Classical Sufism: Foundations of Islamic Mystical Theology* (New York: Paulist Press 2004), pp. 298–26. For a good discussion of the place of the heart in Ghazālī's spiritual psychology, see Ebrahim Moosa, *Ghazālī and the Poetics of Imagination* (Chapel Hill: University of North Carolina Press 2005), pp. 224–27.

70 Muhsin Mahdi points out: "For mystics like Ghazālī (see Shehadi 1964; Sherif 1975), God is unknowable, inaccessible, and wholly unpredictable because He is absolutely free. Even the relative stability and predictability according to which the believer acts in response to the divine law is not a sure passport to heaven or to the vision of God in the hereafter. One needs to be patient and hopeful of God's kindness and mercy, go beyond the strict demands of the law, and practice mystical virtues that culminate in trust and love, the only virtues with which man can counter an utterly unpredictable relation between himself and his Lord." – *Alfarabi and the Foundation of Islamic Political Philosophy* (Chicago: University of Chicago Press 2001), p. 25.

71 Muhsin Mahdi, *Alfarabi and the Foundation*, p. 27.

72 M.G.S. Hodgson, *The Venture of Islam* II, p. 197.

Types of Muslim Esoteric Elitism

Faylasūf Elitism	**Sectarian Elitism, particularly Bāṭinīyya**	**Sufi Elitism**
Forerunners rejected by Rāzī, but developed by al-Fārābī (elements) and Ibn Sīnā (principles)	Principles of *taqīyya* and discipline of *ghulāt* under Ja'far Conspiratorialism of the Ismā'īlīs and other Bāṭinīyya	The argument over al-Ḥallāj; the position of al-Junayd
Ibn Ṭufayl: Falsafah elitism modified by Sufi experience		
Ibn Rushd and the Spanish school most fully represent this attitude in practice		Al-Ghazālī's elitism: *taqlīd* for ordinary believers; *kalām* for ordinary doubters; *taqīyya* for Sufi *'ārif*
The Ibn Ṭufayl–Ibn Rushd positions affect also Jews	*Taqīyya* of Nizārī Ismā'īlīs: after *qiyāma*: unbelievers do not truly exist	Sufi matured positions: Ḥallāj was wrong only in his public avowal *pīrī-murīdī* discipline and the *silsila*
Later Spanish Faylasūfs and Ibn Khaldūn	Merge in Sufi *ṭarīqas*	

In many of his exoteric works, such as *The Foundations of the Articles of Faith* (*Kitāb Qawā'id al-Aqā'id*), Book I. 2 of the *Iḥyā'*), Ghazālī declares very clearly that while esoteric knowledge does not contradict exoteric knowledge, knowledge of the esoteric is restricted to a spiritual elite (*khawāṣṣ*). Why? Because the esoteric dimension "is subtle and beyond the comprehension of most minds. Consequently, its comprehension is restricted to an elite who should not divulge it to those who are unable to grasp it lest, whenever their minds fail to comprehend it or to understand the concealed secrets of the spirit, it becomes a calamity to them."[73]

Ghazālī's strident esotericism in epistemological thought was equally highlighted in the realm of hermeneutics. He was a strong proponent of the theory of the multiple levels of meanings in the Qur'ān, understood to be hierarchically graded – from literal, material exoteric meanings comprehensible to the masses – up to higher, symbolic and anagogic senses apprehended only by adepts.[74] Replying to an objection based on a tradition of the Prophet which states: "Whoever interprets the Qur'ān in accordance with his own opinion shall take his place in the Fire," Ghazālī writes that because of it, "scholars in the exoteric interpretation [of the Qur'ān] have reviled the Sufi interpreters for their metaphorical interpretation (*ta'wīl*) of certain words in the Qur'ān [in a sense] contrary to what was transmitted on the authority of Ibn 'Abbās and other interpreters, and took the position that it amounted to unbelief."[75] Ghazālī refutes this as follows:

> The man who claims that the Qur'ān has no meaning except that which the exoteric exegesis has transmitted is acknowledging his own limitations. He is right in his acknowledgment, but is wrong in his judgement that puts all people on the level to which he is limited and bound. Indeed, reports and traditions [of the Prophet and others] indicate that for men of understanding there is great latitude

73 See Al-Ghazālī, *Kitāb Qawā'id al-Aqā'id* (*Iḥyā'* I.2), trans. Nabih Amin Faris, *The Foundations of the Articles of Faith* (Lahore: Sh. Muhammad Ashraf 1974), p. 39.

74 For an overview of which, see Annabel Keeler and Sajjad Rizvi (eds.), *The Spirit and the Letter: Approaches to the Esoteric Interpretation of the Qur'an* (London: I.B. Tauris in association with the Institute of Ismaili Studies 2017), introduction.

75 *Iḥyā'* I, p. 260; cited by Nicholas Heer, "Abū Ḥāmid al-Ghazālī's Esoteric Exegesis of the Qur'ān," in Leonard Lewisohn (ed.), *The Heritage of Sufism: Classical Persian Sufism: from its Origins to Rūmī* (Oxford: Oneworld 1999), I, p. 238.

> (*muttasa'*) in the meanings of the Qur'ān. Thus, 'Ali said, "[The Messenger of God did not confide to me anything which he concealed from people], except that God bestows understanding of the Qur'ān upon a man." If there were no meaning (*tarjama*) other than that which has been transmitted, what, then, is [meant by] that understanding of the Qur'ān? The Prophet said, "Surely, the Qur'ān has an outward aspect (*ẓahr*), an inward aspect (*baṭn*), an ending (*ḥadd*) and a beginning (*maṭla'*)." This [tradition] is also related as being from Ibn Mas'ūd on his own authority, and he was one of the scholars of exegesis (*'ulamā' al-tafsīr*). What, then, is the meaning of the outward aspect, inward aspect, end and beginning?
>
> 'Alī said, "If I wished I could load seventy camels with the exegesis of the Opening Surah (*al-Fātiḥa*) of the Qur'ān." What is the meaning of this, when the exoteric interpretation [of this surah] is extremely short? Abū al-Dardā' said, "A man does not [truly] understand until he attributes [different] perspectives (*wujūh*) to the Qur'ān." A certain scholar said, "For every [Qur'ānic] verse there are sixty thousand understandings (*fahm*), and what remains to be understood is even more." Others have said, "The Qur'ān contains seventy-seven thousand two hundred sciences (*'ilm*), for every word [in it] is a science, and then that [number] can be quadrupled, since every word has an outward aspect, an inward aspect, an end and a beginning."
>
> The Prophet's repetition of [the phrase] "In the name of God, the merciful, the compassionate" twenty times was only for the purpose of pondering (*tadabbur*) its esoteric meanings (*bāṭin ma'ānīhā*). Otherwise its explanation (*tarjama*) and exegesis (*tafsīr*) are so obvious (*ẓāhir*) *that someone like him would not need to repeat it.* Ibn Mas'ūd said, "He who desires the knowledge of the ancients and the moderns should ponder the Qur'ān," and that is not something that can be attained merely by its exoteric interpretation (*tafsīrihi al-ẓāhir*).[76]

Of course, this delineation and discrimination between those who can comprehend the divine secrets (*asrār*) and realities (*ḥaqā'iq*), that is, the

76 From the *Iḥyā*, trans. Nicholas Heer, "Abū Ḥāmid al-Ghazālī's Esoteric Exegesis of the Qur'ān," in *The Heritage of Sufism*, pp. 238–39.

Sufis using the symbolic mode of allusion (*ishārāt*) in their interpretations,[77] and those who follow the traditional and legal types of exegesis, was by no means original to Ghazālī. The esoteric hermeneutical theory can be traced in Islamic history back as far as the second century, to Ja'far al-Ṣādiq (d. 148/765),[78] in whose works a Sufistic interiorization of Qur'ānic symbolism appears,[79] making him therefore the founder of esoteric Qur'ānic exegesis: both in the Ismā'īlī sense of *ta'wīl* and the Sufi sense of *taḥqīq*, amongst the Shī'ites and Sufis alike.[80] Common to all the mystics and esotericists, from Ja'far al-Ṣādiq, to Sahl ibn 'Abdullāh Tustarī's (d. 283/896) Sufi *Tafsīr*,[81] to 'Abdu'l-Raḥmān Sulamī's (d. 412/1021) *Ḥaqā'iq al-tafsīr*,[82] and finally down to Ghazālī, is their constant citation of certain *ḥadīth* allowing for and announcing the presence of these multiple vertical levels, but basing themselves primarily on the Prophet's celebrated affirmation that, "the Qur'ān has an outward aspect, an inward aspect, an ending and a beginning (*li'l-Qur'āni ẓāhirun wa bāṭinun wa ḥaddun wa muṭṭalaun*)."[83]

According to Ghazālī, the Qur'ān's esoteric meanings should not be divulged to the common masses. Thus, seventh among the ten duties

---

77 For a good discussion of which, see Gerhard Böwering, describing *The Mystical Vision of Existence in Classical Islam: The Qur'ānic Hermeneutics of the Ṣūfī Sahl At-Tustarī (d. 283/896)* (Berlin/New York: Walter de Gruyter 1980), pp. 135–42.

78 Extracts from his Qur'ān commentary are given by Paul Nwyia, "Le Tafsīr mystique attribué à Ja'far al-Ṣādiq," in *Mélanges de l'Université Saint-Joseph*, t. XLIII, fasc. 4, 1967, pp. 181–230. See also Farhana Mayer, *Spiritual Gems: The Mystical Qur'an Commentary ascribed to Ja'far al-Sadiq as contained in Sulami's Haqa'iq al-Tafsir* (Louisville: Fons Vitae 2011).

79 Sells, *Early Islamic Mysticism*, p. 21.

80 Peter Awn, "Sufism," in M. Eliade (ed.) *The Encyclopædia of Religion* XIV, p. 105.

81 *Tafsīr al-Tustarī*, trans. Annabel Keeler and Ali Keeler (Louisville, KY: Fons Vitae 2011), pp. xxvi–xxix. See also Maryam Musharraf and Leonard Lewisohn, 'Sahl Tustarī's (d. 283/896) Esoteric Qur'ānic Commentary and Rūmī's *Mathnawī*: Part 1', *Mawlana Rumi Review* 5 (2014), pp. 180–203.

82 See Abū 'Abdu'l-Raḥmān al-Sulamī, *Tafsīr al-Sulamī wa huwa Ḥaqā'iq al-tafsīr*, ed. Sayyid 'Umrān (Beirut: Dar al-Kutub al-'Ilmīyya 1422/2001), 2 vols.

83 For further discussion of the interior dimensions of meaning in the Qur'ān, see C. Guilliot, *Exégèse, Langue et Theologie en Islam* (Paris: Vrin 1990), pp. 120–25; P. Nwyia, *Exégèse Coranique et Langage Mystique* (Beirut: 1970), *passim.*; Böwering, *op. cit.*, pp. 139–40.

required of the teacher which Ghazālī enumerated in his *Kitāb al-'ilm* in the *Iḥyā'* was that he "give his less competent students only such things as are clear and suitable for them, and should not mention to them that there is anything more complex to follow which he is [for the present] withholding from them. To do so would weaken their desire for what is clear, muddle their minds, and make them imagine that he is stingy in imparting his knowledge, since everyone believes himself capable of every science no matter how complex." Thus, Ghazālī cautions the teacher not to

> confuse the belief of anyone of the common people (*al-'awāmm*) who has bound himself to the religion, and in whose heart the articles of faith handed down from the predecessors (*al-salaf*) are firmly established without anthropomorphisms (*tashbīh*) or metaphorical interpretations (*ta'wīl*), and whose conscience is clear, but whose intellect is not capable of anything beyond that. On the contrary such a person should be left to mind his own business, because if the metaphorical interpretations (*ta'wīlāt*) of the literal [verses] (*al-ẓāhir*) should be mentioned to him, his bonds as a common man [to religion] would be loosened, and it would not be easy to bind him with the bonds of the elite (*al-khawāṣṣ*). The barrier which has prevented him from acts of disobedience will cease to exist, and he will turn into a rebellious Satan who will destroy both himself and others.[84]

In Ghazālī's mind, the deeper meanings of the Qur'ān, the polysemy of its words and its multivalent images and ideas necessarily evoked differences of expression and understanding among Sufis, theologians and philosophers. He often underlined these three groups are saying exactly the same thing but in different words. The reconciliation of opposing academic schools of thought was clearly one positive contribution made by Ghazālī to the catholicity and wider ecumenical concerns of Islamic thought. In his treatise on esoteric knowledge, translated below, he thus explains that the 'rational soul' has been termed various things by various groups, although their meaning is clearly one and the same:

---

84 Nabih Amin Faris, *The Book of Knowledge* (Lahore: Sh. Muhammad Ashraf 1962), pp. 151–52; cited by N. Heer, *art. cit.*, pp. 255–56.

> Every company gives this 'rational soul' (*al-nafs al-nāṭiqa*), that is to say, this substance, its own peculiar name. The philosophers (*al-ḥukamā'*) thus name it the 'rational soul' (*al-nafs al-nāṭiqa*), while the Qur'ān refers to it as the 'serene soul' (*al-nafs al-muṭma'inna*)[85] or the 'Spirit of the Command' (*al-rūḥ al-amrī*);[86] the Sufis call it the 'heart' (*al-qalb*). The difference lies only in the labels and names. In their sense and significance these terms all mean the same thing, in respect to which no differences exist. Hence in our opinion, such terms as 'heart', 'spirit' and 'serene soul' are just different names for the rational soul.[87] The rational soul is a vital living, acting, consciously understanding substance, so whenever we speak of the 'infinite Spirit' (*al-rūḥ al-muṭlaq*) or 'heart', our reference is solely to this substance.[88]

In this passage, one may observe how Ghazālī implies that a supra-rational element in philosophical thinking in Islam, even leniently acknowledging, it appears, that philosophical intuition can also lead to a direct experience of metaphysical truth[89] without recourse to Sufism.

Ghazālī's major and abiding interest, however, was the Sufi tradition. His interest in theology, in canonical jurisprudence and even in philosophy was incidental to his focus on Sufism. His genius was that he had mastered all three disciplines and could speak with authority in all of them. But in the debate between "spiritualization and fundamentalism" as one scholar

---

85 Qur'ān LXXXIX:27.

86 Qur'ān XVII:85.

87 As Farid Jabre astutely notes: "*Il faut absolument entendre nafs dans ce sens réfléchi, pour comprendre les indentiés affirmées par Ghazali: nafs = rūḥ = qalb = 'aql. Pour lui, l'homme est exclusivement un principe connaissant.*" – *Essai sur le lexique de Ghazali*, p. 256.

88 Ghazālī, *Al-Risālat al-ladunī*, pp. 91–92.

89 Osman Bakar, *Classification of Knowledge in Islam: A Study in Islamic Philosophies of Science* (Cambridge, U.K.: Islamic Texts Society 1998), p. 187. Albeit, this view must be qualified with his intense strictures of philosophers' refusal to make reason subservient to revelation in his *Tahāfut al-falāsifa*; on which see *The Incoherence of the Philosophers*, trans. Michael E. Marmura (Provo: Brigham Young University Press 1997).

framed the issue,[90] his impact was patently greater on the former, that is, on the Sufi tradition than on the latter, the narrowly exoteric.[91]

ABŪ ḤĀMID AL-GHAZĀLĪ'S *AL-RISĀLAT AL-LADUNĪ*

The selection that follows features a translation of all of Ghazālī's 'Treatise on Esoteric Knowledge' (*Al-Risālat al-ladunī*). Although a translation of this treatise from the Arabic was made by Margaret Smith many decades ago,[92] my translation is based on a newly published edition of Ghazālī's treatises,[93] in which I attempt to correct certain errors in Smith's translation, modernize and update key English terms of translation used for the

---

90 M. Saeed Sheikh, "Al-Ghazālī (Continued). C. Influence," *A History of Muslim Philosophy* I, p. 639.

91 In Marshall Hodgson's (*The Venture of Islam* II, p. 188) words: "The intellectual foundations of Ghazālī's mission, then, was an expanded appreciation of Sufism. *Kalām* was relegated to a secondary role; and the most valuable insights of *Falsafah* and even of the Ismā'îlî doctrine of *ta'lîm* authority were subsumed into the re-valorized Sufism, which now appeared as guarantor and interpreter of even the Shar'ī aspects of the Islamic faith ... But the *bâṭin* of the Sufis was indispensable. The Islamic faith could not ultimately stand without the continuous re-experiencing of the ultimate truths of the mystics."

92 *Journal of the Royal Asiatic Society* (1938), Part 2, pp. 177–200; Part 3: pp. 353–74. Her translation has been recently reprinted in Seyyed Hossein Nasr and Mehdi Aminrazavi (eds.), *An Anthology of Philosophy in Persia*, vol. 4: *From the School of Illumination to Philosophical Mysticism* (London: I.B. Tauris in association with the Institute of Ismaili Studies 2012), pp. 336–71.

93 I am indebted to Prof. Hermann Landolt for providing me a copy of the edition used here: *Majmū'at Rasā'il al-Imām al-Ghazālī*, ed. Aḥmad Shams al-Dīn (Beirut: Dār al-Kutub al-Islāmīya 1406/1986), III, pp. 87–111. I would also like to thank to Prof. Edmund Bosworth for checking the accuracy of my transliteration and translation against this critical Arabic edition of the text. A Persian translation of the treatise by Zayn al-Dīn Kiyā'ī-Nizhād, *'Ilm-i Ladunī az dīdgāh-i Ghazālī* (Tehran: Mu'assaya-yi Maṭbū'ātī 'Aṭā'ī 1361 A.Hsh./1982) has also been consulted; although generally quite accurate, Kiyā'ī-Nizhād's translation often tends towards paraphrase and abbreviation (sometimes omitting clauses and expressions felt to be extraneous or unappealing). I am indebted to my friend Terry Graham for careful review and insightful comments on my introduction above.

Arabic, and place Ghazālī's thought within the context of Islamic esotericism and theosophy (before and after him) to which it properly belongs. Although its attribution to Ghazālī is still sometimes questioned,[94] today the consensus of learned opinion is that this treatise actually is by him.[95]

There is a ripple of enthusiasm running through this work which one does not find in his expository dissertations in the drier domains of philosophy and jurisprudence. One has a sense, in reading it, that it shows where Ghazālī's focus truly lay; the writer truly feels that he is presenting the core of Islam, the very foundation of his own faith in which the esoteric knowledge which hails from the divine presence (*al-'ilm al-ladunī*) appears as the quintessentially 'Islamic' knowledge, not as the intellectual knowledge of philosophy, nor of canon legality, nor of theology. At the end of the treatise, Ghazālī introduces the "science of the Sufis," which can be understood intuitively through realization of "mystical states (*al-ḥāl*), metaphysical time outside of temporal serial duration (*al-waqt*) and musical audition (*al-samā'*)." The same science of the Sufis is also elaborated in some detail his autobiographical treatise, *Al-Munqidh min al-ḍalāl* (Deliverance from Error), where Ghazālī had introduced his key concept of 'the stage beyond the intellect' (*ṭawr māwarā' 'al-'aql*), explaining that the science of the Sufis is accessed solely through supra-rational means, through the 'mode beyond intellect' (*superintellectualem*) as medieval Christian mystical theologians such as Thomas Gallus (circa 1200–46) defined it.[96] Gnosis (*ma'rifa*) cannot be realized by either sense perception (*'idrāk 'al-ḥawās*) or intellectual perception (*'idrāk 'al-'aql*), but only by access to the level of intelligence beyond ratiocination:

---

94 Treiger thus notes that although its "attribution to al-Ghazālī is still open to doubt ... most of the doctrines presented there are Ghazālian in spirit and the differences that do exist are no more radical than those existing between al-Ghazālī's authentic writings themselves." – *Inspired Knowledge in Islamic Thought*, pp. 73, 147 n. 52.

95 For a good account of various scholars' research and their opinions about its authenticity, see Maurice Bouyges and Michel Allard, *Essai de chronologie des oeuvres de al-Ghazali (Algazel)* (Beirut: Imprimerie Catholique 1959), pp. 124–25.

96 Axel Marc Takás, "Beyond the Intellect: Perpetual Expansion and Transformation in the Antropocosmic Vision of Thomas Gallus and the Akbarian Tradition," *Journal of the Muhyiddin Ibn 'Arabi Society* LV (2014), pp. 71–107.

> Beyond the stage of intellect there is another stage. In this another eye is opened, by which man sees the hidden, and what will take place in the future, and other things, from which the intellect is as far removed as the power of discernment is from the perception of ineligibles and the power of sensation is from things perceived by discernment. And just as one able only to discern, if presented with the things perceptible to the intellect, would reject them and consider them outlandish, so some men endowed with intellect have rejected the things perceptible to the prophetic power and considered them wildly improbable.[97]

The following diagram of "Al-Ghazālī's Scheme of Knowledge," which is based on this treatise,[98] depicts the hierarchical descent of knowledge from the highest level, that of the 'science of disclosure', which is the source of Sufi mystical theology, down to the rest of the sciences. Sufism, as can be seen from the diagram, occupies the supreme level, inferior only to Qur'ānic revelation and its divine self-disclosure.

Devoted to the meaning of knowledge in general, and in particular, to esoteric and 'divine' knowledge, *Al-Risālat al-ladunī* covers a topic that is central to the theme of the anthology, and is divided into eight chapters:

1. On Supersensible Esoteric Knowledge (*al-ʿilm al-ghaybī al-ladunī*)
2. On the Nobility of Knowledge
3. On the Soul and the Human Spirit
4. On the Typologies of Knowledge
   a. The science of the fundamentals of religious faith (*al-uṣūl*)
   b. The science of the corollaries of faith (*ʿilm al-furūʿ*)
5. On the Science of the Sufis
6. An Exposition of Scientific Methodology: On the Paths of Acquisition of Knowledge
   a. The Method of Human Learning
   b. The Method of the Divine Teaching of the Spirit (*al-taʿallum al-rabbānī*)
      i. Revelation
      ii. Inspiration

97 Al-Ghazālī, *Deliverance from Error*, trans. McCarthy, pp. 81–82. On the stage beyond the intellect, see also Treiger, *Inspired Knowledge in Islamic Thought*, p. 53.

98 This diagram is based on the Margaret Smith translation.

GHAZĀLĪ'S SCHEME OF KNOWLEDGE

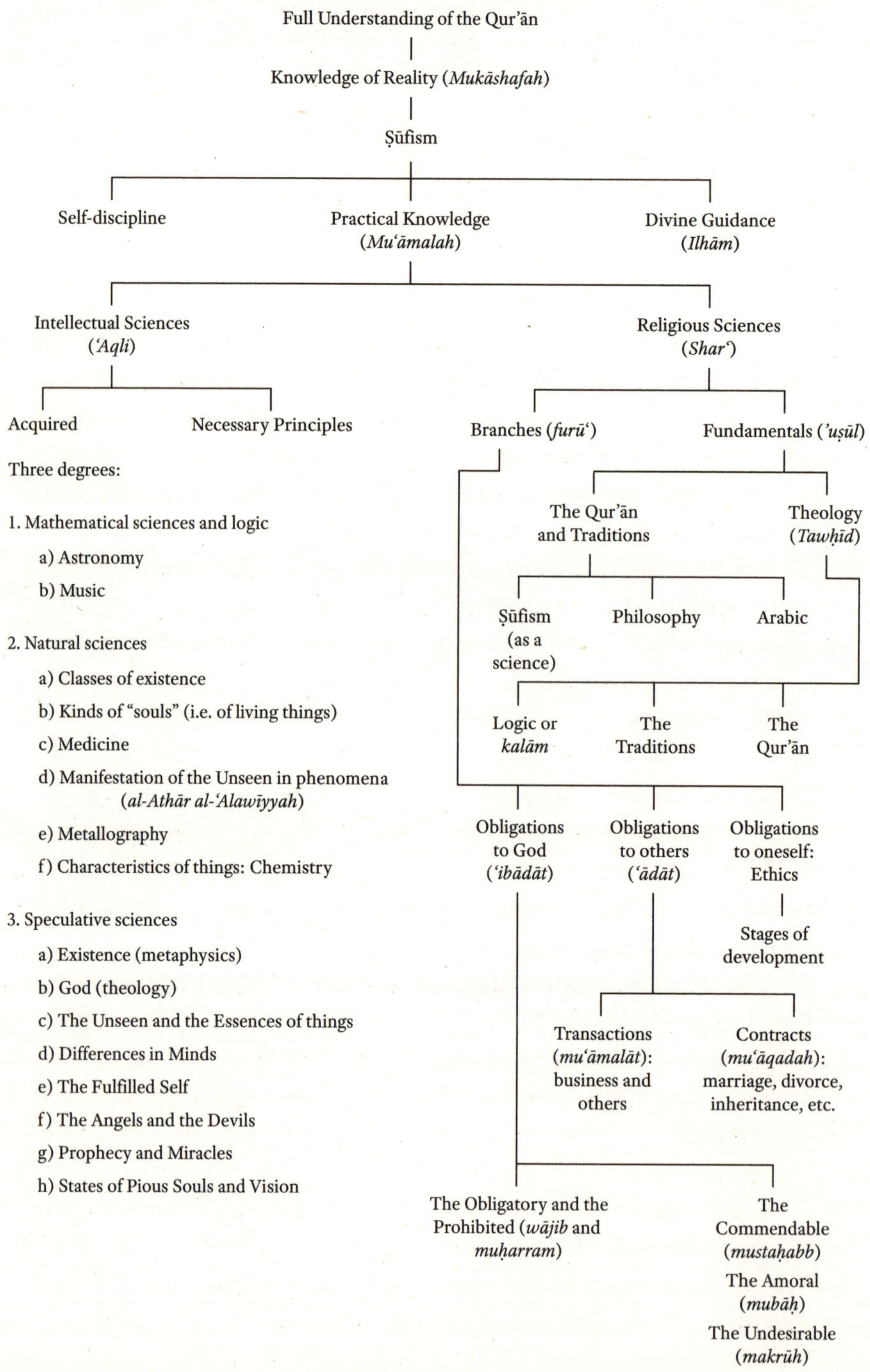

7. On the Hierarchy of Souls in the Acquisition of Knowledge
8. On the Reality of Supernal Esoteric Knowledge and the Means of its Acquisition

Ghazālī's stress in *Al-Risālat al-ladunī* on the primacy of the esoteric vision in this treatise is very much in accord with the anti-sectarian Sufi spirit which sought to establish a humane tolerance of differences of opinion among fellow Muslims in exploring the science of *tawḥīd*. Noting the absurdity of fanatical anathematization of co-religionists on the grounds of doctrinal differences, Ghazālī reflected elsewhere:

> He is a downright fool who, when asked to give his definition of *kufr*, answers: "*Kufr* is anything that is opposed to the Ashʿarite theory, or the Muʿtazilite theory, or the Hanbalite theory or indeed any other theory, (as the case may be)." Such a man is more blind than a blind man, an uncritical follower of authority.[99]

Ghazālī condemned this narrow-minded bigotry, observing that "he who hastens without reflection to the *takfīr*[100] of those who happen to oppose Ashʿarī or anybody else is an ignorant and uncritical man."[101] And of those who would condemn the Islamic rationalists or Muʿtazilites, he wrote:

---

99 From Ghazālī's *Fayṣal al-tafriqa bayna al-īslām wa-al-zandaqa*, ed. Sulaymān Dunyā (Cairo: Dār Iḥyā al-Kutub al-ʿArabīyah 1961), p. 175. This work has been translated into English by R.J. McCarthy as "Appendix 1" in his *Freedom and Fufillment* (Boston: G.K. Hall & co. 1980), and by Sherman Jackson who describes *Fayṣal al-tafriqa* as "the first and by far the most thoughtful and systematic of its type in the history of Islam." – *On the Boundaries of Theological Tolerance in Islam: Abū Ḥāmid al-Ghazālī's* Fayṣal al-Tafriqa (Oxford: Oxford University Press 2002), introduction, p. 5. For further discussion of Ghazālī's theory of *Takfīr*, see Iysa Bello, *The Medieval Islamic Controversy between Philosophy and Orthodoxy:* Ijmāʿ *and* Ta'wīl *in the Conflict between Al-Ghazālī and Ibn Rushd* (Leiden: Brill 1989), pp. 9, 43.

100 The act of declaring their opponents heretics or infidels (*kāfir*). (De Groot, *Religion, Culture and Politics in Iran* [London: I.B. Tauris 2007]. p. 90.)

101 T. Izutsu, *The Concept of Belief in Islamic Theology: A Semantic Analysis of Īmān and Islām* (Tokyo: Keio Institute of Cultural and Linguistic Studies 1965) p. 26.

> It would be wise of you that you restrain your tongue as much as possible from condemning those who pray toward Mekka, and say: "There is no god but God and Muḥammad is His Apostle," without contradicting (by what they say and do) this confession of faith. The sin of leaving alive a thousand *Kāfirs* is far less grave than that of shedding just a few drops of blood of one Muslim.[102]

In the same spirit in this treatise, one can almost hear him asking rhetorically, "What is the point of being a Muslim if one cannot have access to the subtle knowledge that comes directly from the Divine?"[103] Readiness to receive this knowledge requires the devotee's being in the Divine presence, for *ladunī* literally means living in the sapience of 'presential consciousness'. He shows the ways of approaching it, through devotional discipline and meditation, having the comforting confidence that God is the Friend, happy to divulge this knowledge to any devotee of sincerity and good conscience.

The pleasure of this treatise lies in seeing how Ghazālī delights in rolling out his philosophico-theologico-juridical knowledge, then dismissing it in favour of the insights of the Sufis. In this way, he understood that Sufism, as he sees it, is the essence of Islam. One can see exemplified in this treatise the persuasive power Ghazālī was able to bring to bear on the tradition, to take Sufism from an almost ancillary position in the Islamic perspective right to the centre of the Islamic experience, so that in the Muslim world today it is only the most rigidly fundamentalist fringe who do not feel the esoteric teachings of Islam to be at the very heart of their faith.

* * *

102 Izutsu, *The Concept of Belief in Islamic Theology*, p. 29.

103 "For him [Ghazālī], the majority of Muslims are as guilty of uncritical emulation of authority – and therefore as remote the natural disposition (*fiṭra*) as Jews and Christians, etc. The only difference between such Muslims on the one hand, and Jews and Christians on the other is that their opinions, at least some of them, happen to be in line with Islamic teachings and thus, from al-Ghazālī's perspective, 'correct', but they are opinions nonetheless, and not true knowledge." – Alexander Trieger, *Inspired Knowledge in Islamic Thought*, p. 31.

Preface Text

[87] Praise be to God who has beautified the hearts of his elect devotees with the light of Saintship (*nūr al-wilāyat*), nurtured their spirits on the loveliness of divine grace and thrown open the door to Divine Unity to gnostic adepts with the key of formally acquired knowledge (*al-dirāya*). May blessings and peace be upon our lord Muḥammad – leader of all the apostles, master of the Muslim mission in all its pastoral functions, rightly guided director of the Muslim community – and upon his family securely dwelling in the inner sanctum of divine protection.

On Supersensible Esoteric Knowledge (*al-'ilm al-ghaybī al-ladunī*)

I was told by one of my most intimate friends that there is a certain learned scholar who rejected and repudiated the validity of supersensible esoteric knowledge (*al-'ilm al-ghaybī al-ladunī*) which the Sufis hold as a special article of faith[104] and the means by which those who pursue the Sufi Path achieve their aims (for the Sufis believe that such esoteric knowledge is more reliable and superior to all other types of knowledge acquired by instruction or normative didactic means). My friend told me that the poseur claiming this had scoffed, "I am unable to conceive what this 'Sufi science' (*'ilm al-ṣūfī*) is, nor do I think that there is anyone who can discourse on this 'real knowledge' (*'ilm al-ḥaqīqī*) gained by thought and deliberation, without resorting to instruction and making efforts at its acquisition."

"It would seem that this fellow is not acquainted with different methods of obtaining knowledge," I commented, "nor does he seem to have any concrete understanding of the human soul, its various qualities, nor of the different modalities of the soul's aptitude to receive impressions of supersensible phenomena and enjoy knowledge of the angelic realm (*'ilm al-malākūt*).[105]

104 Alternate translation: which is the particular speciality of the Sufis.

105 M. Smith has a long footnote here to Ghazālī's *Iḥyā* where Ghazālī' refers to the divine world (*'ālim malākūt*). See Margret Smith, "Al-Risalat Al-Laduniyya. By Abū Ḥāmid Muḥammad Al-Ghazālī' (450/1059-505/111)," *Journal of the Royal Asiatic Society* (1938), Part 2, p. 189.

"Indeed," my friend replied. "It's just as you say. Knowledge," he claims, "consists solely of jurisprudence (*al-fiqh*), [88] Qur'ānic exegesis (*tafsīr al-Qur'ān*) and scholastic theology (*al-kalām*), and that is it. No knowledge or science beyond these exists, which sciences cannot be learned except by submitting to instruction and applying oneself to their acquisition."

"But," I protested, "how does anyone ever learn the science of Qur'ānic exegesis anyway? The Qur'ān is an ocean comprehending everything. The whole meaning of the Qur'ān and its subtle spiritual realities cannot be found solely in these well-known and celebrated literary compositions in general circulation among the rabble. In fact, Qur'ānic exegesis is quite a different thing from what this poseur supposes."

"Well, I guess he thinks that the only commentaries are the ones well-known and frequently talked about, – such as those of al-Qushayrī, al-Tha'labī, al-Māwardī and others," my friend observed.

"Why, how far wide of the truth he is!" I exclaimed. "Al-Sulamī has assembled so much information in his commentary[106] – gleaned from certain statements made by scholars who have experientially verified their knowledge so that it resembles true spiritual realization – statements the like of which are not mentioned in any other commentaries. But a person like him considers nothing but jurisprudence, scholastic theology and these commonly known commentaries to constitute 'knowledge'. Apparently, he is unable to apprehend all the diverse varieties of knowledge, their subject matter *in extenso*, their epistemological levels and hierarchical degrees, their spiritual realities, their subtle interior expressions and their manifest exterior dimensions. But there is a hackneyed precedent for such behaviour; such is common wont of the ignorant – to reject out of hand that

106 This refers to the *Ḥaqā'iq al-tafsīr* by 'Abd al-Raḥmān al-Sulamī (d. 412/1021), which is discussed by G. Böwering, "The Qur'ān Commentary of al-Sulamī," Wael Hallaq and Donald Little (eds.), *Islamic Studies Presented to Charles J. Adams* (Leiden: Brill 1991), pp. 41–56, who notes (p. 50) that Sulamī "throughout this work assembled only those items of interpretation which he regarded as genuine mystic ways of reading the Qur'ān (*ḥurūf*) in accordance with 'the understanding of the divine discourse on the basis of the language of the People of Reality (*fahm kitābihi 'alā lisān ahl al-ḥaqīqa*)'." See *Tafsīr al-Sulamī wa huwa Ḥaqā'iq al-tafsīr*, ed. Sayyid 'Umrān (Beirut: Dar al-Kutub al-'Ilmīyya 1422/2001), 2 vols.

which they don't comprehend.[107] The poseur has neither drunk of the wine of divine Reality nor apprehended anything of supernal esoteric knowledge (*al-'ilm al-ladunī*), so how can he be expected to admit it exists? Yet neither would I be content for him to simply acknowledge the existence of esoteric knowledge by way of conjecture, surmise or through blind mimesis of someone else's opinion."

"Ha!" said that friend – "I really wish you yourself would compose an account of the different hierarchical degrees of the sciences, and make a critical assessment of this knowledge, tracing it back to your own soul, and set down in writing something about it which would demonstrate it and prove its truth."

"Exposition of the subject you propose is formidably difficult," I said. "What I can do, however, is to embark on some preliminary remarks about the matter as my spiritual feeling directs, following what comes to mind and what seems in harmony with the influx of inspiration at the present moment. Yet I will try to avoid prolixity, for the best type of discourse is that which is brief and gets to the point."[108]

In these chapters I have expounded the desired theme of my learned friend; I pray that God Almighty will grant me His favour and success.

Chapter I: On the Nobility of Knowledge

It should be understood that 'knowledge' consists in the rational soul's perception of the realities of things[109] [88] and their forms abstracted from

107 Exactly the same idea is expressed in verse in the *Mathnawī* V: 3930–32; 3938–41 by Rūmī.

108 Alternate translation of this paragraph: "It would be a formidably difficult task to provide an exposition of this subject that you propose," I replied, "but what I can do is to try, however, is to embark on some preliminary remarks about the matter as my spiritual feeling directs, in harmony with the influx of inspiration that I experience at the present moment, following what comes to mind. I do not wish to be long-winded or verbose, for the best sort of speech is that which is short and direct and gets straight to the point."

109 This definition almost exactly replicates two definitions of knowledge that are cited by F. Rosenthal, *Knowledge Triumphant: The Concept of Knowledge in Medieval Islam* (Leiden: Brill 1970), p. 62, ascribed respectively to Nāṣir-i Khusraw and the *Rasā'il Ikhwān al-Ṣafā*.

matter, in their prototypical natures, qualities, quantities, substances and essences, even though these are simple individual things (*mufradāt*). And the knower (*al-ʿālim*) is one who comprehends, apprehends and perceives (a thing), while the object of knowledge (*al-maʿlūm*) is the essence of the thing itself, the knowledge of which is engraved upon the soul.

The nobility of knowledge is in proportion to the nobility of the object known, just as the rank of the knower is in proportion to the rank of the knowledge that he knows. Without a doubt, the supreme object of knowledge – that which is highest, noblest and most honourable – is God Almighty, who is the Maker, Originator, the Truth and the One. Knowledge of Him – that is to say, knowledge of divine Unity – is the supreme science. It is of highest repute, being totally inclusive. It is necessary that all rational persons acquire it, for according to the dictate of the Lawgiver: "The pursuit of knowledge is incumbent upon every Muslim."[110] He also commanded that one travel in search of knowledge, enjoining: "Pursue knowledge even unto China."[111] Therefore, the most sage and learned of scholars is one who possesses this knowledge. For this same reason, God Almighty has distinguished such sages by mentioning them as having been endowed with the highest rank, saying: "God himself proffers evidence – and so do the angels and *all those endowed with knowledge* – that there is no God but Him, firmly grounded in justice." (III:18).[112]

Now, those who are wise adepts in the science of divine Unity (*ʿilm al-tawḥīd*) are, in the full sense of the term, first of all the prophets, then the learned savants (*ʿulamāʾ*) who are the "heirs of the prophets."[113] Although this science of divine Unity is indeed the supreme science, being in itself perfectly all-inclusive, it does not thereby do away with all the other sciences. Rather, this knowledge of divine Unity cannot be acquired except by means of many premises, and those premises cannot be set properly in order except by means of recourse to many other sciences, such as

---

110 See Javad Nurbakhsh, *Traditions of the Prophet*, vol. I, trans. Leonard Lewisohn (New York: KNP 1981) p. 49.

111 For a good discussion of the motif of travel in pursuit of knowledge in Islam, see Ian Netton, *Seek Knowledge: Thought and Travel in the House of Islam* (London: Curzon 1996). On the two *ḥadīth* cited here, see Bernard Lewis, et al., "ʿIlm," in *EI2* III, pp. 1133ff.

112 Unless otherwise indicated, translations from the Qur'ān are my own.

113 A reference to the ḥadīth of the Prophet: "The learned savants are the heirs of the prophets." See Nurbakhsh, *Traditions of the Prophet*, vol. I, p. 50.

cosmology, the astronomical science as well as all the various natural sciences (*'ilm jamī' al-maṣnū'āt*).[114] Many of the other sciences are to be derived as well from this science of divine Unity, mention of which shall later be made at the proper place.

[90] It should be understood that every sort of knowledge, regardless of its object, is worthy and respectable in itself. Even the science of sorcery, for example, although it be utterly futile and frivolous (*bāṭil*), is in essence worthy and distinguished. This is because knowledge is the contrary of ignorance; ignorance is inevitably associated with darkness; darkness belongs to the domain of moribund sluggishness, while sluggishness in turn approaches pure nullity or negative non-being (*'adam*), under which all that is null, void and false may be subsumed. Ignorance of wisdom falls into the same category as negative non-being or nullity, whereas knowledge of wisdom falls into the category of existence. Existence is better than non-existence, for the course of existence is composed of knowledge, truth and light. Now just as existence excels non-existence, so knowledge surpasses ignorance. Ignorance resembles blindness and darkness, whereas knowledge resembles clear perception and light. "The blind and the seer are not alike, nor the darkness like unto the light."[115] It was to this point that God Almighty alluded when He said: "Are those who know equal to those who do not know?"[116] Therefore, since knowledge is better than ignorance, ignorance a property inevitably associated with physical corporeal matters, and knowledge is one of attributes of the soul, [it follows that] the soul is more excellent, and nobler in rank than the body.

Many are the ways that knowledge can be sought, as those adept in its pursuit will realize; these will be mentioned in a separate chapter. Now that 'knowledge' has been clearly defined for you and its pre-eminence understood, what remains to be clarified is the 'lore of the soul (*ma'rifat al-nafs*)', for the soul constitutes the [Eternally Preserved] Tablet – and abode and habitation – of all knowledge. This is because the body is not the abode of knowledge, for bodies are finite and cannot comprehend and encompass a multitude of sciences; indeed, all bodies can handle are imprinted patterns and silhouetted forms. But [the breadth of] the soul is such that it

114 Literally meaning "the science that comprehends all possible varieties of divine technology and that studies all phenomena formed by God."

115 Qur'ān XXXV:19–20.

116 Qur'ān XXXIX:9.

encompasses all sciences, all knowledge, comprehending these without any hindrance or holdup, tedium or ennui.

We shall now give a brief exposition of the soul:

Chapter II: On the Soul and the Human Spirit

[91] It should be understood that God Almighty has created man from two different things: one, the body that is dark and coarse, subject to generation, corruption and decay; it is composite, made up of various parts, earthy, unable to complete itself without recourse to something else.[117] The other is the soul, a substance that is simple, enlightening, endowed with conscious apprehension, active, moving and capable of completing (material) mechanisms and bodies. God Almighty has assembled the body from dusty grains of food ruled by globules of blood; He has arranged its affairs, shaped its form and fixed for it specific limits. The substance of the soul has been made manifest from His divine Command, which is the Unique (*al-wāḥid*), Consummate (*al-kāmil*), Consummating (*al-mukammil*) and Beneficent (*al-mufīd*).

What I mean by 'soul' here is neither the faculty of appetite that seeks for bodily sustenance, nor the faculty of concupiscence stirring up lustful passions and arousing anger, nor the faculty that resides in the heart and generates life, which is made manifest through sensation and action that proceed from the heart and permeate all the bodily organs – for this faculty is called the 'Animal Spirit (*rūḥ ḥaywānī*)' – (the powers of) sensation, motion, lust and anger composing its legions. This faculty of appetite, which is located in the liver and seeks for bodily sustenance is, through its effective regulation and control, called the 'Natural Spirit (*rūḥ tabī'ī*)', and digestion and excretion can be characterized as being among its traits. Likewise, the faculties of retentive imagination (*al-quwwa al-muṣawwira*), procreation, growth, as well as all the rest of the natural powers, are servants of the body, while the body itself is a servant of the Animal Spirit, whence it receives its power and acts according to its instigation.

117 Plotinus writes: "We know that man is not a thing of only one element; he has a Soul and he has ... a body ... The body [which is] itself too, a composite, cannot for ever hold together; and our senses show it breaking up, wearing out, the victim of destructive agents." Plotinus The Enneads. Trans. Stephen MacKenna (New York: Larson Publications Classic Series 1992), p. 392.

So by the soul (*al-nafs*), I mean solely to designate that perfectly all-inclusive and unique substance (*al-jawhar al-kāmil al-fardī*) unconcerned with any matters but [things that pertain to the faculties of] recollection (*al-tadhakkur*), memory (*al-taḥaffuẓ*), compositive human and animal imagination (*al-tafakkur*), discerning discrimination (*al-tamyīz*) and reflective deliberation (*al-rawī*).[118] It is capable of receiving all types of knowledge and never wearies of its receptivity to supersensory forms abstracted from matter. This substance is the lord of all the spirits and the prince of all the corporeal faculties, such that upon it all of them wait and tend, being subservient to its beck and call.

Every company gives this 'rational soul' (*al-nafs al-nāṭiqa*) – that is to say, this substance – its own peculiar name. The philosophers (*al-ḥukamā'*) thus name it the 'rational soul' (*al-nafs al-nāṭiqa*), while the Qur'ān refers to it as the 'serene soul' (*al-nafs al-muṭma'inna*)[119] or the 'Spirit of the Command' (*al-rūḥ al-amrī*);[120] the Sufis call it the 'heart' (*al-qalb*). The difference lies only in the labels and names. In their sense and significance these terms all mean the same thing, in respect to which no differences exist. Hence in our opinion, such terms as 'heart', [92] 'spirit' and 'serene soul' are just different names for the rational soul.[121] The rational soul is a vital living, acting, consciously understanding substance, so whenever we speak of the 'Infinite Spirit' (*al-rūḥ al-muṭlaq*) or 'heart', our reference is solely to this substance.

118 The following translations reflect those given by Ghazālī in his *Mīzān al-'amal* and *Maqāṣid al-falāsifa*, analyzed by Harry Wolfson in his study of classical Greek, Judeo-Christian and medieval Islamic psychological terminology: "The Internal Senses in Latin, Arabic, and Hebrew Philosophic Texts," *Harvard Theological Review* 28/2 (1935), pp. 103–4. Ghazālī may also have in mind the mystical connotations of these technical terms, which are, respectively: divine commemoration, recollection, meditation, spiritual discernment and vision. (The context does not completely clarify which connotation he here intends.) In translation of these and other related technical terms in Ghazālī's lexicon, reference has also been made below to Farid Jabre, *Essai sur le lexique de Ghazali* (Beirut: L'Université Libanaise 1970), s.v. individual terms.

119 Qur'ān LXXXIX:27.

120 Qur'ān XVII:85.

121 As Farid Jabre astutely notes: "*Il faut absolument entendre nafs dans ce sens réfléchi, pour comprendre les indentités affirmées par Ghazali: nafs = rūḥ = qalb = 'aql. Pour lui, l'homme est exclusivement un principe connaissant.*" *Essai sur le lexique de Ghazali*, p. 265.

On the other hand, the Sufis by 'soul' simply refer the 'Animal Spirit' (*al-rūḥ al-ḥaywānī; anima bruta*), which the Divine Law (*al-shar'*) reaffirms in [the Prophet's] saying: "Your direst enemy is your soul [which lies between your two ribs]."[122] The Lawgiver used the term 'soul' (*al-nafs*) [in this *ḥadīth*] in the absolute sense of the word, and then for emphasis added (this phrase): "*(your soul) which lies between your two ribs.*" And what he wished to indicate by using these terms was that the forces of sexual passion and anger are aroused from the heart that is positioned between the two ribs.

So, now that you have comprehended the difference between these various names and terms, you should know that those who have discussed this subject have proposed diverse interpretations about the reality of this highly refined and exquisite substance, offering a number of different theories concerning it. The scholastic theologians (*al-mutakallimūn*), celebrated for being versed in the art of dialectics and logical disputation, understand the soul to be a body, but they assert it to be a 'subtle body' (*jism laṭīf*), juxtaposed to this coarse physical body (*al-jism al-kathīf*); and according to their opinion there is no other difference between body and spirit except in the respective coarseness of one as compared to the subtlety and refinement of the other. Some of them count the spirit to be a body (a view to which certain physicians also incline), while others view the blood itself as constituting 'spirit'. All of them thus rest content in poor fancies born of their fallible defective vision, without bothering to make any inquiry about the tripartite division (of the spirit).

It should be understood that there are three divisions (to the spirit): [i.] body, [ii.] accident and [iii.] the immaterial individual substance (*al-jawhar al-fard*).

The animal spirit is a subtle body, which is like a lamp that has been kindled and set in the glass of the heart[123] – and by 'heart' here, I mean the cone-shaped organ situated within the chest – with 'life' (*al-ḥayāt*) as the luminous glow

122 A *ḥadīth* frequently utilized by Ghazālī: see Jabre, *Essai sur le lexique de Ghazali*, p. 255.

123 A reference to the Light Verse of the Qur'ān (*āyat al-nūr*, Qur'ān XXIV:35) to the interpretation of which Ghazālī devoted a separate treatise; see al-Ghazālī, *The Niche for Lights* (*Mishkāt al-anwār*), a parallel English–Arabic text, translated, introduced and annotated by David Buchman (Provo: Brigham Young University Press 1998).

cast off by that lamp, blood being its oil,[124] [the powers of] sensation and movement comprising its light, lust its heat, anger its smoke and the faculty [of appetite] that seeks for bodily sustenance (and located in the liver) acting as its servant, sentinel and steward. This 'spirit' can be found in beasts as well as in men, where it effectively functions as a 'body' and its effects behave as 'accidents'. This [animal] spirit neither pursues knowledge, nor understands the path that created beings should take [to God], nor comprehends the rights due [by the creature] to the Creator. It is but a housebound slave chained in fetters, dying when the death of the body overcomes it. If there is an excess of blood within the lamp [of the animal spirit], it will be snuffed out due to excessive heat; whereas if it be short of blood, the lamp will go out from excess of coldness, so that its extinction will be the demise [93] of the flesh. Neither the call and summons of God Almighty nor the Lawgiver's decree can be imposed upon this spirit, for no beast or animal can be found either subject to the summons of the divine ordinances or bound by the rule of the Holy Law.

Man is arraigned by and subject to the beck and call and ordinances of the Divine Law due to another hidden spiritual significance found within him – which in fact is especially peculiar to him – this being his 'rational soul' and the 'spirit of serenity' (*al-rūḥ al-muṭma'inna*). This 'spirit' is neither 'body' nor 'accident' (*'araḍ*), but rather hails from the Almighty's Command, just as God says: "Say, the Spirit hails from the Command of my Lord."[125] He also said: "Soul in serenity – return to your Lord, content and justified in divine confidence."[126] Now, God Almighty's Command is neither corporeal body nor accidental property but rather a divine faculty that resembles the First Intelligence (*al-'aql al-awwal*), the Tablet and the Pen, each of which are simple individual substances, utterly immaterial in nature; in fact, they are intelligible, immaterial radiances, invisible to sense-perception. In our lexicon, both the 'spirit' and the 'heart' are derived from these substances, for they are not susceptible to death and decay; they are indestructible and imperishable.[127] (Upon death) both the heart and spirit

124 The printed text of the treatise here reads r.h.n.h., which is an obvious misspelling, not occurring in any Arabic dictionary; I have corrected it to read d.h.n.h. (*duhnuhu*): 'oil'. I am grateful to Prof. Bosworth for pointing this out and clarifying this reading.

125 Qur'ān XVII:85.

126 Qur'ān LXXXIX:27.

127 Cf. Proclus' Propositions 186: "Every soul is an incorporeal substance and separable from the body" and 187: "Every soul is indestructible and imperishable" E.R. Dodds

separate themselves from the body, remaining waiting to return back to it until Judgement Day, as the Law affirms.

It has been substantiated by means of conclusive demonstrative proofs and irrefutable evidence in the sciences of philosophy that the *spiritus rationalis* (*al-rūh al-nāṭiq*) is neither body nor accident, but rather an eternally existent, immutable substance that is not susceptible of decay. So there is no need to reiterate these demonstrations, or recapitulate these proofs here, or further add to the body of evidence that is already quite well attested and established. Whoever wishes to ascertain these matters for himself should consult the appropriate books that have already been composed on this subject.

Our way, however, is not to adduce proofs or amass demonstrative evidence. Rather, we rely on direct contemplative vision (*al-'iyān*) and put our trust in the vision of faith (*ru'yat al-īmān*), insofar as God Almighty sometimes related the 'Spirit' to His Command and sometimes ascribed it to His Majestic Eminence. Thus, He declared: "I inspired the breath of my Spirit in him"[128] and "Say, the Spirit hails from the Command of my Lord,"[129] and also pronounced, [94] "We breathed into it (Mary's womb) something of our Spirit."[130] God Almighty is far too sublime to co-relate Himself to a body or an accident, which are characterized by baseness, mutability and sudden wasting away. Hence, He declared: "The spirits are like assembled armies,"[131] and "the spirits of the martyrs are in the crops of green birds."[132]

No accident permanently continues to exist after its substance has perished, for the accident is not self-subsistent in essence. Just as the body's composition is compounded of *materia* and form, so to say, it will confront its decomposition and dissolution in exactly the same manner, as is often propounded in texts of philosophy. From such scriptural references, traditions and intellectual demonstrations, we may infer that the Spirit is a simple substance (*jawhar*

(trans.), *Proclus: The Elements of Theology* (Oxford: Clarendon Press 2000 repr.), p. 163.

128 Qur'ān XV:29; XXXVIII:72.

129 Qur'ān XVII:85.

130 Qur'ān LXVI:12; XXI:91.

131 Badī' al-Zamān Furūzānfar, *Aḥadīth-i Mathnawī* (Tehran: Dānishgāh-i Tihran 1335 A.Hsh./1956; repr. Amir Kabir 1361 A.Hsh./1982), no. 132.

132 This well-known *ḥadīth* is cited in Jalāl al-Dīn al-Suyūṭī, *al-jāmi' al-ṣaghīr fī aḥādīth al-bashīr al-nadhīr* (Beirut: Dār al-fikr, n.d.), vol. I, p. 335.

fard), essentially alive and vital in itself, effectively generating either the soundness or unsoundness of one's religious faith. The natural and animal spirit (*al-rūḥ al-tabī'ī wa'l-ḥayawānī*) as well as all the other physical faculties and drives may be counted amongst its legions. Furthermore, this simple substance is able to apprehend both the forms of objects of knowledge as well as the supra-formal spiritual realities of living beings (*ḥaqā'iq al-mawjūdāt*) directly, without being preoccupied with their individual essences and peculiarities. Likewise, the [rational] Soul is capable of comprehending the inner reality of humanity without ever having visibly apprehended any human being, just as it apprehends angels and devils without needing to see their individual selves – the more so as the sensory perception of most people cannot behold these beings. Hence it is that certain of the Sufis profess that the heart possesses its own organ of vision (*oculus cordis*) just like the body, so that just as the ocular eye beholds outward things, the intellectual eye (*'ayn al-'aql*) perceives inward things, the esoteric spiritual realities (*al-ḥaqā'iq*). Hence, the dictum of the Prophet of God: "There is no devotee except that he have two eyes in his heart"[133] – [organs] by which he perceives the Arcanum (*al-ghayb*). Thus, when God Almighty wishes a devotee happiness, He opens the eye of his heart to that which is hidden from his ocular sight.

Now, this Spirit does not perish and pass away with the death of the body, for God has summoned it unto His Gate, as according to His Word: "Return to your Lord."[134] It has but separated and purposely disengaged itself from the body, as a consequence of which its animal powers have ceased to function and its natural activities have become quiescent. This quiescence is dubbed 'death'. Those who follow the spiritual Path (*ahl al-ṭarīqa*), that is to say, the Sufis, depend far more upon the Spirit and the heart than they do on their merely individual selves (*al-shakhṣ*).

[95] Now the Spirit, which derives from the God Almighty's creative Command, inhabits the body like a stranger in a foreign land, being as an alien and outcast in the flesh, its face being turned Yonder to its original homeland and ultimate place of emigration, so that when it is strong and

133 This is apparently a *ḥadīth*, reference needs be traced. Cf. St. Paul's reference (Epistle to the Ephesians I:18) to "the eyes of your heart being enlightened: that ye may know (*illuminatos oculos cordis vestri, ut sciatis*)." Cited by Frithjof Schuon, *The Eye of the Heart: Metaphysics, Cosmology, Spiritual Life* (Indiana: World Wisdom Books 1997), p. 6, n. 8.

134 Qur'ān LXXXIX:27.

unsullied by natural impurities, from Thence it reaps more grace and gain than from its selfhood it ever did obtain. Now that it has been understood that the Spirit is an immaterial individual substance (*al-jawhar al-fard*), that every body requires place and locus, that no accident [i.e. the flesh] may survive and subsist without a substance [i.e. the Spirit], it should be known that this 'substance' does not abide in any locus nor reside in any 'place', for the body is not the abode of the Spirit nor a site and habitation where the heart can abide. Rather, the body is but an implement utilized by the heart and the mount upon which the soul rides. Likewise, the Spirit is not essentially attached to any of the body's limbs and members nor yet detached from them. Rather it is favourably disposed towards the body, bestowing its beneficence and grace upon it.[135]

The first light radiated and projected by the Spirit illuminates the brain, for the brain is the Spirit's specific visible ground of appearance. The Spirit then selects the anterior lobe of the brain as its sentinel and sentry; the middle lobe as its vizier and director; and takes the posterior lobe as its treasury and exchequer, and from its other bits and pieces chooses its infantry and cavalry. The animal spirit (*al-rūḥ al-ḥayawānī*) it co-opts as its servant, the natural spirit it takes as its commissioner, while the body it adopts as a steed on which it mounts, and the entire world becomes its riding field. Life itself provides the Spirit with its property and chattels, motion furnishes its trade, knowledge its revenue, and the Hereafter provides its objective

135 Margaret Smith (in her translation) notes a similarity in ideas between this passage and chap. V.1.10 of the *Enneads.* See Margret Smith, "Al-Risalat Al-Laduniyya. By Abū Ḥāmid Muḥammad Al-Ghazlllịi (450/1059-505/111)," *Journal of the Royal Asiatic Society* (1938), Part 2, p. 199. This is where Polotinus describes two dimensions of the soul. Expanding on his views of these dimensions, the first of which is "the reasoning phase of the Soul [that needs] no bodily organ for its thinking but maintaining, in purity, its distinctive Act that its thought may be uncontaminated ... We may not seek any point of space in which to seat it; it must be set outside of all space: its distinct quality, its separateness, its immateriality, demand that it be a thing alone, untouched by all of the bodily order." Of the second dimension, Plotinus clarifies that "... The admonition to sever soul from body is not, of course, to be understood spatially [but] ... to an attitude of alienation from the body in the effort to lead up and attach to the over-world, equally with the other, that phase of soul seated here and, alone, having to do with body, creating, moulding, spending its care upon it." *The Enneads*, trans. Stephen MacKenna (New York: Larson Publications 1992), V.I.10, p. 433.

and final destination. The Holy Law of Islam (*al-shar'*) provides its course and way, the base passionate soul (*al-nafs al-ammāra*) functions as captain and sentinel, the reproaching soul (*al-lawwāma*) acts the role of a vigilant counsellor; (the faculties of) the senses behave as its spies and bodyguards, religion as its coat of mail, reason behaves as its instructor and sense-perception is its pupil. Towering above and beyond all of these stands the Lord, ever-watchful, on guard.[136]

The soul (*al-nafs*),[137] then, being endowed with such traits and having these implements at its disposal, pays no regard to this tawdry physical form, but being essentially detached from it, behaves toward it with gracious beneficence. Its countenance remains fixed upon its Maker, in order to heed and execute His Command and Will, as benefit demands, until its appointed term be reached. During the period of this journey, the Spirit also does not occupy itself in anything except the pursuit of knowledge – for knowledge will be its ornament in the life hereafter – insofar as ("wealth and children are) an ornament of the life of the world (but good deeds that endure are better in thy Lord's sight.").[138]

In the same way that the eye is occupied with things that its gaze beholds and objects visible to it and the ear is occupied in audition of sounds, and the tongue is primed to discourse with words, and the animal spirit is a votary of the delights of violent passion, and the natural spirit is a lover of the pleasures of eating and drinking, [96] so the 'serene spirit (*al-rūḥ al-muṭma'inna*),[139] that is to say, the heart, all lifelong is not desirous of anything else but knowledge and learning. Thus, it seeks to ornament itself with knowledge all of its days until its demise. If the serene spirit turns its attention to aught but knowledge, it does so out of expedience, because that happens to be in the body's interests and needs, not because it concords with its essential desires or concurs with its principal passion or love.[140]

---

136 *Al-mirṣād* is here meant as an allusion to Qur'ān LXXXIX:14.

137 Here Ghazālī alludes to the 'rational soul' (*al-nafs al-nāṭiqa*).

138 Qur'ān XVIII:46.

139 Identical with the 'serene soul' (*al-nafs al-muṭma'inna*) mentioned above by Ghazālī.

140 Alternate translation: Even if it concentrates on something else besides knowledge, it does this only because it happens to be necessarily expedient to the needs of the body, not because it accords with its own essential desire and love.

Now that you have understood the conditions of the Spirit, its immortality, its love and passion for knowledge, it is necessary that you apprehend the varieties of knowledge. Yet since these are manifold and diverse, we will enumerate them but briefly here:

Chapter III: On the Typologies of Knowledge

It should be understood that knowledge can be sub-divided into two categories: one, religious (*shar'ī*), and the other, rational (*'aqlī*), even though according to those intimately versed in its lore, most religious knowledge is also 'rational', and hence, "to whomsoever God assigns no light, he has no light."[141]

The first type of knowledge, which is religious knowledge, in turn is subdivided into two categories, the first of which is

(I) The science of the fundamentals of religious faith (al-uṣūl)

This science, which is that of divine Unity (*al-tawḥīd*), focuses on the divine Essence, the eternal divine Attributes, the creative Attributes and the Attributes of the divine Essence,[142] which have many diverse names, as has been already mentioned. It also investigates the circumstances of the prophets, the Imāms and, after them, the Prophet's Companions. Eschatology as well features as a subject of this science, examining the circumstances that prevail in the hereafter upon the Day of Resurrection, the Great Awakening, the Judgement of the Dead and how the Vision of God Almighty is beheld. Adepts (*ahl al-naẓar*) in this lore first of all rely and have recourse to the verses of God in the Qur'ān, then the Prophetic Traditions, then refer to intellectually proven inferences (*al-dalā'il al-'aqlī*) and demonstrations based on logical categories of syllogistic reasoning (*al-barāhīn al-qiyāsī*).

---

141 Qur'ān XXIV:40.

142 That is to say, the divine Attributes in respect to eternity *a parte ante* (*al-ṣifāt al-qadīmīyya*), in regard to their dynamic active creativity (*al-ṣifāt al-fa'līyya*) and in their operation as modes of the divine Essence (*al-ṣifāt al-dhātīyya*). Perhaps the best account of Sunni *Uṣūl* thought was that composed by Ghazālī's teacher, Imām al-Ḥaramayn al-Juwaynī in his work *Kitāb al-irshād ilā qawāṭī' al-adilla fī uṣūl al-i'tiqād*, which has been translated by Paul Walker: *A Guide to Conclusive Proofs for the Principles of Belief* (Reading: Garnet Publishing 2000).

They took on board the basic premises of dialectics and logical disputation, both their standard and complex syllogistic varieties, from the logical philosophers, but by using words in the wrong place [97] they ended up incorrectly applying their terminology. In their discourse, they employed such terms as 'substance' and 'accident', 'logical demonstration (*al-dalīl*)', 'theoretical speculation (*al-naẓar*)', 'circumstantial argumentation (*istidlāl*)' and 'demonstrative proof (*al-ḥujja*)'. Now, all these terms vary in meaning according to the different groups using them, so that the term 'substance' among the philosophers has one significance, another meaning amongst the Sufis, another meaning to the scholastic theologians, and so on and so forth. But since it is not the purpose of this treatise to investigate the meaning of each of these terms according to the views of all these various groups, we will forego this discussion and concern ourselves no further with it.

The particular group who engages in the study of Theology (*Kalām*) and specialize in the investigation of the fundamentals of faith and the science of divine Unity are called the 'Scholastic Theologians (*Mutakallimūn*)', the study of *Kalām* thus being celebrated as the study of the science of divine Unity. The science of Qur'ānic exegesis (*al-tafsīr*) is also a branch of the science of the fundamentals of faith, insofar as the Qur'ān is valued tremendously as a book of grand repute and sublime excellence. In it are also to be found many abstruse difficulties that are beyond the grasp of the common man's intelligence, so that only those to whom God Almighty has vouchsafed grace of understanding may fathom it. As the Prophet of God declared, "There is no verse of the Qur'ān that does not have an outward sense, an inward sense, and a more inward, esoteric sense within that inward sense, and so forth up to seven esoteric senses."[143] He also affirmed that, "Not a verse of the Qur'ān is revealed but it has [an exoteric dimension (*ẓahr*) and an esoteric dimension (*baṭn*), and every word has] a limit (*ḥadd*), and every limit has a point of ascent (*muṭṭala'*)."[144] God Almighty has informed us that

143 A good discussion of this *ḥadīth* in the context of Sufi Qur'ān commentary can be found in Pierre Lory, *Les Commentaires ésotériques du Coran d'après 'Abd al-Razzāq al-Qāshānī* (Paris: Le Deux Oceans 1980), pp. 14ff.

144 This is a non-canonical *ḥadīth* (certain portions of which [placed here within brackets] Ghazālī strangely omits), for a good study of which, see Jamal Elias, *The Throne-Carrier of God: The Life and Thought of 'Alā ad-Dawla as-Simnānī* (Albany: SUNY Press 1995), pp. 107–110. Another similar *ḥadīth*: "The Qur'ān has an outward aspect, an

all sciences are to be found gathered together in the Qur'ān and all living beings, both visible and invisible, great and small, sensible and intelligible, all throng therein, for, according to His word: "there is no thing, be it fresh or withered, but it is recorded in a Book Manifest."[145] The Almighty likewise spoke of ["a scripture that We have revealed to thee, blessed] that its adepts may meditate on its verses, and take heed."[146]

Now, insofar as the Qur'ān is a matter of such mighty consequence, which exegete may possibly do justice to it? Which learned savant, which theologian is there who can possibly discharge its obligations as rightly demanded in respect to it? Indeed, all the various commentators' interpretations of the Qur'ān were but tailored to the measure of the reach and range of their minds' understanding, testifying to their respective intellectual powers and the variable quantity of the amount of their knowledge. So if they all said something, in reality, they have said nothing!

Now, the science of the Qur'ān serves as corroboration of the science of fundamentals [98] and derivatives of faith (*'ilm al-uṣūl wa'l-furū'*), and as confirmation of both religious (*shar'ī*) and rational types of knowledge (*'aqlī*). If a commentator's work of interpretation is to achieve direct experiential verification (*al-taḥqīq*), it is incumbent upon him or her that he view the book from a broad number of perspectives, approaching it from the standpoints of lexicology, metaphorical expressions, grammar, [its relation to] Arabic customs and the principles of philosophy and Sufi mystical theology. Any other less holistic approach will end up being limited to one perspective. If he restrict himself solely to one perspective, and content himself with an exposition of only one angle or one science, he cannot be

---

inward aspect, an ending and a beginning (*li'l-Qur'āni ẓāhirun wa bāṭinun wa ḥaddun wa muṭṭala'un*)" is cited in *The Mathnawí of Jalálu'ddín Rúmí*, trans. and ed. R.A. Nicholson, Gibb Memorial Series N.S., 8 vols. (London: E.J.W. Gibb Memorial Trust 1924–40), s.v. Nicholson's commentary on III: 4244–49. For further discussion of the interior dimensions of meaning in the Qur'ān, see C. Gilliot, *Exégèse, Langue et Theologie en Islam* (Paris: Vrin 1990), pp. 120–25; P. Nwyia, *Exégèse Coranique et Langage Mystique* (Beirut: 1970), p. 141. For a good summary of all these *aḥadīth* in the context of Ghazālī's other works, see Nicholas Heer, "Abū Ḥāmid al-Ghazālī's Esoteric Exegesis of the Qur'ān," in Leonard Lewisohn (ed.) *The Heritage of Sufism*, vol. I: *Classical Persian Sufism from its Origins to Rumi* (Oxford: Oneworld 1999), pp. 238ff.

145 Qur'ān VI:59.

146 Qur'ān XXXVIII:29.

said to have adequately responsibly discharged his obligations regarding its exposition.

Another branch of the science of fundamentals is the science of traditions. The Prophet said, "I am the most eloquent of the Arabs and the Persians."[147] He was a teacher to whom revelation was vouchsafed from God Almighty, his intelligence comprehensively and inclusively embracing all beings, both in the upper and lower realms of being. Since lurking beneath every single word of his discourse, indeed, couched within every syllable of his speech, one may discern oceans of mystery and treasuries of secrets cached, knowledge of his traditions and in-depth penetration into his sayings is a matter of great consequence and momentous concern. No one has the ability to understand comprehensively the science of the Prophet's words except if he discipline his soul through devout obedience to the Lawgiver, and struggle to straighten out his heart's crooked ways by staunch adherence to the Holy Law.

However, it is incumbent upon anyone who wishes to discourse or discuss the interpretation of the Qur'ān, and engage in exposition of its hidden hermeneutical sense, and also to be accurate in what he says, to first be thoroughly versed in philology (*'ilm al-lugha*, the science of the [Arabic] language),[148] and well grounded in the subject matter of Arabic: in the conjugation of verbs, declension (of nouns and adjectives), as well as the various patterns of inflection. This is because the science of the [Arabic] language (*'ilm al-lugha*) is like a ladder and flight of stairs ascending up to all the other sciences, so that if someone doesn't know the language, there is no way for him to apprehend any of the other sciences, just as someone must first make use of a staircase to go up to the roof of a house, climbing up it step by step. Thus, since the science of the [Arabic] language is a utensil of such supreme import for knowledge of, and the grand staircase leading up to, the sciences, no student may ever dispense with the study of its precepts, the science of the [Arabic] language being the fundamental principle of everything.

---

147 I have been unable to trace the source of this *ḥadīth.*

148 This term literally signifies 'the science of words', but in classical Arabic usage can also mean 'variant readings', 'dialectical features', and usually refers to lexicology and philology. As is apparent from the ensuing discussion, Ghazālī here uses the term to signify every aspect of general knowledge relating to Arabic language studies.

This science commences with the knowledge of grammatical particles[149] as they appear in separate words, then proceeds on to the science of verbs, in their triliteral, quadriliteral and other root forms. The lexicologist should also examine Arabic poetry, the foremost and most perfect genre of which is pre-Islamic Arabic poetry (*al-Jāhilī*), for the poetry of that period instils one with a sense of serenity and brings rest and refreshment to the soul. After the study of this poetry, grammatical particles and nouns, it is necessary to study grammar and syntax (*al-naḥw*), insofar as the science of [the Arabic] language may be likened to a balance on which one weighs [99] gold and silver. Just as in philosophy, logic (functions as its balance), in poetry, prosody (also plays the part of balance), and for (tailoring) clothes there is the metre bar, and for (weighing) grain, there is the bushel measurement, likewise, anything that is not weighed in a balance cannot be really assessed as to whether it exceeds the right measure or falls short of it. Hence, it should be understood that knowledge of (Arabic) lexicology (*al-lugha*) paves the way to grasp the science of Qur'ānic exegesis (*'ilm al-tafsīr*), Prophetic Traditions (*al-akhbār*), and Science of the Qur'ān itself. Knowledge of the Traditions in turn directs one towards knowledge of divine Unity (*'ilm al-tawḥīd*) which is the sole science by which a devotee may attain salvation, and be delivered from the fears of the life to come. This then, is an explanation *in extenso* of the science of the fundamentals of faith (*'ilm al-uṣūl*).

Now, to address the second category of religious knowledge, this is constituted by:

(II) The science of the corollaries of faith ('ilm al-furū' *[derived from those fundamentals])*

The reason underlying this typology is that knowledge is either a matter of intellectual theory (*'ilm*) or practical application (*'amal*). Thus, the science of the fundamentals of faith (*'ilm al-'uṣūl*) is a theoretical matter, while the knowledge of the corollaries of faith is practical by nature. This practical science imposes three different sorts of obligation upon a person:

1. The first consist of duties that God Almighty charges man to perform, comprising such things as the elements of religious worship: ritual purifications and prayers, alms-giving, pilgrimage, spiritual struggle

149 That is, such things as prefixes, suffixes, definite and indefinite articles.

(*al-jihād*), various sorts of supplication (*al-adhkār*), feast days observances, Friday prayers, as well additional practices relating both to supererogatory spiritual exercises and ordinary religiously obligatory acts (*nawāfil wa farā'iḍ*).

2. In the second place are the obligations to which devotees are bound in respect to one another, these being composed of standard practices and precedents that are subdivided into two other categories as follows:
   i. The first of these concern transactions (*al-mu'āmala*[150]) such as buying and selling, corporate business associations, charitable donations, loans and debts, lawful and just retaliation, as well as the different divisions of blood-money.
   ii. The second of these concern legally binding contractual agreements (*al-mu'āqada*), such as marriage and divorce, bondage and emancipation of slaves, as well as all the obligations and matters pertaining to these obligations.

   The term 'Jurisprudence' (*al-fiqh*) designates both the above sorts of legal obligations. Jurisprudence is a noble and distinguished science that is not only useful but indispensable for the majority of people because of its universal application.
3. The third sort of obligation concerns responsibilities that man holds towards himself,[151] denoting in this respect the Science of Ethics (*'ilm al-akhlāq*). By 'Ethics' is meant either moral qualities that are reprehensible, which must be repudiated and foresworn, or else commendable moral qualities that one should strive to obtain so as to adorn one's character with them. Both the reprehensible and commendable types of moral qualities

---

150 In Ghazālī's thought one can distinguish two distinct usages of the term *al-mu'āmala:* a juridical significance focused on the religious motives underlying human relations, and a technical religious usage of the term treating the relationship between the devotee and his Lord. Ghazālī divides objects of religious activity into (a) those relating to the science of unveiling (*mukāshafa*), the Object of which is purely spiritual (God, His attributes, acts, etc.) and (b) those relating to the science of transactions, the object of which is directed towards one's life in the world and perfecting practical human conduct. (Jabre, *Essai sur le lexique de Ghazali*, pp. 200–1, 209–11.) Ghazālī refers here exclusively to the second, juridical usage of the term.

151 *Ḥaqq al-nafs* may mean both the right that the soul may exercise over oneself (i.e. the soul has a right to eat), as well the obligations that the soul imposes upon man in regard to others; it is the second sense that Ghazālī here intends.

have been set forth in the Scripture of God Almighty and in the Traditions of the Prophet. Indeed, whoever succeeds in actualizing *even one* of these moral qualities has already entered paradise.

[100] As for the second sort of knowledge or science (mentioned at the beginning of this chapter) – rational knowledge (*al-ʿilm al-ʿaqlī*) – it is a difficult, problematic science, in which truth and falsehood stand cheek by jowl.[152] There are three levels of subject matter to this science.[153]

The first and most elementary level comprises the sciences of mathematics and logic. As for Mathematics, it embraces Arithmetic, which is concerned with computation; Geometry, which is the science of measurements and figures; Astronomy, that is to say, the science of celestial bodies; Astrophysics, and the computation of terrestrial distances, and all that relates thereunto. Branching off as corollaries of these sciences one finds Astrology, and the basic principles of (calculating the stars of) nativity and ascendant, as well as Music, which is concerned with the apposition of notes and chords (i.e. tonal harmony).

As for Logic, it deals with the definition and description (*al-ḥadd wa'l-rasm*) of things apprehended by way of intellectual conception or representation (*al-taṣawwur*),[154] considering things by way of the categories of syllogistic argumentation and apodeictic demonstration in order to arrive at a knowledge that is judged to be verifiable and certain (*al-taṣdīq*).[155] The science of Logic follows this method, being first concerned itself with simple individual concepts, then with complex composite concepts, then with propositions (*qaḍāyā*), then with the

---

152 Alternate translation: Now, to treat the second type of knowledge (mentioned at the beginning of this chapter) – rational knowledge (*al-ʿilm al-ʿaqlī*) – this is a difficult, enigmatic science, which is liable to lead one both into falsehood and truth.

153 Ghazālī's discussion here echoes that given in his *al-Munqidh min al-Dalāl* (ed. Farīd Jabre (Beirut: 1969), p. 20ff., trans. by R.J. McCarthy, *Deliverance from Error: An Annotated Translation of al-Munqidh min al-Dalāl and other relevant works of al-Ghazālī* (Louisville: Fons Vitae, n.d.), pp. 63ff.

154 On *taṣawwur* in Ghazālī's thought, see Jabre, *Essai*, p. 144; R.J. McCarthy, *Deliverance from Error*, pp. 65, 110, n. 97a.

155 On this term, used elsewhere by Ghazālī with the same sense, see Jabre, *Essai*, pp. 24–27 (14 c.A. a).

syllogism (*al-qiyās*),[156] then with various forms of the syllogism, and finally with the presentation of the proof (*al-burhān*), at which point the science of Logic culminates.

The second and intermediate level of 'rational knowledge' is that of Natural Science (*al-'ilm al-ṭabī'ī*).[157] The natural scientist concerns himself with 'absolute body' (*al-jism al-muṭlaq*),[158] the foundational structure of the universe, substances and accidents, motion and rest, celestial mechanics, and the actions and reactions of things. Out of this science is generated the theoretical study and examination of the ontological levels of living beings (*marātib al-mawjūdāt*), the various classes of human souls and natural humours, the number of sensory faculties and the modalities of their apprehension of objects of sense-perception. From this science is further derived theoretical reflection on the science of Medicine, which is the study of physical bodies, their infirmities, drugs and remedies, and all matters relevant thereunto. Among the other branches of Natural Science is the science of Meteorology, Mineralogy, and knowledge of the distinctive properties of things. The summation of this science is the science of the Alchemical Art, which concerns the refinement of base metals located in subterranean mines.

The third and supreme level of rational knowledge comprises consideration of what exists in being (*al-mawjūd*), which is divided into the study of the necessary and possible (modes of being); then speculation upon the Creator, His Essence, His divine Qualities and Activities, His Command, Decree, [101] Providential Will, and the hierarchical procession of the manifestation of living beings from Him. After that comes contemplation of the higher realms of being, the immaterial individual substances, the

---

156 On *qiyās* in Ghazālī, see Jabre, *Essai*, pp. 239ff; on the syllogism's diverse forms (hypothetical, disjunctive, etc.), see Jamīl Ṣalībā, *Farhang-i Falsafa*, trans. M.S. Durrahbīdī (Tehran: Intishārāt-i Ḥikmat 1366 A.Hsh./1987), pp. 521ff.

157 'Natural Science' here refers to the physical sciences, biological sciences and faculty psychology. For a good discussion of Ghazālī's classification, see Osman Bakar, *Classification of Knowledge in Islam: A Study in Islamic Philosophies of Science* (Kuala Lumpur: 1992), chap. 9.

158 It would seem that Ghazālī is here referring to 'the material world in toto' and the study of physical matter in general rather than to the Peripatetic philosophical distinction between absolute and particular bodies.

abstract celestial intelligences and the perfect souls, followed by study and consideration of the angels and devils.

At the summit of these considerations, and crowning them, is found study of the science of Prophecy, the phenomenon of miracles (*al-muʿjizāt*), the conditions sustaining and surrounding charismatic powers (*al-karāmāt*), scrutiny of the spiritual states of sanctified souls in bliss, the consciousness experienced in sleep during dreams and the various spiritual degrees of visions (*al-ruʾyā*). Ramifications of this science include the science of talismans (*al-ṭalismāt*) and [white] magical techniques (*nīranjāt*)[159] and all matters relevant thereunto. Within each of these sciences are found minute details subject to further analytical elaboration, as well as incidental characteristics and hierarchical degrees, all of which would demand a great deal of explanation, yet this brief summary must for the present suffice.

Chapter IV: On the Science of the Sufis

It should be understood that rational knowledge (*al-ʿilm al-ʿaqlī*) (discussed in the last chapter) is a science that is, in essence, simple and indivisible, from which is derived another complex, composite science, within which all the characteristics of the two other simple indivisible sciences are found. This complex and composite science is that of the Sufis (*ʿilm al-ṣūfiyya*) and their method of realizing mystical states. They have their own distinct and particular science with a patent method and clear path which synthesizes and combines both types of knowledge.[160] Their science comprises (the study and cognizance of) mystical states (*al-ḥāl*), metaphysical time outside of temporal serial duration (*al-waqt*), musical audition (*al-samāʿ*), ecstasy and yearning (*al-wajd wa'l-shawq*), intoxication and sobriety (*al-sukr wa'l-ṣaḥw*), establishment and obliteration (*al-ithbāt wa'l-maḥw*), sainthood and disciplic devotion

159 My translation has corrected the original printed text which reads *al-nabaranjāt*, obviously a misprint. On this term, see T. Fahd, "Nīrandj," *EI2* VIII, p. 51, which he says designates "the operations of white magic, comprising prestidigitation, fakery and counter-fakery, the creating of illusions and other feats of sleight-of-hand." I am grateful to Prof. Bosworth for this emendation and reference.

160 Here Ghazālī seems to be alluding to the fact that the synthetic spiritual method of the Sufis combines the aforementioned two categories of religious (*sharʿī*) and rational (*ʿaqlī*) knowledge.

(*al-wilāyat wa'l-irādat*), and master and disciple (*al-shaykh wa'l-murīd*), as well as other things connected to their mystical consciousness[161] along with related derivative matters (*al-zawā'id*),[162] moral qualities of character, and the spiritual stations (*al-maqāmāt*). We will have more to say of these three sciences[163] in a book to be especially dedicated to this topic – *Deo volente* – but for now our aim in this treatise is solely to enumerate the sciences and their various classifications, in which respect we have limited ourselves to making a concise and compact summary. Whoever wishes for more than this and would have a more detailed exposition of these Sufi sciences may refer to the relevant books on the subject.

Having come to the end of this exposition devoted to giving an account of the various classifications of the sciences, you should know for certain that there are a number of provisions and stipulations incumbent on any seeker who would acquire any of these skills and crafts and sciences, the

---

161 On the terms *ḥāl, maqāmāt, waqt, faqr,* see Javad Nurbakhsh, *Spiritual Poverty in Sufism* (London: KNP 1984), trans. Leonard Lewisohn, chaps. 4,6,1; on *samā'*, see Leonard Lewisohn, "The Sacred Music of Islam: *Samā'* in the Persian Sufi Tradition" in the *British Journal of Ethnomusicology* VI, 1997, pp. 1–33; on *wajd* and *shawq*, see Leonard Lewisohn, "Wa̱dj̱d," "Shawḳ," *EI2*, s.v.; on *fanā'*, *sukr* and *saḥw*, see Javad Nurbakhsh, *Sufism: Fear and Hope, Contraction and Expansion, Gathering and Dispersion, Intoxication and Sobriety, Annihilation and Subsistence,* trans. William Chittick (New York: KNP 1982), chap. 5; on *maḥw* and *ithbāt*, see *idem.*, *Sufi Symbolism: The Nurbakhsh Encyclopædia of Sufi Terminology,* trans. Terry Graham (London: KNP 1997), VIII, pp. 90–92; on *walāyat*, see Hermann Landolt, "Walāyah," *Encyclopedia of Religion*, ed. M. Eliade (New York: Simon and Schuster Macmillan 1995), XVI, pp. 316–23; on *irādat*, master and disciple, see Javad Nurbakhsh, *In the Tavern of Ruin: Seven Essays on Sufism* (London: KNP, 4th edn: n.d.), chap. 7. Shorter treatments of most of these terms are also given by Hujwīrī, *Kashf al-maḥjūb*, chaps. 10–11.

162 *Al-zawā'id* (sing. *zā'ida*) has two meanings: i. extra, superadded things, appendage, appendix; and ii. excess of light in the heart – Hujwīrī, *Kashf al-maḥjūb*, ed. Zhukovskī (Tehran: Ṭahūrī 1375/1996), p. 500, l. 10. Despite the Sufi context of this passage, I think that it is unlikely that Ghazālī had anything but the first connotation in mind.

163 Ghazālī's tripartite division here refers to the science of religion (*al-'ilm al-shar'ī*), rational or intellectual science (*al-'ilm al-'aqlī*), and the science of Sufism (*'ilm al-taṣawwuf*).

terms of which he must stamp and impress upon his soul.[164] After enumeration of the sciences, it is also incumbent on you to obtain an understanding of the various educational methods and ways of acquiring knowledge, for the methods and ways of procuring knowledge [102] are quite specific. These we will now expound at length and analyze in detail.

Chapter V: An Exposition of Scientific Methodology: On the Paths of Acquisition of Knowledge

It should be understood that human knowledge is acquired by two methods. The first of these is through submission to human instruction (*al-taʿallum al-insānī*); the second vouchsafed through the divine teaching of the Spirit (*al-taʿallum al-rabbānī*).[165]

I. The Method of Human Learning

As for the first method, it is the customary time-honoured path that is accessible to the senses of all intelligent folk. Regarding the learning of the Spirit, it has two aspects, one of which is from outside: through acquiring knowledge through study and learning (*al-taḥṣīl bi'l-taʿallum*), and the other, from within: by engaging in meditative reflection and contemplative thought (*al-ishtighāl bi'l-tafakkur*), internal reflection and contemplation

164 Alternate translation: Now that the discourse devoted to enumerating the classification of the sciences has come to an end, you should know for certain that there are a number of provisions and stipulations incumbent on any seeker who would acquire any of these skills, crafts and sciences, the rules of which he must stamp and impress upon his soul.

165 Modelling himself on this text, Mullā Ṣadrā virtually copies Ghazālī here: "you should also know that man acquires knowledge in two different ways. The first is the way of learning, submitting to being taught and the voluntary acquisition of learning (*al-taʿallum wa'l-kasb*). The second is by way of grace of God and divine attraction (*al-wahb wa'l-jadhba*), vouchsafed by means of divine communication." Ṣadr al-Mutā'allihīn Shīrāzī, *Mafātīḥ al-ghayb* (*Keys to the Invisible Realm*), trans. into Persian by Muḥammad Khwājū'ī (Tehran: Intishārāt-i Mullā 1363 A.Hsh./1984), *Miftāḥ* III; *Mashad* 8, p. 336.

from within in this regard performing the same function as does external exoteric study and learning from without.

However, while acquiring knowledge through study and learning demands the use of a particular person (as a teacher), meditative reflection and contemplative thought (*al- tafakkur*)[166] involves the soul's obtaining succour (directly) from the Universal Soul, insofar as there is no influence more potent than that of the Universal Soul; for its pedagogic strength and didactic power excels the learning and teaching skills of all the world's learned professors and wise savants. All these aforementioned sciences[167] exist *in potentia* within the soul's original principle just as a seed that is buried in the bowels of the earth, a pearl immersed in the depths of the sea, or a gem secreted within the heart of a mine. The acquisition of knowledge through study and learning (*al-ta'allum*) can be defined as the quest to unearth and extract that thing and to nurse it from a state of potentiality into a condition of actuality. The imparting of instruction – teaching – also consists in bringing forth that thing from potentiality into actuality. For this reason, the soul of the pupil resembles the soul of the teacher, so that the former approaches the latter by means of this (pedagogic) relationship, the teacher being like a farmer (sowing seeds), whilst the pupil, who reaps the benefit from him, is like the earth (in which the seeds are sewn). Knowledge *in potentia* may be likened to a seed, knowledge *in actu* may be likened to a green plantlet that has sprouted up, and the soul of the pupil that has reached perfection may be said to resemble a large bough laden down with fruit, or a pearl that has been hauled out from the ocean depths.

Now whenever the corporeal, bodily faculties come to predominate in the soul, the student will experience an even greater need for study and learning, and in his pursuit of the benefits of learning must devote more time to it, enduring greater hardship and toil for its sake. However,

---

166 "Reflection is the beginning of – and the key to – all good ... it is the search for the gnosis which is desired ... as the stone strikes upon the iron and brings forth from it fire, whereby the place is illuminated and the eye is able to see after it was unseeing, and the limbs are stirred to activity, so also the flint-stone of the light of gnosis is Reflection ... and the heart is changed because of this light ... so the fruit of reflections is knowledge and mystics 'states'." Ghazālī's *Iḥyā'* (iv., p. 364; l. 12), cited by Margaret Smith, *Journal of the Royal Asiatic Society* (1938), Part 3: 361.

167 The printed text reads here *al-'ūm* – an obvious printing error that should read *al-'ulūm*, as the translation has stated.

whenever the light of reason (*nūr al-ʿaql*) predominates and prevails over sensuality and the qualities of sense, by making use of an ounce of reflection, the student can dispense with a whole bushel of study, for the receptive soul in a single hour by means of meditative reflection (*al-tafakkur*) may realize that which another soul that is inactive, ossified and uptight [103] could not realize in a whole year's course of study.[168]

So some folks obtain knowledge by means of study and submitting to being taught (*al-taʿallum*) whereas others learn by way of meditative reflection. Study too demands meditative reflection, for the human being cannot simply learn things, whether particular and universal, nor acquire all the various subjects of knowledge; but rather, one learns one thing by means of study and then deduces another thing by means of reflection from the knowledge already apprehended. In fact, most of the speculative sciences and practical arts and crafts may be said to have been inferred by wise souls through their highly refined clairvoyant minds, their powers of contemplative reflection (*fikr*) and their sharp-witted intuitive conjecture (*ḥads*), without recourse to excessive pedagogic learning or any enterprise of grandiose scholarly study.

Indeed, if man were unable to initially infer certain things by means of meditative reflection concerning various subjects of knowledge, this whole business would have become intolerably long and tedious for men and women, nor would the darkness of ignorance ever depart from their hearts. The reason for this is that the soul is unable to apprehend all the matters important for it to know, whether particular or general, simply by means of study and education. Rather, it apprehends certain things by academic study (*al-taḥṣīl*), other things through rational speculation (*al-naẓar*), as is, one sees, the normal convention and wont among people. Certain other things the soul deduces from its inner consciousness by clear insights born of meditative reflection, which is the proven method and wont of men and women of learning, and in this manner the basic premises and principles of knowledge are established.

Even the geometrician, for example, does not learn the whole of what he will need to know for the rest of his life all at once, but rather he first learns the general principles of his science and its axioms, then afterwards, he

168 Alternate version: This is because the receptive soul by means of meditative reflection (*al-tafakkur*) in the space of a single hour can realize that which the stuffy, lethargic and inactive soul could not attain through a whole year's course of study.

draws his own inferences and deductions. Similarly, it is beyond the capacity of any physician to study and learn all the individual diseases of every particular person and their various remedies. Rather, he meditates and reflects upon the general knowledge that he already has, then proceeds to cure all his patients according to their individual constitutions. It is the same with the astrologer. Having learned the general principles of astrology, he ponders and reflects before delivering his judgement (regarding a person's horoscope) basing himself on the various properties of the stars. The same goes for the lawyer and man of letters (*al-faqīh wa'l-adīb*), as well as for (craftsmen engaged in) the making of exquisitely modelled handicrafts such as musical instruments like the lute (*'ūd*). The lute was first invented by way of careful reflection and meditation (*tafakkur*), then another instrument was derived from that instrument by a process of deduction. All the other arts and crafts, whether manual and intellectual, operate in exactly the same manner: their preliminaries are at first learned and absorbed through study, their remaining portions discovered and brought forth through thought and reflection.

Once the door of this kind of creative thinking (*bāb al-fikr*) opens to the soul, it apprehends the nuances of the reflective method (*ṭarīq al-tafakkur*), and how to return, by way of intuitive conjecture, to the basic propositions of the subject under examination. In this fashion one's heart opens, one's scope of vision is expanded and broadened so that everything that formerly existed *in potentia* in the soul is realized *in actu* without much labour and travail.

II. The Method of the Divine Teaching of the Spirit (al-ta'allum al-rabbānī)

As for the second method, it has two modes:

2.a. Revelation

The first is through the imparting of revelation (*ilqā' al-waḥy*), which is experienced when the soul becomes so perfected in its essential substance that the foul blemishes [104] of nature that defiled it and the ugly smut of longings and greedy desires for transient things are all dissolved away. At this point, the soul turns to face its Maker and Originator, and takes recourse in the bounty of its primordial Creator, relying upon His grace and His effusive radiance of light. Then God Almighty regards this soul with His fair favour, granting it full welcome and total acceptance, beholding it with His divine regard. He then draws forth a tablet from the human soul and takes up a pen from the Universal Soul, and upon the human soul's slate traces the inscription of all knowledge. At this point, the Universal Mind (*al-'aql al-kullī*) becomes, as it were, the soul's teacher, the Sanctified Soul like unto its student, enabling the soul to obtain all knowledge without recourse to study or reflection, so all forms become impressed upon it.[169] God Almighty's statement to His Prophet that "God taught you that which you knew not,"[170] down to the end of the verse, was uttered by way of confirmation of this phenomenon.

It should be understood that among all the types of knowledge known to humankind the supreme and noblest degree of science is that known to the prophets, which is a knowledge they realize and understand directly from God Almighty without mediation. A detailed exposition of this can be found in the story of Adam and the angels. Now, the angels spent an entire lifetime devoted to knowledge, so that by a variety of methods and means they had learned all the arts and sciences. At last, they became the most learned of all beings, the most knowledgeable of living creatures. Now, Adam was unlearned; he was not a scholar because he had not undertaken any study under any teacher. So the angels vied with him, vaunting themselves over him haughtily, setting themselves boastfully above him, protesting (to God), "[Will You set one on there (on earth) as will work corruption and spill blood, whereas] we hymn Your praise and extol Your holiness?"[171] "We comprehend the interior spiritual realities of things," the angels also claimed.

So Adam went back to the door of his Maker, and casting all created beings out of his heart, he faced his Almighty Lord and entreated Him for help, so that God taught him all the names.[172] "And then He displayed them (the Names) to the angels, and said, 'So inform me of (the content of) these names if your claim be true.'"[173]

---

169 This passage is copied by Mullā Ṣadrā (*Mafātīḥ al-ghayb*, trans. Khwājū'ī, p. 338) almost verbatim. See the present anthology, p. 349.

170 Qur'ān III:113.

171 Qur'ān II:30.

172 Referring to Qur'ān II:31, "And He imparted to Adam the names, all of them."

173 Qur'ān II:31.

After this, Adam became disillusioned about the angels' so-called "higher consciousness." Their "knowledge" now seemed so trite and insignificant to him. The august sanctity of their lofty ship shattered in two, drowning in a sea of powerlessness.

"The angels then said, "Glory be to You! We have no knowledge of anything but that which You have taught us."[174] [105]

"O Adam, inform them of their names," God Almighty said.[175]

So Adam taught the angels all the occult modes of knowledge and the secrets of the innermost arcanum of the divine Command (*amr*).[176]

Among the intelligent and sagacious people, it is a well-established fact that esoteric supernatural knowledge (*al-'ilm al-ghaybī*) which derives from divine revelation (*al-waḥy*) is more reliable in strength and more integrally all-inclusive than any of the sciences obtained through fields of knowledge that are acquired (*al-'ulūm al-muktasaba*). The knowledge of divine revelation has become the patrimony bequeathed by the prophets. It is the very truth and reality of the apostles. But the door to divine revelation has been barred and bolted shut ever since the age of our lord Muḥammad, who was the Seal of the Prophets (*khātam al-nabīyyīn*), the most learned of mankind,

---

174 Qur'ān II:32.

175 Qur'ān II:33.

176 God's legislating activity and 'decree' hails from the realm of the Angels (*malakūt*), which is also the *mundus invisibilis* (*ghayb*) in which the hidden supersensible realities are found. Farid Jabre (*Essai sur le lexique de Ghazali*, p. 5) commenting on the term *amr* (decree, command), cites Ghazālī's commentary on Qur'ān XXVII:85 ("They will ask thee concerning the Spirit. Say: 'The Spirit is by the command of my Lord, and you have been given but little knowledge of it."): "But it should be known that the Command of God does not signify a 'command' which one might contrast to an interdiction or prohibition. That sort of command is a spoken utterance, whereas the Spirit is not simply utterance. One should not understand the Command as an act or deed (*al-sha'n*), as if one were to say that it is solely a creation (*khalq*) of God. That is in fact the general situation which can be extended to all created beings. This is because the world is twofold: the world of the Command, and the world of Creation, both of which belong to God. Now, bodies, which are subject to quantity and dimension, belong to the world of creation – creation in fact etymologically denotes measurement – and every living being that is free of quantity and dimension belongs to the world of the Command. (*Iḥyā'* III, 326)."

the most eloquent of the Arabs and non-Arabs (*afsaḥ al-ʿArab waʾl-ʿajam*),[177] as he himself declared: "My Lord educated me with good manners (*adabanī rabbī*), so most excellent are my manners!"[178] He also said to his community: "I am the most learned of you, and the most god-fearing towards God Almighty amongst you." Now, the Prophet's knowledge was more perfectly all-inclusive, nobler, firmer and stalwart than all others because it was gotten through the divine teaching of the Spirit (*al-taʿlīm al-rabbānī*), for he never occupied himself with acquiring knowledge through human study and learning. Thus God said, "[this inspiration] is something that one mighty in power taught him."[179]

2.b. Inspiration

The second mode (of the divine teaching of the Spirit) is inspiration (*al-ilhām*). Inspiration is the Universal Soul's (*al-nafs al-kullīyya*) rousing awake the particular human soul (*al-nafs al-juzʾīyya al-insānīyya*) in proportion to the soul's lustral clarity, receptivity and spiritual capacity. Furthermore, inspiration is the effect of Revelation. Revelation is the manifest declaration of the arcane divine Command, while inspiration is an intimation derived thereof. Knowledge (*al-ʿilm*) realized through revelation is called 'prophetic knowledge', whereas that gained by inspiration is called 'supernal esoteric knowledge' (*ʿilm ladunī*). Now, esoteric knowledge is obtained directly, without any causal intermediary being juxtaposed

177 A reference to the *ḥadīth* cited above, pp. 124–5.

178 A *ḥadīth* commonly cited in Sufi texts (cf. Chittick, *The Sufi Path of Knowledge*, p. 175). On the place of *adab* in Islam, see Nuha Alshaar (ed.) *The Qur'an and Adab: The Shaping of Literary Traditions in Classical Islam* (Oxford: Oxford University Press in association with the Institute of Ismaili Studies). On *adab* in Sufism, see Gerhard Böwering, "The *Adab* Literature of Classical Sufism: Anṣārī's Code of Conduct," in Barbara Metcalf (ed.) *Moral Conduct and Authority: The Place of Adab in South Asian Islam* (Berkeley: University of California Press 1984), pp. 62–87; Abū ʿAbd al-Raḥmān al-Sulamī, *A Collection of Sufi Rules of Conduct* (translation of Sulamī's *Jawāmiʿ Ādab al-Ṣūfīyya*), trans. Elena Biagi (Cambridge: Islamic Texts Society 2010); Camille Helminski, *The Book of Character: Writings on Character and Virtue from Islamic and Other Sources* (Bristol, U.K.: The Book Foundation 2004), s.v. "Courtesy (*Ādāb*)," pp. 362–75.

179 Qur'ān LIII:5.

between the soul and its Maker.[180] It can be likened to the radiance cast by the lamp of the Supersensible Realm, the rays of which shine upon a heart that has been refined and released (from worldly accoutrements).

The reason for this is that all knowledge and science is known to be obtained and realized within the substance of the Primordial Universal Soul (*jawhar al-nafs al-kullīyya al-awwalīyya*) that is immanent within primal abstracted (non-material) substances. The Universal Soul's relation to the First Intellect resembles that of Eve to Adam.[181] As has been already elucidated, the Universal Intellect is nobler in rank, more perfectly all-inclusive, superior in strength and nearer to its Maker than the Universal Soul.[182] Yet the Universal Soul is mightier, more refined and nobler in nature than all other created beings. Hence, revelation[183] is generated whenever the

---

180 Ghazālī's concept of the intimate connection of Universal Intellect to God echoes Plotinus' idea of the Intellectual Principle's direct apprehension of the One: "What then are we to think of the All-Perfect but that it can produce nothing less than the very greatest that is later than itself? This greatest, later than the divine unity, must be the Divine Mind, and it must be the second of all existence, for it that which sees the One on which alone it leans while the First has no need whatever of it. The offspring of the prior to Divine Mind can be no other than that Mind itself and thus is the loftiest being in the universe, all else following upon it – the Soul, for example, being an utterance and act of the Intellectual-Principle as that is an utterance and act of The One. But in soul the utterance is obscured, for soul is an image and must look to its own original: that Principle, on the contrary, looks to the First without mediation – thus becoming what it is – and has that vision not as from a distance but as the immediate next with nothing intervening, close to the One as Soul to it." *The Enneads*, trans. Stephen MacKenna (New York: Larson Publications 1992), V.I.6 (p. 429).

181 Cf. the last sentence of Proclus' Proposition 167: "the higher Intelligence is identical with its object, whereas the lower is identical with its own content but not with the prior Intelligible – for the unconditioned Intelligible is distinct from the intelligible in the knower." E.R. Dodds (trans.), *Proclus: The Elements of Theology*, p. 147.

182 "Yet the offspring of the Intellectual-Principle must be a Reason-Principle ... such then is that [higher Soul] which circles about the divine Mind, its light, its image inseparably attached to it: on the upper level united with it, filled from it, enjoying it, participant in its nature, intellective with it, but on the lower level in contact with the realm beneath itself ..." Plotinus, *The Enneads*, V.I. 7 (p. 430).

183 The printed Arabic text here reads *al-ilhām*. I assume that this is a printing error, and that the original must have been *al-waḥy*, which is demanded by the context. Prof. Bosworth recommends consulting a MS.

Universal Intellect bestows its effusive grace down (upon the soul), and inspiration is generated whenever the Universal Soul illuminates (the soul). [106] So revelation is the ornament of the prophets while inspiration is the adornment of the saints (*al-awliyā'*).

However, respecting knowledge of divine revelation (*'ilm al-waḥy*), just as the soul is inferior to the intellect, the saint is inferior in rank to the prophet, so inspiration is below revelation (the former being weaker in comparison to the latter), yet stronger than vision (*al-ru'yā*).[184] While knowledge of inspiration belongs to both the prophets and saints, knowledge of revelation is the peculiar distinctive trait of the apostles (*rusul*), being reserved exclusively for them, as is apparent (in the Qur'ānic accounts) from Adam, Moses, Abraham and Muḥammad – peace be upon them all, as well as other of the apostles among them.

As for the distinction between prophethood (*al-nubuwwat*) and the office of the apostle (*al-risālat*): prophethood is the Sanctified Soul's (*al-nafs al-qudsīyya*) reception of the spiritual realities of objects of knowledge and intelligible percepts (*ḥaqā'iq al-ma'lūmāt wa'l-ma'qūlāt*) and conveying them to those who can benefit from these things and who have aptitude to absorb them.[185] Sometimes it happens that some soul or other is able to receive (these objects and intelligible matters), yet is unable, due some extenuating circumstance or cause, to transmit them to anyone.

As for supernal esoteric knowledge (*al-'ilm al-ladunī*), it belongs to both prophets and saints. It was possessed by al-Khiḍr, and mention of this was made by God Almighty when He stated, "We had taught him [al-Khiḍr] a knowledge from our presence (*'allamnāhu min ladunnā 'ilman.*)."[186] (Referring to this same esoteric knowledge as well), the Commander of the Faithful 'Alī b. Abī Ṭālib – may God's benevolence grace him – confessed, "He (the Prophet) placed his tongue inside my mouth, and a thousand chapters of knowledge (*bāb min al-'ilm*) opened in my heart, and another thousand other gates within each of those gates."[187] He also pronounced, "If

---

184 On the Sufi significance of *ru'yā*, see J. Nurbakshsh, *Sufi Symbolism* (London: KNP 1993), VII, pp. 24ff. On the different senses of *ru'yā* in Ghazālī' thought, see Jabre, *Essai sur le lexique de Ghazali*, pp. 104–5.

185 This is what is known as the phenomenon of Prophetic revelation or *al-waḥy*.

186 Qur'ān XVIII:65.

187 Cited by Ḥusayn Wā'iẓ-i Kāshifī Sabziwārī, *Futuwwat-nāma-yi sulṭānī*, ed. Ja'far Maḥjūb (Tehran: Bunyād-i farhang-i Īrān 1350 A.Hsh./1971), p. 173. Another textual

a cushion were be to set down for me,[188] I would recline on it and administer justice out to the followers of the Torah according to the Torah, pass judgment on the followers of the Gospel according to the rule of the Gospel, and arbitrate amongst the followers of the Qur'ān according to the Qur'ān's law."[189]

Now, this degree is not attained simply by submission to human instruction (*al-ta'allum al-insānī*), but rather, this rank is only realized by a man through the power of esoteric knowledge. 'Alī also said that the exegesis of Moses' scripture would amount to some forty camel-loads [Speaking of the day and age of Moses], then adding "Were God to give me permission to compose a commentary on the meanings of the *Fāṭiha*, I could expand my exegesis to such a sum – that is to say, up to forty camel-loads."[190] Now, this sort of comprehensive amplitude, copious breadth and opening-up of knowledge cannot be achieved by anyone except it come from a highly esoteric, divine and celestial supernal source (of knowledge).

---

variant of this statement, often quoted by Shī'ite thinkers, goes: "The Prophet taught 'Alī a thousand chapters (or 'a thousand sayings' or 'a thousand words'), each of which gave access to a thousand others." Cited by Amir-Moezzi, *The Divine Guide in Early Shi'ism: The Sources of Esotericism in Islam*, trans. David Streight (Albany: SUNY Press 1994), p. 75. "With the growth of Sufi doctrine in the fourth/tenth and fifth/eleventh centuries, increasing emphasis was placed on 'Alī's possession of secret or esoteric knowledge (*'elm al-ladonī*) transmitted to him by the Prophet; many considered it virtually boundless, since he was believed to have even been granted participation in the *ghayb* (e.g. by being granted knowledge of future events ...)" – E. Kohlberg, "'Alī b. Abī Ṭāleb," *EIr* I, p. 846.

188 Setting down a "cushion" for someone often designates a special place of honour given to a person in Middle Eastern societies, often constituting the post or position held by a dignitary, similar to the judge's "bench," magistrate's "chair," or minister's "desk" in contemporary Western society.

189 On the various sources of this saying by Imām 'Alī, see Arzina Lalani (ed. & trans.), *Degrees of Excellence: A Fatimid Treatise on Leadership in Islam (A New Arabic Edition and English Translation of Aḥmad b. Ibrāhīm al-Naysābūrī's Kitāb ithbāt al-imāma)* (London: I.B. Tauris in association with the Institute of Ismaili Studies 2010), p. 82, n. 85.

190 For a discussion of this saying and its sources, see Reza Shah-Kazemi, *Justice and Remembrance: Introducing the Spirituality of Imam 'Alī* (London: I.B. Tauris in association with the Institute of Ismaili Studies 2006), p. 25, n. 68.

Thus, whenever God wishes well for His devotee, He lifts up the veil hanging between his soul and the (Universal) Soul, which is the Pre-eternal Tablet (*al-lawḥ*), so that the mysteries of certain created things are manifested upon it and their interior spiritual meanings inscribed upon its surface. The soul then interprets and explains these mysteries according to its own delight and deserts to whomsoever it wishes amongst His devotees.

Now, the reality [107] of sapiential lore (*ḥaqīqat al-ḥikma*) is attained through supernal esoteric knowledge (*al-ʿilm al-ladunī*), and unless a man attains this degree, he shall never become wise, since wisdom – gnostic sagesse (*al-ḥikmat*) is the Almighty's gift. "He grants wisdom unto whom He wishes; and to whomsoever wisdom has been granted, has received abounding goodness. But none take heed but those who possess deep understanding."[191] The reason for this is that those who succeed in reaching the rank of supernal esoteric knowledge are free to dispense with the pursuit of much learning and need not take the trouble of undergoing teaching and tutorials, so their study is but slight while their teaching is great; their labour is little and their leisure long-lasting.

It should be understood that when revelation (*al-waḥy*) became cut off and the door of the apostolate (*al-risalat*)[192] was bolted shut, people then became free of the need for any further apostles[193] and could dispense with the propagation of further calls to faith (*daʿwat*) after the validation of its proofs[194] and the religion (of Islam) had been made fully complete. As God Almighty said, "Today, I have completed your religion for you."[195] Thus, to proclaim something that provides no added boon and benefit, for which no

191 Qur'ān II:269.

192 Literally signifying the 'sending of the apostles', this term alludes to the legislative, law-giving aspect of prophecy, since in Qur'ānic usage, the *rasūl* is always provided with a book. See A.J. Wensinck, "Rasūl," *EI2* VIII, pp. 454–55.

193 Alternate version: could then dispense with needing.

194 Seven alternate versions of this phrase: after the supporting evidence for it was ascertained to be sound / After the corroboration of proofs / After its evidence had been ratified as being incontrovertible / After its proofs had been incontrovertibly ascertained / After its supporting evidence had been corroborated / After conclusive evidence for it had been adduced and authenticated / Following upon the incontrovertible corroboration of the supporting evidence for the authenticity of the Islamic faith.

195 Qur'ān V:3.

real need exists, would have been unwise and fallen short of the mark of wisdom, for there is no wisdom in manifesting and bringing something to notice when it does not satisfy any need.

The Gate of Inspiration (*bāb al-ilhām*), however, is not shut. Due to the constant, ineluctable demand and need of human souls for invigoration, renewal and reminder, the grace and favour of the light of the Universal Soul (*al-nafs al-kullī*) has not been withdrawn. Despite the fact that people may now dispense with further apostles and prophetic summons, because of their preoccupation with these temptations and their avid desire and voracity for these sensual lusts, they still have the need to be reminded, disciplined and awakened.

It is for this reason that when God Almighty closed the Gate of Revelation (*bāb al-waḥy*) – and that is still a waymark (*āyat*) for devotees – He opened up, out of His mercy, the Gate of Inspiration, that affairs might be arranged and the ontological levels of being set in order, so that people may comprehend that "God behaves with gracious mildness towards His servants, and provides for whomsoever He will," ... "without stint."[196]

Chapter VI: On the Hierarchy of Souls in the Acquisition of Knowledge

It should be understood that knowledge is embedded in all human souls, all of whom are capable of absorbing all the sciences. One soul, however, may be deprived of its proper share of knowledge due to some unforeseen accident or extraneous condition [108] that befalls it,[197] as the *dictum* of the Prophet affirms, "All people were created upright believers (*ḥunafā*)[198], but Satan perverted them." Likewise, he said, "Every infant is born in a state of sound equilibrium in his original nature (*al-fiṭra*) [then his parents make him a Jew, Christian or Zoroastrian]."[199]

196 Qur'ān XLII:19 and II:212.

197 Alternate versions: unforeseen accident / foreign factor / outside factor / extrinsic emergency / condition.

198 On the meaning of this term, see W. Montgomery Watt, "Ḥanīf," *EI2* III, pp. 165–66.

199 A good discussion of the various connotations of *Fiṭra* in Ghazālī's thought is given by Farid Jabre, *Essai sur le lexique de Ghazali*, pp. 222–24. For this *ḥadīth* in particular, see *Essai sur le lexique de Ghazali*, p. 223 and D.B. Macdonald, "Fiṭra," *EI2* II, pp. 931–32.

The 'human rational soul' (*al-nafs al-nāṭiqa al-insānī*) is therefore worthy to be enlightened and to experience the illumination of the Universal Soul (*al-nafs al-kullī*), and is disposed to absorb and appropriate the images of intelligible things from it by virtue of its primordial purity and attributes.[200] However, in this world, due to a variety of accidents and circumstances, some souls have become ill, and so are prevented from taking cognizance of these spiritual realities. Other souls, by contrast, continue to maintain their original, pristine state of health without ever being affected by infirmity and unsoundness, remaining like this as long as they are alive.

However, it is the prophetic souls, who are the recipients of God's revelation and strengthening support (*al-nufūs al-nabawwī al-qābila li'l-waḥy wa'l-ta'yīd*), that are the truly 'sound souls', for they are capable of manifesting miracles and controlling the outcome of events in this nether world by the force of their spiritual will (*taṣarruf*). It is such souls who continue to abide in their original sound state of health and whose humours do not alter when subjected to the corrupting influence of (psychological) illnesses and the failures and vicissitudes of (life's) contretemps.[201] Hence it is that the prophets have become physicians of the soul, summoning people (to realize) the soundness and equilibrium of their original nature (*ṣiḥḥat al-fiṭra*).

However, in this base world the sick souls are ranked in different classes. For some of them, the effect of their sickness is altogether miniscule: it is as though a fine cloud of forgetfulness had settled on their minds, causing them to occupy themselves in study, so that whenever they seek to regain their original, pristine state of health, their ailment can be removed with but little effort and the least of remedies and the clouds of forgetfulness may be dispersed with a small bit of recollection. On the other hand, others may spend an entire lifetime assimilating learning and practising intellectual discipline, yet not gain any understanding at all because of their corrupt natural disposition, for when once one's nature becomes corrupted, it is no longer susceptible of cure. Others there are who alternately remember and

200 Echoing Plotinus' description of the "irradiation of the Intellectual-Principle upon" the understanding, which is a "pure phase of the Soul" and which, in turn, "welcomes to itself the images implanted from its prior." Plotinus, *The Enneads*, V.3. 3 (p. 441).

201 Translator's note to himself: This phrase "vicissitudes of the contretemps (of nature)" took about an hour to invent after lengthy research on the relevant technical terms!

forget: they subject their souls to discipline and humiliation, thus acquiring a little light and some feeble illumination.

Now, these differences between souls arise from their differing propensities and proclivities towards the world, (their conditions alternating) according to the strength or weakness of their absorption in it, such that they are either always like a sick person in the process of recovering his health or like a healthy person who is continually falling sick! Whenever this psychological complex (*al-'uqda*) is resolved, souls shall then acknowledge the existence of supernal esoteric knowledge (*al-'ilm al-ladunī*), for then they will realize that they were conscious, intelligent and wise in their primordial nature (*awwal al-fiṭra*), and that they were in a pure and pristine condition when initially generated. They have only succumbed to ignorance because of their association with this gross, coarse, corporeal frame and residence in this dark dwelling and dismal abode.

By the pursuit of learning [109] these souls seek neither to generate a knowledge that is non-existent, nor to contrive to create an intelligence that is missing. Rather, they wish to restore and restitute the sort of knowledge that is original and innate – insofar as the sickness that afflicted them was due to their absorption in the material ornaments of the body and their preoccupation in preserving bodily functions and maintaining its bases in harmonious order. Similarly, when a kind and doting, loving father who wishes to devote himself to his son's care becomes so completely preoccupied with him that he is oblivious of all his own affairs, focusing on a single matter: that which concerns his son; the same goes for the soul that is intensely enamoured and concerned with this bodily frame, preoccupied with its maintenance, and careful of its welfare. Being immersed and sunk down in the ocean of Physical Nature due to its weakness and fractured personality, throughout its life it needs to study and be vouchsafed teaching (*al-ta'allum*), in this way seeking to recover and recollect what it has forgotten.

Now, the process of study and learning is nothing else but the soul's return to its own substance (*jawharihā*), its retrieval and salvaging forth what lies in its substratum (deposited therein *in potentia*), while searching for its essential perfection, so as to realize its proper happiness and felicity.[202] Of course, whenever they are debilitated and weakened, souls cannot

202 Alternate version: Now, the process of study and learning is nothing else but the soul's return to its own substance (*jawharihā*), and salvaging forth what lies deposited in its own substratum, so as to attain happiness.

actualize this potential nor realize the reality of their substance, so they are obliged to resort to a teacher who is wise and sympathetic, taking recourse in him so that he will aid them in gaining their objectives and aid the fulfilment of their heart's hopes. Such souls are like infirm folk ignorant of how to remedy their malady, only knowing that health is virtuous, commendable and worthy of pursuit. Hence they take betake themselves to a friendly and amicable physician, revealing to him the symptoms of their malady, that he may remove their ailment and purge them of their illness.

We have even seen how certain physicians, when afflicted with a particular illness, such as a chest or head infection, may have all their knowledge and learning vanish from their minds, so that they forget everything they had known. Everything becomes cloudy and confused for them, so that everything they had gained and realized over the course of their life throughout their previous experience becomes, to their impaired powers of memory and recollection, as it were, shrouded in darkness. Then, once the physician recovers his health and his amnesia evaporates, his soul recalls what it lost. It has its learning and knowledge restored. Upon recovering from its amnesia, the soul recollects all the learning it had forgotten during its malady.[203]

Thus, we learn that that the knowledge was not eradicated but merely forgotten,[204] since there is a difference between obliteration (*al-maḥw*), and

---

203 The Platonic substratum of Ghazālī's *Risāla* is quite evident in this reference to the doctrine of *anamnesis* or recollection. Learning is not just reception of instruction from a teacher, Plato taught, but involves a process of 'salvaging', 'excavating' or 'bringing up' from within what the soul knew before birth and then forgot (see his two key dialogues: *Meno* 82B ff. and *Phaedo* 73A). The Christian Platonist philosopher Boethius (480–525) provides a description of *anamnesis* almost identical to Ghazālī's words in this passage, where in his *The Consolation of Philosophy* (Bk. I.2) he describes himself as afflicted by a sickness when Lady Philosophy approaches him, descending from on high ... "she gently laid her hand on my breast and said, 'It's nothing serious, only a touch of amnesia that he is suffering, the common disease of deluded minds. He has forgotten for a while who he is, but he will soon remember once he has recognized me. To make it easier for him I will wipe a little of the blinding cloud of worldly concern from his eyes'." – Victor Watts (trans.), *Boethius: The Consolation of Philosophy* (London: Penguin Books 1969; repr. 1999), p. 6.; also cf. III.11.

204 Alternate translation: For this reason, we may understand that knowledge does not become eradicated but only forgotten/ Thus, we learn that that knowledge does not become destroyed but only overlooked and forgotten.

oblivion or forgetfulness (*al-nisyān*). Obliteration consists in the complete annihilation of the material patterns (*al-nuqūsh*) and signs (*al-rusūm*) (of a thing), whereas oblivion denotes merely the obscuring of (something's) appearance, like a cloud or fog covering the light of the sun from onlookers: it (oblivion) is not the (total) decline and setting of the sun below the earth's horizon.

Hence, by its preoccupation with study and learning the soul is able to dissolve the disease with which it was afflicted and relieve itself of the illness befallen it, so as to return to that which it originally understood in its primordial [110] nature (*awwal al-fiṭra*).

Thus, by occupation with study and learning the soul relieves itself of the illness and dissolves the disease with which it had been afflicted in its substance, thence returning to that which it had known, earlier, in its primordial nature (*awwal al-fiṭra*), its pristine state of (of well-being and) purity. Hence, once you have grasped the cause and purpose of learning, and realized the reality of the soul and its substance, then you should understand that the sick soul has need of learning and is in dire need of spending its life engaged in the pursuit and acquisition of knowledge (*taḥṣīl al-ʿulūm*).

However, when there's but little sign of infirmity in the soul, its sickness being but minute and its illness slight, the clouds (of its delusion) tenuous and its temperament sound, it doesn't need much instruction (*al-taʿallum*), nor need it resort to long travail and strenuous exertions. On the contrary, only a small amount of speculation (*naẓar*) and meditative reflection (*tafakkur*) will suffice it to return back to and restitute its original, pristine state (of knowledge), to direct its gaze back to its source-spring and reality, and to make that which was secreted within it emerge from a state of potentiality into a condition of actuality, thus becoming ornamented with what had been always implanted within it. Thus, in this fashion, its affairs are consummated and work completed, so that in the minimum amount of time it can apprehend the maximum amount of things,[205] and hence is able to express things and interpret objects of knowledge in a fashion commensurate (with their intelligible contents).

In this fashion, the soul becomes learned and wise, perfectly accomplished and articulate. It tries to find enlightenment by turning its attention towards the Universal Soul, and in response the Universal Soul effuses its

205 Alternate version: In this fashion it finds the perfect fulfilment of its affairs, so that in the minimum amount of time it can apprehend the maximum amount of things.

sovereign superabundant grace upon the particular soul. The particular soul in turn, by means of the love which it holds for its own Principle, tries to assimilate itself to it. So it (the particular soul) lops off the branches of jealousy, severs the roots of hatred, and refrains from the world's vanities and idle pageantry. When it attains this degree, it has become indeed most sage and wise. It has realized salvation and that is the ultimate goal of all humanity.

Chapter VII: On the Reality of Supernal Esoteric Knowledge and the Means of its Acquisition

It should be understood that supernal esoteric knowledge, which is the all-permeating diffusion of the light of inspiration (*nūr al-ilhām*), comes into existence only after equipoise (of soul) (*al-taswiya*) is attained, just as God Almighty says, "by the soul and that which gave it equipoise."[206] Yet the restitution of this equipoise can only be realized through three things:

Firstly, by studying the sciences so as to acquire ample and sufficient knowledge of most of them.

Secondly, through exercise of genuine self-discipline and proper self-control. The Prophet alluded [111] to the inner reality of this when he remarked, "He who puts into practice what he knows, God will bequeath him knowledge of that which he doesn't know."[207] The Prophet stated as well, "He who devotes himself to God for forty mornings, God Almighty will cause springs of wisdom to gush forth upon his tongue from his heart."[208]

---

206 Qur'ān XCI:7.

207 Alternate version: God bequeaths knowledge of that which he doesn't know to him who puts into practice what he does know. This *ḥadīth* is not in Arend Jan Wensinck's *Concordance et indices de la tradition musulmane* (Leiden 1933), but is cited in Ghazālī's *Munqidh*; see R.J. McCarthy, *Deliverance from Error: An Annotated Translation of al-Munqidh min al-Dalāl and other relevant works of al-Ghazālī* (Louisville: Fons Vitae, n.d.), p. 86.

208 *Aḥadīth-i Mathnawī*, no. 624, p. 196. Ghazālī also composed a separate treatise called "The Book of the Etiquette of Seclusion" (*K. Adab al-'uzla* as part of his *Iḥyā' 'ulūm al-dīn*) on the practice of the forty-day retreat or *khalwa*.

Thirdly and lastly, by meditative reflection (*al-tafakkur*).[209] This is a practice whereby the soul first submits itself to being taught and endures the discipline of study, then meditates and reflects on the facts and objects of knowledge it knows according to the conditions required by meditative reflection. The gate to hidden spiritual insights (*al-bāb al-ghayb*) is thereby opened to it. The contemplative here is like a businessman, an entrepreneur who takes control of certain properties by force and drive of personal business initiative so that the gates of profit and gain are opened for him, whereas if he had taken the wrong course and adopted bad business practices, his fortune would have been despoiled and laid to waste. Thus, when the reflective and contemplative person (*al-mutafakkir*, lit. 'the thinker') fares upon the highroad of Virtue, he becomes endowed with profound heart-intelligence (*dhū'l-lubāb*) so that a window to the invisible spiritual realities of the *mundus invisibilis* opens up in his heart. Thus, he becomes a sage, one perfectly accomplished, a wise savant, endowed with inspiration and blessed by divine corroboration. Hence, the Prophet said, "An hour of meditative reflection is better than sixty years of religious devotion."[210]

However, we will give a more polished exposition of the different provisions, qualities and required characteristics – as well as the deeper reality of meditative reflection – in another treatise, since it is quite an abstruse subject matter, requiring a lot of additional elucidation and commentary – (that hopefully I will compose) with God Almighty's assistance. But here we must conclude our treatise. For those adept in the art of meditation a few words suffice anyway, "and whomsoever God appoints no light is without any illumination."[211]

---

209 On the place and significance of meditative reflection or contemplation (*tafakkur*) in Ghazālī's thought, see Giuseppe Celentano (trans.), *Al-Ghazālī: il libro della Meditazione (Kitāb al-Tafakkur dall'Iḥyā' 'ulūm ad-dīn)* (Trieste: Società Italiana Testi Islamici 1988), and Farid Jabre, *Essai sur le lexique de Ghazali*, p. 225; M.I. Waley, "Contemplative Disciplines in Early Persian Sufism," in Leonard Lewisohn (ed.) *The Heritage of Sufism*, vol. I: *Classical Persian Sufism from its Origins to Rumi* (Oxford: Oneworld 1999), pp. 541ff. For an overview of Persian Sufi doctrines of *tafakkur*, see Leonard Lewisohn, *Beyond Faith and Infidelity*, ch. 7.

210 A well-known *ḥadīth* utilized by Sufis from time immemorial; see Hujwīrī, *Kashf al-maḥjūb*, ed. V.A. Zhukovskii (St. Petersburg: 1899; repr., Leningrad: 1926), p. 135/8.

211 Qur'ān XXIV:40.

"God is the Friend of the Faithful."[212] In him we put our trust. May God's blessings and peace rest upon our lord Muḥammad, his family and companions. "God suffices for us; what a great Guardian is He,"[213] for there is no might and "no strength except through God, the Exalted and Almighty,"[214] upon Whom I rely in every instant, every circumstance.

May God – Lord of all the worlds – be praised!

212 Qur'ān III:68.

213 Qur'ān III:173.

214 Qur'ān XVII:39.

III

ESOTERIC PSYCHOLOGY AND KNOWLEDGE OF THE HEART

Selections from Rashīd al-Dīn Maybudī's (d. 520/1126) *Kashf al-asrār wa 'uddat al-abrār*

Apart from the semi-legendary authors of the ancient world – Homer, Aesop and the like – certainly very few writers of such a vast work have come down to us with virtually no information about his life in the way that Rashīd al-Dīn Maybudī has in historical times. In fact, all we know of this author for certain is that he began work on his grand-scale mystical exegesis of the Qur'ān, *The Unveiling of Mysteries and Provision of the Pious* (*Kashf al-asrār wa 'uddat al-abrār*), in 520/1126, and that he was probably the disciple of the master who provided the foundation for this work, Khwāja 'Abdu'llāh Anṣārī (d. 481/1089), whose words often spice the narration of the text.[1] The genealogical lineage of his surname – *nisba* – al-Maybudī, refers to the town of Maybud, located fifty kilometres north-west of Yazd, where, according to the author of the only definitive study of Maybudī's life and works,[2] he was born, his father having been a certain eminent Sufi scholar, Jamāl al-Islām Abū Sa'd b. Aḥmad b. Mihrīzād (d. 480/1087).

The Unveiling of Mysteries, which appears in ten volumes,[3] is one of the most important Sufi commentaries ever written on the Qur'ān, and certainly the most celebrated one in Persian. Here, Maybudī expands on and amplifies a (no longer extant) Qur'ānic commentary by his spiritual master. Among Persian commentaries on the Qur'ān, it is one of the longest, being

1 Although for this only circumstantial evidence exists: see Gerhard Böwering's Foreword to Annebel Keeler, *Sufi Hermeneutics: The Qur'ān Commentary by Rashīd al-Dīn Maybudī* (Oxford: Oxford University Press in association with the Institute of Ismaili Studies 2006), p. xix.

2 Keeler, *Sufi Hermeneutics*, pp. 12–13.

3 Rashīd al-Dīn Maybudī, *Kashf al-asrār wa 'uddat al-abrār*, ed. 'Alī Aṣghar Ḥikmat (Tehran: Intishārāt-i Dānishgāhī 1952–60), 10 vols.

only second in length to that by Abū'l-Futūḥ al-Rāzī (flourished twelfth century).[4] William Chittick rightly describes the *Kashf al-asrār* as "the most detailed and important twelfth-century source for Sufi teachings in the Persian language."[5]

Throughout his commentary, Maybudī utilizes the poetic lexicon of Persian Sufism, drawing on the ambiguity of the highly erotic Sufi terminology wherein the raptures of divine love are couched in the language of human passion, elaborating his key mystical ideas by way of allusion and metaphor.[6] Maybudī's commentary is steeped in the rich tradition of Persian love mysticism,[7] drawing heavily upon the *Sawāniḥ* of Aḥmad Ghazālī (d. 520/1126), the Sufi poetry of Sanā'ī (d. 525/1131), and the *Rawḥ al-arwāḥ* of Aḥmad ibn Manṣūr Sam'ānī (d. 535/1140).[8] In respect to the present anthology, perhaps the most significant aspect of the work is its lucid exposition of Sufi technical terminology.

Maybudī's Qur'ānic hermeneutics drew upon the fully mature tradition of Islamic Qur'ān commentary that had commenced two centuries earlier with Abū Ja'far al-Ṭabarī (d. 310/923) and which culminated in the grand pro-Mu'tazilī commentary by Abū'l-Qāsim al-Zamarkhsharī (d. 538/1144) during Maybudī's own day.[9] His commentary is important in several respects: for having established Persian Sufi *tafsīr* as a separate literary genre, thus serving as "the model for many later mystical *tafsīr*s in Persian,"[10]

---

4 Keeler, *Sufi Hermeneutics*, p. 19.

5 William Chittick, *Divine Love: Islamic Literature and the Path to God* (New Haven: Yale University Press 2013), p. xvi.

6 Cf. Keeler, *Sufi Hermeneutics*, p. xxv.

7 As Keeler puts it: "In Khorasan the late fifth/eleventh century and early sixth/twelfth centuries saw both a development and crystallization of the Sufi doctrines of love, and an evolution of the Persian literary language for the expression of mystical experience. Each of these developments is much in evidence in the mystical sections of the *Kashf al-asrār*." – *Sufi Hermeneutics*, p. 15.

8 Keeler, *Sufi Hermeneutics*, pp. 14–15. Chittick points out that "From the beginning of the commentary on Surah 17 to the end of the book, Maybudī frequently draws from his [Sam'ānī's work], sometimes verbatim." – *Divine Love*, p. xix.

9 For an overview of the key preceding commentaries utilized by Maybudī, see Keeler, *Sufi Hermeneutics*, pp. 3–10, 21–22, as well as her article on "Exegesis. iii. In Persian," *Encyclopædia Iranica* IX, pp. 119–23.

10 Annebel Keeler, "Exegesis. iii. In Persian," *Encyclopædia Iranica* IX, p. 121.

for being the first Qur'ānic commentary composed mostly in Persian, for combining exoteric with esoteric exegesis within one work,[11] and for providing a rich lexicon of erotic mystical terminology utilized by later Persian poets such as Ḥāfiẓ (d. 791/1389).[12]

Each chapter of his exegesis contains one or more Qur'ānic passages interpreted according to three different hermeneutic 'levels' or 'semantic shifts' (*nawba*), each of which constitutes a separate section:

Shift I features the literal Persian translation of the Arabic Qur'ānic text. Shift II provides an exoteric commentary incorporating linguistic, grammatical, historical, juridical, ethical and general exegetical matters, being a summary of earlier Arabic commentaries which discussed similar themes, as well as of the teachings of Anṣārī himself. Significant portions of this section, which take up between eight to ten pages in the published text, are in Arabic. Shift III comprises the Sufi (esoteric) commentary, being an exposition of selected verses of the Qur'ānic passage in question, constituting approximately three printed pages in the published edition, very small portions of which are also written in Arabic.[13]

In Shift III, however, the commentary is entirely mystical, and includes sayings, poetry and stories of the Sufi masters which Maybudī marshals up to aid his exegesis. This *nawba* "boasts a far more artistic style, rich in metaphor and embellished with metred and rhyming prose, and numerous verses of love poetry."[14] Maybudī makes ample use of the *Subtleties of Symbolic Allusions* (*Laṭā'if al-ishārāt*), the Sufi Qur'ān commentary by Abū'l-Qāsim al-Qushayrī (d. 465/1074),[15] informing us that this shift is consecrated to "the allegories of mystics (*rumūz-i 'ārifān*), the allusions of the Sufis (*ishārāt-i ṣūfiyān*), and the subtle associations of preachers (*laṭā'if-i*

11 Keeler, *Sufi Hermeneutics*, p. xxi and p. 10.

12 In his *'Irfān u rindī dar shi'r-i Ḥāfiẓ* (Tehran: Nashr-i Markaz 1381 A.Hsh./2003; 3rd printing), pp. 68–139, Dāryūsh Āshūrī demonstrates the dependence of much of Ḥāfiẓ's imagery on Maybudī's lexicon.

13 According to Keeler (*Sufi Hermeneutics*, pp. 19–20) only between 5 and 10% of the Shift III is in Arabic.

14 Keeler, *Sufi Hermeneutics*, p. 19.

15 Chittick, *Divine Love*, p. xix.

mudhakkirān)."[16] Many of the original *munājāt*, poetry and prose of Anṣārī also are found in this section.[17]

Since it is with esoteric Sufi texts that we are concerned here, in the selections below I have concentrated on the 'third shift', examining several important passages of esoteric exegesis and providing a translation thereof in the anthology. My first selection concerns the theme of the Four Levels of the Heart & The Three Types of Divine Light. This is Maybudī's interpretation of Qur'ān: XXXIX:22–23, expounding the four levels of Sufi esoteric psychology or knowledge of the heart, and discussing the three types of divine light which respectively illuminate tongue, heart and body.[18] The verse in questions is as follows:

> Is he whose breast (*ṣadr*) has been expanded for Submission (*islām*), such that he walks in a divine light from his Lord (like one who sees not)? Then woe unto those whose hearts are hardened against the remembrance of God. They are plainly astray in error.[19]

In this passage, the notion of following or walking in divine light, as 'Abdu'llāh al-Bayḍāwī (d. 685/1286) in his commentary on this verse in his *Anwār al-tanzīl wa asrār al-ta'wīl* observed, is metaphorical of having one's heart opened to spiritual knowledge (*ma'rifa*) and guidance. According to the *ḥadīth* of the Prophet, "When light enters the heart, it expands and it becomes spacious." When asked what the mark of that was, he responded, "Constant turning to the Abode of Eternity, shunning the abode of delusion, and preparing for death before it arrives."[20]

---

16 Cited by Keeler, *Sufi Hermeneutics*, p. 19.

17 See my "Preface: Ansari and Early Persian Erotic Spirituality," in Nahid Angha (trans.), *Ansari's* Hundred Fields: *An Early Persian Treatise on the Sufi Way* (London: Archetype 2010), p. 8 for a discussion of these *munājāt*.

18 Rashīd al-Dīn Maybudī, *Kashf al-asrār wa 'uddat al-abrār*, ed. 'Alī Aṣghar Ḥikmat (Tehran: Intishārāt-i Dānishgāhī 1952–60), VIII, pp. 412–14.

19 *The Glorious Qur'ān*, trans. Marmaduke Pickthall (London: Allen & Unwin 1976), XXXIX:22–23 (with modifications).

20 See S.H. Nasr, et al. (eds.), *The Study Quran* (New York: HarperOne 2015), p. 1123, n. 22.

The four divisions of the heart and their respective veils, which are elaborated below by Maybudī, are traditional elements of Sufi teachings. The foremost Persian Sufi master of the Timurid period, Shāh Niʿmatullāh Walī (1330–1431)[21] practically reproduces this passage, but regards the heart's core or *fu'ād* as the locus of gnosis (*maʿrifat*) rather than (like Maybudī here) the site of contemplation of God.[22] The Kubrawī Sufi theosopher Najm al-Dīn Rāzī (d. 654/1256) likewise describes seven levels (*ṭawr*) of the heart (*aṭwār al-qalb*), in the following order: breast (*ṣadr*), heart (*qalb*), pericardium (*shaghāf*), heart's core (*fu'ād*), heart's grain (*ḥabba al-qalb*), heart's arcanum (*suwaydā'*), heart's blood (*muḥjat al-qalb*).[23]

Perhaps the most comprehensive study of the spiritual heart is that by Abū Ḥāmid al-Ghazālī in the *Book of the Elaboration of the Marvels of the Heart* (*Kitāb Sharḥ 'ajā'ib al-qalb*, which is Book XXI of his *chef d'oeuvre*, the *Iḥyā' 'ulūm al-dīn*). Here, the great Sunni mystical theologian elucidates that the heart discussed by the Sufis is not the physical "lump of flesh that has no value," but rather "a subtle thing" which "is the essence [true nature] of man. In man it is what perceives, knows, is aware [cognizant], is spoken to, punished, blamed, and responsible." He explains that the connection of this subtle spiritual organ of perception to the physical heart "resembles the connection of accidents with bodies and of qualities with the qualified, or the connection of the user of a tool with the tool, or the connection of something in a place with the place."[24] Ghazālī likewise

21 For further information about Shāh Ni'matallāh Walī, see Reza Tabandeh, "Ni'matallāh Valī, Shāh," in *Encyclopaedia of Islam* III, eds. Kate Fleet, Gudrun Krämer, Denis Matringe, John Nawas and Devin J. Stewart, consulted online 8 November 2023.

22 *Risālahā-yi Ḥaḍrat-i Sayyid Nūr al-Dīn Shāh Nimatu'llāh Walī*, ed. Javād Nūrbakhsh (Tehran: Intishārāt-i Khānaqāh-i Nimatu'llāhī 1975), vol. I, p. 219. For a translation of Shāh Nimatu'llāh's version of this passage, see Nūrbakhsh, *Sufi Symbolism* (London: KNP 2000), XV, p. 121.

23 Rāzī, *Mirṣād al-'ibād*, ed. M.A. Riyāḥī (Tehran: Intishārāt-i 'ilmī u farhangī 1372 A.Hsh./1994), pp. 195–97. See Nūrbakhsh, *Sufi Symbolism* (London: KNP 1999), IX, pp. 91–92, for a translation of this passage, and pp. 85ff. for other relevant terms concerning the heart. For a fuller discussion of the psychology of the heart, see Javād Nūrbakhsh, *The Psychology of Sufism*, trans. Terry Graham et al. (London: KNP 1992).

24 Trans. Richard McCarthy, *Al-Ghazali: Deliverance from Error: Five Key Texts Including His Spiritual Autobiography, al-Munqidh min al-Dalal* (Boston: Twayne 1980),

underlines that, depending on specific technical donnotations, theological connotations and contexts, the terms heart (*qalb*), spirit (*rūḥ*), intellect (*'aql*) and soul (*nafs*) can often have synonymous meanings. In part 10 of this work (An Exposition of Religious Texts testifying to the Correctness of the Sufis' Method in Acquiring Knowledge, not by Learning or from the Customary Method), Ghazālī cites the same verse commented on by Maybudī (XXXIX:22) as a proof-text of the authenticity of the gnostic insight of the Sufis.

As would be expected of a commentary on the Muslim missal, Maybudī's work is peppered with frequent citations from the Qur'ān. Although the passionate spiritual romanticism of his literary style echoes that of his master Anṣārī, the actual description of the various veils (*parda*) of the heart in this passage is replete with original inspired insights not found in other Sufi texts. Like Anṣārī, Maybudī has a peculiar penchant for using ternary phrases, and, as can be seen in his theories of the three kinds of divine light,[25] and the three robes of divine honour vouchsafed the Sufi, his elucidation of mystical experience is usually characterized by a tripartite structure. The motif of gluttony as the central cause of hardness of the heart at the end of the passage is found in many other Sufi texts of the twelfth century.[26]

Appendix V, p. 311. For a fuller translation of this text, see John Renard, *Knowledge of God in Classical Sufism: Foundations of Islamic Mystical Theology* (New York: Paulist Press 2004), pp. 298–331.

25 There are many theories in Sufism concerning divine lights generated from the heart. One of the most ancient is that elaborated by Ḥakīm al- Tirmidhī (d. circa 300/912) in his *Bayān al-farq bayn al-ṣadr wa'l-qalb wa'l-fu'ād wa'l-lubb* (An Exposition of the Difference between the Breast, Heart, Heart's Core and Heart's Kernal) in Kenneth L. Honerkamp (trans.), *Three Early Sufi Texts*: Two texts from the Path of Blame by Abū 'Abd al-Raḥmān al-Sulamī al-Naysabūrī (d. 412/1021) and *A Treatise on the Heart,* attributed to Al-Ḥakīm al-Tirmidhī (d. c.300/912), trans. Nicholas Heer (Louisville: Fons Vitae 2003); see Heer's translation of "The Lights of the Heart," pp. 40–45.

26 The most elaborate treatment available on this is found in T.J. Winter (trans.), *Al-Ghazālī on Disciplining the Soul, Kitāb Riyāḍat al-nafs, & On Breaking the Two Desires, Kitāb Kasr al-shahwatayn,* Books XXII and XXIII of *The Revival of the Religious Sciences* (Cambridge: Islamic Texts Society 1995), chapters 23.1–23.2.

SELECTIONS FROM RASHĪD AL-DĪN MAYBUDĪ'S COMMENTARY ON QUR'ĀN XXXIX:22–23

The Four Levels of the Heart and the Three Types of Divine Light

It should be understood that four different types of veil (*parda*) lie within the heart of man.

The first veil is that of the breast (*ṣadr*), which is site of the Testament of Islam (*'ahd-i Islām*), to which the Almighty's word testifies, "Is he whose breast (*ṣadr*) has been expanded for Submission (*islām*) ..."[27]

The second veil is that of the heart (*qalb*) itself, which is the site of the Light of Faith (*nūr-i īmān*), as indicated by God Almighty's word, "He has written faith upon their hearts."[28]

The third veil, that of the heart's core (*fu'ād*),[29] acts as the seraglio of *Contemplatio Deo* (*mushāhada-yi Ḥaqq*),[30] according to God's word: "The heart (*fu'ād*) did not lie in what it saw."[31]

---

27 Qur'ān XXXIX:22. Alternate versions: The first veil is that of the breast (*ṣadr*), which is the permanent locus/repose / permanent dwelling of the testament/covenant of Islam // The first veil is that of the breast (*ṣadr*), which is the permanent locus of the covenant of Islam (*'ahd-i Islām*).

28 Qur'ān LVIII:22.

29 The *fu'ād* is one of the subtle centres of the heart's vision. Ismā'īl Ḥaqqī (d. 1724), the great Turkish Sufi exegete, commenting on this passage, cites an anonymous poet's verse, "His heart was within his eye, and his eye was within his heart," and interprets the vision of the *fu'ād* as suprasensory in nature (*Tafsīr Rūḥ al-bayān* [Istanbul: 1970]), IX, p. 223. Rūzbihān Baqlī (d. 606/1210) in his *Commentary on the Paradoxes of the Sufis* (*Sharḥ-i shaṭḥiyyāt*), ed. Henry Corbin (Tehran: Institut Français d'Iranologie de Téhéran 1981), p. 502, cryptically writes, "The letter 'm' of the 'dominion' (*mīm* of *mulk*) of the *fu'ād* of Muḥammad is extracted from the Light of divine Contentment ... This discourse is a mystery of those who have realized intoxication, who are stricken dumb by God's overawing power, and in their infatuation speak words of ecstasy in neither Arabic or Persian!" A good overview of the meanings of *fu'ād* in early Muslim mysticism is given by Bernd Radtke and John O'Kane (trans.), *The Concept of Sainthood in Early Islamic Mysticism: Two Works by Al-Ḥakīm Al-Tirmidhī* (London: Curzon Press 1996), pp. 50–51.

30 Alternate version: behaves as the gateway to divine contemplation.

31 Qur'ān LIII:11.

The fourth veil is that of the pericardium (*shaghāf*), which is the abode of love, according to God's word, "He enamoured her (*shaghafa*) with love."[32]

Each of these four veils has its own distinctive features, God focusing His attention on each veil in a different way.[33] Whenever the Lord of the Worlds wishes to rope in the astray who has wandered far, by casting around him the lasso of His Mercy and summoning him back to the right path of His faith, He first fixes His gaze upon his breast, so that his bosom may become purified of passions and of aberrant opinions, and so his progress according the usages sanctioned by Prophetic tradition (*sunna*) may be made straight and direct.[34]

Next, He focuses His regard upon his heart in order to purify it of the defilements of the world and to purge it of the vices which constitute bad character, such as conceit, envy, arrogance, hypocrisy, avarice, malice, and foolish hauteur, in this manner swiftly conveying the heart on the path of holy abstinence (*wara'*).[35]

Then He focuses His gaze on his heart's core, dispelling his partiality and fondness for worldly things and created beings.[36] He opens the sluices of the spring of knowledge and wisdom in his heart,[37] so that the Light of divine

32 Qur'ān XII:30.

33 Alternate versions: God scrutinizing each veil with a different kind of look / and God fixes His gaze on each veil with a separate regard.

34 Alternate versions: Whenever the Lord of the Worlds desires to recall and rope in with His Mercy's lasso a runaway, // a drifter who has strayed with the lasso of His Mercy // escapee/fugitive/runaway bringing him back into the path of His faith /// When it happens that the Lord of all the Worlds deigns to restrain a runaway fugitive and recall him back into the right path of His faith, casting around him the lasso of His Mercy, He first fixes His gaze/focuses His attention on his breast, so that his bosom may become purified of passions and aberrant opinions, so that his steps may be guided aright on the way of Prophet's Sunna / that his progress according to the customary procedure and usage sanctioned by Prophetic tradition may be straight and direct.

35 Alternates: worldly contamination/the squalid polluting influences of the world, expurgating. In this manner, the heart may move swiftly on the path of holy abstinence (*wara'*).

36 Alternate versions: driving away/out his fondness and partiality for the world and created beings.//dispersing/driving out his affective ties to.

37 Alternate version: He opens up the spring of knowledge and wisdom in his heart.

Guidance is vouchsafed to the site of his insight, "such that he walks in a divine light from his Lord ..."[38] as He has declared.

Finally, He focuses His regard – ah! what a regard! – on the pericardium. His gaze thereon is like a lovely mistress beholding the face of the soul, causing fruits to blossom and multiply on the tree of joy, whereupon He makes the eyes of ecstasy and pleasure wakeful and alert.[39] His regard is like a tree widespreading its branches, under whose shade can be found the Friend's company. His loving gaze is wine and the gnostic's heart its cup.[40] When this gaze penetrates the pericardium, it extricates him from the mud and mire (of material existence), so that he steps up into the quarter of annihilation (*fanā'*).

Three things in three things are made naught – seeking dissolved in the Sought, knowing annihilated in the Known, and loving in the Beloved obliterated.[41]

The Master of the Sufi Path (*pīr-i ṭarīqat*)[42] pronounced: "Both this world and next in loving have been lost. Loving also in the Friend has disappeared. I dare not say now either that 'I am I', or that 'He is He.'"

The eyes I have are all full of the face of the Friend.
I'm content with my eyes as long as the Friend is in them.

38 Qur'ān XXXIX:22.

39 Alternate versions: Like a lovely mistress in beholding the face of the soul, His gaze makes fruits to flourish and burst open on the tree of joy, and the eyes of ecstasy and pleasure by Him become alert and awake. His gaze makes the fruits multiply on the tree of mirth // Fruits flourish and burst open on the tree of joy through His regard // His gaze and regard makes the tree of joy and mirth grow fruitful/Fruits // His gaze and regard cause fruits to blossom and multiply upon the tree of joy, and eyes of ecstasy and pleasure by Him are made alert and awake.

40 The Persian text reads "*pīrayih*" (ornament), which I assume to be a scribal error for "*piyālih*" (wine-cup), which vis-à-vis the bacchanalian symbolism of the passage makes far more sense.

41 Alternate version: Three things are annihilated and dissolved in three things: seeking becomes dissolved in the Sought; knowing annihilated in the Known, and loving is dissolved in the Beloved.

42 Maybudī here is quoting his own master, Khwāja 'Abdu'llāh Anṣārī of Herat (d. 481/1089).

To distinguish between one's eyes and the Friend is no good thing:
Either let Him be in lieu of these eyes, or the eyes in lieu of Him.[43]

In regard to what God said, "he walks in a divine light from his Lord ..."[44] (it should be known that) there are three kinds of light: upon the tongue, in the body and in the heart.

The light upon the tongue is the light of divine unity and the profession of Muslim faith (*nūr-i tawḥīd'ast u shahādat*).

The light of the body is service and obedience [to God] (*khidmat u ṭā'at*), while the light of the heart is longing and love (*shawq'ast u maḥabbat*).

The light of the tongue brings one to the Garden (*jannat*), according to His word, "For what they profess, God has rewarded them with gardens ..."[45]

The light of the body raises one up to Paradise (*firdaws*), as His word declares, "But those who have faith and do good deeds shall be awarded with Gardens of Paradise."[46]

The light of the heart leads one to the *visio dei*, which is the encounter with God's Countenance (*liqā'*),[47] as His word proclaims, "Faces shall be resplendent that day, gazing upon their Lord."[48]

Whoever in this world attains these three lights, is also gifted with three robes of honour.[49] The first (robe given him) is that of an awe-inspiring majestic bearing, inspiring reverential respect (*mahābat*) without making

43 This famous *rubā'ī* has been ascribed to a number of poets and mystics, including Abū Sa'īd ibn Abī'l-Khayr (d. 440/1048), Rashīd Vaṭvāṭ (d. 573/1177) and Awḥād al-Dīn Kirmānī (d. 635/1238). For its attribution to the first, see Sa'īd Nafīsī (ed.), *Sukhanān-i manẓūm-i Abū Sa'īd Abū'l-Khayr*, 2nd edn (Tehran: Intishārāt-i Kitābkhāna-yi Sanā'ī: n.d.), p. 15 (n. 102); for the second, see S. Aḥmad Bihishtī Shīrāzī, *Rubā'ī-nāma: Guzīda-yi Rubā'iyāt az Rūdakī Samarqandī tā imrūz* (Tehran: Intishārāt-i Rawzāna 1372 A.Hsh./1993), p. 179 (n. 1605).

44 Qur'ān XXXIX:22.

45 Qur'ān V:85.

46 Qur'ān XVIII:107.

47 A good overview of all the various meanings of *liqā'* (compared to *naẓar*, *ru'yat*, etc.) in Islamic theology and Sufism is given by Naṣrullāh Pūrjavādī, *Ru'yat-i māh dar āsimān: bar-rasī-yi tārīkhī-yi masa'la-yi liqā' Allāh dar kalām u taṣawwuf* (Tehran: Nashr-i Dānihsgāhī 1375 A.Hsh./1996), pp. 193–96, 188–90 (on the vision of the heart).

48 Qur'ān LXXV:22–23.

49 Alternate versions: receives also/is granted as well // three mantles/robes of honour.

people afraid of him.[50] The second is a delightfully sweet humour (*ḥalāwat*) which makes people seek him out, although they have no particular reason to be with him. The third is love (*maḥabbat*), which makes people adore him, although they have no kinship or family connection with him.[51]

The Master of the Sufi Path (*pīr-i ṭarīqat*) declared, "That awe-inspiring majestic bearing, that sweetness of humour and that love all derive from light of divine propinquity, kindled and kept ever lit in his heart, so that the all-discerning vision of the Friend directly scrutinizes and contemplates the eye of his heart."[52]

God also said, "Then woe unto those whose hearts are hardened against the remembrance of God."[53]

It should be understood that this hardness of heart comes from the profusion of sin,[54] which in turn arises from an excessive amount of lust, which in turn arises from filling one's stomach to the full. 'Ā'isha the Honest[55] in this context remarked, "The first innovation (*bid'a*) to appear among

---

50 Cf. Emerson's remark, "Fear God, and where you go, men shall think they walk in hallowed cathedrals." – "Worship," in *Emerson: Essays and Lectures*, ed. Harold Bloom (New York: Library of America 1983), p. 1071.

51 Alternate versions: without being either kith or kin with him/although they share no ties of blood with him/without their being bound by any ties of blood, or sharing any family connection with him.

52 Alternate versions: "That awe-inspiring majestic bearing, that sweet humour and that love all derive/the light of closeness to God / from the light of proximity to God that is kindled/aflame / that is kept ever lit and burning in his heart, so that the Friend's perspicacious vision fixes its sights upon his heart's eye." // which in his heart is kindled and kept ever lit, so that the perspicacious vision of the Friend turns its regard/in clear view contemplates his heart's eye/and surveys.

53 Qur'ān XXXIX:22.

54 Alternate versions: an excessive amount of sin/an abundance of sin/great quantity of sin/excessive sin/a great amount of sin.

55 'Ā'isha bint Abī Bakr (d. 58/678) was the third and most dearly adored of the Prophet's wives, on whom see W. Montgomery Watt, *EI2* I, pp. 307–8 (s.v.). Her saying is also found in Ghazālī's *Iḥyā'* XXIII. See T.J. Winter (trans.), *Al-Ghazālī on Disciplining the Soul, Kitāb Riyāḍat al-nafs, & On Breaking the Two Desires, Kitāb Kasr al-shahwatayn*, Books XXII and XXIII of *The Revival of the Religious Sciences* (Cambridge: Islamic Texts Society 1995), p. 122, with a different translation and full annotation to the *ḥadīth* sources given.

people after the Apostle of God passed away, was that they began eating to the point of satiety. People indulged themselves until they were fully sated, at which point both their internal and external libidinous passions (*shahwathā*) were aroused, so they turned refractory and rebelled."

Dhū'l-Nūn Miṣrī (d. 60/859) said, "I have never eaten my fill without then committing a sin."[56] Abū Sulaymān Dārānī (d. 215/830)[57] also said, "Six vices appear within whoever eats to his fill. Firstly, he loses the sweetness of devotion; secondly, he suffers from lapses in his ability to commit words of wisdom to memory; thirdly, he is disbarred from feeling compassion for people (since he imagines that everyone else is like himself, fully sated); fourthly, his lust increases and overwhelms him; fifthly, he feels obedience and worship of God to be burdensome; and sixthly, while the rest of the believers make their way to the mosque and retire to their oratories for prayer, he spends his time in the latrine, making ablutions."

It is related that the Prophet (blessings and peace be upon him) said, "Quicken your hearts with eating but little, and purify them with hunger, so that they become sound and clear." He also said, "Whoever lets his stomach

56 Born in Upper Egypt of Nubian parents, he lived most of his life in Cairo. Nicholson calls him "the man who, more than any other, deserves to be entitled the founder of theosophical Ṣúfism." R.A. Nicholson, "A Historical Enquiry concerning the Origin and Development of Sufism, with a list of definitions of the terms '*ṣūfī*' and '*taṣawwuf*, arranged chronologically," *Journal of the Royal Asiatic Society*, Part I (1906), p. 309. Jāmī says that "He is the head of this sect; they all descend from, and are related to, him. There were Shaykhs before him, but he was the first that explained this Sufi symbolism (*ishārat bā 'ibārat āward*) and spoke concerning this 'path'." ("A Historical Enquiry," p. 309.) He was the first to give a systematic teaching concerning the mystical states and spiritual stations (*aḥwāl u maqāmāt*) of Sufism. He was also the first Sufi to discourse on mystical knowledge or *ma'rifat* and distinguish it from academic knowledge or *'ilm*. This same saying is likewise cited in the *Iḥyā'* XXIII: see T.J. Winter (trans.), *Al-Ghazālī* ..., p. 122 with a different translation and full annotation to the *ḥadīth* sources given.

57 Also cited in the *Iḥyā'*, see T.J. Winter (trans.), *Al-Ghazālī* ..., p. 126 with a different translation and full annotation to the *ḥadīth* sources given; and in 'Aṭṭār, *Tadhkirat al-awliyā'*, ed. M. Isti'lāmī. (3rd edn) (Tehran: Zawwār 1365/1986), p. 279. On Dārānī, who belonged the earliest generation of ascetic Sufis, see Hujwīrī, *Kashf al-Maḥjūb*, abridged trans. by R.A. Nicholson (London: Luzac & Co. 1936), pp. 112–113. Cf. another of his sayings, "The night of the faithful believer descends at that time when his stomach is full of food." – 'Aṭṭār, *Tadhkirat al-awliyā'*.

go hungry increases the insight and sagacity of his heart, and mightily amplifies his mental powers of thought."[58] Shiblī (d. 334/945),[59] "I never went hungry without a fresh sort of wisdom being infused in my heart and learning some new spiritual lesson."[60]

The Prophet said, "The noblest in rank among you before God are those who hungered and meditated the longest, and the most abhorrent in God's sight are those who slept at night (after) eating and drinking. Eat and drink until your belly is half-full, for that is a part of prophethood (*nubuwwat*)."[61]

---

58 Both sayings cited in the *Iḥyā'* XXIII: see T.J. Winter (trans.), *Al-Ghazālī* ..., p. 118 with a different translation and full annotation to the *ḥadīth* sources given.

59 One of the leading members of the School of Baghdād, he was known for his ecstatic utterances and drunken spirituality, praised by Junayd as "the Eye of God among people on the earth." ('Aṭṭār, *Tadhkirat al-awliyā'*, p. 618); for a good account of whom, see J. Nūrbakhsh, *Shiblī: mast-i ḥaqq va majdhūb-i ḥaqīqat* (London: Khānaqāh-i Ni'matu'llāhī Publications 1376 A.Hsh./1997).

60 This saying is also cited in the *Iḥyā'* XXIII: see T.J. Winter, *Al-Ghazālī* ..., p. 118 with a different translation and full annotation to the *ḥadīth* sources given.

61 These sayings are also cited in the *Iḥyā'* XXIII: see T.J. Winter, *Al-Ghazālī* ..., pp. 108–9 with a different translation, slightly different texts, and full annotation to the *ḥadīth* sources given.

IV

TYPOLOGIES OF GNOSIS AND KNOWLEDGE

Selections from Rashīd al-Dīn Maybudī's Commentary on Qur'ān V:98 in his *Kashf al-asrār*

In the selection below, Maybudī explains the difference between the three main types of knowledge in Islam: the academic-homiletic (*'ilm-i ta'līmī*), logical-circumstantial (*'ilm-i istidlālī*), and the divinely infused esoteric (*'ilm-i ladunī*). He then elaborates the ten different branches of Islamic learning: the science of divine Unity (*'ilm-i tawḥīd*), the science of jurisprudence (*'ilm-i fiqh*), the science of preaching and the academic sermon (*'ilm-i wa'ẓ*), the science of interpretation (of dreams and visions) (*'ilm-i ta'bīr*), the science of medicine (*'ilm-i ṭibb*), the science of astronomy (*'ilm-i nujūm*), the science of scholastic theology (*'ilm-i kalām*), the science of earning a livelihood (*'ilm-i ma'āsh*), the science of philosophy (*'ilm-i ḥikmat*) and the science of divine Reality (*'ilm-i ḥaqīqat*).

The very definition of the highest type of knowledge – which Maybudī calls 'knowledge of divine Reality' (*'ilm-i ḥaqīqat*) – here is very significant. "Divinely infused esoteric knowledge (*'ilm-i ladunnī*)," he explains, "is knowledge of divine Reality which is 'ecstatic realization' (*'ilm-i ḥaqīqat yāft ast*). It is particular to gnostics and sincere adepts. It is to them that the divine Word alludes in the verse: "We had taught him [Khiḍr] a knowledge from our presence (*'allamnāhu min ladunnā 'ilman*)."[1]

The Persian sentence *'ilm-i ḥaqīqat yāft ast* is deceptively simple. On closer examination it is clear that the Persian Sufi term *yāft* (attainment, realization) used here translates into Persian the Arabic term *wajd* (ecstasy), derived in Arabic from the trilateral root WJD, from which are derived some of the following conjugations: i. *wajd*: (a) 'finding' (b) 'ardour, ecstasy'; ii. *wijdān* (the verbal noun, emphasizing the active aspect of *wajd*): (a) 'the find' (b) 'feeling, sentiment, ecstasy'; iii. *wājid* (the active participle): (a) 'the finder' (b) 'an ecstatic'; iv. *wujūd* (the abstract noun): (a) 'findingness' (b) 'existence' (c) 'realized ecstasy'; v. *mawjūd* (the passive participle):

1 Qur'ān XVIII:65.

(a) the 'Found One' (b) the 'Existent One' (a name of God); vi. *tawājud*, (a gerund) meaning 'imitative ecstasy' or 'affecting ecstasy'.[2] So when Maybudī writes that *'ilm-i ḥaqīqat yāft ast*, he actually means to say something like "the esoteric knowledge of divine Reality is only understood by rapture wherein ecstasy is found," and it is only there that "real existence is understood."

Elsewhere in this selection, Maybudī repeatedly underlines the significance of esoteric knowledge for the Muslim religious life. His epistemology continually privileges mystical intuition and consciousness over all other types of knowledge, affirming that "it is one's mystical consciousness and influx of inspiration at the present moment (*aḥwāl va awqāt*)" that determines the quality of one's knowledge. By adopting such specifically Sufi terminology – in effectively declaring that all science and knowledge are spiritual requirements only in regard to one's particular spiritual state of mind and heart (*aḥwāl*) and connection with God within (or rather 'outside' the serial process of) various moments in time (*awqāt*), Maybudī ultimately implies that *knowledge is a function of mystical consciousness, not vice-versa*.[3] However, since there is no *via illuminativa* and visionary journey (*sayr*) without undergoing a *via purgativa* by way methodical progress on the spiritual path (*sulūk*), such a mystical consciousness must have a moral basis, and is inconceivable without the practice of the virtues, he writes that "it is incumbent upon every Muslim to keep in the forefront of consciousness those things that appertain to the heart, since it is forbidden to harbour envy, hypocrisy, conceit, rancour, hostility or suspicion against other Muslims."

Although he discusses the significance of altogether ten different sciences, three receive Maybudī's censure: the sciences of earning a living (*'ilm-i ma'āsh*), (certain branches of) astronomy and scholastic theology (*'ilm-i kalām*). The latter he considers to be absolutely Satanic; to which end, Shāfi'ī's celebrated maxim: 'Knowledge of scholastic theology is ignorance, and ignorance of scholastic theology is knowledge' (*Al-'ilm bi'l-kalām jahl wā'l-jahl bi'l-kalam 'ilm*) is cited approvingly. Maybudī's wholesale condemnation of *Kalām* is typical of the thought of his master Anṣārī, who composed an entire treatise attacking and condemning

2 For an extended analysis of these six connotations of WJD, see my "Principles of the Philosophy of Ecstasy in Rūmī's Poetry," in Leonard Lewisohn (ed.), *The Philosophy of Ecstasy: Rumi and the Sufi Tradition* (Bloomington, Indiana: World Wisdom 2014), pp. 35–80.

3 For an overview of *aḥwāl* and *awqāt*, see Dr. Javad Nurbakhsh, *Spiritual Poverty in Sufism*, trans. Leonard Lewisohn (London: KNP 1984), pp. 63–80, 93–120.

Kalām rational theology entitled Condemnation of Scholastic Theology and its Scholars (*Dhamm al-kalām wa ahlihī*).[4] As Keeler remarks:

> No serious study of Maybudī's commentary can ignore the fact that it presents what at first sight appear to be two contradictory doctrinal perspectives: that of a strict and dogmatic traditionalist, who insists that knowledge can only be derived from the Qur'an and the sayings of the Prophet and the pious predecessors, and who disallows all metaphorical interpretations of the Scripture; and that of an ecstatic love mystic, who sets forth allusive, poetic, and often allegorical interpretations of the Qur'anic verses.[5]

The particular Qur'ānic verse that has prompted that Maybudī's exposition of the varieties of knowledge in this selection is: "Know that God is severe in retribution and that God is All-forgiving and All-merciful."[6] Why this particular verse should have inspired such a long excursus on the branches of Islamic sciences and the varieties of knowledge remains obscure, insofar as this verse caps off a series of divine commandments and prohibitions in the Surah Al-Mā'idah ('The Table Spread') relating to performing the pilgrimage to Mecca,[7] and its theme is largely unconcerned with the subject of knowledge, whether exoteric or esoteric.

EXCERPT FROM MAYBUDĪ'S COMMENTARY ON QUR'ĀN V:98

> Know that Allah is severe in punishment,
> but that Allah (also) is Forgiving, Merciful[8]

4 For a good discussion and selected translation of which, see A.G. Ravan Farhadi, *'Abdullāh Anṣārī of Herāt (1006–1089 C.E.): An Early Ṣūfī Master* (London: Curzon Press 1996), pp. 36–40.

5 *Sufi Hermeneutics*, p. xxvi. For a fuller discussion of his attitude, see *Sufi Hermeneutics*, pp. 17–18.

6 Qur'ān V:98. See Maybudī's *Kashf al-asrār* III, pp. 241–43.

7 See S.H. Nasr, et al. (eds.), *The Study Quran*, p. 327, n. 98 for the historical context of the verse and a discussion of these prohibitions and commands.

8 Muhammad Pickthall (trans.), Qur'ān V:98.

In the above verse, God Almighty enjoins one to "Know ...,"[9] and it should be understood that the meaning of knowledge (*'ilm*) is cognizance (*dānish*).[10] The locus of knowledge is the heart. Furthermore, it should be understood that there are three types of knowledge: academic-homiletic knowledge (*'ilm-i ta'līmī*),[11] ratiocinative knowledge (*'ilm-i istidlālī*),[12] and divinely infused esoteric knowledge (*'ilm-i ladunī*).

(The first type, which is) Ratiocinative knowledge is a result of reason, a consequence of experimentation, and (exemplifies) the realm of discrimination (*tamyīz*, i.e. between good and evil) through which humankind becomes honoured by (God's word) "We have honoured the Children of Adam ..."[13]

Academic-homiletic knowledge is heard by people from God through the literal form of revelation (*tanzīl*). It is heard from Muḥammad through his summons to faith (*balāgh*), as well as learned from teachers through instruction. The learned men of the world are cherished and celebrated in different ways, being accorded various degrees, because of their possession of this knowledge, as (the Scripture) indicates: "God will exalt those who have faith and knowledge to high degrees."[14]

Divinely infused esoteric knowledge is knowledge of divine Reality (*'ilm-i ḥaqīqat*) which is 'ecstatic realization' (*yāft*). It is particular to gnostics and sincere adepts. It is to them that the divine Word alludes in the verse: "We had taught him [Khiḍr] a knowledge from our presence (*'allamnāhu min ladunnā 'ilman*)" (XVIII:65).

It has been said that there are ten different branches of knowledge:

---

9 Qur'ān V:98.

10 The Persian term *dānish* is synonymous with the Arabic word *'ilm* (science or knowledge).

11 Ordinary exoteric knowledge acquired by instruction and teaching through normal academic channels of education.

12 This refers to philosophical knowledge of a purely intellectual nature acquired by rational methods, via logical demonstrations, proofs and argumentation.

13 This phrase should be read in the context of the entire verse: "We have honoured the Children of Adam and borne them over land and sea, and provided sustenance of delicious and sweet things for them, and graced them with far greater favours than most else that We created." (XVII:70)

14 Qur'ān LVIII:11.

First, comes the science of divine unity (*'ilm-i tawḥīd*); second, the science of jurisprudence (*'ilm-i fiqh*); third, the science of preaching and the academic sermon (*'ilm-i wa'ẓ*),[15] fourth, the science of interpretation (of dreams and visions) (*'ilm-i ta'bīr*),[16] fifth, the science of medicine (*'ilm-i ṭibb*), sixth is the science of astronomy (*'ilm-i nujūm*), seventh is the science of scholastic theology (*'ilm-i kalām*), eighth is the science of earning a livelihood (*'ilm-i ma'āsh*), ninth is the science of philosophy (*'ilm-i ḥikmat*) and tenth is the science of divine Reality (*'ilm-i ḥaqīqat*).

The science of divine Unity is life. The science of jurisprudence is medicine. The science of preaching and the academic sermon is food. The science of dream-interpretation is supposition. The science of medicine is cunning artifice. The science of astronomy is a trial. The science of scholastic theology is perdition. The science of earning a livelihood is the work of the rabble. The science of philosophy is a mirror. The science of divine Reality is ecstatic realization.

Of the science of divine Unity, God Almighty said: "[We have never sent other than inspired men before you as apostles.] Ask the followers of (earlier) divine reminders if you have not yet understood (this)"[17] and "Are those who know equal to those who do not?"[18]

Of the science of jurisprudence, He said: "and [the faithful] shall devote themselves to acquiring a deeper knowledge of the Faith (*li-yatafaqqahū fi'd-dīn*)."[19]

---

15 For a good discussion of the genesis and development of this science in classical Islam, see George Makdisi, *The Rise of Humanism in Classical Islam and the Christian West* (Edinburgh: Edinburgh University Press 1990), pp. 173–93.

16 "The science of interpretation of visions is that in which the correspondences between psychically based imagination and hidden suprasensible matters are understood, so that one comprehends by it how the former become translated into the latter, thus deducing from the dream experience that it conveys either something of personal advantage or else a message of caution in respect to one's *état d'âme* in the outer world or regarding one's external worldly circumstances." – *Kashf al-ẓunūn* cited in 'Alī Akbar Dihkhudā, *Lughat-nāma*, eds. M. Mu'īn and M. Ja'far Shahīdī (Tehran: Mu'assasa-yi Lughat-nāma Dihkhudā & Tehran University Press 1373 A.Hsh./1994), s.v. "Ta'bīr."

17 Qur'ān XVI:43.

18 Qur'ān XXXIX:9.

19 Qur'ān IX:122.

Of the science of preaching and the academic sermon, He said: "Become a man of God[20] [by your continuous teaching of the Scripture and your deep study thereof]"[21] and also referred to "those among them who are able to investigate and elicit matters (pertaining to the truth)."[22] The principle of this science lies in the art of conveying divine threats without disheartening and discouraging, and in relaying divine promises without giving (a false sense of) security to the audience. It demonstrates one's spiritual knowledge (*ma'rifat*).

Of the science of interpretation (of dreams and visions), God said: "And he [Joseph] said to him of the two that he supposed[23] [to be saved, 'Mention me in your Lord's presence.']"[24] The principles of this science are supposition (*ẓann*), conjecture (*qiyās*) and speculative suggestion (*khāṭir*). But when in reality it (the dream) actually came to pass, he (Joseph) said: "My Lord has made it (my dream) come true."[25]

Of the science of medicine, He said: "[God] taught man that which he knew not."[26] The principle of this science is experimentation and cunning artifice. It is permissible (*mubāḥ*), good and should be viewed favourably. Shāfi'ī said: "The sciences of the scholars are (twofold): the science of religions and the knowledge of medicine."[27]

---

20 The Qur'ān's exhortation is to become a "spiritual (*rabbānī*)," i.e. one who is engaged in the "work of the Lord (*al-rabb*)."

21 Qur'ān III:79.

22 Qur'ān IV:83.

23 On the basis of his analysis of their two very different dreams, the Qur'ān relates that Joseph "supposed" that one of his two cell-mates would be saved and the other executed. Maybudī propounds a deeper interpretation of the verb 'suppose' (*ẓanna*: also meaning 'to deem', 'consider', 'guess', 'imagine') used in this verse. In a flight of philological fancy, Anṣārī uses Joseph's 'supposition' to coin his own theosophical pun, stating that the study and analysis of dreams is itself in essence mere guesswork. Obviously, Maybudī's understanding of this science presupposes a careful study and reading of Surah XII.

24 Qur'ān XII:42.

25 Qur'ān XII:100.

26 Qur'ān XCVI:5.

27 *Al-'ilm 'ulamān 'ilm al-adyān wa 'ilm al-abdān.* Alternative translations: The sciences of the learned are the sciences of religions and of bodies / Scholars' knowledge pertains to sciences concerned with religions and sciences / The sciences of the learned are the

Of the science of astronomy, God declared: "For it is by the stars that people navigate and find their way."[28] This science is of four sorts:

1. The first type, which is a religious requirement (*wājib*), is the science of reckoning the correct direction to face in prayer (*qibla*) and of calculating the correct times of prayer.
2. The second type, which is religiously permissible and good, is the science of navigation – over both land and sea – of which God says: "And it is He who has set up the stars for you that you might be guided by them through the darkness of land and sea."[29]
3. The third type, which is reprehensible, is the science of (knowing the astrological bases of) the natural humours (*ṭabāyi'*) by (studying) the stars and constellations.
4. The fourth type, which is forbidden by religion, and is utter heresy and philosophy (*falāsifa*), is the science of the principles of astrophysics (*'ilm-i aḥkām ast bi-sayr-i kawākib*).

God Almighty made reference to the science of scholastic theology in mentioning how "satanic evil impulses[30] inspire their cronies to dispute with you,"[31] and spoke of "false speech over-flourished with beauty,"[32] and in the verse (about hypocrites), "and if they speak, you (O prophet) lend an ear to their speech"[33] also referred to the same thing. To practise this science is to set the text of the Qur'ān and the Sunna of the Prophet aside while engaging in exaggerated controversies about marginal exoteric matters;[34] it is to exercise discretion (*istiḥsān*) in applying independent legal judgment (*ijtihād*) while basing oneself on a biased rational opinion that is a prey to

science of faiths and religions and of bodies of flesh / The sciences of the learned are those of religions and those of material bodies.

28 Qur'ān XVI:16.

29 Qur'ān VI:97.

30 Following Muhammad Asad's rendition of *shayāṭīn* as 'evil impulses': see his notes to this verse as well as to II:14; VI:112 and XIV:22 in his *The Message of the Qur'ān* (Gibraltar: Dar al-Andalus 1980).

31 Qur'ān VI:121.

32 Qur'ān VI:112.

33 Qur'ān LXIII:4.

34 Alternative version: petty externalities.

passion. *Knowledge of this science is essentially ignorance.* Hence, Shāfi'ī's dictum: "Knowledge of scholastic theology is ignorance, and ignorance of scholastic theology is knowledge."

Of the science of earning a livelihood (*'ilm-i ma'āsh*), God said: "They comprehend only the superficial appearance of the life of the world,"[35] and pointed out exactly the same in saying: "[So avoid those who turn away from remembrance of Us] and desire only the life of the world. That is the full sum of their knowledge."[36] Among the common people, there are different modes of acquiring this knowledge, either by intelligent expertise or ardently relishing its pursuit. Some persons pursue it moderately while others go after it with avid cupidity, but the whole of this knowledge consists in mere convention and dull habitude.

Of the science of philosophy,[37] God Almighty declared about it: "[As for these parables,] no one understands them save the wise."[38]

As for the science of divine Reality, concerning which God pronounced: "We had taught him [Khiḍr] a knowledge from our presence,[39] it is exactly what He referred to in (Khiḍr's rebuke to Moses later on in the same chapter): "[And how will you be able to patiently forebear with] that which is beyond the scope of your knowledge?"[40]

A full exposition of these last two types of knowledge will be offered elsewhere – *Deo volente.*

---

35 Qur'ān XXX:7.

36 Qur'ān LIII:30.

37 In normal Islamic usage the concept of *philosophy* was usually expressed by the term *ḥikmat*, which literally means 'wisdom', since the Greek terms *falsafa* and *faylasūf* mostly had bad 'heretical' connotations. In Anṣārī/Maybudī's lexicon, the term *ḥikmat* connotes 'theosophy' as well as 'philosophy'. Henry Corbin notes, "the word *ḥikmah* is identical to the Greek *sophia*, and term *ḥikmat ilāhīyah* corresponds literally to the Greek *theosophia*." – *Histoire de la philosophie islamique* (Paris: Gallimard 1964), p. 14. In the lexicon of Muslim Peripateticism, the term *ḥikmat* was also often utilized to denote Greco-Islamic 'philosophy'. Therefore, both the followers of revelation and the votaries of reason in Islam – ratiocentric sage and mystic saint alike – have been often denominated by the same term '*ḥakīm*' (*theosophos*). For an extended discussion of the various meanings of *ḥikmat* in Islam, see A.M. Goichon's article on "Ḥikma," *EI2* III, pp. 377–78.

38 Qur'ān XXIX:43.

39 Qur'ān XVIII:65.

40 Qur'ān XVIII:68.

As for that sort of knowledge about which Muḥammad said: "The search for knowledge is incumbent upon every Muslim,"[41] the scholastic theologians claim that it is scholastic theology, through which (they say) knowledge of God Almighty can be obtained. The jurists assert it is the science of jurisprudence, by which the lawful from the unlawful in the Canon Law is distinguished. The traditionalists (*aṣḥāb al-ḥadīth*) maintain it is the science of the holy scripture and the Sunna since this is the fundamental source of all the sciences of the religious Law. The Sufis claim it to be the science of the mystical states of the heart (*'ilm-i aḥwāl-i dil*), insofar as the devotee's lasting felicity depends upon pursuit of this path of devotion.

However, adepts who have experientially verified and personally realized the truth (*muḥaqqiqān*) prefer not to interpret this tradition as referring, in the exclusive sense, to any one of these sciences. In any case, not all of above-mentioned sciences are religiously obligatory or necessary (*wājib*) to know. One may say rather that whatever type of science or knowledge the devotee needs to know becomes in fact 'necessary' or 'obligatory' at that time that he needs to know it. So the true meaning of the tradition is that it is incumbent on the devotee to pursue whatever particular type of knowledge that he is required to put into practice.

Now, the first of these is the science or knowledge of divine gnosis and Sunni doctrine (*'ilm-i ma'rifat-i khudā va i'tiqād-i ahl-i sunna*). Next comes the science of ritual prayer and purification (*namāz u ṭahārat*) – or as much of it as religion makes obligatory, for it is also a legally binding custom that one possess knowledge of the Prophetic practice (*sunna*). Thus, for instance, when the month of Ramaḍān arrives, keeping the fast is a religious duty, or if a legatee receives some money, after a year is up, it is obligatory for him to know how much alms he must give away – and to whom they should be given, and what specific conditions are legally binding regarding this charity. Likewise, when it comes to knowledge of the Pilgrimage (*ḥajj*), it is incumbent for him to know what are its fundamentals, various ritual duties and binding conditions, and when the proper period of travel comes about.

The same goes for all the other chores and tasks that confront him, whether these relate to marriage, business transactions, earning a salary, or artisanship – whichever of these is learnt, it is necessary to understand which conditions apply, what is to be accepted and allowed, and what is to be rejected and forbidden. Furthermore, above and beyond these things it

41 *Aḥādīth-i Mathnawī*, p. 209.

is incumbent upon every Muslim to keep in the forefront of consciousness those things that appertain to the heart, since it is forbidden to harbour envy, hypocrisy, conceit, rancour, hostility or suspicion against other Muslims.

Therefore, while it is evident that there is no Muslim who may presume to be self-sufficient or autonomous when it comes to the need for knowledge and science, at the same time, not all sorts of knowledge are required by religion. Rather, as we have explained, it is one's mystical consciousness and influx of inspiration at the present moment (*aḥwāl va awqāt*) that determines whether a particular type of knowledge be necessary or religiously required (*wājib*) or not.

V

GNOSIS AND THE *VIA NEGATIVA*

ʿAyn al-Quḍāt Hamadānī (executed 525/1131) on Gnosis[1]

The following selection comprises an extract from the *Prognostications* or *Tamhīdāt* by ʿAyn al-Quḍāt Hamadānī. A Persian Sufi master executed for heresy in 525/1131[2]), he figures as the founding father of speculative metaphysics in Sufism. As a mystical theologian, ʿAyn al-Quḍāt possesses a uniquely original authorial voice which is unlike that of any other writer in the entire Sufi tradition.[3] The personality of his prose is as charismatic, full of conviction and certitude as that of St. Teresa de Avila (d. 1582). His drunken transports recall Richard Rolle (d. 1349), while his inspired visionary insights evoke St. John of the Cross (d. 1591). His prophetic voice is characterized by startling paradoxes and wild antinomian doctrines, the likes of which only a William Blake could have conceived.

---

1 I am grateful to Mohammed Rustom for his very helpful comments on this chapter.

2 Although the charges that led to his trial and execution concerned with his theological views, as several scholars have recently shown, the political machinations of his enemies were the immediate cause of his death: see Omid Safi, *The Politics of Knowledge in Premodern Islam: Negotiating Ideology and Religious Inquiry* (Chapel Hill: University of North Carolina 2006), chap. 6; and Carl Ernst, *Words of Ecstasy in Sufism* (Albany: SUNY Press 1985), pp. 110–17; Mohammed Rustom, *Inrushes of the Spirit: The Mystical Theology of ʿAyn al-Quḍāt* (Abany: SUNY Press 2023), s.v. 'Execution.'

3 This aspect of his style is also highlighted by Salīma Maqṣūdlū, "ʿAyn al-Quḍāt Hamadānī" in *Dānishnāma-yi zabān va adab-i fārsī*, ed. Ismāʿīl Saʿādat (Tehran: Farhangistān-i zabān va adab-i fārsī 1391 A.Hsh./2012), vol. IV, p. 704. As Christiane Tortel puts it: "*L'esthétique soufie, chez ʿAyn al-Quzāt, est construite sur une vision sans stereotype, totalement subjective. C'est un esthétique non normative.*" – *Les Tentations Métaphysiques (Tamhidāt)*, presentation, traduction du persan et de l'arabe, et notes par Christiane Tortel (Paris: Les Deux Océans 1992), p. 25.

He was born circa 490/1097[4] during the early effloresce of the Sufi tradition, belonging to the generation following the towering figures such as Abū Ibrāhīm Mustamlī Bukhārī (d. 434/1042–43), 'Ali b. 'Uthmān Jullābī Hujwīrī (d. 463/1071), Abū'l-Qāsim al-Qushayrī (d. 465/1074), Khwāja 'Abdullāh Anṣārī of Herat (d. 481/1089) and Abū Bakr Nassāj al-Ṭūsī (d. 487/1094), who composed many of the foundational texts in that tradition. The progenitors of several of the great Persian Sufi Orders: 'Abd al-Qādir Jilānī (d. 527/1133), founder of the Qādirīyya; Abū'l-Najīb al-Suhrawardī (d. 563/1168), founder of the Suhrawardīyya; and the Naqshbandī Order's founder Abū Ya'qūb Yūsuf Hamadānī (d. 535/1140) – a native of Hamadān like 'Ayn al-Quḍāt – were contemporaries.[5]

He was the foremost Sufi disciple of Aḥmad al-Ghazālī (d. 520/1126),[6] author of the important Persian treatise on mystical love, *Sawāniḥ*,[7] and famed as the "Sultan of the Sufi Path" among other towering spiritual figures in this period.[8] 'Ayn al-Quḍāt was also the intellectual follower of the latter's elder brother, the illustrious theologian Abū Ḥāmid al-Ghazālī (d. 505/1111), whose *summa theologica* of Islamic Sufi piety, the *Revivification of the Sciences of Religion* (*Iḥyā' 'ulūm al-dīn*) rescued him from a crisis of scepticism during his early twenties.[9] And yet, "the thought of 'Ayn al-Quḍāt," as Massignon put it, "awakened in mysticism by the powerful romanticism of

4 Salīma Maqṣūdlū, "'Ayn al-Quḍāt Hamadānī" p. 702; Alireza Zekavati Gharagozlou, "'Ayn al-Quḍāt Hamadānī" in *Encyclopedia Islamica* III, p. 944.

5 For a comprehensive overview of 'Ayn al-Quḍāt's biography, see Omid Safi, *The Politics of Knowledge in Premodern Islam: Negotiating Ideology and Religious Inquiry* (Chapel Hill: University of North Carolina 2006), chap. 6.

6 For his Sufi chain of initiation, see *Les Tentations Métaphysiques (Tamhidât)*, presentation, traduction du persan et de l'arabe, et notes par Christiane Tortel (Paris: Les Deux Océans 1992), p. 318. For the relation between Aḥmad Ghazālī and 'Ayn al-Quḍāt, see G. Böwering, "'Ayn al-Qożāt Hamadānī," *EIr* III, pp. 140–43.

7 See Leonard Lewisohn, "Sawanih," in *Encyclopædia of Love in World Religions*, ed. Yudit Greenberg (New York: Macmillan Reference & Thomson Gale 2007), II, pp. 535–38.

8 See Leonard Lewisohn, "Al-Ghazali, Ahmad," in *The Encyclopedia of Philosophy*, ed. Donald Borchert (New York: Macmillan Reference & Thomson Gale 2006; 2nd edn), vol. I: 117–18.

9 On the relationship between 'Ayn al-Quḍāt and elder Ghazālī, see Naṣrullāh Pūrjavādī, *'Ayn al-Quḍāt va ustādān-i ū* (Tehran: Intishārāt-i Asāṭīr 1374 A.Hsh./1995), pp. 135–77.

Aḥmad Ghazālī, led to a stronger spirituality than that of the two Ghazālī brothers."[10]

As an adolescent he participated in Sufi musical séances (*samā'*) in the company of his father,[11] and in his late teens, he became a devotee of several Sufi masters who were deeply immersed in the Khurāsānī tradition of Persian Sufism which emphasized that there was no way of acquiring gnosis (*ma'rifat*) save through submitting to a spiritual master (Arabic: *shaykh*; Persian: *pīr*), giving the latter absolute power and control over the direction of one's inner life. Since inner vision (*baṣīrat*) is "exclusively possessed by gnostics (*al-'ārifun*)," the disciple must refer to the gnostic *shaykh* who is one who possesses supernal esoteric knowledge (*'ilm al-ladunnī*), insofar as he is incapable of realizing God directly, but "capable of doing so through a *pīr*. Therefore whatever they need to know they should learn through the hearts of the *pīrs*."[12] As he relates in an autobiographical passage in his earliest extant composition, it was only due to his encounter with his master

---

10 Louis Massignon, *The Passion of al-Ḥallāj: Mystic and Martyr of Islam*, trans. Herbert Mason (Princeton: Princeton University Press 1982), II, p. 168.

11 Maqṣūdlū, "'Ayn al-Quḍāt Hamadānī," p. 702. On his practice of *Samā'*, see Najīb Māyil Haravī, *Khāṣiyat-i āyinigī: naqd-i ḥāl, guzāra-ārā, va guzīda-yi āthār-i fārsī-yi 'Ayn al-Quḍāt Hamadānī* (Tehran: Nashr-i Nay 1374 A.Hsh./1995), introduction, p. 4.

12 Forugh Jahanbakhsh, "The *Pīr-Murīd* Relationship in the Thought of 'Ayn al-Quḍāt Hamadānī," in Sayyid Jalāl al-Dīn Āshtiyānī, Hideichi Matsubara, Takashi Iwami, Akiro Matsumoto (eds.), *Consciousness and Reality: Studies in Memory of Toshihiko Izutzu* (Leiden: Brill 2000), pp. 130–31, with reference to *Nāmahā-yi 'Ayn al-Quḍāt al-Hamadānī*, vol. 1, eds. 'Alīnaqī Munzawī and 'Afīf 'Usayrān (Tehran: Intishārāt-i Zawwār 1362 A.Hsh./1983), p. 279. Many examples in his writings of his devotion to spiritual teachers, including Aḥmad Ghazālī, are cited in my "In Quest of Annihilation: Imaginalization and Mystical Death in the *Tamhidat* of 'Ayn al-Qudat Hamadani," in Leonard Lewisohn (ed.), *The Heritage of Sufism*, vol. I: *Classical Persian Sufism from its Origins to Rumi* (Oxford: Oneworld 1999), pp. 288–92.; *Nāmahā-yi 'Ayn al-Quḍāt al-Hamadānī*, vol. 3, ed. 'Alīnaqī Munzawī (Tehran: Intishārāt-i Isāṭīr 1377 A.Hsh./1998), p. 389 (§190); *Nāmahā-yi 'Ayn al-Quḍāt al-Hamadānī*, vol. 2, p. 109 (§156: "Here you will understand what 'seeing God in the mirror of the soul of the spiritual master' means"). See also Naṣrullāh Pūrjavādī, *'Ayn al-Quḍāt va ustādān-i ū* (Tehran: Intishārāt-i Asāṭīr 1374 A.Hsh./1995).

Aḥmad Ghazālī that his eye of inner vision itself was opened.[13] It is this eye of interior vision that allows one to access and apprehend what he called the ontological "domain beyond reason" (*al-ṭawr warā'a al-'aql*).[14] The theory of knowledge inaccessible to the human intellect, that is 'beyond the stage of reason', was first elaborated in detail by 'Ayn al-Quḍāt Hamadhānī in two of his works: *Zubdat al-ḥaqā'iq*,[15] and *Shakwa gharīb*[16] where he explains that this sort of knowledge is grasped by visionary unveiling (*al-kashf*), in contrast to the stage of reason where objects of knowledge can only be known by evidence adduced by demonstrative argumentation (*istidlāl*).

'Ayn al-Quḍāt's thought and writings were subject to numerous intellectual and spiritual influences, but space allows only a few of these to be mentioned here. First and foremost, he followed, advocated and propagated the teachings of the radical martyr of love Manṣūr Ḥallāj (d. 310/922), who he dubbed "the master of lovers, chief of gnostics,"[17] accurately predicting that he would be martyred like him.[18] A key transmitter of Ḥallāj's

13 This passage is cited in full in Lewisohn, "In Quest of Annihilation," pp. 291–92. See also Firoozeh Papan-Matin, *Beyond Death: The Mystical Teachings of 'Ayn al-Quḍāt Hamadhānī* (Leiden: Brill 2010), pp. 147–49.

14 See Toshihiko Izutsu's brilliant study of this aspect of his thought: "Mysticism and the Linguistic Problem of Equivocation in the Thought of 'Ayn al-Quḍāt Hamadanī," in Toshihiko Izutsu, *Creation and the Timeless Order of Things* (Ashland, OR: White Cloud Press 1994), pp. 98–118.

15 *Zubdat al-ḥaqā'iq*, ed. 'Afīf 'Usayrān (Tehran: 1340 A.Hsh./1961), chap. 16.

16 *Shakwa gharīb al-awṭān ilā 'ulamā' al-buldān*, ed. 'Afīf 'Usayrān (Tehran: 1341 A.Hsh./1962), pp. 44ff.

17 *Tamhīdāt*, ed. 'Afīf 'Usayrān (Tehran: Intishārāt-i Manūchihrī 1341 A.Hsh./1962), p. 235. Louis Massignon, somewhat hyperbolically but not inaccurately, writes that "'Ayn al-Quḍāt describes Ḥallāj as a kind of knight-errant of divine love, an insurgent of sanctity, a rebel against legal formalism, a herald of love's paradise." – *The Passion of al-Ḥallāj: Mystic and Martyr of Islam*, trans. Herbert Mason (Princeton: Princeton University Press 1982), II, pp. 168–69. On the impact of Ḥallāj's teachings on 'Ayn al-Quḍāt's thought, see my *Beyond Faith and Infidelity: The Sufi Poetry and Teachings of Mahmud Shabistari* (London: Curzon Press 1995), pp. 276–83; Carl Ernst, *Words of Ecstasy*, pp. 73–84; Peter Awn, *Satan's Tragedy and Redemption: Iblīs in Sufi Psychology* (Leiden: Brill 1983), pp. 134–41.

18 *Tamhīdāt*, p. 236.

sayings, 'Ayn al-Quḍāt is central to the survival and continuity of the Ḥallājian legend and legacy.[19]

Likewise, "one of the founders of Persian Sufi poetry,"[20] Abū'l-Majd Majdūd ibn Ādam Sanā'ī (d. 525/1131) had a huge influence on 'Ayn al-Quḍāt's poetic vision and expression.[21] Like Sanā'ī, 'Ayn al-Quḍāt made use of the symbolism of heresy, just like the early *malāmatī* masters of Nishapur, to express the highest reaches of faith. The verse, ideas and symbols of Sanā'ī's series of poems called 'wild-man lyrics' (*qalandariyyāt*)[22] written on antinomian themes, 'Ayn al-Quḍāt frequently quoted in his writings.[23]

Similarly, 'Ayn al-Quḍāt Hamadānī also made use of the poetry of Ismā'īlī poet and philosopher Nāṣir-i Khusraw (d. 469/1077) to illustrate his ideas, while sometimes taking a more nuanced view of the Ismā'īlī doctrine of the infallibility of the Imām than that of his mentor Abū Ḥāmid al-Ghazālī.[24]

He was also acquainted with and influenced by the thought of Avicenna (Ibn Sīnā, d. 428/1037). Although he may have read the criticisms levelled at the Peripatetic thinker by Abū Ḥāmid al-Ghazālī in various works, in contradistinction to Ghazālī, 'Ayn al-Quḍāt, who often questioned the bodily resurrection in his writings,[25] eschewed Ghazālī's anti-philosophy

---

19 On which, see Massignon, *The Passion* II, pp. 166–69.

20 J.T.P. de Bruijn, *Persian Sufi Poetry: An Introduction to the Mystical Use of Classical Poems* (London: Curzon 1997), p. 35.

21 On which, see Hamid Dabashi, *Truth and Narrative: The Untimely Thoughts of 'Ayn al-Quḍāt Hamadhānī* (Richmond, UK: Curzon 1999), pp. 190–91.

22 J.T.P. de Bruijn, 'The *Qalandariyyāt* in Mystical Poetry, from Sanā'ī Onwards,' in Leonard Lewisohn (ed.), *The Heritage of Sufism*, vol. 1: *Classical Persian Sufism from its Origins to Rumi* (Oxford: Oneworld 1999), pp. 75–86.

23 See Rustom, *Inrushes of the Spirit*, chap. 1.

24 Hermann Landolt, "Early Evidence for the Reception of Nāṣir-i Khusraw's Poetry in Sufism: 'Ayn al-Quḍāt's Letter on the Ta'līmīs," in *Fortresses of the Intellect: Ismaili and other Islamic Studies in Honour of Farhad Daftary*, ed. Omar Ali-de-Unzaga (London: I.B. Tauris and the Institute of Ismaili Studies 2011), pp. 369–86.

25 Maqṣūdlū, "'Ayn al-Quḍāt al-Hamadānī, p. 704. For a good summary of 'Ayn al-Quḍāt's own nuanced and complex position on the resurrection of the body vs. soul, see *Nāmahā-yi 'Ayn al-Quḍāt al-Hamadānī*, vol. 2, pp. 35–42.

views and embraced Avicenna's teachings in respect to eschatology and the resurrection of the soul.[26]

His writings are also replete with quotations of the maxims and sayings of the great Sufi teachers of both the schools of Baghdad and Khurasan, such as Fuḍayl ibn 'Iyāḍ (d. 187/803),[27] Ma'rūf al-Karkhī (d. circa 199/815),[28] Abū'l-'Abbās Qaṣṣāb (d. unkn.),[29] Bishr Ḥāfī (d. 226/841),[30] Bāyazīd Bisṭāmī (d. ca. 261/875),[31] Sahl ibn 'Abdullāh Tustarī (d. 283/896),[32] Ibrāhīm Khawāṣṣ (d. 291/904),[33] Abū'l-Ḥusayn Nūrī (d. 295/907),[34]

---

26 The various references to Avicenna in the *Tamhīdāt* (see pp. 167, 289, 349–50) reveal that 'Ayn al-Quḍāt understood him to be an illuminated visionary thinker (e.g. "may a thousand souls of false claimants be sacrificed to that person [Ibn Sīnā] who has lifted the veil and given us a sign of the roadless way! – *Tamhīdāt*, p. 350), certainly not the benighted, misguided, heretical intellectual depicted by Abū Ḥāmid al-Ghazālī, although recent research has revealed that Ghazālī himself clearly adopted many of his own visionary doctrines concerning revelation, prophecy and inspiration from Avicenna, while carefully disguising their source; on which, see Alexander Treiger, *Inspired Knowledge in Islamic Thought: Al-Ghazālī's Theory of Mystical Cognition and its Avicennian Foundation* (London: Routledge 2012). I would agree with Papan-Matin that he "identified with Avicenna's brave approach to knowledge and regards it as a new paradigm in philosophical thought," approaching him as a "visionary philosopher ... who is in immediate contact with the truth that is disclosed to him at the highest stage of reason, which borders the terrain of visionary insight." – *Beyond Death*, pp. 54–55. For a good discussion of their relationship, see also Najīb Māyil Haravī, *Khāṣiyat-i āyinigī: naqd-i ḥāl, guzāra-ārā, va guzīda-yi āthār-i fārsī-yi 'Ayn al-Quḍāt Hamadānī* (Tehran: Nashr-i Nay 1374 A.Hsh./1995), pp. 74–77; Hermann Landolt, "'Ayn al-Quḍāt: 1. Life and Work," EI[3] (online).

27 *Nāmahā-yi 'Ayn al-Quḍāt al-Hamadānī*, vol. 2, p. 117.

28 *Nāmahā-yi 'Ayn al-Quḍāt al-Hamadānī*, vol. 3, p. 373; *Tamhīdāt*, p. 256.

29 *Nāmahā-yi 'Ayn al-Quḍāt al-Hamadānī*, vol. 2, p. 173. Qaṣṣāb was an associate of Abū'l-Qāsim al-Qushayrī (d.), see Martin Nguyen, *Sufi Master and Qur'an Scholar: Abū'l-Qāsim al-Qushayrī and the Laṭā'if al-ishārāt* (Oxford: Oxford University Press in association with the Institute of Ismaili Studies 2012), p. 70.

30 *Nāmahā-yi 'Ayn al-Quḍāt al-Hamadānī*, vol. 3, p. 368.

31 *Tamhīdāt*, pp. 24, 62, 67, 77, 94, 95, 119, 159, 214, 274, 298, 313, 314.

32 *Tamhīdāt*, pp. 83, 147, 248, 250, 268.

33 *Nāmahā-yi 'Ayn al-Quḍāt al-Hamadānī*, vol. 2, pp. 118, 221.

34 *Tamhīdāt*, pp. 261, 306.

Abū'l-Qāsim Junayd (d. 297/910),[35] Manṣūr al-Ḥallāj,[36] Abū Bakr Shiblī (d. 334/945),[37] Abū'l-Ḥasan Kharaqānī (d. 426/1034)[38] and Abū Sa'īd ibn Abī'l-Khayr (d. 440/1048),[39] and even verses from his contemporary, the poet Sanā'ī (d. 525/1131),[40] who he constantly cites in support of his own ideas. 'Ayn al-Quḍāt's works are both the product of direct visionary insight and prodigious scholarship and learning. Every other sentence of his prose usually features a quotation from either the Qur'ān, *ḥadīth* or one of the maxims of the Sufis, his memory evidently having been steeped in the rich theosophical and theological teachings of Islamic Sufism.

'Ayn al-Quḍāt also possessed a comprehensive knowledge of Arabic poetry, was an excellent stylist in both Arabic prose and verse,[41] and judging by his writings, had memorized the Qur'ān, which he constantly cites, and even composed a work of Qur'ānic commentary that is no longer extant.[42] His frequent references to the sciences of jurisprudence (*fiqh*) and citation of numerous Prophetic Traditions (*ḥadith*), demonstrates his expertise in both fields. His mastery of apologetic theology (*Kalām*) is evident in his Arabic-language *Shakwā al-gharīb*, 'Complaint of a Stranger in Exile',[43] where he also displays great prowess in Arabic grammar, linguistics and prosody.

---

35 *Tamhīdāt*, pp. 253, 314, 332.

36 *Tamhīdāt*, pp. 22, 62, 91, 119, 122, 129, 223, 235, 247–48, 251, 257, 260, 266, 274, 284, 295; *Nāmahā-yi 'Ayn al-Quḍāt al-Hamadānī*, vol. 2, p. 187.

37 *Tamhīdāt*, pp. 79, 82, 114, 136, 217, 234–35, 238, 243, 256, 316, 332.

38 *Nāmahā-yi 'Ayn al-Quḍāt al-Hamadānī*, vol. 3, p. 402; vol. 2, pp. 119, 249; *Tamhīdāt*, pp. 129, 134, 317.

39 *Tamhīdāt*, pp. 155, 211, 285, 349, 350.

40 *Nāmahā-yi 'Ayn al-Quḍāt al-Hamadānī*, vol. 2, p. 243.

41 On which, see Dabashi, *Truth and Narrative*, pp. 193–99.

42 In one of his letters, he writes, in reference to Muslim formalist exegetes: "I don't wish to foolishly tear the skin off anybody so as to make myself out as somehow superior to someone else, but I myself know the exoteric interpretation of the Qur'ān much better than those so-called exegetes." – *Nāmahā-yi 'Ayn al-Quḍāt al-Hamadānī*, vol. 2, p. 50, §66. See also Hermann Landolt, "'Ayn al-Quḍāt al-Hamadhānī, 1. Life and Work," in EI[3].

43 A.J. Arberry (trans.), *A Sufi Martyr: The Apologia of 'Ain al-Quḍāt al-Hamadhānī* (London: Allen & Unwin 1969). For the original Arabic, see *Zubdat al-ḥaqā'iq-i 'Ayn*

He authored a number of works,[44] his earliest being a short treatise on philosophical mysticism entitled *The Quintessence of Spiritual Realities* (*Zubdat al-ḥaqā'iq*), written in 516/1122 at age twenty-four.[45] From the time of his meeting with Aḥmad Ghazālī in 512/1118 at age 21, to his execution ten years later in 1131, 'Ayn al-Quḍāt also wrote a series of epistles to disciples and friends[46] that have been edited and published in three volumes, which are as valuable for fathoming the scope and depth of his thought as his formal compositions.[47] An avid, prolix letter-writer, the autobiographical intimacy and warm personality of his correspondence in places recalls to mind Seneca's Epistles. Elsewhere his fiery conviction, passionate sincerity, combined with learned eloquence reminds one of Marsilio Ficino's lengthy letters penned to fifteen-century Italian princes, philosophers, and popes. In one of his letters, he records: "For some time now I have been so wrapped up in this passion that I compose four or five different letters every day and night. Each letter contains some eighty lines and every word therein a priceless gem."[48]

Closely related to these epistles, and in some cases exactly reflecting their content, is his *Prognostications* (*Tamhīdāt*),[49] 'Ayn al-Quḍāt's *chef de*

al-Quḍāt al-Hamadānī, ed. 'Afīf 'Usayrān, with Persian translation and introduction by Mahdī Tadayyun (Tehran: Markaz-i Nashr-i Dānishgāhī 1379 A.Hsh./2000).

44 For a full list, see Gharagozlou, "'Ayn al-Quḍāt Hamadānī," p. 947.

45 Omar Jah (trans.), *The Zubdat* al-*ḥaqā'iq of 'Ayn al-Quḍāt al-Hamadhānī* (Kuala Lumpur: ISTAC 2000), introduction, p. 9.

46 For Aḥmad Ghazālī's correspondence with 'Ayn al-Quḍāt, see *Makātibāt-i Khwāja Aḥmad Ghazālī bā 'Ayn al-Quḍāt al-Hamadānī*, ed. Naṣrullāh Pūrjavādī (Tehran: Intishārāt-i Khānaqāh-i Niʿmatullāhī 2536 Shāhanshāhī).

47 *Nāmahā-yi 'Ayn al-Quḍāt al-Hamadānī*, vol. 1 and 2, eds. 'Alīnaqī Munzawī and 'Afīf 'Usayrān (Tehran: Intishārāt-i Zawwār 1362 A.Hsh./1983); vol. 3, ed. 'Alīnaqī Munzawī (Tehran: Intishārāt-i Isāṭīr 1377 A.Hsh./1998).

48 See *Nāmahā-yi 'Ayn al-Quḍāt al-Hamadānī*, vol. 2, p. 81; cf. Lewisohn, "In Quest of Annihilation," p. 294.

49 On this work, see Rustom, *Inrushes of the Spirit*, chap. 1.

oeuvre and the subject of numerous studies[50] and commentaries.[51] The published critical edition of Persian text of Hamadānī's *Tamhīdāt,* which runs to 354 pages, shows this to be his longest and most mature philosophical work. Ranking as a major classic in the world's literature, the work includes major chapters on such topics as Prophetology, Saintship, Faith, Love, the Heart, the Spirit, Faith and Infidelity, Satanology, Qur'ānic Exegesis, Poetic Symbolism, Contemplative Disciplines, Eschatology, Epistemology, as well as the author's view of Anthropology and Comparative Religion. *Prognostications* is also a vast treasury of Islamic theosophical thought, which influenced – in fact, created certain literary models within – Islamic literature in Mughal India.[52] It is highly original both in thought and literary expression and in its extraordinary daring of vision and the bold expression of fresh antinomian doctrines may best be compared to William Blake's *The Marriage of Heaven and Hell* in the Christian mystical tradition.

Insofar as the author is bereft of himself, drowned in rapture,[53] his utterances are those of ocular inspiration, the reader himself must either have some acquaintance with the mystical states (*aḥwāl*) that animate his prose or else have a background of study in the Sufi theosophical tradition that inspires the masterpiece. 'Ayn al-Quḍāt's pattern of thinking is simultaneously rational and meta-rational, discursive and mystically inspired, as Toshihiko Izutzu observed:

> His thought is structured in reference to two different levels of cognition at one and the same time. That is to say, the process of philosophic thinking in Hamadānī is as a rule related to two levels of discourse, one referring to the domain of empirical experience based on sensation and rational interpretation, and the other referring to a

---

50 For an excellent overview of its contents, see the editor's ('Afīf 'Usayrān) lengthy introduction to the *Tamhīdāt,* as well as the 'Alīnaqī Munzawī's 250-page introduction into *Nāmahā-yi 'Ayn al-Quḍāt al-Hamadānī,* vol. 3. Rustom's *Inrushes of the Spirit* provides a comprehensive study of the *Tamhīdāt.*

51 See Papan-Matin, *Beyond Death,* pp. 177–90.

52 For the impact of his thought on Sufism in India, see Papan-Matin, *op. cit.*, chap. 5: "The Legacy of 'Ayn al-Quḍāt."

53 See my "In Quest of Annihilation," pp. 295–303, for a discussion of the ecstatic character of 'Ayn al-Quḍāt's compositions.

> totally different kind of understanding which is peculiar to the "domain beyond reason." ... He visualizes the "domain of reason" (*ṭawr al-'aql*) and the "domain beyond reason" (*ṭawr warā'a al-'aql*) as two contiguous regions, the latter being directly consecutive to the former. This means that the last stage of the "domain of reason" is in itself the first stage of the "domain beyond reason" by having exhausted all the rational resources of thinking, are able to step into the domain of the trans-rational faculty of the mind. The latter domain discloses itself to a man when, at the extremity of his rational power, an all-illuminating light suddenly emerges in his interior. The appearance of this "inner light" (*nūr fī al-baṭin*) transforms the vision of the world into something which man has never dreamt of. He is now an *'ārif*, a gnostic, whereas he has been – being confined to the "domain of reason" – an *'ālim*, a rational thinker.[54]

As pointed out above, 'Ayn al-Quḍāt himself informs us that it had been an outcome of his practice and application of the disciplines of the Sufi Path, for only through discipleshood to Aḥmad al-Ghazālī did he obtain his enlightenment. Understanding his thought thus presupposes a thorough acquaintance with the terminology and theosophy of Sufism.[55] 'Ayn al-Quḍāt's declaration in his *Apologia* is thus equally applicable to his *Prognostications*: "Every expression of mine occurring in these anecdotes requires the preparation of rules and the laying down of fundamentals of the science of Sufism, so that its meaning may be fully realized."[56]

The eight pages (56–64, §77–87) of this work translated below comprise a short chapter on self-knowledge that treats the subject of gnosis (*ma'rifat*). The author argues that gnoselogy presupposes prophetology and that only by comprehending the soul of the Prophet Muḥammad can anyone attain to any gnosis of the Divine Essence (*ma'rifat-i dhāt Allāh*). He divides gnosis of God respectively into knowledge of the divine Essence, attributes and decrees. The final degree is attained when the gnostic (*'ārif*), and gnosis (*ma'rifat*) are both obliterated in the Object of Gnosis (*ma'rūf*). Ultimately, however, he admits that knowledge of God is ineffable, and can only be

54 Izutsu, "Mysticism and the Linguistic Problem of Equivocation," pp. 120–22.

55 For further discussion of which, see Lewisohn, "In Quest of Annihilation," pp. 292–94.

56 Cited in Lewisohn, "In Quest of Annihilation," p. 294.

expounded through esoteric language, "by cryptic sign and symbol (*ramz*)," which pertains to the domain beyond reason.

'AYN AL-QUḌĀT'S *TAMHĪDĀT*

On the Principle of the Fourth Prognostication: "Know Yourself so You May Know God"

(76) Listen, my dear and noble friend! Although various conditions and circumstances have conspired against me putting my affairs in order to write about the Tradition – "One who knows himself knows his Lord"[57] – that prompted your query, what can I do? "God prevails in His purpose."[58] In previous prognostications (*tamhīdhā*) you already have heard a discussion of certain types of gnosis (*ma'rifat*). Certain other types in the tenth prognostication shall be described in their entirety, or a part and a bit thereof as they are vouchsafed to me.

(77) Once a man attains a spiritual station (*maqām*) in which he becomes intoxicated by the wine of gnosis (*sharāb-i ma'rifat*), so that he realizes the farthest degree of intoxication and the ultimate limit of his 'soul' (*khwud*), the soul of Muḥammad (*nafs-i Muḥammad*) is manifested to him, for [as the verse attests], "There has come to you a messenger from amongst yourselves."[59] All the days of his life then become like a garment whose embroidery is the "delight and peace of one who witnesses it." This must needs a fortune above and beyond which no higher fortune exists. Whoever obtains self-knowledge, realizing gnosis of his own soul (*ma'rifat-i nafs-i khwud*) also obtains knowledge and gnosis of Muḥammad's soul. Whosoever gains gnosis of the soul of Muḥammad sets the foot of his

57 An allusion to the tradition of the Prophet: *Man 'arafa nafsahu faqad 'arafa rabbahu*. – Badī' al-Zamān Furūzānfar, *Aḥādīth-i Mathnawī* (Tehran: Dānishgāh-i Tihrān 1335 A.Hsh./1956; Rprt. Amīr Kabīr 1361 A.Hsh./1982), p. 167. For a discussion of this *ḥadīth*, see also A. Altmann, "The Delphic Maxim in Medieval Islam and Judaism," *Studies in Religious Philosophy and Mysticism* (Ithaca: Cornell University Press 1969), pp. 1–40; Michael Sells, *Mystical Languages of Unsaying* (Chicago: University of Chicago Press 1994), pp. 103.

58 Qur'ān XII:21. Trans. A.J. Arberry.

59 Qur'ān IX:128.

aspiration upon gnosis of the Divine Essence (*ma'rifat-i dhāt Allāh*). This is the meaning of (the Prophet's saying) "Whoever has seen me, has seen God,"[60] for whoever does not have self-knowledge or gnosis of himself does not have knowledge of Muḥammad, so how can he ever become a knower, a gnostic of God?[61] Once gnosis of the Light of Muḥammad (*ma'rifat-i nūr Muḥammad*) is obtained, so that oath of "Lo! those who swear allegiance unto thee (Muḥammad), swear allegiance only to God"[62] is confirmed, then the work of this wayfarer (*sālik*), both in this world and the Next, is completed, and as (the Qur'ān) attests: "This day I have perfected your religion for you."[63] Then, it is announced to him that, "The culmination of the bounty of your gnosis has been reached and has ripened. And yet, the gnosis of Muḥammad is not exclusively reserved for you, but is also comprehended by the common folk, for 'God has shown grace to the believers by sending unto them a messenger of their own who reciteth unto them His revelations.'"[64]

(78) Although it is incumbent upon this spiritual traveller (*mard-i sālik*) to offer up thanks for this bounteous grace, yet he cannot. So they offer up thanks for him instead. Alas, he has been vouchsafed so much self-knowledge, so much gnosis of himself through knowledge of his Lord that he neither knows (himself as) the gnostic nor (Him as) the Object of Gnosis (*ma'rūf*)! Did not Abū Bakr Ṣāddiq (may God be pleased with him!) say concerning this that "the inability to apprehend [the process of] apprehension is itself apprehension (*al-'ajz 'an dark al-idrāk idrāk^{un}*)"?[65] This maxim

60 Furūzānfar, *Aḥādīth-i Mathnawī*, p. 63.

61 The Persian text, which is slightly less formal and polished, literally reads: "Whosoever knows not himself is not a knower of Muḥammad, so how can he be a knower of God?"

62 Qur'ān XLVIII:10.

63 Qur'ān V:3.

64 Qur'ān III:164.

65 This is an oft-cited Sufi maxim, a good analysis of which is given by Maḥmūd Shabistarī (d. after 737/1337) in his *Risāla Ḥaqq al-yaqīn* as follows: "The summit of knowledge (*'ilm*) – which is 'conscious apprehension' (*idrāk-i idrāk*) – is inapprehension (*'adam-i idrāk*), for whereas the Real 'Object-of-Apprehension' (*mudrak*) is infinite, knowledge (*'ilm*) is finite. This inapprehension is a type of apprehension without consciousness of either apprehension or inapprehension, and at this point one falls into a dumbfounded stupor (*ḥayrat*) and [is confronted by] absorption of the apprehending

means that gnosis (*ma'rifat*) and apprehension (*idrāk*) are what entirely consume the gnostic (*'ārif*), so that he cannot apprehend whether he is the one-who-apprehends (*mudrik*) or not.

(79) [As the adage goes]: "Glory be to Him who has not appointed any other way to gnosis of Him but incapacity to know Him!"[66] Not just anyone is given access to gnosis of His ineffable Essence (*ma'rifat-i dhāt-i bīchūn-i ū*). For whoever desires to acquire knowledge and gnosis (*ma'rifa*) of the Divine Essence must make the soul of the interior reality of his self (*nafs-i ḥaqīqat-i khwud*) into a mirror, so that gazing thereupon, he will recognize the soul of Muḥammad. Then, he shall make the soul of Muḥammad into a mirror. "And I saw my Lord during the Night Ascension in the fairest of

---

subject (*mudrik*) in the (divine) 'Object-of-Apprehension' (*mudrak*). Insofar as the perceiver is endowed with inapprehension, his condition resembles (ordinary) ignorance and heedlessness – although the possessor of this mystical state is, in fact, veiled from such [ignorance]. "You would have thought them awake, as they lay sleeping." (Qur'ān XVIII:18). In Ṣamad Muwaḥḥid (ed.), *Majmū'a-i āthār-i Shaykh Maḥmūd Shabistarī* (Tehran: Kitābkhāna-i Ṭahūrī 1365 A.Hsh./1986), p. 287. Elsewhere, 'Ayn al-Quḍāt explains this maxim as follows: "When a man becomes completely drunk, does he know at all that he is drunk? Never! As long as one iota of a man is left that allows him to perceive that he is drunk and others sober, he is still stranded in the realm of [sober] discrimination, whereas perfect drunkenness consists in a man's existence becoming ransacked and plundered ... That is why Abū Bakr Ṣāddiq said that 'the inability to apprehend [the process of] apprehension is itself apprehension'. What he meant is that apprehension is that your entire being be consumed, such that you cannot apprehend that you are an apprehender." – *Nāmahā-yi 'Ayn al-Quḍāt al-Hamadānī*, vol. 2, pp. 27–28. A list of other Sufi texts and authors who have elucidated this maxim is given in Bāqir Ṣadrniyā, *Farhang-i māthūrāt-i mutūn-i 'irfānī* (Tehran: Surūsh 1380 A.Hsh./2001), p. 321, no. 65. The doctrine of *de docta ignorantia* (learned ignorance) taught by Nicholas de Cusa (d. 1464) in his treatise *On the Vision of God* (*De visione Dei*) is quite similar: "Therefore, I thank you, my God, because you make clear to me that there is no other way of approaching you except that which to all humans, even the most learned philosophers, seems wholly accessible and impossible. For you have shown me that you cannot be seen elsewhere than where impossibility confronts and obstructs me." – *Nicholas of Cusa: Selected Spiritual Writings*, trans. H. Lawrence Bond (New York: Paulist Press 1997), p. 251.

66 A well-known Sufi adage, on which see Ṣadrniyā, *Farhang-i māthūrāt*, p. 272, no. 27.

forms,"[67] alludes to this mirror. Find within this mirror: "faces on that day resplendent looking towards their Lord,"[68] and send the cry that "they measure not the power of God with a true measure"[69] out into the world, for (as the Prophet said) "we have not known God as He truly deserved."[70] But this spiritual station is exalted and rare: not just anyone realizes it and not just anyone comprehends it.

(80) My cherished friend! Edify yourself through gnosis of your self, for gnosis in this world is the seed (which sprouts up into) the *Visio Dei* hereafter. What have you heard? I say: whoever possesses gnosis (*ma'rifat*) today will perceive the divine Vision (*ru'yat*) tomorrow.[71] Listen to it from God: "Whoever has been blind here in this world will be blind in the Hereafter and even further astray."[72] So whoever is blind in respect to gnosis of God in this world, will be blind regarding the Vision of God in the Hereafter. Listen to Muḥammad – peace be upon him – who pronounced: "On the Day of Resurrection (*qiyāmat*), someone will cry out 'O Lord!', and the call will be returned to him: "Invoke me not, for as you did not know me in the world, so how will you recognize me in the hereafter?" "They forgot themselves so He has forgotten them"[73] indicates this precisely. Whoever forgets his own soul (*nafs-i khwud*) has forgotten Him as well and whoever remembers his soul has remembered God as well. (Hence, the two adages:) "One who

67 This *ḥadīth* which, as Schimmel noted, "the majority of Muslims of course refuted vehemently" (*And Muhammad is His Messenger* [Chapel Hill: University of North Carolina 1985], p. 164), is often cited in connection with the Sufi practice of "looking at young men" (*naẓar ilā' al-aḥdāth*). For a comprehensive discussion of this issue, with references to the views of Ḥallāj, 'Ayn al-Quḍāt, 'Irāqī, Jāmī, and other Sufis, see Hellmut Ritter, *The Ocean of the Soul: Men, the World and God in the Stories of Farīd al-Dīn 'Aṭṭār*, trans. John O'Kane (Leiden: Brill 2003), pp. 484–502.

68 Qur'ān LXXV:22–23.

69 Qur'ān VI:91.

70 *Aḥādīth-i Mathnawī*, p. 465.

71 For further discussion of 'Ayn al-Quḍāt's views on the question of the vision of God in this world vs. that in the hereafter, see Naṣrullāh Pūrjavādī, *Rū'yat-i māh dar āsimān: barrasī-yi tārīkhī-yi mas'ila-yi liqā' Allāh dar kalām va taṣawwuf* (Tehran: Markaz-i Nashr-i Dānishgāhī 1375 A.Hsh./1996), p. 155.

72 Qur'ān XVII:72.

73 Qur'ān IX:67.

knows himself knows his Lord,"[74] and "Whoever is incapable of self-knowledge will in the end be incapable of knowing his Lord."[75] Eternal felicity is inextricably tied to human self-knowledge: every person's portion of felicity will be in the same measure as his or her self-knowledge or gnosis of self (*maʿrifat-i khwud*).

(81) The knowledge or gnosis of God Almighty is of three types: One is knowledge of the divine Essence (*dhāt*); another knowledge of the divine Attributes (*ṣifāt*); and another knowledge of the divine actions and decrees (*afʿāl u aḥkām*). And yet, my friend, knowledge of God's actions and decrees can only be obtained through self-knowledge, by gnosis of one's own soul (*maʿrifat-i nafs*). (For, as these two Qur'ānic verse attest:) "And in yourselves (are the signs of God). Can you not then see?"[76] "We shall show them our signs on the horizons and within themselves."[77] As much as one's knowledge of the soul develops and is perfected, one's knowledge of God's actions develops and is perfected. One only acquires knowledge of the divine Attributes in proportion to realizing knowledge of the soul of Muḥammad (*nafs-i Muḥammad*), for "from amongst yourselves (*anfusikum*) there has come a messenger."[78] Yet who has the courage to discourse on the knowledge of His Essence – in its sublimity – since, as the Prophet's dictum enjoins: "Reflect upon God's bounties and blessings (*ālāʾ*), but do not reflect upon his Essence,"[79] it is prohibited to expound upon the knowledge of God (*maʿrifat-i khudā*) except by way of cryptic sign and symbol (*bi-ramz*).

(82) Dear friend, know that God's actions may be divided into two types: those appertaining to the material realm (*mulkī*) and those appertaining to the spiritual kingdom (*malakūtī*). This present world and all that lies herein is called the material realm (*mulk*); that world and all therein is called the spiritual realm (*malakūt*), whilst all else besides this present

74 Furūzānfar, *Aḥādīth-i Mathnawī*, p. 167.

75 This Arabic sentence seems to be based on the *ḥadīth*, "He who knows himself knows his Lord," which is in turn a Sufi Muslim version of the celebrated Delphic Maxim (see ch. VI, n. 81). The sentence may also be rendered: "Whoever is unable to realize gnosis of himself will in the end be incapable of realizing gnosis of his Lord."

76 Qur'ān LI:21.

77 Qur'ān XLI:53.

78 Qur'ān IX:128.

79 *Aḥādīth-i Mathnawī*, p. 142.

world and that world beyond is called the supraformal realm (*jabarūt*). So long as you do not understand and transcend the material realm, you will not reach the spiritual realm; and as long as you do not understand and transcend the spiritual realm, you will never reach the supraformal realm. Now, in each of these triune worlds, God – Almighty and Holy – with whom "are the treasures of the heavens and the earth,"[80] has a treasury, although not everyone knows this. O friend, I swear by the majestic power of the Eternal Being, that you must engage in spiritual practice (*sulūk*)[81] with so much ardour that from the material realm you will advance to the spiritual realm. Then, you must engage in so much spiritual practice that you journey from the lower to the upper echelons of the spiritual realm.

(83) And so one must continue on, proceeding and *progressing* (*sulūk*) until the beauty of this verse: "So glory be unto Him in whose hand lies the dominion of everything, and unto Him you will be returned,"[82] reveals itself. One will then see the beauty of the Creator of the spiritual realm within this verse, so that (the meaning of) "... knows his Lord,"[83] will reveal itself. And yet, this (understanding of) "... knows his Lord" is imperfect so long as one does not emerge from behind the veil of Lordship (*rubūbīyyāt*) to reach behind the veil of the beauty of Divinity (*jamāl-i ilāhīyyāt*), and then emerge from behind veil of Divinity to reach within the veil of His Exclusive Power (*'izzat*), and then emerge from the behind the veil of His Exclusive Power to reach within the veil of His sublimity (*'aẓamat*), and then from the veil of His sublimity reach inside the veil of His august magnificence (*kibriyā*). Within the veil of God's august magnificence, then one will perceive both this world and the Next as having been obliterated, for "all that lies thereupon is perishing,"[84] whereupon one is commanded to "regard the

80 Qur'ān LXIII:7.

81 On the various connotations of this technical term in Sufism, see my article on "Sulūk," *EI2* IX, pp. 861–63, as well as my "The Spiritual Journey in Kubrawi Sufism," in Todd Lawson (ed.), *Reason and Inspiration in Islam: Theology, Philosophy and Mysticism in Muslim Thought, Essays in Honour of Hermann Landolt* (London: I.B. Tauris and the Institute of Ismaili Studies 2005), pp. 364–79.

82 Qur'ān XXXVI:83.

83 This is the second part of the first *ḥadīth* cited at the beginning of this selection: "One who knows himself knows his Lord."

84 Qur'ān LV:26.

beauteous countenance of God,"[85] so that at last, "there remains nothing but the countenance of the Lord."[86]

(84) Here, nothing remains of the gnostic (*'ārif*), and gnosis (*ma'rifat*) is obliterated as well. All becomes the Object of Gnosis (*ma'rūf*) for "Unto God all affairs come home"[87] attests. At this spiritual station, "He loves them, and they love Him"[88] appear to be identical.[89] This mystical point then exposes itself on the wide expanse of the supraformal realm. When Ḥuṣayn confessed "I am the Truth,"[90] when Bāyazid announced, "How great is my glory!"[91] what else have they said but this? No 'wayfarer' (*sālik*) any longer exists here! The Creator (*khāliq*) Himself is the wayfarer! What station can ever transcend this station? What fortune ever exceed this fortune? As if to ask forgiveness for (the neglect of) this, a hue and cry goes up throughout the material and spiritual realms: "When we will, we can replace them (human beings), bringing others like them in their stead."[92]

(85) Alas, what do you hear? Is it not aught than the time has not yet come for the human condition (*basharīyyat*) to be overthrown and turned on its head! Else, one might fear that divine Reality (*ḥaqīqat*) would

---

85 I could not find this particular verse in the Qur'ān, but for a very similar verse, see XXX:50.

86 Qur'ān LV:27.

87 Qur'ān XLII:53.

88 Qur'ān V:54. For a long discussion of this celebrated verse of central significance in the erotic theology of both Hamadānī and the Brothers Ghazālī, see my "Sufism's Religion of Love, from Rābi'a to Ibn 'Arabī," in Lloyd Ridgeon (ed.), *The Cambridge Companion to Sufism* (Cambridge: Cambridge University Press 2014), pp. 150–80.

89 'Ayn al-Quḍāt Hamadānī here implies that divine love or God's love for man (= "He loves them") merges with human love or man's love of God (= "they love Him) within the transcendental unity of Beloved (God), Lover (man) and Love. For further discussion of this theoerotic doctrine, see my "Divine Love in Islam," in *Encyclopædia of Love in World Religions*, ed. Yudit Greenberg (New York: Macmillan Reference & Thomson Gale 2007), vol. I, pp. 163–65.

90 For references to the many Sufi sources who have cited or expounded this celebrated saying (*Anā al-Ḥaqq*) of Manṣūr al-Ḥallāj (d. 304/922), see: Ṣadrniyā, *Farhang*, pp. 88–89, no. 791.

91 For Sufi commentators on this famous ecstatic saying (*Ṣubḥānī mā a'ẓama sha'nī*) of Bāyazid Basṭāmī (d. 261/875), see Ṣadrniyā, *Farhang*, p. 272, fn. 34.

92 Qur'ān LXXVI:28.

overturn the Muslim Canon Law (*sharī'at*)! Alas! You have just heard the verse: "When we will, we can replace them (human beings), bringing others like them in their stead."[93] – but what is its meaning? *Become me* for just a moment (*yik sā'at marā bāsh*) so you will know what "bringing ... in their stead (*tabdīlān*)" really is! It is the Light of God infused into the devotee's interior being. And when it comes and shines, nothing of substance remains to a man that, through himself, he might see himself. Thus, "We hurl the truth against falsehood and it prevails over it, and behold, falsehood vanishes away."[94] Ah, what an alchemical transmutation! From whence and unto whither?! "... Such that he follows in a divine light from his Lord ..."[95] That light unites with light while the darkness flees away, just as when the rays of the sun shine forth, encompassing [and enshrouding] the light of the stars, the stars abdicate their influence and sway. Here, the wayfarer gambles his own desire away for the sake of all desires; he loses his own sight for the sake of all eyesight: all becomes Vision. During *samā'*, Abū al-'Abbās Qaṣṣāb[96] always used utter these verses:

Within the sight of the eye we've placed a vision,
  Giving it nourishment by means of the eye.
Then by chance we passed down the street of Beauty:
  Now, we are free from both eye and seeing of sights.

(86) Dear friend! Hearken to the debate between the bodily frame (*qālib*) and the heart (*dil*). Listen to what the physical frame tells it – for what does the physical frame know what's befallen the heart? Most of the time the

---

93 Qur'ān LXXVI:28.

94 Qur'ān XXI:18.

95 Qur'ān XXXIX:22. To contextualize his meaning, the entire verse should be cited here: "Is he whose breast (*ṣadr*) has been expanded for Submission (*islām*), such that he follows in a divine light from his Lord (like one who sees not)? Then woe unto those whose hearts are hardened against the remembrance of God. They are plainly astray in error."

96 His full name is Abū'l-'Abbās Aḥmad b. Muḥammad Qaṣṣāb (death-date unknown), he was a master of Abū Sa'īd ibn Abī'l-Khayr (d. 440/1048). See Muḥammad Ibn Munawwar, *The Secrets of God's Mystical Oneness*, trans. John O'Kane (Costa Mesa: Mazda 1992), index, s.v. Abū'l Abbās Qaṣṣāb.

heart simply pulls the wool over the eyes of the physical frame – for what should the heart reply to the physical frame? Listen:

What gall had you, O Heart, to desire that friend,
  the one who's slain so many others like you?
The Heart replied: "Just wait till we all are *one*."
  The affair I had in mind was of that kind.

(87) Yet who in the world understands this discourse except for adepts and confidants of divine intimacy, those liberated from human attributes, having realized the divine Qualities, so that their interior reality perpetually hymns these verses to their human nature (*basharīyyat*):

In love, there aren't any tales of Adam and Eve.
  Whatever comes of Adam and Eve is not of us.
They say to me that these words are not at all fair,
  Well, the sun's a stranger here: none has vision there.

No more than this may be said at the present moment. Further exposition of "One who knows himself knows his Lord" can be found in subsequent chapters of these *Prognostications*. Seek it in earnest until you find it, and apprehend it as having been heard from me until you understand.

VI

THE INITIATIC SCIENCE OF UNVEILING

Selections from Ibn 'Arabī's (d. 638/1240) *Al-Futūḥāt al-Makkīyya*

Muḥyī al-Dīn Ibn 'Arabī (d. 638/1240) was a seminal genius whose effect on esoteric, and particularly Sufi, currents of thought in Islam can be felt down to the present day.[1] Known as the Shaykh al-Akbar (*Magister Maximus*), from whom the so-called "Akbarian" school of Sufism and mystical gnosis originates, his writings constitute by far the most elaborate philosophy of religion and religious life in the Islamic world to date. In the words of J.W. Morris, they present us "a comprehensive metaphysics which offered an all-encompassing justification and explanation for the observed diversity of religions, philosophic, and spiritual 'paths' to God – whether within the multiple sects and schools of later Islamic culture, or in the wider, even multi-confessional context of the Ottoman, Safavid and Mughal empires."[2]

Scholarship and study of Ibn 'Arabī's thought has progressed tremendously over recent decades. The landmark studies of William Chittick and Gerald Elmore in English, the monographs of Michel Chodkiewicz and Claude Addas in French, and as well as the on-going proliferation of critical editions of Ibn 'Arabī's works in Arabic, and translation of the same into European languages has meant that today we have a much clearer picture of both his historical personality and theosophical doctrine. Coupled with the journal published by the Ibn 'Arabī Society in England, over sixty volumes of which have been published to date, a greater understanding of his thought has been obtained in the last forty years than could be had over the past four hundred. His prodigious literary achievements are presently being reciprocated by the wonder-working reproductions and studies of his works in European and Oriental languages. Indeed, the latter half of the twentieth

1 See Ṣamad Muwaḥḥid (ed.), *Majmū'a-i āthār-i Shaykh Maḥmūd Shabistarī* (Tehran: Kitābkhāna-i Ṭahūrī 1365 A.Hsh./1986) introduction, p. 10; 'Abd al-Ḥusayn Zarrīnkūb, *Justujū-yi dar taṣawwuf-i Īrān* (Tehran: Amīr Kabīr 1357 A.Hsh./1978), p. 313.

2 J.W. Morris, "... Except His Face: The Political and Aesthetic Dimensions of Ibn 'Arabī's Legacy" *Journal of the Muhyiddin Ibn 'Arabi Society* XXIII/1998, p. 23.

century and the first half of the twenty-first have been as important to Western understanding of Ibn 'Arabī's thought as the last half of the fifteenth century was for the comprehension of Plato's philosophy.

In the history of esotericism in fact, the figures of Plato and Ibn 'Arabī are eminently comparable in the influence they have had on the development of metaphysics in Christianity and Islam respectively. As one scholar recently observed, "Paraphrasing Whitehead's famous remark about Plato – and with something of the same degree of exaggeration – one could say that the history of Islamic thought subsequent to Ibn 'Arabī (at least down to the eighteenth century and the radically new encounter with the modern West) might largely be construed as a series of footnotes to his works."[3] Another modern-day commentator on the Shaykh has maintained that, "his influence is so penetrating that it is impossible to understand the history of Islamic thought after the thirteenth century without a good understanding of Ibn 'Arabī. Especially in the Sunni world, where rational theology (*kalām*) suffered gradual ossification and 'Hellenistic' philosophy (*falsafa*) disappeared, it is not an exaggeration to say that *Ibn 'Arabī's thought became the only theology and philosophy*."[4]

The course of both mystical and philosophical thought, whether in the Shī'ite theosophical schools of Safavid Persia or amongst the Sufi gnostics of Sunni Islam, was forever altered by the advent of Ibn 'Arabī. His vast corpus of writings reigned with practically undisputed authority over a vast extent of "Muslim geographical space – from the Maghreb to the Far East ..."; over the face of entire Islamic world, "the stamp of akbarian teaching is not only printed on 'intellectual' Sufism, but may also be detected in the world of brotherhoods which embrace the most diverse social classes and cultural levels."[5] His teachings also had a momentous impact on the literary expression of Sufism, such that he became "the most influential theorist in all of Sufism."[6] Intellectual discourse, both in

3 J.W. Morris, "Ibn 'Arabī and his Interpreters. Part II: Influences and Interpretations," *J.R.A.S.*, 106/4 (1986), p. 733.

4 Masataka Takeshita, *Ibn 'Arabī's Theory of the Perfect Man and its Place in the History of Islamic Thought* (Tokyo 1987), p. 1.

5 Michel Chodkiewicz, "The Diffusion of Ibn 'Arabī's Doctrine," *Journal of the Muhyiddin Ibn 'Arabi Society* IX/1991, pp. 37.

6 Cyrus Ali Zargar, "The Poetics of *Shuhūd:* Ibn al-'Arabī's 'Intuitive, Enamored Heart' and the Composition of Erotic Poetry," *Journal of the Muhyiddin Ibn 'Arabi Society* XXXV (2013), pp. 13–36 [p. 13].

prose and verse, became subject to the influence of his literary style and imbued with his highly sophisticated metaphysical terminology. This was mostly because, in William C. Chittick's words, "he brought Sufism into the mainstream of serious intellectual speculation," from the thirteenth century onwards, employing "all the tools of the theologians, philosophers, grammarians, and other specialists."[7] He found his greatest and most enthusiastic supporters among the educated Persian dervish population, many of the greatest names of which counted themselves as disciples or interpreters of his doctrines. These include the likes of Awḥād al-Dīn Kirmānī (d. 635/1238), Ṣadr al-Dīn Qūnawī (d. 673/1274), Fakhr al-Dīn 'Irāqī (d. 688/1289), Sa'īd al-Dīn al-Farghānī (d. 699/1299), 'Azīz al-Dīn Nasafī (d. circa 699–700/1300), Mu'ayyid al-Dīn Jandī (d. 700/1301), 'Abd al-Razzāq al-Kāshānī (d. 740/1339 or 736/1335–6), 'Alā al-Dawla Simnānī, Dāwūd Qayṣārī (d. 751/1350) and Rukn al-Dīn (Bābā Ruknā) Mas'ūd Shīrāzī (d. 768/1367), not to mention Maḥmūd Shabistarī (d. after 740/1339), Muḥammad Shīrīn Maghribī ("Ibn 'Arabī's faithful interpreter"[8]), Khwāja Muḥammad Pārsā (d. 822/1419), Ṣā'īn al-Dīn Turkah Iṣfahānī (d. 830/1427) and Shāh Nimatu'llāh Walī (1330–1431). His intellectual legacy also extended to mystical poets and thinkers in the West such as Dante and Ramon Llull (d. 1316).[9]

Born in 560/1165 in Murcia, Spain, Ibn 'Arabī's family moved to Seville when he was eight,[10] where he was brought up. A child prodigy in matters

7 *The Sufi Path of Knowledge: Ibn al-'Arabī's Metaphysics of Imagination* (Albany: SUNY Press 1989), p. 289.

8 Annemarie Schimmel, *Mystical Dimensions of Islam* (Chapel Hill: University of North Carolina 1975), p. 167. On Maghribī relation to Ibn 'Arabī, see Leonard Lewisohn (ed.), *Dīwān-i Muḥammad Shīrīn Maghribī* (Tehran: Tehran University Press in association with SOAS Publications, University of London 1372 A.Hsh./1993), Persian introduction, pp. 9–15.

9 On Llull and Ibn 'Arabī, see Jereer El-Moor, "The Fool for Love (*Foll Per Amor*) As Follower of Universal Religion," Part 1" *Journal of the Muhyiddin Ibn 'Arabi Society* XXXV (2004), pp. 47–74, and "The Fool for Love (*Foll Per Amor*) As Follower of Universal Religion," Part 2: XXXVI (2004), pp. 85–125; Maria Rosa Menocal, *Shards of Love: Exile and the Origins of the Lyric* (Durham, N.C.: Duke University Press 1994), pp. 59–62; J.N. Hillgarth, *Ramón Lull and Lullism in Fourteenth-Century France* (Oxford: Oxford University Press 1971), pp. 43ff.

10 William Chittick, "Ibn al-'Arabī," *Encyclopædia Iranica* VII, p. 664.

of the Spirit, in an autobiographical account he relates that, when he was about fifteen, he experienced an illumination after a period of solitary retreat. Subsequently, he was brought by his father to meet the famous philosopher Averroes, where he found that the sage's understanding could not match his interior vision.[11]

His private mystical experiences were deepened by practical training and experience in the Sufi Path under a series of teachers during his twenties. These teachers are enumerated in fascinating detail in his autobiographical treatises, where he describes in detail some seventy odd masters, vividly portraying the intensity of his spiritual practice and the originality of his visionary experiences.[12] He specialized in *ḥadīth*, was known for his intense piety, firm in his detachment from all worldly interests. Rank and status, women and wealth held for him absolutely no interest. His interior guide was Jesus, from whom he received numerous revelations; the Prophet Muḥammad his refuge in face of temptations. These and many other details of his remarkable spiritual life and intellectual development are recorded with sensitive erudition in *Quest for the Red Sulphur: The Life of Ibn ʿArabī* by Claude Addas.[13]

Although later he did benefit from following the methodical guidance (*sulūk*) of several spiritual teachers, Ibn ʿArabī traversed the stages of the Sufi Path under the sway of divine attraction (*jadhba*). For this reason, in his writings, one finds speculations about theosophical issues and intricacies of theology intertwined with stories of his personal encounters with saints, clairvoyant séances with pre-Islamic prophets, raptures, ecstasies and transports out of the body. In 597/1200 he left Spain permanently in order to make the Ḥajj. Once in Mecca, he began writing the most detailed and intricate account of his teachings – *Al-Futūḥāt al-Makkīyya* in the following year.[14] In 1204, he set out from Mecca travelling through central Islamic lands, and finally settling in Damascus in 620/1223, where he lived and taught until he died in 638/1240.

---

11 Henry Corbin, *Creative Imagination in the Sufism of Ibn ʿArabī*, trans. R. Manheim (Princeton: Princeton University Press 1969), pp. 40–43.

12 Ibn ʿArabī, trans. R.W.J. Austin, *Sufis of Andalusia, the Rūḥ al-Quds and al-Durrat al-Fākhirah* (Sherborne: Beshara 1988).

13 Translated by Peter Kingsley (Cambridge: Islamic Texts Society 1993), pp. 39–40.

14 Chittick, "Ibn al-ʿArabī," *EIr*, p. 664.

A prolific author, Ibn 'Arabī composed some 850 works, of which 700 are extant, and at least 450 genuine.[15] From his innumerable treatises and tracts, his most famous work is a short (180 pages) and original treatise on prophetology, entitled *The Bezels of Wisdom* (*Fuṣūṣ al-ḥikam*), comprising twenty-seven chapters, each of which is devoted to the divine wisdom revealed in a particular prophet and specific divine word. Each of these prophets represents a different mode of knowing: each prophet in his human setting is a kind of bezel, a gemstone in which "each kind of wisdom is set, thus making of each prophet the signet or sign, by selection, of a particular aspect of God's wisdom."[16] The prophets start with Adam in chapter one and conclude with Muḥammad in chapter twenty-seven without any apparent intervening chronological order.

Ibn 'Arabī also authored a *Dīvān*, a large body of Arabic mystical poetry, the most famous collection of which is called the *Tarjumān al-ashwāq*.[17]

However, his major work was *The Meccan Illuminations* (*al-Futūḥāt al-Makkīyya*) which covers 2,580 pages in its common edition (published in Cairo 1911; repr. Beirut: Dār Ṣādir, n.d., that has been used for the present translation), but which in its new critical edition is projected to cover thirty-seven volumes of about 500 pages each. Consisting of 560 chapters – the same number of words as is in the Surah *Al-Fatḥ* (hence the title of the book *al-Futūḥāt*)[18] – this book has been described as "a sort of all-encompassing encyclopaedia of Islamic thought, especially in the domain of spiritual practice, and perhaps the most penetrating and profound of all commentaries on the Qur'an and traditions of the Prophet."[19] The *Futūḥāt* is full of

15 Chittick, "Ibn al-'Arabī," *EIr*, p. 665.

16 R.J.W. Austin (trans.), *Ibn al-'Arabī: The Bezels of Wisdom* (New York: Paulist Press SPCK 1980), p. 16.

17 *The Tarjumān al-Ashwāq: A Collection of Mystical Odes by Muḥyi'iddīn Ibn al-'Arabī*, trans. R.A. Nicholson (London: RAS 1911, repr. London: Theosophical Publishing House 1978). See also Michael Sells, *Stations of Desire: Love Elegies from Ibn 'Arabī* (Jerusalem: IBIS 2000).

18 As M. Chodkiewicz points out in his study of "The *Futūḥāt al-Makkiyya*: some Unresolved Enigmas," in Leonard Lewisohn (ed.), *The Heritage of Sufism*, vol. II: *The Legacy of Mediæval Persian Sufism* (Oxford: Oneworld 1999), p. 231.

19 James Morris, "... Except His Face: The Political and Aesthetic Dimensions of Ibn 'Arabī's Legacy" *Journal of the Muhyiddin Ibn 'Arabi Society* XXIII/1998, p. 22.

references to other Islamic thinkers such as Ghazālī, and citations of the Qur'ān and *ḥadīth* also abound.

The inspired nature of the *Futūḥāt* is quickly apparent from even the most cursory study. Of its inspiration, he boasts that, "neither this particular book nor any of my other works have been composed in the way that ordinary books are composed, and I do not write them according to the habitual method of authors." ... "I have not written one single letter of this book other than under the effect of divine dictation."[20] Elsewhere in the text he declares, "The books we have composed – this and others – do not follow the route of ordinary compositions, nor do we follow the route of ordinary authors ... My heart clings to the door of the Divine Presence, waiting mindfully for what comes when the door is opened. My heart is poor and needy, empty of every knowledge ... When something appears to the heart from behind that curtain, the heart hurries to obey and sets it down in keeping with the commanded bounds."[21]

Thus Ibn 'Arabī was not a philosopher in the modern sense of the word. Although he commented that Plato had "tasted" the states of the Sufis, and understood "unveiling;" he rejects Greek rationalism, saying: "the meaning of 'philosopher' is lover of wisdom, since *sophia* in Greek is "wisdom" and *phil* is "love," every man of intelligence loves wisdom." As for the Islamic Peripatetics, he concludes, "if while loving wisdom, they had sought it from God, not from reflection, they would have hit the mark in everything."[22] The popularly vulgarized conception of Ibn 'Arabī as a philosopher who wove together the truths and maxims of Sufism into a philosophical 'system' concocted out of his own personal delusions and fantasy, could not be farther from the truth, for as he says:

> The Folk of Allah do not follow the authority of their reflections, since a created thing should not follow the authority of another created thing. Hence they incline toward following God's authority.

20 Cited from the *Futūḥāt* by Michel Chodkiewicz, "The *Futūḥāt al-Makkiyya* ...," p. 225.

21 *Futūḥāt* I 59.12. Cited by Chittick, *The Sufi Path of Knowledge* (Albany: SUNY Press 1989), p. xv.

22 *Futūḥāt* II 523.2, cited by Chittick, *Sufi Path*, p. 203.

> They come to know God through God, and He is as He says about Himself, not as meddlesome reason judges.[23]
>
> Sound knowledge is not given by reflection, nor by what the rational thinkers establish by means of their reflective powers. Sound knowledge is only that which God throws into the heart of the knower ... He who has no unveiling has no knowledge (*man lā kashf lah lā ʿilm lah*).[24]
>
> Is there anything which cannot be reached by way of unveiling and finding? We say that there is nothing, and we forbid reflection totally, since it makes its possessor heir to deceit and lack of sincerity. There is nothing whose knowledge cannot be attained through unveiling and finding. In contrast, occupying oneself with reflection is a veil.[25]

In what follows, six different selections from the Meccan Illuminations (*Al-Futūḥāt al-makkīyya*) of Ibn ʿArabī are features that concern the difference between knowledge (*ilm*), visionary unveiling (*kashf*), and gnosis or inspired knowledge (*maʿrifat*). For Ibn ʿArabī, 'knowledge' in essence is revelatory and visionary, obtained through the practice of contemplative exercises.[26] It can only be obtained by visionary unveiling or disclosure (*kashf*), not by reason (*ʿaql*) or deliberation (*naẓar*) since neither of the latter are ultimately valid authorities for the attainment of truth. Ibn ʿArabī explicitly refers to his own mystical method as that of unveiling (*kashf*), intuitive tasting (*dhawq*), opening (*fatḥ*), insight (*baṣīrat*), and witnessing

---

23 *Futūḥāt* II 298.2; Chittick, *Sufi Path*, p. 166.

24 *Futūḥāt* II 290.25; Chittick, *Sufi Path*, p. 170.

25 *Futūḥāt* II 523.2;

26 "In Ibn ʿArabī's various works, four actions are described which lead to inspired knowledge [*maʿrifa*]: retreats, spiritual exercises, spiritual efforts and ritual invocation (*adhkār*) ... Sufi masters such as al-Kalābādhī, in his book *Kitāb al-Taʿarruf lī madhhab ahl al-taṣawwuf*; Ibn ʿAlī Sarrāj al-Ṭūsī in his *Kitāb al-Lumaʿ*; al-Qushayrī, the author of *al-Risāla*; Abū Ṭālib al-Makkī, author of *Qūt al-qulūb*, and al-Ghazālī in his *Iḥyāʾ ʿulūm al-dīn*, agree unanimously that spiritual exercises are necessary to acquire the sciences of the heart, which is why these actions precede spiritual knowledge and are the cause of it – and Ibn ʿArabī approves of their claims in numerous passages." – Souad Hakim, "The Paths of God: A Journey through the Spiritual Experience of Ibn ʿArabī and his Writings," in *Journal of the Muhyiddin Ibn ʿArabi Society* LIX (2016), pp. 71–93 [pp. 78–79].

(*shuhūd, mushāhada*). Each of these terms possesses a different technical meaning in respect to the acquisition of gnosis (*ma'rifat*). "We are not one to quote the words of philosophers," asserts the Shaykh, "nor the words of anyone else, since in this book and in all our books we only write that which is given by unveiling and dictated by God."[27]

KNOWLEDGE IS A DYAD: VISIONARY UNVEILING VS. RATIOCINATION[28]

This short selection from chapter 65 of the *Futūḥāt* (I. 319.26–320.2) illustrates Ibn 'Arabī's view that knowledge is essentially *à deux*, and explains why the methods of obtaining knowledge are basically binary and dyadic.

The first way is *esoteric*; it is all revelatory and intuitive: it is that of visionary unveiling (*ṭarīq al-kashf*), pertaining to the Sufis. The knowledge obtained in this manner requires no proof of its truth, being by way of intuitive sapiential 'taste' (*dhawq*). Ibn 'Arabī's belief in heart-savour's intuitive taste (*dhawq*) and the independence of its insights from rational proof and demonstration was disputed by many of the later theosophers of the seventeenth-century School of Iṣfahān, who tended to combine philosophical speculation with mystical intuition. One such thinker in particular, 'Abd al-Razzāq Lāhījī (see chapter X below), asserted that only the latter can establish the verity of the former, that reason is ultimately revelation's best advocate. Hence Lāhījī's assertion that "the judgment passed on the intrinsic truth of visionary disclosure is *dependent* on rational demonstration (*burhān*)." Ibn 'Arabī, of course, found such a doctrine, permitting reason to determine the true limits of revelation, simply unacceptable (see p. 215 "Epistemological Foundations of Sufi Gnosis" below).

The second way is *exoteric;* it is all intellectual and ratiocinative, attained through reflection and circumstantial reasoning using rational demonstration (*tarīq al-fikr wa al-istidlāl b'al-burhān al-'aqlī*). The latter is the preferred method of theologians and philosophers. And of course, as befits the *Magister Maximus* of the Sufi Shaykhs, the first way, which neither

27 *Futūḥāt* II 432.8; Chittick, *The Sufi Path of Knowledge*, p. xv.

28 This is a short passage from chapter 65 of the *Futūḥāt* (I. 319.26–320.2); all translations from the Qur'ān are mine. The page numbers in the Arabic printed edition are bracketed in the translation.

scruples may waylay nor doubts assay, towers far above the second in its efficacy, accuracy and truthfulness.[29]

* * *

[319.26] God Almighty says: "God will exalt those who have faith among you and elevate to a high degree those who have been vouchsafed knowledge" (LVIII:11).

Now, the ways of acquiring knowledge of God are twofold; there is no third. Anybody who professes the unity of God in any other manner besides these two ways but blindly and slavishly follows religious precedent in his profession of divine Unity (*muqallid fī tawḥīdahu*).

The first way is that of visionary unveiling (*al-kashf*), the knowledge of which is intuitively self-evident (*'ilm ḍarūrī*) through visionary disclosure appearing within his soul. It admits no doubts. He has no power to parry and repel it. Nor is he aware of any evidence or proof which might substantiate it, beyond that which he finds within himself.[30]

However, some Sufis dispute this. They say that both the demonstrative proof (*al-dalīl*) and the meaning that is demonstrated are to be found together within his visionary unveiling, since that truth which is not recognized except through a proof must, of course, be disclosed by means of that same proof. Our friend Abū 'Abdu'llāh al-Kattānī of Fez was of this opinion. I myself heard him express this view. He let us know about his own mystical state in this and so spoke truthfully. But he erred in the matter (of visionary unveiling) itself in thinking that it always must be like that, for others discover the same thing in their souls by way of intuitive sapiential 'taste' (*dhawq*) without having any 'proof' at all about it disclosed to them. Otherwise, the same knowledge can be realized through the divine illumination (*tajallī ilāhī*), which is vouchsafed to its adepts – who are the Apostles, Prophets, and some of the saintly Friends of God (*al-rusul, al-anbiyā', al-awliyā'*).

---

29 Part of this selection has been translated by Chittick, *Sufi Path*, p. 169. I would like to thank Muhammad Reza Jozi for carefully checking and providing helpful editorial comments on my translation.

30 For this doctrine in Rūmī, see *Mathnawī-yi ma'nawī*, ed. R.A. Nicholson (London: Luzac 1925–1940), I:116.

Now, the second way (of acquiring knowledge) is that of reflection and demonstration by logical methods of reasoning and argumentation (*ṭarīq al-fikr wa'l-istidlāl bi'l-burhān al-'aqlī*). This way is inferior to[31] the former one though, since doubts and misgivings may intrude upon those who engage in speculation based on demonstrative proofs (*ṣāḥib al-naẓar fī al-dalīl*) and thus these proofs may become undermined and impaired. Painstaking efforts are then required to dispel these doubts and get hold of a legitimate perspective that would approach one's objective properly.

In any case, besides these two ways there is no third course.[32]

Only those who are adept in these two ways of knowledge profess divine Unity [320]. Amongst the class of scholars learned in divine Unity, those who are the most eminent and celebrated adduce many demonstrations and intellectually based considerations about the science of divine Unity (*'ilm 'alā al-tawḥīd*) – that is to say, the divine Unity of the Essence – which they substantiate by incontrovertible proofs. But this science is not vouchsafed to all those who are adept in visionary unveiling: only to some of them.[33]

ON THE THREE TYPES OF SCIENCES[34]

The second selection from Ibn 'Arabī gives a summary of his typology of knowledge. Here, in the Introduction to the *Futūḥāt* (I. 31.8–25), the Shaykh al-Akbar subdivides the sciences into (i) rational science (*'ilm al-'aql*), (ii) the science of mystical states (*'ilm al-aḥwāl*), and (iii) the sciences of mysteries (*'ulūm al-asrār*).

Mystical states are Janus-faced.

On the one hand, their light dispels the murk and gloom of the mystic's selfhood, dulls the bite of the gnarling sorrows of the anxious ego with its

---

31 Alternate versions: inferior to / far below / quite beneath / lower than.

32 That is, there are only two ways to realize knowledge of God: that of the Sufi and the Philosopher.

33 *Al-Futūḥāt al-Makkīyya* I, p. 320.2.

34 From the introduction to the *Futūḥāt* (I. 31. 8–25). A small part of this selection has been translated by Chittick, *Sufi Path*, pp. 169–70. I would like to thank Muhammad Reza Jozi for carefully checking and providing helpful editorial comments on my translation.

perpetual lust and concern for "self" improvement, and dissolves the constant cloying of sensual desire. These higher states of consciousness are free boons of divine grace which are *felt;* they are *savoured* by intuitive sapiential 'taste' (*dhawq*);[35] they are beyond intellectual cognition.

On the other hand, their spiritual sustenance is purely temporary, and their light as often waylays the wayfarer as guides him on the Path.[36] Because they belong to the realm of fluctuation (*talwīn*) and lack stability (*tamkīn*), of course they cannot totally efface the selfhood of the seeker. Their gnosis is but temporal. When the state passes, the knowledge it bestowed likewise perishes. For this reason, in the final selection translated below (VI. "Savouring the Taste Divine"), Ibn ʿArabī denies that true Sufis have any mystical states at all.

The highest level of gnosis and the pinnacle of Sufi apophatic theology is called the "sciences of mysteries" by Ibn ʿArabī. This science is known only by a kind of holy infusion of the Spirit. Particularly reserved for the Sufi saints and the prophets, it is beyond the level of reason; no mental deliberation can apprehend it. The theory of a knowledge that is inaccessible to the human intellect or 'beyond the stage of reason', propounded here by Ibn ʿArabī under the rubric of the science of mysteries, was first elaborated in detail by ʿAyn al-Quḍāt Hamadhānī (see the previous chapter) in two Arabic works: *Zubdat al-ḥaqā'iq*,[37] and *Shakwa gharīb al-awṭān ilā ʿulamā' al-buldān*.[38] Exactly like Ibn ʿArabī, ʿAyn al-Quḍāt explained that

---

35 A keyword in Ibn ʿArabī's lexicon, for good studies of which see Lewisohn, *Beyond Faith and Infidelity*, pp. 41–42, 176–78; W.C. Chittick, *The Sufi Path of Knowledge*, p. 392, n. 36; For the study of *dhawq* in other Islamic intellectual (and esoteric) traditions, see R.J. McCarthy (trans.), Al-Ghazali: *Deliverance from Error: Five Key Texts ...* (Louisville: Fons Vitae, n.d.), pp. 114–15, n. 162; Ormsby, Eric L. "The Taste of Truth: The Structure of Experience in al-Ghazālī's *Al-Munqidh Min Al-Ḍalāl*," in *Islamic Studies Presented to Charles J. Adams*, eds. W.B. Hallaq and D.P. Little (Leiden: Brill 1991).

36 For a good discussion of the theory of mystical states in Sufism, see Javad Nurbakhsh, trans. Leonard Lewisohn, *Spiritual Poverty in Sufism* (London: KNP 1984), pp. 65–80.

37 Edited by ʿAfīf ʿUsayrān (Tehran: 1340 A.Hsh./1961), chap. 16. See the translation by Omar Jah, *The Zubdat al-Ḥaqā'iq of ʿAyn al-Quḍāt Al-Hamadānī* (Kuala Lumpur: International Institute of Islamic Thought 2000).

38 Edited by ʿAfīf ʿUsayrān (Tehran: 1341 A.Hsh./1962), pp. 44ff. See the translation by A.J. Arberry, *A Sufi Martyr: The Apologia of ʿAin al-Quḍāt al-Hamadhānī* (London: Allen & Unwin 1969).

supra-rational knowledge is apprehended through visionary unveiling (*al-kashf*), in contrast to rational knowledge where objects of knowledge can be known by evidence adduced by demonstrative argumentation (*istidlāl*).

* * *

[I.31.8] Abū Yazīd[39] said, "You take your knowledge from the dead, who in turn have taken their knowledge from another dead person, whereas we have taken our knowledge from One who is Living, who shall never die." So it should be understood that those who are possessed of high spiritual aspiration (*al-ṣāḥib al-himmat*),[40] during the course of their solitary retreat with God, through the mighty grace of His generous gift-giving and by strength of His favour, obtain a type of knowledge, the interior mystical consciousness of which is concealed from all scholastic theologians (*mutakallim*) in general, and indeed, from all speculative and logically minded thinkers (*ṣāḥib naẓar wa burhān*), since this knowledge surpasses theoretical intellectual vision based on rational speculation (*al-naẓar al-ʿaqlī*).

The sciences are constituted of three hierarchical degrees or levels (*marātib*):

The first degree is that of rational science (*ʿilm al-ʿaql*), which consists of any sort of knowledge that you can obtain by immediate, *a priori* evidence (*ḍarūrat*), or which follows upon theoretical consideration of

39 Bāyazīd Bisṭāmī (d. 261/875) is probably the most celebrated mystic in the history of Sufism. Louis Massignon (*Essay on the Origins of the Technical Language of Islamic Mysticism*, p. 185) calls him "a figure without peer ... the model of the perfect Muslim ascetic." He was the author of about 500 oral sayings, most of which are of dubious and spurious origin, and many of which were compiled about a hundred years after his death in a book entitled *Kitāb al-nūr fī kalimāt Abī Yazīd Ṭayfūr*, at the same time when his first disciples appeared. Nicholson ("A Historical Enquiry concerning the Origin and Development of Sufism, with a list of definitions of the terms '*sufi*' and '*taṣawwuf*', arranged chronologically', *Journal of the Royal Asiatic Society*, Part I, 1906, p. 326) remarked that "Báyazíd, unless I am mistaken, became the legendary hero of Persian Sufism just because he was in reality a thorough Persian and true representative of the religious aspirations of his countrymen."

40 On Ibn ʿArabī's notion of *himmat*, see Corbin, *Creative Imagination*, p. 222.

demonstrative proofs adduced (to substantiate something), on the condition that one is technically specialized in this art (of thinking) sufficiently enough to discover that proof's internal contextual sense and significance, and (also be able to discern) any dubious, suspect proofs of the same kind (as the true proof) within that particular intellectual cosmos. It is for this reason that they have always said that there are two kinds of rational speculation (*al-naẓar*)[41]: the sound or healthy (*ṣaḥīḥ*), and the unsound or corrupt (*fāsid*) kinds.

The second degree is the science of mystical states (*'ilm al-aḥwāl*), to which no way exists except by intuitive sapiential 'taste' (*dhawq*). The rationalist thinker (*al-'āqil*) is incapable of measuring the bounds of this science, nor can he produce any evidence or proof that would demonstrate (that he has) the knowledge of it, for it is like the knowledge of the sweetness of honey, the bitterness of patience, the joy of sexual intercourse, love, ecstasy, longing, and similar forms of knowledge. For it is impossible that anyone can ever comprehend such sciences without becoming properly endowed with them (through realization) and without realizing them by intuitive experiential 'taste'. The likeness of this type of knowledge – that is known (only) to adepts in intuitive sapiential taste – resembles the case of someone in whom the bilious humour preponderates,[42] so that honey tastes bitter to him or her (being unable to relish it), although the actual taste of honey is not bitter. However, since gall predominates in his humour all he tastes seems like bitter bile.

The third degree is the sciences of mysteries (*'ulūm al-asrār*), which is a type of lore 'beyond the stage of reason' (*al-'ilm alladhī fawq al-ṭawr al-'aql*), that derives from the divine breath of inspiration conveyed through the Holy Spirit to the (human) spirit (*'ilm nafth rūḥ al-quds fī al-rūḥ*).[43] This

41 For a good discussion of the meaning of *al-naẓar* in Ibn 'Arabī's thought, see Chittick, *Sufi Path*, p. pp. 159–60.

42 According to traditional Islamic medicine, four 'humours' operate in the process of digestion. These are blood, phlegmatic, bilious and atrabilious humours. For an accessible and largely authentic account of the Sufi theory of these humours, see Shaykh Hakim Moinuddin Chishti, *The Book of Sufi Healing* (Rochester, Vermont: Inner Traditions 1991), chap. 5.

43 Cf. The similar remarks made by 'Izz al-Dīn Maḥmūd Kāshānī in his *Miṣbāḥ al-hidāya wa miftāḥ al-kifāya* on the first of his tripartite division of esoteric knowledge, which is the science of divine revelation (*waḥy*), in which dicta were spoken to the Prophet by

science, which is the exclusive prerogative of the prophet (*al-nabī*) or saintly friend of God (*al-walī*), is of two kinds:

1. The first kind, just like the first grade of knowledge mentioned above,[44] can be apprehended through the reason. However, its knower does not acquire it through rational speculation (*naẓar*); but rather, the very (existential) level (*martaba*) of this knowledge vouchsafes it to the knower.[45]
2. The second kind, which is related to the second grade of knowledge mentioned above[46] (although its quality excels and is far more distinguished than that grade) is constituted of the sciences of (Prophetic) reports (*'ulūm al-akhbār*), within which things both true and false can be found, unless the truthfulness of the reporter's assertions has been established and the infallibility (*'iṣma*) of the reports that he delivers and declares has been confirmed by those who receive these reports. Such are the reports given by the prophets from God, as in their reports of the Garden of Paradise and all that lies therein. Therefore, the declaration of the Prophet concerning what exists in Paradise comes from the 'Science

mediation of Gabriel's descent or by means of his inspiration (*nafth*), translated below in this volume (see chapter six, p. 193).

44 I.e. rational science based on reason (*'ilm al-'aql*).

45 In Ibn 'Arabī's lexicon as W.C. Chittick points out, the word 'level' (*martaba*) is generally synonymous with the term divine 'Presence' (*ḥaḍra:* of which there are five in number). "In general the word 'Presence' is synonymous with 'level' (*martaba*), a term which carries a more philosophical and less religious connotation. Ibn al-'Arabī's followers often speak of the 'levels of existence' (*marātib al-wujūd*), which they consider to be infinite in number but whose general categories (*kulliyāt*) may be reduced to five or six, i.e. the Divine Presences ... The first is the Presence of Knowledge or of the Inward (*ḥaḍrat al-bāṭin*). It embraces God's Names and Attributes as well as the immutable entities. Facing the First Presence in the opposite position is the World of Sense-Perception, or the Presence of the Outward (*ḥaḍrat al-ẓāhir*). Between these two is the Central Presence, which comprehends the two sides and pertains exclusively to the Perfect Man. Then on the right side is the Central Presence, between it and the Divine Unseen, is the Presence of the Spirits. Finally, on the left side of the Central Presence, between it and the Visible World as such, is the World of Image-Exemplars." "The Five Divine Presences from al-Qūnawī to al-Qayṣarī," *The Muslim World*, LXXII/2 (1982): pp. 109, 112.

46 I.e. the science of mystical states (*'ilm al-aḥwāl*).

> of (Prophetic) Reports', whereas his statement concerning the Resurrection, that there can be found a pool there, the taste of which is sweeter than honey, pertains to the science of mystical states, which is the science of intuitive heart-savour (*'ilm al-dhawq*). But his saying that "God was [or is] and nothing was [or is] with him"[47] and other such sayings belongs to the rational sciences (*'ulūm al-'aql*), which is apprehended by means of rational speculation (*al-naẓar*).

Now, the last [third] kind science – that is, the science of mysteries (*'ilm al-asrār*) – is such that its knower comprehends and encompasses all other sciences *in toto*, whereas those who comprehend the other sciences (by other means) are not like that. Hence, there is no science superior to and nobler than this comprehensively all-inclusive science, the scope of which comprehends and embraces all subjects of knowledge. However, the sage who relays the knowledge of science of mysteries must be truthful and impeccable (*'iṣma*) in the opinion of those who hearken to him. This is a condition that everyone cites.[48]

KNOWLEDGE (*'ILM*) VS. GNOSIS (*MA'RIFA*)[49]

The third selection from Ibn 'Arabī discusses the difference between esoteric and exoteric forms of knowledge. Medieval thinkers both in classical Islam and the Christian West took a good deal of care for terminology. Their general exactitude in the use of abstract terms was probably higher than is ours today, when science and learning is based more on the direct examination of phenomena than the splitting up of terminology. Among

47 A good discussion of the references and use of this *ḥadīth* by Ibn 'Arabī and by writers in the earlier Sufi tradition is provided by Chittick, *Sufi Path*, p. 393, n. 13; also cf. *idem.*, *The Self-Disclosure of God: Principles of Ibn 'Arabī's Cosmology* (Albany: SUNY Press 1998), s.v. "Index of Hadiths and Sayings," p. 435.

48 Ibn 'Arabī, *Al-Futūḥāt al-Makkīyya* (Cairo: 1911; repr. Beirut: Dār Ṣādir, n.d.), I, p. 31: 13–25.

49 From chapter 177 ("On the Station of Gnosis") of the *Futūḥāt* (II. 318.30–319.4). I would like to thank both Muhammad Reza Jozi and Dr. Nader al-Bizri for carefully checking and providing helpful editorial comments on my translation. A few lines from this selection are also translated by Chittick, *Sufi Path*, p. 149.

Islamic thinkers who endorsed the reality of esoteric knowledge, debates over terminology inevitably figured highly, with thinkers of different schools differing in whether to refer to the esoteric mode of sapience as *ʿilm* or *maʿrifa*, for both terms can mean 'knowledge'.[50] Many Sufis, as William Chittick notes, "placed *maʿrifa* at a higher stage than *ʿilm*, and in this context it would be fair to translate the first as gnosis and the second as knowledge. Then *maʿrifa* is equivalent to the direct knowledge called unveiling, witnessing and tasting"[51] (treated in the first selection translated above). Ibn 'Arabī refuses to take a stand in this terminological debate, and considers the divergence of views among scholars and mystics on these two words merely to be a matter of individual preference, and in this selection devoted to the relation of knowledge (*ʿilm*) to gnosis (*maʿrifa*), he explains why.

* * *

On the designation of this Station of Gnosis (*maqām al-maʿrifa*) and the one endowed with it, who is named the "gnostic" (*al-ʿārif*).

Our companions have disagreed about the Station of Gnosis and the gnostic, the Station of Knowledge (*maqām al-ʿilm*) and the man of knowledge (*al-ʿālim*). One group asserts that the Station of Gnosis is lordly (*rabbānī*), and that of Knowledge is divine (*ilāhī*). It is a view that I myself profess, as well as certain other mystics who have personally realized their knowledge, such as Sahl al-Tustarī,[52]

50 See Reza Shah-Kazemi, "The Notion and Significance of *Maʿrifa* in Sufism," *Journal of Islamic Studies* XIII/2 (2002), pp. 155–81.

51 Chittick, *Sufi Path*, p. 148.

52 An early Sufi connected to the Sufi School of Baghdad, who hailed from Shushtar in southwestern Iran, Sahl ibn 'Abdullāh Tustarī (d. 283/896) was the author of one of the earliest mystical Qur'ān commentaries: *Exegesis of the Tremendous Qur'ān* (*Tafsīr al-Qur'ān al-azīm*), ed. Muḥammad Basīl (Beirut: Dār al-Kutub al-'Ilmīyya 1423/2001); see also Sahl ibn 'Abdullāh al-Tustarī, *Tafsīr al-Qur'ān al-ʿaẓīm*, ed. M.B. al-Naʿsānī al-Ḥalabī (Cairo: Maṭb'a Sa'āda 1329/1908); and the recent English translation of this text by Annabel and Ali Keeler, *Tafsīr al-Tustarī* (Louisville, KY: Fons Vitae 2011). On

Abū Yazīd (Bisṭāmī),[53] Ibn al-'Arīf[54] and Abū Madyan.[55]

Another group assert that the Station of Gnosis is divine and that the Station of Knowledge is inferior to it. This is a view that I also profess, insofar as what they denote as "knowledge," we interpret to be "gnosis," and what they designate as "gnosis" we interpret as "knowledge." So our disagreement is merely verbal.

The basic issue here concerns God Almighty's declaration: "When they hear what has been bestowed upon the Apostle from on high, you can see their eyes overflowing with tears because of the Truth that they recognize therein (*mimma 'arafū min al-Ḥaqq*)."[56] So God has (in this verse) designated them as "gnostics" (*'ārifīn*) not as "scholarly men of learning" (*'ulamā'*).

---

his impact on Ibn 'Arabī, see Binyamin Abrahamov, *Ibn al-'Arabī and the Sufis* (Oxford: Anqa 2014), pp. 53–62.

53 See n. 39, above. On Abū Yazīd and Ibn 'Arabī, see Abrahamov, *Ibn al-'Arabī and the Sufis*, pp. 35–52.

54 Ibn al-'Ārif was the most famous disciple of Ibn Barrajān, founder of the Andalusian Sufi 'School of Almeria', both of whom were executed for heresy in 536/1141. Ibn al-'Ārif exerted a great influence on the development of Ibn 'Arabī's thought. See Claude Addas, *Quest for the Red Sulphur: The Life of Ibn 'Arabī*, trans. [from the French by] Peter Kingsley (Cambridge, UK: Islamic Texts Society 1993), pp. 52–54; and Abrahamov, *Ibn al-'Arabī and the Sufis*, pp. 139–44.

55 Abū Madyan (d. 590/1194) is one of the most frequently cited Sufi masters in Ibn 'Arabī's works. He was born in Seville, Spain, but passed most of his life in Fez, Morocco: see Vincent Cornell, *The Way of Abū Maydan: Doctrinal and Poetic Works of Abū Maydan Shu'ayb ibn al-Ḥusayn al-Anṣārī* (Cambridge, UK: Islamic Texts Society 1993). On his influence on Ibn 'Arabī, see Abrahamov, *Ibn al-'Arabī and the Sufis*, pp. 157–64.

56 Qur'ān V:83. To contextualize Ibn 'Arabī's arguments, it will be helpful here to cite the three verses under discussion: "(83) When they hear what has been bestowed upon the Apostle from on high, you can see their eyes overflowing with tears because of the Truth that they recognize therein. They say: 'O our Lord, we have faith, so inscribe us amongst the witnesses'. (84) And how should we not have faith in God and the truth that has been given us, and be desirous that (our Lord admit us into the company of the righteous)? (85) God has rewarded them for what they confess with gardens (through which rivers flow)" [Trans. LL].

Then, God, (continuing in the same verse) mentions them, recalling that, "They say: 'O our Lord, we have faith, so inscribe us amongst the witnesses.'" Hence, the verse states, "O our Lord (*rabbanā'*)," but it does not state, "O our God (*ilāhanā*)." Thus, the verse pronounces, "we have faith (*āmanā*)," but it does not say, "we have knowledge (*'alamnā*)," nor does it say, "we bear witness (*shāhidnā*)." Then (to the verse), it is added, "so inscribe us amongst the witnesses," but it does not announce, "we are amongst the witnesses."

And He said (the verse continues): "And how should we not have faith in God [319.1], and the truth that has been given us, and be desirous that [our Lord admit us into the company of the righteous]?" But He did not say, "Apportion us admittance to the company of the righteous, O Lord ...," nor did He say, "O God, among the company ...," nor did He say, "amongst your devotees who are righteous," as the prophets have said. Rather, concerning this "company" whose attributes have been just described, God declared, "God has rewarded them for what they confess with gardens (through which rivers flow)."[57] (V:85), which is a site of sensual enjoyment for all souls, and in this manner God bestows upon them a station that best suits their just deserts.

We have elaborated on the distinction between gnosis and knowledge in our book entitled *The Orbits of the Stars* (*Mawāqi' al-nujūm*),[58] where we explained that if one were to ask a person who believes in the superiority of the station of gnosis about it, he would reply in exactly the same manner as his adversary and rival who maintains the superiority of the station of knowledge. Therefore, the disagreement between the two viewpoints is merely linguistic and terminological. It is not in respect to the actual meaning. [319.4]

57 Qur'ān V:85.

58 Composed in 596/1200, its full title is *Mawāqi' al-nujūm wa maṭālī' ahillat al-asrār wa-l-'ulūm* (*The Settings/Orbits of the Stars and the Risings of the Crescents of the Mysteries of Knowledge*) (Beirut: Al-Maktaba Al-'Aṣrīyyah 2004). For more on this work, see Gerald T. Elmore, *Islamic Sainthood in the Fullness of Time: Ibn al-'Arabī's Book of the Fabulous Gryphon* (Leiden: Brill 1999), p. 49.

THE LIGHT OF KNOWLEDGE AND FAITH[59]

The following short passage from chapter 177 of the *Futūḥāt* (II.305.35 - 306.9), entitled "On the Station of Gnosis," explains the meaning of sapiental taste (*dhawq*), and its relation to the Light of Faith and the Light of Knowledge. In Sufism, faith (*imān*) is conceived of as the product of the heart's illumination.[60] The cardiological basis of faith in all schools of Islamic theology is axiomatic, and a common feature of religious language worldwide. S.H. Nasr observes:

> It is in the heart that intelligence and faith meet and where faith itself becomes saturated with the light of sapience. In the Quran both faith (*imān*) and intelligence (*'aql*) are explicitly identified with the heart (*al-qalb*), while in Hinduism the Sanskrit term *sraddhā*, which is usually translated as faith, means literally knowledge of the heart. In Latin also the fact that *credo* and *cor/cordis* are derived from the same root points to the same metaphysical truth.[61]

This selection reiterates a constant theme in Ibn 'Arabī's works: that Faith is a kind of *a priori*, self-evident knowledge which "a person finds in his heart and is not able to repel."[62] Faith in God is not realized by miracles, nor by the furnishing of proofs.[63] Since knowledge is attained by virtue of the heart's illumination with "Light of Faith," the gnostic who is secure in his vision is one who follows his own inner light, adhering to the invisible *credo* realized within his inner being. Hence, Rūmī describes the wise and

---

59 The following passage is from chapter 177 of the *Futūḥāt* (II.305.35 – 306.9), entitled "On the Station of Gnosis." I would like to thank Muhammad Reza Jozi and Dr. Nader al-Bizri for carefully checking and providing helpful editorial comments on my translation (the first paragraph of which was also translated by Chittick, *Sufi Path*, pp. 196–97).

60 In his treatise on esoteric knowledge translated in this volume, Ghazālī explains: "it is that certain of the Sufis profess that the heart possesses its own organ of vision (*oculus cordis*) just like the body, so that just as the ocular eye beholds outward things, the intellectual eye (*'ayn al-'aql*) perceives inward things, the esoteric spiritual realities (*al-ḥaqā'iq*)."

61 S.H. Nasr, *Knowledge and the Sacred*, p. 150.

62 Cf. *Futūḥāt* II. 259.1ff., translated by W. Chittick, *The Sufi Path of Knowledge*, p. 194.

63 Chittick, *The Sufi Path of Knowledge*, p. 194.

intelligent man (*'āqil*) as one who follows his own inner light. Such a person alone is the true "believer," for faith is obedience to this inner illumination with utter selflessness.[64] So "the man of faith is a believer in himself (*mu'min-i khwīsh*), and bases his faith upon that Light by which his soul subsists,"[65] exactly as Ibn 'Arabī asserts here. It is this light which is, as Rūmī says, the "Master-Intelligence (*pīr – pīr-i 'aql bāshad*) of the Sufi wayfarer,"[66] which distinguishes the realized spiritual adept (*muḥaqqiq*) from the intellectual poseur (*muqallid*) who merely mimics the sayings of the saints and adduces proofs and reasons for their expressions,[67] and so must rely on an external guide (*pīr*) in his blindness. The Shaykh explains that there are three groups of those who aspire to this Knowledge of the "Light of Faith (*nūr al-īmān*)."

The first group are those actually illuminated by this Light, whose vision and conviction in the Prophet is incontrovertible, being based on the sapience and savouring *dhawq* of prophetic consciousness itself. Literally meaning 'taste', *dhawq* in Ibn 'Arabī's view constitutes the aesthetic organ of the Spirit, by means of which the spiritual drunkard relishes realities that are supersensual and directly apprehends by intuitive feeling divine truths that to dry reason appear to be but the ravings of a madman. One cannot reason about spiritual matters; one can only taste them. Just as the ways and means of poetic inspiration are invisible to all but the poet and the seer, to the eyes of reason there is no divinity within rhyme, but only a mathematical harmony to which the thinking head keeps tune, although such a theory to every poet but exhibits the intellectual's own disgusting 'tastelessness'.

The second group are theologians and savants who rely on the "light of their knowledge about Him," yet who do not actually possess any interior faith. Their understanding of God is purely based on rational considerations that are all "foreign, but of true desert / Plays round the head, but come not to the heart."[68] They may or may not, depending on their sincerity, attain to

---

64 *Mathnawī-yi ma'nawī*, ed. R.A. Nicholson, IV: 2189.

65 *Mathnawī-yi ma'nawī*, ed. R.A. Nicholson, IV: 2190.

66 *Mathnawī-yi ma'nawī*, ed. R.A. Nicholson, IV: 2163.

67 *Mathnawī-yi ma'nawī*, ed. R.A. Nicholson, IV: 2167–79.

68 From Pope's 'Essay on Man' (IV: 253-58). All fame is foreign, but of true desert, / Plays round the head, but comes not to the heart: / One self-approving hour whole years out-weighs / Of stupid starers and of loud huzzas; / And more true joy Marcellus exil'd feels, / Than Caesar with a senate at his heels.

the light of faith. Even if verbally they bear witness to the truth of the Prophet's mission, their knowledge is but mnemonic: of the 'head', not the 'heart', lacking all interior illumination and personal realization.

The third group are uneducated savants who know God simply by virtue of the inner purity of their heart and mind. It was of such mystics that Alexander Pope wrote:

> See! the sole bliss which Heav'n could on all bestow;
> Which who but feels can taste, but thinks can know:
> Yet poor with fortune, and with learning blind,
> The bad must miss; the good, untaught, will find;
> Slave to no sect, who takes no private road,
> But looks thro' Nature, up to Nature's God ...[69]

These are unlettered adepts whose enlightenment is their very learning, a state of grace being all they know. And it is to them that these verses on "Faith" by George Herbert (1593–1633) also refer:

> If bliss had lien in art or strength
> None but the wise and strong had gained it.
> Where now by Faith all arms are of a length;
> One size doth all conditions fit.
>
> A peasant may believe as much
> As a great Clerk, and reach the highest stature.
> Thus dost thou make proud knowledge bend and crouch
> While grace fills up the uneven nature.[70]

* * *

[305: 35] According to the intuitive, sapiential 'taste' (*dhawq*)[71] that characterizes our Path, it is not possible to ascertain the veracity of the Prophet

69 Pope, "Essay on Man," IV, 327–32.

70 "Faith," in *George Herbert: The Country Parson, The Temple*, ed. John Wall Jr. (Classics of Western Spirituality Series, London: SPCK 1981), pp. 164–65.

71 On this term, see my *Beyond Faith and Infidelity: The Sufi Poetry and Teachings of Maḥmūd Shabistarī* (London: Curzon Press 1995), pp. 176–78.

(*taṣdīq*) by means of rational arguments adduced from demonstrative evidence (*al-dalāla*). [306] Rather, God must illumine and enlighten the heart through His divine Name "Light" (*al-nūr*). It is only when one's subtle inner being (*bāṭin*) becomes coloured with the hue of that Light that one can ascertain the truth of the Prophet. It is this that is called the 'Light of Faith (*nūr al-īmān*)'.

Others there are who have procured nothing of this Light within themselves, who, although they knowledgeably affirm (the Prophet's) truthfulness by means of demonstrative evidence and proofs, since they do not have that Light that is cast into the heart, they are still in denial (of the Prophet) despite their knowledge. God Almighty said [in regard to such folk]: "in their iniquity and pride they rejected (our signs), although their souls were convinced of their truth."[72]

On the same level, but just beneath them, are those about whom God states: "God let him go astray despite having a knowledge."[73] The "knowledge" referred to here is the light of knowledge *about* Him, not the light of Faith. Therefore, when such a person affirms the veracity of the Prophet and makes his affirmation plainly manifest [i.e. through the formal verbal confession of faith], he relies on his reason because it guided him towards God-the-Truth (*al-Ḥaqq*). This is the case even though he has not obtained even a glimmer of the light of Faith that might enlighten him. Such a person doesn't realize that it was by means of that very light [of Faith], and not by means of the light of his own knowledge, that he has affirmed the Faith [in the Prophet],[74] not the light of knowledge which may also be possessed by persons who have rejected the Prophet even while they are cognizant of the truth of his mission. Yet nonetheless, when such an 'affirmer' relies on his own reason and accordingly comes at last to be counted amongst those who affirm the Prophet's veracity, at this point God reveals (*kashafa Allāh lahu*) to him [the inner meaning of] the light of his Faith and the light of his Knowledge which then becomes all "Light upon Light."[75]

---

72 Qur'ān XXVII:14.

73 Qur'ān XLV:23.

74 The meaning here is that the rationalist believer has forgotten that all knowledge in Islam originates in Faith begotten of interior enlightenment, rather than bequeathed by rational demonstration.

75 Qur'ān XXIV:35.

(Aside from these groups), there is a third type. Such a person possesses nothing of the light of speculative knowledge (*nūr al-'ilm al-naẓarī*), nor does he understand the correct context by which one must substantiate the miracle [of the Prophet]. Nonetheless, despite possessing nothing of the light of speculative knowledge, God casts the light of Faith into his heart, so that he did believe and thus affirmed the veracity of the Prophet, for his conscience is pure, his mind fit and apt, and the temple of his body enlightened. Although alien to rational reflection (*al-fikr*), he hurries to accept and acknowledge (the truth of the Prophet).

EPISTEMOLOGICAL FOUNDATIONS OF SUFI GNOSIS

The following passage (II. 297.33–299.6) from chapter 177 of *Al-Futūḥāt al-Makkīyya* concerning "The Station of Gnosis" addresses the relation of gnosis (*ma'rifa*) to spiritual practice (*'amal*), making it clear that the pursuit of gnosis is not purely a theoretical preoccupation with the abstractions of faith, but involves spiritual practice as well, being realized through active devotion to God and service to people. For Ibn 'Arabī only knowledge combined with spiritual practice is effectual.[76] He also elucidates the difference between those who follow human directions, obeying their own reason (*'aql*), and those who are obedient to divine authority (*taqlīd*), and thus rightly guided. Ibn 'Arabī believes that there is no escape from following authority. Since man by the very nature of things always sees through a glass darkly, it is best to follow the divinely inspired authority of the Qur'ān: it is always safer if one conforms oneself to the testaments of Faith and the prophetic vision.[77]

Since conformism (*taqlīd*) pervades all spheres of life: one either servilely adheres to the dictates of sense-perception, or else follows logical proofs based on intellectual speculation, or is nourished on reasons weak or strong. All these methods of acquiring knowledge are equally susceptible to error. The only escape from the dilemma of sensory and rational

76 See also Chittick, *Sufi Path*, pp. 151–52.

77 Some parts of this selection have been translated by Chittick, *Sufi Path*, pp. 149, 167–69, and in *idem*, *The Self-Disclosure of God: Principles of Ibn al-'Arabī's Cosmology* (Albany: SUNY Press 1998), pp. 8–9. I would like to thank Muhammad Reza Jozi for his careful review of and comments on my translation.

agnosticism is to acquire knowledge directly from God by following the authority of the Apostle (Muḥammad) and Scripture (Qur'ān) of God. In this fashion, one apprehends the truth directly from God. Alluding to the famous *ḥadīth al-nawāfil*: "My servant does not cease drawing near to He by works of supererogative piety ... so that when I love him, I become the ear, eye, foot, hand, and tongue (by which he hears, sees, walks, grasps and talks),"[78] Ibn 'Arabī claims that he followed this practice "until God Himself became our very eyes and ears! Until we comprehended and understood things through God Himself ..."

Ultimately, however, because the Sufi's *imitatio Muhammadi* is exercised through visionary unveiling and contemplative vision (*kashf*), being personally verified, it is certain and incontestable. Conformism to authority of this sort thus produces a clairvoyant intuitive vision in the soul, assuring the mystic that his audition and vision have become graced by and immersed in the hearing and sight of God.

Ibn 'Arabī explains that although God is revealed equally in the macrocosm as in the microcosm, the best revelation is that which is subjectively verified within the heart of the seer, insofar as the "Kingdom of God comes not with observation ... for behold, the Kingdom of God is within you."[79] Since both knowledge derived from the senses as well as the certitudes of reason are susceptible to falsification and error in his opinion, only contemplative visionary unveiling (*kashf*) grants any ultimate certitude. In this, his views are identical to those of Ghazālī.[80]

In the final part of this selection, Ibn 'Arabī returns to what he calls the "customary method" of treating the topic, namely to a discussion of the Islamic version of the Delphic Maxim ("He who knows (*'arafa*) himself knows his Lord"),[81] treating the principle of cosmological antonymy, the

---

78 *Aḥādīth-i Mathnawī*, no. 42.

79 Luke XVII:20–21.

80 See *Al-Ghazālī, Al-Munqiḏ min aḍalāl (Erreur et Délivrance)*, ed. (traduction française avec introduction et notes) Farid Jabre (Beirut: Commission Libanaise Pour La Traduction des Chefs-d'oeuvre 1969), pp. 35–44; also in *Freedom and Fulfillment, Al-Ghazali: Deliverance from Error*, trans. Richard McCarthy (Louisville, KY: Fons Vitae, n.d.), pp. 77–87.

81 On the Greek origin of this *ḥadīth*, see Franz Rosenthal, *Greek Philosophy in the Arab World* (Hampshire: Variorum Reprints 1990), II, pp. 409–10; on its role in Sufi theories of knowledge, see *idem., Knowledge Triumphant*, pp. 137–38. For a good discussion of

famous analogy between macrocosm and microcosm. He then turns to exegesis of the renowned Qur'ānic verse concerning the "horizons" and the "selves,"[82] arguing that our "objective" knowledge of externals (the "horizons" being everything outside us) is ultimately a reflection of our "subjective" knowledge of ourselves. Ibn ʿArabī's doctrine here is by no means original. It was prefigured in a tale about Rābiʿa al-Adawīyya (d. ca. 162–176/788–92), paraphrased in verse as follows by Rūmī in his *Mathnawī-yi maʿnawī*:[83]

Once in a garden, as the Sufis do,
  A Sufi laid his head upon his knee,
And seeking spiritual expansion, delved
  So deep in meditation, he seemed asleep.
A busybody by his lethargic form
  Was bored and cried, "What's all this somnolence?
Look up and see these leafy vines and trees,
  This vernal sward, these signs of God's designs!
Hear God's command to 'contemplate and gaze'[84]
  – So look upon these signs of divine mercy!"

The Sufi said: "You say they're 'signs'? Those 'signs'
  Are in the heart. This is your gluttony!

---

this *ḥadīth*, its variants and sources in early Platonism, neo-Platonism and early Christianity, and various versions of it given by Ibn ʿArabī, see Dom Sylvester Houédard, "Notes on the More Than Human Saying: 'Unless You Know Yourself You Cannot Know God'," *JMAIS* XI (1992): pp. 1–10.

82 Qur'ān XLI:53.

83 Rūmī had adopted the tale from Farīd al-Dīn ʿAṭṭār (d. 618/1221) before him, who had narrated it in prose: "One day in Spring she entered the house and did not come out. Her servant girl said, "Lady! Come outside and contemplate God's effects in creation!" (Paraphrasing the verse: *Fānaẓar ilā athar raḥmat Allāh kayfa yaḥyā al-arḍ baʿd mūtahā* (XXX:49) Rabīʿa replied, "Rather, enter within and see the Maker Himself. I am too preoccupied with beholding the Maker to regard the handiwork." (*Shaghaltanī mashāhadat al-Ṣāniʿ ʿan maṭālaʿat al-maṣnūʿ*). – *Tadhkirat al-awliyā'*, ed. Muḥammad Istiʿlāmī. (3rd edn, Tehran: Zawwār 1365/1986), p. 82.

84 "Gaze upon the signs of God's mercy in creation (and contemplate) how He quickens the earth after her death." – Qur'ān XXX:50.

What's outside merely are the 'signs of the signs.'
This garden and greenery you see
Are in the soul's deepest essence, yet
Outside, like water in a flowing brook
The garden's likeness is reflected there.
It's but a garden's phantom that you see
Cascading by grace of the water there.
They're gardens in the heart and orchards there
All full of fruit. Their images are
Reflected on this water, earth and air."[85]

While the passage translated below tends to lend credence to the doctrine "the primacy of the self," as William Chittick observes,[86] it also is a simple reinstatement of the doctrine of God's effects (*vestigial ... Dei*), the signs (*āyāt*) of God's existence beheld by the visionary's eye throughout all creation, having been placed there by God.[87] At the final stage, the gnostic realizes that the knowledge of God granted by consideration and contemplation of the horizons (*al-naẓar fī'l-afāq*), is identical to what was vouchsafed by contemplation of himself (*al-naẓar fī'l-anfūs*).

* * *

It should be understood that gnosis (*ma'rifat*) is a divine attribute (*na't ilahī*), and amongst the divine Names there is nothing essentially like it in terms of words. Its locus is the level of exclusive divine Unity (*aḥadīyya*)[88] and it does not concern itself with anything but the Divine One (*al-wāḥid*).

85 *The Mathnawí of Jalálu'ddín Rúmí*, ed. R.A. Nicholson (London: E.J.W. Gibb Memorial Trust 1924 –40), IV: 1358–65.

86 William Chittick, *The Self-Disclosure of God: Principles of Ibn al-'Arabī's Cosmology* (Albany: SUNY Press 1998), p. 8. See Prof. Chittick's entire discussion here ("Selves and Horizons"), pp. 6ff.

87 Cf. Annemarie Schimmel, *Deciphering the Signs of God: A Phenomenological Approach to Islam* (Albany: SUNY Press 1994), p. 227.

88 In Ibn 'Arabī's lexicon, the level of 'exclusive divine Unity' (*aḥadīyya*) excludes all kinds of multiplicity, whereas 'inclusive divine Unity' (*waḥidīyya*) embraces all the modes of Being, and *includes* the realities of things. *Aḥadiyyya* has thus been described as "the Supreme Unity unknowable by creatures as such by distinctive cognition, since

For the Sufis (*al-qawm*),[89] gnosis is a practical path, a methodical way (of spiritual practice) (*maḥajja*), and thus gnosis involves every kind of knowledge that may be obtained through spiritual practice (*'amal*), god-fearing piety (*taqwā*),[90] and through faring the (Sufi) path of ethical conduct (*sulūk*),[91] since it is been obtained through visionary unveiling experientially verified and personally realized (*kashf muḥaqqiq*), to which no doubts or misgivings penetrate.[92]

Such gnosis is in contradistinction [298] to the sort of knowledge gained through purely rational considerations or speculative thinking (*al-naẓar al-fikrī*)[93] which is never free from being pried apart by doubts and misgivings and bewilderment, and depreciation of the means of obtaining it.

---

there is nothing outside of it, but knowable by the extinction (*al-fanā'*) of the creature in It, in which case It knows Itself through Itself, derived from the Name: 'the One', *al-Aḥad* which is the name of the absolute transcendence of God, the absolutely indivisible Divine Essence, impersonal and supraontological, and to be distinguished as such from the ontological principle, *al-Waḥdānīyya*." Ibn 'Aṭā'illāh, *Ṣūfī Aphorisms* (*Kitāb al-Ḥikam*), trans. Victor Danner (Leiden: Brill 1973), p. 70.

89 For Ibn 'Arabī, the two terms *qawm* 'a people' and *ṭā'ifah* 'a group' used here more or less identically refer to the Muslim mystical elite or the Sufis. As Martin Lings observes, it was by virtue of the Qur'ān's reference to a spiritual minority who "keep vigil nearly two thirds of the night, or its half or a third. Thou and a group who are with you" (LXXIII:20) that "the Sufis often refer to themselves as 'the group' (al-*ṭā'ifah*), as mentioned in the above verse." – "The Qur'ānic Origins of Sufism," *Sufi* 18 (1993), p. 7.

90 On this term, see Leonard Lewisohn, "Taḳwā" in *EI2*, Supplement.

91 On this term's meaning, see Leonard Lewisohn, "Sulūk," in *EI2* IX, pp. 861–63.

92 This paragraph has also been translated and discussed by Chittick, *Sufi Path*, p. 149.

93 "Consideration (*naẓar*) refers to the specific activity of reason when it employs reflection. It is the investigation of phenomena as well as the thought processes whereby reason reaches conclusions. In this meaning *naẓar* is practically synonymous with *fikr*. However, the latter term designates a specific faculty possessed by reason, while the term *naẓar* is used in a wide variety of other meanings in keeping with its literal sense of 'to look'. Thus it is employed to refer to the gaze of the physical eye, reason, or the heart, that is, to sensory, the rational, and the supra-rational levels. The terms 'reflective consideration', 'reflection', and 'consideration' all refer especially to the endeavours of the rational thinkers, such as the philosophers and the proponents of Kalām." (Chittick, *Sufi Path*, pp. 159–60).

One should realize that although knowledge cannot be properly validated or established to be sound unless one apprehends things in their essences, most everyone who apprehends something knows it through something *extraneous* to the essence of the thing itself. Such a person is but a conformist (*muqallid*), imitatively following the knowledge that extraneous thing gives him about it (rather than intimately knowing the thing itself). And yet, throughout all of existence, no one has any knowledge of things in their essence except for the One (*al-wāḥid*). All knowledge other than that possessed by the Divine One – be it a knowledge of things or of empty nothings – is merely sham conformism. It is a travesty (of that true divine knowledge: i.e. *taqlīd*).

Since it has been confirmed that all other knowledge but God's knowledge is but sham, imitative and second-hand, let us then follow God's suit, and let us adhere to divine precedent, especially in matters relating to knowledge of Him.

But how is it that we profess that knowledge of any matter that beings other than God possess is pure sham and servile conformism?

It is because man cannot know anything except by means of the faculties that God gives him, that is, by his senses and his reason. Therefore, man has no choice but to adhere to and follow the dictates and data provided to him by his senses.[94] Sometimes the data given to him by senses is in error; other times it is sound and accords with the facts on the ground. Hence, man is obliged to follow whatever data his reason provides him, whether this be immediately evident propositions (*ḍarūrat*) or intellectual speculations (*naẓar*). Now, reason (*al-'aql*) also obeys the authority of rational, reflective thinking (*al-fikr*), some of which is sound and quite correct, other of which is weak and corrupt, since reason's knowledge of events and things is but occasional and fortuitous.

Thus, nothing exists but blind belief and servile conformism (*taqlīd*)!

Since the circumstances are as we have said, the intelligent man who wishes to know God should accept and follow that which God has testified about Himself in His scriptures and on the tongues of His apostles. When he wishes to understand things, he should not recognize them by means of knowledge given to him by his faculties [both sensory and rational], but rather exert himself in works of supererogatory devotion until (he reaches

94 Alternate version: than to imitate and believe in the authority of the data with which his senses provide him.

a point that) God becomes his hearing, seeing and other faculties,[95] so that he recognizes everything through God Himself and knows God through God Himself as well. Thus, while there is no way to escape from blind imitation and the slavish following of precedent (*taqlīd*), when you know God *through* God and recognize everything else *through* God, then neither ignorance, doubts, vagueness nor misgivings can interfere with and disturb that knowledge.

And here I have given you an admonition the like of which has never struck your ear!

The intelligent and wise among those who engage in theological speculation (*al-ʿuqalāʾ min ahl al-naẓar*) imagine that they possess knowledge by virtue of what their intellectually based considerations, sense-perception and reason have given them, whereas their station is merely one of conformism (*fī maqām al-taqlīd*) to these faculties. Every faculty that exists is subject to error, and although they themselves understand this, they fall into error by trying to distinguish between what sensory perception, reason and rational reflection can and cannot get wrong and be mistaken about,[96] attempting to arbitrate and discern what the difference between these various types of error are. They don't realize that what they suppose to be error may in fact be true and correct!

This is a malady without any remedy that can never be alleviated and eliminated except by one whose knowing is *through* God, and not through any other way or means. Now, since God Almighty knows everything through His Essence, not by any superadded means thereof, it behoves you to become learned through that which God Himself has taught you, since (in this case) you will be following someone who is knowledgeable and not ignorant, who follows no external authority in knowledge. Whoever imitates and follows aught but God, has followed that which is prone to

95 An allusion to the famous *ḥadīth al-nawāfil:* "My servant does not cease drawing near to He by works of supererogative piety ... so that when I love him, I become the ear, eye, foot, hand, and tongue (by which he hears, sees, walks, grasps and talks)." – Furūzānfar, *Aḥādīth-i Mathnawī*, no. 42.

96 That is to say, they suppose that there to be different *degrees* of error granted by sense perception and those given by reason, and think these various degrees can be discerned, delineated and so separated apart, when, as a matter of fact, both sensory and rational modes of understanding are almost equally fallible and susceptible to error.

error, susceptible to mistakes, and which is correct only by chance and accident.[97]

If someone objects to me in this, saying: "How can you know this? It is entirely possible that you yourself have been mistaken in these classifications,[98] that you yourself follow authority in a conformist manner as well, and are equally prone to the same errors of reason and reflection as those others whom you criticize."

To this I would reply: "Indeed, you're right;" but since we perceive that there is no way of getting beyond conformism and following precedent, we have preferred to follow the authority of what's called the 'Apostle' (*rasūl*) and 'God's Word' (*kalām Allāh*), and to conform ourselves to their authority regarding our knowledge. And that we did until God Himself became our very sight and hearing! Until we comprehended and understood things through God Himself, and gained our understanding of these classifications[99] through God Himself as well!

But the fact that our judgment was sound and that we hit it right in this imitative following of precedent was but an accidental grace of fortune (*bi'l-ittifāq*). This is because, as we stated earlier, whenever reason or one of the faculties hits upon something that is, according to the dictates of its own essence, right and true, that is but fortune and chance. It is not the case that they are mistaken in every circumstance. All we said was that we cannot tell the difference between their right and wrong, or distinguish their veracity from falsehood.

But when the faculties of a person all 'become God'[100] such that he recognizes and understands things through God, then he will discern and understand in what things the faculties are right and in what amiss. And none may deny what we profess here, for it is something that he will encounter within himself.

---

97 This doctrine is elaborated in quite similar terms by Rūmī, *The Mathnawí of Jalálu'ddín Rúmi*, ed. R.A. Nicholson (London: Luzac 1925–1940), IV: 3487–93.

98 That is, perhaps you are mistaken in your elaboration of the above classification concerning the universal fallibility of the faculties of sense perception, reason and reflection.

99 In other words, these classifications, being the outcome of visionary unveiling (*kashf*), not mere rational investigation, have been intuitively verified beyond all doubt.

100 An allusion to the *ḥadīth al-nawāfil* cited in n. 56 supra.

Now that this point has been settled, you must occupy yourself in that which God Almighty has commanded you to do in respect to spiritual practices: in works of obedience, in contemplative vigilance over your heart's thoughts, in contrition and compunction before God, in halting before, and not transgressing beyond, His prescribed limits, in dispassionately exercising detachment through Him while effacing yourself in preference of Him over all, until God Himself 'becomes' your very faculties, until all your affairs are apperceived through the heart's vision (*ʿalā baṣīrat*).

I have counselled you thus insofar as we have seen that God informs us about certain matters concerning Himself – matters which rational demonstrations and sound reflective considerations deny and reject – even though [at the same time] these same reasoning powers also establish proofs that substantiate through demonstrations (the messages brought by) the prophetic reporter and make it a requirement that one have faith in him. So follow the suit and conform to the authority of your Lord – since there is no way to escape from imitation and following authority – but do not blindly follow the authority of your reason in its interpretation (*ta'wīl*). For your reason here concurs with you in accepting the soundness of this report, in confessing that it is from God,[101] so no room for disputation, in which reason could make objections to you, can exist here. Again, do not blindly follow the authority of your reason in matters of hermeneutical interpretation (*ta'wīl*), but rather – render this knowledge back unto God, its Professor![102]

You should then engage yourself in spiritual practices until your standing in this knowledge becomes like that of God Himself. Then you will become a gnostic adept (*ʿārif*). For this intimate knowledge (*maʿrifa*) is what is ultimately besought of all since it is a sound knowledge that fallacy cannot faze or error ambush.[103]

Now that this matter has been settled, we may return to what is the customary method when treating this topic, that which is employed by

---

101 Alternate versions of this sentence: For your reason concurs with you in its acceptance of the soundness of this report, concurring that it is from God / For your reason and yourself are both in concord and concur in accepting the soundness of this report, and professing that it is from God.

102 For a different translation of the last few paragraphs, see Chittick, *Sufi Path*, pp. 167–68.

103 Alternate version of this phrase: which is not fazed when faced by fallacy nor circumscribed by error.

those adept in it – insofar as the method I have informed you of is exotic and unprecedented.

[In this respect, it is worth mentioning that Abū 'Abd Allāh al-Ḥarīth] Muḥāsibī [d. 243/857] remarked that gnosis (*al-ma'rifa*) comprises knowledge of four things: Allāh, the soul (*al-nafs*), the world, and Saṭan.[104] The Prophet of God (God's blessings and peace be upon him) similarly stated that there is no way to obtain intimate knowledge of God (*ma'rifat Allāh*) except through knowledge of one's own soul; thus, His word (the *ḥadīths*): "He who knows himself knows his Lord," and "He who knows Himself best knows his Lord best."[105] So He made you into an evidential demonstration, establishing your self-knowledge – your gnostic insight into your self – as a guide to knowledge of Him. This "evidential demonstration" which *you are*, exists either by way of the fact that He has endowed you, out of His Essence and Attributes, with the same qualities that He gave Himself, while appointing you as His deputy and viceroy (*khalīfa*) on earth,[106] or else, because He made you, in your very being, indigent and poor towards Him; or else by virtue of both of these being combined together by force of necessity.

In the same manner, we see that God, apropos of the sort of divine knowledge known as 'gnosis' (*al-ma'rifa*), declares that, "We will show them Our Signs on the horizons and within themselves, until it is clear to them that it is the Truth."[107] Thus, God has committed us to the "horizons (*al-afāq*)," which comprises everything that is external to us and has also referred us back to our "selves," which comprises everything with and within us. Now, when we become cognizant of both these matters (that is, understand what is both external and internal to us), then we become cognizant of Him (*'arafnāhu*) and it becomes "clear" that "He is the Truth

---

104 Muḥāsibī's fourfold division of knowledge is found in his *Risālat fī'l-mūrāqaba wa inqiṣāmiha* (*Treatise on Meditation and its Circumstances*), a good summary of which is found in Margaret Smith's study of *Al- Muḥāsibī: An Early Mystic of Baghdad* (Lahore: Islamic Book Foundation [repr.] n.d.), p. 53; also cf. R. Arnaldez, "Al-Muḥāsibī," *EI2* VII: 466–67.

105 These two *ḥadīth* were the subject of the previous chapter, dedicated to 'Ayn al-Quḍāt Hamadānī's view of esoteric knowledge. See Furūzānfar's *Aḥādīth-i Mathnawī*, p. 167.

106 An allusion to two verses of the Qur'ān II:30 and XXXVIII:26, where man is described as God's viceroy on earth.

107 Qur'ān XLI:53.

(*al-Ḥaqq*)." Hence, that God's evidential demonstration is more comprehensive and complete (than all other demonstrations and proofs)!

This is because when we initially look into our own selves (lit. 'souls', *nufūs*), we will not understand whether the knowledge that we have been given by speculative consideration of the world 'outside' us – [299] which is, as His dictum asserts, "on the horizons" – endows us with any knowledge of God that is not conferred (equally) by (the speculative consideration of) our own "self" – "soul," or what is within it. Granted this is the case, then when we contemplate our own "self" – "soul," (it can be said) that we should obtain the same knowledge that is gained by gazing upon "the horizons."

In this respect, the Legislator (*al-Shāriʿ*) knew that the soul comprehensively envelops all the spiritual realities of the world,[108] and thus out of the keenness of his aspiration and concern for you, he rallied you to turn back to yourself, just like God said regarding him that "[he is] anxious about, and solicitous of, your welfare."[109] In this way, he wished you to approach this 'evidential demonstration' (within the soul) so you would succeed in illuminating yourself with knowledge of God, and thus find ultimate happiness.

Now, the reason why God mentioned the "horizons" was to caution you regarding what we said (above), lest you suppose that something had been left over (outside) upon the "horizons" that would be capable of conferring a knowledge of God not already offered you by yourself (*nafsika*: your soul). So he committed you to the "horizons" (*al-āfāq*), so that when you did become cognizant of (the existence of) exactly the same 'evidential demonstration' of God provided by them, you would then gaze within your soul and find exactly the same thing there too. Thus (you would understand), that the knowledge of God granted by consideration and contemplation of the horizons (*al-naẓar fī'l-āfāq*), is identical to what was vouchsafed by contemplation of yourself.

108 This passage may be suitably compared with ʿAbd al-Razzāq Lāhījī's view that "the mirror of the rational soul's cosmic universality (*mirāt-i jāmaʿīyyat-i nafs-i nāṭiqa*)," when purged "of the rusty smudges of the contretemps of his natural humours," is able to behold "the forms of the spiritual realities of things." For the full text, see chapter 10 on Lāhījī below.

109 Qur'ān IX:128.

Henceforth, neither doubts may remain nor misgivings penetrate into you. For there is nothing but God, yourself, and what is outside you – and that is the world.[110]

SAVOURING THE TASTE DIVINE[111]

The sixth and last selection from Ibn ʿArabī is on the relation of sapiental taste (*dhawq*) to knowledge of God, Ibn ʿArabī discusses the meaning of gnosis (*maʿrifa*), stressing that it is obtained by means of *dhawq* alone. The gnostic, who is immersed in God and thus reflects the higher ethic of God's own nature, is effectively "beyond truth and error." At this spiritual station, which is that of obliteration (*mahw*) and annihilation of self (*fanā'*), the gnostic's consciousness is alien and estranged even from gnosis itself. Being of self bereft, his is knowledge *de docta ignorantia*, which transcends both knowing and unknowing.

Text

[316.5] God does not choose ignoramuses for friends. If someone apprehends all the subject matter of gnosis (*maʿrifat*) along with its various *differentia*, such a person may be then explicitly called a 'gnostic' (*ʿārif*). Furthermore, if someone gains knowledge of God (*al-ʿilm bi'llāh*), enabling him to discern between what is permissible and what is forbidden and fraudulent, distinguishing between God's knowledge of His divine Essence and God's knowledge of His creation, such a station is characteristic of the 'divine theologians' (*al-ʿulamā' bi'llāh*), but it is not typical of gnostics (*al-ʿārifīn*).

[This is because] Gnosis is both the Destination and the Way (*al-maʿrifa maḥajja wa'l-ṭarīq*), whereas knowledge (*al-ʿilm*) is the direct evidence (*ḥujjat*) thereof. Furthermore, knowledge is a divine attribute, whereas gnosis is a magisterial psychical lordly quality (*naʿt kiyānī nafsī rabbānī*), and it is to gnosis to which the present chapter is devoted.

110 *Al-Futūḥāt al-Makkīyya* II. 299.6.

111 From chapter 177 ("On the Station of Gnosis") of the *Futūḥāt* (II.316.5 – 316.18). A few sentences from this passage are translated by Chittick, *Sufi Path*, p. 149.

Those of our companions amongst God's adepts (*ahl Allāh*) give the name 'gnostics' to God's adepts (i.e. to themselves). They designate as "gnosis (*ma'rifat*)" the knowledge of God that is obtained by way of intuitive experiential heart-savour (*ṭarīq al-dhawq*). In defining this station, they take into account the properties inevitably associated with it and the results achieved from it, the qualities which become manifest within its adepts.

Junayd was once asked about gnosis and the gnostic. He quipped, "The water is dyed by the hue of its glass."[112] The gist of this adage is that the gnostic assumes divine ethics, modelling himself on the moral nature of God, until it appears as if the gnostic *is* Him, while at the same time, he is *not* Him – and yet, he *is* Him!

Amongst the Sufis, the gnostic is one renowned for his imposing presence, dignified demeanour, total lack of attachment, dispassion, come what may. In the beginning, gnosis is established and granted by God, but in the end, it is infinite and endless. The heart of gnosis cannot be affected by the intrusion of either 'truth' or 'untruth'. If concentration upon invocation of God (*dhikr al-Ḥaqq*) so overpowers the gnostic that he is enraptured and transported outside himself, so that he is made absent from himself, still he contemplates only God, paying no regard to anything else. For he is alive through his Lord, not through his heart, such that even if gnosis intrudes upon his heart, the spiritual frame of mind that he enjoys would thereby suffer and be altered to the worse. By this is meant that his mystical state would revert back to God – not that it would vanish and disappear. The condition of the gnostics in this respect is similar to that which God Almighty spoke of, discoursing through the tongue of Bilqīs, the Queen of Sheba: "Verily, when kings enter a city they lay it waste, abasing the honour of its inhabitants, ruining their reputation. This is how they will behave."[113] However, according to us, it is not like this at all, in the sense that the notables among them (the gnostics) are glorified *through God*, after having been glorified through *what's other than God*, although [in reality] their loss of honour was [actually] by means of God, not by what's other than God).

Amongst the Sufis, there is in fact no (such thing as a) 'mystical state' (*ḥāl*). The gnostic (*al-'ārif*) undergoes effacement of his attributes (*maḥw*

112 A famous saying of Junayd (d. 297/910) frequently quoted by Ibn 'Arabī. See Chittick, *Sufi Path*, pp. 149, 229.

113 Qur'ān XXVII:34.

rusūm),[114] dissolution of personal identity (*fanā' huwīyya*), and experiences absence from all traces of selfhood (*ghaybat atharahu*). This is because gnosis is not perfectly complete so long as the devotee experiences (any sense of having self-) independence through God (*istighnā' bi'llāh*). For the gnostic is dumbstruck and mute; sundered (from selfhood); he is incoherent, subdued, rendered powerless and incapable of uttering any praise of the One that he knows. He feels fearful, vexed and annoyed while still subsisting in this bodily frame. [316.18]

---

114 In his *Kitāb Iṣṭilāḥāt al-ṣūfīyya*, under the rubric of "effacement of the heart's adepts" (*maḥw arbāb sarā'ir*), 'Abd al-Razzāq Kāshānī describes this process as follows: "It is the removal of the veil of theoretical knowledge and all its afflictions, and countering these with the affirmation of constant communion. This is achieved by eliminating the attributes of the seeker and characteristic habits of his nature and behaviour, and irradiating him with the attributes of the Truth and its nature and behaviour. As it has been said [in the Sacred Tradition]: 'I become his hearing, by which he heard, and his seeing, by which he saw." al-Qāshānī, *A Glossary of Sufi Terms*, trans. Nabil Safwat (London: Octagon Press 1991), no. 187, p. 41 (with minor changes). For a lengthy exposition by various Sufi authors on the doctrine of *Maḥw*, see Javad Nurbakhsh, *Sufi Symbolism* (London: KNP 1997), vol. XII, pp. 85–100.

VII

THE TYPOLOGY OF KNOWLEDGE IN SUFISM

Selections from ʿIzz al-Dīn Maḥmūd Kāshānī's (d. 735/1334) *Miṣbāḥ al-hidāya wa miftāḥ al-kifāya*

ʿIzz al-Dīn Maḥmūd Kāshānī's (d. 735/1334) *The Lamp of Guidance and the Key of Sufficient Knowledge* (*Miṣbāḥ al-hidāya wa miftāḥ al-kifāya*)[1] is justly celebrated as one of the foremost doctrinal treatises in the Persian Sufi tradition. As a Persian manual of Sufism, the *Miṣbāḥ al-hidāya* is comparable in its importance to the *Kashf al-maḥjūb* by ʿAlī ibn ʿUthmān Hujwīrī (d. 463/1071) and the *Mirṣād al-ʿibād* of Najm al-Dīn Rāzī (d. 654/1256). Having said that, it is a far more impersonal and academic work that either of these two texts.[2] In respect to its literary style, although the *Miṣbāḥ al-hidāya* is overly Arabized and often replete with turgid Arabic terminology,[3] one can also find lovely passages composed of rhymed Arabic

1 *Miṣbāḥ al-hidāya wa miftāḥ al-kifāya*, ed. Jalāl al-Dīn Humāʾī (Tehran: Intishārāt-i Kitābkhāna-yi Sanāʾī, 2nd edn, n.d.).

2 One commentator on the *Miṣbāḥ al-hidāya* thus complained: "It would seem that the author intended for his readers, who were, in the first instance, Sufi novices, to read the book so as to discover answers to their spiritual questions therein. However, the literary style of the *Miṣbāḥ al-hidāya* is far from the common recognized literary style of other Sufi prose works. We don't find in the book the normal clarity of language wherein an author's personal mystical states and spiritual revelations are revealed – of that there is no sign. In the fullest sense, the work is an academic text written to expound and explain the principles and terminology of the Sufis." – ʿĀbidī, "Miṣbāḥ al-hidāya," p. 46.

3 As Dhabīḥu'llāh Ṣafā (*Tārīkh-i adabiyāt-i Īrān* [Tehran: Intishārāt-i Firdaws 1373 A.Hsh./1994, 13th edn], vol. III, Part 2, p. 1265) complains: "although the author professes he wrote the book for people who did not know Arabic, the work is nonetheless excessively full of Arabic phraseology and constructions, with long sentences in Arabic, along with Arabic verse." See also ʿĀbidī, "Miṣbāḥ al-hidāya," p. 47.

and Persian prose poetry (*nathr-i musajja'*).[4] In certain chapters, its composition has a simple, fluent style reminiscent of Seljuk Persian writing.[5]

Although Kāshānī's *Miṣbāḥ al-hidāya* is often considered to be merely a Persian translation of the *'Awārif al-ma'ārif*, the classic Arabic work on Sufism by Shihāb al-Dīn Abū Ḥafṣ 'Umar Suhrawardī (d. 632/1234) – perhaps the most celebrated manual of Sufi discipline, doctrine and practice ever composed[6] – Kāshānī clarifies that this is not really the case, asserting in his introduction that he had received a calling from the Invisible World to compose an independent work based on the words of the great masters while incorporating his own inspirations and spiritual conquests (*futūḥāt*), "such that most of the roots and branches of the *'Awārif al-ma'ārif* would be included."[7]

The most Sufi popular works during the age that 'Izz al-Dīn Kāshānī flourished – late thirteenth and early fourteenth centuries – were Suhrawardī's *'Awārif al-ma'ārif* and the erotic *qaṣā'id* of 'Umar ibn Fāriḍ of Egypt (d. 633/1235), the supreme Arab Sufi poet.[8] At the same time, the writings of the *Magister Maximus* (Shaykh al-Akbar) Ibn 'Arabī (d. 638/1240) were everywhere being taught in Sufi circles. While the influence of Suhrawardī's *'Awārif* and Ibn Fāriḍ's poetry are quite visible in Kāshānī's

4 Nīkū'ī, "'Izz al-Dīn Kāshānī," p. 622, with reference to Jalāl al-Dīn Humā'ī's introduction to the *Miṣbāḥ al-hidāya wa miftāḥ al-kifāya*, pp. 25–48; see also *Miṣbāḥ al-hidāya wa miftāḥ al-kifāya*, ed. 'Iffāt Karbāsī and Muḥammad Riḍā Barzigar-Khāliqī (Tehran: Intishārāt-i Zavvār 1385 A.Hsh./2006), introduction, p. xii.

5 It should not be forgotten that its heavily Arabized diction was typical of other works of a similar style such as the *Tārīkh-i jahāngushā-yi Juwaynī* and the *Tārīkh-i Waṣṣāf*, which were composed during the same day and age. – Maḥmūd 'Ābidī, "Miṣbāḥ al-hidāya," *Dānishnāma-yi zabān va adab-i fārsī*, ed. Ismā'īl Sa'ādat (Tehran: Farhangistān-i zabān va adab-i fārsī 1391 A.Hsh./2012), vol. IV, p. 47.

6 Schimmel (*Mystical Dimensions*, p. 245) refers to it as "one of the standard works taught in Indian *madrasas* in courses on Sufism."

7 *Miṣbāḥ al-hidāya*, pp. 7–8. Referring to the dissimilarity of the two works, William Chittick points out: "Comparison of the tables of contents of *'Awāref* and *Meṣbāḥ* is enough to show that the two works bear little resemblance in structure, while those passages which are indeed based upon the *'Awāref* (often indicated by reference to 'Shaykh-al-eslām') have usually been expanded and/or rewritten." – William Chittick, "*'Awāref al-Ma'āref*," *Encyclopædia Iranica* III, p. 115.

8 Cf. to the *Miṣbāḥ al-hidāya*, Humā'ī's introduction, pp. 45–46.

Miṣbāḥ al-hidāya, no sign of any interest in the Shaykh al-Akbar's doctrines, terminology or works appear in the work.

About the life and times of 'Izz al-Dīn Kāshānī, we have very little information.[9] No date of his birth has been recorded in any historical source.[10] We do know, however, that he was born in Naṭanz,[11] and most all scholars concur however that he died in 735/1334. He was evidently well versed in all the normal sciences of the day, and particularly renowned for his expertise in Arabic and Persian literature, Philosophy, Sufism, Scholastic Theology (*kalām*), and *Ḥādīth*.[12] He belonged to the Suhrawardī Sufi Order, being a disciple of two masters of this order: Nūr al-Dīn 'Abd al-Ṣamad Iṣfahānī (d. 699/1299) and Ẓahīr al-Dīn 'Abd al-Raḥmān ibn Shaykh Najīb al-Dīn 'Alī Buzghush Shīrāzī (d. 716/1316).[13] In turn, both of these masters were disciples of Shaykh Najīb al-Dīn 'Alī Buzghush Shīrāzī (d. 678/1279), who in turn was a disciple of Shihāb al-Dīn Abū Ḥafṣ 'Umar Suhrawardī (d. 632/1234), the founder-progenitor of the Suhrawardī Order.[14] Both 'Izz al-Dīn and 'Abd al-Razzāq Kāshānī (d. 730/1329), who wrote the famous commentary on Anṣārī's *Manāzil al-sā'irīn* and composed the celebrated *Treatise on Sufi Terminology* (*Risālat Iṣṭilāḥāt al-ṣūfīyya*), were fellow disciples of Nūr al-Dīn 'Abd al-Ṣamad Iṣfahānī and Ẓahīr al-Dīn 'Abd al-Raḥmān ibn Shaykh Najīb al-Dīn 'Alī Buzghush Shīrāzī.[15]

In juridical affiliation (*fiqh*) Kāshānī followed the Sunni Shāfi'ī school of Jurisprudence, and in Apologetic Theology (*Kalām*) adhered to the Ashā'rite School. In a Sufi spirit, however, he professed his own original

9 Māšā-Allāh Ajūdānī, "'Ezz-al-Dīn Kāšānī," *EIr* IX, p. 132.

10 'Alī Riḍā Nīkū'ī, "'Izz al-Dīn Kāshānī," *Dānishnāma-yi zabān va adab-i fārsī*, ed. Ismā'īl Sa'ādat (Tehran: Farhangistān-i zabān va adab-i fārsī 1391 A.Hsh./2012), vol. IV, pp. 621–22.

11 A town located in central Iran, north of Iṣfahān, today with a population of about 13,000 souls.

12 Nīkū'ī, "'Izz al-Dīn Kāshānī," p. 621.

13 J.S. Trimingham, *The Sufi Orders in Islam* (Oxford: Oxford University Press 1971), p. 36; Erik Ohlander, *Sufism in an Age of Transition: 'Umar al-Suhrawardī and the Rise of the Islamic Mystical Brotherhoods* (Leiden: Brill 2008), p. 316.

14 Nīkū'ī, "'Izz al-Dīn Kāshānī," p. 621; *Miṣbāḥ al-hidāya wa miftāḥ al-kifāya*, ed. 'Iffāt Karbāsī and Muḥammad Riḍā Barzigar-Khāliqī (Tehran: Intishārāt-i Zavvār 1385 A.Hsh./2006), p. vii.

15 *Miṣbāḥ al-hidāya*, ed. Karbāsī and Barzigar-Khāliqī, introduction, p. vii.

interpretations of many doctrines in both these sciences, rejecting many of the hardline dogmatic positions and fundamentalist interpretations of both schools.[16] Nonetheless, as can be seen from the selections translated below, 'Izz al-Dīn Kāshānī is very much a Sharī'a-centric Sufi, emphasizing the need for strict adherence to regular devotional practices, invocations, supplications, and other acts of worship. In this respect, his writings precisely echo those of Suhrawardī, to whose Order he adhered.[17] The following passage reveals his nomocentric spirit tempered by the universalistic gentility of his Sufi ethics:

> Since the Sufi possesses certitude (*yaqīn*), he witnesses all phenomena as coming from God Almighty by way of the light of divine Unity. He is content no matter what happens, enjoying immunity from the effects of anger within himself; all depression and sorrow, perfidy and guile being removed far away from him ... And how could there be any place for perfidy and guile within the Sufi's heart, when the ground of all these is love of the world, and that is banished from him? The only time anger ever manifests itself within him is when he sees aspersions cast upon holy and sacred things ... Hence, the words and deeds of the Sufi are all weighed upon the scales of the Canon Law of Islam (*mīzān-i shar'*) so you will never find any abusive or lewd words issuing from his mouth ...[18]

In Persian Sufi literature, Kāshānī's *Light of Guidance* generated quite a legacy. The Persian Sufi poet 'Imād al-Dīn Faqīh Kirmānī (773/1364) set in verse (of 2770 couplets) its key themes in ten chapters. Named the "Epistle on the Sufi Path" (*Ṭarīqat-nāma*), each chapter of 'Imād al-Dīn's *mathnawī* poem is also subdivided like Kāshānī's work into ten parts.[19] The *Miṣbāḥ*

16 Nīkū'ī, "'Izz al-Dīn Kāshānī," p. 622, with reference to Jalāl al-Dīn Humā'ī's introduction to the *Miṣbāḥ al-hidāya wa miftāḥ al-kifāya*, pp. 25–48; *Miṣbāḥ al-hidāya*, ed. Karbāsī and Barzigar-Khāliqī, introduction, p. ix.

17 This is particularly visible in the various subchapters on ritual prayer, hours of devotion, supplications to be made during the day and night, & etc. in the Eighth Gateway (*Bāb*).

18 *Miṣbāḥ al-hidāya*, ed. Humā'ī, pp. 355–56. See also Humā'ī's introduction, pp. 46–47.

19 *Ṭarīqat-nāma*, ed. Rukn al-Dīn Humāyūn-Farrakh (Tehran: Intishārāt-i Asāṭīr 1374 A.Hsh./1995). 'Imād al-Dīn's work was not simply a verse-paraphrase of Kāshānī's Sufi

al-hidāya was later used by a number of well-known Sufis of the Naqshbandī Sufi Order, such as Muḥammad Pārsā (d. 822/1419)[20] and Jāmī, who copied large swathes from it into his *Nafaḥāt al-uns*.[21] Today in Iran and Afghanistan, the *Light of Guidance* is one of three texts that function as 'required reading' among certain Sufi Orders, the other two being Lāhījī's commentary on the *Garden of Mystery* (*Gulshan-i rāz*) of Maḥmūd Shabistarī and the *Mathnawī* of Rūmī.

Like the chapter by 'Ayn al-Quḍāt Hamadānī translated above, much of Kāshānī's exposition is devoted to the idea that the Prophet is the origin of all exoteric and esoteric knowledge in Islam. Other key subjects covered in the selected passages from Kāshānī's *Miṣbāḥ al-hidāya* include:

- The difference between Exoteric and Esoteric Knowledge & Scholarship, and between Guiding Reason (*'aql-i hidāyat*) and Practical Reason (*'aql-i ma'āsh*)
- The difference between the divine scholar (*'ālim-i rabbānī*), the savant of the Life hereafter (*'ālim-i ukhravī*), and the worldly scholar (*'ālim-i dunyavī*)
- The Prophet as the Origin of all Exoteric and Esoteric Knowledge in Islam.
- The difference between knowledge gained through instruction (*'ilm-i dirāsat*) and knowledge conveyed by divine bequest (*'ilm-i varāthat*)
- The two kinds of birth (*vilādat*): the formal-physical (*ṣūratī*) and spiritual (*ma'navī*) birth
- The relation between the (exoteric) Islamic sciences (*'ulūm-i islāmī*) and the (esoteric) sciences of faith (*'ulūm-i īmānī*)
- The three degrees of certitude (*yaqīn*): theoretical knowledge of certitude (*'ilm al-yaqīn*), ocular certitude (*'ayn al-yaqīn*), and the reality of certitude (*ḥaqq al-yaqīn*)

---

manual, but also drew on the *'Awārif al-ma'ārif* of Suhrawardī and the *Kitāb al-Ta'arruf* of Abū Bakr Kalābādhī al-Bukhārī. See *Ṭarīqat-nāma*, Humāyūn-Farrakh's introduction, pp. xx–xxiii.

20 Pārsā cited it in his *Faṣl al-khiṭāb*; see 'Ābidī, "Miṣbāḥ al-hidāya." p. 47.

21 See *Miṣbāḥ al-hidāya*, Humā'ī's introduction, p. xxxiii. Also see 'Abd al-Raḥmān Jāmī, *Nafaḥāt al-uns min ḥaḍarāt al-quds*, ed. Maḥmūd 'Ābidī (Tehran: Intishārāt-i Iṭalā'āt 1370 A.Hsh/1991), p. 3, where lines 7–8 (as mentioned in the *Ta'līqāt*, p. 640) are taken by Jāmī from the *Miṣbāḥ al-hidāya* (ed. Humā'ī), p. 426.

- The relation between the light of faith (*nūr-i īmān*) and the light of certitude (*nūr-i yaqīn*). On Esoteric or Divinely infused Knowledge (*'ilm-i ladunnī*)
- On Esoteric or Divinely infused Knowledge (*'ilm-i ladunnī*).[22]

KĀSHĀNĪ'S *MIṢBĀḤ AL-HIDĀYA*

The Difference Between Exoteric and Esoteric Knowledge

By knowledge (*'ilm*) is meant a light derived from the Niche of Prophecy (*mishkāt-i nubuwwat*) that shines within the heart of the faithful devotee, by means of which he finds the way to God, or to a godly deed or to a divine precept. Such knowledge is the distinguishing characteristic of man (*waṣf-i khāṣṣ-i insān*) and man's powers of sensory and intellectual apprehension are divorced from, and excluded access to, this knowledge.

Now, the difference between Reason (*'aql*) and such knowledge is that Reason is a light innate within the soul (*nūrī'st fiṭrī*) by means of which virtue and vice, good and evil are distinguished. Whereas Reason is shared in common betwixt the Muslim faithful (*mu'min*) and infidels (*kāfir*) alike, knowledge pertains exclusively to faithful Muslim believers. The 'Reason' shared in common amongst believers and unbelievers only discerns between probity and improbity in affairs of this world, and as such, may be possessed by both the faithful and the infidel alike, but the Reason which can discern between probity and improbity in the affairs of the Hereafter is peculiar to Muslim believers. There exists an intrinsic connection between it and 'knowledge'. The eyesight of this Reason is illuminated with the Light of Guidance (*nūr-i hidāyat*) and dyed with the eye-shadow (*kuhl*) of the Canon Law (*sharī'at*).

Although Reason is a single entity in essence, it has two sides. One side faces the Creator, being designated at the Guiding Reason (*'aql-i hidāyat*). This is particular to the Muslim believers. The other side faces creation, is communal in nature, and is called Practical Reason (*'aql-i ma'āsh*). Adepts in faith (*ahl-i īmān*), seekers of God and those in pursuit of Truth (*Ḥaqq*) and the life hereafter always keep their Practical Reason subservient to their

22 Translations from selected passages on pp. 56–62, 65–67, 75–79, 80–82, 90, 92–94, 98, 101–3 have been given here.

Guiding Reason. Whenever Practical Reason is in agreement and accord with Guiding Reason, they consider it reliable, and act according to its dictates, but whenever Practical Reason stands in opposition to the dictates of Guiding Reason, they discredit and disregard it. It is for this reason that worldly folk impute feeble-mindedness to them and accuse them of want of intellect, not knowing that beyond their ordinary reason, they possess another 'Reason': a 'higher intelligence'.

Now, knowledge is of three types. First comes the knowledge of divine Unity (*'ilm-i tawḥīd*), as is indicated by the verse: "So know that there is no deity save God."[23] The second is the knowledge of the works of God, as respecting annihilation and creation, proximity and distance, death-wielding and life-giving, resurrection and renewal, rewards and punishments, and other matters. The third is the knowledge of the precepts of the Canon Law of Islam, with all its various prescriptions and prohibitions.

And each of these three types of knowledge has its own type of distinct seeker or wayfarer (*sālik*) who pursues it. The wayfarer on the first path is called a divine scholar (*'ālim-i rabbānī*), within whose knowledge is contained the last (second and third) two types of knowledge, but not vice-versa. The wayfarer on the second course is called a savant of the Life hereafter (*'ālim-i ukhrawī*), within whose knowledge is contained some of the knowledge of the Canon Law and its obligations, but not the other way round. The wayfarer pursuing the third course is called a worldly scholar (*'ālim-i dunyawī*). Such a scholar knows nothing of the former two types of knowledge: "they know only the outward appearance of the life of the world, and are unaware of the hereafter."[24] Of course, if such scholars had any awareness of the hereafter, they would put what they know into practice, for negligence in action denotes weakness of faith. If they had faith in God and the hereafter in their hearts, they would have not neglected to perform any good deed.

Although the divine scholars possess certitude concerning the Unity of God Almighty and have faith in the Hereafter and its divine affairs, they are also obedient and submissive to the religious mandates of Islam. They are those who excel and are foremost in the virtues of the spiritual life

---

23 Qur'ān XLVII:19.

24 Qur'ān XXX:7.

(*al-sābiqūn*).[25] Although the Sufis (*ahl-i taṣawwuf*) and the savants of the Life hereafter have faith in the circumstances of the next life, they also possess a sufficient amount of learning in the other Islamic sciences, which they put into practice as well. They are the righteous (*abrār*), the "companions of right hand."[26] Yet the worldly scholars know only the exoteric dimension of the Islamic sciences, so their knowledge, being acquired by mere rote-learning (*taʿallum*), bestows no benefit upon them.

... Just as there is no one superior to the divine scholars and the savants of the Life hereafter, so none are worse-off than the worldly scholars, as the *ḥadīth* attests: "Indeed the best of the righteous are the virtuous scholars and the worst of villains are the wicked scholars." The reason for this is that there is nothing better than knowledge if pursued for the sake of God, but nothing more harmful than it when pursued for worldly aims and gains. The more benefit there is in something, the more harm exists within it as well.[27]

The Benefits of Esoteric Knowledge to the Heart

Whenever the temperament of the heart becomes corrupted by love of, and inclination towards, the world, so that the various parts of one's being are surfeited by negative moral characteristics (*akhlāq-i radīyya*), knowledge only results in an increase of the disease of passion (*maraḍ-i hawā*). One's natural humours become subject to and overwhelmed by moral infirmities such as pride, conceit, jealousy, envy, and other vices, and these then cast one down into perdition. Behold this grand sham – whereby an act meant to lead one to salvation becomes instead a cause of perdition! See how the same scholar, by means of whom those who have fallen into a pit of passion

25 Referred to in the Qur'ān, LVI:10, and elsewhere, meaning those who go first and outstrip others to win a race. On this term, see S.H. Nasr, et al. (eds.), *The Study Quran* (New York: HarperOne 2015), p. 1321, n. 10, commenting on Qur'ān LVI:10. See also John Penrice, *A Dictionary and Glossary of the Kor-ân* (London: Curzon Press 1873; repr. 1979), p. 66.

26 Referred to in the Qur'ān, LVI:8 (*aṣḥāb al-maymana*), where the term is associated with "righteousness and blessedness." – *The Study Quran*, p. 1320, n. 8, commenting on Qur'ān LVI:8.

27 Kāshānī, *Miṣbāḥ al-hidāya*, ed. Humā'ī, pp. 56–58.

could have been rescued from the hell-fire of human nature, becomes himself bound hand and foot by the shackles of passion!

> If a morsel of food sticks in the throat,
> a sip of water suffices as remedy;
> But what's to be done
> with one who chokes on water?

One sign of truly beneficial knowledge is that it increases one's piety and humility and it amplifies the sense of 'nothingness' (*nīstī*) in one's soul, so that the flame of ardent longing and seeking for God burns even brighter. The proof of this is found in a legal edict and the text of the prophetic tradition which states:

> Whoso seeks knowledge for the sake of God will not obtain from it success in anything but that which increases his sense of lowliness of soul, humility towards people, fear of God, and spiritual struggle in religion. Such a one benefits from knowledge, so let him pursue it. But whoso pursues knowledge for the sake of the world, seeking to obtain thereby a high degree among men or political rank among rulers, will not obtain from it any success except in that which increases pride of soul, arrogance towards people, delusion vis-à-vis God, and further torment in the world. Such a one does not benefit from knowledge, so let him desist and refrain from pursuing it, for on the Day of Judgement that knowledge will become an argument that is used against his own soul and a cause of woe and misery to him.[28]

Now, knowledge is of benefit and delight only for one who focuses on (strengthening) his spiritual resolve (*'azā'im*), rather than following the permitted dispensations permitted (*rukhṣa*).[29] ... Beneficial knowledge is

28 I have not been able to trace the source of this tradition. Neither Karbāsī/Barzigar-Khāliqī nor Humā'ī in their editions of the *Miṣbāḥ al-hidāya* provide a reference to any source.

29 For a good study of *rukhṣa* in Sufism, see I.R. Netton, "'The Breath of Felicity': *Adab, Aḥwāl, Maqāmāt* and Abū Najīb Suhrawardī," in Leonard Lewisohn (ed.), *The Heritage of Sufism*, vol. 1: *Classical Persian Sufism from its Origins to Rumi (700–1300)* (Oxford: Oneworld 1999), pp. 457–82.

that which succours the life of the heart so much so that its disassociation from the heart becomes a cause of the heart's death. Once Fatḥ Mawṣilī (d. 220/835)[30] posed this question to a gathering,

"Is it not the case with men that when one withholds food and drink from them, they die?"

"Yes," they replied.

"Well, it's the same with the heart," he commented, "if one deprives it of wisdom (*al-ḥikmat*) and knowledge (*al-'ilm*) for three days, it dies as well."

And the Commander of the Faithful 'Alī – peace be upon him – pronounced:

"The scholars (*al-'ulamā'*) are the lamplights of their age, each scholar being the lamp of his age from whom his contemporaries receive enlightenment."[31]

From these statements it is evident that the presence of divinely learned scholars (*'ulamā-yi rabbānī*) is the greatest of God's blessings, and their absence is a divine punishment, being the cause of the darkness of infidelity and error (*ẓulmat-i kufr u ḍalālat*).

Now the source of knowledge (*'ilm*) is the heart, and its manifestation therein depends on carefully observing the correct spiritual comportment vis-à-vis God Almighty.[32]

Prophetology and Epistemology: The Prophet Muḥammad as Origin of Exoteric and Esoteric Knowledge in Islam

Know that the origin (*maṣdar*) and source (*mansha'*) of all the sciences (*'ulūm*) is the Divine Presence. Now, the first source-spring from which the pre-eternal divine knowledge showered its grace was the pure heart of Muḥammad, whose pure prophetic soul, by means of a divine purification and purgation, had been purged of the murky blemishes of passional desire

30 Abū Naṣr ibn Sa'īd Fatḥ al-Mawṣilī (d. 220/835) was a well-known early Sufi. See T.J. Winter's translation of the *Iḥyā*'s Books XXII and XXIII: *Al-Ghazālī: On Disciplining the Soul* (*Kitāb Riyāḍat al-nafs*) *& On Breaking the Two Desires* (*Kitāb Kasr al-shahwatayn*) (Cambridge: Islamic Texts Society 1995), p. 215.

31 Humā'ī says that this *ḥadīth* is cited in the first *juzw* of Ghazālī's *Iḥyā' al-'ulūm*, where it is preceded by the phrase: "Some of them say" (*qawl ba'ḍahum ...*).

32 Kāshānī, *Miṣbāḥ al-hidāya*, ed. Humā'ī, pp. 58–60.

and the infirmities of nature ... And from the enlightened heart and pure soul of the Prophet flowed all the grace of the sciences (*'ulūm*), mystical states (*aḥwāl*), and all the ethics (*akhlāq*) and [performance of] meritorious deeds (*a'māl*) into the hearts and souls of the rest of the Muslim community (*ummat*).

However, the conduits and *wadis* of hearts and souls vary in their receptive capacity to apprehend the grace of his revelation. Some could only be receptive to practical works (*a'māl*). Such were the devotees (*'ubbād*). Some could only be receptive to ethical instruction (*akhlāq*) and practical works. Such were the ascetics (*zuhhād*). Some were receptive to practical works, morality and mystical states (*aḥwāl*) all together. Such were the Sufis, who through perfect obedience to the Prophet – peace and blessings be upon him – achieved the supreme aptitude of spirit (*isti'dād-i tamām*).

Hence, it is evident that the existence of the Lord of the Universe (Muḥammad) – may supreme blessings be upon him – is the original source (*ma'khadh*) of all the sciences, that the derivation of the lights of the both the exoteric and esoteric sciences (*'ulūm-i ẓāhira va bāṭina*) is all from the niche of the perfect words and the lamps of his exemplary works (*a'māl*), ethics (*akhlāq*) and mystical states (*aḥwāl*). Every scintillation of light not derived from the Lamp of his Prophethood (*nubuwwat*) cannot in reality be called 'knowledge' (*'ilm*), for the sciences (*'ulūm*) of all the learned scholars (*'ulamā'*) are but a drop of water derived from the grace of his knowledge.

Each person according to the measure of his own capacity receives benefit from him. "He sends down water from the heavens, so the *wadis* flow each according to their measure."[33] Whereas the exoteric scholars (*'ulamā'-yi ẓāhir*) receive a benefit from the apparent literal sense (*ẓāhir*) of his words, the esoteric scholars (*'ulamā'-yi bāṭin*) receive a benefit from their interior spiritual sense (*bāṭin*). This is because each word of the Qur'ān and prophetic traditions (*ḥadīth-i nabawi*) possesses both an exoteric and esoteric dimension, the former being the lot of the exoteric scholars and the latter the portion of the esoteric scholars.[34]

---

33 Qur'ān XIII:17.

34 Kāshānī, *Miṣbāḥ al-hidāya*, ed. Humā'ī, pp. 60–62.

Faith and Works: The Relation of Pedagogic Knowledge to Prophetic Lore

Knowledge gained through instruction (*'ilm-i dirāsat*) is the prolegomenon to works (*'amal*), whilst knowledge conveyed by divine bequest (*'ilm-i varāthat*)[35] is the fruit of those works. Knowledge (*'ilm*) without works (*'amal*) is fruitless, sterile and unproductive, while works without knowledge are faulty and defective.[36] The marriage of knowledge and works, which results in the knowledge conveyed by divine bequest, is the fruit of soundness of faith (*īmān*).

Knowledge without works indicates a weakness in faith, for laxity in works of piety arises from deficiency in faith. By 'works' here are meant austerity (*zuhd*) and god-fearing piety (*taqwā*). By means of the burnishing tool of austerity and god-fearing piety, the devotee must polish clean his inner self (*ẓāhir va bāṭin-i Khwud*), expurgating from his character all hue and taint of passional desire and material nature (*tab'*), so that the form of the spiritual realities of faith (*ḥaqā'iq-i īmān*) may radiate forth from within him.

When God Almighty declares: "And fear God. God is teaching you ...,"[37] He first ordained pious God-fearing piety (*taqwā*). Only afterwards was added to this the particulars of instruction (*ta'līm*), thus indicating that 'knowledge conveyed by divine bequest' cannot be obtained except through the avant-propos of knowledge gained through instruction. This knowledge cannot be conveyed purely by means of the practice of external works: it will only be obtained when combined with 'interior works' (*'amal-i bāṭin*), that is, when graced by the *reality* of austerity and god-fearing piety.[38]

---

35 Literally meaning divinely bequeathed knowledge gained by prophetic inheritance.

36 The Karbāsī/Barzigar-Khāliqī edition's text here reads *saqīm*, which I have followed, rather than *safīm*, which Humā'ī's text cites, and which is obviously a typographical error.

37 Qur'ān II:282.

38 Cf. John Bunyan: "This sign should have been first, but first or last it is also false; knowledge, great knowledge may be obtained in the mysteries of the Gospel, and yet no work of grace in the soul. Yea, if a man have all knowledge, he may yet be nothing, and so consequently be no child of God. When Christ said, 'Do you know all these things?' And the disciples answered, 'Yes', he added, 'Blessed are ye if ye do them.' He doth not lay the blessing in the knowing of them, but in the doing of them. For there is knowledge

Scholars who are "inheritors of the prophets"[39] have received knowledge of the realities of faith (*'ilm-i ḥaqā'iq-i īmān*) by divine bequest through rectifying their 'spiritual connection' (*nisbat-i ma'nawī*) which is a cause of their (reception of the) spiritual legacy (*mīrāth-i ma'nawī*). Insofar as the prophets act as 'spiritual fathers' and the divine scholars (*'ulamā'-yi rabbānī*) behave as their spiritual sons and descendants, this 'spiritual connection' has its own particular paternity and filiation.

There are two kinds of birth (*wilādat*): a formal-physical (*ṣūratī*) and a spiritual (*ma'nawī*) birth. Formal-physical birth involves the emergence of the embryo of the human spirit from the placenta of the world of the invisible (*'ālam-i ghayb*) into the open expanse of the present visible world (*'ālam-i shahādat*) through (intercourse with the mother by) the physical father. For this birth, a physical connection of kinship (*nasab-i ṣūratī*) is required, from which the formal bequest of material assets and properties ensues.

But the spiritual birth is contrary to this. It involves the emergence of the embryo of the spirits of believers (*arwāḥ-i mu'minān*) from the placenta of this present visible world (*'ālam-i shahādat*) into the wide-open spaces of the supernatural world (*'ālam-i ghayb*) through mediation of the spiritual

---

that is not attended with doing: he that knoweth his master's will and doth it not. A man may know like an angel and yet be no Christian ... Not that the heart can be good without knowledge; for without that the heart is naught: there is therefore knowledge, and knowledge. Knowledge that resteth in the bare speculation of things, and knowledge that is accompanied by with the grace of faith and love, which puts a man upon doing the will of God from the heart: the first of these will serve the talker, but without the other the true Christian is not content." *The Pilgrim's Progress*, ed. R. Sharrock (London: Penguin Books 1985 rpt.), pp. 129–30. In this context, W.C. Chittick points out that "In English, 'faith' is normally understood as volitional rather than cognitive. People think of faith as related to supposition and opinion rather than knowledge and certainty. In contrast, faith in Islam pertains primarily to knowledge and the commitments that people make on the basis of knowledge. It stands above knowledge, not below it. It adds to knowledge a dimension of personal commitment, an engagement with the truth that one knows." – *Faith and Practice of Islam: Three Thirteenth Century Sufi Texts* (Albany: SUNY Press 1992), p. 7.

39 An allusion to a famous *ḥadīth*: "The men [and women] of learning are inheritors of the prophets." For its references, see William Chittick, *The Sufi Path of Knowledge: Ibn 'Arabī's Metaphysics of Imagination* (Albany: SUNY Press 1989), p. 377 and p. 413, n. 21.

father. A spiritual affiliation (*nasab-i maʿnawī*) must be established for this birth, from which the spiritual bequest of sapiental knowledge and mystical states (*ʿulūm wa aḥwāl*) ensues.

Such a birth occurs when the spirit completely detaches itself from its worldly entanglements and its affectionate regard for the world and its denizens, and makes contemplation of the state of the life hereafter and supernatural realities the focus of its vision. This is the same 'second birth' to which Jesus referred when he said: "Unless a man is born again, he cannot see the Kingdom of Heaven."[40] In the same way that formal-physical birth requires a drop of sperm in a womb, within which its (the embryo's) limbs and the spirit's quickening breath is shaped, so the 'spiritual birth' requires a 'word of faith', which must abide in the heart where it is shaped by faith-filled spiritual realities – such as repentance (*tawba*), asceticism (*zuhd*), trust in God (*tawakkul*), patience (*ṣabr*), gratitude (*shukr*), contentment (*riḍā*), love (*maḥabbat*), yearning (*shawq*), consignment of one's affairs to God (*tafwīḍ*), submission (*taslīm*), annihilation of self (*fanāʾ*), subsistence (*baqāʾ*), the eye of certitude (*ʿayn al-yaqīn*) and the truth of certainty (*ḥaqq al-yaqīn*) – and the insufflation of the spirit of divine Unity (*ruḥ-i tawḥīd*) upon the form of the harmonious shape of Faith.

Therefore, neither exit from the present material world (*ʿālam-i mulk u shahādat*) nor obtaining refuge in the supersensory realm of the divine Kingdom (*ʿālam-i malakut u ghayb*) can occur except through faith in what is invisible or supernatural. This is because whenever one's interior being (*bāṭin*) becomes illuminated by the light of faith and certitude, by accustoming oneself to continual contemplation of supersensory affairs and refraining from paying attention to the world and its business, their invisible realities become all sensibly present to it, so that sensory existence becomes transformed into a supernatural existence ... Whoever does not utterly turn his back on the world, abstaining from all its affairs and devoting his attention to the hereafter, is indicative that the reality of faith has still not entered his heart – even though he may still continue with the appearance of performing the outer rites of Islam by blind imitation. This is a condition which the word of God referred in stating: "The wandering Arabs say: 'We believe.' Say (unto them, O Muhammad): 'You don't believe', but say rather 'We submit', for faith has not yet entered your hearts."[41]

40 John III:3.

41 Qur'ān XLIX:14.

The relationship of (the formal religion of) 'Islām' to Faith (*īmān*) is that of the body to the Spirit: the (exoteric) Islamic sciences (*'ulūm-i islāmī*) are to the (esoteric) sciences of faith (*'ulūm-i īmānī*) what rinds are (to a kernel). By 'rind' is meant all those sciences gained through instruction (*'ilm-i dirāsat*) which are the prolegomenon to works (*a'mal*), the (esoteric) sciences of faith (*'ulūm-i īmānī*) being their kernel and synopsis. Hence, the kernel is knowledge conveyed by divine bequest (*'ilm-i warāthat*) which has been passed down to the divine scholars (*'ulamā'-yi rabbānī*) and the Sufis from the Prophet (peace and blessing be upon him) by virtue of the spiritual affiliation enjoyed from their second birth.[42]

The Degrees of Certainty[43]

By certainty (*yaqīn*) is meant the appearance of the light of Reality whilst experiencing a lifting of the veils of the human condition (*basharīyyat*). This is found through the testimony of ecstatic experience (*wajd*) and heart-savour (*dhawq*) rather than by inferential proofs based on ratiocination (*'aql*) and scholastic tradition (*naql*). As long as this light appears from behind a veil, it is called the 'light of faith' (*nūr-i īmān*), but whensoever the veil is lifted, it is called the light of certitude (*nūr-i yaqīn*). In reality, however, it is but one light: for that same light of faith, being stripped of the veils of the human condition and becoming the heart's usher, is transformed into the light of certitude.

But as long as (the delusion of) self-existence persists, a cloud of human qualities from the ground of humanity (*basharīyyat*) rises up, beshrouding the countenance of Reality's bright sun. Yet, on certain occasions, the

42 Kāshānī, *Miṣbāḥ al-hidāya*, ed. Humā'ī, pp. 65–68. The final passages of this selection are similar to the description of the second spiritual birth in the Ismā'īlī tradition expounded in "Divine Epiphany and Spiritual Birth in Ismailian Gnosis" (trans. Ralph Manheim) by Henry Corbin in his *Cyclical Time and Ismaili Gnosis* (London: Kegan Paul International 1983), pp. 59–150; see esp. pp. 135–40.

43 For a good summary of the three stages of certainty in classical Sufism, see Javad Nurbakhsh, *Sufi Symbolism: The Nurbakhsh Encyclopædia of Sufi Terminology*, trans. Terry Graham et al. (London: KNP 1997), vol. III, pp. 173ff.; on other various mystical senses of *Yaqīn*, see also Farid Jabre, *Essai sur le lexique de Ghazali* (Beirut: L'Université Libanaise 1970), s.v. "Yaqīn."

clouds dissipate so that one obtains a gleam of that light, which, by way of rapture (*wajd*) vouchsafes the mystic's heart a certain sapiential intuitive taste (*dhawq*). One becomes like a man afflicted with cold, upon whom the warm rays of sunlight are of a sudden cast, so that he feels delight and relief by basking in the warmth of its glow and heat.

By 'sun' here should be understood the reality of divine truths (*ḥaqīqat-i ḥaqā'iq*), the light from which – when shining from behind a veil – is the light of faith, and when piercing through and dissolving the veil – is the light of certitude. The 'man stricken with cold' is analogous to a person veiled by human qualities. Thus, the 'Light of Faith' is immutable and unchanging, while the 'Light of Certitude' is subject to flashes and shimmerings that fluctuate and come and go, just as the *ḥadīth* relates: "Faith is stable while certitude is subject to oscillation."[44]

Certitude has three dimensions. First, there is the theoretical knowledge of certitude (*'ilm al-yaqīn*) which can be likened to a person who is certain about the sun's existence by way of rational deduction, and through observing its rays and sensing its warmth.

The second is ocular certitude or the eye of observational certitude (*'ayn al-yaqīn*) which is analogous to a person who, through directly viewing the solar orb, thus becomes certain of the sun's existence and no longer has any doubts about it.

The third dimension is that of certain truth or the reality of certitude (*ḥaqq al-yaqīn*) which is analogous to a person who finds certitude in the sun's existence through the total dissolution of his optical vision and obliteration of the light of his eye in the light of the sun.

Thus, in 'theoretical knowledge of certitude' what was previously an object of knowledge becomes intimately realized and clearly evident, whilst in ocular certitude it becomes directly observed and objectively witnessed. Finally, in the 'reality of certitude' the duality between observer and object of perception, beholder and beheld, vanishes and is eliminated. The seer becomes the object of sight, the object of sight the seer. However, even those who have realized spiritual perfection and consummation only but rarely achieve this condition in any permanently durable manner: the experience resembles flashes of lightning that suddenly flare up out of nowhere

44 This is similar to this *ḥadīth*: "Faith is stable in heart while certitude is subject to oscillation." Nadīm Mar'ashlī and 'Usāma Mar'ashlī, *kanz al-'amāl fī sunan-i al-aqwāl wa al-af'āl* (Beirut: limu'asisa al-risālah 1986), vol. III, p. 739.

and then immediately dissipate. If it were to last more than a moment, the entire frame and constitution of the wayfarer would be annihilated and all the features of his being would dissolve away. It is to this moment's breath (*dam*) that the *ḥadīth*: "I have a moment with God in which no archangel nor any prophet sent on a mission can be contained alongside me"[45] alludes.

There is no cure
 for lovers but this:
To stitch up shut their lips,
 then fix their gaze on you.

There is no place
 for them to dwell
At your gate. They ring the bell,
 then pass along the way.

Therefore, faith is the fundamental principle of certitude (*īmān aṣl-i yaqīn buvad*), in respect of which (the three stages of certitude:) theoretical knowledge of certitude, ocular certitude and the 'reality of certitude', are but derivatives. Since some people excel others in faith, God Almighty has ordained that believers must 'keep the faith', as the verse, "O you who have faith ..."[46] attests.

Faith has many degrees, insofar as "It is He who has sent down the *Sakīna* into the believers' hearts, that they might add faith to their faith,"[47] In this context, the term 'peace' or *Sakīna* designates the certitude which lays to rest the distress of doubt that afflicts the heart[48] and to which the Canon Law refers as 'faith'. As the *ḥadīth* states: "Faith is all certitude."[49]

45 See Badī' al-Zamān Furūzānfar, *Aḥadīth-i Mathnawī*, 3rd edn (Tehran: Intishārāt-i Amīr Kabīr 1361 A.Hsh./1982), no. 100; see also W. Chittick, *The Self-Disclosure of God: Principles of Ibn al-'Arabī's Cosmology* (Albany: SUNY Press 1998), p. 437.

46 Qur'ān IV:136.

47 Qur'ān XLVIII:4; trans. A.J. Arberry, *The Qur'ān Interpreted* (Oxford: Oxford University Press 1983), with modifications.

48 An alternate translation would be: "indicates the certitude which assuages the doubts that torment the heart ..."

49 This is similar to this *ḥadīth*: "Certitude is all faith." Muḥammad al-Sa'īd ibn Basyūnī Zaghlūl, *Al-musū'a al-kubrā l-'aṭrāf-i al-ḥadīth al-nabawwī* (Beirut: Dār al-kutub al-'ilmīyah 2021), vol. 50, p. 555.

Thus, whatever is apprehended by methods of rational supposition (*istidlāl ʿaqlī*) is far from being even a theoretical knowledge of certitude (*ʿilm al-yaqīn*), for that knowledge is purely ratiocinative (*istidlālī*), while this knowledge is spontaneously intuitive (*ḥālī*). The lamp of reason (*chirāgh-i ʿaql*) will never dissolve the dreary shades of doubt unless the sun of Reality cast its aurorial glow upon it, for, as the adage goes: "snuff out the lamp when the dawn breaks." Still, it is God Who effects success.[50]

On Esoteric or Divinely infused Knowledge (*ʿilm-i ladunī*)

Esoteric knowledge is a sort of knowledge understood and apprehended by those drawn nigh to God (*ahl-i qurb*), which is imparted to them by way of divine instruction and inculcation, not through rational proofs (*dalāʾil-i ʿaqlī*) nor by testimonies based on theological proofs and narratives (*shawāhid-i naqlī*). Describing the case of Khiḍr – peace be upon him – the Eternal Word of God declared: "And we taught him knowledge from Our Presence."[51] Now, the difference between theoretical knowledge of certitude (*ʿilm al-yaqīn*) and esoteric knowledge is that the former involves apprehension of the light of the divine Essence and Attributes, whereas the latter is the direct apprehension of spiritual realities and words (*maʿānī wa kalamāt*) from God without any human intermediary.

Esoteric knowledge (*ʿilm-i ladunī*) is of three sorts: divine revelation (*waḥy*), inspiration (*ilhām*) and cardiognosy (*firāsa*).[52]

---

50 The above selection comprised a translation of the whole of chapter 9 "On Knowledge of Certainty," in Kāshānī, *Miṣbāḥ al-hidāya*, ed. Humāʾī, pp. 75–76.

51 Qurʾān XVIII:65. This passage merits comparison with Rashīd al-Dīn Maybudī's interpretation of the concept of 'esoteric knowledge' (*ʿilm-i ladunī*) or 'knowledge by divine inspiration' (*min ladunnī*) in his exegesis of the same verse (see his *Kashf al-asrār* V, p. 728).

52 For further discussion of *firāsa*, see Annemarie Schimmel, *Mystical Dimensions of Islam* (Chapel Hill: University of North Carolina 1975), p. 193; Chittick, *Sufi Path*, p. 304, who also points out that "the word *firāsa* is also applied to the science of physiognomy" (p. 409, n. 16). Gerald Elmore translates the term as "intuitive discernment" in his *Islamic Sainthood in the Fullness of Time: Ibn al-ʿArabī's Book of the Fabulous Griffin* (Leiden: Brill 1998), p. 617n.

Revelation (*waḥy*) appertains exclusively to prophets; it is of two types: the Divine Word (Logos = Qur'ān; *kalām-i ilahī*) and the Prophetic traditions (*ḥadīth-i nabawī*). All the Prophet's dicta were revelation, as the verse states: "He does not speak of his own desire. It is naught but a revelation revealed."[53] The divine word was sent down to the Prophet's heart, through the mediation of the Angel Gabriel; it was "brought down by the Trustworthy Spirit."[54] Some of the dicta of the Prophet (*ḥadīth-i nabawī*) descended without the mediation of the Angel Gabriel in the locus of epiphanic vision (*maḥal-i shuhūd*), as the verse "there was revealed to his servant that which he revealed"[55] indicates. Some dicta were spoken by mediation of Gabriel's descent, others by means of his inspiration (*nafth*)[56] to the Prophet's heart, as the *ḥadīth*: "Gabriel cast the breath of inspiration into my heart" establishes. By the "descent of Gabriel" (*nuzūl-i Jibra'īl*) is meant the epiphanic divulgement (*tanazzul*)[57] of his angelic form in a human shape. By 'inspiration' (*nafth*) is meant the casting of a revealed divine truth into the heart of a prophet, traversing the veils shrouding the Unseen without any imaginalized form (*tamaththul-i ṣūratī*).

Now, if someone asks what distinction is there between the Divine Word and Prophetic traditions – since both of them are by-products of revelation – our reply will be that in the case of the Qur'ān, both its morphological appearance and literal form (*ṣūrat*) as well as its inner content (*ma'nā*) were a revelation from on high, but in the case of the Prophet's traditions or sayings, their content was the direct result of revelation while their literal form was the Prophet's own word and discourse.

... The wisdom behind God Almighty's assignment of Gabriel to act as the Agent of His Word lies in the fact that because divinity and humanity have no mutual bonds of relationship (*nisbat*) between them, and no colloquy between any two persons can occur unless there is some

53 Qur'ān LIII:3–4.

54 Qur'ān XXVI:193.

55 Qur'ān LIII:10.

56 *Nafth* literally means 'expectoration, spitting out or discharge', and is often used to describe curses uttered by demonic imprecation (as in the "blowing on knots" mentioned in Qur'ān CXIII:4). Here, however, its connotation here is positive, referring to the divine breath of inspiration conveyed through angelic mediation.

57 Literally, a 'divulgement by descent'.

correspondence and comparability between them, Divine wisdom thus assigned Gabriel – one of whose faces (*rūy*) is turned toward the [supra-formal] realm of divine power and the other of which is turned towards the [formal] realm of divine wisdom – to act as an agent between Himself and the human nature of the Prophet – peace be upon him. In this fashion, through his face turned towards the realm of divine power, Gabriel was able to receive revelation, while through the other face turned towards the realm of divine wisdom, he could epiphanize himself in a human form (*maẓhar-i ṣūrat-i basharī*) so that a homological affinity (*mujānasat*) and dialogue [between God and man] might formally occur. It was for this reason that Gabriel imaginalized himself in human form whenever he appeared.

In this mundane phenomenal realm, the situation resembles the case of a person who wishes to teach a parrot to speak – despite the fact that there is absolutely no reciprocity of relationship (*tanāsub*) between man and parrot. A mirror is thus placed in front of the parrot, and from behind that, the trainer addresses it. Beholding in the mirror a fowl of its own kind and likeness speaking to it, the parrot supposes that everything it hears comes from the form of the other parrot speaking to it.

In exactly the same way, by agency of the human form of Gabriel, God Almighty spoke to Muḥammad, and through the human form of the Prophet also spoke to men in that manner. For men hearken only to men. The Prophet's human form was thus assigned to act as an agent between Him and humankind; it was His mirror-image from behind and beyond which veil, He alone acted as Speaker (*mutakallim*). One proof of this is this verse in the Qur'ān (XVIII:110) "Say: 'I am only a mortal like you. It is revealed to me'..."

It is interesting to note that the degrees of understanding (of revelation) mentioned in the verse:

> It belongs not to any mortal that
> God should speak to him, except
> by revelation, or from behind a veil
> or that He should send a messenger
> and he reveal whatsoever He will,
> by His leave ...[58]

58 Qur'ān XLII:51, trans. Arberry, *The Qur'ān Interpreted*, p. 504.

– correspond quite well with the various degrees of revelation (*marātib-i waḥy*) described above. Traditions of the Prophet narrated *without* the agency of Gabriel conform to revelation in the absolute sense of the word, whereas those traditions received by the Prophet's heart by and *with* the agency of Gabriel's inspiration, correspond to the divine Word that was revealed "from behind a veil." While the Qur'ān and *ḥadīth*, which both come to the Prophet by medium of Gabriel's epiphany, are congruous with the revelation of the prophetic mission itself – that is, with Gabriel['s mission] – any exposition of this spiritual truth, except by way of symbolic allusion and innuendo, cannot be contained within the discursive scope of this brief treatment.

Inspiration (*ilhām*), however, is particular to God's elect friends (*khawāṣṣ-i awliyā'*), and is a kind of true and reliable knowledge which God Almighty hurls into the hearts of elect Friends of God (as the verse states) "Say: 'My Lord hurls the truth – He is Knower of the Unseen.'"[59] This is what the Sufis call a thought of truthful inspiration (*khāṭir-i ḥaqqānī*) – which will be discussed later on in the chapter on 'passing thoughts' (*khawāṭir*) – God-willing.

As for cardiognosy (*firāsa*), that is a kind of knowledge revealed from the Unseen through perspicacious examination (*tafarrus*) of the traces of the form of something.[60] It is shared among the elect believers, as the tradition: "Beware of the cardiognosy of the man of faith, for he sees by the light of God."[61]

Now the difference between cardiognosy and inspiration is that in the former occult matters are uncovered by means of perspicacious examination of the visible traces of something's form, whereas in the latter, no such formal medium is necessary. The difference between revelation and

59 Qur'ān XXXIV:48.

60 Hence, the application of *firāsa* to the science of physiognomy.

61 Furūzānfar, *Aḥadīth-i Mathnawī*, no. 33. See also Chittick, *The Sufi Path*, p. 340; Schimmel, *Mystical Dimensions*, p. 205. In his *Kashf al-asrār* (vol. V, p. 334), Maybudī explains that there are three kinds of cardiognosy: "experimental cardiognosy (*firāsat-i tajārubatī*; i.e. intellectual intuition) which all people of discernment have; deductive cardiognosy (*firāsat-i istidlālī*) which all intellectual types of people possess; and cardiognosy *per se* – appertaining to the vision of the heart, that is to say, clairvoyance (*firāsat bi-naẓar-i dil*) by way of that light which the believer has in his heart, as the Prophet said: Beware ..."

inspiration is that inspiration follows, and is dependent on, revelation, whereas revelation does not follow nor depend on inspiration. That is to say, the saints or friends of God enjoy the degree of inspiration they possess by virtue of their obedience to the prophets, whereas the prophets' revelations depend upon no one (but God). And God knows best.[62]

62 The foregoing selection comprised a translation of the better part of chapter 10: "On Esoteric Knowledge" in Kāshānī, *Miṣbāḥ al-hidāya*, ed. Humā'ī, pp. 76–79.

VIII

EPISTEMOLOGICAL DELIBERATIONS ON GNOSIS AND VISIONARY UNVEILING

A Chapter on Esoteric Knowledge from Sayyid Ḥaydar Āmulī's (d. after 787/1385) *Kitāb Naṣṣ al-Nuṣūṣ* (*fī Sharḥ Fuṣūṣ al-Ḥikam*)

Chapter eight features a translation of the chapter on esoteric knowledge in the *Kitāb Naṣṣ al-nuṣūṣ* [*fī Sharḥ Fuṣūṣ al-ḥikam li-Muḥyī al-Dīn Ibn al-ʿArabī*] by Bahā al-Dīn Ḥaydar b. ʿAlī ʿAlawī Ḥusaynī (720/1320–787/1385). Sayyid Ḥaydar Āmulī, as he was popularly known, was a Shīʿite Sufi theologian acclaimed for his integration of Imāmite Shīʿism, Sufism and the thought of Ibn ʿArabī into a coherent system of philosophical mysticism.[1]

Born and raised in Āmul in Ṭabaristān, south of the Caspian Sea, he came from a long line of Iranian Shīʿite Sayyids, that is, descendants of the Prophet. He was educated in the usual sciences of his day in diverse cities throughout Khurāsān and Central Iran, Iṣfahān in particular. He worked in different governmental posts in Ṭabaristān, and eventually became the chief Vizier of Fakhr al-Dawla Shāh Ghāzī b. Ziyār, sovereign of the province.[2]

At thirty years of age, in 750/1349, he had a conversion experience that caused him to set his governmental career aside, sever all worldly attachments and address himself to the life of the heart and spirit. Abandoning kith and kin, and hearth and home, he set out on a pilgrimage to Mecca. Midway in his journey he stopped in Iṣfahān where he encountered a certain Nūr al-Dīn Ṭihrānī, to whom he became a devoted disciple. From there, he went on to Baghdād where he was forced to remain for a long period due to

---

1 Ṣamad Muwaḥḥid, *Dā'irat al-maʿārif-i buzurg-i Islāmī* (Tehran: 1374 A.Hsh./1995), II, s.v. "Āmulī," pp. 214–15.

2 Sayyid Ḥaydar Āmulī, *Kitāb Naṣṣ al-nuṣūṣ fī Sharḥ Fuṣūṣ al-ḥikam li-Muḥyī al-Dīn Ibn al-ʿArabī*, ed. H. Corbin and Osman Yahya as *Le Texte des textes* (Tehran: Intishārāt-i Ṭūs, 2nd edn 1367 A.Hsh./1988), French introduction, p. 2; Sayyid Ḥaydar Āmulī, *Jāmiʿ al-asrār va maba'a al-anwār* (Tehran: Intishārāt-i ʿilmī wa farhangī 1384 A.Hsh./2005).

sickness and lack of facilities for travel. He finally managed to successfully execute his pilgrimage in 751/1350. Shortly thereafter he made his way north. He settled in Najaf in southern Iraq, which was a famous centre of Shīʿite learning even in that period. He remained in Najaf for most of the rest of his life, studying under a variety of Shīʿite scholars, and composing most of his major works.

A prolific author, he wrote about forty works on a vast diversity of topics, seven of which are today extant.[3] The following six of these works concern the more esoteric dimensions of Islamic thought:

1. *Asrār al-sharīʿa wa aṭwār al-ṭarīqa wa anwār al-ḥaqīqa* (*Mysteries of the Divine Law, Levels of the Spiritual Path and Lights of Divine Reality*).[4]
2. *Amthalat al-tawḥīd wa abniyat al-tajrīd* (*Exemplars of Divine Unity and Principles of Detachment*).[5]
3. *Al-Baḥr al-khiḍamm fī tafsīr al-Qur'ān al-aʿẓam* (*The Vast Oceanic Exegesis on the Tremendous Qur'ān*).
4. *Jāmiʿ al-asrār wa manbaʿ al-anwār* (*The Compendium of Mysteries and Source-spring of Illuminations*).[6] In this book, Āmulī attempts to show the unity between Sufism and Shīʿism, as he himself says in its introduction (p. 3): "This book is based on the statements of the true scholars who have experientially verified their knowledge, being men of God known as 'Sufis'. It is in accordance with the faith of the Imāmī Shīʿites and establishes a concordance with the principles and rites of both groups." Later on in the same introduction (pp. 5, 9) he adds: "From my early youth, or rather from childhood until now when I have reached old age, I was preoccupied in striving to acquire true knowledge of my pure

---

3 See E. Kohlberg, "Āmolī, Sayyed Bahā' al-Dīn Haydar b. ʿAlī b. Ḥaydar al- ʿObaydī al-Ḥosaynī," *EIr* I, p. 983. See Muwaḥḥid, "Āmulī," for a comprehensive bibliography of his works.

4 This work by Āmulī is available in English translation: *Inner Secrets of the Path*, trans. Asadullah ad-Dhaakir Yate (Qum: Ansariyan Publications 2000).

5 This Persian treatise is modelled after the *Lamaʿāt* of Fakhr al-Dīn ʿIrāqī.

6 Sayyid Ḥaydar Āmulī, *Jāmiʿ al-asrār wa-manbaʿ al-anwār* (*La philosophie shiʿite*: 1: Somme des doctrines ésotériques (*Jāmiʿ al-asrār*) 2: Trité de la connaissance de l'être (*Fī maʿrifat al-wojūd*: *inẓimām-i Risālat naqd al-nuqūd fī maʿrifat al-wujūb*, publiés avec une double introduction et index par Henry Corbin et Osman Yahia (Tehran: Institut Franco-Iranien de Recherceh 1969).

ancestors, who were those 'Immaculate Imāms'. I pursued this lore exoterically – by following the particular canon law (*sharī'a*) of one Islamic religious denomination, namely the Imāmī Shī'ites – as well as esoterically, by adhering to that 'interior reality' (*ḥaqīqat*) especially known to the group of the Sufis who are among the sovereign adepts of divine Unity. I was continually attempting to show the unity and concordance of both these camps. Whilst undertaking this task I had no other purpose and intention but to foster the betterment and advancement – both internally and externally – of the faith of my pure forefathers and ancestors.[7] Most Sufis imagine out of ignorance that the immaculate Imāms were devoid of all mystical or gnostic qualities, while Shī'ites have been deluded into thinking that the character of the Imāms was exclusively restricted to the conventional sciences of their day."

5. *Al-Muḥīṭ al-a'ẓam fī ta'wīl kitāb Allāh al-'azīz al-muḥkam*, a book on esoteric hermeneutics, devoted to interpreting the famous *ḥadīth* which ascribes seven levels of meaning to the Qur'ān.[8] The work was apparently modelled after Najm al-Dīn Rāzī's *Baḥr al-ḥaqā'iq wa manba' al-daqā'iq*. As explained below, Āmulī remarked that this work was of the same place and significance in his own oeuvre as was the *Fuṣūṣ al-ḥikam* in the writings of Ibn 'Arabī (who had claimed to have received that work as a revelation from the Prophet directly).
6. *Kitāb Naṣṣ al-nuṣūṣ* [*fī Sharḥ Fuṣūṣ al-ḥikam li-Muḥyī al-Dīn Ibn al-'Arabī*], a commentary on the *Fuṣūṣ al-ḥikam* of Ibn 'Arabī. "If we wish to gain an adequate representation of Islamic thought and spirituality following the thirteenth century, and in particular of Shi'ite or imāmite spirituality," writes Henry Corbin, "it is indispensable that we acquire comprehension of this work."[9]

---

7 Āmulī was a "Sayyid," that is, a descendant of the Prophet, and he alludes by the adjective 'pure' here to the Shī'ite belief that certain elect members of the Prophet's family, the "twelve Imāms" in particular, were characterized by infallibility and purity (*ma'ṣūmīyyat*).

8 See Muwaḥḥid, "Āmulī," p. 215 for a description of this work – not to be confused with his *Al-Baḥr al-khiḍamm fī tafsīr al-Qur'ān al-a'ẓam*.

9 Sayyid Ḥaydar Āmulī, *Kitāb Naṣṣ al-nuṣūṣ fī Sharḥ Fuṣūṣ al-ḥikam li-Muḥyī al-Dīn Ibn al-'Arabī*, ed. H. Corbin and Osman Yahya as *Le Texte des textes* (Tehran: Intishārāt-i Ṭūs, 2nd edn 1367 A.Hsh./1988), French introduction, p. 2.

As Corbin reveals,[10] the last three monumental oeuvres are of immense significance in the history of Shīʿite philosophy, theology and theosophy. In the "*histoire métaphysique*" – as Corbin calls it – of post-Ibn ʿArabī theosophy, Āmulī occupies a special place due to the spiritual relation of his own works to those of the Shaykh al-Akbar on the one hand and to the Prophet's "two books" on the other. That is to say, just as Ibn ʿArabī found himself juxtaposed "between two books": (1) the *Fuṣūṣ al-ḥikam* (*The Bezels of Wisdom*), which he claimed had been handed to him by the Prophet directly in a vision, and (2) *Kitāb al-Futūḥāt al-Makkīyya* (*The Meccan Illuminations*), which he claimed to have been divinely inspired to him by God, the first book having been "descended upon him (*al-nāzil ʿalay-hi*)" and the second book having been "emanated from him (*al-ṣādir min-hu*)," the Prophet likewise was juxtaposed "between two books" – the first being the revelation of the Qur'ān vouchsafed to him by the Angel Gabriel, and the second being the *Fuṣūṣ al-ḥikam* which he bestowed upon Ibn ʿArabī. In a similar sense, Ḥaydar Āmulī too, found himself placed between two commentaries: (1) his own Qur'ān commentary (*Al-Muḥīṭ al-aʿẓam*) and (2) his commentary on Ibn ʿArabī's *Bezels of Wisdom*, namely the *Kitāb Naṣṣ al-nuṣūṣ*. Describing this peculiar mystical condition of being placed "between two books," he wrote:

> And we also have found ourselves given two books without peer or likeness ... There is one book, which was bestowed *upon* us from on-high (*al-fā'id ʿalaynā*) and another book that has emanated *from* us ... The former is the *ta'wīlāt* (spiritual hermeneutics) of the holy Qur'ān, which comprehends the most precious and venerable divine sciences and doctrines of the Qur'ān, wherein the symbols and particular figures of the Prophet, the subtle doctrines and Muḥammadan metaphysical realities have been assembled ... This esoteric commentary (*tafsīr ʿirfānī*) may be likened as being to us what the *Fuṣūṣ al-ḥikam* was to the Shaykh (Ibn ʿArabī), and what the Qur'ān was to the Prophet.
>
> ... As for the other book that has emanated *from* us: this is the present commentary, the *Naṣṣ al-nuṣūṣ*, which is not devoid of possessing a certain divine dispensation, insofar as it is a *summa* (*jāmiʿ*) of diverse types of knowledge and multiple doctrines. As we have explained, it is organized into twenty-seven (more exactly twenty-eight) diagrams,

10 Āmulī, *Kitāb Naṣṣ al-nuṣūṣ*, French introduction, p. 3.

> and arranged into chapters and sections that cover a number of different categories, with many different subdivisions. This book is to us (from whom this commentary has emanated) what the *Fuṣūṣ* is to the Prophet (from whom it emanated), and corresponds to the *Futūḥāt* in relation to Ibn 'Arabī (from whom that book emanated).
>
> ... Just as the basis (*asās*) of the precedence of our Prophet [over other prophets] rests upon the two books in question (the Qur'ān and the *Fuṣūṣ*), the basis (*asās*) of the precedence the Shaykh (Ibn 'Arabī) lies in the two above-cited works (the *Fuṣūṣ* and the *Futūḥāt*), and similarly, the pre-eminence with which we have been favoured rests on the two books that are in question here (namely, our spiritual commentary on the Qur'ān and the present commentary on the *Fuṣūṣ*).[11]

The structure of Āmulī's spiritual claims regarding his own oeuvre can be paraphrased as follows: Just as God revealed the Qur'ān to the Prophet, the latter revealed the *Fuṣūṣ* to Ibn 'Arabī; just as the Prophet revealed the *Fuṣūṣ* to Ibn 'Arabī, the latter received the *Futūḥāt* from God; and just as God revealed the *Al-Muḥīṭ al-a'ẓam* to Ḥaydar Āmulī, the latter bestowed the *Naṣṣ al-nuṣūṣ* upon all humanity.[12] The following diagrams also serve to illustrate these claims:

Qur'ān ← **The Prophet** → *Fuṣūṣ al-ḥikam*
Fuṣūṣ al-ḥikam ← **Ibn 'Arabī** → *Al-Futūḥāt*
Al-Muḥīṭ al-a'ẓam ← **Ḥaydar Āmulī** → *Naṣṣ al-nuṣūṣ*

Qur'ān	*Fuṣūṣ al-ḥikam*	*Al-Muḥīṭ al-a'ẓam*
The Prophet	Ibn 'Arabī	Ḥaydar Āmulī
Fuṣūṣ al-ḥikam	*Al-Futūḥāt*	*Naṣṣ al-nuṣūṣ*[13]

11 Āmulī, *Kitāb Naṣṣ al-nuṣūṣ*, French introduction, p. 6.

12 Adapted from Corbin, *Kitāb Naṣṣ al-nuṣūṣ*, French introduction, pp. 6–7.

13 Adapted from Corbin, *Kitāb Naṣṣ al-nuṣūṣ*, French introduction, p. 7.

Āmulī ardently wished his *Naṣṣ al-nuṣūṣ* to take first place amongst the other commentaries on the *Fuṣūṣ*, and to be so comprehensive as to render theirs obsolete.[14] As the title of the work indicates, this book is advertised as being the quintessence of all commentaries on the *Fuṣūṣ al-ḥikam* of Ibn 'Arabī (on which literally hundreds of glosses and commentaries were written). He compared the spiritual rank of his commentary to the Qur'ān's pre-eminence over the prior revelations of scripture: the Torah, the Psalms and the Gospels – whence the appellation of his book: "The Texts of [all] Texts." Unfortunately, the commentary in its entirety is no longer extant; all that exists today is the remarkable Prolegomenon of the commentary published by O. Yahya and H. Corbin, and from which some extracts have been translated below so as to give a taste of his thought.

His Prolegomenon, itself comprising an integral work in its own right regardless of the lost commentary, follows a tripartite structure found in a number of other works belonging to the school of Ibn 'Arabī. Each discussion is treated under three different rubrics: philosophical rationalism or reason (*'aql*), theology or tradition (*naql*) and mystical insight or intuition (*kashf*), corresponding to the threefold division between the literal revelation of the Law (*sharī'at*), the Sufi Path (*ṭarīqat*) and spiritual realization (*ḥaqīqat*).[15] The work itself is divided up into Prognostications (*tamhīdāt*), Principles (*arkān*) and Diagrams (*dawā'ir*).

Āmulī, as with many Sufis of his day and age, took Ibn 'Arabī's claim that the *Fuṣūṣ al-ḥikam* had been handed to him in a vision by the Prophet very seriously, but the spiritual import of the *Fuṣūṣ* was only to be realized experientially by the elite. While Ibn 'Arabī's *Fuṣūṣ* like all the other divine sciences (*'ulūm ilāhī*) in Islam had been 'vouchsafed' to humankind as part of the divine trust or dispensation (*amānat*), "penetration into the metaphysical realities and subtleties of this work [*Fuṣūṣ al-ḥikam*] is a degree reserved for the elect among the adepts in matters divine (*al-khawāṣṣ min ahl Allāh*), for the book is intended only for the most perfect adepts and initiates who have reached perfection. These adepts are known as the 'Friends of God' (*awliyā' Allāh*), 'those drawn nigh' (*al-muqarribīn*) or 'the Pivots' (*aqṭāb*). The Shaykh (Ibn 'Arabī) alludes to this matter in the first

14 *Naṣṣ al-nuṣūṣ*, Arabic text, Ā48; Corbin, *Kitāb Naṣṣ al-nuṣūṣ*, French introduction, p. 16.

15 *Naṣṣ al-nuṣūṣ*, Arabic text, Ā46; Corbin, *Kitāb Naṣṣ al-nuṣūṣ*, French introduction, p. 16.

chapter [of the *Fuṣūṣ*] where he states, 'This subject is not something which one's reason can comprehend by way of mental dialectics (*'aql bi-ṭarīq naẓar fikrī*); rather this science entails a direct apprehension which one cannot obtain except through divine visionary unveiling (*kashf ilāhī*).'"[16]

For Āmulī, Ibn 'Arabī's work represents the zenith of Islamic esotericism. The 'visionary revelation' of the *Fuṣūṣ* to Ibn 'Arabī neither contradicted the Muslim *sharī'at*, nor brought a new *sharī'at*, but rather the book comprised "everything *esoteric* in any *sharī'at*."[17] The cycle of the 'Friends of God' (*walāya*) which succeeded the epoch of the prophets, the last of whom was Muḥammad, shall be, he avers, never-ending; it is a *revelatio continuata* complementing the exoteric dimension of the Muḥammadean Truth (*ḥaqīqat Muḥammadīyya*) that the Prophet incarnated during his lifetime. After his death, both the Shī'ite Imāms and the highest Sufi adepts have continued to gain access this revelation, perpetually recurring in the *mundus imaginalis*, by way of their powers of meditative reflection (*mufakkira*); in this manner the revelation of the *esoteric* book continues forever.[18]

Quoting from Abū Ḥāmid al-Ghazālī's treatise on esoteric knowledge (translated in ch. 2), Āmulī argues that all knowledge is a product of ecstatic consciousness (*al-wajdānīyyat*) understood through intuitive sapiential taste (*al-dhawqīyyat*). He then details the various types of gnostics, respectively: those whose lore derives through conjectural deductive reasoning (*istidlāl*), those whose knowledge is an infusion of divine grace, citing verses from 'Umar ibn Fāriḍ of Egypt (d. 633/1235),[19] the greatest of the Arab mystical poets, to illustrate the thesis. His theory of *kashf* is heavily reliant on both Ghazālī and Ibn 'Arabī, although it is totally uninfluenced, in this selection at least, so far as I can tell, by any specifically Shī'ite theological tenets.[20]

16 *Naṣṣ al-nuṣūṣ*, Arabic text, Ā82; Corbin, *Kitāb Naṣṣ al-nuṣūṣ*, French introduction, p. 20.

17 Corbin, *Kitāb Naṣṣ al-nuṣūṣ*, French introduction, p. 22.

18 Corbin, *Kitāb Naṣṣ al-nuṣūṣ*, French introduction, pp. 22–23.

19 For further information on 'Umar ibn Fāriḍ, see Th. Emil Homerin (trans.), *'Umar ibn al-Fāriḍ: Sufi Verse, Saintly Life* (New York: Paulist Press 2001).

20 Thus L. Gardet's claim that his idea of *kashf* represents "the applying of the Ṣūfī *kashf* to the Shī'ī search for the hidden meanings of things." ("Kashf," *EI2* IV, p. 698) is quite unwarranted so far as the present text is concerned.

For Āmulī the Shīʿite doctrine of a never-ending esoteric *walāya* led directly to Ibn ʿArabī's esoteric teachings in the *Fuṣūṣ*.[21] One of the very few ideas on which Āmulī criticizes the Shaykh al-Akbar concerns the latter's claim to be the 'Seal of the Saints', which obviously is irreconcilable with the author's own Shīʿite tenets. In the second *tamhīd* of his *Text of Texts*, devoted to proving the superiority of Ibn ʿArabī over all the other saints and friends of God down to Āmulī's own day ("without this infringing on the pre-eminence of the rank of the caliphs, the Prophet's companions or the Imāms"), he juxtaposes his own theory of *walāya* to that of Ibn ʿArabī.[22]

Although Āmulī's works are seldom studied today outside of religious seminaries and departments of Islamic Studies in universities, he remains a thinker of major significance, if not universal importance for his anti-sectarian vision that transcended the Shīʿite–Sunni divide and for his Sufi ecumenism. Etan Kohlberg characterizes his significance as follows:

> He was an early proponent of the thesis that Imamite Shiʿism, which combines *šarīʿa*, *ṭarīqa*, and *ḥaqīqa*, is identical with Sufism. Every true Shiʿite (referred to by Āmolī as *mo'men momtaḥan* ("a believer put to test") is also a Sufi, and vice-versa. The Imams, who are invested with mystical knowledge, are the guides not only of the Shiʿite community, but also of all those who seek the mystical path. Āmolī is equally critical of Shiʿites who reduce their religion to a legalistic system and of Sufis who deny that their origins and doctrines go back to the Imams.[23]

21 Corbin, *Kitāb Naṣṣ al-nuṣūṣ*, French introduction, p. 23.

22 For a good overview of the general meanings of *walāyah*, see Hermann Landolt, "Walāyah," *Encyclopedia of Religion*, ed. Mircea Eliade (New York: Simon & Schuster Macmillan 1995), vol. 15, pp. 316–23. For Āmulī's critique of Ibn ʿArabī's theory of *walāyah*, see Henry Corbin, *En Islam iranien: Aspects spirituels et philosophiques*, vol. I: *Le shī'ism duodécimain* (Paris: Éditions Gallimard 1971), pp. 61, 272; *idem.*, *Kitāb Naṣṣ al-nuṣūṣ*, French introduction, pp. 22–23; Hermann Landolt, "Ḥaydar-i Āmulī et les deux *miʿrājs*," *Studia Islamica*, no. 91 (2000), pp. 91–106.

23 E. Kohlberg, "Āmolī," pp. 984–85.

The translation presented here is from the third section of the third part[24] of the *Naṣṣ al-nuṣūṣ*, entitled "The Pillars" (*arkān*). The third and last "pillar": (*rukn*) among these pillars concerns gnoselogy (that is, speaking in the true sense of the word, despite modern agnostic philosophy which has reduced the scope and parameters of this science to mere 'epistemology'), the real subject matter of this pillar is "the metaphysics of cognition," as Henry Corbin insightfully informs us.[25]

Some of the subjects covered in this section include the difference between esoteric knowledge (*al-'ilm al-ladunī, al-ma'rifat*) and ordinary book learning (*al-'ilm*), visionary unveiling (*al-kashf*) contemplative vision (*al-mushāhada*) and the five Levels of the divine Presence of Knowledge (*al-ḥaḍrat al-'ilmīyyat*). The author attempts to differentiate between the traditional divine sciences and the conventional sciences that are acquired by exterior means. Only the first type, the 'divine sciences' constitute knowledge in the real sense of the word; the second type constitute knowledge in but the metaphorical, figurative sense of the word, these being known in today's parlance as the 'human sciences' or the 'humanities'.[26] The first type of knowledge pertains to the Sufis, to the true men of God.[27] The second belongs to philosophers and scholastic theologians (*ḥukamā', mutakallimūn*), who are opposed to and ridicule the former.[28]

In the chapter on "The Sciences of the People of God Amongst the True Sufis, and on Sapiental Understanding of Their Knowledge" translated here, Āmulī outlines the difference between *al-'ilm al-ladunī*, *al-'ilm* and *al-ma'rifat*, *al-kashf*, *al-mushāhada*, and the five levels of the Presence of Knowledge (*al-ḥaḍrat al-'ilmīyyat*). Since a good abstract of the contents of the whole selection translated here (comprising his own summary of this

24 This third part is subdivided into three pillars, the first two explore respectively: (i) the metaphysics of divine Unity (*tawḥīd*), discussing the *tawḥīd* of the Essence (*dhāt*), the divine Attributes (*waṣf*), and Activities (*fa'l*), and (ii) the metaphysics of the absolute Being (*wujūd muṭlaq*) along with the mysteries of esoteric *tawḥīd*.

25 Corbin, *Kitāb Naṣṣ al-nuṣūṣ*, French introduction, pp. 27, 30–32.

26 Corbin, *Kitāb Naṣṣ al-nuṣūṣ*, Arabic text, §53.

27 On Ḥaydar Āmulī's close relationship with Sufism, see Shahrām Pāzūkī, "Sayyid Ḥaydar Āmulī: jāma'-yi taṣawwuf va tashayya'," in *idem.*, *'Irfān va hunar dar dawra-yi mudirn* (Tehran; Nashr-i 'Ilm 1393 A.Hsh./ 2015), pp. 279–302.

28 Pāzūkī, "Sayyid Ḥaydar Āmulī: jāma'-yi taṣawwuf va tashayya'."

'third pillar') is provided by Ḥaydar Āmulī himself in his own introduction to the *Kitāb Naṣṣ al-nuṣūṣ* (§80) it will be useful to cite it here:

> The intention of the third pillar is discussion of the meaning of the various sciences, investigating them according to their tripartite divisions into rational, traditional and visionary ways (*al-'aqlīyya wa'l-naqlīyya wa'l-kashfī*). This pillar further differentiates between those sciences which are the result of inspiration and interior illumination (*al-'ulūm al-ilāhīyya al-ladunīyya al-kashfīyya*) and those conventional sciences that are vain and unreal, having been acquired by individual striving and effort (*al-'ulūm al-kasbīyya al-rasmīyya al-majāzīyya*). Here we also assert that this knowledge is impossible to grasp or apprehend except by the way of the knowledge of the divinely infused sciences (*al-'ulūm al-ilāhīyya al-ladunīyya*). The seeker of such sciences should use proper methods for their acquisition, that is to say, he must engage in ascetic discipline (*al-riyāḍat*), practise bouts of solitary isolation (*al-khalwat*) and spiritual warfare (*al-mujāhadat*). He should strive to totally focus his attention on God, practise voluntary death (*al-mawt al-irādī*), and aspire to mystical annihilation (*fanā' al-'irfānī*) which will lead him to eternal life (*al-baqā' al-abadī*). Our prayer is that God Almighty through the truth of Muḥammad and his pure offspring, will enable us to attain this degree.[29]

Several pages of the "pillar," the exposition of which lean heavily on Ibn 'Arabī's son-in-law and successor Ṣadr al-Dīn Qūnawī, are devoted to explaining the difference between knowledge (*al-'ilm*), gnosis (*al-ma'rifat*) and wisdom (*al-ḥikmat*). Mentioning a number of different definitions of knowledge, he endorses the view that true knowledge is what is immediately self-evident (*ḍarūrī*). Knowledge thus "depends on something *beyond* definition and description, which is immediately conceptualized in the mind." He concludes that knowledge is ultimately equivalent to the act of mystical unveiling (*kashf*): "'Knowledge' may be designated as 'the perfect and complete rending the veil (*al-kashf al-tām*) off the face of the object of knowledge specific to the science subject to scrutiny.'" So as far as I know this definition of knowledge is unique and original to Ḥaydar Āmulī. There

29 *Kitāb Naṣṣ al-nuṣūṣ*, Arabic text, §80.

is nothing even faintly similar to it in the various definitions of knowledge provided by Franz Rosenthal in his comprehensive work *Knowledge Triumphant*.[30]

ESOTERIC KNOWLEDGE IN THE *KITĀB NAṢṢ AL-NUṢŪṢ*

Concerning the Sciences of the People of God Amongst the Elect True Sufis, and Knowledge of their Insights, subdivided into Several Chapters[31]

No doubt it is extremely difficult to define what knowledge (*'ilm*) is, since, according to the opinion of some, knowledge is obtained without any prior premeditation (*badīhī*); it is 'found' through a process of spontaneous self-realization (*wajdānī*), while according to others it is something either acquired through personal exertions (*kasbī*) or is something immediately self-evident (*ḍarūrī*), apprehended as the capacity of each individual allows. Hence, according to the opinion of both these groups, there is no single absolute definition of knowledge since it must encompass the knowledge of both the Necessary Being and that of Possible beings. From whence it is apparent that the definition of knowledge pertaining to the Necessary Being is quite distinct from the definition of knowledge pertaining to possible beings. The reason for this is that knowledge of the Transcendent Necessary Being is essential, active, true and eternal, whereas possible beings' knowledge is subject to the stimuli of external influences, accidental, unreal and obtained by making efforts at its acquisition.

A useful definition of knowledge, however, is as follows:

30 See F. Rosenthal, *Knowledge Triumphant: The Concept of Knowledge in Medieval Islam* (Leiden: Brill 1970), pp. 52–69, where most of the main Sufi definitions of knowledge are presented.

31 *Kitāb Naṣṣ al-nuṣūṣ fī Sharḥ Fuṣūṣ al-ḥikam li-Muḥyī al-Dīn Ibn al-'Arabī* by Sayyid Ḥaydar Āmulī, ed. H. Corbin and Osman Yahya (Tehran: Ṭūs, 2nd edn 1367 A.Hsh./1988), pp. 472–78. I am deeply indebted to Muhammad Reza Jozi, who has translated the entire *Naṣṣ al-nuṣūṣ* into Persian, for reviewing my English translation and offering many useful elucidations of its various subjects.

> According to them (the true Sufis), 'knowledge' is that which is disclosed in a special manner by God through revelation (*waḥy*), inspiration (*ilhām*) and visionary unveiling (*kashf*).

By visionary unveiling is meant rending the veil off the face of the object of knowledge that is pursued – whatever its condition.

In their view, knowledge belongs to the category of things apprehended by intuition (*al-wajdānīyya*) and sapiential taste (*al-dhawqīyya*), rather than by the usual means of individual striving and effort. Alluding to this idea, some scholars have said that "Knowledge, like Existence, has no finite limitation and definition, but is a quality found out about through intuition (*min al-ṣifāt al-wajdānīyya*)." But they differ as to whether there really exists a knowledge within the person of the knower that has a form (accurately) corresponding to the object of knowledge, or whether such knowledge is merely something relational between the knower and the object of knowledge.[32] But the opinion that is soundest and closest to the truth is that knowledge is a quality that necessarily requires the knower be related to the object of knowledge. Thus, just as it is correct to say that knowledge is something related to existence, so one can also assert that knowledge is related to nonexistence. By this is meant that, for example, we know that the sun will rise tomorrow although the 'object' of our knowledge is now non-existent. In this respect, it has been said that "one can know everything by means of knowledge," but if and when we want to know 'knowledge' by means of 'knowledge', this necessarily results in a vicious circle (*al-dawr*), whereas if we wish to understand what knowledge is by means of something *other than* knowledge, this necessarily results in an infinite regress (*al-tasalsul*). On the other hand, if we would understand what knowledge is by means of another knowledge – well, there is nothing other than knowledge but ignorance, and there is no way one can define knowledge by means of ignorance! Therefore, there is no other choice but to say that knowledge belongs to the category of things apprehended by ecstatic consciousness

32 Ḥaydar Āmulī's discussion below seems to be partially indebted to 'Allāmah al-Ḥillī's (d. 726/1325) analysis of knowledge in his *Anwār al-malakūt fī Sharḥ al-Yāqut*, ed. Najmī-Zanjānī (Tehran 1338 A.Hsh./1959), pp. 12ff., cited by F. Rosenthal, *Knowledge Triumphant: The Concept of Knowledge in Medieval Islam* (Leiden: Brill 1970), p. 49.

(*al-wajdānīyya*) and intuitive sapiential taste (*al-dhawqīyya*), as is the opinion of the Muslim theosophists (*ahl Allāh*).[33]

But having understood this, we will now proceed to cite and expound their words concerning this subject. First of all, we may cite the definition of knowledge given by Muḥammad al-Ghazālī in his treatise "On Esoteric Knowledge" (*al-Risālat "al-'ilm al-ladunī"*),[34] where he states,

> Knowledge is the rational soul's perception of the realities of things[35] and their forms abstracted from matter in their prototypical forms, qualities, quantities, substances, and essences, whether these be simple individual things (*mufrada*), or complex composite things (*murakkaba*). And the knower (*al-'ālim*) is one who comprehends, apprehends and perceives (a thing), while the object of knowledge (*al-ma'lūm*) is the essence of the thing itself, knowledge of which is engraved upon the soul.
>
> The nobility of knowledge is in proportion to the nobility of the object known, just as the rank of the knower corresponds to the rank of the knowledge that he or she knows. Without a doubt, the supreme object of knowledge, and that which is highest, noblest and most honourable, is God Almighty – the Maker, the Genetrix, the Truth, the One. And knowledge of Him – that is to say, knowledge of divine Unity – is the supreme science, which is of highest repute, being totally all-inclusive. It is incumbent upon every individual to learn this science and necessary that every rational person acquire it. Thus, according to the dictate of the Lawgiver: "The pursuit of knowledge is incumbent upon every male and female Muslim;"[36] and he also commanded that one travel in search of knowledge, enjoining:

---

33 Cf. mystical definitions of knowledge cited by Franz Rosenthal, *Knowledge Triumphant*, pp. 67–69 (L).

34 The indented passage cited here is from the first chapter of Ghazālī's treatise, all of which is translated in chapter two above.

35 This is almost exactly the same as two definitions of knowledge that are cited by Rosenthal (*op. cit.*, p. 62) which are ascribed to Nāṣir-i Khusraw and the *Rasā'il Ikhwān al-Ṣafā'*.

36 See Javad Nurbakhsh, *Traditions of the Prophet*, vol. I, trans. Leonard Lewisohn and Terry Graham (New York: KNP 1981) p. 49.

> "Pursue knowledge even unto China."[37] Therefore, the most sage and learned of scholars is he or she who knows this knowledge. For this same reason, God Almighty has distinguished such sages by mentioning them as having been endowed with the highest rank, saying: "God himself proffers evidence – and so do the angels and all those endowed with knowledge – that there is no god but Him, firmly grounded in justice."[38]
>
> Now, those who are wise adepts in the science of divine Unity (*'ilm al-tawḥīd*) in the full sense of the term, are first of all the prophets, then the saints, followed by the learned savants (*'ulamā'*) who are the "heirs of the prophets."[39]

Another spiritual master (*min al-mashāyikh*) who has expounded this subject, reconfirming Ghazālī's statements, pronounced:

> Gnosis (*al-ma'rifa*) is finer and more selective than knowledge (*al-'ilm*), because gnosis is ascribed to two concepts (*ma'nā*), each of which constitutes a different kind of knowledge. The first of these is a kind of knowledge that is a purely internal matter (*al-'ilm bi'amr bāṭin*) circumstantially deduced from something external. When a description of a certain person, for instance, is provided, you recognize who it is internally by means of certain external signs that are provided, as in the case where God addresses his Prophet, saying "You will recognize them [the hypocrites] by their countenances and you will recognize them by their tone of voice."[40]

The second of these is a kind of knowledge that has been previously established and known over the course of time. For example, when you see again a person whom you had seen a long time ago, you understand him to be the

---

37 For a good discussion of the motif of travel in pursuit of knowledge in Islam, see Ian Netton, *Seek Knowledge: Thought and Travel in the House of Islam* (London: Curzon 1996). On the two *ḥadīths* cited here, see Bernard Lewis, et al., "'Ilm," in *EI2* III, pp. 1133ff.

38 Qur'ān III:18.

39 A reference to the ḥadīth of the Prophet: "The learned savants are the heirs of the prophets." See Nurbakhsh, *Traditions of the Prophet*, p. 50.

40 Qur'ān XLVII:30.

same person you had previously known, so you say: "After so many years, I still recognized him." Therefore, the first kind of object of knowledge known is absent (from sight and mind), whilst the second kind is present (to sight and mind).

So (the question arises) is there really any difference between these (two) types of knowers or gnostics, except in respect to the two different kinds of objects that are known or recognized? On the one hand, there is the type of gnostic who has no other way to obtain gnosis of God Almighty except by means of conjectural deductive reasoning (*istidlāl*) proceeding from His Activities to His Qualities, from His Qualities to His Names, and from His Names to His Essence. "Such are called to from afar."[41] On the other hand, there is another type of gnostic to whom pre-eternal divine mercy has been vouchsafed, by means of which he soars into the sanctuary of divine vision (*shuhūd*), beholding there once again – after his previous vision of God in the place of *Alast*[42] – the known Object, that is, God Almighty. The latter gnostic knows God *through* His divine Essence, Names and Qualities, in contradistinction to (the deductive knowledge of) the first type of gnostic.

Between these two types of knowers or gnostics lies a wide gap. Insofar as the object of knowledge is absent unto the first type of gnostic, he is like a dreaming man who sees strange fantasies that do not correspond to reality, whereas the second gnostic, to whom the object of knowledge is actually present, is like a man who is fully awake and his vision accords with reality. And it is to this distinction that Ibn al-Fāriḍ alludes in his poem:

To obtain knowledge of my divine Names from my Essence
 is wakefulness and vision
But to find knowledge of my divine Essence from my Names
 is just sleep and dreaming;
Likewise, one who seeks to reach knowledge of my Essence
 through my Activities in reality is ignorant;

41 Qur'ān XLI:44.

42 An allusion to the dialogue and covenant in pre-eternity between God and man, the time when God asked the 'Children of Adam', future human beings, whether he was their Lord (*alastu bi-rabbikum*) and they replied affirmatively (referring to Qur'ān VII:172): "Indeed we bear witness to it (*balā shahidnā*)."

Whereas if he proceeds from knowledge of my Essence to
my Activities, he is a true gnostic.[43]

God in His august grandeur and transcendent majesty is a Unity in respect to His Essence, Qualities, Names and Activities. This means that all the things that are predicated as related to His Essence, Qualities, Names and Activities are but unreal and fictional in their relation (to Him), since all things are in reality merely reflections of the brilliant theophanic illuminations of the one Essence, pre-eternal Qualities and divine Names which shine upon the phenomenal forms of creation. Yet, at the same time, there is nothing but Him in these phenomenal forms of creation: they are just like forms that appear as brilliantly reflected in a mirror.

Therefore, this 'audition' and 'vision' and suchlike qualities in reality all belong to Almighty God alone – whatever beings they are temporarily predicated to – for "He is the Hearer and the Seer," as the Almighty pronounces in a verse which indicates that these divine Names and Qualities must be reserved exclusively for Him. Now, the reason why God Almighty has revealed the mystery of His divine Essence and Qualities in the phenomenal manifestation of his Acts is not due to the fact that these things were previously concealed to Him. Rather, as Ibn Fāriḍ also relates of his Beloved in his poem, who declaims in the tongue of divine Unity:

These are but theatres and forms wherein I present myself,
Though I am displayed therein yet I was not concealed
from myself prior to my epiphany in them.[44]

Rather, it is God Almighty who manifests Himself in the divine Name 'The Outward' (*al-ẓāhir*) after all, just as He manifested Himself in the divine Name 'The Inward' (*al-bāṭin*) to begin with. But the marvel of marvels is that everything within which God Almighty has manifested Himself is also

43 These verses belong to his *Tā'iyya*, and are found in Sa'īd al-Dīn Farghānī's commentary on the poem entitled: *Mashāriq al-darārī: Sharḥ-i Tā'iyya-yi Ibn Fāriḍ*, ed. Jalāl al-Dīn Ashtiyānī (Mashhād: Dānishgāh-i Firdawsī 1357 A.Hsh./1978), pp. 437–38.

44 I was unable to locate this verse in the *Mashāriq al-darārī*, although it appears in R.A. Nicholson, *Studies in Islamic Mysticism* (Cambridge: Cambridge University Press 1980 repr.), v. 545, p. 250.

a veil concealing Him, and that there is no phenomenon in which God is concealed, in which He is not also manifest and revealed!

> She showed herself by veiling herself in phenomena, and she was hidden by the objects in which she was manifest, assuming tints of diverse hue in every appearance.[45]

Yet, this but demonstrates His handiwork's skilful arrangement, the superior force of His wisdom and the all-inclusiveness of His epiphany, for "such is the measurement of the Almighty, the Wise"[46] as God declares.

But since the purpose of citing the words of these two great spiritual teachers was something entirely different, let us set this matter aside for the moment.

What we intended to demonstrate was that gnosis (*al-ma'rifa*) to them (the true Sufis) is something quite different from knowledge (*al-'ilm*), and that gnosis, whether vis-à-vis the Necessary Being or of anything else, is of a higher degree than knowledge. The reason for this is that there are only two modes of knowledge; there is (i) either a kind of knowledge concerning the Necessary Being and what pertains to that, or else (ii) a kind of knowledge concerning possible beings and what pertains to them. Outwardly there are no more than these two things. Our discussion here, of course, concerns (knowledge of) outwardly existing living creatures, rather than nonentities of a mental character (*al-ma'dūmāt al-dhihnīyya*).[47]

Now, it is impossible to obtain any knowledge of the Necessary Being except by way of visionary unveiling and contemplative vision (*al-kashf wa'l-mushāhada*). Likewise, if one attempts to verify, hermeneutically speaking, the situation for oneself, it also becomes readily apparent that no knowledge of possible beings can be obtained except through this same visionary mode of understanding, since, as was stated above, the reality of the possible being is nothing else than God Almighty himself, whose reality cannot be apprehended except by this method. Therefore, everything (both

45 *Mashāriq al-darārī*, p. 264. The translation is adapted, with modifications, from R.A. Nicholson's rendition of the *Tā'īyya* in his *Studies in Islamic Mysticism*, p. 222 (v. 545).

46 Qur'ān XXXVI:38.

47 Alternate versions: mental abstractions which are purely 'naught and non-existent'/ non-existent creatures of fancy / imaginary beings that don't exist.

knowledge and gnosis) goes back to visionary unveiling and contemplative vision – which is also our purpose here. Apropos of which, the poet (Ibn Fāriḍ) says:

> You are the reality of every living being;
> And all the world's being,
> all its fantasy, all its fancy.

One must struggle to understand this: it is quite a subtle and refined point. The great Shaykh Ṣadr al-Dīn Qūnawī, the supreme spiritual Pole (*a'ẓam aqṭāb*) of this path, while making a spiritual inquiry into the distinction between knowledge (*al-'ilm*), gnosis (*al-ma'rifa*) and wisdom (*al-ḥikma*) in his book entitled *The Keys of the Invisible Realm* (*Mafātīḥ al-ghayb*)[48] expressed himself in a language both beauteous and subtle, sophisticated and terse, noting:

> It should be understood that the Presence of Omniscience (*al-ḥaḍrat al-'ilmīyya*)[49] embraces and comprehends various universal levels of

48 The correct and full title of this work is *Miftāḥ al-ghayb al-jam' wa al-jūd* (*The Key to Spiritual Synthesis and Generosity*). It has been described as "an exposition on the ontological rank and defining characteristics of the Perfect Human Being (*al-insān al-kāmil*) [which was] perhaps the most influential of Ṣadr al-Dīn's works. It became a basic text in both Ottoman and Persian domains, read by both Sunni and Shī'ite followers, and attracted a number of commentaries." – Jane Clark, "Towards a Biography of Ṣadr al-Dīn Qūnawī," *Journal of the Muhyiddin Ibn 'Arabi Society* XLIX (2011), p. 27.

49 William Chittick provides a crisp summary of the theory of the divine presences according to al-Qūnawī as follows: "In general the word 'Presence' is synonymous with 'level' (*martaba*), a term which carries a more philosophical and less religious connotation. Ibn al-'Arabī's followers often speak of the 'levels of existence' (*marātib al-wujūd*), which they consider to be infinite in number but whose general categories (*kulliyāt*) may be reduced to five or six, i.e. the Divine Presences ... The first is the Presence of Knowledge or of the Inward (*ḥaḍrat al-bāṭin*). It embraces God's Names and Attributes as well as the immutable entities. Facing the First Presence in the opposite position is the World of Sense-Perception, or the Presence of the Outward (*ḥaḍrat al-ẓāhir*). Between these two is the Central Presence, which comprehends the two sides and pertains exclusively to the Perfect Man. Then on the right side is the Central Presence, between it and the Divine Unseen, is the Presence of the Spirits. Finally, on the left side

multiplicity, these being: the Presence of Knowledge (*ḥaḍrat al-ʿilm*), the Presence of Gnosis (*ḥaḍrat al-maʿrifa*), the Presence of Wisdom (*ḥaḍrat al-ḥikma*), the Presence of divine Providence and Fate (*ḥaḍrat al-taqdīr wa'l-qadr*).

By 'knowledge' is meant the disclosure of the fully distinct comprehension of each and every object of knowledge along with all their concomitants, and all that these concomitants demand.

By 'gnosis' is meant knowledge of the underlying realities of those objects of knowledge from the point of view of their substantial reality while abstracted from all their concomitants and all that these concomitants require, and their hierarchical arrangement into various levels.

By 'wisdom' is denoted the knowledge of the 'hierarchical levels' (*al-ʿilm bi'l-marātib*),[50] the spiritual realities of these levels, and the hierarchy situated between the realities of the objects of knowledge, and their concomitants and accidents. By 'wisdom' is also meant knowledge of the spiritual abodes and mystical states (*al-mawāṭin wa'l-aḥwāl*).[51]

As for the Presence of Providence and Fate: this is consequential and subordinate to the Presence of Knowledge. By this Presence (of Providence and Fate) is meant the ordination of the quantities of spiritual realities and their various particularities in the divine knowledge according to the scale of gradation that each possesses. For Providence is the measurer of God Omnipotent (*al-taqdīr muqaddir al-Qadīr*) [which is allocated] according to the Almighty's foreordained degree and the rank in knowledge of that degree.

Whoever succeeds in penetrating into and exposing these majestical presences, in comprehending their spiritual truths, both in regard

---

of the Central Presence, between it and the Visible World as such, is the World of Image-Exemplars." "The Five Divine Presences from al-Qūnawī to al-Qayṣarī," *The Muslim World*, LXXII/2 (1982): pp. 109, 112.

50 Here, Qūnawī is referring to the ontological levels (*marātib al-wujūd*) of the universe in which all beings participate vis-à-vis the Divine Presence.

51 Spiritual states (*aḥwāl*) in Sufism are held to be fleeting modes of consciousness which are constantly fluctuating, and these diverse states are usually juxtaposed and contrasted to 'stations' (*maqāmāt*) or 'abodes' (*mawāṭin*) in which one settles down and resides.

to what distinguishes and what unites them in common, is indeed a supreme hermeneut.

May God in his wisdom and grace place all of us among those given such revelations! Indeed, He is omnipotent over all which He wills!

The conclusion one can reach from this is that knowledge is more general and common than gnosis, while gnosis is more particular and exclusive than knowledge, although both of them (*al-ʿilm* and *al-maʿrifa*) can be designated as (modes of) 'knowledge'. So in respect to us (humanity), 'knowledge' means the visionary disclosure of the fully distinct and effectively passive circumambience (of man by God), while in respect to the Necessary Being 'knowledge' signifies the full and absolute visionary disclosure of the effective Agency of the Essential Reality, as was mentioned above as well. This then is an exposition of the reality of knowledge couched in the language of sapiential heart-savour (*lisān al-dhawq*), so far as this spiritual degree permits.

However, so far as conventional linguistic expression and normal parlance goes, knowledge has been defined as "something that is by itself necessarily self-evident, which in reality is openly apparent to everyone, such that there is no need to explain it through definition and reveal it by exposition." On the other hand, others – who constitute the majority opinion – have said: "Knowledge demands definition and description to verify its meaning and to distinguish it from other quiddities."

Those who advocate the former viewpoint, however, argue that each of us is herself or himself conscious and aware of being 'knowledgeable', and thus we can distinguish our knowledgeability from conjecture, scepticism and doubt. Nor is there anything more evident and clear to man than what he discerns within himself.[52] In the same way that man does not need to know the definition of hunger, thirst, pain or pleasure into order to apprehend them, so he does not need to have the definition of knowledge on hand to discern what it is. Likewise, if every thing else also demanded a definition and description, this would necessarily lead to either a vicious circle or an infinite regress, both of which are fallacies.

52 Alternate version: Nor is there anything clearer and more obvious to man than what he discerns within himself.

Hence, it is now obvious that knowledge of things depends on some thing *beyond* definition and description, but which is immediately conceptualized in the mind. Now, there is nothing more clear and evident than sensible objects, and things innately apprehended from within (*al-maḥsūsāt wa'l-wajdāniyyāt*).[53] 'Knowledge' belongs to the category of things innately apprehended from within, and therefore does not in principle require any definition for it to become manifest. Of course, there are certain cogent proofs that can be adduced to reply (to objections), but this is not the place to present them.

Those who advocate the latter viewpoint, however, argue that the reality of knowledge is not some sort of immediately evident conception (*ghayr mutaṣawwirat bi'l-ḍarūrat*), although they differ and disagree as how to interpret it. Some of them profess that knowledge is conviction (*i'tiqād*) about something to one's own satisfaction (*sukūn al-nafs*).[54] Some of them say that knowledge is cognition of the object of knowledge as it is (*ma'rifat al-ma'lūm alā mā huwa bih*).[55] Others of them say that knowledge is that thing through which one becomes learned when one's essence becomes conjoined with it,[56] or else it is some thing which allows one's essence to validate its own evaluations and certitudes about things.

Although these expressions vary in form and substance, what they share in common is that they all agree that knowledge is a concept (*ma'nā*) subsistent in the very essence of the knower, which causes him to become characterized as having 'knowledge', and by means which things are disclosed and revealed.

Therefore, knowledge is something through which 'the act of becoming unveiled' (*al-inkashāf*) occurs, a process that some have interpreted as

53 In Islamic philosophy, sensible objects or objects of sense perception (*al-maḥsūsāt*) are held to be apprehended by the five external senses, in contrast to "things directly apprehended from within" (*al-wajdāniyyāt*) which are understood by means of the internal senses. For a further study of the term, see Jamīl Ṣalībā, *Farhang-i Falsafī*, translated from Arabic to Persian by Manūchihr Ṣāna'ī Durrabīdī (Tehran: Intishārāt-i Ḥikmat 1366 A.Hsh./1987), p, 659.

54 Cf. similar definitions given by F. Rosenthal, *Knowledge Triumphant*, p. 55, 63.

55 Cf. similar definitions given by F. Rosenthal, *Knowledge Triumphant*, pp. 53 (B.2), 58 (D. 3).

56 Cf. similar definitions given by F. Rosenthal, *Knowledge Triumphant*, pp. 52–53 (A. 2).

'unveiling' (*al-kashf*) itself,[57] insofar as a thing becomes disclosed through unveiling, just as motion occurs through moving, and literacy is acquired by learning. (Of course, there are certain arguments and discussions that arise here, which will be treated in their proper places when discussing the opinions of the mystical philosophers and scholastic theologians.) Following deep investigation and speculation on the matter, however, the sum and substance of all their words is that 'knowledge' may be designated as "the perfect and complete rending the veil (*al-kashf al-tām*) off the face of the object of knowledge specific to the science subject to scrutiny."[58] This definition is in accord with statements on the subject given by the Muslim theosophists (*ahl Allāh*), different aspects of which have already been cited above.

57 According to the *Definitions* of Jurjānī: *Kitāb al-ta'rīfāt*, ed. Ibrāhīm al-Abyārī (Beirut 1985), p. 237, the word *kashf* "literally means 'rending the veil', but in [Sufi] terminology it applies to obtaining consciousness of invisible spiritual conceptions or ideas and matters relating to such 'truths', by means of direct vision (*shuhūd*) or presential awareness (*ḥuḍūr*)."

58 This definition of knowledge seems to be original to Ḥaydar Āmulī. There is nothing even faintly similar to it in the various definitions of knowledge provided by Rosenthal (*Knowledge Triumphant*, pp. 52–69).

IX

THE SEVEN STAGES OF THE SPIRITUAL HIERARCHY

Ṣā'īn al-Dīn Turkah Iṣfahānī's (d. 830/1427) *Risāla-yi Shaqq al-qamar va sā'at*

In the history of Islamic esotericism, Ṣā'īn al-Dīn 'Alī ibn Muḥammad Turkah Iṣfahānī (d. 830/1427) was a thinker of extraordinary originality whose mystical thought played a formative and fundamental role in the development of later theosophical doctrines, but which has hardly been studied by modern scholars, whether Iranian or Western. As S.H. Nasr points out, "in his integration of illuminationist theosophy with Peripatetic thought and philosophical mysticism (*'irfān*)," he is "perhaps the most important figure in Islamic philosophy after Nāṣir al-Dīn Ṭūsī, figuring as the key link in the chain (of philosophical thought stretching) between Mullā Ṣadrā, Suhrawardī and Ibn Sīnā."[1] The profound originality of Ṣā'īn al-Dīn's Persian prose style, Nasr adjudicates as well, "puts him in the same rank as Nāṣir Khusraw, Suhrawardī, Bābā Afḍal, Naṣīr al-Dīn Ṭūsī and Quṭb al-Dīn Shīrāzī."[2]

Born circa 761/1360 in Iṣfahān, Ṣā'īn al-Dīn spent his youth travelling through Syria, Egypt and the Hijāz in pursuit of learning. It is known that he learned the fundamentals of jurisprudence at the hand of an older brother who was a juridical authority.[3] His journeys would certainly have taken place after preliminary study in a Shāfi'ite madrasa in Iṣfahān, which was still a predominantly Sunni city on the eve of the Safavid Shī'ification when it was established as the Iranian capital under that dynasty in the early sixteenth century.

1 Ṣā'īn al-Dīn Turkah, *Risālah-i i'tiqādāt* in Sayyid 'Alī Musavī Bihbahānī & Sayyid Ibrāhīm Dibājī (eds.), *Chārdah Risāla-yi Farsī Ṣā'īn al-Dīn ... Turkah Iṣfahānī* (Tehran: Chāpkhāna-yi Firdawsī 1351 A.Hsh./1972), introduction by S.H. Nasr, pp. b, j.

2 Ṣā'īn al-Dīn Turkah, *Risālah-i i'tiqādāt*, S.H. Nasr's introduction, p. j.

3 Muḥammad Taqī Bahār, *Sabk-shināsī* (Tehran: Chāp-i Tābān, n.d.), III, p. 230.

In an Egypt undergoing a Sunnite restoration, he studied with Sirāj al-Dīn 'Umar b. Raslān Bulqīnī (d. 805/1403), the most important Shāfi'ite jurisprudent of the day,[4] with an eminence far beyond the posts he held officially, such as the vital *Qāḍi al-'askar*, supreme judge of the military. Sirāj al-Dīn was also a Shādhilī Sufi, indicating the notable interconnection between Shāfi'ite jurisprudence and Sufism, but he was also a conservative, being amongst those who condemned Ḥallāj in a debate with the restorer of the Shādhilīyya in Egypt, Shams al-Dīn Muḥammad Ḥanafī (d. 847/1443), a supporter of the martyr.[5]

The little that is known of his life's history, apart from sketchy references to his education, really begins in his adulthood, where he is seen serving as a legal counsellor in the courts of one princeling or another. Though a Shāfi'ite in Sunni jurisprudence, he would cite the school of Abū Ḥanīfa with equal authority. His qualifications provided for service as chief justice under various regimes.

Ṣā'īn al-Dīn was the author of some thirty books and treatises in Arabic and Persian.[6] While the literary style of his autobiographical works is

---

4 'Abd al-Raḥmān Ibn Khaldūn, *The Muqaddimah*, trans. F. Rosenthal, Bollingen Series XLIII (Princeton: Princeton University Press, 1958/1967), III, p. 12, where the author states that the Shāfi'ite leadership was assumed by the present Shaykh of Islam in Egypt, Sirāj al-Dīn al-Bulqīnī, describing him as "the greatest Shāfi'ite in Egypt today and, indeed, the greatest Egyptian religious scholar." (The Persian secondary sources that discuss Turkah misspell the man's surname, making it appear to be Bū'lqīnī. He is actually from the Egyptian town of Bulqīn.) I am grateful to Terry Graham for clarifying the identity of Bulqīnī.

5 Louis Massignon, *The Passion of al-Hallāj*, Bollingen Series XCVIII (Princeton: Princeton University Press, 1982), II, pp. 37, 38 and 51. Massignon indicates the divisions in the Shāfi'ite camp over the correctness of Ḥallāj's position, the martyr himself having been an adherent of this school. Thus, Bulqīnī was consistent with one of the two positions, his going back to Ḥallāj's associate Junayd, a Sufi master who was also a Shāfi'ite authority. On the other hand, his adversary Ḥanafī, a member of the school indicated by his name, was among the few adherents of that school to endorse the martyr.

6 His Arabic works include: *Sharḥ Fuṣūṣ al-ḥikam* (a commentary on Ibn 'Arabī's *Fuṣūṣ*), *Kitāb Mafāḥaḍ* (on numerology); *Risāla Bā'īyya* (on Numerology and Divination); *Risāla Anzālīyya* (on Revelation in Sunni Kalām Theology); *Risāla Muḥammadīyya* (on the numerological significance of the name Muḥammad, a Ḥurūfī

relatively simple and straightforward, his works on esoteric Islamic spirituality, such as the treatise translated here, are typical of the period to which he belonged in being written in "an ornate literary style filled with rhyming prose (*saj'*) and other signs of painstaking labour in their composition (*takallufāt*). His peculiar prose style is not original but follows that of 'Aṭā Malik Juwaynī; being only slightly more eloquent and somewhat less pretentiously laboured."[7] Nonetheless, his prose is filled with pleasant fluency, original metaphors and charming sweetness.

ṢĀ'ĪN AL-DĪN TURKAH AND PERSIAN SUFISM

As a Sufi, there is some evidence that he was a close associate of the master and Founder of the Ni'matu'llāhī order-founder Shāh Ni'matu'llāh Walī Kirmānī (d. 732/1332).[8] In Herat, the Timurid capital under the rule of Shāhrukh (r. 1408–1447), the son of Tamurlane, he was certainly a close

---

tract); *Hawāshī wa Iṣṭilāḥāt* (on Marginalia and Technical Terms); *Risāla Mihr Nabuwwat* (on Prophetology); *Risāla Tamḥīd fī Sharḥ Qawā'id al-tawḥīd* (a commentary on the famous theological work by Ṭūsī); *Risāla mukhtaṣar*; *Risāla Bismala*; *Risāla Manāhij* (on Logic); *Sharḥ Tā'īyya Ibn Fāriḍ* (commentary on Ibn Fāriḍ). His Persian works include: *Sharḥ Tā'īyya Ibn Fāriḍ* (commentary on Ibn Fāriḍ), *Asrār al-ṣalāt* (on the mysteries of prayer); *Dar Aṭwār thalatha-yi taṣawwuf* (on Sufism); *Tuḥfa 'Alā'īyya* (On the Principles and Customs of Sunni Islam); *Madārij afhām al-afwāj* (on marriage); *Risālah-i i'tiqādāt* (on Belief); *Munāẓara-yi bazm u razm* (a literary tract); *Risālah dar Sharḥ-i Lama'āt-i 'Irāqī* (a commentary on 'Irāqī's *Lama'āt*); *Risālah Shaqq al-qamar va biyān-i sā'at* (translated below); *Risālah Anjām* (on Sufism); *Risālah Nuqṭah* (interpretation of the ḥadīth "I am the dot under the letter B"); *Risālah dar ma'nī-yi dah bayt* (commentary on a poem by Ibn 'Arabī); *Risālah dar Mabdā' va ma'ād* (on Eschatology); *Risālah Su'āl al-mulūk* (on Numerology); *Risālah Sullam-i dār al-salām* (on the five pillars of Islam); *Tarjuma-yi ḥādīthī az Ḥaḍrat Amīr al-Mu'minīn 'Alī* (commentary on some *ḥadīth*s of 'Alī); *Risālah-i Khawwāṣ-i 'ilm-i ṣarf* (a Sufi interpretation of Arabic grammar). See Bahār, *op. cit.*, III, pp. 236–38.

7 Bahār, *op. cit.*, III, p. 238.

8 See 'Abd al-Razzāq Kāshānī, *Manāqib-i Ḥaḍrat-i Shāh Ni'mat Allāh-i Walī* in *Majmu'a dar tarjuma'-i aḥwāl-i Shāh Ni'mat Allāh-i Wall-yi Kirmānī*, ed. Jean Aubin (Bibliotheque Iranienne no. 7; Paris: Librairie d'Amérique et d'Orient 1982;1956 ed. rpt.), pp. 70–71. I am grateful to Terry Graham for bringing this connection to my attention.

associate of Shāh Ni'matu'llāh's chief khalifa, Shāh Qāsim-i Anwār (d. 837/1433–34), so much so that, like the latter, he was implicated in the abortive assassination of the monarch in 830/1426–27 engineered by the politically radical Ḥurūfī movement, though, unlike Shāh Qāsim, he was more quickly exonerated and avoided the latter's punishment of exile.[9] Despite his reservations about formal Sufism (see below), some evidence exists to indicate that Ṣā'in al-Dīn may also have actually been affiliated to the Naqshband, in the person of Muḥammad Pārsā (d. 822/1419). In fact, his copious mention of this Naqshbandī master – the only living authority to which he refers, the others being long-dead authors of Sufi doctrinal works – and the earnest presentation of him as emphasizing the importance of the canon law and the Prophetic Custom in Sufism, provides rather robust circumstantial evidence of a possible disciplic connection.[10]

While Ṣā'īn al-Dīn seems to have made his living as a jurisprudent, his prime occupation outside his profession was as an esoteric thinker fusing the thought of the schools of Ibn 'Arabī (d. 638/1240) and Suhrawardī. He penned a commentary on the *Fuṣūṣ al-ḥikam* by Ibn 'Arabī in 831/1427, while his major work on ontology, the *Tamhīd al-qawā'id*, "paraphrases Jandī's *Fuṣūṣ* commentaries."[11] He inherited his interest in theosophy and philosophy from his father, Ṣadr al-Dīn Turkah, who introduced him to the study of the Ishrāqī, or 'Illuminationist', school founded by Suhrawardī.[12] In the first decade of the fourteenth century, Ṣā'īn al-Dīn Turkah served in the court of Mīrzā Iskandar in Iṣfahān, who later rebelled against Shāh Rukh (in 817/1414). Shāh Rukh as a consequence conquered Iṣfahān and Fars. Although Ṣā'īn al-Dīn Turkah retired from public service, he was not immune from attacks of those envious of his position. He travelled twice to meet Shāh Rukh in Khurāsān, where he composed several treatises in the prince's honour, in which he complains about the stratagems that his rivals had used against him. Although at one

9 Bahār, *op. cit.*, III, p. 233.

10 Turkah, *Risāla-yi nafathat al-maṣdūr-i awwal* in *Chahār risāla-yi fārsī-yi Ṣā'in al-Dīn Turka-yi Iṣfahānī*, pp. 172, 186–87, 193. See also Dr. Jalīl Misgar-nizhād (ed.), *Muḥammad Pārsā: Sharḥ-i Fuṣūṣ al-ḥikam* (Tehrān: Nashr-i Dānishgāhī 1366 A.Hsh./1987), introduction, p. 16.

11 W.C. Chittick. *Encyclopædia Iranica* "Ebn al-'Arabī," VII, p. 668.

12 Sayyid 'Alī Mūsawī Bihbihānī, *Aḥwāl u āthār-i Ṣā'in al-Dīn Turkah Iṣfahānī*, in H. Landolt and M. Mohaghegh (eds.), *Collected Papers on Islamic Philosophy and Mysticism* (Tehran: Tehran University Press 1971)," p. 101.

point, Shāh Rukh put Ṣā'īn al-Dīn Turkah in charge of the judiciary (*qaḍāwat*) of province of Yazd, his rivals at court persisted in intriguing against him, accusing him of being a Sufi, thereby obliging Ṣā'īn al-Dīn to travel to Herat to defend the orthodoxy of his Sunni beliefs, and his association with the kind of esotericism connected with the Ḥurūfiyya, in whose letter-occultism he certainly did have an open interest.

But he still seemed to have been tarred by the brush of heterodoxy for his open espousal of Sufism, so that in the wake of the wave of anti-esotericism following the assassination attempt on Shāh Rukh, he was forced to defend his Sufi principles in a treatise, the "Profession of Faith" or "Tract on Religious Belief" (*Risālah-i iʿtiqādāt*), Then he carried the argument further in another treatise, in which he goes so far as to state that Sufism is not a matter of belief but of perception and revelation.[13] Devoted to elucidating his views on Sufism and its compatibility with orthodox Sunnism, these semi-autobiographical confessional treatises were all dedicated to Shāh Rukh. The two most important of these treatises are entitled "First Expectoration," or "Inspired effusions in relief of chest pain, I" (*nafthat al-maṣdūr-i awwal*), or "An Initial Letting off of Some Steam" – more colloquially rendered – composed in two parts, the second being entitled "A Secondary Letting off of Some Steam" (*Nafthat al-maṣdūr-i duwam*).

Although the first treatise, composed when he was fifty-nine years old, is full of much important autobiographical information, for the purposes of the present essay, its main importance lies in the light it casts on his attitude to Sufism in general and esoteric Islam in particular. For the last fifteen years, he claims in this treatise, "I have not been occupied in teaching any other sciences but Qur'ānic commentary (*tafsīr*), *ḥadīth*, the Principles of Theology (*uṣūl*), and Jurisprudence (*fiqh*), nor have I ever stepped even one hairs'-breadth outside the bounds of the exoteric Law (*ẓāhir-i sharʿ*)."[14] He goes on to say that he has already defended himself previously before Shāh Rukh against similar charges of heresy that others had levelled against him, having publicly confessed at that time his adherence to the Sunni faith.[15]

---

13 Zarrīnkūb, 'Abd al-Ḥusayn, *Dunbāla-yi justujū-yi dar taṣawwuf-i Irān* (Tehran: Amīr Kabīr 1983), p. 131. See below (p. 322), where the relevant passage is translated.

14 Ṣā'īn al-Dīn Turkah, *Nafthat al-maṣdūr awwal*, in *Chahārdah Risāla-yi Farsī Ṣā'īn al-Dīn ...*, p. 170.

15 Ṣā'īn al-Dīn Turkah, *Nafthat al-maṣdūr awwal*, in *Chahārdah Risāla-yi Farsī Ṣā'īn al-Dīn ...*, p. 172.

In the beginning of his 'Tract on Religious Belief', Ṣā'īn al-Dīn casts a coldly disdainful eye on different Islamic sects and theological doctrines. Just as he is highly critical of the Mu'tazilite denial of the vision of God in the hereafter, so he rejects the philosophers' (*falāsafa*) view that creation expresses that final extent of God's Power and Will, while attacking the Shī'ite doctrine that God's Nature obliges Him to vouchsafe grace upon anyone who worships and obeys Him, and to display His wrath to all to those who sin and trespass against Him.[16]

At the end in his 'Tract on Religious Belief', he characterizes himself as a Sunni Sufi.[17] He begins another smaller autobiographical tract on the same subject with these words:

> The belief (*i'tiqād*) of this *faqīr* has never been anything other than that which the leaders of the Sunni sect (*a'imma-yi sunnat u jamā'at*) – may God's grace accompany all of them – profess, and at the present moment, it is still the same. [Then, after detailing some of the spiritual and intellectual reasons for this affiliation] ... And whoever follows a religious affiliation (*madhhab*) other than this is lost and gone astray.[18]

From this passage and other biographical particulars that he relates about his life in other autobiographical writings, we can now correct an important misunderstanding of his thought promulgated by Henry Corbin, who mistakenly conceived his philosophy to be representative of a kind of *Shī'ite* gnostic spirituality.[19] His cool if not downright cold attitude towards

16 Ṣā'īn al-Dīn Turkah, *Risālah-i i'tiqādāt* in *Chahārdah Risāla-yi Farsī Ṣā'īn al-Dīn ... Turkah Iṣfahānī*, p. 227.

17 "This then is the full mystery of the doctrinal beliefs of this dervish, and those of everyone following him in the Sunni religious denomination (*madhhab-i sunnat va jamā'at*)." Ṣā'īn al-Dīn Turkah, *Risālah-i i'tiqādāt*, p. 229.

18 Ṣā'īn al-Dīn Turkah, *I'tiqādīyya*, in *Chahārdah Risāla-yi Farsī Ṣā'īn al-Dīn ...*, p. 267.

19 It would appear that the primary reason why Henry Corbin insists in his *Histoire de la philosophie islamique* (Paris: Gallimard 1964, p. 63) against so many autobiographical statements (to the contrary by Ṣā'īn al-Dīn) that he was a Shī'ite, is that the mystic's Persian works were as yet unpublished when Corbin composed his history. The collection of fourteen Persian essays by Ṣā'īn al-Dīn, published in Tehran by Dr. Bihbahānī in 1972 (*Chahārdah Risāla-yi Farsī Ṣā'īn al-Dīn*: see note 1 above) clearly reveals that his

sectarian Shī'ism is reflected in the following passage found in another of his Persian works, where he wrote:

> The Shī'ites and the Mutazilites are in agreement in many of their theological principles, and the opinion of both these groups are mostly in accordance with those of the Philosophers. *All these three groups are enemies of the Sunnis (sunnat u jamā'at). All the Sufi shaykhs follow the Sunni denomination. In fact, no one who is* ***not*** *a member of the Sunni denomination can grasp this science (of Sufism).* Hence, anyone who comes to a Sufi master (*murshid*) in pursuit of this science will not be offered any spiritual direction until he or she converts to Sunnism.[20]

Ṣā'īn al-Dīn here directly links the esoteric tradition of Sufism with exoteric Sunni theology, implying by extension that Shī'ites, Mutazilites and Peripatetic philosophers are all misled and astray in their faith.

Despite Ṣā'īn al-Dīn's evident unwillingness to publicly confess himself an affiliate of any contemporary Sufi *ṭarīqa*, his deep sympathy and devotion for the great classical Sunni Sufi esoteric tradition and its masters is everywhere in evidence in his writings. Given the political climate, he was at pains to stress that Sufism was not an ideology, like Ḥurūfism, making it clear that, as a Sufi, he was not a member of an organization of a sort that

---

sectarian affiliation was to the Sunni community. Yet bias in viewing Turkah as a Shī'ite continues to persist, to the point that an eminent British scholar in the mid-1990s (John Cooper, "From al-Ṭūsī to the School of Iṣfahān," in S.H. Nasr and Oliver Leaman, eds., *History of Islamic Philosophy* (London: Routledge 1996), I, 591 (italics mine) described him as "one of the first to seek to unify the Peripatetic, *ishrāqī*, and Akbarian strands in the perspective of *Shī'ī* esotericism." Nor does the fact that Ṣā'īn al-Dīn's *Kitāb al-tamhīd al-qawā'id* is today still used as a teaching text of gnosis (*'irfān*) and Sufism (*taṣawwuf*) in Shī'ite madrasahs in Qum in Iran (S.H. Nasr, "The Traditional Texts used in the Persian Madrasahs," *Islamic Quarterly* XIX/3 & 4; 1975, pp. 172–86) make him a Shī'ite thereby, as some Iranian scholars have argued, viewing his own patent confessions of Sunnism purely as pious dissimulation or *taqīyya*. I find it rather repugnant to think a man of such great religious sincerity could exhibit such an extreme depth of dissemblance, which would make him the author of two contradictory, exoteric teachings.

20 Ṣā'īn al-Dīn Turkah, *Nafthat al-maṣdūr awwal*, in *Chahārdah Risāla-yi Farsī Ṣā'īn al-Dīn* ..., p. 175. Italics and bold type mine.

might threaten the socio-political establishment. In his *Nafthat al-maṣdūr awwal*, Ṣā'īn al-Dīn points out that Sufism cannot be classified as a heresy. The bias maintained by so-called orthodox theologians against the study of Sufism appears absurd when contrasted and compared to the unbalanced support given by the Timurid State to the teaching of the profane sciences. If monarchs are willing to fiddle away their time and demean their dignity by attacking the so-called heresy of Sufism, "why is it they never bother to castigate the science of astronomy, which is clearly a type of religious infidelity (*kufr*) since so many of its principles contradict the Qur'ān?"

> And if astronomy is infidelity, then so is astrology also infidelity, since it is grounded in astronomy, yet one sees that most of the discussions that take place in royal assemblies revolve around astrology, especially during the present day when this science has been revived with a fresh vigour, with edicts continually being issued to erect new observatories, the like of which no rulers in past epochs ever founded.[21]

Noting that "it is a common trait of petty-minded fault-finders to try to pigeonhole people by labelling them with names," he observes how some mullahs, whom he refers to derogatively as 'turbanites' [*ahl-i dastār*], characterizing them as quarrelsome meddlers constantly engaged in disputing and fighting with each other, are especially engaged in refutation of the Sufis, and so have accused him of being a Sufi as well:

> They have continuously tried to drag this *faqīr* into (belonging to) the Path of Sufis such as Junayd and Shiblī and Bāyazīd and Khwāja Muḥammad 'Alī Ḥakīm Tirmidhī and Shaykh Sa'd al-Dīn Ḥamuya, the light and grace of each of whose mausoleums has filled all four quarters of the world with luminosity and the fragrance of the Sacred.[22]

As can be seen by the enthusiastic and flowery epithets attached to classical heroes of the Sufi tradition cited here, Ṣā'īn al-Dīn was by no means

21 Ṣā'īn al-Dīn Turkah, *Nafthat al-maṣdūr awwal*, in *Chahārdah Risāla-yi Farsī Ṣā'īn al-Dīn ...*, pp. 173–74.

22 Stating, "These are the beliefs then of this *darvīsh*." *Risālah-i i'tiqādāt*, p. 224.

displeased in having the label 'Sufi' attached to his name. In fact, he characterized himself as a "dervish" in one place of the same tract.[23] His dominant sympathy, however, hovers with the *elect* among the great Sunni Sufis, with whom he stands shoulder to shoulder in opposition to the popular exoteric Sunni theologians, their common enemy. In his treatise on his 'Profession of Faith' he writes sarcastically that one of the reasons that he set pen to paper

> ... was because it had been heard that my contemporaries in general, and the turbanites (*ahl-i dastār*) in particular (insofar as their noble nature requires that the scissors of spiteful self-interest be continually employed in hostile contact and engaged in animosity with one another by setting afire and shredding each other's character) had been relating these sort of (spiteful) tales about the religious doctrine of the dervishes (*dar bāb-i iʿtiqād-i darvīshān*), while standing, as it were, before the pedestal of their throne ... However, the reason why these turbanites repudiate and reject the dervishes is that there are certain types of complex and difficult sciences pertaining to the works of the prophets and the mysteries of God's saints (*awliyā'*) that still exist down to the present day, the understanding of which is beyond the comprehension of most people. None but smart intelligent folk (*zīrakān-i hūshmand*), who by virtue of their obedience [of the Prophet], and Masters of the Sufi Path (*pīrān-i ṭarīqat*) who have traversed this path, with the help of being befriended by divine favour after subjecting themselves to a multitude of ascetic exercises and learning many sciences, can traverse this arena on the swift foot of Thought. No one else has the ability to understand these sciences.[24]

Ṣā'īn al-Dīn's admiration for the great representatives of the Persian Sunni Sufi tradition, whom he classifies as constituting the elect intelligentsia (*khawāṣṣ*) of esoteric Islamic thought is here quite evident. Authorities such as Ghazālī and Anṣārī are the true saints, he declares, the "smart intelligent folk" who follow the true Prophet, the real masters of the *ṭarīqat*. In fact, Ṣā'īn al-Dīn observes that the lack of understanding of these esoteric sciences on the part of the common rabble is the main reason why Imām

23 Ṣā'īn al-Dīn Turkah, *Risālah-i iʿtiqādāt*, p. 229.

24 Ṣā'īn al-Dīn Turkah, *Risālah-i iʿtiqādāt*, p. 223.

Muḥammad Ghazālī and Shaykh 'Abdu'llāh Anṣarī ("who bore away the ball of intellectual pre-eminence from their contemporaries in arena of their day and age") have been attacked and criticized for their works. Ṣā'īn al-Dīn here uses the term "intelligent person" (*hūshmand*) in a general mystical sense, defining it as "someone who is capable of making use of the sound assets of the present moment (*naqd al-waqt*), not one who is heedless of his own present moment of inspiration (*waqt-i khwud*), preoccupied with another moment, whether of the past or future."[25]

Esotericism is a time-honoured mode of intellectual and religious discourse, he argues in defence of Sufism. If an idea's literary expression contains several levels of interpretation and degrees of meaning, most of which are erroneous, but one of which is correct and true, then the idea itself cannot be condemned as constituting error or construed as blasphemy:

> First of all, it is possible to make a full explanation and to formulate an esoteric exegesis (*ta'wīl*) for *all* the words and discourses delivered by the Sufi shaykhs. The legal authorities that specialize in Islamic jurisprudence (*a'immih-yi fiqh*) all agree that if within one discourse several different connotations can be found, all of which are blasphemous except for that (non-blasphemous), one, then the fair judge must chose the connotation that *isn't* blasphemous, and adjudicate that the words are *not* to be interpreted in a heretical sense.
>
> What a strange tale all this is!
>
> On the one hand, all those masters who uttered these statements clearly asserted that their intention in such sayings had nothing to do with the formal, exoteric dimension (*ẓāhir*). On the other hand, one finds two other groups, that is, the Mu'tazilites and the philosophers, who actually substantiate by demonstration their heretical opinions, arbitrarily and persistently adducing arguments in defence of these opinions. Nobody objects to anything they say, while they are allowed to pursue and persecute these Sunni (Sufi) shaykhs.
>
> How well Ḥāfiẓ Shīrāzī sums up the situation:

> Lift up the tulip-cup, the eyes'
>   drunken narcissus gaze;

25 Ṣā'īn al-Dīn Turkah, *Risālah-i i'tiqādāt*, p. 227.

And set on me the label 'pervert'.
  With so many judges
That are set upon me,
  O Lord, who shall I take to be my judge?[26]

The real enemies of religion, continues Ṣā'īn al-Dīn, are thus the crypto-Shī'ites and crypto-philosophers, who, disguised as Sunnis, attack the Sufis as infidels. "And the reason why they do this is to defend their own sect, instead of attacking those two other heresies (i.e. Mu'tazilite philosophy and the natural scientists)."[27] At this juncture, Ṣā'īn al-Dīn clarifies what he perceives to be the inseparable relationship between Sufism and Sunnism, while pointing out some of the shortcomings of the former:

> Although it is clearly the case that this company of the Sufis are the highest dignitaries of the Sunni denomination, since any Sunni who attains to the degree of perfection in knowledge and its application is designated as a 'Sufi', two ugly flaws have appeared as a by-product of the words and behaviour of this group (the Sufis).
>
> The first is that they have uttered a few words and spoken discourses inspired by sapiential 'taste' and an influx of inspiration born of mystical consciousness (*az sar-i dhawq u ḥāl*), the exterior sense (*ẓāhir*) of which appears to be blasphemous. Then along comes a troupe of vain and errant folk who have not transcended their brute animal natures who latch onto these words, adopting them to further their own fallible ends, saying that 'everything is God' (*hamah-yi chīz khudā'st*) – Heaven forfend! – and so become apostates and heretics. They imagine that the rhyme and verse of the great masters such as Shaykh Aḥmad Jām, Mawlānā Rūm, 'Irāqī and others convey this (pantheistic) sense, and so announce in public that these masters followed their faith. Then up walks a company of nobles and princes who are too bewildered and confused to know whether or not their words are truthful. Why? Because they have heard how the

26 Ṣā'īn al-Dīn Turkah, *Nafthat al-maṣdūr awwal*, in *Chahārdah Risāla-yi Farsī Ṣā'īn al-Dīn ...*, p. 174. The line is from Ḥāfiẓ, *Dīvān*, ed. Parvīz Nātil Khanlarī (Tehran: Intishārāt-i Khwārazmī 1359 A.Hsh./1980), 335: 4.

27 Ṣā'īn al-Dīn Turkah, *Nafthat al-maṣdūr awwal*, in *Chahārdah Risāla-yi Farsī Ṣā'īn al-Dīn ...*, p. 175.

jurisprudents (*fuqaha*) condemn and excommunicate them, while they have seen for themselves how badly they (the Sufis) conduct themselves. So these princes and notables end up repudiating and denying the Sufis entirely, and in this, they are fully justified! For the words of the Sufi masters are extremely hard to understand, while the disposition and behaviour of this other group who have affiliated themselves to the Sufis, is extremely ugly and repulsive.

What fault of it is mine
That among so many swine
Not one pearl can be found?

It is no secret that the words of the Sufi masters can only be understood by someone who has exerted himself for years in pursuit of knowledge while making efforts in practical works through following the Sunna of the Prophet Muḥammad (peace and blessing be upon him), after which, befriended by divine grace, he becomes the object of the regard of a perfect master who has realized and comprehended the spiritual stations (*maqāmāt*) of this path. Only then, after availing himself of this master and spending many years engaged in his service, only after all of this, will he perhaps understand all of their words – or perhaps not. So how can a band of lewd and dissolute folk whose outward character is utterly soiled with sin, and whose inward nature is filled with all sorts of spite, rancour, envy and malice, who have never taken even one single step outside their soul's lustful passions, ever hope to understand such statements?[28]

The second "ugly flaw" of Sufism is actually neither the fault of the majority of the Sufis nor of the theosophy of Sufism itself, but rather pertains to the fallacies and foibles of certain pseudo-Sufis – charlatan shaykhs advertising their own miracle-working powers, laying claim to incredible ascetic feats, and creating as a consequence, social and political disturbances in the land, says Ṣā'īn al-Dīn.[29]

---

28 Ṣā'īn al-Dīn Turkah, *Nafthat al-maṣdūr awwal*, in *Chahārdah Risāla-yi Farsī Ṣā'īn al-Dīn ...*, p. 176.

29 So far goes the summary of the introduction. The main part of the treatise contains two sections (*waṣl*). The first section concerns various *ḥadīth* relating to harmfulness of

Despite his defence of the esoteric language of Sufism, his maintenance of the orthodox nature of the Sufis' pursuit of the Prophet's Sunna, and his defence of the path of the great classical masters in the above treatise, in other works Ṣā'īn al-Dīn is careful not to endorse the Sufi tradition either in regard to its overall theological doctrine nor in respect to its practical *tarīqat* methods and initiatic lineage. His position regarding direct affiliation with the Sufi tradition he clarifies in another small two-page tract "On Belief" (*I'tiqādīyya*) as follows:

> However, during the days of my youth and pursuit (of knowledge), following the adage that enjoins one to 'Study until the dawn', if I did engage in the study of certain sciences that contradicted or were contrary to these (Sunni) principles, my examination of these sciences was not due to my belief in them, but simply for the sake of obtaining many-sidedness and versatility (*tafannun*),[30] and by way acquiring culture and erudition. Such, after all, is the habit and practice of lovers of knowledge, and is in accordance with the custom of my occupation, for my following of these things was by the example of the religious leaders (may God hallow their innermost mystery) the Proof of Islam (*ḥujjat al-islām*, i.e. Ghazālī) and the pride of mankind (*fakhr al-anām*).
>
> Sinful wretch I am, but I was not the first of Love's criminals –
> Nor me it was who first of all brought
> *Amor*'s games of love into the world.
>
> Likewise, the various things concerning the words of the Sufi masters that were written (by me), which were at the command and entreaty of a group of them, should be considered in the same way. They were

heretical innovation (*bid'at*), monasticism, religious fanaticism, and various other matters. The second section is devoted to the defence of Sufism itself, concentrating on the presenting a synopsis of a mystical treatise by Muḥammad Pārsā, which in turn was composed by way of commentary on a poem by Ibn Fāriḍ. In this part Ṣā'īn al-Dīn actually defends the role of esoteric knowledge in Islam in general and Sufism in particular.

30 On the importance of *tafannun* in Islamic education, see George Makdisi, *The Rise of Humanism in Classical Islam and the Christian West* (Edinburgh: Edinburgh University Press 1990), p. 304.

> not written because I believed in them, since most of those words are not matters bound up with doctrines of religious belief (*iʿtiqādī nīst*).[31]

Commenting on the biographical and political circumstances underlying some of the above-cited passages, Professor Zarrīnkūb notes that while Ṣāʾīn al-Dīn was "no doubt associated with the Sufi movement and with Shāh Qāsim-i Anwār [d. 837/1433–34], because of anti-Sufi conspiracies and prejudices against certain Sufi groups prevailing at the court of Shāh Rukh, he was obliged in his *Risālah-i iʿtiqādāt* to rebut the accusation of affiliation with Sufism that had been levelled against him. In his *Nafthat al-maṣdūr awwal,* he maintains furthermore that whatever he has composed in its chapters should not be interpreted as reflecting his own personal 'belief' (*iʿtiqād*), since Sufism is not a matter of 'belief' but rather an experience realized through direct visionary perception (*kashf*) and insight (*idrāk*)."[32] As Zarrīnkūb here points out, although Ṣāʾīn al-Dīn declines to profess himself fully and formally as an *exoteric* affiliate of the Sufi tradition, he is quite clear about the *esoteric* nature of his understanding and knowledge of this tradition. "My knowledge," he informs us, "has not been obtained by way of supposition and imitation (*gumān u taqlīd*) like that of our contemporaries, but rather verified by real certainty and obtained by a comprehensively perfect knowledge realized through the good graces of obedience to Muḥammad and following his wise discourses ... My knowledge has *not* been obtained by theoretical means of demonstration and rational thought."[33]

ṢĀʾĪN AL-DĪN'S THEORY OF THE ESOTERIC HIERARCHY

Looking at the precise nature of Ṣāʾīn al-Dīn's doctrine of the hierarchy of adepts in esoteric knowledge, one sees that he maintains that there are two different approaches to God. These are the exoteric and esoteric ways, each

31 Ṣāʾīn al-Dīn Turkah, *Iʿtiqādīyya*, in *Chahārdah Risāla-yi Farsī Ṣāʾīn al-Dīn ...*, pp. 267–68.

32 ʿAbd al-Ḥusayn Zarrīnkūb, *Dunbāla-yi justujū-yi dar taṣawwuf-i Īrān* (Tehran: Amīr Kabīr 1362 A.Hsh./1983), p. 141.

33 Ṣāʾīn al-Dīn Turkah, *Risālah-i iʿtiqādāt*, pp. 229–30.

of which is fared properly by two different sorts of wayfarers on the path of religion (*ṭālibān-i rāh-i dīn*):

> The first kind are those who know the way leading to the quarter of Interior Spiritual Reality (*kūcha-yi maʿnā*) and to the farthest reaches of Certitude, who do not allow themselves rest and recline on the portal of the phenomenal form and exoteric appearances (*ṣūrat*).
>
> The second sort are those who do not have the strength to undertake the journey towards the waystations of spiritual realization (*manāzil-i taḥqīq*) and who, despite all their scouring about after knowledge and practical application, are never able to gain access to anything beyond the seraglio of phenomenal form and exoteric appearances.[34]

To first group pertains knowledge of the inner realities of faith (*īmān*) and to the second belongs the outward formalities of ordinary religious practice or 'Islām'. Ṣā'īn al-Dīn's fundamental distinction between esoteric authority based on spiritual realization, and exoteric understanding restricted to knowledge of the literal externals of religion is similar in certain respects to the doctrines and teachings of the Shīʿite philosopher ʿAbd al-Razzāq Lāhījī, who is featured in this volume as well, as the following passage from the *Gawhar-i murād* illustrates:

> It should be also understood that there are but two ways for humankind to approach God: either the exoteric (*rāh-i ẓāhir*) or the esoteric way (*rāh-i bāṭin*). Although one may *know* God through the exoteric way, one can only *reach* God by the esoteric way – and how wide the gap between [theoretically] knowing God and actually reaching Him is! It is because of this that so many allusions have been made to the hardships of the esoteric way, in contrast to the exoteric way which involves much less hardship – being based on rational demonstrations within the reach of every intelligent person capable of discerning cause from effect.[35]

34 Ṣā'īn al-Dīn Turkah, *Risālah-i iʿtiqādāt*, pp. 239–40.

35 *Gawhar-i murād* (*The Essence of Spiritual Intention* or *Crown-jewel of Desire*), ed. Z. Qurbānī Lāhījī (Tehran: 1372 A.Hsh./1993), p. 34.

However, in order to better understand the full scope of Ṣā'īn al-Dīn's esoteric thought, it will be more useful to examine his *Risāla-yi Shaqq al-qamar va sā'at* (*Treatise on Cleaving the Moon in Twain and the Advent of the Final Hour*) in which the various stages and degrees of esoteric knowledge are explained in much greater depth and detail.

The treatise begins with a description of the Qur'ānic verse: "The hour has drawn nigh and the moon is rent twain." (LIV:1) referred to in its title. Given the deeply symbolic nature of both the key images in this verse (moon and hour), it is probably quite appropriate that Ṣā'īn al-Dīn's exegetical discourse should take on the form of an imaginal autobiographical tale set in a visionary academic landscape. The author begins the treatise recounting his chance visit to a religious college where he found a group students gathered around discussing the meaning of this verse according to "the rhetorical expressions of both the literalist exoteric authorities and the lexicon of the scholastic theologians (*mutakallimūn*)."[36]

To Ṣā'īn al-Dīn, whose approach to hermeneutics of the Qur'ān was intensely mystical, this verse contained a deeper esoteric sense that he personified as an 'invisible Witness of Beauty' (*shāhid-i ghaybī*), belonging to the realm of divine beauty.[37] Abstracted from her place in the Ideal

36 All the following citations are from *Risāla-yi Shaqq al-qamar va sā'at,* in Bihbahānī and Dibājī (eds.), *Chārdah Risāla-yi Farsī Ṣā'īn al-Dīn ... Turkah Iṣfahānī,* pp. 101–17.

37 Aḥmad 'Alī Rajā'ī Bukhārā'ī, in his *Glossary of Ḥāfiẓ's Verse* (*Farhang-i ash'ār-i Ḥāfiẓ* (Tehran: Intishārāt-i 'lmī, n.d., 2nd edn, p. 361ff.) devotes several comprehensive pages to the meaning of *shāhid,* citing most of the important authorities that have written on this Sufi technical term. He notes that "literally, the term *shāhid* means 'seer' and 'witness'; in the Sufi lexicon it is used to mean 'the Good' and 'the Beautiful' in an absolute sense, with the connotation that the *shāhid* is one who bears 'witness' to God's artifice." Bukhārā'ī cites Quṭb al-Dīn Manṣūr 'Abbādī's *Al-taṣfiya fī aḥwāl al-mutaṣawwifa* (Tehran 1968; pp. 211–12) on this term: "It should be understood that in Sufi terminology there are many different sorts of (implications to the term) *shāhid.* The *shāhid* is that thing found to be acceptable to the eyes of the heart. It is an interior spiritual reality (*ma'nā*) that becomes attached to heart such that the heart beholds it in all its states, seeking deeper intimacy with it by envisioning it (*bi-dīdār-i ū uns talabad*), and the *shāhid* is that which 'bears witness'. Therefore, that which the spiritual wayfarer's heart becomes intimately attached to beholding, and which it contemplates in all its contemplative moments, such that that thing attests and bears witness to the soundness of its presential awareness-of-heart – that thing is the *shāhid.* As long at wayfarer languishes

Realm, incarcerated in the secular Academe, Ṣā'īn al-Dīn laments her condition as a virgin, subjected to ignorant mullahs' molestation:

> They were putting this lovely virgin from the sacred precincts of prophecy and Qur'ānic inimitability on public display and had decked her out in garments of technical expressions found in the common sciences, – even though she is sequestered from the sight of strangers who reside in the City of Reason (*sharistān-i 'aql*), hidden from the view of those who live in the Lane of Reflection (*kū-y fikr*), while the comprehension of immature men who inhabit the degree of spiritual chivalry and knightliness has never once laid hand on the skirt of her chaste innocence.

Simultaneous with this metahistorical, imaginal apparition of the Sophianic spirit of the verse to the author as a ravishing virgin compromised by the unchaste seductions of undeserving intellectual aliens, the author admits his wish to make his commentary on the verse 'keep up with the times'. So upon contemplation of the spiritual form of the Qur'ānic verse, he re-enters the exigencies of linear historical time, commenting that "the thought seemed then to pass through my feeble fractured consciousness that I should dress her up in apparel suited to the needs of the time and the demands of the age."

The rest of the treatise exemplifies Ṣā'īn al-Dīn's attempt to dress up, or to re-present the verse's esoteric virginal reality in harmony with his own

---

and longs for the sight of it, he is a spectator or observer (*mashāhid*), but as soon as by way of contemplative absorption and annihilation, he loses all personal qualification of self, drowning in the essence of the *shāhid*, he becomes a 'martyr' (*shahīd*; lit. 'one who has borne witness [for his faith]'). So whatever the wayfarer's heart hangs upon is his *shāhid*, whether this be a phenomenal form (*ṣūrat*), a song (*āwāz*), a verse, an idea, or a moment of meditation. As for one who makes his *shāhid* out to be a beautiful face or a child, there is no warrant for this on the Sufi Path (*nih ḥukm-i ṭarīqatī-ast*); rather this belongs to the after-effects of the powers of concupiscence. In this fashion whenever the heart resolves to pursue its 'invisible Witness of Beauty' (*shāhid-i ghaybī*), and the base passional soul (*nafs-i ammara*) is unable to apprehend that reality for itself, it attaches itself to a form in this visible phenomenal world, thus becoming bound and attached to a certain 'pretty face' which is an image of the divine workmanship, and that thing they call the *shāhid*."

esoteric interpretation of the Islamic intellectual tradition. At the beginning of the treatise, he observes,

> Since the hierarchical degrees (of understanding) of every society and people are classed in different gradations according to the amount of their faith and scientific knowledge, we have arranged each of the various categories of apologetic theology (*kalām*) and the principles of theology (*uṣūl*), of this noble discussion into a methodologically systematic order, so that perspicacious and discerning adepts in the ways of manners and morals as well as mature mystics in the stations of the spiritual quest may possess for themselves a decisive, binding and sufficient pattern to emulate.

His treatise covers seven classes of people, who are differentiated by their increasingly refined degree of esoteric comprehension.

The first class are the exotericists or *ahl-i ẓāhir*. These are "specialists in the study of prophetic traditions (*muḥaddithān kalām-i nabawwī*), the guardians of the literal sense of its texts." According to this group, a simple blind acceptance of the external sense of the verse suffices, for "to demand *how* such a cleavage could have occurred is blasphemous and reprehensible. They believe that the signification of 'the splitting of the moon' should be confined solely to this (exoteric dimension)."

The second class are likewise exotericists, *ahl-i ẓāhir*, whom he describes as "having gone beyond the level of blind conformism and having reached the frontiers of direct experiential verification (*taḥqīq*) and certitude (*yaqīn*) through making use of reflective thought and speculation." They are the philosophers of Islam (*ḥukamā'-yi islām*) and the orthodox scholastic theologians (*mutakallimūn*), whose position is in essence identical to the first group, with this significant difference: that they do *not* refrain from the asking of questions. However, since their interpretation of the moon's cleavage rules out any symbolic approach to the problem, they basically are content to argue that since God is a free Agent, He is able to *literally* split the moon, "since the heavenly bodies are sensory objects just like any other bodies, and being composed of material elements, are capable of being split apart and rent in twain." Thus, although they are theologians and philosophers of considerable skill and erudition, their literalistic approach to the verse's imagery restricts their understanding to its most superficial materialistic sense.

Ṣā'īn al-Dīn characterizes the third class as being "exoteric philosophers (*ḥukamā'-yi ẓāhir*) and their latter-day followers." This class, who represent the most simple and primitive kind of Islamic esotericism, insofar as they essentially deny that the verse should be interpreted in the literal sense of the word, for

> they affirm that for each stellar body (*kawkab*) and heavenly sphere (*falak*) (in the exterior sky) there corresponds an invisible esoteric reality (*bāṭin*), which they call the Intellect (*'aql*). Hence, the esoteric reality of the moon they name the "Active Intellect (*'aql-i fa'āl*)." Likewise, another of their principles posits that the farthest degree of human perfection – the degree of the Seal of the Prophets – is that one becomes conjoined, or 'one', with this same "Active Intellect."

In this passage Ṣā'īn al-Dīn refers to the two well-known interpretations about human intelligence's relation to the Active Intellect. According to the first interpretation, an essential *oneness* is said to exist between the two intellects, leading to the confluence and confounding of the soul with the Active Intellect. According to the second interpretation (held by both Avicenna and Suhrawardī), the two minds merely become *conjoined* to one another, while preserving the distinct individuality of both.

The exoteric philosophers maintain that the farthest degree of human perfection is that of the 'acquired intellect' (*'aql-i mustafād*) in which the Active Intellect enters into man and becomes the virtual 'Form' of his knowledge, so that he becomes an inspired philosopher.[38] Based on these philosophical conceptions, according to this group,

---

38 Here, Turkah is evidently referring to al-Fārābī's theory that "the ordinary thinking human mind reaches its perfection when it becomes *'aql mustafād*. Although the *'aql mustafād* is lower in rank than the separate Active Intelligence which has produced it, it is nevertheless pure activity in its own way no longer needing the faculties of the lower soul for its operations. It is, therefore, comparable from this point of view with the Active Intelligence. Moreover, at this stage, it is capable of contemplating the Active Intelligence itself which had so far been only its productive agent. In a few unique cases, when this happens, the Active Intelligence becomes the form of the *'aql mustafād* and the perfect philosopher, or the Imam (or the Prophet) comes into existence. Only, even in these cases, a certain part or degree of the Active Intelligence (called the Holy ghost)

> The 'splitting of the moon' may be thus considered as a metaphor (*kināyat*) for transgressing beyond its exoteric reality and becoming conjoined with its esoteric reality which is the Active Intellect. Now, since there is no higher degree of human perfection than that according to them, and the degree of the Seal of the Prophets constitutes the final entelechy of the human species, for this reason 'rending the moon in twain' exclusively refers to the spiritual level of the Seal of Prophecy. This then is an in-depth analysis of the significance (*taḥqīq*) of the splitting of the moon couched in the language of the exoteric philosophers, who are called Peripatetics, Aristotle having been their teacher and Avicenna their (current) leader and master.

The fourth class are called "the ancient philosophers (*ḥukamā-yi qadīm*)" by Ṣā'īn al-Dīn, and it is with them that the true esoteric tradition of Islam commences. They are the followers of Shihāb al-Dīn Yaḥyā Suhrawardī (d. 587/1191), named "Oriental Theosophers or Illuminationists (*ishrāqiyān*)." Their hermeneutical approach to this verse, however, is based on Illuminationist principles, according to which there are two kinds of light: the first a light totally devoid of any form of corporeal darkness and penumbra; and the second a light intermingled with the darkness of corporeal *materia*. They interpret the cleavage of the moon as symbolic of the irradiation of a combination of both sorts of light, asserting that while

> the moon is a metaphor for the admixture of light with darkness, the actual splitting of the moon can be interpreted as a symbol for the clear manifestation of knowledge and the perfection of its epiphanic function within its interior (*bāṭin*), which being 'split open' has now emerged and become revealed for all the world to see.

For these 'Illuminationists', as for the (third class of) exoteric philosophers, the highest degree of cosmic existence belongs to the Seal of the Prophets (*martaba-yi khatamī*). At this degree, "knowledge becomes exteriorized as it actually is," and therefore "the significance of rending the moon in twain

---

is involved, a part remaining completely beyond and transcendent to man." Fazlur Rahman, *Prophecy in Islam* (Chicago: University of Chicago Press 1958), p. 14.

thus refers exclusively to the spiritual level of the Seal of Prophecy," Ṣā'īn al-Dīn concludes.

The realized adepts in Sufism (*muḥaqqiqān-i ṣūfiyya*) constitute the fifth class. They are "those who are proficient in direct contemplative vision (*ahl-shuhūd*)." According to these advanced Sufi adepts, there are basically two kinds of epiphany and luminous manifestation. The first kind lies in the phenomenal manifestation of the world, "in which the revelation of every thing possible to be becomes totally manifest as it actually is." This first epiphany is designated "Adam" by the Sufis, who is, as Henry Corbin points out in his commentary on this passage, "a compendium of all existence, insofar as all being realizes through and by him the degree of self-consciousness."[39] Through the form of Adam, the celestial Anthropos, "all phenomena enters into the realm of form and manifestation."

The second epiphany is a more intense kind of manifestation appearing through the Seal of the Prophets (*khātam*), in whom the esoteric reality or archetypal meaning (*maʿnā*) of phenomena is revealed. As Ṣā'īn al-Dīn puts it, one who is invested as "the Seal of the Prophets" displays "the esoteric meaning (*maʿnā*) from out of that form which was perfectly inclusive on its own level, and the exhibition of this form to the world."

This epiphany constitutes a kind of theomorphosis of the human soul, which "for the adept is a matter of direct contemplation, without having to have recourse to rational or dialectical constructions."[40] Thus, to the realized adepts among the Sufis, Ṣā'īn al-Dīn states: "the splitting of the moon alludes to the total divulgence of the esoteric sense (*maʿnā*) through that perfect form without the intermediation of any artificial means or the logical arrangement of premisses acquired (through study), in such a manner as to predict the advent of the Seal of the Prophets."

The sixth class are those who practise an arcane sort of symbolic interpretation of the Scripture through 'deciphering the mysteries of the letters of the Qur'ān' (*Ramz-khwānān-i ḥurūf-i Qur'ānī*)." These supreme hermeneuts of the Qur'ān are a group,

> whose knowledge is obtained without recourse to contemplative reflection (*fikr*), spiritual practice (*amāl*) or any other intermediary

39 Henry Corbin, *En Islam iranien*, Tome III: *Les Fidèles d'amour, Shīʿism et soufisme* (Paris: Gallimard 1972), p. 248.

40 Corbin, *En Islam iranien*, Tome III, p. 249.

> means of (intellectual) exertion. Their contemplative perception (*naẓar*) proceeds and derives from the same forms that were revealed to and descended upon the prophets from the hierocosmos and realm of divine Transcendence.

In order to demonstrate the superiority of this esoteric class of adepts over the Sufis and Ishrāqī theosophers, Ṣā'īn al-Dīn explains that "the highest degree of being is the degree of the divine Word (*martaba-yi kalām*)," which enjoys an "all-encompassing epiphanic plentitude (*jāma'a*), insofar as through it all spiritual conceptions or Idea-archetypes (*ma'nāhā*) are made manifest and all spiritual realities (*ḥaqā'iq*) and gnostic lore (*ma'ārif*) by it made explicit and elucidated, clearly recognizable for all the world to see. All the Idea-archetypes which are the ultimate pith and purpose of the Truth, and cherished by the Absolute, are 'all decked out upon this throne.'" This degree of being derives, however, "from the light cast by the epiphany of the divine Name 'The Speaker' (*iqtabās-i nūr-i ẓuhūr az mutakallim mīkunad*)." This Name manifests certain eternally subsistent characters, one of which is the Qur'ān's *written character*, and it is this character which Qur'ān LIV:1 refers to as the "Moon," as Ṣā'īn al-Dīn explains:

> It is this written character, which is simply the Moon (that lies) at the source of all written letters (*aṣl-i ḥurūf*). In this respect, 'cleaving the Moon in twain' is a symbol of the coming forth of the original symbolic archetypal meaning (*ma'nā-yi aṣlī*) from out of the exoteric form of its written character (*ṣūrat-i raqamī-yi kitābī*) without any intermediary means of thought or reflection needed to divulge it, and without any mental exertion, as is normally the case with ideas designated by conventional meanings (*ma'ānī waḍ'ī*) and with the traditional sciences.

Only to these adepts in Qur'ānic numerology is the inner meaning of this written character revealed; these adepts are thus enabled "through visionary experience to split open and divulge, as if by secret ambush, the (written) character, thus laying bare and exposing (the esoteric meaning)."

The final and seventh class of adepts belong to the Family of the Prophet. Ṣā'īn al-Dīn posits that the esoteric significance of the 'splitting of the moon' relates to understanding what he calls "the All-inclusive Word of the

Seal of the Prophets (*kalām-i kāmil-i khātam al-nabuwwa*)." Another term he uses for this 'Word' is the 'Perfect Form' (*kamāl-i ṣūrat*)," which, he says, "harbours and includes the full plenitude of all spiritual meanings (*tamām-i ma'nā*)." The only group of people capable of comprehending and thus able to "disclose the full extent and scope (of this Form)," are "the pillars of the prophetic family (*asāṭīn-i ahl-i bayt*)," who are also called "those who possess inner strength and spiritual vision (*Ulā al-'aydī wa'l-abṣār*),[41] ... who are the elect servants of the Seal of the Prophets, and his perfectly worthy heirs." The highest gnostic in this category is 'Alī ibn Abī Ṭālib (d. 40/661).

According to Ṣā'īn al-Dīn, the most perfect aspect of this seventh degree of gnosis is found in the science of Arithmomancy (*jafr*),[42] "which completely demonstrated the way to expound and expose the esoteric spiritual sense."

This, then, is an overview of the basic hierarchy of knowers and knowledge in the treatise. Being a tract on 'esoteric knowledge', no doubt much still remains that is obscure and even impenetrable despite the above summary. But at least the full translation of the treatise given here helps alerts us to the importance of his mystical philosophy. The essential contours of 'Alī Turkah Iṣfahānī's view of the esoteric hierarchy of adepts is illustrated through the following diagram.

41 *Ulā al-'aydī wa'l-abṣār* is a reference to the Qur'ān: "And call to mind Our servants Abraham and Isaac and Jacob, all possessed of inner strength and vision." (XXXVIII:45), who are also characterized two verses later (in v. 47) as belonging to the "Chosen Elect, the Good."

42 *Jafr* is a science based on speculations about the numerical value of Arabic letters, often involving calculations intended to divine the future, the lore of which was originally said to have been deposited amongst the Shī'ites by prophetic apanage. T. Fahd notes that "the Shī'ī conception of prophecy, closely connected with that of the ancient gnosis made the prophetic afflatus pass from Adam to Muḥammad and from Muḥammad to the 'Alids ... Deviating from its original form of esoteric knowledge of an apocalyptic nature, reserved to the imāms who were the heirs and successors of 'Alī, it [*jafr*] became assimilated to a divinatory technique accessible to the wise whatever their origin." "Djafr," in *EI2*, pp. 375–76.

The Seven Degrees of Gnosis and Gnostics according to Ṣā'īn al-Dīn Turkah

Class I: *Ahl-i ẓāhir*. Exoteric Theologians specializing in *ḥadīth* who forbid all Esoteric Exegesis and Questioning of the Literal Sense of the Scripture.

1. **No Esoteric Reality to the Moon Exists**
   A. **Gnosis** is Knowledge of the Literal Meaning of the Scripture.
   B. **'Splitting of the Moon'** means the Moon was Literally 'Cleft in Twain.'

Class II: *Ahl-i ẓāhir*. Exoteric Islamic Philosophers and Scholastic Theologians, whose Exegesis of the Scripture is Confined to Reflection and Speculation

1. **No Esoteric Reality to the Moon Exists**
   A. **Gnosis** means Intellectual Reflection and Speculation about the Literal Meaning of the Scripture.
   B. **'Splitting of the Moon'** = God is a Free Agent. Because He *can literally split* the Moon, therefore He *did literally split* the Moon.

Class III: *Ḥukamā'-yi ẓāhir*. Exoteric Philosophers Denying the Scripture's Literal Sense

1. **The Esoteric Reality of the Moon is the Active Intellect (*'aql-i fa'āl*)**
   A. **Gnosis** is in Conjunction with the Active Intellect by the 'acquired intellect' (*'aql-i mustafād*) of the inspired philosopher.
   B. **'Splitting of the Moon'** is a Symbol for transgressing beyond its exoteric reality and conjunction with its esoteric reality (the Active Intellect).

Class IV: *Ḥukamā-yi qadīm* (Ancient Philosophers). Esoteric 'Oriental Theosophers' or 'Illuminationists' (*ishrāqiyān*)

1. **The Esoteric Reality of the Moon** = Epiphany of Gnosis
   A. **Gnosis** is the Dissolution of Darkness of the *ẓāhir* of the Scripture; Revelation of the Light of the *Bāṭin* of Prophecy.
   B. **'Splitting of the Moon'** means the clear manifestation of Esoteric Knowledge at the spiritual level of the Seal of Prophecy.

Class V: *Muḥiqqiqān-i ṣūfiyya*. Realized Sufi Adepts and Clairvoyant Visionaries (*Ahl- shuhūd*) abjuring Rational and Dialectical Methods

1. **The Esoteric Reality of the Moon** signifies Exposure of the Esoteric Sense (*maʿnā*) of the Scripture through an 'Ideal Universal Form' (*ṣūrat-i kāmil; ṣūrat-i tāma*)
   A. **Gnosis** is the Theomorphosis of the Human Soul through the Revelation of Seal of the Prophets (*khātam*), in whom the Esoteric Reality/ Archetypal Meaning (*maʿnā*) of Phenomena is Revealed.
   B. **'Splitting of the Moon'** means the total divulgence of the esoteric sense (*maʿnā*) through the revelation of an 'Ideal Universal Form' (*ṣūrat-i kāmil; ṣūrat-i tāma*), without the intermediation of any artificial means or the logical arrangement of premises acquired (through study), in such a manner as to predict the advent of the 'Seal of the Prophets.'"

Class VI: *Ramz-khwānān-i ḥurūf-i Qur'ānī.* Esoteric Qur'ānic Symbolists.
1. **The Esoteric Reality of the Moon** means the Epiphany of the divine Name 'The Speaker' (*al-mutakallim*); this Logos is the Word that lies at the Heart of all Written Characters
   A. **Gnosis** is Direct Vision of the same forms Revealed to and Descended upon the Prophets from the Hierocosmos & Realm of divine Transcendence.
   B. **'Splitting of the Moon'** is a Symbol for the manifestation of the original symbolic archetypal meaning (*maʿnā-yi aṣlī*) from out of the exoteric form of its written character (*ṣūrat-i raqamī-yi kitābī*) without any intermediary means of reflection divulging it, and without any mental exertion, as is normally the case with ideas designated by conventional meanings (*maʿānī waḍʿī*) and with the traditional sciences.

Class VII: *Ulā al-'aydī wa'l-abṣār.* Those who possess Inner Strength and Spiritual Vision. Elect Servants of the Seal of the Prophets and His Perfectly Worthy Heirs, who are Adepts in Qur'ānic Arithmomancy (*jafr*).
1. **The Esoteric Reality of the Moon understood by Arithmomancy**
   A. **Gnosis** is Knowledge of "the full plenitude of all spiritual meanings" through Arithmomancy, inspired by the grace of the All-inclusive Word of the Seal of the Prophets (*kalām-i kāmil-i khātam al-nabuwwa*) = the 'Perfect Form' (*kamāl-i ṣūrat*).
   B. **'Splitting of the Moon'** is a mystery revealed by means of Arithmomancy.

* * *

From the above precis of the treatise and the foregoing it is evident that the entire treatise is devoted to the *devoilement*, the stripping off the veil (*kashf al-ḥijāb*) and revealing invisible esoteric sense underlying the Qur'ānic chapter on the Moon (LIV). The "bride of the Qur'ān" symbolizes the esoteric invisible nature of the spiritual meaning to which the verse bears witness (*shāhid-i ghaybī*), Ṣā'īn al-Dīn availed himself of an image that is of ancient provenance in Persian Sufi poetry. Thus, Sanā'ī describes this same bride of the Qur'ān as "casting off her veil" only when she sees the "kingdom of faith has become secure and free from riot and disturbances."

> The bride of the reverend Qur'ān shall strip off her veil
> Once she sees the state government of Faith free from riot.[43]

According to Ṣā'īn al-Dīn, the bride cannot be perceived by Reason, for Faith does not reside in the city of Reason. Nor can she be apprehended by Reflection, for Visionary Perception is not the result of Reflection. Only (*ishrāqī*) Illumination, (*Ṣūfī*) Vision, decipherment of the (*Ḥurūfī*) Numerological Arcana or Prophetic Revelation can approach her.

In terms of the hierarchical graduation of knowledge in Islamic thought, this implies that for the first two classes of sage, the moon is effectively invisible, that is to say, without any esoteric reality. In other words, insofar as the esoteric reality of the Moon is beyond Reason and Reflection, outside the range of the instruments of *'Aql* and *Fikr*, all exoteric theologians and rational philosophers are spiritually blind and benighted.

The second two classes of sage, respectively the mystical and Illuminationist philosophers, behold the moon through modes of intellectual gnosis. If I have understood Ṣā'īn al-Dīn correctly here, the Ismā'īlī philosophers are to be ranked in class three, belonging to the *Ḥukamā'-yi ẓāhir*, or exoteric philosophers who deny the Scripture's literal sense. There are several important differences however between the Ismā'īlī upright adept (*muḥiqq*), the peripatetic mystical sage and the Ishrāqī visionary. For ordinary mystical philosophers, "rending the moon in twain' exclusively refers to the spiritual level of the Seal of Prophecy," which level of understanding was accessed solely by the Prophet Muḥammad. To the Ishrāqīs, however, esoteric

43 Abū al-Majd Sanā'ī, *Dīwān ḥakīm Abū-l-majdūd ibn Ādam Sanā'ī Qaznawī*, ed. Muḥammad Taqī Mudarris Raḍawī (Tehran: Sanāī publication 1380 A. Hsh./2006), p. 52.

knowledge lies *within the adept's realization* of the level of the Seal of Prophecy, so that the revelation of the light of the *Bāṭin* of prophecy is experienced *within* each adept. In Ismā'īlī thought, however, such gnosis appertains exclusively to the Imām or his appointed representatives, such as the *Ḥujjat*.

The fifth level is that of the highest Sufi adepts, whose realization of gnosis is essentially the same as that of fourth class (the Ishrāqī adepts) with very few differences. The Ishrāqī adepts experience gnosis directly through an illumination of the soul that allows them to realize "the spiritual level of the Seal of Prophecy." The Sufis, however, experience the Prophet's vision by "total divulgence of the esoteric sense (*ma'nā*) through the revelation of an 'Ideal Universal Form' (*ṣūrat-i kāmil*; *ṣūrat-i tāma*)." This form is probably what the Sufis refer to as the *Shāhid* (see n. 37, above) and what the Illuminationist philosophers call "auroral revelation" (*ishrāq*).

The final two levels of mystical adept are respectively those who have penetrated into the inner meaning of the Logos. The occult numerologists who belong to class six are those who, exactly like the Sufis and the Ishrāqī gnostics, obtain their gnosis through access to a higher realm of understanding. For the Ishrāqīs, this higher understanding is realized by means of an epiphany based on Illuminationist principles. The Sufis experience a kind of theomorphosis of the Soul by mediation of the ideal form of the Prophet. The esoteric Qur'ānic symbolists, however, by the epiphany of the divine Name 'The Speaker', the original symbolic archetypal meaning underlying the exoteric form of the Qur'ān's written character, attain to the penultimate level of gnosis.

Each of these last three classes thus lie one degree above the next:

What the Ishrāqīs (I) cannot know by oriental epiphany, the Sufis (II) know through their own particular gnostic revelation of the Prophet's 'Ideal Universal Form'.

What the Sufis cannot grasp through beholding that Form, the esoteric Qur'ānic symbolists (III) realize by their own transcendent access to and visionary experience of the Logos.

Finally, Ṣā'īn al-Dīn describes a seventh class who are the "elect servants of the Seal of the Prophets, and his perfectly worthy heirs." Their supreme rank is identical to that of certain esoteric adepts in the family of the Prophet. They are "the pillars of the prophetic family (*asāṭīn-i ahl-i bayt*)." He then boldly affirms that only this seventh class have any true understanding of the esoteric reality of the Moon, for none except those pillars "has ever beheld its enchanting, heart-ravishing face."

> Indeed, it was from the family of the venerable Seal of the Prophets (salutations and peace be upon them) that is to say, Amīr ('Alī ibn Abī Ṭālib, d. 40/661) and his noble sons (peace be upon them) – that the foundation of something like arithmomancy (*jafr*) was formulated and established, (a science) which completely demonstrated the way to expound and expose the esoteric spiritual sense.

Here, while it would in appearance seem that Ṣā'īn al-Dīn Turkah's doctrine approaches a kind of pious Shī'ite esotericism (and it is this which probably misled Corbin to confuse his thought with Shī'ite mystics such as Ḥaydar Āmulī), examination of his other writings in fact reveals that he is saying that Ḥurūfī mystics are the supreme adepts, excelled only the members of the Prophet's family who were the actual founders of the science of numerology (*abjad*) and arithmomancy (*jafr*).[44] This esoteric orientation is not grounded in some Shī'ite sectarian bias, as Corbin thought, but rather represents an occultist's opinion about prophetic revelation.

Politically speaking, Ṣā'īn al-Dīn Turkah was alleged to have been involved with the attempt on the life of Shāh Rukh and, like his contemporary Qāsim-i Anwār (d. 837/1433–4), was said to have been subject to Ḥurūfī influences. Indeed, the editor of his Persian treatises dubs him "one of the grandees of the Ḥurūfī *ṭarīqat*,"[45] although I have not found any evidence in his works linking him with Faḍl Allāh Astarābādī (740/1340–796/1394),[46] the founder of the Ḥurūfī sect or any of his followers.[47] Ṣā'īn al-Dīn Turkah interprets the epithet 'Ḥurūfī' in the widest possible sense to denote the 'Science of Letters' (*'ilm-i ḥurūf*) which "encompasses every particular or general object of knowledge, and which can be deduced from the patterns made by the forms of the

44 For further information on "Islamicate Occult Sciences," see Liana Saif, Francesca Leoni, Matthew Melvin-Koushki and Farouk Yahya, *Islamicate Occult Sciences in Theory and Practice* (Leiden: Brill 2023).

45 Sayyid 'Alī Musawī Bihbahanī, introduction, *Chārdah Risāla-yi Farsī Ṣā'īn al-Dīn ...*, p. yu.

46 For further information on Faḍl Allāh Astarābādī, see Shahzad Bashir, *Fazlallah Astarabadi and the Hurufis* (London: Oneworld Academic 2005).

47 See A. Bausani, "Ḥurūfiyya," *EI2* III, pp. 600–1.

heavenly constellations and their astronomical transfigurations."[48] His absorption in the occult sciences in general, and the science of numerology, *jafr*, in particular, exerted considerable influence on the subsequent history of Islamic philosophy in Persia.[49] However, since discussion of these sciences and the highly complex philosophical analysis of the 'Science of Letters' given by Ṣā'īn al-Dīn in his various treatises would necessitate much preliminary exposition of, and introduction into, some quite intricate metaphysical discussions outside the scope of this volume, this aspect of his thought unfortunately has had to be excluded from the present study.

In sum, if we examine the entire *Risāla-yi Shaqq al-qamar va sā'at* as a whole, the importance of the equation:

The true Muslim = the gnostic esotericist

For Ṣā'īn al-Dīn Turkah this cannot be overemphasized. These true esotericists furthermore comprise five categories of adept:

1. Peripatetic philosophers (*Ḥukamā'-yi ẓāhir*)
2. 'Oriental Theosophers' or 'Illuminationists' (*ishrāqiyān*)
3. Realized Sufi Adepts and Clairvoyant Visionary Sufis
4. Esoteric Qur'ānic Symbolists
5. Elect Adepts in Qur'ānic Arithomancy

Each of these adepts specializes in a different type of esoteric knowledge; each possesses a higher degree of insight and understanding than the adept inhabiting the degree immediately inferior. Yet all of these will be able to lift the veil off the face of the moon; all will be able to experience the inner truth of *imān*, to apprehend the beauty of Islam, and all may behold the *Shāhid-i ghaybī* of divine Revelation with various degrees of gnosis and understanding. With this elitist division of the Muslim intelligentsia into various hierarchical grades, this treatise gives an excellent idea of the pervasive nature of esotericism in Islamic philosophical thought.

---

48 Bihbahanī, introduction, *Chārdah Risāla-yi Farsī Ṣā'īn al-Dīn ...*, p. yu. For a good summary of this science, see T. Fahd, "Ḥurūf," *EI2* III, pp. 595–96.

49 *Chārdah Risāla-yi Farsī Ṣā'īn al-Dīn ...*, S.H. Nasr's introduction, p. j.

ṢĀ'ĪN AL-DĪN'S *RISĀLA-YI SHAQQ AL-QAMAR VA SĀʿAT*

Praise be God and blessings upon His Prophet Muḥammad!

One day, being assisted by Providence and companioned by good fortune in following the divine dictum: "Say, voyage throughout the land!" (VI:11), while taking in hand the staff of wayfaring and gazing upon every bazaar with an eye to garnering from it spiritual benefit and counsel, I assayed the works of every sect, apprising myself of the justice of their standards. When of a sudden, I chanced to pass by some colleges of traditional religious sciences, where minds exercise themselves in the arena of intellectual competition and experimentation. The floor of debate and disputation having been opened, I saw the scholars there engaged in discussing the significance and investigating the circumstances of 'the splitting of the moon',[50] labouring to demonstrate its spiritual import, while drawing upon the rhetorical expressions of both the literalist exoteric authorities and the lexicon of the scholastic theologians (*mutakallimūn*).

They were putting this lovely virgin from the sacred precincts of prophecy and Qur'ānic inimitability on public display and had decked her out in garments of technical expressions found in the common sciences, – even though she is sequestered from the sight of strangers who reside in the City of Reason (*sharistān-i 'aql*), hidden from the view of those who live in the Lane of Reflection (*kū-y fikr*), while the comprehension of immature men who inhabit the degree of spiritual chivalry and knightliness has never once laid hand on the skirt of her chaste innocence. Inspired by a moment of spontaneous spiritual feeling (*zabān-i waqt*), I heard myself break out in song,

On ground where even garden cypresses on stilts
of wood are forced to strut, we too will make
this silverbodied cypress shape rise up and dance.

Indeed, the thought seemed then to pass through my feeble fractured consciousness that I should dress her up in apparel suited to the needs of the time and the demands of the age, clothing her in a raiment from the

50 A reference to the debate over the meaning of the first verse of *Sūrah* LIV (The Moon): "The hour has drawn nigh and the moon is rent twain."

wardrobe of "I was sent with the all-comprehensive words,"[51] the key to the heritage of which – through the good fortune of keeping the intimate company and following the suit of the Seal of the Prophets – lies in the hand of those humble, lowly devotees who dwell in the Lane of Spiritual Poverty (*kū-y faqr*). I would try to express myself in the language and lexicon of every group that fares the royal highway of Perfection, and thus give sufficient sign of this veiled virgin who lies swaddled in the drapery of the Seal of the Prophet.[52] Thus, I would try to loosen a few bands of the tight girdle of the divine majesty and exclusive chastity which engirthed her,[53] taking the verse, "Verily, the Qur'ān has seven esoteric degrees"[54] as my warrant, so that this bride, swathed and swaddled in her seven golden-embroidered layers of cloths, secreted in the solitary cloister of esoteric meaning, might be displayed in the bridal chamber of seekers' approbation.

A silhouette from
His native nature
Is summoned up – look!
The same in shape and yet
It's cast in mould that's new.
No hand at your table ever has touched
A morsel of text such as this.

---

51 A celebrated *ḥadīth* of the Prophet, full references to which can be found in Chittick, *The Sufi Path of Knowledge: Ibn al-'Arabī's Metaphysics of Imagination* (Albany: SUNY Press 1989), p. 396, no. 38.

52 Alternate version: Couching myself in all the different dialects of the various groups who fare the royal highway of Perfection, I would try to express myself, thus giving some sign and indication of this veiled beauty enfolded within the drapery of the Seal of the Prophet.

53 Alternate version: I would try to loosen a few of the drawstrings on the gown of majesty and purity which engirthed her.

54 Apparently a variant version of the renowned prophetic tradition: *inna li-'l-Qurāni ẓahran wa-baṭnan wa li-baṭnihi baṭnan ilā sabʿati abṭunin* (Verily, the Qur'ān has an outward degree and inward degree, and its inward degrees goes even unto seven inward degrees). Cited by R.A. Nicholson, *The Mathnawí of Jalálu'ddín Rúmí,* Persian text edited and translated by R.A. Nicholson (8 vols. London & Leiden: 1925–40; repr. London: Luzac 1982), in his commentary on III:1897.

Yet by way of explanation, I must needs present an introduction to this 'text'. It is clear that the significance of the *ḥadīth*: "I was sent with the all-comprehensive words" – which conveys peculiar signs that point exclusively of the Seal of the Prophets, the venerable refuge of divine apostleship – is that words of truth[55] act as his interpreter, embracing (as they do) all the levels of being. In other words, just as those who voyage in the realm of divine ideas (*jahān-i ma'nā*) with every moment's breath receive another morsel from the meal cloth of his graces, likewise neither are the prisoners remanded in the pillory of the City of Phenomenal Form entirely disadvantaged either or deprived of all boon and benefit. While in the tavern of direct spiritual self-realization those who swill down seas in every breath quench their thirst on the wine of the graces of divine loveliness sold in the refinery of His perpetually emanating beneficence, so those who imbibe but a dram in the priory of sham knowledge and blind imitation are made giddy-headed by tiny trickles that drop from the goblet of his everlasting perfection.

Another affaire de la coeur
    You conduct with every heart;[56]
One sees your every high street
    Filled with bazaars galore.

Indeed, from the meal cloth of His unstinted mercy each living creature receives a different snippet and scrap according to the measure of their mind and original aptitude of spirit. This is a favour no mortal thanks can match.

If you bring a cup to hand
    you'll take from his cask a cup of wine;
and if you hold up an empty beaker,
    they'll fill your flask to full[57]

55 The Persian expression (*sukhanān-i ḥaqā'iq*) literally means 'discourses based on spiritual realities.'

56 This first half of this couplet is by Rūzbihān Baqlī, and the second half by an unknown author.

57 A verse from a ghazal in the *Dīvān* of Shāh Ni'matu'llāh (d. 834/1431): see *Kulliyāt-i Ash'ār-i Shāh Ni'matu'llāhī Valī* (Tehran: Intishārāt-i Khānaqāh-i Ni'matu'llāhī no. 67, 6th printing 1361 A.Hsh./1982), ed. Javād Nūrbakhsh, p. 352.

Indeed, this maiden confined within the sacred seraglio of Prophecy and Apostleship must be represented to the minds of various groups of people in accordance with their individual powers of comprehension and discernment. Particular, distinct signs of her should be given only in accordance with their individual perceptions and peculiar perspectives of vision.

> Each according to his taste and sight
> Makes a different likeness of your face,
> Striking similes for it to this or that.
> You are apart from all this and that.

Since the hierarchical degrees (of understanding) of every society and people are classed in different gradations according to the amount of their faith and scientific knowledge, we have arranged each of the various categories of apologetic theology (*kalām*) and the principles of theology (*uṣūl*)[58] of this noble discussion into a methodologically systematic order, so that both discerning critics of manners and morals as well as mature adepts[59] in the stations of the spiritual quest may possess for themselves a decisive, binding and sufficient model to follow.[60] This discussion embraces seven classes (*ṭabaqa*) of people:

The first class are the exotericists (*ahl-i ẓāhir*), that is, specialists in the study of prophetic traditions (*muḥaddithān kalām-i nabawwī*). It is they who are the guardians of the literal sense of its texts. They have comfortably rested their backs on the cushion of religious conformism (*taqlīd*) and having retired in peace from all diligent investigation and research, feel contented with themselves. Their doctrine concerning religious belief regarding this problem and other similar matters is simply that they resolve to give their definitive endorsement, for example, to the exoteric sense of the moon's being literally cleft in twain, while considering that to demand *how* such a cleavage could have occurred is blasphemous and reprehensible. According to them, the signification of 'the splitting of the moon' should be confined solely to this (exoteric dimension). And since the understanding

58 For a discussion of the distinctions and similarities of these two sciences, see D. Gimaret, *EI2*, s.v. "*Uṣūl al-Dīn*" and L. Gardet, *EI2*, s.v. "*'Ilm al-Kalām.*"

59 Or: both perspicacious and discerning adepts/ mature mystics in the ways of manners and morals.

60 Or: pattern to emulate.

of majority of the common people hardly surpasses this literal aspect, and they have set themselves up as leaders of this class of people, thus the perfect wisdom of all-knowing Providence has deemed it expedient that their understanding should not surpass this level.

In the garden of her beauty,
exoteric knowledge is but a thorn
How wretched is he who,
before that rose,
is content with a thorn.[61]

The second class are also exotericists (*ahl-i ẓāhir*). They, however, have gone beyond the level of blind conformism and have reached the frontiers of direct experiential verification (*taḥqīq*) and certitude (*yaqīn*) through making use of reflective thought and speculation. These are the philosophers of Islam (*ḥukamā'-yi islām*) and the orthodox scholastic theologians (*mutakallimūn*). The religious belief or credo of most members of this class regarding this problem and other related matters, however, is exactly the same as that of the first group, except with this difference: that they do not forbid the asking of questions. In fact, they even adduce reasons to explain the why and wherefore of the matter. This is because they have already proven, based upon their own principles, that God is Almighty is a free Agent who can do whatever He so wishes by virtue of His own free choice. Furthermore, they have established that the heavenly bodies are sensory objects just like any other bodies, and being composed of material elements, are capable of being split apart and rent in twain.

Now, since these two premises have been agreed upon, it is possible (so they say) that the specific miracle of the Prophet (Muḥammad) amongst the other prophets – salutations upon them all – appeared by his will in that special shape. Whatever reasons philosophers may then bring forth to prove that heavenly bodies are not susceptible of being cleft apart are, in this fashion, rebutted by them and rendered null and void. Since their

61 This verse, which is modelled after two verses in the Dīvāns of 'Irāqī and Maghribī in the same metre and rhyme, employing almost identical imagery. See Leonard Lewisohn (ed.) *Dīwān-i Muḥammad Shīrīn Maghribī* (Tehran: Tehran University Press; London: SOAS Publications 1993), ghazal 186: 13; and *Dīwān-i Fakhr al-Dīn 'Irāqī*, ed. Sa'īd Nafasī (Tehran: n.d.), p. 220.

arguments are all connected and dependent upon the basic principles of belief held by the first class, the perfect wisdom of all-knowing Providence has deemed it expedient that their understanding should not surpass this level.

This is because the basis of their knowledge rests on whatever reason warrants to be correct when evidence can be adduced from the Scripture and the *sunna* to substantiate it accordingly. Now, since in this particular case it has been established by rational evidence that the splitting of the moon is *possible*, and in the Qur'ān one reads: "The hour has drawn nigh and the moon is rent twain," and there have also been narrated *ḥadīth* in corroboration of it, thus they adjudicate that this event *literally happened* by the blessed will of the Prophet in order to confute those deniers who sought a miracle from him.

The round bread loaf of the moon
    that lay in the heavens' inverted bowl
fell broken down when a greedy man asked to have
    a morsel from the meal cloth of his mercy

The third class are the exoteric philosophers (*ḥukamā'-yi ẓāhir*) and their latter-day followers, in whose thinking very clear evidence has been revealed to demonstrate that this sensible material moon cannot be cleft in twain by virtue of the fact that it is part of the celestial vault of heaven (*falak*).[62] The mere force of absurdity can accomplish nothing. Consequently, it has to be admitted that the splitting of the moon mentioned in the Qur'ān has another meaning.

Now, in order to expound this other sense and meaning in their own terms it will be necessary to mention another premiss that can be obtained by a process of spiritual inquiry from their principles. This is that they affirm that for each stellar body (*kawkab*) and heavenly sphere (*falak*) (in the exterior sky), there corresponds an invisible esoteric reality (*bāṭin*), which they call the Intellect (*ʿaql*). Hence, the esoteric reality of the moon they name the Active Intellect (*ʿaql-i faʿāl*). Likewise, another of their principles posits

62 Commenting on this argument, Henry Corbin (*En islam iranien* III, p. 239) explains that "it is in effect an axiom of cosmology that celestial etheric matter cannot possibly ever be subject to the influence of accidents stemming from sublunar terrestrial matter." – *En islam iranien* III, p. 239.

that the farthest degree of human perfection – the degree of the Seal of the Prophets – is that one becomes conjoined, or 'one', with this Active Intellect.[63]

Although differences of opinion are entertained by them regarding this, they call this degree that of the 'acquired intellect' (*'aql-i mustafād*),[64] (maintaining that) anyone who reaches this degree can immediately apprehend any matter to which he turns his attention without producing any fresh mental dialectic. They also maintain that there is no higher degree of human perfection than this.[65]

---

63 *Kih bih 'aql-i fa'āl payvandad va yā bā ū yakī shavad.* Henry Corbin comments that "Ṣā'īn al-Dīn here alludes to two opposing interpretations: *conjunction* with the Active Intellect which safeguards individuality, or *unification* in which the existence of the soul fuses and confounds itself with the Active Intellect. Avicenna and Suhrawardī vigorously maintained the first conception." – *En islam iranien* III, p. 240, n. 66.

64 The three stages of human intellect in Islamic philosophy are usually cited as: material intellect, actual intellect and acquired intellect, each stage of which acts as the matter and substratum of the succeeding stage, which when reached, as Fārābī states, the two become "as one thing in the way that a compound of matter and form is one thing", cited by Herbert Davidson, *Alfarabi, Avicenna & Averroes on Intellect: Their Cosmologies, Theories of Active Intellect, & Theories of Human Intellect* (Oxford: Oxford University Press 1992), pp. 53–54. As with Ṣā'īn al-Dīn here, in Fārābī's usage, notes Herbert Davidson, "acquired intellect designates the ultimate stage in which the human intellect possesses a complete body of knowledge." (*Alfarabi, Avicenna & Averroes on Intellect,* p. 50.) According to Fārābī, "when a man reaches the stage of acquired intellect, and the active intellect joins the acquired intellect as its form, the active intellect 'enters into (*ḥalla fī*) the man. The active intellect sends forth a new 'emanation' on the human subject, rendering him a 'philosopher and man of practical wisdom'. The human soul becomes 'united [*muttaḥid*] as it were' and 'conjoined' (*ittaṣala*) with the active intellect." (*Alfarabi, Avicenna & Averroes on Intellect,* p. 54.) For a good summary of the relation of Active to Acquired Intellect in early Islamic philosophy, see Fazlur Rahman's chapter on "The Doctrine of Intellect," in his *Prophecy in Islam: Philosophy and Orthodoxy* (Chicago: University of Chicago Press 1979).

65 This sentence seems to indirectly paraphrase a passage in Fābābī's *Al-Madīna al-Faḍila,* where he writes that the adept by receiving, through mediation of the Acquired Intellect, the emanation of the Active Intellect, thereby becomes "a wise man and a philosopher and an accomplished thinker who ... warns of things to come and tells of particular things which exist at present." See Richard Walzer's revised text, translation

When and if this premiss is established, the 'splitting of the moon' may be thus considered as a metaphor (*kināyat*) for transgressing beyond its exoteric reality and becoming conjoined with its esoteric reality which is the Active Intellect. Now, since there is no higher degree of human perfection than that according to them, and the degree of the Seal of the Prophets constitutes the final entelechy of the human species, for this reason 'rending the moon in twain' exclusively refers to the spiritual level of the Seal of Prophecy. This then is an in-depth analysis of the significance (*taḥqīq*) of the splitting of the moon couched in the language of the exoteric philosophers, who are called Peripatetics, Aristotle having been their teacher and Avicenna their (current) leader and master.

If Greece is drowned in water,
  become dust on the road of Medina
For Grecian seers are one-eyed
  travellers on this way.

The fourth class are the ancient philosophers (*ḥukamā-yi qadīm*) who, over the course of time, have come to be called the 'Oriental Theosophers' or 'Illuminationists' (*ishrāqiyān*). According to their principles, the 'splitting of the moon' in the literal and objective sense, is also considered as an impossibility. Explanation of the meaning of this according to their method also requires the elaboration of a prolegomena drawn from their principles.

Now, the situation is that they regard light – which can be described as the principial origin of phenomenal manifestation of the world (*aṣl-i paydā'ī-yi 'ālam*) and all that lies therein – as subdivided into two categories. The first category is that of a light totally devoid of any form of corporeal darkness and penumbra, and the second category is that of a light intermingled with the darkness of corporeal *materia*.[66] The first light enables one to obtain knowledge both of universals and spiritual realities abstracted from matter (*'ilm bi kulliyāt u ḥaqā'iq-i mujarrada az māda*), without these having to appear in any way through the medium of concrete particular

(and commentary) of Al-Fārābī's *On the Perfect State* (*Mabādī ārā ahl al-madīnat al-fāḍilah*) (USA: Great Books of the Islamic World 1998), p. 245, §10.

66 The first category of light designates the angelic Intelligences; the second, the celestial Souls, movers of the Spheres, and human souls who have been invested with the governorship of a physical body. (*En islam iranien* III, p. 243.)

entities. The second category of light – which intermixed with darkness, whose rays irradiate outward in every direction – enables one to comprehend and obtain knowledge of both universal and particular realities,[67] once its potentiality has been actualized.

Another of the principles they posit is that in order for the chain of living beings to reach completion and realize its maximum perfection, it is necessary that all knowledge achieve a state of total manifestation, both in regard to universal realities (*kulliyāt*) and particular concrete things (*juz'iyāt*), so that nothing is left in a virtual condition and all stages of potential being are actualized. Having established this premiss, the 'splitting of the moon' may be thus considered to designate in their lexicon a kind of admixture of light with darkness (*nūr-i mumtizaj*) which has the capacity to make manifest *in actu* all knowledge that is secretly retained within it *in potentia*, so that the ultimate perfection of its epiphany and epiphanic function (*kamāl-i paydā'ī va paydākunandigī*) is obtained by the radiance reflected from its rays, such that various types of knowledge are manifested from it as they actually are.[68] Therefore, whereas the moon is a metaphor for the admixture of light with darkness, the actual splitting of the moon can be interpreted as a symbol for the clear manifestation of knowledge and the perfection of its epiphanic function within its interior (*bāṭin*), which being 'split open' has now emerged and become revealed for all the world to see. The symmetrical relations between each of these figures is obvious, and there is no need for any further commentary.

Now, since the final limit and link in the chain of being and the highest degree of existence among the stages of cosmic existence – the stage of the Seal of the Prophets (*martaba-yi khatamī*) – is that knowledge become exteriorized as it actually is, the significance of rending the moon in twain thus refers exclusively to the spiritual level of the Seal of Prophecy, since it is at this level that the everything that exists becomes manifest and revealed.

To sum up all: my essence is the stage
    Where everything that is appears

67 That is to say, to have an understanding both of pure Ideas and the archetypal forms of things as well as of concrete sensible realities (*En islam iranien* III, p. 244.)

68 Alternate versions: so that the ultimate perfection of its epiphany and epiphanic function (*kamāl-i paydā'ī va paydākunandigī*) is realized by medium of the reflexive nature of its light's rays/the radiant reflectivity of its rays of light.

When I contemplate it
I am God's supreme name in truth.

The fifth class are the realized adepts in Sufism (*muḥaqqiqān-i ṣūfīyya*), and those proficient in direct contemplative vision (*ahl- shuhūd*).[69] Explanation of the meaning (of rending the moon in twain) in their lexicon will require the elaboration of a prolegomena, in order to elucidate a few of their principles.[70] The explanation of this may be given as follows:

The cause of the descent of the primordial Source of Being (*tanazzul-i aṣl-i wujūd*) through all the divine hierarchies and worlds, and its subsequent emergence in various forms (of multiplicity) is only unto this purpose: that His revelation and self-manifestation might reach their full perfection.[71] And that perfection is of two sorts, endowed with two degrees.

First comes the degree of divine epiphany and phenomenal manifestation (*ẓuhūr u paydā'ī*) in which the revelation of every thing possible to be becomes totally manifest as it actually is. Although this revelation may appear in any form, it is designated by the symbol 'Adam'[72] in the parlance of the Sufis. By this term they denote a reality that totally comprehends and encompasses all degrees of being, to such an extent that nothing in being,

69 The term *muḥaqqiqān* denotes a personal verification of the truth which is at once experiential and speculative. The *muḥaqqiqān* are 'those who have understood' in the true sense of the word, a designation that corresponds to the true technical sense of the adjective 'hermeneutic', implying an act of understanding that is self-conscious. They are also 'speculative' in the true sense of the word, the 'speculative' being one who speculates, while conscious of the fact that he himself is the *speculum*, the mirror in which he beholds everything, and understands that the image appearing in the mirror is a proper representation of being, since his act of contemplation is supported by personal realization. Hence, the second qualification given to the Sufis in the above passage: they are those vouchsafed with eyewitness experience (*ahl-i shuhūd*), initiates admitted to the contemplation of the mystery. (Henry Corbin, *En Islam iranien* III, p. 247.)

70 Alternate version: that some of their principles may become clear.

71 Alternate version: that the full plentitude of His revelation might become manifest.

72 This is the Sufi version of the gnostic concept of the celestial Anthropos, who is a being perfect in essence, embracing all degrees of being. Adam is a compendium of all existence, insofar as all being realizes through and by him the degree of self-consciousness. (Henry Corbin, *En Islam iranien* III, p. 248.)

whether particular or universal, is outside the scope of its compass.[73] As the verse attests: "there is nothing, be it wet and fresh or dry and withered, but it exists writ in a clear Book" (VI:59). All phenomena enter into the realm of form and manifestation through this reality.

Whatever exists in the world
  is not outside yourself
Seek from yourself all and everything
  that you would.

In every thing, he is its core
  and subtle essence,
Lodged and consigned
  within this compendium.

The second degree of the perfection of Being is that of its epiphanic function and manifestation (*paydākunanigī u iẓhār*), in which all that exists is revealed and exposed as it actually is. In their parlance [this degree, which is that of] the Seal of the Prophets (*khātam*) refers to a person capable of being invested with this position (of theophanic revelation), so that this important function is fulfilled by him. This investiture consists in the divulging and showing forth of the esoteric meaning (*ma'nā*) through a form which, on its own level, is totally complete, and the revelation or showing forth of this form throughout the world.[74]

Having established this premise, according to the above interpretation, the moon is a figure of that 'universal form' (*ṣūrat-i tāma*), insofar as the perfect figure (*ṣūrat-i kāmil*; [that is, of a woman]), found in popular usage common to the literary traditions of all nations, is compared to a moon. As one poet put it:

Lest you drive reason mad,
  veil your face,
    O indoors moon[75]

73 Alternate version: is beyond the range of its embrace.

74 Alternate version: This investiture consists in the emergence of the esoteric meaning (*ma'nā*) from out of that form which was perfectly inclusive on its own level, and the exhibition of this form to the world.

75 Verse by Sa'dī (thanks to M.J. Juzi).

Therefore the splitting of the moon alludes to the total divulgence of the esoteric sense (*maʿnā*) through that perfect form without the intermediation of any artificial means or the logical arrangement of premisses acquired (through study),[76] predicting in this way the advent of the Seal of the Prophets.[77]

> O light of the eyes!
> Now is the cycle of the manifestation of the saints
> Wash away your writings;
> what use have tales here?

The sixth class are those who decipher the mysteries of the letters of the Qur'ān (*ramz-khwānān-i ḥurūf-i Qur'ānī*).[78] They are a group whose knowledge is obtained without recourse to contemplative reflection (*fikr*),

---

76 "This investiture is the apparition and bursting forth of the esoteric sense which had been hidden under that perfect form, that is to say, the apparition of the *Forma Dei* through her, not that she incarnates it in the technical sense of the term 'incarnation' in Christianity Rather, as a mirror carries an image in itself, she bears it in herself ... As in the symbolism of the Ishrāqīs, the mirror here is the symbol of this perfect form, while the cleavage of the moon to which this Qur'ānic verse alludes, is the Hour of Theophany, that is to say, the manifestation of the divinity in the mirror of this form: the theomorphosis of the human form. For the adept, this meditation is a matter of direct contemplation, without having to have a rational or dialectical construction." – Henry Corbin, *En Islam iranien* III, p. 249.

77 Alternate version: in such a manner as to predict the advent of the Seal of the Prophets.

78 Henry Corbin notes that (*En Islam iranien* III, p. 252) this science concerns the kind of spiritual practice "in which the adept contemplates each (Arabic) letter as if it were a symbol or ideogram with a precisely calculated numerical value, thus giving him a direct intuitive perception without recourse to the help of any mental dialectic. This science is also arranged according to the prophetic model." Jean Canteins notes that "the science of letters rests on an esoteric usage and interpretation of letters of the Arabic alphabet considered triply as ideophonic (preponderance of sonoral symbolism), ideographic (preponderance of graphic or 'hieroglyphic' symbolism), and arithmologic (each letter having a numerological value in such a way that the science of letters does not go without a science of numbers." "The Hidden Sciences in Islam," in S.H. Nasr (ed.), *Islamic Spirituality: Manifestations* (New York: Crossroad 1991), II, p. 449.

spiritual practice (*amāl*) or other intermediary means of (intellectual) exertion (*kasb u naẓar*). Their contemplative perception (*naẓar*) proceeds and derives from the same forms that were revealed to and sent down to the prophets from the hierocosmos and realm of divine Transcendence.

Explanation of the meaning of this according to their method, however, necessarily requires some introductory comment. To investigate the matter in depth, it can be said that there are multiple degrees of Being, and these multiple degrees of being differ in their capacity, one from another, to receive Being. Some beings, such as the Spirits that are arranged in different hierarchical degrees, and the some bodies, both the inanimate (*ajsām*) and the animate types (*ajsād*), are provided with autonomous existence and so are independently self-subsistent. Other types of beings, such as physical actions and spoken words and circumstances of this sort, are dependent and deprived of all autonomy.

One of the progenitive sources of these degrees (*ummuhāt-i marātib*) is the degree of the Speech (*martaba-yi kalām*). All that exists throughout the other divine and cosmological degrees of being, whether pertaining to universal or to concrete individual realities, exists within the sphere of this Speech. Furthermore, everything that could *not* exist on those degrees of being, seemingly impossible or else incompatible with phenomenal factuality, is capable of existing here (on this degree of Speech). One of the properties of this degree of being is its all-encompassing epiphanic plentitude (*jāmaʿa*), insofar as through it all spiritual conceptions/idea-archetypes (*maʿnāhā*) are made manifest, and all spiritual realities (*ḥaqāʾiq*) and gnostic lore (*maʿārif*) by it made explicit and elucidated, clearly recognizable for all the world to see. All the entirety of spiritual reality (*tamām-i maʿnā*) which are the ultimate pith and purpose of the Truth, and cherished by the Absolute, are "all decked out upon this throne."[79]

Be still until His mystery is divulged;
Take heed until His works are manifest

However, this degree has no autonomous existence of its own. Rather it derives from the light cast by the epiphany of the divine Name 'The Speaker'

79 A paraphrase of an unknown verse.

(*iqtabās-i nūr-i ẓuhūr az mutakallim mīkunad*), and its own existence from that Name is but derivatively adopted.[80]

The above premise having been made clear,[81] we may now state that the 'Moon' may be interpreted as symbolic of this degree. In the first instance, (this symbolism arises) from the derivative nature of its phenomenal manifestation. That is, just as the Moon shines by the light of the Supreme Luminary (the Sun), without which it would be cast into the outer darkness of non-existence, likewise the Word was made manifest by way of the light cast by the epiphany of the divine Name 'The Speaker (*mutakallim*)'.[82] In the second instance (the appropriateness of the symbolism is found in the fact that), any form which is manifested from this degree (of the Word) is eternally permanent and subsistent, the sensible vestiges and concrete actualizations of Being (*athār va aḥkām-i wujūd*) are more conspicuous and in evidence thereupon. Among its other forms is that of the *written* character (*ṣūrat-i raqamī*), the sound-form of which (*ṣūrat-i nuṭqī-yi au*) does not persist even for a moment, and has no extended duration.[83]

---

80 Corbin, commenting on this passage, observes: "This divine Word is not an autonomous, self-subsistent degree of existence; the epiphanic plentitude that it confers on things through their 'utterance', it borrows from the subject that utters them (the *mutakallim*); it takes its being from the being of its subject." (*En Islam iranien* III, p. 253.)

81 Alternate version: With the above prefatory remarks by way of clarification/ With the above clarification by way of preface.

82 Henry Corbin notes in respect to this passage that "to know a being is to discern under its manifestation (*ẓāhir*), the secret (*bāṭin*) of the divine Word that utters it and that it utters, and which does not in fact subsist autonomously outside its being, seeing that it is its own very being. The Word is not manifested except by the manifestation of the subject that utters it, in the same way that the light of the Moon is nothing else but an epiphany of the light of the Sun." (*En Islam iranien* III, p. 254.)

83 Henry Corbin notes that "although unfortunately the phenomenon of sound-waves is unstable and of short duration, it may reclothe itself in a form more consistent and more persistent than this momentary vibration, a form privileged to it as well because the effects, vestiges and laws of existence have been much better revealed through it than in other forms. That form, that is, the design traced by the scripture, has the result that, if on the one hand, the Word has no existence other than through the subject who utters it, on the other hand, this subtle and fragile mode of existence – that is a 'sound-existence', the vibration provoked by the shock which the beings reading the secret incantation of their being

There is no other form that is outwardly manifest in being other than these two forms.[84]

It is evident[85] that this 'character' (*raqam*) is simply the Moon (which lies) at the source of all written letters (*aṣl-i ḥurūf*). In this respect, 'cleaving of the Moon in twain' is a symbol of the coming forth of the original symbolic archetypal meaning (*ma'nā-yi aṣlī*)[86] from out of the exoteric form of its written character (*ṣūrat-i raqamī-yi kitābī*) without any intermediary means of reflection divulging it,[87] and without any mental exertion, as is normally the case with ideas designated by conventional meanings (*ma'ānī waḍ'ī*)[88] and with the traditional sciences. Those ideas and sciences are revealed by the subject's own conscious acts and rational arrangements, contrary to this group's spiritual realities that are revealed through visionary experience that split open and divulge, as if by secret ambush, the (written) character, thus laying bare and exposing (the esoteric meaning).

How wide apart is what's been sown
  and then grown up
from what's been clogged
  and then togged up.

I saw many blessed people from numerous groups, but I never saw anyone more blessed than Sa'd ibn Mālik.

– obtains in return a durable and stable existence that is always lent it by the recitation of the warnings found within the verbal design of the scripture." (*En Islam iranien* III, pp. 254–55.)

84 These two forms probably refer to the two things mentioned above: (1) the form of the Word made manifest by the light of the epiphany of the divine Name 'The Speaker', meaning the Qur'ān; and (2) the permanent traces of being in the natural world.

85 Literally: "by no means concealed."

86 For an extended discussion of the term *ma'nā* in Sufi poetry and theosophy, see Leonard Lewisohn, *Beyond Faith and Infidelity*, pp. 181–83.

87 Alternate versions: to draw it out/exposing it/to render it transparent.

88 Muḥammad Lāhījī writes that "By *waḍ'* (assignation, designation) is implied the special designation of a word to be equivalent to a certain meaning, so that whenever it is read or heard, that same meaning is inferred from it." *Mafātīḥ al-i'jāz fī sharḥ-i Gulshan-i rāz*, eds. Muḥammad Riḍā Barzgār Khāliqī and 'Iffat Karbāsī (Tehran: Zawwar 1371 A.Hsh./1992), p. 468.

The seventh class pertains to the degree of those who possess inner strength and spiritual vision (*ulā al-ayyadā wa'l-abṣār*).[89] They are those who are the elect servants of the Seal of the Prophets, and his perfectly worthy heirs. The revelation of this level (*ẓuhūr-i īn ṭūr*) only occurs at epoch which is blessed, auspicious and fortunate, "to you I plead in our days of life for (forgiveness of) our sins."[90] As a preface to elucidation of this mystery, it should be stated[91] that the All-inclusive Word of the Seal of the Prophets (*kalām-i kāmil-i khātam al-nabuwwa*) – may the best of benedictions and most complete and inclusive of blessings be upon him – which may be designated by the term 'Perfect Form' (*kamāl-i ṣūrat*), is without doubt that which harbours and includes the full plenitude of all spiritual meanings (*tamām-i maʿnā*). Within it is contained each and every idea or meaning – whatever that may have been, is, or will be. However, none has found the way to disclose the full extent and scope (of this Form). None, except those who are pillars of the prophetic family (*asāṭīn-i ahl-i bayt*), has ever beheld its enchanting, heart-ravishing face.

While certainly there have been numerous perfect spiritual beings cognizant of the realities of the Abode of Final Return, who have, by their tremendous powers of intuitive spiritual taste,[92] divulged vestiges (of the divine) and spiritual lore by direct experiential verification of the Truth (*bih jalā'il-i adhwāq kashf-i āthār un maʿārif-i taḥqīq-i shiʿār*) and thus turned towards the direction of this divine consciousness,[93] nonetheless, while profound ideas of great significance have been indeed divulged to them, the

89 This is a reference to Qur'ān XXXVIII:45 (And call to mind our servants Abraham and Isaac who were endowed with inner strength and spiritual vision.) For a French paraphrase with commentary on this section, see Corbin, *En Islam iranien* III, pp. 259–60.

90 The original is in Arabic. The seventh class refers to the manifestation of certain saints who have the spiritual power to dominate and influence the course of events of the world, and also possess deep spiritual perception and vision.

91 Alternate translation: To introduce the exposition of this mystery / Prefacing this mystery's elucidation, it should be stated.

92 Alternate translation: tremendous heart-savour/momentous mystical perception.

93 Alternate translation: focused their attention in the direction of this act of piety / and have turned towards the quarter of this virtue.

totality and ultimate depth of meaning intended to be conveyed by that Word has never been made clear to any of them.[94]

No one has ever seen your face,
    and yet a thousand
        Door-keepers have arrived.
You are a rose still closed,
    And yet a hundred nightingales have arrived.[95]

Indeed, it was from the family of the venerable Seal of the Prophets (salutations and peace be upon them) that is to say, Amīr ('Alī ibn Abī Ṭālib, d. 40/661) and his noble sons (peace be upon them) – that the foundation of something like arithmomancy (*jafr*)[96] was formulated and established, (a science) which completely demonstrated the way to expound and expose the esoteric spiritual sense.

Having made the above premise clear, it should be made demonstrably evident that splitting the moon in twain according to the expressions which

94 Commenting on this sentence, Henry Corbin observes that "from Ṣā'in al-Dīn's perspective, all the Spirituals have recognized in an all-inclusive fashion what this Perfect Form (the Imām as celestial Anthropos) is, from which emanates the fullness of spiritual meaning. They have not, however, been able to subject it to a detailed analysis that would comprehend all its various circumstances, but at least they have had knowledge of the Final Return and its locus. For example, they have not really been able to comprehend the allusions of eschatology: the rendering of accounts, the Balance, the apparition and typification of human acts." (*En Islam iranien* III, p. 260, n. 8.)

95 *Dīwān-i Ḥāfiẓ*, ed. Parwīz Nātil Khanlarī (Tehran: Sahāmī 'ām 1362 A.Hsh./1983; 2nd edn), no. 64: 1, p. 144. Translation by Robert Bly and Leonard Lewisohn.

96 *Jafr* is a science based on speculations about the numerical value of Arabic letters, often involving calculations intended to divine the future, the lore of which was originally said to have been deposited amongst the Shī'ites by prophetic apanage. T. Fahd notes that "the Shī'ī conception of prophecy, closely connected with that of the ancient gnosis made the prophetic afflatus pass from Adam to Muḥammad and from Muḥammad to the 'Alids ... Deviating from its original form of esoteric knowledge of an apocalyptic nature, reserved to the imāms who were the heirs and successors of 'Alī, it [*jafr*] became assimilated to a divinatory technique accessible to the wise whatever their origin." "Djafr," in *EI2*, pp. 375–76.

are found in the perfect Word of the Qur'ān revealed to the venerable Seal of the Prophets (peace be upon him), where it has been declared: "The hour has drawn nigh and the moon is rent twain"[97] and have shown the way to thereunto and given an indication of it, in a way that both they themselves (Alids) and their devotees understand.

One hint I gave of what
was in this text
and that was it.[98]

No space remains in this treatise to discuss anything further than this. The researcher who seeks to broaden the scope of his spiritual apprehension[99] may refer to more detailed accounts which have been presented in longer tracts. So godspeed unto you.

A Discourse on the Meaning of 'The Hour'

Since both 'the Hour drawing nigh' as well as the 'the moon being cleft' were mentioned in the blessed verse, it will be appropriate to expound the meaning of the "Hour" according to the same sevenfold classification so that the meaning of the entire verse may be completely explained. The verse in question, which is: "The hour has drawn nigh and the moon is rent twain, yet if they see a sign they turn away and say: 'this is powerful sorcery'," (LIV:1–2), literally means that 'the Day of Resurrection (*qiyāmat*) drew near and the moon was cleft asunder, but if hypocrites and infidels perceive

97 Alternate version: "The hour has drawn nigh (92) and the moon is rent twain (283)." The number at the end, 283, is itself the numerology for "*jafr*" indicating to those that are aware; the number 92 in the middle of the *ayat* in question decodes as the numerological spelling of the name Muhammad. We are grateful to Robert Darr for deciphering the numerological calculations in the alternate reading.

98 The second hemistich of the *maṭlaʿ* of a ghazal by Ḥāfiẓ (see *Dīwān-i Ḥāfiẓ*, ed. Khanlarī, no. 157: 1, p. 330); the full couplet of which reads: "How can a mind afflicted with grief be inspired with lovely poetry? I have spoken one point of truth in this book, and that is it."

99 Alternate version: A researcher who seeks to expand the aptitude and capacity of his mystical taste.

a sign (of God) then they turn away and say that 'this is but very strong magic.'" So far goes the literal interpretation.

The term 'the Hour' (*sāʿat*) may be explained as signifying that whatever individual existed in primordial pre-eternity (*awwal-i azal*), along with whoever shall exist unto the latter end of post-Eternity (*ākhir-i abad*), will all be summoned forth to present themselves, along with all their deeds, all of which will be weighed on the scales of true justice, so that the doers of iniquity will be separated (from the righteous), and each one accorded his proper place. From Him it originates and unto Him it returns.

The first class, who are the exoteric jurisprudents and specialists versed in the science of Prophetic traditions, maintain that after death and at that Hour, every limb and organ of the human body which perishes and dissolves will be reassembled and brought to life again. No inquiries into the circumstances of this event must ever be made, they assert; rather it is merely incumbent upon us simply to follow the precedent (*taqlīd*) already handed down to us from the prophets and perfect spiritual beings, exactly as has been expounded, in several places, in the text of the Qur'ān.

The second class are the orthodox scholastic theologians (*mutakallimūn*) and those versed in reason and reflective thought (*ahl-i ʿaql u fikr*). On problems such as this and related matters they do not content themselves with the imitative following of religious precedent (*taqlīd*). Instead, they maintain that God Almighty is a free Agent able to do whatsoever He wills; hence, the limbs of man scattered and split asunder at the time of death can be reassembled (by God), so that an individual, exactly the same in his every particular, may be recreated again, just as he was created at first when he was as yet nothing.[100] Thus they give the reply to the philosophers who profess that it is impossible to recreate a being that has perished exactly in the same form as it was previously. Some of the insightful orthodox scholastic theologians maintain that original limbs of man, by virtue of which his body survived and subsisted, are quite sufficient for that individual to be created anew.

The third class are the peripatetic philosophers (*ḥukamā-yi mashāʾī*). They maintain that it is the *Spirits* of men which are brought back on the Day of Judgement. The Spirit is an abstract immaterial substance (*jawharī mujarrad*), that is to say, it is the individual's very *being* that is independent

100 Alternate version: the same person, exactly the same in his every individual particular, may be created again just as he was created at first when nothing at all.

of matter.[101] It cannot be quantified, given colour, formal shape or physical locus,[102] having been created independent of all these. For this reason, the Spirit is the locus of the knowledge and understanding of everything, and its ultimate perfection is that everything should become manifest in it from earliest pre-eternity to the furthermost end of post-eternity, such that it understands it. Whenever the Spirit realizes[103] this degree, it has regained its own final destination (*ma'ād-i aṣlī-yi khwud*), which is the supersensory realm far removed from the blemishes of this bodily condition and the taint of corporeality. There, everything is in a state of intelligent consciousness and self-realization (*dānandih va yābandih*); ignorance and mental impairment cannot be found there.

If you could find the street
 on which my mistress has her flat
every door and wall there you'll see
 is full of soul and animate.

The fourth class are the Illuminationist philosophers (*ḥukamā'yi ishrāqiyān*), according to whom the destined entelechy (*bāz-gasht*, i.e. of man in the world hereafter) is a matter also pertaining to that Eternally Existent Spirit. According to them this Spirit may be defined as a light linked and coupled to the darkness of the world of corporeal bodies. One of the properties of light is whenever it reaches something that is so darkly opaque that it cannot penetrate through it, it casts down a shadow, so that the light bounces back with its luminosity enhanced through the power of the light's reflection.[104]

In the same way, that Existential Light (*nūr-i wujūdī*) when coupled together with the world of corporeal bodies – which they call 'the Human Spirit (*rūḥ-i ādamī*)' and the '*anima rationalis* (*nafs-i nāṭiqa*)' – must also

101 Alternate version: without the need for any material substance.

102 Alternate version: susceptible of quantification, colouration, shape or physical locus / endowed with quantity, colour, shape or place.

103 Alternate versions: attains/reaches.

104 This is based on the ancient Platonic theory of light which says that a ray of light, when it reaches a dark body reflects back in the same direction as the source of light.

reflect back with rays projected by way of contrast[105] and shine with enhanced luminosity. The Light of Being's enhanced luminosity lies in the fact that whereas at first it could only comprehend universals, after it becomes conjoined (with the realm of corporeal bodies) it can accommodate and comprehend the world's particulars as well.[106] Whenever it realizes its own perfection upon this degree, it becomes such that no living creature is invisible to it, whether those pertaining to universal realities (*kullīyyāt*) hailing from the world Yonder or those belonging to particular concrete things (*juz'īyyāt*) of this lower world, so that the sense of the verse "on a day that unconscious thoughts will all be disclosed"[107] informs his degree. Thus

> All that was and all that ever will exist
> You can find within yourself.[108]

The fifth class are the Sufis, who maintain that all things return to their own origin. They hailed from Yonder and to There they will eventually return. To verify the truth of this[109] it may be asserted that (the Hour occurs) whenever the Form of the Truth (*ṣūrat-i ḥaqq*)[110] is manifested in its totality in

---

105 Alternate versions: must also emit a contrasting luminosity / must also reflect back with rays projected by way of contrast/be contrastingly reflective.

106 Alternate versions: This enhanced luminosity/This enhancement and increased luminosity lies in this that at the outset it can only comprehend universals, whereas after becoming conjoined (with the realm of corporeal bodies) it is able to penetrate and understand the particulars of the world / that it can at first only accommodate and comprehend universals consists in the fact that in the beginning / lies in this that it can at first only accommodate and comprehend universals / consists in the fact that in the beginning/at the outset it can only comprehend universals, whereas after becoming conjoined (with the realm of corporeal bodies) it is later able to penetrate and understand the particulars of the world.

107 "Verily God is able to return him back again/ on a day all unconscious thoughts will be disclosed." (LXXXVI:8–9).

108 Alternate version:

> Find within you all that is
> and all that ever will exist.

109 Alternate version: By way of spiritual inquiry into this notion we may state that.

110 This is a technical term often used in the lexicon of school of Ibn 'Arabī, one of the celebrated interpreters of whom, 'Abd al-Razzāq Kāshānī (d. 736/1335), defines it as

such a manner that whatever existed in virtual condition and *in potentia* becomes manifest and revealed. In the same way, the epoch of its manifestation (*zamān-i iẓhār*) was from the time of Adam (peace be upon him) until Muḥammad the Arab (salutations and peace be upon him), who was the Seal of the Prophethood.[111]

By the term 'Prophet' is implied a person who can establish the Form of the Truth. Now, Muḥammad (salutations and peace be upon him) became the Seal of the Prophets because the foundation that he laid and that form which was sent down (by revelation) to him was effectively all-inclusive and complete. It was an integrally perfect form[112] (*ṣūrat-i kāmila*).[113] If, hypothetically speaking, a form more all-inclusive and perfect than his could exist, then whoever that form was revealed to would himself be the Seal. Such 'all-inclusive perfection of form' consists in the fact that no interior spiritual signification or idea (*maʿnā*) secreted within the innermost recesses of Infinity and suprasensory Invisibility remained hidden to it. On the other hand, it revealed and exposed everything in a form that represents and exposes those spiritual realities.

Thus – having established this premise – whoever apprehends this integrally perfect form, manifesting and displaying the fullness of spiritual meaning and reality (*tamām-i maʿnā*), will contain everything that was or will be, from earliest pre-eternity to the furthermost end of post-eternity, within himself.

Yesteryear and yesterday, tomorrow and today,
All four are one: you too become one.[114]

"the Muḥammadean Reality, which is also the conjunction of the two oceans of Necessary and Possible being." *Laṭā'if al-aʿlām fī ishārāt-i ahl al-ilhām*, ed. Majīd Hādīzādih (Tehran: Mirāth-i Maktūb 2000), p. 357.

111 "Each thing, each being, returns to its origin. The return to the origin for the human form (the imminent Hour, the Resurrection) occurs at the moment that it assumes the fullness of its theophanic function." (Henry Corbin, *En Islam iranien* III, p. 249.)

112 Alternate versions: consummate/immaculate, complete/perfect form.

113 The adjective *kāmila* or *kāmil*, which is here translated as 'integrally perfect', may also convey other connotations of 'consummate, plenary, all-inclusive, completely mature, ripened.'

114 Alternate translation:

Today, yesteryear, yesterday and tomorrow, all four
Become one and the same – you too become singular.

The sixth class are adepts in the science of letters (*arbāb-i ʿilm-i ḥurūf*) who also maintain [like the Sufis] that all things return to their own origin. The form in which the things return, however, is a sacred celestial form free from the blemishes of this bodily condition and not subject to the controls of created beings,[115] and that (form) is those twenty-nine letters that descended (by way of divine revelation) to the Seal of the Prophets. Whenever the symbolic archetypal meanings of those letters are brought out and exposed, freed from being determined by conventional usages and implications and disengaged from (irrelevant) comparisons and connections that have been attached to them from outside themselves, so that the signification of the verse: "the moon was rent in twain," which is a sign of the final hour drawing nigh, is elucidated, then of course, the full interior spiritual sense of that verse will be exposed in such a manner that everything from earliest pre-eternity to the furthermost end of post-eternity will be revealed and no secret remains hidden.

> If substance there was beyond vowels and letters
> Then that would descend in the place of the letters.

The seventh class pertains to the degree of those who possess inner strength and spiritual vision who are specifically distinguished by belonging to this present temporal dispensation that our founder [Muḥammad] (may God's salutations be upon his blessed and distinguished forefathers) has brought to light and manifested. And it is this that certain perfect spiritual beings and realized adepts have understood in a summary manner: that the revelation of all spiritual ideas and realities (*tamām-i maʿānī*) occurs by medium of this integrally perfect form (*ṣūrat-i kāmila*). However, direct realization of its conditions and circumstances was beyond them and they were unable to make even an indirect inference about it in any detail. Although they could expose and clarify something of the meaning of the Abode of Final Return and the ultimate source of divine emigration (*bāz-gasht u maʿād*), they were powerless to apprehend anything of the Day of Judgement, the Balance, the Examination of Deeds, or the Fountain of nectar in Paradise. (Apprehension of) such things is specially reserved to the Amīr (ʿAlī ibn Abī Ṭālib), peace be upon him, and the method of disclosing the interior

115 Alternate translations: untainted/unaffected/beyond the sway of created beings // and exempt from/not subject to the domination of created beings.

spiritual significance (*maʿnā*) within the literal letters without the operation (*kasb*) and mediation (*taʿammul*) of the Person (i.e. ʿAlī) who is the principal source and debut of everything, was not made clear to them.

A thousand enigmas subtler, finer spun than
A strand of hair lies here.
– Not everyone
Who shaves his scalp can understand the *qalandar*.[116]

Divine directives can be found to expand on all these matters through the same method.[117] It should be understood that there are poems which I composed on the term 'the Hour' in a style and way that can be understood by those who are their (the true ʿAlids) devotees.

Salutations and peace be upon Muḥammad, his virtuous descendants and pure family, and praise be to God, Lord of all the worlds.

This treatise was finished on the 18th of Rabīʿ al-awwal in the year 829 A.H. (5 February 1426).

116 *Dīwān-i Khwāja Shams al-Dīn Muḥammad Ḥāfiẓ*, ed. Parvīz Nātil Khānlarī (Tehran: Intishārāt-i Khawārazmī 1359 A.Hsh./1980), ghazal 174: 6–7.

117 Alternate versions (with a quite different meaning): It should be known that through the same method one may be guided to expand on these brief remarks / It should be known that one can expand on these brief remarks through the same divinely guided method.

X

VISIONARY UNVEILING AND THE ESOTERIC SCIENCES

Selections from Mullā Ṣadr's (d. 1045/1636) *Mafātīḥ al-ghayb*

The following selection is from Mullā Ṣadrā's *Mafātīḥ al-ghayb* (*Keys to the Invisible Realm*). S.H. Nasr describes the contents of this work as "combining gnostic doctrines on metaphysics, cosmology and eschatology and containing ample references to the Quran and *Ḥadith*."[1] Known as *Ṣadr al-Muta'allihīn* (Chief of the Mystical Theosophers), Ṣadrā Shīrāzī was the greatest Persian mystical philosopher of the Safavid period and central thinker of what has come to be known as the 'School of Transcendental Theosophy' (*al-ḥikmat al-muta'ālīyya*). A member of the seventeenth-century School of Iṣfahān of Persian Neo-Platonists, his remarkable genius, as Henry Corbin commented, combined the constructive and summative force of a St. Thomas Aquinas with the intuitive vision of a theosopher like Jacob Boehme.[2]

However, not a great deal is known about the terrestrial life of the Shīrāzī sage. What we do know is that he was born around 979/1571[3] into an aristocratic family in Shiraz in southwest Persia. His full name is cited as Ṣadr al-Dīn Muḥammad Ibn Ibrāhīm al-Shīrāzī.[4] After elementary

1 S.H. Nasr, *Ṣadr al-Dīn Shīrāzī and his Transcendent Theosophy: Background, Life and Works* (Tehran: Imperial Iranian Academy of Philosophy 1978), p. 43.

2 *En Islam iranien: Aspects spirituels et philosophiques*, vol. IV: *L'École d'Isfahan, L'École Shaykhie, Le Douzième Imâm* (Paris: Éditions Gallimard 1972), p. 56.

3 Ḥāmid Nājī Iṣfahānī (ed.), *Majmū'a-yi Rasā'il-i falsafī-yi Ṣadr al-Muta'allihīn* (Tehran; Intishārāt-i Ḥikmat 1375 A.Hsh./1996), introduction, p. v; Corbin, *En Islam iranien* IV, p. 54.

4 In what follows, I will be generally following the accounts given by Henry Corbin, *En Islam iranien* IV, pp. 54–121; S.H. Nasr, "The School of Iṣfahān," and "Ṣadr al-Dīn Shīrāzī (Mullā Ṣadrā)," in M.M. Sharif, *A History of Muslim Philosophy* (Wiesbaden: Harrassowitz 1966), vol. II, pp. 904–32 and 932–61; *idem.*, "Spiritual Movements, Philosophy and

schooling there, he moved to Qazwīn and then Iṣfahān, the cultural, intellectual, scientific and political capital of Iran.[5] In Iṣfahān, we know that he studied under the mystical theologian Shaykh Bahā' al-Dīn 'Āmilī (Shaykh Bahā'ī, d. 1030/1621),[6] who held the position of Shaykh al-Islām there under Shāh 'Abbās I (reigned 1588–1629) and was the author of the finest Persian Sufi *mathnawīs* of the Safavid period.[7] He also was a student of Mīr

Theology in the Safavid Period," *The Cambridge History of Iran*, vol. VI: *The Timurid and Safavid Periods* (Cambridge: Cambridge University Press 1968), pp. 656–97; *idem.*, "Mullā Ṣadrā: His Teachings," in S.H. Nasr and Oliver Leaman (eds.), *History of Islamic Philosophy* (London: Routledge 1996), I, pp. 643–70; *idem.*, *Ṣadr al-Dīn Shīrāzī and His Transcendent Philosophy* (Tehran: Iranian Academy of Philosophy 1978); James Winston Morris, *The Wisdom of the Throne: An Introduction to the Philosophy of Mullā Ṣadrā* (Princeton University Press 1981); Fazlur Rahman, *The Philosophy of Mullā Ṣadrā* (Albany 1975); Hossein Ziai, "Mullā Ṣadrā: His Life and Works," in S.H. Nasr and Oliver Leaman (eds.), *History of Islamic Philosophy* (London: Routledge 1996), I, pp. 635–42; Ḥāmid Nājī Iṣfahānī (ed.), *Majmū'a-yi Rasā'īl-i falsafī-yi Ṣadr al-Muta'allihīn* (Tehran; Intishārāt-i Ḥikmat 1375 A.Hsh./1996), introduction, pp. iii–liii; Henry Corbin, *History of Islamic Philosophy*, trans. [from French] by Liadain Sherrard (London: KPI in association with the Institute of Ismaili Studies 1993), pp. 342–45; Fazlur Rahman, "Mullā Ṣadrā," in M. Eliade (ed.) *The Encyclopædia of Religion* (New York: Simon and Schuster Macmillan 1995), vol. X, pp. 148–53; Ibrahim Kalin, "Mullā Ṣadrā: Addendum," in *The Encyclopedia of Philosophy*, 2nd edn, ed. Donald Borchert (New York: Macmillan Reference & Thomson Gale 2006), vol. VI, pp. 419–21, and a number of other encyclopedia articles on the sage.

5 Corbin, *En Islam iranien*, vol. IV, p. 57; Hossein Ziai, "Mullā Ṣadrā: His Life and Works," in S.H. Nasr and Oliver Leaman (eds.), *History of Islamic Philosophy* (London: Routledge 1996), I, p. 636.

6 For a good overview of his relationship with both Shaykh Bahā'ī and Mīr Dāmād, see Sayyid Muḥammad Khāminahī, "Zindigī, shakhṣiyat va maktab-i Ṣadr al-Muta'allihīn, Part 2: Ṣadrā va Shaykh Bahā'ī," in *Khirad-nāma-yi Ṣadrā*, no. 2 (1374 A.Hsh./1995), pp. 20–32; *idem.*, "Zindigī, shakhṣiyat va maktab-i Ṣadr al-Muta'allihīn, Part 3 (1375 A.Hsh./1996): Ṣadrā va Mīr Dāmād," pp. 32–39.

7 See his three *mathnawīs*: *Shīr u shakar*, *Nān u panīr*, *Nān u ḥalwā*, published in Mihdī Tawḥīdīpūr (ed.), *Kulliyāt-i ash'ār-i Farsī, va Mūsh u Gurba Shaykh Bahā'ī* (Tehran: Intishārāt-i Kitābfurūshī-yi Maḥmūdī 1336 A.Hsh./1957).

Dāmād (d. 1041/1631), "the central figure in the school of Iṣfahān,"[8] and possibly of Mīr Abū al-Qāsim Findiriskī (d. 1050/1640–1) as well.[9] The latter was a Sufi philosopher[10] known for his ecumenical temperament,[11] who was actively involved in the ongoing translation movement of Hindu classics into the language of Persian Sufism, as exemplified by his Persian translation of the *Yoga Vasiṣtha* by Niẓām al-Dīn Pānipatī.

During the next period of his life, which lasted between seven and fifteen years,[12] Mullā Ṣadrā retreated to the village of Kahak, some thirty kilometres southeast of the town of Qumm,[13] where he spent his time in contemplation, invocation, prayer, and engaged in composition of some his minor

---

8 S.H. Nasr, "The School of Iṣfahān," in M.M. Sharif, *A History of Muslim Philosophy* (Wiesbaden: Harrassowitz 1966), II, p. 909.

9 Corbin (*En Islam iranien*, vol. IV, p. 58), however, notes that Mullā Ṣadrā's affiliation to Findiriskī cannot be verified for certain, having never been confirmed in any of the author's works.

10 "As a Sufi," S.H. Nasr points out, "in spite of his having advanced very far upon the Path and having reached the state of pure contemplation and illumination, he [Findiriskī] mingled with the common people and wore the coarsest wool, and yet he was one of the most respected men in the Ṣafawid court. His manner resembled that of the Hindu Yogīs with whom he had had so much contact. He was a real man among men and one of the most striking Sufis of his time. While completely detached from the world and even from purely formal learning, he composed several important treatises including one on motion (*al-ḥarakah*), another on the arts and sciences in society (*ṣanā'īyyah*) ... *Uṣūl al-fuṣūl* on Hindu wisdom, and a history of the Ṣafawids." – S.H. Nasr, "The School of Iṣfahān," p. 922. For more on Mīr Findiriskī and Sufism, see my "Sufism and the School of Iṣfahan: *Taṣawwuf* and *'Irfān* in Late Safavid Iran ('Abd al-Razzāq Lāhījī and Fayḍ-i Kāshānī on the Relation of *Taṣawwuf, Hikmat* and *'Irfān*)," in Leonard Lewisohn and David Morgan (eds.), *The Heritage of Sufism*, vol. III: *Late Classical Persianate Sufism: The Safavid and Mughal Period* (Oxford: Oneworld 1999), pp. 99–101.

11 On which, see Akbar Hādī, *Sharḥ-i ḥāl-i Mīr Dāmād va Mīr Findiriskī* (Iṣfahān: Intishārāt-i Mītham Tamār 1363 A.Hsh./1984), p. 57.

12 The precise amount of time he spent there is unclear. See Corbin, *En Islam iranien*, vol. IV, p. 60; Hossein Ziai, "Mullā Ṣadrā: His Life and Works," p. 637; 934–35; S.H. Nasr, "Ṣadr al-Dīn Shīrāzī (Mullā Ṣadrā)," in M.M. Sharif, *A History of Muslim Philosophy* (Wiesbaden: Harrassowitz 1966), II, p. 934.

13 "Mullā Ṣadrā," *Dānishnāma-yi zabān va adab-i fārsī*, ed. Ismā'īl Sa'ādat (Tehran: Farhangistān-i zabān va adab-i fārsī 1391 A.Hsh./2012), vol. IV, pp. 181–82.

treatises,[14] which were to lay "the ground work for most of his major works."[15] During this period of his life, he was vouchsafed interior illumination (*ishrāq*), and attained – in the words of Corbin – "to that personal spiritual realization which for philosophy is an indispensable point of departure, without which, for him as well as for his fellow mystics, philosophy is naught else but a sterile and illusory enterprise."[16]

During the third and last period of his life, after receiving an invitation from the governor of Fars, the province of southwest Persia Allāhwirdī Khān (d. 1022/1613), he moved back to his hometown Shīrāz, known as the 'Portal of Knowledge' (*dār al-'ilm*) due to the international reputation enjoyed by its famous philosophers, theologians, Sufis and poets,[17] where he assumed a professorial position at the Madrasa Khān, a newly founded college for religious studies. He spent the remainder of his life in Shīrāz teaching and writing.[18] During this final period of his life he also made seven pilgrimages to Mecca, during the last of which he died in Basrā in 1045/1636.[19]

---

14 D. MacEoin, "Mullā Ṣadrā Shīrāzī," *EI2* VII, p. 547.

15 Ziai, "Mullā Ṣadrā: His Life and Works," p. 637.

16 Corbin, *En Islam iranien*, vol. IV, p. 61.

17 Corbin, *En Islam iranien*, vol. IV, pp. 61–62. On Ṣadrā and Shīrāz, see Qāsim Kākā'ī, "Shīrāz: Mahd-i 'irfān, zādgāh-i Mullā Ṣadrā," *Khirad-nāma-yi Ṣadrā*, no. 2/Serial 2 (1374 A.Hsh./1995), pp. 63–69. On Ṣadrā and the School of Shīrāz, see S.H. Nasr and Mehdi Aminrazavi (eds.), *An Anthology of Philosophy in Persia*, vol. V: *From the School of Shiraz to the Twentieth Century* (London: I.B. Tauris in association with the Institute of Ismaili Studies 2015), pp. 162–221. On the pre-Safavid School or Schools of Shīrāz in general, see Corbin *Histoire de la philosophie islamique* (Paris: Gallimard 1986), pp. 459–61; Reza Pourjavady, *Philosophy in Early Safavid Iran: Najm al-Dīn Maḥmūd al-Nayrīzī and His Writings* (Leiden: Brill 2011), chap. 2.

18 Corbin, *En Islam iranien*, vol. IV, p. 61; Nasr, "Ṣadr al-Dīn Shīrāzī (Mullā Ṣadrā)," p. 935; MacEoin, "Mullā Ṣadrā Shīrāzī," *EI2* VII, p. 547. For a discussion of this professorial appointment, see Mullā Sadrā, *Kasr aṣnām al-jāhilīyya fī al-radd 'alā mutasawwafa*, ed. Muḥammad Taqī Dānishpazhūh (Tehran: Dānishkadih-i 'Ulūm-i ma'qūl va manqūl 1340 A.Hsh./1962), introduction, pp. ii–iv.

19 Ḥamīd Riḍā Ṭālibzāda, "Mullā Ṣadrā," *Dānishnāma-yi zabān va adab-i fārsī*, ed. Ismā'īl Sa'ādat (Tehran: Farhangistān-i zabān va adab-i fārsī 1391 A.Hsh./2012), vol. IV, p. 181.

As Mohammad Rustom, Carl Ernst[20] and several other scholars have shown,[21] most of Mullā Ṣadrā's works exhibit a thorough knowledge of the Sufi tradition, his writings being peppered with references to early Sufis such as Ḥallāj, Ibn 'Aṭā', Abū Bakr Wāsiṭī, Abū Sa'īd Abū'l-Khayr, Bisṭāmī, Junayd and 'Abdu'llāh Anṣarī, as well as to later Sufis such as Ghazālī and Ibn 'Arabī, and to Persian Sufi poets such as Farīd al-Dīn 'Aṭṭār and Jalāl al-Dīn Rūmī.[22] Respecting the Sufi tradition, Mullā Ṣadrā is similar to Ḥaydar Āmulī in his adherence to the School of Ibn 'Arabī and Ṣadr al-Dīn Qūnawī (d. 673/1274), the stepson of Ibn 'Arabī and the foremost interpreter and systematic proponent of his teachings to the Persian-speaking world),[23] whose views he endorsed and supported on a number of important issues including the imaginal world, the eternal archetypes, afterlife states, eschatology, as well as his hermeneutical approach to the Qur'ān.[24] In his *Four Spiritual Voyages*, Mullā Ṣadrā quotes Ibn 'Arabī more often than

---

20 Mohammed Rustom, *The Triumph of Mercy: Philosophy and Scripture in Mullā Ṣadrā* (Albany: SUNY Press 2012), pp. 41–42, citing Carl Ernst's "Sufism and Philosophy in Mullā Ṣadrā," *Islam-West Philosophical Dialogue: papers presented at the World Congress on Mulla Sadra* (Tehran 1999), vol. I (1999), pp. 173–92. I am grateful to Prof. Ernst for providing me his revised version of this essay that is at the time of writing forthcoming in *It's Not Just Academic! Essays on Sufism and Islamic Studies* (New Delhi: Yoda Press in collaboration with Sage Publications 2017).

21 In the introduction to his encyclopaedic *Farhang-i iṣṭilāḥāt-i Mullā Ṣadrā* (*Philosophical Glossary of Mullā Ṣadrā*), Ja'far Sajjādī (Tehran: Intishārāt-i Vizārat-i farhang-i irshād-i Islāmī 1379 A.Hsh./2000) provides a full list of the various mystics, theologians and philosophers cited throughout Mullā Ṣadrā's major works; the roster of which includes fifteen Greek philosophers, twenty-four Muslim Peripatetic thinkers, nineteen Sufis, eleven Muslim scholastic theologians (*mutakallimūn*) and twenty-one exegetes of the Qur'ān (pp. xii–xv)!

22 See my "Sufism and the School of Isfahan," pp. 95–98; Rustom, *The Triumph of Mercy*, p. 45.

23 "In fact, the whole body of Mullā Ṣadrā's transcendental theosophy functions as the rational structure and logical articulation of Ibn 'Arabī's teaching." – M.R. Jozi, "The Influence of Ibn 'Arabī's Doctrine of the Unity of Being on the Transcendental Theosophy of Ṣadr al-Dīn Shīrāzī," in Leonard Lewisohn and David Morgan (eds.), *The Heritage of Sufism*, vol. III: *Late Classical Persianate Sufism: The Safavid and Mughal Period* (Oxford: Oneworld 1999), pp. 266–72 [p. 267].

24 Juzi, *op. cit.*

any other Sufi author (227 times in fact); only two other figures – both philosophers – are more frequently cited (Suhrawardī at 253 times, and Ibn Sīnā at 767 times) than Ibn 'Arabī in his masterpiece.[25]

There are of course many other influences on Mullā Ṣadrā's thought aside from Sufism. His philosophy fits squarely within the Islamic Peripatetic tradition (drawing on al-Kindī, al-Fārābī, Ibn Sīnā, etc.), while taking the key inspiration for its epistemology and its metaphysics (of light) from the post-Illuminationist *Ishrāqī* tradition in Islamic philosophy, since he wrote glosses both on Avicenna's *Shifā'* and Suhrawardī's *Ḥikmat al-ishrāq*.[26] He was also an accomplished exegete on the Qur'ān, a skilled Shī'ite scholastic theologian, and a (albeit mediocre) poet in Persian. Like other members of the School of Iṣfahān, Mullā Ṣadrā's thought thus comprised a synthesis of Sufism, Shī'ite Imāmology and theology, Islamic Platonism (*Ishrāqī* theosophy), and Peripatetic rationalism (if we keep in mind, as Corbin reminds us,[27] that Aristotle was understood by them to have been the author of a mystical *Theology* based on the Enneads of Plotinus[28]).

Mullā Ṣadrā authored over fifty major works and minor treatises,[29] most of which were composed during the final period of his life.[30] The most important of these, for which he is primarily known, is his magnum opus, "monument de la pensée islamo-iranienne,"[31] is the *Asfār al-arba'ah* (Four Spiritual Voyages), which, writes S.H. Nasr, is "comparable in dimension and scope to the *Shifā'* and the *Futūḥāt al-Makkiyah* and in a way stands midway between the Peripatetic encyclopaedia of Ibn Sīnā and the compendium of esoteric sciences of Ibn 'Arabī."[32] The following

25 Ernst, "Sufism and Philosophy in Mullā Ṣadrā," pp. 5–8.

26 Ziai, "Mullā Ṣadrā: His Life and Works," p. 640.

27 *Histoire de la philosophie islamique*, p. 463.

28 See Peter Adamson, *The Arabic Plotinus: A Philosophical Study of the 'Theology of Aristotle'* (London: Duckworth 2002).

29 On his various works, see Nasr, "Ṣadr al-Dīn Shīrāzī (Mullā Ṣadrā)," pp. 935–36; Mullā Ṣadrā, *Risāla-yi Sih aṣl*, ed. S.H. Nasr, published "by the effort" of Muḥammad Riḍā Jūzī (Tehran: Intishārāt-i Rawzāna 1377 A.Hsh./1998), Nasr's introduction, pp. 10–11; Ḥāmid Nājī Iṣfahānī (ed.), *Majmū'a-yi Rasā'il-i falsafī-yi Ṣadr al-Muta'allihīn*, pp. xiii–xv.

30 Nasr, "Ṣadr al-Dīn Shīrāzī (Mullā Ṣadrā)," p. 935.

31 Corbin, *En Islam iranien*, vol. IV, p. 67.

32 Nasr, "Ṣadr al-Dīn Shīrāzī (Mullā Ṣadrā)," p. 937.

lovely summary by Henry Corbin gives a good overview of the mystical structure underlying this huge Arabic work (nine volumes, each approximately 500–900 pages long in the recent critical edition published in Tehran[33]), which has been described as "the most advanced work in Islamic philosophy"[34]:

> The *Four Spiritual Voyages* in its title makes reference to the traditional terminology of the mystical gnosis of Islam. The *first* of these voyages commences in the creaturely realm and terminates in God (*mina'l-khalq ilā'l-Ḥaqq*). The issues discussed and the ground covered here include problems involving the composition of existent beings, the entire physical realm, matter and form, substances and accidents. At the end of the first voyage the wayfarer is raised up to the supersensible plane of divine realities. The *second* voyage is then a voyage setting off to God, in God and by God (*fi'l-Ḥaqq bi'l-Ḥaqq*). Here the wayfarer does not abandon the ground of the metaphysical realm; he is initiated into the *Ilāhiyāt* (*Divinalia*): the problems of the divine Essence, divine Names and divine Attributes. The *third* voyage then proceeds along a mental course that is the inverse of the first: the traveller 'redescends' from God back to the creaturely realm, but 'with God' or 'by God' (*mina'l-Ḥaqq ilā'l-khalq bi'l-Ḥaqq*). This voyage follows the order of the procession of beings that spring from the Light of Lights: the wayfarer is initiated into the knowledge concerning the hierarchic Intelligences, into the multitudes of supersensible universes, whose planes superimpose themselves on those of the physical world of sensible perception. Here, all is cosmogony and angelology. Lastly, there is the *fourth* voyage undertaken 'with God' or 'by God' in this same creaturely realm (*bi'l-Ḥaqq fī'-khalq*). The wayfarer here is essentially initiated into the knowledge of the soul, that is to say, knowledge of his self (illuminative 'oriental' knowledge); he is initiated into esoteric *tawḥīd*, such that he recognizes that nothing exists but God, in the sense of the maxim: "He who knows his soul (that is to say, himself) knows his Lord." Finally,

33 *Al-asfār al-arba'a*, ed. Sayyid Muḥammad Khāminahī and Ghulām Riḍā A'vānī (Tehran: Bunyād-i Ḥikmat-i Mullā Ṣadrā 1383 A.Hsh./2004), 9 vols.

34 S.H. Nasr, "Mullā Ṣadrā," *The Encyclopedia of Philosophy*, 2nd edn, ed. Donald Borchert (New York: Macmillan Reference & Thomson Gale 2006), vol. VI, p. 418.

> this amounts to an initiation into the prospects of eschatology; the Grand Return (*Ma'ād*) takes place, that is to say, which prospects of what infinite worlds present themselves to man from the very moment that he crosses the threshold of death.[35]

The legacy of Mullā Ṣadrā's thought was continued by his two most famous students (also sons-in-law). The first, 'Abd al-Razzāq b. 'Alī b. Ḥusayn Lāhījī (d. 1072/1661–2), was one of the central theologians, philosophers and poets of the School of Iṣfahān.[36] The second, Mullā Muḥsin Fayḍ-i Kāshānī (d. 1090/1679–80) was an equally "eminent theologian, philosopher, jurisprudent and mystic of the Safavid period, known for his prolific compositions in subjects ranging from Peripatetic philosophy to Ishrāqī 'Oriental' theosophy, mysticism (*'irfān*) and both speculative and practical Sufism (*taṣawwuf-i naẓarī wa 'amalī*)."[37]

Today, following upon the initial groundbreaking studies and early critical editions and translations of Mullā Ṣadrā's works made by Henry Corbin and S.H. Nasr during the 1960–70s, his writings generated their own separate industry in the academic world. A Persian journal (*Khirad-nāma Ṣadrā*) devoted exclusively to his philosophy was launched in Iran in the 1990s, which has appeared in multiple volumes, followed by *Transcendent Philosophy: An International Journal for Comparative Philosophy and Mysticism*, launched in London in the year 2000, each issue of which has usually featured several articles concerning Mullā Ṣadrā's philosophy. There is a plethora of works available today in Persian, Arabic and a number of European languages devoted to various aspects of his philosophy. Mullā Ṣadrā's 'School of Transcendental Theosophy (*al-ḥikma al-muta'āliya*)' still flourishes in Iran today, with many active thinkers. Indeed, the last chapter

---

35 Corbin, *En Islam iranien*, vol. IV, p. 67.

36 On him, see my "Sufism and the School of Iṣfahan: *Taṣawwuf* and *'Irfān* in Late Safavid Iran ('Abd al-Razzāq Lāhījī and Fayḍ-i Kāshānī on the Relation of *Taṣawwuf*, *Hikmat* and *'Irfān*)," pp. 101–12; S.H. Nasr and Mehdi Aminrazavi (eds.), *An Anthology of Philosophy in Persia*, vol. V, pp. 222–60.

37 *Muntakhabātī az āthār-i ḥukamā'ī ilāhī-yi Īrān az 'aṣr-i Mīr Dāmād u Mīr Findariskī tā zamān-i ḥāḍir*, edited, introduced and annotated by Sayyid Jalāl al-Dīn Ashtiyānī; French introduction by Henry Corbin (Paris/Tehran: 1975), II, p. 118 from Ashtiyānī"s Persian introduction.

of this book is consecrated to a member of Mullā Ṣadrā's school: Ḥājjī Mullā Hadī Sabziwārī (d. 1289/1873).

* * *

The following passages[38] from Mullā Ṣadrā's *Mafātīḥ al-ghayb* have been translated below:

1. The eighth 'temple of theophany' (*mashhad*) on "demonstration of the spiritual sciences which are termed 'esoteric' (*ladunnī*)," which is a sub-chapter within the third chapter or 'key' (*miftāḥ*) (pp. 334–42) on "the essence of the sciences and their significance, expounding the nobility, grandeur and superiority of knowledge."
2. The first 'scene' on "the kinds of supersensory interior unveilings (*mukāshafa*) explained in brief" (pp. 343–46) which is the first sub-chapter within the fourth chapter or key on "the hierarchical degrees of visionary unveiling (*kashf*) and their causes, and on the varieties of inspiration, passing thoughts and satanic temptations (*al-ilhāmāt wa 'l-khawāṭir wa 'l-wasāwas*) and the demonic and angelic causes of these phenomena, within which are certain 'temples of theophany'."

As can be seen from the above précis, the translated passages concern Ṣadr al-Muta'allihīn's mystical epistemology, in respect to which he is generally counted a follower of Shihāb al-Dīn Suhrawardī, the Master of Illuminative Theosophy (*Shaykh al-ishrāq*), basing himself on Suhrawardī's doctrine of knowledge by presence (*'ilm-i huḍūrī*).[39] The Safavid theosopher thus

---

38 *Mafātīḥ al-ghayb* (*Keys to the Invisible Realm*) by Ṣadr al-Mutā'allihīn (Tehran Mu'assisāt-i Muṭala'āt va taḥqīqāt-i farhangī 1363 A.Hsh./1984); also published with an introduction and translation into Persian by Muḥammad Khwājū'ī (Tehran: Intishārāt-i Mullā 1363 A.Hsh./1984; 2nd edn 1371 A.Hsh./1992). I would like to thank Prof. Hermann Landolt for supplying me with copies of the relevant pages in the Arabic text of the *Mafātīḥ* edited by Muḥammad Khwājū'ī (Beirut: Mu'assasat al-tārīkh al-'Arabī 1499/1999: based on the lithograph copy of 1282 A.H. plus two good manuscripts), vol. 1, pp. 220–27, from which I have translated these passages.

39 On this doctrine, see Mehdi Ha'iri Yazdi, *The Principles of Epistemology in Islamic Philosophy: Knowledge by Presence* (Albany: SUNY Press 1992); Mehdi Amin Razavi, *Suhrawardi and the School of Illumination* (Richmond, UK: Curzon 1997), pp. 103–13;

described knowledge as light – the light of knowledge and faith which discloses the realities of the world just as sunlight reveals the features of the material world.[40] His pronouncement in this chapter that "Knowledge is the presential form of the realities of things within the substratum of the knower" (*al-'ilm ... al-ṣūrat al-ḥāḍarat li-ḥaqā'iq al-ashyā 'ind al-jawhar al-'āqil*)" is of course not particularly original, and many such definitions of knowledge given by previous thinkers and theologians in Islam might be cited,[41] but the adjective 'presential form' (*al-ṣūrat al-ḥāḍarat*) does expose the *Ishrāqī* tint colouring his epistemology.

One of the interesting aspects of Mullā Ṣadrā's treatment of knowledge is his citation of a number of traditions concerning 'Alī ibn Abī Ṭālib's endowment with esoteric knowledge. On reading these references to Imām 'Alī, readers unfamiliar with 'Alī's position as the founding father of Sufism[42] might immediately invoke 'Shī'ite tendencies' as the source of Mullā Ṣadrā's inspiration. In fact, by a close comparative reading of chapters two and nine, it is clear that Mullā Ṣadrā had simply plagiarized all these so-called 'pro-Shī'ite traditions' verbatim from the *Treatise on Esoteric Knowledge*, (translated in chapter two of this collection) by the famous Sunni Sufi theologian, the 'Proof of Islam' of Abū Ḥāmid al-Ghazālī. His imitation of Ghazālī, which can hardly be interpreted as a privileging of the Shī'ite over the Sunni Muslim tradition, is just another indication of the mutually inherited tradition of Islamic *ḥikmat* theosophy, and the commonly shared

---

Henry Corbin, *En Islam iranien: Aspects spirituels et philosophiques*, vol. II: *Sohrawardî et les Platoniciens de Perse* (Paris: Éditions Gallimard 1971), pp. 63–65; on Mullā Ṣadrā's use of Suhrawardī's doctrine, see *idem.*, *En Islam iranien*, vol. IV: *L'École d'Isfahan, L'École Shaykhie, Le Douzième Imâm*, pp. 65–66.

40 Mullā Ṣadrā, *Risāla-yi Sih aṣl*, ed. S.H. Nasr (Tehran: Tehran University Press 1340 A.Hsh./1961), pp. 6–7. My exposition here is much indebted to Shahram Pazouki's unpublished essay: "Sufi Knowledge in Mulla Sadra" lent to the author.

41 It is in the vein of twenty other similar definitions of knowledge – as being a form, concept, meaning or process of mental verification – cited and compared by F. Rosenthal, *Knowledge Triumphant*, pp. 60–63 (cf. particularly E: 5, 14, 16).

42 This is treated in detail in my article: "'Alī ibn Abī Ṭālib's Ethics of Mercy in the Mirror of the Persian Sufi Tradition," in M.A. Lakhani (ed.), *The Sacred Foundations of Justice in Islam* (Vancouver, Canada: Sacred Web 2006), pp. 109–45.

esoteric ground[43] which, in spite of outward sectarian differences, Mullā Ṣadrā stands on and shares with a number of Sunni Sufi divines, Ghazālī, Suhrawardī and Ibn ʿArabī included.

In fact, *every one of the ideas without exception* expounded in the first ten pages of Mullā Ṣadrā's work (all of 'Eighth Temple of Theophany' down to the section entitled "the fourth key to the Invisible World") constitutes a paraphrase, if not outright plagiary, of Sufi ideas found in Ghazālī's treatise on esoteric knowledge! One of the main reasons that this translation is included in this anthology is to show how esoteric thought in Islam comprises a literary inheritance as well as a divine inspiration. The tremendous impact of Ghazālī's Sufi theosophy upon Mullā Ṣadrā is highlighted by ʿAbd al-Ḥusayn Zarrīnkūb:

> In reality, in his *Asfār* and other works Mullā Ṣadrā repeatedly directly quotes the words of Ghazālī, thus demonstrating that he – like his own teacher Mīr Dāmād – believes in and extols Ghazālī. There are many instances of Ghazālī's influence on his writings; one might mention Mullā Ṣadrā's citation of Ghazālī when discussing the issue of the divine Unity of the Elect (*tawḥīd-i khawwāṣ*), which occurs on the level of annihilation in divine Unity (*fanā dar tawḥīd*), where, the tone and tenor of his quotation from Ghazālī make it sound as if he considers the latter's words to be a kind of 'proof-text', such that the mere citation of Ghazālī's words should, it would seem, suffice to dispel the doubts of all who might call his ideas into question. Likewise, the literary style of Ghazālī's *Munqidh min al-ḍalāl* is clearly reflected in Ṣadrā's preface to the *Asfār*. The manner that he elucidates his own intellectual and spiritual journey which is also similar to that of Ghazālī. This is revealed in his vast oeuvre, the *Asfār al-ārbaʿa*, which he based on the four spiritual journeys of wayfarers on the Sufi *ṭarīqat*, where he establishes and elaborates his philosophical teachings on this same foundation of the gnosis of the Sufis ...[44]

43 Henry Corbin thus astutely comments: "*En derniére analyse, un Mollâ Sadrâ ne peut être expliqué que par lui-meme, car nous pouvons toujours collectioner les "sources," les citations ou les allusions, cela ne donnera jamais un Mollâ Sadrâ, si tout d'abord il n'existe pas un Mollâ Sadrâ pour les rassembler dans l'ordre d'une structure qu'il était seul à pouvoir leur donner.*" – *En Islam iranien*, vol. IV, p. 64.

44 ʿAbd al-Ḥusayn Zarrīnkūb, *Dunbāla-yi Justujū-yi dar taṣawwuf-i Īrān* (Tehran: Amīr Kabīr 1362 A.Hsh./1983), pp. 249–50.

Composed in defence of "the occult science (*al-'ilm al-ghaybī*) on which the spiritual wayfarers and gnostics rely and depend," Mullā Ṣadrā opens the 'Eighth Temple of Theophany' copying Ghazālī virtually word-for-word, revealing how his theories stood in the shadow (or rather, basked in the light of) his great Sunni Sufi ancestor. Following further in the footsteps of Ghazālī's chapter three ("On the typologies of knowledge"),[45] Mullā Ṣadrā divides up knowledge into religious and rational types (*shar'īyya wa 'aqlīyya*), citing the very same *hadīth*s and Qur'ānic verses that had been given by Ghazālī to demonstrate exactly the same points about the science of the Qur'ān. He then gives a précis of Ghazālī's lengthy exposition of the various types of rational sciences, before skipping over Ghazālī's short chapter 4 "On the Sciences of the Sufis," to continue to closely follow the substance of the latter's argument. In his treatment of the superiority of esoteric, divinely infused knowledge to exoteric learning taken from a human teacher, Mullā Ṣadrā's imitation of Ghazālī's treatise reaches a crescendo. Juxtaposing the following three passages, we witness the overwhelming debt of the Safavid Supreme *Ḥakīm* to the Seljuk *Shaykh al-Islām*:

> **Ghazālī:** It should be understood that human knowledge is acquired by two methods. The first of these is through submission to human instruction (*al-ta'allum al-insānī*); the second vouchsafed through the divine teaching of the Spirit (*al-ta'allum al-rabbānī*).
>
> **Mullā Ṣadrā:** Man acquires knowledge in two different ways. The first is the way of learning, submitting to being taught and the voluntary acquisition of learning (*al-ta'allum wa'l-kasb*). The second is by way of grace of God and divine attraction (*al-wahab wa'l-jadhba*), vouchsafed by means of divine communication.
>
> * * *
>
> **Ghazālī:** [The second method is learning] from within by engaging in meditative reflection and contemplative thought (*al-ishtighāl bi'l-tafakkur*), internal reflection and contemplation from within in this regard performing the same function as does external exoteric study and learning from without. However, while acquiring knowledge

45 Ṣadrā skips chapter two of Ghazālī's *Al-Risālat al-ladunī* here, proceeding directly on to paraphrase chapter three of the text.

through study and learning demands the use of a particular person (as a teacher), meditative reflection and contemplative thought (*al-tafakkur*) involves the soul's obtaining succour (directly) from the Universal Soul, insofar as there is no influence more potent than that of Universal Soul; for its pedagogic strength and didactic power excels the learning and teaching skills of all the world's learned professors and wise savants.

Mullā Ṣadrā: [The second] method is learning from within (*al-ta'allum min al-dākhil*), which involves engaging oneself in contemplative reflection (*al-tafakkur*), insofar as learning is to the exterior personality (*al-ẓāhir*) what reflection is to the interior psyche (*al-bāṭin*). The only difference between the two modes of learning is that whereas the process of (outward) learning involves one particular person benefiting from the teaching of another particular person, reflection involves the soul availing itself of the weal of the Universal Soul – and that makes a far greater impact and more powerful impression in terms of transmission of a teaching than all the tutorials of all the scholars and sages combined together!

* * *

Ghazālī: [The method of the divine teaching of the Spirit] has two modes: The first is through the imparting of revelation (*ilqā' al-waḥy*), which is experienced when the soul becomes so perfected in its essential substance that the foul blemishes [**104**] of nature that defiled it and the ugly smut of longings and greedy desires for transient things are all dissolved away. At this point, the soul turns to face its Maker and Originator, and takes recourse in the bounty of its primordial Creator, relying upon His grace and His effusive radiance of light. Then God Almighty regards this soul with His fair favour, granting it full welcome and total acceptance, beholding it with His divine regard. He then draws forth a tablet from the human soul and takes up a pen from the Universal Soul, and upon the human soul's slate traces the inscription of all knowledge.

Mullā Ṣadrā: [The sciences of visionary disclosure (*'ulūm kashfiyya*) have two modes]: The first sort is that inspired through revelation (*ilqā' al-waḥy*), Such knowledge is obtained whenever the soul is cleansed of the filth of human nature and the dirt of sin, purged and purified of the vileness of the *la condition humaine*. At this juncture the soul, placed *vis-à-vis* the divine visage, puts its trust in divine Providence, while relying and depending on divine grace. Gazing upon the soul with His goodwill and favour and grace, God Almighty then turns completely towards it. He selects the soul to be a slate, takes the Universal Intellect as a Pen, and then inscribes upon it the totality of the knowledge of all the sciences (*jamī' al-'ulūm*) by way of a 'divine infusion from Him' (*min ladunahu*).

Exactly the same pedagogic metaphor utilized by Ghazālī regarding (what might be called) 'academic husbandry' (the student's soul compared to a seed and the teacher to the farmer who sows knowledge within him, bringing the lore existent *in potentia* within him into actuality) Mullā Ṣadrā proceeds to slavishly copy and mimic Ghazālī's simile that likened the Universal Soul's relation to the Universal Intellect as that of Eve to Adam. He echoes Ghazālī's definition of prophethood down to the very letter.[46] Defining the meaning of esoteric knowledge (*al-'ilm al-ladunīyya*), he adduced the celebrated tale, cited five hundred years earlier by Ghazālī in his treatise on this subject, that the Prophet had conveyed his inner lore to 'Alī b. Abī Ṭālib by a deep kiss. He also relates several other traditions linking 'Alī to the possession of esoteric knowledge cited by Ghazālī before him.

In the final four pages of the selection, however, Mullā Ṣadrā veers away from following Ghazālī to give an account of interior unveilings (*mukāshafa*). His speculations here are quite similar to the views of Kubrawī Sufis such as Najm al-Dīn Rāzī (d. 654/1256) on the topic.[47] He first defines, and then discusses the differences between, sensory interior

46 Cf. Ghazālī: "prophethood is the Sanctified Soul's reception of the spiritual realities of objects of knowledge and intelligible percepts (*ḥaqā'iq al-ma'lūmāt wa'l-ma'qūlāt*)" – with Ṣadrā: "prophethood signifies the sanctified soul's (*nafs-i qudsī*) reception and acknowledgement of the spiritual truths of objects of knowledge (*ḥaqā'iq al-ma'lūmāt*) from the substance of the Universal Intellect by means of a spiritual address and a holy converse."

47 See Najm al-Dīn Rāzī, *Mirṣād al-'ibād*, ed. M.A. Riyāḥī (Tehran: Intishārā-i 'Ilmī va Farhangī 1374 A.Hsh./1995), pp. 289–315.

unveilings (*al-mukāshafat al-ṣūrīyya*) and visionary unveiling abstracted from the forms of spiritual realities (*al-kashf al-ma'nawī al-mujarrad min ṣuwar al-ḥaqā'iq*). Both these experiences are fed by man's own resinous heart (like Ghazālī before him, he identifies the heart with the *anima rationalis* (*nafs al-nāṭiqa*) illuminated by the practical intelligence or applied reason (*al-'aql al-'amalī*).

The influence of Ibn 'Arabī can be seen in his assertion that interior unveilings of all kinds and shapes constitute theophanies of divine names (*tajalliyyāt ismā'īyya*):

> Everything beheld by the eye (during such interior unveilings) is thus a theophany of the divine name 'the Seer' (*al-Baṣīr*); everything heard by ear is a theophany of the divine name 'the All-Hearing (*al-Samī'*), and so forth with the rest of the divine names. Each one of these names is subservient to its own Lord, while all of them are subjects of the divine name 'the Omniscient' (*al-'ālīm*).

In Ibn 'Arabī's thought, the presence of God is epiphanized in all things through the theophanies of His divine Names. Just as the process of creation takes place by means of the epiphany of various divine Names, the mystical experience of God within the soul is through the visionary unveiling (*kashf*) of these same Names. From this passage, it is clear that, as Carl Ernst points out, there is a "greater degree of approximation between Mullā Ṣadrā and Sufism on the question of mystical vision."[48]

The selection concludes with Mullā Ṣadrā's profoundly fascinating discussion of the relationship of thought (*fikr*) to unveiling (*kashf*). His view of the place of 'intuitive conjecture' (*ḥads*) in the act of mystical unveiling and contemplative meditation particularly merits attention, insofar as he understands it as divinely illuminated by the sacrosanct light (*al-nūr al-qudsī*).[49] In contradistinction to Ghazālī, who had considered *ḥads* merely as a higher form of meditative reflection (*al-tafakkur*), Mullā Ṣadrā views it as a kind of supra-rational intuition, involving the immediate grasping of

48 Carl Ernst, "Sufism and Philosophy in Mullā Ṣadrā," typescript lent by the author, p. 5.

49 A good discussion of *ḥads* in Mullā Ṣadrā's mystical epistemology is given by Ibrahim Kalin, *Knowledge in Later Islamic Philosophy: Mullā Ṣadrā on Existence, Intellect, and Intuition* (Oxford; Oxford University Press 2010), pp. 154–57.

spiritual realities without recourse the normal categories of rational reflection that takes place when "the mind turns away from incidental problems towards the fundamental elements or first principles." In this, his view is similar to that of Avicenna (who had theorized that it was the presentation of the middle term of a syllogism without any search or effort on the part of the mind.[50] The difference is that whereas for Avicenna *ḥads* is a kind of 'quick wit', for Mullā Ṣadrā it is "an exceptional faculty of the soul, which connects it to the 'Sacred Angelic world'."[51] In the *Asfār*, he thus explains:

> Know that the source of all knowledge is the world of the sacred but the capacities of human souls are different. In the case of perfect capacity, there is no difference in abundance between primary and secondary intelligibles. In perceiving the primary intelligibles, man is like that when he understands the middle term [of a syllogism] in perceiving theoretically matters in such a way that understanding takes place as if without a cause whereas the existence of something without a cause is impossible. But the cause is sometimes outward and visible and sometimes inward and hidden. That which dictates knowledge to capable souls is in reality the very cause hidden from the senses.[52]

This definition of *ḥads* also echoes that of Jurjānī in his *Ta'rīfāt* who had defined it as "the mind's swift transference from preliminary matters to basic issues. It stands in contrast to thought (*al-fikr*). Intuitive conjecture is the lowest degree of visionary unveiling (*al-kashf*)."[53] Yet Ṣadrā designates *ḥads* by the Ishrāqī (rather than Peripatetic) philosophical definition, according to which it "represents the elevation of the human spirit towards transcendental principles in such a manner that the soul becomes transmuted into mirror burnished bright facing the divine Truth, which fills it with overflowing light. It occupies itself with that light, without however, the Truth being completely incarnated in the soul. This becoming filled up

50 Alexander Treiger, *Inspired Knowledge in Islamic Thought: Al-Ghazālī's Theory of Mystical Cognition and its Avicennian Foundation* (London: Routledge 2012), pp. 74–80.

51 Kalin, *Knowledge in Later Islamic Philosophy*, p. 154.

52 Cited by Kalin, *Knowledge in Later Islamic Philosophy*, pp. 154–55.

53 *Ta'rīfāt*, ed. Ibrāhīm al-Abyārī (Beirut: Dār al-Kitāb al-'Arabī 1405 A.H./ 1984), s.v. *ḥads*.

with light is termed a 'visionary unveiling of the spirit (*kashf-i rūḥī*)' or 'inspiration (*ilhām*)'."[54]

This selection concludes with a brief discussion of inspiration (*al-ilhām*) and 'spiritual contemplation' (*al-shuhūd al-rūḥī*).

SELECTIONS FROM MULLĀ ṢADR'S *MAFĀTĪḤ AL-GHAYB*

THE EIGHTH TEMPLE OF THEOPHANY[55]

In proof of the Theosophical Sciences that are designated as 'divine esoteric knowledge'[56]

It should be understood – may God bestow guidance upon you – that most of those who are renowned as scholars repudiate the occult science (*al-'ilm al-ghaybī*) on which the spiritual wayfarers and gnostics rely and depend, despite the fact that this science is more reliable and trustworthy than other sciences. They affirm that there is no other meaning to knowledge (*'ilm*) but that which is acquired through instruction, reflective thinking, speculation and intellectual study. Some even imagine that real knowledge is restricted solely to Islamic jurisprudence (*fiqh*), the exoteric sense of Qur'ānic exegesis (*ẓāhir al-tafsīr*) and scholastic theology (*kalām*), claiming that beyond these there is not any other kind of knowledge. But such an opinion is corrupt and unsound. Anyone who professes such a view has not, so to speak, apprehended any meaning at all from the Qur'ān. He or she has not yet verified for himself the reality of the fact that the Qur'ān is an ocean circumscribing and accommodating all spiritual realities (*jamī' al-ḥaqā'iq*).

---

54 Jamīl Ṣalībā, *Farhang-i Falsafī*, translated from Arabic to Persian by Manūchihr Ṣāna'ī Durrabīdī (Tehran: Intishārāt-i Ḥikmat 1366 A.Hsh./1987), p. 303.

55 Ṣadr al-Mutā'allihīn al-Shīrāzī, *Mafātīḥ al-ghayb*, ed. Muḥammad Khwājū'i (Beirut: Mu'assasat al-tārīkh al-'Arabī 1499/1999), pp. 220–27; see also *Tarjuma-yi Mafātīḥ al-ghayb*, ed. and trans. [from Arabic into Persian] Muḥammad Khwājū'i (Tehran: Intishārāt-i Mullā 1363 A.Hsh./1984; 2nd edn 1371 A.Hsh./1992), pp. 334–46.

56 The term translated as theosophy here is *'ulūm al-rabānīyya* which means divine sciences' and the term *al-'ulūm al-ladunī:* referring to divinely infused esoteric knowledge mentioned in Qur'ān XVIII:65: "We had taught him [Khiḍr] a knowledge from our presence (*'allamnāhu min ladunnā 'ilman*)."

This is because the whole meaning of the Qur'ān is not contained in these general works of exegesis that are celebrated as attributed to the likes of al-Qushayrī,[57] al-Tha'labī,[58] al-Wāḥidī, al-Zamakhsharī[59] and others.

The approach of such folk to deny every kind of subject matter that is beyond their understanding. These sham imitators of tradition have never even tasted a draught of the pure wine of spiritual truth. They are afflicted with this chronic illness: they have become hung up at the level of blind imitation of religious precedents (*taqlīd*) of their fathers and elders; they are frozen in stasis at the degree of hollow *verbatim* narration of texts. Thus they repudiate and deny the validity of everything besides common hearsay. This illness in them has so become firmly entrenched in them that they can neither remedy it nor cut off its nutritive substances. On the other hand, those in whom this illness has not taken firm root may remedy it by first of all by betaking themselves to various types of sciences, along with the source-springs and advantages those sciences furnish. In this fashion, they will come to apprehend what such divine esoteric knowledge (*al-'ilm al-ladunnīyya*) is, and what is its purpose, until at last they affirm its actual existence.

Thus, we affirm that "Knowledge is the presential form of the realities of things within the substratum of the knower."

Knowledge is of two types: the first concerns things canonical (*shar'ī*: pertaining to regulations determined by the religious law) and second concerns things rational-intellectual (*'aqlī*: pertaining to judgments made by human reason). Of course, most of what pertains to the Canonical Sciences (*shar'īyya*) according to its scholars is also *rational-intellectual*, while most of what pertains to the intellectual sciences according to its scholars is also *canonical* (determined by the religious law). "And for one whom God has not appointed light, there is no light."[60]

However, as for the Canonical Sciences or Sciences of the Religious Law (*'ulūm-i shar'īyya*), these are subdivided into two types: the science of

---

57 'Abd al-Karīm al-Qushayrī (d. 465/1074) was the author of a famous treatise (*Risāla*) on Sufism as well as a Sufi Qur'ān commentary.

58 Tha'labī (d. 427/1035) authored a famous commentary: *al-Kashf wa'l-bayān 'an tafsīr al-Qur'ān*.

59 Abū'l-Qāsim Maḥmūd ibn 'Umar al-Zamakhsharī (d. 538/1144) was the author of a famous Mu'tazilite commentary entitled *Al-Kashshāf 'an ḥaqā'iq ghawāniḍ al-tanzīl*.

60 Qur'ān XXIV:40.

principles and fundamentals (*uṣūl*) and the science of the branches and secondary aspects (*furū'*).

The former pertain to the sciences or knowledge of divine unity (*tawḥīd*), the Messengers' mission (*risālat*), the Scripture (*kitābat*), prophecy (*nubuwwat*), leadership of the Muslim community (*imāmat*), and ultimate emigration to the divine source (*ma'ād*). The true believer is one who understands these sciences either by certain theosophical knowledge born of visionary disclosure (*'irfān yaqīn kashf*) or else through rational demonstration (*burhān*). To this matter God Himself has attested in stating: "The Messenger has faith in what was sent down to him from his Lord, and the believers as well: all of them have faith in God and His angels, and in His Books and His Messengers – we set no distinction between any one of His Messengers. They say, 'We hear and obey. Grant us your forgiveness – O our Lord – for the wayfaring is all unto You.'"[61]

The science of 'the branches and secondary aspects' pertains to knowledge of juridical judgments, directives, ordinances, the rulings and rites of marriage and so forth. The Qur'ān is an ocean encompassing all such sciences, within which are to be found such a vast number of intricate problems that no mind can ever comprehend them – except for one whom God has vouchsafed an understanding of His Scripture and granted intellectual penetration into (the meaning of) religion, so that his knowledge reaches the degree of certainty. According to the celebrated *ḥadīth*, each 'lectio' (*ḥarf*) of the Qur'ān has a limit (*ḥadd*) and each limit a point of transcendency (*maṭla'*).[62] Thus God Almighty has given an exposition of *all* of the sciences which in turn give an exposé of the realities of things – whether sensible or intelligible, visible or invisible, large or small. As His Word attests: "Not a leaf falls but He knows of it; not a grain lies in the bowels of

61 Qur'ān II:285.

62 For a good discussion of the background and use of various versions this *ḥadīth* in both Muslim theology and Sufism, see G. Böwering, *The Mystical Vision of Existence in Classical Islam: The Qur'ānic Hermeneutics of the Ṣūfī Sahl at-Tustarī (d. 283/896)* (Berlin: Walter de Gruyter 1980), pp. 139ff; Nicholas Heer, "Abū Ḥāmid al-Ghazālī's Esoteric Exegesis of the Qur'ān," in Leonard Lewisohn (ed.), *The Heritage of Sufism*, vol. I: *Classical Persian Sufism from its Origins to Rumi (700–1300)* (Oxford: Oneworld 1999), pp. 237–39.

the earth, and naught is there of what is wet or what is dry, but that it has been writ in a clear scripture."[63]

However, regarding the second type of knowledge – pertaining to things rational-intellectual – this is a particularly difficult sort of lore to fathom and distinguish what is sound and correct from what is corrupt and incorrect therein. Yet, one who does comprehend this science as it deserves, will understand that its premises are, in reality, all based on legal principles of the Sacred Law (*uṣūl-i sharīʿat*) and that its branches likewise all devolve upon branches of the Sacred Law.

The principles and fundamentals of rational-intellectual knowledge are of two sorts: theoretical and practical. As for the theoretical sort, its subject matter comprises three degrees in proportion to its proximity or distance from physical bodies of the cosmos.[64] The supremely highest degree of theoretical philosophy relates to spiritual or divine things (*al-ilahiyyāt*, that is, Theology) the intermediate degree relates to the Exact Sciences (*al-riyāḍiyāt*, that is, Mathematics), and on the lowest degree one finds the Natural Sciences (*al-tabīʿiyāt*).

As for the latter (Practical Philosophy), this also comprises three degrees. First and foremost is the science of refinement of moral character (*ʿilm tahdhīb al-akhlāq*, that is, Ethics), followed by household management (*ʿilm tadbīr al-manzil*, that is, Economics[65]), and finally, the science of government (*ʿilm tadbīr al-madanīyya*, that is, Political Science). The branches and secondary aspects of these sciences are manifold, but this is hardly the proper place to discuss them in detail.

These premises having been understood by you, you should also know that man acquires knowledge in two different ways. The first is the way of learning, submitting to being taught and the voluntary acquisition of learning (*al-taʿallum wa'l-kasb*). The second is by way of grace of God and divine attraction (*al-wahab wa'l-jadhba*), vouchsafed by means of divine communication. Learning (*al-taʿallum*) is either acquired from without or within.

---

63 Qur'ān VI:59.

64 That is to say, theoretical knowledge becomes refined in proportion to degrees of increasing immateriality.

65 For an excellent discussion of the development of this technical term, see Reza Pourjavady, "Risāla-yi Tadbīr-i manzil dar *Jāmaʿ al-ʿulūm* Fakhr-i Rāzī," *Maʿārif* XVII/1 (July 2000), pp. 23–52; for a good overview of its meaning in Islamic practical philosophy, see also W. Heffening and G. Endress, "Tadbīr," *EI2* X, pp. 52–53.

The former method – which is the customary way among people who conduct themselves through sense-based appearances – involves the inculcation of certain audible words and expressions from a human teacher, then the writing of those words and expressions down. The second method is learning from within (*al-taʿallum min al-dākhil*), which involves engaging oneself in contemplative reflection (*al-tafakkur*), insofar as learning is to the exterior personality (*al-ẓāhir*) what reflection is to the interior psyche (*al-bāṭin*). The only difference between the two modes of learning is that whereas the process of (outward) learning involves one particular person benefiting from the teaching of another particular person, contemplative reflection involves the soul availing itself of the weal of the Universal Soul – and that makes a far greater impact and more powerful impression in terms of transmission of a teaching than all the tutorials of all the scholars and sages combined together!

The reason for this is that all the sciences (*al-ʿulūm*) are concentrated in the ground of the soul (*aṣl al-nafs*), where they are rooted like a seed in the earth or an image suspended in an unburnished and smudged mirror. Teaching is the bringing out and excavation *in actu* of the thing deposited there *in potentia*. The teacher, in bestowing the benefit of instruction on others, resembles a farmer, while the student's soul resembles the cultivated and tilled earth in which the student's potential knowledge is sewn like a kernel or seed. By means of irrigation with the water of his pedagogy and constantly flowing instruction, the teacher causes this seed to ripen and bear fruit. But to do this properly, the teacher must prune and trim back the thorns of doubt choking the budding plant and then trim away and snip off any scraggy offshoots of corrupt and erroneous opinions and beliefs that sprout off from the sapling so that the student's soul when it develops to its full maturity will be like a tree heavy-laden with fruit, or like a mirror burnished bright and clear, sparkling with brilliance vis-à-vis the object of its desire.[66] At this time – during late childhood – when the student becomes

66 This is a universal doctrine common to many wisdom traditions of the world and Mullā Ṣadrā's words here bear comparison to this passage from the Northern Buddhist treatise *Tsungmi*: "Just as it is in the nature of the mirror to shine, so all beings at their origin possess spiritual illumination. When, however, the passions obscure the mirror, it becomes covered over, as if with dust. When false thoughts, under the direction of the master, are overcome and destroyed, they cease to proclaim themselves. Then is the Intellect illumined, in accordance with its nature, and nothing remains unknown. It is

liberated from the condition of potentiality, he is like iron that is freshly molten. Then, once that iron has (hardened and) been polished so that the rust of sin, supposition and doubt are completely burnished away, he then becomes like a mirror that has regained its original condition. After the veil of blind imitation of religious precedents (*taqlīd*) is lifted off, he is like a mirror removed from its casing. Then, when its surface is placed before the divine Truth (*al-ḥaqq*), he becomes like a mirror facing the direction of the divine Form (*al-ṣūrat*).[67]

However, when the bodily faculties' infatuations and drives, such as anger, lust and similar passions, overwhelm and subdue the soul, the educated person will be obliged to redouble his efforts and spend more time in striving for knowledge and increasing his learning. But when the Intellect (*al-ʿaql*) manages to vanquish and subdue sensuality and its cravings, the seeker will find that a small amount of meditative reflection (*qalīl al-tafakkur*) suffices him far more than a great deal of studious learning (*kathīr al-taʿallum*) ever did. How many sages there are for whom an hour of meditative reflection far excels an entire year of studious learning by the ignorant.[68]

---

like the polishing of a mirror ..." Cited by Titus Burckhardt, *Mirror of the Intellect: Essays on Traditional Science and Sacred Art*, trans. W. Stoddart (Cambridge: Quinta Essentia 1987), p. 118.

67 Mullā Ṣadrā, using the same mirror metaphor, expounds this doctrine as follows in his *Asfār*: "If the heart is illuminated by the light of gnosis and faith, and emerges from potentiality to actuality by the [spiritual] discipline, act of service [to God] and the purification from the dirt of sins of filth of the sensuous appetites – like the iron when melted by the fire its dirt and filth leaves it, and from it the polished mirror is obtained – it becomes a sound eye illuminated by the light of the highest celestial kingdom. Then each of the organs of awareness becomes informed by the great signs from His Lord, it becomes a door to the gnosis of His Exalted Lord, and he is able to abstract sensible meanings from the particular sensible forms, and understand from them the divine secrets." – *Spiritual Psychology: The Fourth Intellectual Journey in Transcendent Philosophy: Volumes VIII & IX of the Asfar by Mullā Ṣadrā Shīrāzī*, trans. [from Arabic to English] by Latimah-Parvin Peerwani (London: ICAS Press 2008), p. 652.

68 This sentence is adopted from the celebrated *ḥadīth*: "An hour of contemplation is better than a year of prayer." Cited by Javad Nurbakhsh, *Traditions of the Prophet*, trans. Leonard Lewisohn and Terry Graham (New York: KNP 1983), vol. 2, p. 1.

It is therefore clear that some people acquire knowledge through study and learning (*al-taʿallum*), while others acquire it through meditative reflection and contemplative thought (*al-tafakkur*), but whereas study and learning do require reflection, vice-versa does not apply.

Regarding spiritually transmitted instruction or the teaching of the Spirit (*al-taʿlīm al-rabbānī*) that is conveyed without any causal intermediary means – this transcends all these other sciences since it is the knowledge of things hereafter, that is, it pertains to the sciences of eschatology (*ʿulūm ukhrawīyya*). Those who successfully apply themselves to this science become scholars of the life hereafter who shun and renounce this world. Worldly scholars (*ʿulamāʾ al-dunyā*) have been forbidden access to this science by God. These are the sciences of visionary disclosure (*ʿulūm kashfīyya*)[69] which cannot be apprehended except through the spiritual intuition born of the heart's sapiential 'taste' and enraptured apprehension (*dhawq wa wijdān*). Like the knowledge of the quality of the relish of intoxication,[70] these sciences cannot be realized by means of any simple or bare description. Only one who tastes them knows them. They are of two sorts:

69 According to the Definitions of Jurjānī (*Kitāb al-taʿrīfāt*, ed. Ibrāhīm al-Abyārī, Beirut 1985; p. 237), the word *kashf* "literally means 'rending the veil', but in [Sufi] terminology it signifies obtaining consciousness of invisible spiritual conceptions or ideas, and matters relating to divine 'truths' by means of interior vision (*shuhūd*) and presential intellectual vision (*ḥuḍūr*)."

70 The Arabic text here reads *al-sukr* (intoxication) but this could well be a scribal error for *al-shakkar* (sugar's sweetness). Mullā Ṣadrā's comparison of the ineffable clarity of the truth of *kashf* to the indescribable certainty of the taste of sugar or rapture of intoxication is of ancient provenance in Sufi texts. In the beginning of the introduction to the *Futūḥāt*, Ibn ʿArabī describes the science of mystical states (*aḥwāl*) as consisting of a kind of knowledge "which cannot be reached except through direct tasting. No man of reason can define the states, nor can any proof be adduced for knowing them, naturally enough. Take for example knowledge of the sweetness of honey, the bitterness of aloes, the pleasure of sexual intercourse, love, ecstasy, yearning, and similar knowledges. It is impossible for anyone to know any of these sciences without being qualified by them and tasting them." Cited and translated by William Chittick, *Ibn ʿArabī's Metaphysics of Imagination: The Sufi Path of Knowledge* (Albany: SUNY Press 1989), p. 169.

The first sort is that inspired through revelation (*ilqā' al-waḥy*). Such knowledge is obtained whenever the soul is cleansed of the filth of human nature and the dirt of sin, purged and purified of the vileness of the *la condition humaine*. At this juncture the soul, placed *vis-à-vis* the divine visage, puts its trust in divine Providence, while relying and depending on divine grace. Gazing upon the soul with His goodwill and favour and grace, God Almighty then turns completely towards it. He selects the soul to be a slate, takes the Universal Intellect as a Pen, and then inscribes upon it the totality of the knowledge of all the sciences (*jamī' al-'ulūm*) by way of a 'divine infusion from Him' (*min ladunahu*), according to the divine writ: "We had taught him [Khiḍr] a knowledge from our presence (*'allamnāhu min ladunnā 'ilman*)."[71] Thus the Universal Intellect (*al-'aql al-kullī*) is as the teacher, the soul in its sacral state or the sanctified soul (*nafs-i qudsī*) is like its student who obtains all the sciences from the Universal Intellect, so that *without any study* it can gain a conception of spiritual truths.[72] Thus when addressing His Prophet (peace be upon him and his family), God says: "You knew nothing of what the Scripture was, nor what was Faith, but we made a light, whereby We guide whom We will of Our servants."[73] God also said: "He taught you that which you knew not."[74] This type of knowledge far transcends all the sciences belonging to the mass of society since it is obtained directly from God without any intermediary means. Thus the wisest of all

---

71 Qur'ān XVIII:65.

72 This philosophical doctrine is shared both by Peripatetic thinkers such as Ibn Sīnā and Al-Fārābī and Ishrāqī theosophers like Mullā Ṣadrā. As Zailan Morris explains: "Both Ibn Sina and al-Farabi hold the view that at the level of the acquired intellect, man is capable of contemplating the Active Intellect itself. In its highest perfection, the acquired intellect attains union with the Active Intellect ... without it being essentially identified with the latter ... Through union with the Active Intellect, the acquired intellect becomes the prophetic intellect which is the receptacle of divine knowledge or revelation. In the union of the acquired intellect of the Prophet with the Active Intellect, the prophetic intellect receives knowledge from the latter. This transcendent knowledge is revelation (*wahy*)." *Revelation, Intellectual Intuition and Reason in the Philosophy of Mulla Sadra* (London: Routledge 2003), p. 41.

73 Qur'ān XLII:52.

74 Qur'ān IV:113.

humankind (the Prophet) – may God's peace be upon him and his family – declared: "My Lord taught me courtesy, and how fair is my courtesy!"[75]

The second sort of teaching of the Spirit is inspiration (*ilhām*) which is the liberal exuberance of the soul as befits its spiritual quality and aptitude via the divine Tablet (*al-lūḥ*). Inspiration is the effect and consequence of revelation (*al-waḥy*), the difference between them being that revelation is sounder and stronger than inspiration. Whereas the latter is designated as a prophetic knowledge (*'ilm-i nubuwwīyya*), the former is called "from the divine presence (*ladunīyya*)." Inspiration is as a radiance cast from the lantern of the invisible supernal realm into the heart that is purely undefiled and serenely detached. This is because all the sciences can be found immanent within the Universal Soul (*al-nafs al-kullī*) that belongs among the primordially pure and abstract substances (of the cosmos).

The Universal Soul's relation to the Universal Intellect resembles the relation of Eve to Adam.

It is apparent that the Universal Intellect is superior to the Universal Soul. Revelation is born from the overflowing emanative grace of the Universal Intellect, but inspiration is the offspring of the radiant epiphany (*ishrāq*) of the Universal Soul.

In the traditions of the Imāms (peace be upon them) it is related that Marwān bin Muslim narrated from Yazīd who narrated from Abī Ja'far (Imām Bāqir) who narrated from Abī 'Abdu'llāh (Imām Ṣādiq) (when he was asked about the interpretation) of the Word of God Almighty ("We never sent any Messenger (*rasūl*) or Prophet (*nabī*) before you but that Satan during the recitation of his message cast profane insinuations on his aims, but God renders null and void what Satan inspires, and then God confirms His signs. God is All-knowing and All-wise."[76] that:

> May God make me your ransom and sacrifice! This (exoteric meaning) is not our reading of this verse. What is the significance of [the terms] messenger, Prophet and transmitter of Prophetic traditions (*muḥaddith*)? He (then) said: 'The messenger is one to whom an angel is revealed, with which he converses. The Prophet is one who beholds the angel in his dreams. It is possible that prophethood

75 A *ḥadīth* commonly cited in Sufi texts. See Chittick, *The Sufi Path of Knowledge*, p. 175.

76 Qur'ān XXII:52.

(*al-nubuwwat*) and messengership (*al-risālat*) be combined in one individual. The transmitter of Prophetic traditions is one who hears a (celestial) sound without seeing any (angelic) form. In this sense, the soul of the Saint (*al-walī*) acquires knowledge of different sciences (*al-'ulūm*) from an angel, who is the bearer of knowledge, and yet, does not behold the angel's countenance, for that is what befits the degree of the Prophet insofar as he is a Prophet.

To sum up: inspiration (*al-ilhām*) is that which is shared in common among prophets and saints, while revelation (*al-waḥy*) is particular to the prophets whose remit encompasses both messengership and prophethood. Thus, prophethood signifies the sanctified soul's (*nafs-i qudsī*) reception and acknowledgement of the spiritual truths of objects of knowledge (*ḥaqā'iq al-ma'lūmāt*) from the substance of the Universal Intellect by means of a spiritual address and a holy converse. Messengership signifies the conveyance (*tablīgh*) of this address and converse to its worthy recipients and disciples. On occasion it may happen that the sanctified soul receives spiritual truths directly without it having received the conveyance of any message, as in God Almighty's word regarding Khiḍr (peace be upon him) attests: "We had taught him [Khiḍr] a knowledge from our presence."[77]

The Commander of the Faithful (*Amīr al-mu'minīn*) declared: "The Prophet (may the salutations of God be upon him and his family) stuck his tongue in my mouth. Suddenly a thousand doors (or 'chapters') of knowledge in my heart were opened, and within each door another million doors (or 'chapters') opened up."[78] He also said: "Would that they were to set up a chair (of judgment) for me, that I might judge the people of the Torah by their Torah, the people of the Gospels by their Gospels, and the people of the Qur'ān by the Qur'ān."[79] It is clear that this degree cannot be procured by anyone simply by medium of human instruction; rather it is obtained by

---

77 Qur'ān XVIII:65.

78 For an excellent discussion of the esoteric sense and intellectual context of this tradition, see Mohammad Ali Amir-Moezzi, *The Divine Guide in Early Shi'ism: The Sources of Esotericism in Islam*, trans. David Streight (Albany: SUNY Press 1994), pp. 75–77, p. 195, n. 381.

79 The Shī'ite theory that the Imāms possess knowledge of all the revealed books of previous revelations, is discussed in detail by Amir-Moezzi, *The Divine Guide in Early Shi'ism*, pp. 73ff.

strength of the divinely infused esoteric knowledge (*al-ʿilm al-ladunīyya*). He also pronounced: "It is related that in the time of Moses that he had written forty commentaries on his scripture. But if God were to command me, I could write a commentary on the meaning of the (first) letter – *Alif* – of the Surah al-Fāṭihā (the Opening Chapter of the Qur'ān), which would surpass that in size." [80] – And that is to say, forty commentaries. So it is obvious this sort of commodious breadth and expansively open purview of knowledge would be impossible except through divinely infused esoteric inspiration (*ilhāmiyān laduniyyān*).

An Admonition

It should be understood that the difference between revelation and inspiration can be approached in another way, although the source and debut of the two (as was mentioned above) are one and the same thing.[81] That is to say, while inspiration is obtained from God Almighty directly without any angelic intermediary in a special, particular manner that accompanies every living creature, revelation, on the other hand, is obtained by medium of an

---

80 ʿAlī's saying cited by Mullā Ṣadrā is taken directly from Ghazālī's *Al-Risālat al-ladunī*, who quotes it in slightly different format: "Were God to give me permission to compose a commentary on the meanings of the *Fāṭiha*, I could expand my exegesis to such a sum – that is to say, up to forty camel-loads." On this saying and its sources, see Reza Shah-Kazemi, *Justice and Remembrance: Introducing the Spirituality of Imam ʿAlī* (London: I.B. Tauris in association with the Institute of Ismaili Studies 2006), p. 25, n. 68.

81 Kalin's summary of the place of revelation in Mullā Ṣadrā's epistemology, and the relation between *waḥy* and *ilhām* is helpful here: "While Ṣadrā holds fast to the categorical distinction between revelation (*waḥy*) and inspiration (*ilhām*), he is aware of the implications of revealed knowledge for the validity of non-rational forms of knowledge. As a Muslim philosopher, he could not have remained indifferent to the epistemic challenge of revelation to philosophy. Unlike the Farabian attempt to humanize the process of revealed knowledge, Ṣadrā takes revelation to be a special case of knowledge to be understood in its own terms ... In short, the foundation of metaphysics is neither reason nor even intuition but revelation and what the prophets and philosophers have deduced from it." – *Knowledge in Later Islamic Philosophy*, pp. 204–5. On Mullā Ṣadrā's doctrine of revelation, see also Fazlur Rahman, *The Philosophy of Mullā Ṣadrā* (*Ṣadr al-Dīn Shīrāzī*) (Albany: SUNY Press 1975), pp. 184–88.

angel. Thus, although the 'Sacred Traditions' (*al-ḥadīth al-qudsīyya*),[82] are considered to be the 'Word of God', they are not designated as being (on par with either) 'Revelation' and the 'Qur'ān.[83]

The reason for this is that when the Prophet (may the blessing of God be upon him and his family) contemplated the form of all things in the cosmos and their genesis, because of the consummate perfection of the substance of his prophecy, the boundlessness of his soul, the expansiveness of his heart, and the general strength of his faculties, wit and intelligence, the Angel bearing divine revelation was imaginalized (*fayatamaththul lahu*) for him both in the esoteric *mundus imaginalis* (*'ālam al-tamaththul al-bāṭinī*)[84] and within his internal sense (*al-ḥiss al-dākhilī*). The Prophet then recognized the Angel there (in the *mundus imaginalis* and within his internal sense) as well as in the pure uncreated spiritual realm. [The saint (*al-walī*)], on the other hand, does not apprehend any of the veridical sciences except at the station of the spiritual beings disengaged from the *mundus imaginalis* (*al-arwāh al-mujarrada 'an 'ālam al-tamaththul*). For this reason, because of the strength of its influx and the intensity of its unveiling, the interior vision of the Angel and his audition to the divine Word, the first (form of divine communication experienced by the Prophet) is termed "Revelation," whereas the second (form of divine communication experienced by the saint) is merely termed inspiration and inspired utterance (*ilhām wa taḥaddīsān*).

---

82 These are theopathic sayings uttered by the Prophet Muḥammad on behalf of God, which are often considered to be on the same par and level of revelation as verses of the Qur'ān.

83 Zailan Moris explains this doctrine as follows: "Mulla Sadra postulates that the gap between divine revelation and human reason can be effectively bridged by intellectual intuition or 'unveiling' [*kashf*]. According to Mulla Sadra, intellectual 'unveiling' occurs as a result of the intellect being illuminated by the Active Intellect or the Holy Spirit which is identified with the archangel Gabriel who is the instrument of revelation. Thus, there is an important and necessary relation between revelation and intellectual illumination or 'unveiling'. It is through revelation that the human intellect is able to actualize itself. Intellectual illumination is not separate or independent of revelation." – *Revelation, Intellectual Intuition and Reason in the Philosophy of Mulla Sadra*, p. 177.

84 On the *mundus imaginalis*, see Henry Corbin, "*Mundus Imaginalis*, or the Imaginary and the Imaginal," in *idem.*, *Swedenborg and Esoteric Islam*, trans. Leonard Fox (W. Chester, Pennsylvania: Swedenborg Foundation 1995). pp. 1–33.

Revelation entails contemplative unveiling (*al-kashf al-shuhūdī*) along with spiritual unveiling (*al-kashf al-ma'nawī*), whereas inspiration consists only of spiritual unveiling. Another difference is (as was mentioned before) that Revelation, due to its connection to exoteric matters (*al-ẓāhir*), is the particular characteristic of prophethood, whereas inspiration is the particular reserve of the esoteric cycle of the saints or friends of God (*al-wilāyat*). Similarly, unlike inspiration, Revelation also requires active service in the public propagation of Faith (*al-tablīgh*).

* * *

THE FOURTH KEY OF THE INVISIBLE WORLD

On the hierarchical degrees of visionary unveiling (*kashf*) and their cause; and on varieties of inspiration, passing thoughts and satanic temptations (*al-ilhāmāt wa 'l-khawāṭir wa 'l-wasāwis*) and the demonic and angelic causes of these phenomena, within which are certain temples of theophany

THE FIRST TEMPLE OF THEOPHANY

On the kinds of interior unveilings (*mukāshafa*) in brief

As was indicated before, it should be understood that there are two sorts of visionary unveiling: sensory visionary unveiling and supersensory visionary unveiling, or those pertaining to sensory forms and those pertaining to spiritual realities (*ṣūrī wa ma'nawī*).

Visionary unveiling in sensory forms relates to things realized in the *mundus imaginalis* (*'ālam al-mithāl*) through the medium of the five external senses, detailing the causes of which would require a long-drawn-out discourse. It is obvious that the soul (*al-nafs*) in its essence comprises (the senses of) hearing, seeing, smelling, tasting, and touching.

Sensory interior unveilings (*al-mukāshafat al-ṣūrīyya*) sometimes occur visually by way of the sight of eye, as in that kind of vision that takes off the veil from the form of spirits incarnated in bodies (*ṣuwar al-arwāḥ al-mutajasadat*) or like seeing the lights of spiritual beings.

Sometimes they occur by way of the sense of hearing, as in the Prophet's audition of divine revelation (*al-waḥy*) that came down upon him in the shape of words arranged in a harmonious pattern[85] or like the sound of the rattling[86] of a chain or the drone of honey-bees. As has been related in the traditions of the Prophet (peace be upon and his family), he actually heard the sounds of these things, by which is meant that he grasped their purport and understood their meaning.

Sometimes these sensory interior unveilings occur by way of smell, in which he imbibed the scent and aroma of heavenly breezes and the sweet smell of divine success and favour, as from the Prophet has been related when he said: "Divine breezes from your Lord waft through the days of your life. Hearken to them!"[87] and also in his statement: "Verily, I scent the breeze of the All-merciful from the direction of Yemen."[88]

Sometimes they occur through the sense of touch, which happens through the conjunction of two lights or two imaginal bodies. Regarding this phenomenon, Ibn 'Abbās related that the Prophet of God (peace be upon him and his family) said:

"I beheld my Lord – *Gloria in Excelsis Deo* – in the fairest of forms."

Then He asked, "What argument took place in the transcendent realm, O Muḥammad!"

Then the Prophet said twice: "O my Lord, You are more knowledgeable," adding: "God placed His hands between my two shoulders such that I could feel their coolness between my breasts. At that, I understood everything there was throughout the heavens."

Then he recited this verse: "So also did We show Abraham the spiritual realm of the heavens and the earth, that he might be among those that have certitude."[89]

Sometimes they occur through the faculty of taste, as though one sees various types of foodstuffs, tasting and partaking of each of them, so that one becomes conscious of a supersensory reality. The Prophet thus said: "In a dream, I saw that I was drinking milk, so much so that the moisture

85 Alternate versions: harmonious words/harmonious rhythmical words.

86 Alternate versions: jingling/clinking.

87 Badī' al-Zamān Furūzānfar, *Aḥādīth-i Mathnawī* (Tehran: Amīr Kabīr 1361 A.Hsh./1982), 3rd edn, p. 20.

88 Furūzānfar, *Aḥādīth-i Mathnawī*, p. 73.

89 Qur'ān VI:75.

of it came out from under my fingernails. I interpreted this to mean knowledge."

Although some of these interior unveilings (*mukāshafa*) may sometimes be combined with other types, or at other times occur isolated and alone, they all constitute theophanies of divine names (*tajalliyyāt ismā'īyya*). Everything beheld by the eye (during such interior unveilings) is thus a theophany of the divine name 'the Seer' (*al-Baṣīr*); everything heard by ear is a theophany of the divine name 'the All-Hearing (*al-Samī'*), and so forth with the rest of the divine names. Each one of these names is subservient to its own Lord, while all of them are subjects of the divine name 'the Omniscient' (*al-'ālīm*).

So it can be said that the different varieties of interior unveilings in sensory forms (*al-kashf al-ṣūrī*) relate and pertain, in the first instance, to occurrences and phenomena in the external world, in which case they are designated as partaking of 'monasticism' (*rahbānīyya*). However, if unrelated to occurrences and phenomena in the external world, these unveilings are considered to be sound and trustworthy. Those who are adept at progress in the spiritual life (*ahl al-sulūk*) have a sort of knowledge which, because of the inattention of their lofty aspiration to worldly concerns and affairs, refuses to pay any heed to these sensory types of interior unveilings. Their attention rather focused upon the affairs of the world to come, so that they regard these types of unveilings as being but false wizardry (*al-istidarāj*)[90] or divine deceit (*al-makr*) vis-à-vis the devotee. Neither do most of such adepts pay any heed to the interior unveilings of the life

90 In his glossary of Muslim technical terms, Al-Tahānawī (*Kashāf iṣṭilāḥāt al-funūn*, ed. M. Wajih, Abd al-Haqq and Gholam Kadir, with W. Nassau Lees [Calcutta: 1862], I, p. 463) describes this term as meaning a type of miracle or marvel performed by a non-Muslim or an impious person, an interpretation supported by Hujwīrī in his *Kashf al-maḥjūb* (*The "Kashf al-maḥjūb:" The Oldest Persian Treatise on Sufism*, trans. R.A. Nicholson, Gibb Memorial Series, no. 17. 1911; reprinted London: 1976, p. 224) who defines it as belonging to "miracles performed by those who pretend to godship." Mīr Sayyid Sharīf Jurjānī in his *Ta'rīfāt*, ed. Ibrāhīm al-Abyārī (Beirut: Dār al-Kitāb al-'Arabī 1405 A.H./ 1984), s.v., describes the term as connoting divine wrath in the form of divine grace, so that one is eventually and 'gradually lead' to perdition and goes astray by worldly success. For another treatment of the term, see Maryam Musharraf and Leonard Lewisohn, Maryam Musharraf and Leonard Lewisohn, "Sahl Tustarī's (d. 283/896)

hereafter. For they are those whose ultimate aim and final purpose is to achieve annihilation in God (*al-fanā' fi'llāh*) and to realize obliteration of their Selfhood in the Divine One (*al-mahw fī janābihu*).

These sorts of sensory interior unveilings (*al-mukāshafat al-ṣūrīyyat*) are mostly accompanied with an increased awareness and consciousness of supersensible realities disclosed from the *mundus invisibilibis*. In fact, many of them involve visionary unveilings of spiritual realities (*al-mukāshafat al-ma'nawīyyat*) as well. The highest degree of these unveilings – and that which is graced with the most certitude – is that which makes a synthesis between the formal and supraformal, the sensory and the spiritual levels.

Now, the source of all these interior unveilings is the human heart, that is to say, the *anima rationalis* (*nafs al-nāṭiqa*)[91] which is illuminated with the practical intelligence or applied reason (*al-'aql al-'amalī*) and which employs all five of the (internal) spiritual senses. As was mentioned above, "the soul (*al-nafs*) in its essence comprises (the senses of) hearing," etc., just as God indicated: "For it is not the eyes that grow blind, but rather it is the hearts, within the breasts, that are blind"[92] – and in traditions of the Prophet much can be found in the way of support of this.

Now, since it is those internal spiritual senses that constitute the principle and fountain head of these external physical senses,[93] when the veil is lifted from between (the heart) and what lies on the outside, the principle (the heart's internal senses) is then made one and conjoined with the branch (the external senses), so that what is perceived by these (internal)

Esoteric Qur'ānic Commentary and Rūmī's *Mathnawī*: Part 2," *Mawlana Rumi Review* VII (2016), pp. 106–127 [pp. 107–9].

91 Mullā Ṣadrā's son-in-law 'Abd al-Razzāq Lāhījī, thus points out (see the text translated in the following chapter, p. 381) that the *nafs-i nāṭiqa* "in lexicon of the holy law and in the technical terminology of Sufism is called the 'heart' (*qalb*). Here he also apparently is repeating Ghazālī's identification of the two terms (in the treatise translated above in chapter 2, the section "On the Soul and the Human Spirit", pp. 91–92.)

92 Qur'ān XXII:46.

93 For an excellent treatment of the fundamental theories of the external and internal senses in Islamic faculty psychology, see Harry Wolfson's "The Internal Senses in Latin, Arabic, and Hebrew Philosophic Texts," *Harvard Theological Review* XXVIII/2 (1935), pp. 69–133.

senses is also witnessed by those (external senses). The Spirit (*al-rūḥ*) at this juncture directly witnesses this occur in its own essence. This is because these spiritual realities were all united on their own level of existence (the Spirit) at the station of the Intellect (*fī maqām al-ʿaql*). The Intellect is itself the whole of Existence, as has been proven in regard the speculative sciences (*al-ʿulūm al-naẓarīyya*)[94] where we have adduced rational demonstration in proof (*burhān*) of this point, with discussion suitable to discerning speculative thinkers (*ahl al-naẓar*). Our exposition here has not resorted to adducing rational proofs, although further demonstration of these premises can be found in our other books and discourses.

However, so far as visionary unveiling abstracted from the forms of spiritual realities (*al-kashf al-maʿnawī al-mujarrad min ṣuwar al-ḥaqāʾiq*) is concerned: this is realized by the theophany of the divine name 'the Sage Omniscient One' (*al-ʿālim al-ḥakīm*). This sort of unveiling is the manifestation of hidden supernatural spiritual meanings and the revelation of

94 S.H. Nasr's succinct summary of Ibn Sīnā's views puts Mullā Ṣadrā's seemingly radical pronouncement on the Intellect (based on Avicenna's cosmological principles regarding it and his psychological theories regarding the soul) into context and so merits citation here: "The manifestation of the Intellect on the microcosmic level depends upon the hierarchy of the faculties which man possesses, including those of the kingdoms below him in the hierarchy of cosmic existence. The human soul (*al-nafs al-nāṭiqah*), which is given to each human being by the Active Intellect, has, in addition to the powers of the vegetative and animal souls, the faculties of action (*ʿamal*) and speculation (*naẓar*) which stand between the world of form and matter and the world of pure forms and which are able to turn to both this world and the next. Man stands between the sensible and the intelligible worlds. Through his senses he receives impressions which by means of various faculties of the animal soul reach the level of ratiocination. He also possesses the rational soul, which, with the aid of the Active Intellect, can lead him beyond this world to the angelic realm of the pure Intelligences ... [The soul's] felicity lies in uniting itself with the Intellect and in leaving the sensible world in favour of the Intelligible. This is its entelechy and deliverance. As the Universe is generated by God's contemplation and intellection of Himself, so does it become integrated in its Divine archetype in the act of intellection within man which results in the return of the sensible world to the intelligible one." S.H. Nasr, *An Introduction to Islamic Cosmological Doctrines* (London: Thames and Hudson 1978), pp. 257–59.

realities of the divine Essence: It is hierarchically divided into several degrees:

First occurs the manifestation of spiritual realities within the faculty of thought without recourse to any preliminary studies or prolegomena and without the gradation of things according to logical categories of syllogistic reasoning. Rather, the mind turns away from incidental problems towards the fundamental elements or first principles – a process which is designated as 'intuitive conjecture' (*ḥads*)[95] – and then (those spiritual realities become manifest) through the faculty of intellection that is employed by the faculty of thought. This is designated as the light of holiness or sacrosanct light (*al-nūr al-qudsī*). Intuitive conjecture constitutes glittering effulgences (*lawāmaʿ*)[96] cast from its rays and represents the lowest degree of visionary unveiling.

Then (the manifestation of spiritual realities occurs) on the level of the heart, which is called inspiration (*al-ilhām*). Inspiration signifies the manifestation of one idea (*maʿnā*) from among others – not one intelligible reality from among other such realities or one spiritual being from among various spiritual beings – in which case it would be termed 'a visionary experience of the heart' (*mushāhadat qalbīyyat*).

Then (the manifestation of spiritual realities occurs) at the spiritual station of the Spirit (*maqām al-rūḥ*). This is termed 'spiritual contemplation' (*al-shuhūd al-rūḥī*), and resembles a brilliant sun illuminating the heavens of the ontological levels of the Spirit (*marātib al-rūḥ*) and the terrestrial realms of the ontological levels of the body (*al-jasad*). The Spirit thus apprehends veridical intelligible realities by its own essence directly from God, the Sage Omniscient, according to the measure of its own aptitude and without any recourse to causal intermediaries. That is to say, the Spirit has received all this by its own innate power of receptivity, lavishing

---

95 *Ḥads* is defined as "the capacity of the mind to draw immediate inferences from the data presented to it or to see through a kind of mental illumination the necessary connection between premises and conclusion." –M. Saeed Shaikh, *A Dictionary of Muslim Philosophy* (Lahore: Institute of Islamic Culture 1981), s.v. *ḥads*. See note 1057.

96 "As a technical term in Sufism, 'glittering effluences' refer to radiant lights which shine upon novices pure in soul. These lights are reflected from the imagination (*khiyāl*) to the *sensus communis* (*ḥiss-i mushtarik*) and then apprehended by the external senses." See Al-Tahānawī, *Kashāf iṣṭilāḥāt al-funūn* II, p. 1299.

its grace down upon all that lies beneath – as well the faculties superior and inferior to – the heart.[97]

97 Alternate version: That is to say, by its primordial power of receptivity, the Spirit apprehends all this, and then lavishes its grace down upon everything else below – as well as all the faculties superior and inferior to – the heart.

XI

ESOTERIC AND EXOTERIC PATHS OF KNOWLEDGE IN ISLAM

Selections from ʿAbd al-Razzāq Lāhījī's (d. 1072/1661–2) *Gawhar-i murād*

A central member of the seventeenth-century School of Iṣfahān, ʿAbd al-Razzāq b. ʿAlī b. Ḥusayn Lāhījī (d. 1072/1661–2)[1] has been described as "the most famous authority on Shiʿi *kalām* during the Safavid period."[2] In his youth, he became a follower of Mullā Ṣadrā, migrating to the village of Kahak, southeast of the town of Qumm, where the Safavid sage had retreated to spend several years studying and

1 On Lāhījī, see Jalīl Misgarnizhād's introduction to his edition of *Dīvān-i Fayyāḍ Lāhījī* (Tehran: Dānishgāh-i ʿAllāma Ṭabāṭabāʾī 1373 A.Hsh./1994), and the excellent edition with a comprehensive introduction of the same *Dīvān-i Fayyāḍ Lāhījī* (Tehran: Dānishgāh-i Tihrān 1372 A.Hsh./1993) ed. Amīr Bānūʾī Karīmī. Other accounts include: Muḥammad ʿAlī Mudarris Tabrīzī, *Rayhānat al-adab* (Tehran 1331 A.Hsh./1952), IV, p. 361; Riḍā Qulī Khān Hidāyat, *Riyāz al-ʿārifīn*, ed. Mehr ʿAlī Gurkānī (Tehran: n.p., n.d.), p. 382; Mīrzā Muḥammad Bāqir al-Musavī al-Iṣfahānī, *Rawḍat al-jannat* (Qum: 1391/1971), IV, p. 196; Ādharbīgdilī, *Ātashkada*, ed. Ḥasan Sādāt Nāṣirī (Tehran: Amīr kabīr 1336 A.Hsh./1957), II, p. 846 (sources also utilized by Karīmī and Misgarnizhād in their introductions). See also Ṣamad Muwaḥḥid, "ʿAbd al-Razzāq Lāhījī," *Dānishnāma-yi zabān va adab-i fārsī*, ed. Ismāʿīl Saʿādat (Tehran: Farhangistān-i zabān va adab-i fārsī 1391 A.Hsh./2012), vol. IV, pp. 557–60. On Lāhījī's philosophical views and Sufism, see my "Sufism and the School of Iṣfahān: *Taṣawwuf* and *ʿIrfān* in Late Safavid Iran (ʿAbd al-Razzāq Lāhījī and Fayd-i Kāshānī on the Relation of *Taṣawwuf, Ḥikmat* and *ʿIrfān*)," in Leonard Lewisohn and David Morgan (eds.), *The Heritage of Sufism*, vol. III: *Late Classical Persianate Sufism: The Safavid and Mughal Period* (Oxford: Oneworld 1999), pp. 101–12.

2 S.H. Nasr, in S.H. Nasr and Mehdi Aminrazavi (eds.), *An Anthology of Philosophy in Persia*, vol. V: *From the School of Shiraz to the Twentieth Century* (London: I.B. Tauris in association with the Institute of Ismaili Studies 2015), p. 223.

writing.[3] He acted there as a scribe for many of Mullā Ṣadrā's works, such as the *Asfār* and the *Shawāhid al-rubūbīyya*, studying these texts with him personally.

'Abd al-Razzāq eventually ended up becoming Mullā Ṣadrā's son-in-law, who bestowed upon him the pen-name 'Fayyāḍ' ('Bestower of Spiritual Grace')[4] – echoing the pen-name *Fayḍ* ('Grace') vouchsafed by Mullā Ṣadrā to his other – first – son-in-law, Muḥsin Fayḍ-i Kāshānī (d. 1091/1680), the eminent Safavid mystical theologian. His poetic panegyrics in praise of Mullā Ṣadrā show him to have been a devoted and loving follower of the great mystical philosopher, and as far as his works and biographical notices about Lāhījī permit us to estimate, his affection was reciprocated by his father-in-law. 'Fayyāḍ' composed several *qaṣā'id* celebrating and honouring his teacher Mullā Ṣadrā,[5] where he often extols him in hyperbolic terms. The following verses are typical:

> He's chief of the world's assembly (Ṣadr[6]), a universe of kindness (*iḥsān*), the Universal Intellect (*'aql-i kull*). From him, Perfection itself is honoured and Learning has worth.
>
> He adorns the niche of Intelligence by virtue of his thought; he gives light to the Lamp of the Law by example of his learning.
>
> Thinkers think straight due to his insight; down to Judgement Day he provides a staff to guide the hand of thought.
>
> Whenever he makes his epiphany, the mirrors of the interior being of all visionaries (*ahl-i shuhūd*) are burnished bright and clear.
>
> His consciousness animates the solitary retreat of the Platonists; he possesses the most sagacious judgement in the Debating Hall of the Aristotelians.[7]

---

3 *Dīvān-i Fayyāḍ Lāhījī*, ed. Amīr Bānū'ī Karīmī (Tehran: Dānishgāh-i Tihrān 1372 A.Hsh./1993), p. vii.

4 *Dīvān-i Fayyāḍ Lāhījī*, ed. Amīr Bānū'ī Karīmī, p. viii.

5 In a long *qaṣīda* entitled *Mu'jazat al-shawq* in reply to 'Urfī Shīrāzī's qaṣīda *Tarjumat al-shawq*, Fayyāḍ penned a panegyric to Mullā Ṣadrā; see *Dīvān-i Fayyāḍ Lāhījī*, ed. Jalīl Misgarnizhād (Tehran: Dānishgāh-i 'Allāma Ṭabāṭabā'ī 1373 A.Hsh./1994). pp. 423–24. He also wrote three other separate *qaṣīda*s in praise of Mullā Ṣadrā, *Dīvān-i Fayyāḍ Lāhījī*, pp. 458–60, 462–64, 465–68.

6 Alluding to Mullā Ṣadrā's proper name: Ṣadr al-Dīn.

7 *Dīvān-i Fayyāḍ Lāhījī*, ed. Karīmī, p. 121.

'Abd al-Razzāq Lāhījī travelled widely within the borders of Persia, and although Qumm was his preferred place of residence – he worked as Professor of Intellectual Sciences (*ma'qūlāt*) in the Madrasa Maṣūmīyya there[8] – allusions to his frequent visits to Kāshān, Tabrīz, Iṣfahān, Mashhād and Shīrāz appear in his *Dīvān.*[9] Lāhījī trained many students in Islamic mystical philosophy (*ḥikmat*), perhaps the most famous of whom was Qaḍī Sa'īd Qummī (1103/1691).[10] Two of Lāhījī's sons – Ḥasan and Ibrāhīm Lāhījī – became renowned theologians and philosophers in their own right.[11]

'Abd al-Razzāq Lāhījī was an intimate associate of several Shī'ite monarchs of the Safavid period, such as Shāh 'Abbās II (1642–1666) and Shāh Ṣafī I (1038/1628–1052/1642), writing occasional political panegyrics in praise of them, and being closely associated with the Safavid Shī'ite state.[12] However, a careful reading of these praise-poems reveals them to have been by and large penned as courtly formalities, and often filled with testimonies excusing himself from their service so as to spend time in spiritual retreat and religious study.[13]

Lāhījī authored numerous Arabic works, including marginal annotations to the *Commentary on Ibn Sīnā's Philosophical Allusions* (*Sharḥ-i Ishārāt*) by Nasīr al-Dīn Ṭūsī; the *Flashes of Inspiration* (*Shawāriq al-ilhām fī tajrīd al-kalām*, a commentary on another of Ṭūsī's works (*Tajrīd al-'aqā'id*); and a treatise on the Temporality of the World (*Risāla Ḥudūth*

8 *Dīvān-i Fayyāḍ Lāhījī*, ed. Karīmī, p. xi.

9 *Dīvān-i Fayyāḍ Lāhījī*, ed. Karīmī, pp. ix–x.

10 On whom, see S.H. Nasr and Mehdi Aminrazavi (eds.), *An Anthology of Philosophy in Persia*, vol. V: *From the School of Shiraz to the Twentieth Century* (London: I.B. Tauris in association with the Institute of Ismaili Studies 2015), pp. 327–553.

11 For a brief selection and translation from the works of both Lāhījī and Lāhījī's son Ḥasan, see S.H. Nasr and Mehdi Aminrazavi (eds.), *An Anthology of Philosophy in Persia*, vol. V: *From the School of Shiraz to the Twentieth Century* (London: I.B. Tauris in association with the Institute of Ismaili Studies 2015), "The Two Lāhījīs," pp. 222–60.

12 His political affiliations are discussed by Sajjad Rizvi, "A Sufi Theology Fit for a Shī'i King: The *Gawhar-i Murād* of 'Abd al-Razzāq Lāhījī," in A. Shihadeh, ed. *Sufism and Theology* (Edinburgh: Edinburgh University Press 2007), pp. 83–98. My approach to Sufism in Lāhījī's writings significantly differs from Rizvi's, who emphasizes the political context of his writings over their spiritual dimension.

13 See *Dīvān-i Fayyāḍ Lāhījī*, ed. Karīmī, pp. xxi–xxii.

al-'ālam). He was also the author of a number of philosophical works in Persian, the most famous of which is his *Gawhar-i murād* (*Crown Jewel of Desire*), a general work on philosophical theology, apologetic theology (*Kalām*), ontology, Sufism (*taṣawwuf*) and mystical theology (*'irfān*), parts of which are translated below.[14]

In terms of his philosophical thought, Lāhījī is usually classified as a Peripatetic philosopher. This is not, however, quite the case. Although Avicenna is the most frequently cited author in the *Gawhar-i murād*, making Lāhījī appear to be a strict follower of his Peripatetic doctrine – contrary to Madelung[15] – his interpretation of the *Shaykh al-Ra'īs* rather reflects the tradition of mystical Islamic *ḥikmat* found in the "Waystations of the Gnostics," the last chapter of Avicenna's *Book of Philosophical Allusions*.[16] In ontology, he favoured Aristotle's view of the absolute materiality of substances over Mullā Ṣadrā's theory of trans-substantial motion (*ḥarakat-i jawharī*);[17] he also was opposed in some works (for one, in the *Gawhar-i murād*) to his father-in-law's doctrine of the primacy of existence (*aṣālat al-wujūd*).[18]

His *Dīvān*, which is quite sizeable (over 12,000 couplets), contains all the normal forms of Persian poetry (*qaṣīda, tarkīb-band, mathnawī, sāqī-nāma, ghazal, rubā'ī*, etc.). Over half of the collection consists of panegyrics (in *qaṣīda* form) to the twelve Shī'ite Imāms, the Prophet, Fāṭima, etc. In these panegyrics he largely imitates the great classical Persian *qaṣīda* poets such as Anvarī (d. circa 582/1186), Mas'ūd Sa'd Salman (d. 515/1121), Sanā'ī (d. 525/1131 or 545/1150), Sa'dī (d. circa 691/1292), Ẓahīr Fāryābī (d. end of sixth/twelfth century), and 'Urfī (d. 1000/1591).[19] Some of his best *Qaṣīda*s are those in which he imitates Sanā'ī. He also penned a *Sāqī-nāma* in which he assails the arid austerities (*zuhd-i khushk*) of ascetics. His poetry is replete with abstruse theological and philosophical terminology, reflecting his own

14 A full list of his works can be found in Muwaḥḥid, "'Abd al-Razzāq Lāhījī," pp. 557–58 and *Dīvān-i Fayyāḍ Lāhījī*, ed. Karīmī, p. xxiii.

15 W. Madelung, "'Abd al-Razzāq Lāhījī," *Encyclopædia Iranica* I, p. 157.

16 For further discussion of this, see my "Sufism and the School of Iṣfahān," pp. 101–12.

17 *Dīvān-i Fayyāḍ Lāhījī*, ed. Karīmī, p. xvii; Nasr and Aminrazavi (eds.), *Anthology* V, p. 222.

18 On which, see Megawati Moris, *Mullā Ṣadrā's Doctrine of the Primacy of Existence* (*aṣālat al-wujūd*) (Kuala Lumpur: ISTAC 2003).

19 Examples of his imitations are given by Karīmī (ed.), *Dīvān-i Fayyāḍ Lāhījī*, pp. xxv–xxvii.

scholarly preoccupations with theology and philosophy;[20] stylistically speaking, his verse is heavily influenced by the 'Indian Style' (*sabk-i Hindī*), which was all the rage during the seventeenth century; the chief influences and objects of emulation and imitation in his ghazals are Rūmī, Sa'dī, Ḥāfiẓ, Kamāl Khujandī, Ṭālib Āmulī, Naẓīrī, and particularly Ṣā'ib (the latter was a close personal friend).[21] Although his verse occasionally displays originality, his genius lay in mystical philosophy rather than his poetry, which is generally but a pale reflection of the great classical authors; as a consequence, his verse is seldom featured in anthologies of the significant poets of the period.[22]

* * *

The ensuing translation features a lengthy extract from 'Abd al-Razzāq Lāhījī's *Crown Jewel of Desire* (*Gawhar-i murād*).[23] In terms of treatment of the differing forms of esotericism in Islam, Lāhījī's work is undoubtedly the most lucid and wide-ranging of all the texts presented in this collection, definitely demonstrating the basic premise of this anthology: that the 'esoteric way' constitutes the common ground of the Islamic intellectual tradition. The ecumenical scope of his presentation of the esoteric way is visible in his corralling of the chapter on the "Stations of the Gnostics" by Avicenna in support of Sufi mystical doctrines and appropriation of a

20 *Dīvān-i Fayyāḍ Lāhījī*, ed. Karīmī, p. xxviii.

21 See the examples given by Karīmī, *Dīvān-i Fayyāḍ Lāhījī*, pp. xviii–xlii See also selections from his ghazals cited by Dhabīḥu'llāh Ṣafā, *Tārīkh-i adabiyāt-i Īrān* (Tehran: Intishārāt-i Firdaws 1373 A.Hsh./1994, 13th edn), V/2, pp. 1231–33.

22 *Dīvān-i Fayyāḍ Lāhījī*, ed. Karīmī, pp. xxvi–xxviii.

23 I have used the (2nd) edition, edited by Z. Qurbānī Lāhījī [Tehran: 1372 A.Hsh./1993; 2nd edn, Tehran: Nashr-i Sāyih1383 A.Hsh./2004], the introduction of which (see esp. pp. 8–10) is unfortunately very misleading, using this philosopher as a propaganda tool for the so-called 'Islamic Republic' of Iran (cf. pp. 12ff.), and thus omits all references to the pro-Sufi passages in the *Gawhar-i murād* which I have translated here. Although pp. 8–10 of this introduction, for example, are devoted to 'Abd al-Razzāq's *'irfān*, no reference is given to any of the (apparently politically incorrect] pro-Sufi passages in the *Gawhar-i murād* translated here. The same religious bias and partisanship is also evident in Jalīl Misgarnizhād's introduction to Fayyāḍ's *Dīvān* where the one section (on pp. 30–33) devoted to Lāhījī's "Kalām, 'Irfān and Taṣawwuf" utterly fails to deliver on the subtitle's promise – neglecting to mention the latter subject at all!

number of other authors to elucidate these same doctrines, such as Naṣīr al-Dīn Ṭūsī's famous commentary on that chapter and Anṣārī's *Ṣad maydān*.

In order to show the common ground shared by the thinkers in this anthology it will be useful to digress briefly and compare and contrast the various esoteric doctrines expressed by Lāhījī in his *Gawhar-i murād* with those propounded by Ṣā'īn al-Dīn Turkah Iṣfahānī in his *Risāla-yi Shaqq al-qamar va sā'at*.[24] Although both thinkers flourished in historically different milieus in fifteenth- and seventeenth-century Persia, there is much in the way of mystical theology that unites these two Iṣfahānī thinkers in respect to theosophical doctrines and ideas, poetic taste and mystical vision – commonalities which concern moreover their esoteric rather than exoteric doctrines. Particularly in regard to matters relating to the interior dimension of religious thought, visionary contemplation, the hierarchy of gnostic adepts, and their common view that gnosis is superior to rational philosophy, they share some quite similar principles and premises.

Lāhījī advocated a kind of gnostic Sufism devoid of many of the key elements of the classical Sufi tradition. He disdained the master-disciple relationship obtained in *khānaqāh*-based *ṭarīqat*s, and believed, for instance, the Sufis should really be philosophers as well.[25] In one place, when referring to the Sufis, he claims that "those who have personally verified the Truth among the Sufis (*muḥiqqīn az Ṣūfīyya*)"[26] are alone able to comprehend the doctrine of *fanā'*. This statement indicates, as Henry Corbin points out,[27] that Lāhījī was indebted to the spiritual typology proposed in Ṣā'in al-Dīn Turkah Iṣfahānī in his *Risāla-yi Shaqq al-qamar*. These *muḥaqqiqīn*

---

24 See my "Sufism and Theology in the Confessions of Sa'in al-Din Turka Isfahani (d. 830/1437)" in A. Shihadeh, ed. *Sufism and Theology* (Edinburgh: Edinburgh University Press 2007), pp. 63–82.

25 "Sufis and Qalandars who do not have a firm grounding in discursive theosophy (*ḥikmat-i baḥthīyya*), who lack acquaintance with philosophical theology, traditional commentaries and exoteric knowledge concerning the ontological origin and end of creation (*mabda' u ma'ād*), while introducing themselves as masters (*murshid*) and spiritual guides of people – as do the *aqṭāb* of our own period and [some in] previous epochs – are nothing but brigands who waylay the common folk." Cited in *Muntakhabātī az āthār-i ḥukamā'ī ilāhī-yi Īrān az 'aṣr-i Mīr Dāmād u Mīr Findariskī tā zamān-i ḥāḍir*, edited, introduced and annotated by Sayyid Jalāl al-Dīn Ashtiyānī, French introduction by Henry Corbin (Paris/Tehran: 1972), I, pp. 290–91.

26 *Gawhar-i murād*, p. 33.

27 *En Islam iranien* III, p. 247.

az Ṣūfiyya – Lāhījī's supreme Sufi adepts – are in fact technically identical to Turkah's fifth class of esotericist (called *Muḥaqqiqān-i ṣūfiyya* [Realized Sufi Adepts]). The following two diagrams depict their respective approaches to esotericism, the varieties of sciences and adepts who are learned in them.

'Abd al-Razzāq Lāhījī's Hierarchy of Adepts

5. Adepts who've realized the Truth among the Sufis (*muḥaqqīn az Ṣūfiyya*) = Gnostics (*'urafā'*) = the true scholar who has experientially verified and personally realized his knowledge (*'ālim-i muḥaqqiq*). These are also called the true 'believers', 'sincere devotees', 'righteous servants' and 'pietists' (*mu'minīn va mukhliṣīn va ṣāliḥīn va muttaqīn*).

4. Peripatetic Philosophers who have direct experiential verification (*muḥaqqiqīn-i ḥukamā'*) of the mystical teachings Avicenna outlined in the "Waystations of the Gnostics" (*Fī maqāmāt al-'ārifin*), interpreted in the light of Ṭūsī's commentary.

3. Ishrāqī Theosophers (*ishrāqī*).

2. Scholastic Theologians (*mutakallim*).

1. Devotees (*'ābid*) or Ascetics (*zāhid*) who are not gnostics (*ghayr al-'ārif*).

Ṣā'īn al-Dīn Turkah's Spiritual Typology of Gnostic Esotericists

5. Elect Adepts in Qur'ānic Arithomancy (*Ulā al-'aydī w'al-abṣār*).

4. Esoteric Qur'ānic Symbolists (*Ramz-khwānān-i ḥurūf-i Qur'ānī*).

3. Realized Sufi Adepts and Clairvoyant Visionary Sufis (*Muḥiqqiqān-i ṣūfiyya*).

2. 'Oriental Theosophers' or 'Illuminationists' (*ishrāqīyān*).

1. Primitive Islamic Esotericists: The Peripatetic Philosophers (*Ḥukamā'-yi ẓāhir*).

'Abd al-Razzāq Lāhījī's Four Sciences of *Theosophia* (*Ḥikmat*)

The Two Exoteric Ways

1. Peripatetic Philosophy (*mashshā*)	2. Scholastic Theology (*kalām*)

The Two Esoteric Ways

3. Illuminationism (*ishrāq*)	3. Sufism (*taṣawwuf*)
Preceded by Study of	Preceded by Study of
1. Philosophy (*ḥikmat*)	2. Scholastic Theology (*kalām*)

***Theosophia* (*Ḥikmat*) Sacred and Profane**

I. *Theosophia* (*Ḥikmat*) dependent on revelation (*waḥy*), relying on either

a. rational methods of demonstration (*'aql, burhān, baḥth, tafakkur*)
→ Way of Scholastic Theology (*kalām*)

or –

b. visionary disclosure and presential vision (*kashf u shuhūd*)
→ Way of Sufism (*taṣawwuf*)

II. *Theosophia* (*Ḥikmat*) independent of revelation, relying on either

a. rational methods of demonstration (*'aql, burhān, baḥth, tafakkur*)
→ Way of Peripatetic Philosophy (*mashshā'ī*)

or –

b. visionary understanding and presential vision (*kashf u shuhūd*)
→ Way of Oriental Theosophy, Illuminationism (*ishrāqī*)

Both Lāhījī and Ṣā'īn al-Dīn Turkah discriminated between exoteric and esoteric ways and wayfarers to God; both maintain these two ways are distinguished by an emphasis on intellectual theory and outward appearances in the exoteric approach, as contrasted with knowledge and true Reality in the esoteric *via mystica*. Ṣā'īn al-Dīn Turkah's and Lahījī's thought may also be both compared and contrasted in respect to their similar but dissimilar approaches to visionary understanding and presential vision (*kashf u shuhūd*). But unlike his father-in-law's plagiary of the Sunni *Shaykh al-Islam* Ghazālī, Lāhījī's imitation of the Shafi'ite divine is not only far more creative and dynamic, but bears the stamp of being the product of an original existential vision. For the Ṣā'īn al-Dīn, rational and dialectical methods of knowledge are denigrated in a manner quite similar to that of classical Sufi sages such as 'Aṭṭār and Rūmī. For him, the Bride of Faith simply does not ever reside in the City of Reason. For 'Abd al-Razzāq, however, the gnostic vision is an integral part of his rationalist philosophical vision, the two approaches differing only in the superior clarity of the mystical over the philosophical vision.[28] Furthermore, according to Lāhījī, the mystical vision simply reaffirms the rationalist theologian's theoretical knowledge. Lāhījī identifies the true Sufis as *'urafā'* such as Avicenna, concluding, with passages which he claims express the highest truths of Sufi ontology, his *Crown Jewel of Desire* with citations from Avicenna's *Maqāmat al-'arifīn*, in which he places the science of the gnostics (*'urafā'*) above philosophy (*ḥikmat*).

Their attitudes towards the abstruse Arcana of Islamic esotericism may also be contrasted. The highly occult and arcane esotericism of Ṣā'in al-Dīn Turkah Iṣfahānī's thought often reminds one of similar cryptic language employed by Western mystics such as Jacob Boehme. The gnosis obtained at the highest two tiers of his esoteric hierarchy, for instance, properly pertains to the subject matter of the occult sciences (*'ulūm-i ghaybī*), which are quite outside the normal curriculum of the intellectual sciences in Islam. Lāhījī's esoteric hierarchy on the other hand is far less exclusivistic; on its highest tier simply dwell the true Sufis; here he is in accord with a wide diversity of Muslim thinkers, from Ghazālī to Ibn 'Arabī, who had also endorsed the supremacy of the Sufi adepts among the *'ulamā*.

---

28 Emphasizing the complementary nature of the esoteric Sufi Path of Love and the exoteric Religio-philosophical Way of Reason, in these verses from a *qaṣīda* Lāhījī writes: "Know the Paths of Reason (*rāh-i 'ishq u 'aql*) and Love are not separate / What's Exoteric (*ẓāhir*) and Esoteric (*bāṭin*) hold hands together – the one to veil the other. // Love is the Esoteric of the Qur'ān and its occult mysteries / Reason is the Exoteric Law (*ẓāhir-i shar'*) and a clear proof. // The suit of the Canon Law is cut to a man's size and height: / Love is its esoteric and Reason its exoteric being. // ... Though both are same in kind and their work is one / Yet Love's in the background and Reason's in the foreground. // Reason shows you the path to Placelessness (*lā-makān* = Utopia), / yet Love shall make you yourself placeless like the Friend." – *Dīvān-i Fayyāḍ Lāhījī,* ed. Amīr Bānū'ī Karīmī, p. 107.

Lāhījī includes Sufism among what he calls the various 'esoteric ways' in the Islamic *theosophia* (*ḥikmat*) tradition. The subtitle of the second subject of discussion (*maṭlab*) in his introduction (pp. 33–37) to the *Gawhar-i murād*, "An Exposition of the Path to God and its Division into the Exoteric and Esoteric Ways (*rāh-i ẓāhir u rāh bāṭin*)," (the first selection translated in the anthology) explains why these esoteric ways enable man to actually have a direct experience of God while exoteric ways solely permit man to know Him by theoretical means:

> It should be understood that there are but two ways for humankind to approach God: either the exoteric (*rāh-i ẓāhir*) or the esoteric way (*rāh-i bāṭin*). Although one may *know* God through the exoteric way, one can only *reach* God by the esoteric way – and how wide the gap between [theoretically] knowing God and actually reaching Him is! It is because of this that so many allusions have been made to the hardships of the esoteric way, in contrast to the exoteric way which involves much less hardship – being based on rational demonstrations within the reach of every intelligent person capable of discerning cause from effect.[29]

Pursuit of the esoteric way, states Lāhījī, demands divine revelation, direction and guidance of a prophet, unlike the exoteric way, for the prophet has not been ordained to guide people "on the exoteric path and the way of logical demonstration (*rāh-i ẓāhir u istidlāl*)."[30] He notes that the exoteric and esoteric paths in Islam are fundamentally opposite (*bar 'aks*) to each other; while the former relies on reason, reflection, argumentation and deliberation, the latter negates all rational means entirely:

> On the one hand, the wayfarer on the exoteric way of ratiocinative reasoning proceeds stage by stage through establishing proofs for things, before finally ending up in establishing a proof for a cause that itself has no cause ... On the other, the wayfarer on the esoteric way of progression proceeds by disavowing and negating things stage by

29 *Gawhar-i murād*, p. 34. This passage is also discussed in my "Sufism and the School of Iṣfahān," pp. 108–9.

30 *Gawhar-i murād*, p. 34.

> stage, until he finally attains the eternally subsistent being impenetrable to perishability and impervious to dissolution and destruction.[31]

The esotericists consider the use of rational means to understand God as "hindrances" that interfere with realization of "the pleasures of spiritual contemplation (*mushāhada*)."[32] But both the theosophers (*ḥukamā'-yi ilahī*) and the highest Sufi adepts join in sharing the same entelechy and objective, which is pursuit of these contemplative pleasures, for

> It is this pleasure (of contemplation) that the theosophers (*ḥukamā'-yi ilahī*) designate as 'true felicity' (*sa'ādat-i ḥaqīqī*), and which those who have personally verified the Truth among the Sufis (*muḥiqqīn-i Ṣūfīyya*) dub 'union and annihilation in God' (*wuṣūl u fanā'*), and in this lies the joy that is the consolation of the prophets and the delight of the saints.[33]

If compared to the levels of the esoteric hierarchy proposed in the *Risāla-yi Shaqq al-qamar*, in this passage Lāhījī appears to have combined classes four and five of Ṣā'īn al-Dīn Turkah's hierarchy into a single degree of esoteric wisdom, so that the *Ḥukamā-yi qadīm* (Ancient Philosophers) and Esoteric 'Oriental Theosophers' or 'Illuminationists' (*ishrāqiyān*) are united with the *Muḥiqqiqān-i ṣūfīyya*, Realized Sufi Adepts, and Clairvoyant Visionaries (*Ahl-i shuhūd*) abjuring Rational and Dialectical Methods, as fellow adepts in gnosis and travellers on the same mystical highway. However, in the next chapter of the *Gawhar-i murād* ("On the Difference Between Scholars, and Exposition of the Purpose and Use of the Science of Scholastic Theology [*Kalām*] and Mystical Philosophy [*ḥikmat*]"), Lāhījī explains in greater depth and detail what he means. Sufis and theosophers are not simply identical to each other. He notes that are basically only two schools of scholastic theology (*mutakallimīyyat*) and mystical philosophy (*ḥakīmīyyat*)[34] which concentrate on mystical theology or modes of divine knowledge (*ma'ārif-i ilahī*) in Islamic thought. By *mutakallimīyyat* Islamic apologetic theology (*Kalām*) is obviously implied, and by *ḥakīmīyyat* the

31 *Gawhar-i murād*, p. 35.

32 *Gawhar-i murād*, p. 35.

33 *Gawhar-i murād*, p. 35.

34 *Gawhar-i murād*, p. 38.

science of philosophy evidently meant, inclusive of both the Peripatetic and Illuminationist branches. And alongside scholastic theology and mystical philosophy is found the central esoteric tradition in Islam: Sufism.

"The reality of Sufism (*ḥaqīqat-i taṣawwuf*)," asserts Lāhījī next, "relates to one's conduct on the esoteric way (*sulūk-i rāh-i bāṭin*) alone." The relation of exoteric with esoteric knowledge in Sufism is clarified as follows:

> Having said that, it should be added the mode of conduct maintained upon the exoteric way should pave the way for and precede progress on the esoteric way (*masbūq-ast bar sulūk-i rāh-i ẓāhir*). Hence, the Sufi must first be either a mystical philosopher (*ḥakīm*) or a scholastic theologian (*mutakallim*). Claiming competence in Sufism (*ida'ā-yi taṣawwuf*) before being firmly grounded in mystical philosophy (*'ilm-i ḥikmat*), Kalām and, generally speaking, before being perfectly accomplished in rational theoretical methods (*ṭarīq-i naẓar*), whether these be according to the lexicon of the orthodox theologians (*'ulamā'*) or not, is nothing but imposture and deliberately pulling the wool over the eyes of the common people.[35]

The term Sufism (*taṣawwuf*) is used here in the most general sense of the word, as an Islamic *via mystica* shorn of association or identification with any particular *silsila*, *pīr*, *ṭarīqat* or even doctrines technically defined as 'Sufi':

> Our discourse here does not concern either the term *taṣawwuf* (Sufism) or the word *ṣūfī*. Rather, our intention is to elucidate the meaning of 'spiritual conduct' (*sulūk-i ma'nawī*), the quest for true union and the self-denying annihilation of all but Him, thus becoming eternal in His Eternity. The *ḥadīth* (in which God declares) "I am his ear ... and eye" alludes to this degree, and this is what is referred to as wholehearted devotion (*ikhlāṣ*) and god-fearing piety (*taqwā*) in the Canonical Law of Islam (*shar'*). Whatever the Sufis profess to have attained through interior intellectual revelations (*mukāshafāt-i 'ilmīyya*), their intention is not the attainment of speculative knowledge (*'ilm-i naẓarī*) without proofs and demonstrations – since it is impossible to acquire speculative knowledge without certain

35 *Gawhar-i murād*, p. 38. This passage is also discussed in my "Sufism and the School of Iṣfahān," pp. 109–10.

> intermediary means. Rather, their purpose is a kind of contemplation (*mushāhada*) which is the result of rational demonstration (*burhān*) without the interference of fantasy and delusive imagination.[36]

In this passage, Lāhījī is careful to note that the methods of rational proof and demonstration (*burhān*) by no means contradict the outcome and vision born of Sufi contemplation (*mushāhada*). In fact, the latter is in some sense the product of the former. His ideas expressed here seem to be aimed at elucidating the classic Sufi position on the correlation of *burhān* (rational demonstration) to *jadhba* (divine attraction). This doctrine is enunciated by Shabistarī in his *Garden of Mystery*, where he writes that "If illumination is vouchsafed the seeker either by grace of divine attraction or through the reflection cast by rational demonstration/ His heart, through the light of God, will enjoy a mysterious communion so that he can return back the way he came. / Thus he will find the way to a faith based on certainty either by divine attraction or through the certitude of rational demonstration."[37] Muḥammad Lāhījī (d. 912/1507) in his celebrated commentary on this poem explains how rational demonstration may assist spiritual realization as follows:

> Whereas rational demonstration (*burhān*) involves corroborative reasons (*dalīl*), the method of adducing reasons is the opposite of that of divine attraction (*jadhba*); the latter being realized *without* any accessory means, while demonstration depends upon the support of means and instrumental accessories ... Thus, one might say that 'the reflection cast by rational demonstration' [in the verse] refers here to that very light of knowledge which shines upon and illumines the gnostic adept's heart by way of the reflection cast by rational proofs and demonstrations.[38]

---

36 *Gawhar-i murād*, p. 38.

37 *Gulshan-i rāz*, in *Majmū'a-yi āthār-i Shaykh Maḥmūd Shabistarī*, ed. Ṣamad Muwaḥḥid (2nd printing. Tehran: 1371 A.Hsh./1982), p. 80: v. 326–28. *Mafātīḥ al-'ijāz fī sharḥ-i Gulshan-i rāz*, ed. R. Khāliqī and 'I. Karbāsī (Tehran: Zawwār 1371 A.Hsh./1992), pp. 215–16.

38 *Mafātīḥ al-'ijāz fī sharḥ-i Gulshan-i rāz*, ed. R. Khāliqī and 'I. Karbāsī (Tehran: Zawwār 1371 A.Hsh./1992), pp. 215–16.

The close connection and relation between rational demonstration (*burhān*) and visionary disclosure (*kashf*) is clarified by ʿAbd al-Razzāq Lāhījī as follows:

> Now, the meaning of unveiling or visionary disclosure (*kashf*) is precisely this: that one contemplates and perceives things without any veil (*bī-pardih*). It is therefore apparent that whatever is understood by means of direct visionary disclosure is the same as that which is understood through rational demonstration (*burhān*), so there is no difference between the two except in the clarity and obscurity of their respective perceptions. It may be said that certain things are understood by means of visionary disclosure *before* they're understood through rational demonstration (*burhān*), but the judgement passed on the intrinsic truth of visionary disclosure is of course *dependent* on rational demonstration (*burhān*).
>
> Therefore, if anyone claims that there is some sort of valid (knowledge obtained through) visionary disclosure that stands in contradiction to the requirements of rational demonstration, his claim is to be rejected and repudiated.[39]

The ultimate objective of this intellectually enlightened and philosophically oriented *via mystica*, affirms Lāhījī, is that the adept attain to purity of contemplative vision, realizing such a degree of knowledge "where no veil or curtain hangs betwixt to shroud the object from sight, a situation which corresponds to the contemplative insight of the gnostic (*mushāhada-yi ʿārif*) who has been trained in the ascetic discipline of shunning conventional precedents and customs, who rigorously adheres to the practice of dispassionate separation and detachment of intelligible realities (*tajrīd va tanzīh-i maʿānī*) from the coverings and veils of phantasy and imagination. This situation varies as well in proportion to the strength or weakness of the degree of ascetic discipline exerted."[40]

But only two types of savants, each distinguished from the other by their degrees of lesser and greater understanding, are capable of realizing this contemplative insight. The first, the conventional scholar's understanding, is undeveloped compared to that of the second, the esotericist or gnostic.

39 *Gawhar-i murād*, p. 40.

40 *Gawhar-i murād*, p. 39.

> The conventional traditionalist scholar (*'ālim-i rasmī*) apprehends things with certainty, but it is still through a veil, while the true scholar who has experientially verified and personally realized his knowledge (*'ālim-i muḥaqqiq*), shunning and avoiding conformity with conventional manners and customs, contemplates things independent of all veils. The condition of the former type of scholar in relation to the latter resembles the relation of hearsay to direct vision.[41]

According to Lāhījī's syncretistic vision, the adept who has personally verified the Truth among the Sufis (*muḥaqqiq-i Ṣūfiyya*), and the true scholar who has experientially verified and personally realized his knowledge (*'ālim-i muḥaqqiq*) share essentially the same theosophical realization and insight. Thus, the Sufi merges with enlightened philosopher savant in the person of the gnostic (*'ārif*).

Lāhījī clarifies his position on *Ishrāqī* Platonism by labelling it an esoteric tradition (or more precisely "a path of conduct on the esoteric way" – *sulūk-i rāh-i bāṭin*) parallel to Sufism. Like Sufism, it should also be preceded by progress upon the exoteric way. However, whereas the prerequisite for Sufism is the study of scholastic theology, the prerequisite for Ishrāqī theosophy is the study of philosophical mysticism (*ḥikmat*).[42]

In sum, according to Lāhījī, there are four principal ways of Islamic knowledge, two esoteric and two exoteric. The two esoteric ways are Sufism and Ishrāqī Platonism, and the two exoteric ways are philosophical theology and Peripatetic philosophy.

> It is well known that the 'Path of Illuminationism' has been classified as a type of philosophy (*ḥikmat*), that philosophy in turn can be

---

41 *Gawhar-i murād*, p. 39.

42 *Gawhar-i murād*, p. 40. Paraphrasing Lāhījī's views here, Henry Corbin notes that the situation of Ishrāqī philosophy "in relation to Peripatetic philosophy corresponds to that occupied by the Sufis in relation to the *kalām*. An *ishrāqī* can be considered a Sufi in the broad sense of the word, and he is certainly closer to the Sufis than he will ever be to the *mutakallimūn* or to the rationalist philosophers. Nevertheless, he cannot be considered purely and simply as a Sufi." Henry Corbin, *History of Islamic Philosophy*, trans. Liadian Sherrard (London: KPI in association with the Institute of Ismaili Studies 1993), p. 283.

> divided up into the Illuminationist and Peripatetic schools. Sufism likewise is to be accounted an entirely separate way dedicated to the acquisition of gnosis (*ma'rifat*). The truth of the matter is that Peripatetic philosophy (*ḥikmat-i mashshā'ī*) can be compared to philosophical theology (*'ilm-i kalām*), and the 'Path of Illuminationism' can be compared to the Path of Sufism. The former two ways relate to progress on the exoteric path, and the latter two ways relate to progress upon the esoteric way.[43]

The sole difference between the two esoteric ways is that Sufism depends on observation of the *Sharī'a*, which the Ishrāqī way does not; similarly, with the two exoteric ways: the study of philosophical theology (*kalām*) depends on observation of the Law, which Peripatetic philosophy does not. The diagram given above (see p. 368) illustrates these distinctions.

As the careful reader will note, the passages translated in this anthology Lāhījī's work comprise the most lucid expositions of the necessity for esotericism, and one of the most original defences of Sufism from a philosophical standpoint that can be found in all Islamic philosophical literature.[44]

SELECTIONS FROM LĀHĪJĪ'S *CROWN JEWEL OF DESIRE*

An Exposition of the Path to God and its Subdivision into Exoteric and Esoteric Ways

It should be understood that the *via mystica* which leads to God Almighty is a way upon which none should imagine any methodical progress (*sulūk*) can ever be made except by means of humble entreaty and self-abnegation

43 *Gawhar-i murād*, pp. 40–41.

44 I have translated the second section of Lāhījī's Introduction (pp. 33–37) on "Exposition of the Path to God and its Division into the Exoteric and Esoteric Ways (*rāh-i ẓāhir u rāh-i bāṭin*)," and select passages on *Ḥikmat* (pp. 38–42) from the third section "On the Difference Between Scholars, and Exposition of the Purpose and Use of the Science of Scholastic Theology (*Kalām*) and Mystical Philosophy (*ḥikmat*);" as well as the second section of the book's conclusion "On Mention of the Paths of the Sages Amongst the Scholars of the *Sharī'at*, Who are the Sufis and Gnostics (*'urafā'*), Whether or Not They be Designated by this Name" (pp. 686–93).

(*'ajz va nīstī*). Indeed, what relation does a clod of dust and dirt have to the pure Creator?[45] What likeness does an earthborn being have with the Lord of Lords? For there is no kinship between the creature and the Creator, between the possible and the Necessary Being, the temporally created and the Eternal Being, and the perishing and the Everlasting One, such that one should, by betaking oneself to the former, be able to attend the latter's Court. The only way (to that Court) is through negation of all relationships (*ṣalb-i hama-yi nisbathā*), for when all relationships and ties are abolished, and the veils of fantasy and imagination are dislodged from one's sight, such that one utterly despairs of all things, then the good tidings of hope in all things is issued. When the dust settles and the air clears, then what's visible is clearly evident to the eye. Now all beings through their phenomenal contingency are like a swirling cloud of dust polluting the atmosphere of thought, so that as long as the cloud does not settle nothing but dust can be seen.

Thus, the object of those who have personally verified the Truth among the Sufis (*muḥaqqīn az Ṣūfīyya*) in professing the 'Unity of Being' (*waḥdat-i wujūd*) and complete self-annihilation (*fanā'-yi muṭlaq*) cannot be anything above and beyond this idea that is here alluded to. Whatever else you hear about this matter, beware, pay it no heed! In a word, the path to God (*rah-i khudā*) is a straight and narrow one; it can neither be discovered by self-will nor traversed solely with the aid of reason (*pāyimardī-yi 'aql*). One can only hope in divine grace, that by His Beneficent Mercy He will open the way to his servants. Although he has sent the prophets to reveal this way, after they expounded and exposed it, one still must traverse the way which has been shown to one. Nonetheless, although one must proceed on the way oneself [by freewill], unless He conduct you [by divine attraction], traversing it will be impossible.

It should be also understood that there are but two ways for humankind to approach God: either the exoteric (*rāh-i ẓāhir*) or the esoteric way (*rāh-i bāṭin*). Although one may *know* God through the exoteric way, one can only *reach* God by the esoteric way – and how wide the gap between [theoretically] knowing God and actually reaching Him is! It is because of this that

45 This sentence is a direct paraphrase of Shabistarī's hemistich in *Gulshan-i rāz*, ed. Ṣamad Muwaḥḥid, *Majmū'a-i āthār-i Shaykh Maḥmūd Shabistarī* (Tehran: Kitābkhāna-i Ṭahūrī 1365 A.Hsh./1986) pp. 71–72, v. 125. "What relation does dust have to the pure realm: for apprehension is nothing but [to realize one's] incapacity to apprehend."

so many allusions have been made to the hardships of the esoteric way, in contrast to the exoteric way which involves much less hardship – being based on rational demonstrations within the reach of every intelligent person capable of discerning cause from effect.

But the way of rational demonstration should precede the way of spiritual conduct (*sulūk*),[46] for as long as a person does not know that there are posting houses on a road he never will make a journey to any destination.[47] Now, the prophet's mission is *not* in order to guide people on the exoteric path and the way of logical demonstration, because this (esoteric) way all depends upon having a prophet's spiritual direction. If it were the case that the conscience's acquiescence and assent to the fact that the Prophet is an emissary of God (*taṣdīq-i paygambar*) depended upon (first) knowing God, it would necessarily end up in a vicious circle. Said differently: the work of the prophets in guiding others on this path is for the sake of waking up the sleeping. When a sleeping person who is endowed with sound vision is woken up by someone, upon waking he will inevitably see things through his own individual eyesight. Nor will the one who wakes him bother to meddle further with him after waking him. It is even entirely possible that the person may wake up by himself and see things of his own accord, since 'waking up' does not necessarily depend on another's awakening.

In the same vein, people are fast asleep in an infatuated state of negligence (*ghiflat*[48]) and what sleep is to the eye of the senses, so negligence is to the eye of Reason. Upon this way all the work and labour of the prophets is dedicated to waking people up from the sleep of negligence (although it

46 *Sulūk* denotes 'methodical progress on the '*via mystica*' or *ṭarīqa*, the process of ascension and advancement – psychical, ethical and spiritual – which the Sufi 'wayfarer' (*sālik*) experiences in his pursuit (*ṭalab*) of God. For further discussion of this term in Sufism, see Leonard Lewisohn, *EI2*, s.v. "*sulūk*."

47 *Gawhar-i murād*, pp. 33–34. In his French introduction to the *Muntakhabātī az āthār-i ḥukamā'ī ilāhī-yi Īrān* (I, p. 124), Henry Corbin underlines that this passage, which is also cited there, demonstrates the author's "secret and profound inclination for Sufism."

48 The term *khwāb-i ghiflat* literally means 'sleep of heedlessness', but here refers to what the English mystic William Law (1686–1761) called "a strange infatuated state of negligence which keeps people from considering what devotion is" – William Law, *A Serious Call to a Devout and Holy Life*, ed. P. Stanwood (London: SPCK 1978), p. 205.

is also entirely possible that a person will of his own accord wake from sleep). Therefore, if upon waking up from the sleep of negligence, people were to put their Reason – having now rent its veil of negligence – to work, they would certainly be able to know God. But if after waking up from the sleep of negligence they still do not know God, it is simply because they have not put their mind to the task and set their Reason to work – just like someone who wakes from sleep yet will not open his eyes to see the things lying about him.

It is for this reason that God Almighty in the Qur'ān refers to those who did not confess their faith after the prophets' mission and wakening summons as "those who are in denial and inimical obstinacy (*ahl-i juḥūd va 'inād*)." For being in denial consists in knowing something yet professing to know nothing about it. A person who wakes up but won't open his eyes, protesting that 'there's nothing to see', is of course only being stubborn and obstinate. For this reason, a note of surprise creeps in in many places in the Qur'ān when such stubborn types are mentioned, such as "Can you not then see?"[49]; "Have you no reason?"[50]; "Will you not take thought?"[51]; "Will then they not reflect [on the Qur'ān]?"[52] and so on. Therefore, if human reason had no independence in its conduct in exoteric matters and ratiocinative reasoning, so many expressions of wonder would have been out of place.

It is necessary to understand that the exoteric and esoteric paths of progression are contrary to one another. On the one hand, the wayfarer on the exoteric way of ratiocinative reasoning proceeds stage by stage through establishing proofs for things, before finally ending up in establishing a proof for a cause that itself has no cause. For instance, through scrutiny of an effect, he proves that this effect may have an effective agent, and since he perceives marks of 'being effected' upon that effective agent, he will conclude that it also has another effective agent behind it, until, by the same analogy, he ends up demonstrating that there is an effective agent that has no marks of 'being effected' on it.

On the other hand, the wayfarer on the esoteric way of progression proceeds by disavowing and negating things stage by stage, until he finally

49 Qur'ān XLIII:51.

50 Qur'ān II:76.

51 Qur'ān VI:50.

52 Qur'ān IV:82.

attains the eternally subsistent being impenetrable to perishability and impervious to dissolution and destruction. For instance, since the wayfarer understands by rational proofs that the Cause and Creator of things must be beyond destruction and deprivation and must not show any marks of 'being effected' within itself, he will reject everything that he perceives as having traces of destruction and deprivation in it, until he reaches a perfect being in which no destruction exists. After this, he cannot (seriously) cast a glance at anything else but this being, and naturally everything which hinders him from contemplation of that perfect being becomes his enemy and foe. So he resolves to forswear all such hindrances so that he may remain forever immersed in the pleasures of spiritual contemplation (*mushāhada*). Not only will he not hearken to anything else, he will not even bother to betake himself away from that pleasure to what has been made pleasurable – which is his own very essence. And it is this pleasure that the theosophers (*ḥukamā'-yi ilahī*) designate as 'true felicity' (*sa'ādat-i ḥaqīqī*), and which those who have personally verified the Truth among the Sufis (*muḥaqqīn-i Ṣūfiyya*) dub 'union and annihilation in God' (*wuṣūl u fanā'*), and in this lies the joy that is the consolation of the prophets and the delight of the saints.

The whole purpose of the mission of the prophets and messengers is to summon people to this pleasure, to urge them on to realize this supreme degree. In traversing this way, it is impossible for the reason of anyone to be entirely independent, for even if a human being may be endowed with a character that is inclined towards perfection, in many other respects he is afflicted with corrupt vices and flaws of character that the demanding drives of lust and anger (*shahwat va ghaḍab*) arouse and propagate in him. These propagandists of vice do not permit him even to conceive of perfection, much less pursue it. If the punishments of the Canon Law and all the threats and promises of the Lawgiver did not exist to drive men, by constraint and force, to enter this way, no one would have ever been able to venture upon it.

Although the farthest limit of the exertions and efforts of Reason is to know the sense, significance, and universal properties of things, the attainment of select and specific knowledge of particular modes of conduct, works and deeds. Precisely what things will bring one near or cause one to become alienated from God – is not within the measure and command of human reason. Therefore, divine wisdom made it requisite that prophets be dispatched in order that certain things might be made mandatory and loved (whatever is a cause of attention to, or stimulates an increase in concentration upon, the Real Objective, or else a means of avoidance of, or a greater aversion to, everything other than the Real Objective), and certain other things be made forbidden and hated (whatever is a cause of preoccupation or further engagement in what is other than the Real Objective, or else a means of avoidance of or a greater aversion to the Real Objective). Divine wisdom also dictated that the *sine qua non* for performance of all good deeds be simply and solely realization of closeness to God and total sincerity, so that the wayfarer never becomes listless and neglectful of the Real Objective, whatever may befall him. Divine wisdom also dictated that immersion in permitted indulgences should be regarded as reprehensible, and forbade debauchery and vanity (albeit, there is no permitted indulgence which cannot be seen as manifesting, when regarded from a certain point of view, a kind of intention to realize closeness to God and a dedication to sincerity).

If while being swept up in the surging course of his various mystical states and practical works, the aspiring wayfarer manages to concentrate his sights upon this sublime pattern of conduct which the holy Lawgiver had laid down (particularly so if he be conscious, even in a summary way, of the hidden esoteric sense and purpose of these practices), such that the mirror of the rational soul's cosmic universality (*mirāt-i jāmaʿīyyat-i nafs-i nāṭiqa*)[53] – which both in lexicon of the holy law and in the technical terminology of Sufism is called the 'heart' (*qalb*) – and the ontological level of the Ithmus (*martaba-yi barzakhīyyat*) that acts as a mediator between [the sensory and supersensory] worlds are permanently established within him, the dictates of the world of the senses, which exercised their control over him through nature's sway, become truly refined and polished clear, as it were, of the rusty smudges of the contretemps of his natural humours and the darkness of sensuality from him is purged all away. In this fashion, the forms of the spiritual realities of things – the wherewithal of the perception of the intellectual conceptions of which had been acquired by means of demonstrative reasoning (*istidlāl*) during the journey on the exoteric way (*safar-i rāh-i ẓāhir*) – and all the capital assets of experiences bequeathed him during the hum and bustle of the esoteric journey's daily bazaar, are exposed to light, so that form of each one of those spiritual

53 Just like the heart, the rational soul possesses a kind of all-encompassing universality or global reality that transcends human material identity and personality.

realities becomes a mirror of the Beauty-with-Perfection of that Real Perfection. At this juncture, the wayfarer faces plunging into the abyss of divine Union (*lujja-yi vuṣūl*), which in the lexicon of the Canon Law is known as 'the Artesian Well of Plenty' (*artūwā-yi kawthar*), while the food-cloth of true felicity (*mā'ida-yi sa'ādat-i ḥaqīqī*) – which can be interpreted according to the technical terminology of philosophical mysticism (*ḥikmat*) by the Qur'ānic verse "No soul what is what comfort and joy is stored up for them as a reward for that which they used to do,"[54] and by the Prophetic tradition: "The eye has not seen, nor the ear heard ..."[55] – is laid down for him, whereupon the correspondence between the technical terminology of adherents of exoteric legalistic religion (*ahl-i sharī'a*) and adepts in the esoteric divine Reality (*ahl-i ḥaqīqat*) in respect to all these ideas also becomes explicit.

It has been clearly demonstrated that the way to God is subdivided into two types: the exoteric and esoteric ways, and that the exoteric way has been discovered and realized by means of reason (*'aql*), fared thereupon by rational means, whereas on the esoteric way God is the Guide, and the prophets have been delegated as escorts and pilots. Now, finding this esoteric way – and observing those conditions that *allow one to find it* and then progress upon it so as to realize its veridical (ultimate) stage – depends (first) on finding the exoteric way and proceeding along it in such a fashion that fulfils its conditions. Therefore basing ourselves on this premise, our purpose in the following brief treatise is the exposition of the characteristics of formal conduct on the course of the exoteric way, in demonstration whereof we intend to arrange and adduce rational arguments, but in such a fashion that anyone with a normal amount of discernment – succoured of course by probity of character – will be able to obtain a great conviction of its truth without being inconvenienced by having to take cognizance of any scholarly technical terminology, and so be directed towards the principles

---

54 Qur'ān XXXII:17.

55 An allusion to the *ḥadīth-i qudsī* (sacred tradition): "I have provided for my righteous devotees that which neither the eye has seen, nor the ear heard, nor has ever passed through the heart of man." – Badī' al-Zamān Furūzānfar, *Aḥādīth-i Mathnawī* (Tehran: Amīr Kabīr 1982), p. 93. N.B. This tradition is obviously an Islamic paraphrase of I Corinthians ii, 9: "But as it is written: "Eye hath not seen, nor ear heard, neither have entered into the heart of man, the things which God hath prepared for them that love him."

of the sacred sciences, shattering the shackles of blind mimesis of tradition.

On the Difference Between Scholars, and Exposition of the Purpose and Use of the Science of Scholastic Theology (*kalām*) and Mystical Philosophy (*ḥikmat*)[56]

It should be understood that the sort of differences which exist among scholars regarding modes of theological knowledge (*ma'ārif-i ilahī*) are restricted to (two schools of) scholastic theology (*mutakallimīyyat*) and philosophical theosophy (*ḥakīmīyyat*). Two further divisions exist within the field of scholastic theology, namely the Mu'tazilites and Ash'arites.

The path of Sufism, however, is not splintered by any such divisions because differences of this kind exist only among those who pursue the exoteric way (*sulūk-i rāh-i ẓāhir*) and the path of rational speculation and demonstration (*ṭarīqa-yi naẓar va istidlāl*), whereas the reality of Sufism (*ḥaqīqat-i taṣawwuf*) relates to one's conduct on the esoteric way (*sulūk-i rāh-i bāṭin*) alone. While the final objective of the former is obtaining knowledge (*ḥuṣūl-i 'ilm*), the ultimate aim of the latter is Union with the divine Essence (*wuṣūl-i 'ayn*).

Having said that, it should be added the mode of conduct maintained upon the exoteric way should pave the way for and proceed progress on the esoteric way (*masbūq-ast bar sulūk-i rāh-i ẓāhir*). Hence, the Sufi must first be either a mystical philosopher (*ḥakīm*) or a scholastic theologian (*mutakallim*). Claiming competence in Sufism (*ida'ā-yi taṣawwuf*) before being firmly grounded in mystical philosophy (*'ilm-i ḥikmat*), Kalām and, generally speaking, before being perfectly accomplished in rational theoretical methods (*ṭarīq-i naẓar*), whether these be according to the lexicon of the orthodox theologians (*'ulamā'*) or not, is nothing but imposture and deliberately pulling the wool over the eyes of the common people.

Our discourse here does not concern either the term *taṣawwuf* (Sufism) or the word *ṣūfī*. Rather, our intention is to elucidate the meaning of 'spiritual conduct' (*sulūk-i ma'nawī*), the quest for true union and the self-denying annihilation of all but Him, thus becoming eternal in His Eternity. The

56 *Gawhar-i murād*, pp. 38–42.

ḥadīth (in which God declares) "I am his ear ... and eye"[57] alludes to this degree, and this is what is referred to as wholehearted devotion (*ikhlāṣ*) and god-fearing piety (*taqwā*) in the Canonical Law of Islam (*shar'*). Whatever the Sufis profess to have attained through interior intellectual revelations (*mukāshafāt-i 'ilmīyya*), their intention is not the attainment of speculative knowledge (*'ilm-i naẓarī*) without proofs and demonstrations – since it is impossible to acquire speculative knowledge without certain intermediary means. Rather, their purpose is a kind of contemplation (*mushāhada*) which is the result of rational demonstration (*burhān*) without the interference of fantasy and delusive imagination.[58]

Now, to expand on these brief remarks. However so much the rational soul (*nafs-i nāṭiqa*) is infiltrated by lust and anger and other corporeal faculties, the mind's apprehension of intelligible realities (*ma'qūlāt*) will become more tarnished and contaminated through veils of imagination and phantasy. Likewise, in proportion to the mind accustoming itself to abandoning habitual convention and relinquishing its wonted routine, the more it will gain independence from phantasy and the senses, and the intellect's contemplation of abstract ideas will become that much clearer.

Any object of knowledge apprehended by the untrained mind immersed in conventional precedents and customs and entangled in technical terminology and literalistic expressions, is only of a conceptual nature, and since such conceptions are, in any case, grasped by the mind by means of various phonetic forms, literal expressions, grammatical conditions and terminological definitions, these conceptions will not be devoid of certain accidental impedimenta arising from the senses and imagination. Therefore, the mind's apprehension of the reality of things through such conceptions becurtained by accidental impedimenta of particular phenomena is just like a person's perception of sensory objects through a curtain suspended before his eye. Ultimately, his perception will fluctuate in clarity and obscurity according to the differing texture of the veil, its transparency and

57 "When I love a servant, I, the Lord, am his ear so that he hears by Me, I am his eye, so that he sees by Me, and I am his tongue so that he speaks by Me, and I am his hand, so that he takes by Me." Cited by Annemarie Schimmel, *Mystical Dimensions of Islam* (Chapel Hill: University of North Carolina 1975), p. 43.

58 *Muntakhabātī az āthār-i ḥukamā'ī ilāhī-yi Īrān* I, pp. 287–88; *Gawhar-i murād*, pp. 38–39.

opacity, thinness and thickness, so that the clarity of the objects perceived will be in exact proportion to the subtlety and thinness of the texture of the veil.

Finally, a degree is reached where no veil or curtain hangs betwixt to shroud the object from sight, a situation which corresponds to the contemplative insight of the gnostic (*mushāhada-yi 'ārif*) who has been trained in the ascetic discipline of shunning conventional precedents and customs, who rigorously adheres to the practice of dispassionate separation and detachment of intelligible realities (*tajrīd va tanzīh-i ma'ānī*) from the coverings and veils of phantasy and imagination. This situation varies as well in proportion to the strength or weakness of the degree of ascetic discipline exerted.

Therefore, it can be said that even if the conventional traditionalist scholar (*'ālim-i rasmī*) apprehends things with certainty, it is still through a veil, while the true scholar who has experientially verified and personally realized his knowledge (*'ālim-i muḥaqqiq*),[59] shunning and avoiding conformity with conventional manners and customs, contemplates things independent of all veils. The condition of the former type of scholar in relation the latter resembles the relation of hearsay to direct vision.

Now, the meaning of unveiling or visionary disclosure (*kashf*) is precisely this: that one contemplates and perceives things without any veil (*bī-parda*). It is therefore apparent that whatever is understood by means of direct visionary disclosure is the same as that which is understood through rational demonstration (*burhān*), so there is no difference between the two except in the clarity and obscurity of their respective perceptions. It may be said that certain things are understood by means of visionary disclosure *before* they're understood through rational demonstration (*burhān*), but the judgement passed on the intrinsic truth of visionary disclosure is of course *dependent* on rational demonstration (*burhān*).

Therefore, if anyone claims that there is some sort of valid (knowledge obtained through) visionary disclosure that stands in contradiction to the requirements of rational demonstration, his claim is to be rejected and repudiated. However, everything said here refers only to visionary disclosures of the intelligible realm (*kashf-i 'ilmī*). Debate and discussion about other particular types of visionary disclosures, and prescience of the phenomena of the invisible realm, which belong to the category of

59 For a good discussion of the term *muḥaqqiq*, see H. Corbin, *En Islam iranien* III, 247.

'charismatic powers (*karāmat*)', will be discussed in another, more suitable place.

The Illuminationist path (*ṭarīqa-yi Ishrāq*) does not in reality lie amongst the ways of normative didactic knowledge achieved through education (*'ilm-i taḥṣīlī*). Rather it is a path of conduct on the esoteric way (*sulūk-i rāh-i bāṭin*) which [like Sufism] should first be preceded by progress upon the exoteric way (*masbūq-ast bar sulūk-i rāh-i ẓāhir*). There is no difference between illuminationism and Sufism except that Sufism may be juxtaposed to the discourse of the scholastic theologians (*takallum*) whereas illuminationism (*ishrāq*) may be juxtaposed to philosophical mysticism (*ḥikmat*).[60] That is to say, whenever the mystic's spiritual conduct on the esoteric path comes after his conduct on the exoteric path (pursued according to the principles of philosophical mysticism [*ḥikmat*]) – then it is known as the 'Path of Illuminationism' (*ṭarīqa-yi ishrāq*); but if his conduct on the esoteric path comes after his conduct on the exoteric path (followed according to the principles of philosophical theology [*kalām*]) – then it is known as the 'Path of Sufism'.

Both the *Ishrāqī* sages' condemnation of the Peripatetics and the Sufis' censure of philosophical theologians and conventional religious scholars stem from the fact that both [those denounced] groups have limited themselves to purely formal conduct on the course of the exoteric way (*sulūk-i rāh-i ẓāhir*). They have based their studies on mere acquisition of intellectual concepts while disregarding and casting aside the essential goal – spiritual conduct on the esoteric path and quest for divine Union. [On the other hand], the Peripatetic philosophers and the philosophical theologians' censure of the *Ishrāqī*s and Sufis stem from the fact that the latter groups have set foot on the esoteric path without the adequate provision of exoteric knowledge and in-depth inquiry according to methods based on logical inference (*ṭarīq-i burhān*). But in reality, both groups are right in what they say, for true comprehensiveness (*kamāl-i ḥaqīqī*) lies in the transformation of both one's inner and outer being, and, just as disregarding the inner being

60 Paraphrasing Lāhījī's statement here, Henry Corbin notes that the situation of Ishrāqī philosophy "in relation to Peripatetic philosophy corresponds to that occupied by the Sufis in relation to the *kalām*. An ishrāqī can be considered a Sufi in the broad sense of the word, and he is certainly closer to the Sufis than he will ever be to the mutakallimūn or to the rationalist philosophers. Nevertheless, he cannot be considered purely and simply as a Sufi." *History of Islamic Philosophy*, p. 283.

and contenting oneself with formal learning constitutes aberration and arrogance, so undertaking the interior journey without observing the proprieties of conduct in exoteric matters (*sulūk-i ẓāhir*) is a deviation and defect.

It is well known that the 'Path of Illuminationism' has been classified as a type of philosophy (*ḥikmat*), that philosophy in turn can be divided up into the Illuminationist and Peripatetic schools. Sufism likewise is to be accounted an entirely separate way dedicated to the acquisition of gnosis (*ma'rifat*). The truth of the matter is that Peripatetic philosophy (*ḥikmat-i mashshā'ī*) can be compared to philosophical theology (*'ilm-i kalām*) and the 'Path of Illuminationism' can be compared to the Path of Sufism. The former two ways relate to progress on the exoteric path, and the latter two relate to progress upon the esoteric way, as has already been explained.

However, the difference between Islamic philosophical theology (*kalām*) and philosophy (*ḥikmat*) lies in the following. Since it is understood that reason (*'aql*) enjoys complete independence in the acquisition of the divine sciences (*ma'ārif-i ilahī*) as well as in other intellectual matters, and that observation of the *Sharī'a* is not requisite in these matters, therefore the acquisition of the veridical sciences of Divine Reality (*ma'ārif-i ḥaqīqī*) and demonstration of the precepts of certitude (*ithbāt-i aḥkām-i yaqīnīyya*) regarding the individual essences of existing beings – in such a way that is in accordance with the thing itself, by means of inferential proofs (*dalā'il*) and intellectual demonstrations (*barāhīn*) that terminate in original insights (*badī'hiyyāt*) which no mind may dare desist or tarry in accepting, without this either being discordant or concordant with any particular condition or circumstance and without it being under the impact or influence of [the doctrines of] any nation – this is the way of the philosophers (*ṭarīq-i ḥukamā'*). The knowledge obtained through this way is called 'the science of philosophy (*'ilm-i ḥikmat*)' in the terminology of those who are learned. Although it is not impossible that such a science be in agreement with genuine religious laws (*sharayi'-i ḥaqqīyya*) – since the truth of the *Sharī'at* itself depends on verification [of its principles] through rational demonstration (*burhān-i 'aqlī*) – but when it comes to adducing *proofs* of philosophical problems this concordance [of religious law and philosophy] plays no function, since the demonstration of these [philosophical rules] does not depend upon the law.

If on occasion a conflict between an axiom of philosophy, which is definitively demonstrated by valid proofs, and a rule of religious law arises, it is required that a hermeneutic exegesis (*ta'wīl*) upon that religious rule be made. If, however, the religious rule be a matter of such solid certainty (*thubūt*) that it cannot be subjected to any hermeneutic exegesis, and if furthermore, that axiom of philosophy does not constitute a basis for proof of any matter pertaining to the religious law (*sharī'at*), then it is apparent there is something defective in the method used to demonstrate the said axiom of philosophy. Furthermore, it is quite possible that no rational and intelligent mind will be able to ascertain the truth of any such matter that is not subject to demonstration by religious law.[61]

However, if that axiom of philosophy is something also used as a basis for proof of a matter pertaining to the religious law, then it is obvious that there was something wrong in the way that the axiom was approached. Nonetheless, it is not allowed that there should exist (for example) the agreement of all intelligent minds on that matter along with the absence of anyone successfully proving and realizing the truth of it; otherwise, this would necessarily lead to the disestablishment of the religious law.

The first situation is exemplified by the question of the temporal eternity of the world (*qidam-i zamānī-yi 'ālam*),[62] the contrary of which (that is: creation in time – if affirmed) cannot be used as the basis for proof of a matter pertaining to prophecy (*nubuwwat*), and therefore it is allowable that all intelligent minds on this subject should agree. The second situation is exemplified by the question of the negation of God's knowledge of particulars, the contrary of which (that is: God's knowledge of particulars – if affirmed) is something that inevitably can be employed as the basis for the proof of prophecy, and therefore agreement of all intelligent minds on this is impossible.

---

61 That is to say, even with the light of faith and the grace of God, it is hard enough to penetrate into the mysteries of the universe, but deprived of such light, it is quite possible that revelation of certain matters of science will always remain beyond the scope of human reason.

62 A reference to the discussion about the world's temporal or eternal nature in Islamic philosophy, discussed for instance by Ghazālī in his *Tahāfut al-falāsifa*, trans. Michael Marmura, *The Incoherence of the Philosophers* (Utah: Brigham Young University Press 1997), pp. 12ff.

This then is our exposition of the true significance of the science of philosophy or philosophical mysticism (*ḥaqīqat-i 'ilm-i ḥikmat*).

On the Paths of the Sages Amongst the Scholars of the *Sharī'at*, who are the Sufis and Gnostics (*'urafā'*), Whether or Not They be Designated by this Name[63]

It should be understood that the point *d'appui* of man in his totality and the perfections of the rational soul (*nafs-i nāṭiqa*) – after acquiring knowledge of theoretical philosophy (*ḥikmat-i naẓarīyya*) – is the acquisition of Justice as a natural disposition (*malaka-yi 'idālat*). By 'Justice' is meant adopting the *via media* in all one's conduct and behaviour, in such a manner that one does not tend to go to any extreme, be it of excess or paucity. Inevitably, this depends on both the understanding of, and the concrete amount of the effect of, all of one's acts and behaviour upon the soul, both in terms of quantity and quality. It is certainly not within the natural capacity of man to acquire this virtue *in extenso*: Rather it depends on divine communication and instruction conveyed through the mission of prophets and apostles and through the subsequent establishment of canonical laws and regulations. Therefore, the acquisition of the virtue of Justice and the gaining of a civilized character (*tahdhīb-i akhlāq*) depends upon the existence of the prophets and their direction and guidance. This need of man to obtain a refined, civilized character is but another singular way of demonstrating the necessity of Prophecy (*nubuwwat*), just as the need of man for civilization (*tamaddun*) is another way to approach this subject, as was stated above.

All in all, the proper amount of exertion that one needs to expend, whether in regard to doing or abstaining from an action, cannot be apprehended except by medium of the prophets. As the Shaykh in his 'Treatise on Ethics', after giving an account of the different types of virtues, propounds: "and yet the proper appraisal and determination of these virtues should be apprehended from the eminent leaders of every nation (*arbāb al-milal*)."

And from this it is apparent that the significance of the Balance on the Day of Resurrection, which is an instrument for the weighing of

63 This section is a translation of the concluding chapter of the *Gawhar-i murād*, pp. 686–93.

deeds and actions,[64] is nothing but the prophets and the deputies of the prophets (peace be upon them), as was pointed out above. Therefore, the objective of the mission of the prophets is naught else but the refinement of the character of (men's) rational souls and the acquisition of the virtuous disposition of 'Justice' in human nature, just as the chief and last of the prophets affirmed: "I have been sent to perfect nobility of character."[65]

Thus, the diligent efforts made in pursuit of canonically obligatory actions and deeds should be of the sort that causes one to become bedecked with virtuous traits of character and to be shorn of vice, to acquire traits of moral excellence and transform habits of vice into virtues. Such spiritual realities as these needs must require perfect prognostication, full conscious awareness, occupation with monitoring one's own mystical states (*aḥwāl*), while being acquainted and informed of one's own interior psycho-spiritual affairs (*umūr-i bāṭin*) and the fluctuating transformations of the heart, as well as insight into the minute details of perilous passions that plague the soul. It also requires making a supreme effort to practise acts of devotion with complete sincerity, while purifying one's spiritual resolve of all flaws and blemishes. However, inevitably it is extremely difficult if not nigh impossible for most, if not all, people to engage in contemplation of these spiritual realities while caught up in the enjoyment of, and association and preoccupation with, the conventional requirements, social customs and while involved in the entanglements of worldly affairs.

---

64 A reference to the scholastic debate about weighing and reckoning of one's deeds on the Judgement Day or the Day of Rendering of Accounts (*yawm al-ḥisab* or *yawm al-dīn*). One of the key questions discussed by scholars concerned the true meaning of the Qur'ān's many references to the weighing (*al-wazn*) of deeds in the hereafter and the Scales or Balance (e.g. XLII:17; LV:6–8; LVII:25). According to popular tradition, the instrument used for the weighing of deeds will be a "Balance" or "Scales" (*mizān*), which is interpreted both by the Mu'tazilites and Ash'arites as being metaphorical. For a good discussion of these debates, see Ch. Pellat, *EI2* III:465–68, s.v. "*Ḥisab.*"

65 This *ḥadīth* can be found in the standard collections such as Bukhārī, Muslim, Tirmidhī, etc. For a good discussion of medieval Islamic theories on and the topos of *makārim al-akhlāq*, see Majid Fakhry, *Ethical Theories in Islam* (Leiden: Brill 1994), pp. 143ff.

It is for this reason that many of the religious scholars who are experientially versed in *Sharīʿa*-matters (*muḥaqqiqān az ʿulamāʾ-yi sharīʿat*),[66] as well as the sage philosophers throughout the land during all times and periods, have chosen – after learning the sciences of sapiential certitude (*ʿulūm-i yaqīnīyya*), acquiring a disposition graced with intellectual virtues, and perfecting the powers of speculation and theory – to retire into seclusion and reduce their frequenting of wanton company and mixed society. Likewise, they incited and encouraged their followers and students to follow their course in this, without however directly denoting their conduct with any specific name, or thinking it incumbent that they single themselves out as following some conventional position or form of behaviour.[67] In the early days of Islam, there were also a number of the devoted Companions of the Prophet and perfect adepts among their later followers who behaved in the same fashion, praising seclusion from society for God's sake and lauding the practise of retirement in order to pursue worship and devotion.

But not long thereafter there appeared a company of people who in blind imitation of their practice established original and unusual customs and rites, who togged themselves up in special costumes, considering it necessary to give themselves special names, enacting peculiar rituals and coining their own separate terminology. In this fashion, the [customs of] 'masterhood and discipleship' (*pīrī va murīdī*) have become prevalent: good has been combined with evil, and wet with dry compounded. However, in relation [to the spiritual life] the closest thing to rectitude is to content oneself with worshipping and serving God without presuming to adopt any but the most ordinary names and denominations – such as 'believers', 'sincere devotees', 'righteous servants', and 'pietists' (*muʾminīn va mukhliṣīn va ṣāliḥīn va muttaqīn*) – all terms mentioned in the Qurʾān and the sacred Tradition (*sunna*), and that one not presume to adopt any other apparel and appearance than that of [simple] spiritual poverty and

66 Alternate version to consider: Many of the spiritual scientists among the legal scholars.

67 Alternate versions to consider: They also encouraged and incited their students and followers to act likewise/to do the same, although they refrained from denoting their conduct with any specific name/epithet, nor did they think it necessary or incumbent to single themselves out as following some conventional position or form of behaviour in this respect.

self-denial (*faqr va fanā'*), whatever its outer dress may be, as was the custom of the Companions and followers of the Prophet.

The spiritual scientists (*muḥaqqiqīn*) belonging to this class[68] are lords of high aspiration whose sights are fixed exclusively on the Unique Divine Essence, and whose attention is focused on no dimension but the divine Aspect. In the path of their spiritual wayfaring to God (*sulūk-i rāh-i khudā*) this group have delineated certain spiritual stations (*maqāmāt*), the first of which, after awakening (to the Quest), is repentance (*tawba*) from abandoning devotional practices and indulgence in sin, and the last is forsaking everything other than God, and repenting from the real sin (*gunāh-i ḥaqīqī*) – which is one's fictional self-existence (*wujūd-i majāzī*), for it has been said "Your existence is a sin worse than all other sin."[69]

A myriad of these spiritual stations has been delineated. Some of the adepts of this [Sufi] sect have calculated their number to be one thousand. In his book entitled *Manāzil al-sā'irīn* (Stations of the Wayfarers)[70] Khwāja 'Abdu'llāh Anṣārī [d. 481/1089] presented one hundred spiritual stations which are bases of all the other stations; these hundred stations were in turn subdivided into ten parts, each of which constitutes another separate station in itself, altogether comprising a thousand parts (stations). The last of these stations – which involves transcending and casting aside all but God – is called the station of annihilation (*martaba-yi fanā'*). By *fanā'* is not meant annihilation *within* that station, rather this station implies annihilation *from* annihilation. For at this level the depths of divine Union are made manifest and the wayfarer becomes qualified with all the divine Qualities, becoming eternal in God's own Eternity.

In his *Book of Philosophical Allusions* (*Kitāb al-Ishārāt*), Shaykh Abū 'Alī bin Sīnā (Avicenna) composed an entire chapter devoted to these "Waystations of the Gnostics (*Fī maqāmāt al-'ārifīn*)," and as Imām Fakhr-i Rāzī pointed out in his commentary on these *Philosophical Allusions*: "this

68 *Ṭabaqa:* i.e. the class of scholars versed in *Sharī'a* learning as well as the lore of the *Ḥaqīqa*.

69 For an extended discussion of the various philosophical implications and the religious contexts of these passages, see Leonard Lewisohn, "Sufism and the School of Iṣfahān," pp. 104–7.

70 See A.G. Ravan Farhadi, *'Abdullāh Anṣārī of Herāt (1006–1089 C.E.) An Early Sufi Master* (London: Curzon Press 1996), pp. 73–77.

chapter contains the most important and valuable subject matter of this book, because in it the author has organized the sciences of the Sufis in a far better manner than any of his forebears and, to tell the truth, better than anyone subsequent to him."

In the beginning of this chapter, the Master (Avicenna) declares:

> There are certain spiritual stations and degrees relating to the knowledge of God and how one may traverse the way to Him that are particularly exclusive to the gnostics, and none but them can reap any benefit from these stations and degrees. These things are granted to them especially, to enjoy during the course of their life in the world while their souls are still attached to their bodies. It is as if while they are still draped in the veil and vestment of the body, they are *not within* this veil and vestment; rather that they have stripped off that vestment and thrown it away.[71]

In another section of that chapter,[72] it is stated:

> Gnosis (*'irfān*) commences with detachment from materiality (*tafrīq*), [then proceeds to] disassociation from material things (*nafḍ*), renunciation (*tark*), negation (*rafḍ*), before becoming deeply absorbed in unitive consciousness (*jam'*), which for the sincere disciple signifies the gathering together of divine Qualities [within him]. Finally in the One (*al-wāḥid*), it culminates and halts.

71 After citing Avicenna's Arabic text, a Persian translation of this passage – translated here – is provided by Lāhījī. Both the Arabic text and the commentary by Ṭūsī on this passage (the ninth *namaṭ*) can be found in Sulaymān Dunyā's edition of *Al-ishārāt wa'l-tanbīhāt* (Cairo: Dār al-Ma'ārif al-Miṣr 1960), pp. 789ff. A more exact translation from the Arabic is as follows: "In their life in this world, the gnostics possess certain spiritual stations and degrees which are particularly exclusive to them, which can be found in no one but them. It is as if the gnostics enjoy such a state that, while still behind the veil of their bodies, they have been transported outside of themselves and have set foot in the realm of immateriality and divine sanctity."

72 This section is actually the nineteenth "allusion" of the next (tenth) chapter (*faḍl*) of the *Al-ishārāt*, ed. S. Dunyā, pp. 838–40.

In his commentary on this passage,[73] Muḥaqqiq (Naṣīr al-Dīn) Ṭūsī (d. 672/1273) observed:

> All the "Waystations of the Gnostics," have been summed up and subsumed within this one section, which may be summarized as follows:
>
> The acquisition of knowledge (*taḥṣīl al-ma'rifat*), which is the perfection of rational soul (*nafs al-nāṭiqa*) (the soul's knowledge being imperfect and only potentially 'acquired') can be realized by two things: purgation (*takhallī*) and illumination (*taḥallī*), just as a sick person is treated through the two methods of expurgation and abstention. The first sort of treatment is entirely negative and the second type is positive and affirmative, following the first. Each of these respective methods has several hierarchical degrees, as follows:
>
> The degrees of purgation involve (firstly) the gnostic's detaching his soul from everything that distracts him essentially from the divine Truth. Such detachment (*tafrīq*) implies distinguishing between things, while not preferring one [worldly] thing over another.
>
> This is followed by disassociation (*nafḍ*) from the after-effects and traces of worldly attachments, such as desires and inclination towards various passions. In this way his essence becomes detached from those things and unites itself with the Truth. Such disassociation (*nafḍ*) signifies the vigorous motion of one thing away from another thing that is considered to be contemptible to oneself, just as one shakes the dust off of clothes.
>
> Next, renunciation (*tark*) signifies the pursuit of perfection for its own sake, that is, it consists in purgatively eliminating (*takhallī*) and severing (*inqiṭā'*) something away.
>
> Then comes total negation (*rafḍ*), which signifies carefree abandonment and complete disregard for everything.

73 Ṭūsī's commentary (*Sharḥ al-Ishārāt*) is reproduced in the form of marginal notes to S. Dunyā's published edition of the *Al-ishārāt*. Hamid Dabashi offers a good discussion of the significance of this commentary in Islamic philosophy in his essay on "Khwāja Naṣīr al-Dīn al-Ṭūsī: The philosopher/vizier and the intellectual climate of his times" in Oliver Leaman and S.H. Nasr (eds.), *History of Islamic Philosophy* (London: Routledge 1996), I, pp. 546ff.

As for the degrees of illumination (*taḥallī*), these may be summarized as follows:

When the gnostic severs his ties from his selfhood (*nafs*) and unites himself with the divine Truth, he sees all forms of power absorbed and enveloped in the divine Power, all forms of knowledge immersed and drowned in the divine Knowledge, from which no being is concealed, and all powers of will immersed within the divine Will, whose sway no being can evade. In fact, he perceives all existence and all perfections in existence to be proceeding by way of emanation from within Him.

Thereupon the divine Truth (*ḥaqq* = God) becomes his eye through which he gazes, his ear by which he hears, his strength by which he acts, his knowledge by which he understands, and his existence through which he gains being. And at this time the gnostic truly becomes "qualified with the Qualities of God."[74]

So this is the significance of (what Avicenna referred to as the) apprehension of mystical gnosis (*'irfān*) during the gathering together of divine Qualities within the inner nature of the disciple through force of sincerity. Subsequently these and other divine Qualities (e.g. Power, Knowledge, Will) although distinct and separate from one another, are all united in respect to their source in the One (*al-wāḥid*). Indeed, God's essential Knowledge is completely identical to His Will, and so on (with the other Qualities). And since there is no other essential being but God, neither is there any distinction between His Qualities and Essence, nor separation between the Essence and the Qualities. Rather, they are all one. As God Almighty says: "Verily, God is One."[75] And this Oneness is itself God, and nothing else besides Him exists.

And this same meaning is found in the statement of Shaykh (Ṭūsī, commenting on Avicenna's words that): "It (gnosis) culminates in the One," (where Ṭūsī states) "and there, neither the person who characterizes nor the

74 An allusion to the alleged ḥadīth: *takhallaqū bi-akhlāq Allāh.*

75 These exact words do not occur in the Qur'ān, but their sense is echoed in many similar verses, such as for example: V:73.

Object characterized, neither gnostic nor the Object of gnosis, remains, and this is the spiritual station of 'halting' (*maqām al-wuqūf*)."[76]

Now, there is nothing strange or cryptic about this matter. These words are just another way of expressing (*taqrīr-i dīgar*) the doctrine of the 'Unity of Being' (*waḥdat-i wujūd*), which is the most cherished delight[77] of the gnostics and the fruit fostered by the hearts of the saints.[78] And this statement also contains an allusion to the famous sacred tradition of the Prophet (*ḥadīth-i qudsī*): "My devotee, by performing acts of superogatory devotion, keeps approaching me, until I love him. When I love him, I am the ear by which he hears, the eye by which he sees, the tongue by which he speaks, the hand by which he grasps."[79] It is clear that this sublime matter is completely in accordance with both the [doctrines of the] philosophers (*ḥukamā*) and the esteemed Canon Law of Islam (*sharī'at*).

From what has been mentioned above, it is evident that the degree of gnosis (*ma'rifat*) is higher than that of philosophy (*ḥikmat*) and the Object sought by the gnostics (*'urafā'*) is dearer than that of the philosophers (*ḥukamā'*). For the latter aims to detach the rational soul from corporeality and attach it to the heavenly pleroma and the realm of pure immateriality. The aim of the gnostics, on the other hand, is to accomplish severance of their attention from all but God and to actually realize the station of annihilation (*fanā'*), merging into the World of Eternal Subsistence (*'ālam-i baqā'*).

Yet, the aims of both the gnostics and the philosophers are more exalted than those of the ascetics and religious devotees (*zuhād va 'ubbād*), for the latter group does not aim to transcend corporeality, but only struggles to overcome the physical pleasures of the flesh in the hope of obtaining the

---

76 *Al-ishārāt*, ed. S. Dunyā, p. 841.

77 Literally "the light of the eyes (*qurrat al-'ayn*)."

78 Although it may appear strange that the doctrine of the Unity of Being, which is usually ascribed to Ibn al-'Arabī, is held by Lāhījī to be here paraphrased by Ṭūsī, this is not entirely improbable, since "in his later years Ṭūsī turned towards Sufism," as Hermann Landolt points out in "Khwāja Naṣīr al-Dīn Ṭūsī (597/1201–672/1274), Ismā'īlism, and Ishrāqī Philosophy," in N. Pourjavady and Zh. Vesal (eds.) *Naṣīr al-Dīn Ṭūsī: Philosophe et savant du XIIIc siecle* (Tehran: Presses Universitaire d'Iran 2000), p. 30.

79 Cited in J. Nurbakhsh, *Traditions of the Prophet (Ahadith)*, trans. Leonard Lewisohn (New York: KNP 1981), p. 15.

joys of the hereafter. Explaining the difference between the ascetic (*zāhid*) and the religious devotee (*'ābid*) in his "Waystations of the Gnostics," Avicenna observes:

> The word 'ascetic' (*zāhid*) is a term used to denote someone who renounces and refrains from pursuit of the wares and passions of this world. The word 'devotee' (*'ābid*) is a term particularly used to designate one who is fastidious in practising acts of worship such as prayer, fasting, and so forth. The word 'knower' or 'gnostic' (*'ārif*) is a term used to refer to one who concentrates his thoughts upon the all-powerful sacrosanct realm of the Spirit (*quds al-jabarūt*), being continuously receptive to the effulgent radiance of the light of the Truth within his secret transconscious self (*sirr*),[80] and in this (spiritual work) there are some gnostics who subserviently follow others.[81]

In his exposition of the difference between the aims of the ascetic (*zāhid*), the religious devotee (*'ābid*) and the gnostic (*'ārif*) in the "Waystations of the Gnostics," Avicenna goes on to elaborate these matters further:

> For the non-gnostic (*ghayr al-'ārif*), asceticism (*zuhd*) is merely a sort of business transaction (*mu'āmalat*) in which one makes use of the wares of this world to purchase the goods of the hereafter. According to the gnostic, however, asceticism consists in the interior purification (*tanazzuh*) of his transconscious self (*sirr*) of all else but the Truth (God, *al-Ḥaqq*) and disdainfully considering (*takabbur*) everything but God to be insignificant.

---

80 This word literally means 'mystery', but here refers to the superconscious source of awareness within which the converse between God and man is held; in Sufism, it specifically "designates the intimate and ineffable centre of consciousness, the 'point of contact' between the individual and his Divine principle" as Titus Burckhardt in his *An Introduction to Sufi Doctrine*, trans. D. Matheson (Northamptonshire: Thorsons Ltd. 1976), p. 125, explains. Shams Inati's translation in *Ibn Sīnā and Mysticism* (Remarks and Admonitions: Part Four) (London: KPI 1996), pp. 81–82, of this word as "the innermost thought" is incorrect.

81 *Al-ishārāt,* ed. S. Dunyā, pp. 799–800.

> For the non-gnostic, worship of God (*'ibādat*) is merely a type of business transaction done, it would seem, merely for the sake of some reward and recompense gleaned in the world hereafter.
>
> But to the gnostic, worship is a sort of asceticism that is exercised by the will and powers of estimation and imagination in order to familiarize, focus and train them on the Truth and turn them away from the direction of pride. As a result, when experiencing the epiphany of the Truth (*yastajallā al-Ḥaqq*), his interior transcious self remains tranquil and without any obstruction, finding freedom in the illumination of resplendent aurorial lights, which then become a permanent predisposition within him. In this fashion, whenever his transconscious self wishes to gain access to the Light of Truth (*nūr al-Ḥaqq*) without being bothered by (variable) desires and designs – or rather, in fact, with their assistance – he may view this light and so wend his way totally absorbed in the path of holiness.[82]

In the first-cited passage above, he had observed that "there are some gnostics who subserviently follow others," – meaning that while it isn't requisite for every ascetic and devotee to be a gnostic, every gnostic must be of course both a devotee and an ascetic, yet also making clear that both asceticism and devotional worship are found to exist within the gnostic. In the second passage, he clarified the distinction between the gnostic and non-gnostic's form of asceticism and worship. The asceticism of non-gnostic is in reality a type of buying and bartering of the ephemeral wares of this world for the immutable wares of the hereafter; likewise, the non-gnostic's worship is a business transaction similar to that of a person who works with his eyes only fixed on the wage.

In contrast to this, the gnostic's asceticism is a means to purify and lustrate away everything except for God Almighty (from his heart) so that the interior psyche (*bāṭin*) is never distracted from its preoccupation with the Almighty. His asceticism is likewise a 'display of arrogance' (*takabbur*), in the sense of belittling and treating with contempt – for the sake of God – everything except God Almighty. Similarly, the gnostic's worship involves ascetically disciplining and training the powers of will and other faculties in

82 *Al-ishārāt*, ed. S. Dunyā, pp. 801–2.

order that while focusing (his thought in) his inner being on God Almighty, the interior psyche will be subservient and submissive and not create any disturbance for him, so that he not fall prey to the distractions of desire and passion. In the final chapter,[83] Avicenna goes on to say:

> When asceticism reaches its culmination, the gnostic's inner being becomes as it were a burnished mirror juxtaposed to the Face of God Almighty. Then the traces of divinity are presented to the mirror of the gnostic's inner being, so that he is showered with true raptures and delights. Inevitably he finds joy in himself. Having one regard fixed on himself and another focused on God, he still wavers irresolutely between these two.[84]

And so he continues in the final chapter:

> When the gnostic reaches such a station where sometimes his gaze is focused God and other times on himself, he must strengthen his will, resolving never to have any regard for himself any more, but rather to become absent from 'self', utterly annihilated from everything but God. All his attention and contemplation should be exclusively focused on the hierocosmos. If he does regard himself, however, it should be because he sees himself as endowed with such an [advanced] degree and fine distinctions. Now, when the gnostic

83 *Al-ishārāt*, ed. S. Dunyā, p. 833.

84 After citing Avicenna's Arabic text (see *Al-ishārāt*, ed. S. Dunyā, p. 833), Lāhījī provides a Persian translation-paraphrase of this passage. It is the latter that I have translated here, rather than Avicenna's original Arabic, which, however, may be more exactly translated as: "When [the gnostic's] asceticism reaches its culmination, his transconscious self (*sirr*) becomes a burnished mirror which faces God (*al-Ḥaqq*). Sublime delights are showered down upon him, so that his soul is enraptured with itself through what it has [been vouchsafed] of God's manifested traces. While he has his gaze fixed on God on the one hand, and his regard focused on himself on the other, he still wavers irresolutely [between these two]."

realizes this spiritual station, he certainly has attained the reality of 'Union'.[85]

– May God cause me and all seekers of Truth to realize this station!
May salutations and blessing of peace be upon
Muḥammad and his family!

85 This passage immediately follows the preceding citation from Avicenna's *Al-ishārāt* (ed. S. Dunyā, pp. 834–35), with Lāhījī again providing a Persian paraphrase of the passage, which I have translated here. Avicenna's original Arabic is far more succinct (as well as slightly different from the Persian rendition) and may be translated as follows: "Then he becomes absent from himself, solely focusing his sights on the hierocosmos. If he does perceive himself, it is simply because he is the one who sees, not to adorn and present himself in a favourable light. And this indeed is Union with God (*al-wuṣūl*)." See Lenn Goodman's (*Avicenna*, pp. 168–71, 189), for a good discussion of the meaning of *wuṣūl* in this passage.

XII

THE REALITY OF VISIONARY UNVEILING

Selections from Sabziwārī's (d. 1289/1873) Correspondence

Ḥājī Mullā Hādī Sabziwārī (d. 1289/1873) was the leading Persian philosopher of the nineteenth century, responsible for reviving the thought of Mullā Ṣadrā and establishing his school as the dominant influence in traditional circles in Persia down to the present day.[1] Although there were a number of other thinkers during the Qājār period, such as Mullā 'Alī Nūrī, Mullā 'Abdu'llāh Zunūzī, and Muḥammad Riḍā Qumsha'ī who taught and wrote on the works of Mullā Ṣadrā, Sabziwārī today remains the most popular and famous of them all. This is mostly due to his Arabic poem, *The Rhyme of Philosophy* (*Manzūma-yi ḥikmat*) and his commentary thereon (*Sharḥ-i Manzūma-yi ḥikmat*), in which he versified the fundamental ideas of Mullā Ṣadrā in a manner easily accessible and comprehensible to all students of Islamic philosophy.[2]

Hadī Sabziwārī was born in 1212/1797 in the town of Sabziwār in Khurāsān, Iran. At an early age he went to Mashhād where he studied

---

1 As S.H. Nasr observes: "Sabziwārī is the best known *ḥakīm* of the Qajar period and the only one about there are a few works in European languages." – "The Metaphysics of Ṣadr al-Dīn Shīrāzī and Islamic Philosophy in Qājār Iran," in *Qajar Iran: Political, Social, and Cultural Change, 1800–1925*, ed. Edmond Bosworth and Carole Hillenbrand (Costa Mesa: Mazda 1992), pp. 176–98 [p. 190]. Sajjad Rizvi points out that "it was the contribution of Sabzawari to the intellectual history of the Qajar period that established the school of Mulla Sadra, to the exclusion of other intellectual trends." – '*Hikma Muta'aliya* in Qajar Iran: Locating the Life and Work of Mulla Hadi Sabzawari (d. 1289/1873)', *Iranian Studies* 44/4 (2011), pp. 473–96 [p. 475].

2 Toshihiko Izutsu and Mehdī Muḥaqqiq (trans.), *Sharḥ al-Manẓūmah fī al-ḥikmah* (*The Metaphysics of Sabzawārī*) (Delmar, NY: Caravan 1977). For a good exposition of his philosophy, see Toshihiko Izutsu, "The Fundamental Structure of Sabziwārī's Metaphysics," in M. Mohaghegh and T. Izutsu (eds.), *Sharḥ-i Ghurur al-farā'id* (*Sharḥ-i Manẓūna-yi ḥikmat*) (Tehran: Dānishgāh-i Tehran and Montreal: Institute of Islamic Studies 1969), Part One; Metaphysics, pp. 1–151.

Arabic, jurisprudence, logic and Islamic law for a period of ten years.[3] In his early twenties, he travelled to Iṣfahān, which was the dominant centre for the study of philosophy, known as the 'Portal of Sciences of Persia', *Dār al-'ulūm-i Īrān*,[4] where he studied Mullā Ṣadrā's metaphysics under several of the leading representatives of that school, including Mullā 'Alī Nūrī (d. 1246/1830) and Mullā Ismā'il Isfahānī (d. 1268/1853), among several other teachers.[5] After remaining in Iṣfahān for eight years, Sabziwārī returned to his native province of Khurāsān, where he remained, teaching jurisprudence, principles of Islamic theology (*uṣūl al-dīn*), and philosophy in Mashhād for approximately five years (1826–31). After a brief visit to Sabzawār, he set out on a pilgrimage to Mecca.[6]

Upon his return from Mecca to Iran in 1834, due to the dangerous political circumstances and societal unrest throughout Persia, he first went to eastern Iran, where remained for a year working incognito as janitor in a madrasa in Kirmān.[7] Eventually, he made his way back north to his native Khurāsān, where he settled in Sabziwār with his family. There he was to spend the remaining forty years of his life teaching the throngs of students who now flocked to study with him from all corners of the Islamic world the sciences of jurisprudence, logic, metaphysics, theology, and Qur'ānic commentary, eventually dying at age seventy-seven in 1289/1873.

Hadī Sabziwārī was the author of a huge volume of works (some fifty-two books and treatises in both Arabic and Persian[8]) on diverse subjects such as philosophy (*ḥikmat*), logic, music jurisprudence, ethics, physics,

---

3 S.H. Nasr, "Hādī Sabzavārī," *EIr* XI, pp. 437–41 [p. 437]. A good general account of Sabzawārī's biography was penned by his grandson, Asrārī Sabzawārī, *Sharḥ-i zindigī-yi Ḥāj Mullā Hādī Sabzawārī*, published as an appendix to *Dīvān-i Mullā Hadī Sabzawārī (Asrār)*, ed. Aḥmad Karamī (Tehran: Intishārāt-i Tālār 1375 A.Hsh./1996), pp. 197–283.

4 Riḍā Qāsimī, "Ḥājj Mullā Hadī Sabziwārī," *Sufi* [Persian version] (London 1374 A.Hsh./1995), No. 27, pp. 6–15 [p. 7].

5 S.H. Nasr, "*Ḥājī Mulla Hādī Sabzawārī*," in *A History of Muslim Philosophy*, ed. M.M. Sharif (Wiesbaden: Otto Harrassowitz 1963), vol. 2, pp. 1543–58 [p. 1544]; Rizvi, "*Hikma Muta'aliya* in Qajar Iran," p. 478.

6 Nasr, "*Ḥājī Mulla Hādī Sabzawārī*," p. 1544; Rizvi, "*Hikma Muta'aliya* in Qajar Iran," p. 479; Qāsimī, "Ḥājj Mullā Hadī Sabziwārī," p. 7.

7 Qāsimī, "Ḥājj Mullā Hadī Sabziwārī," p. 7.

8 Nasr, "Hādī Sabzavārī," *EIr* XI, p. 438. Full titles of his works are given by Nasr, '*Ḥājī Mulla Hādī Sabzawārī*', pp. 1544–45; more detailed bibliographical information is

eschatology, Arabic grammar, Persian literature, Imāmology and Qur'ān commentary. Sabzawārī also held an extremely high rank as a mystical poet in the Sufi tradition of the gnostic ghazal (*ghazal-i 'ārifāna*), despite his meagre poetic output and the small size of his *Dīvān*. His poetry is still celebrated and sung among dervish séances in Iran today. His lyrics are particularly influenced by, and have been compared by eminent Iranian writers such as Sayyid Muḥammad 'Alī Jamālzādeh to the ghazals of Ḥāfiẓ (d. 791/1389).[9] Sabziwārī also composed an important philosophical commentary on the *Mathnawī* of Jalāl al-Dīn Rūmī (d. 672/1273).[10]

Although Ḥakīm Sabzawārī often identified himself as a dervish, his precise relationship with the Sufi *ṭarīqas* in Qājār Persia is a matter of dispute. According to one source, he was initiated into Sufism by the Ni'matullāhī Sufi master Munawwar 'Alī Shāh (d. 1301/1884).[11] He also was

---

furnished in Rizvi, '*Hikma Muta'aliya* in Qajar Iran', pp. 484–87, and Qāsimī, "Ḥājj Mullā Hadī Sabziwārī," pp. 9–12.

9 See Qāsimī, "Ḥājj Mullā Hadī Sabziwārī," p. 13. On Sabzawārī's imitation of Ḥāfiẓ, see Bahman Solati, *The Reception of Ḥāfiẓ: The Sweet Poetic Language of Ḥāfiẓ in Nineteenth and Twentieth Century Persia* (Leiden: Leiden University Press 2013), pp. 91–93. Ḥāfiẓ's influence is also discussed in 'Alī Falsafī's introduction to the *Dīvān-i Mullā Hadī Sabzawārī* (*Asrār*), ed. Aḥmad Karamī (Tehran: Intishārāt-i Tālār 1375 A.Hsh./ 1996), pp. 18–23.

10 Eliza Tasbihi, "Sabzawārī's *Sharḥ Asrār:* A Philosophical Commentary on Rūmī's *Mathnawī*," *Mawlana Rumi Review VII* (2106), pp. 175–96; John Cooper, 'Rūmī and *Ḥikmat:* Towards a Reading of Sabzawārī's Commentary on the *Mathnawī*', in *The Heritage of Sufism*, vol. I: *Classical Persian Sufism from its Origins to Rūmī (700–1300)*, ed. Leonard Lewisohn (Oxford: Oneworld 1999), pp. 409–33.

11 The Ni'matullahī master Dr. Javad Nurbakhsh (d. 2008) relates how "Ḥāj Mullā Sabzawārī received the *Yūnisīyya* litany to repeat from [the Ni'matullāhī master] Munawwar 'Alī Shāh [d. 1301/1884]. After several years it was then suggested [by Munawwar 'Alī Shāh] that he should be initiated with another invocation (*dhikr*). He [Sabzawārī] declared: 'The Yūnisīyya litany suffices me'." – Unpublished typescript of a discourse addressed to "the dervishes of Īrān," dated VII/1/1366 A.Hsh./1987 (author's personal archive). The 'Yūnisīyya' is a litany repeated 110 times based on Qur'ān XXI:88; for the its description and esoteric meaning, see Javād Nūrbakhsh, *Dar bihisht-i ṣūfiyān* (London: Intishārāt-i Khānqāh Ni'matullāhī 1362 A.Hsh./1983), pp. 143–44.

a close associate with the Dhahabī Sufi master Rāz-i Shīrāzī (d. 1286/1869),[12] who met him in 1854 and claimed that the Ḥakīm later sent "some ten to fifteen of his students to study as well as his son Ākhūnd Mullā Muḥammad to me. At his behest I inculcated and instructed them in the practice of *dhikr* (silent invocation of God)."[13] Another of Sabzawārī's famous students was the Ni'matullāhī-Gunabadī Sufi master Hajjī Muḥammad Kāẓim Tanbākū-furūsh (Sa'ādat 'Alī Shāh, d. 1289/1872).[14] His relationships to these Sufi masters alone constitutes adequate circumstantial evidence, I think, to establish that he was an initiate and practitioner of the Sufi tradition, a postulation supported by numerous verses in his *Dīvān*, such as the following:

> There's nothing true, all's false and counterfeit
> In the coinage of this universe. True coin alone exists
> In the alchemical glance of perfect dervishes.
>
> Nor is fire found in the burning bush that Moses
> In the Valley of Peace has seen. No, fire alone exists
> In the conflagration found in the hearts of dervishes.[15]

The biography of Ḥakīm Sabzawārī written by his grandson provides further evidence of his Sufi character, as can be seen from the following

12 On Sabzawārī's connection with Rāz-i Shīrāzī, see my "The *Qawā'im al-anwār* of Rāz-i Šīrāzī and Shi'ite Sufism in Qajar Persia," in Denis Hermann and Fabrizio Speziale (eds.), *Islam in the Indo-Iranian World during the Modern Epoch* (Berlin: Klaus Schwarz Verlag-IFRI. Collection Islamkundliche Untersuchungen: 2010), pp. 247–71 [p. 250].

13 Rāz-i Shīrāzī, *Qawā'im al-anwār wa tawālaʿ al-asrār*, ed. Khayru'llāh Maḥmūdī (Shīrāz: Intishārāt-i Daryā-yi nūr 1383 A.Hsh./2004), pp. xxiv–xxv.

14 On Sa'ādat 'Alī Shāh, see my "An Introduction to the History of Modern Persian Sufism," a 2-part study in *The Bulletin of the School of Oriental & African Studies* (vol. 61, pt. 3, Oct. 1998), pp. 437–64. [pp. 449–56]. On Sabzawārī and Sa'ādat 'Alī Shāh, see Nasr, "Hadī Sabziwārī," *EIr* XI, p. 439; Rizvi, '*Hikma Muta'aliya* in Qajar Iran', p. 484.

15 *Dīvān-i Mullā Hadī Sabzawārī* (*Asrār*), ed. Aḥmad Karamī (Tehran: Intishārāt-i Tālār 1375 A.Hsh./ 1996), pp. 88–89.

vignette where his piety and practical dervish ethics are extolled by his grandson:

> All during his life, his practice was to spend the last third of the night awake, entreating and beseeching God, reciting the supplication of *Jawshan-i kabīr*, and praying. His weeping and crying were so intense during that part of the night that his family, who were sleeping in the chamber upstairs, would be woken up upon hearing his nocturnal cries and lamentation ... The late Asrār[16] was so indifferent to the world and all therein – so abstinent from and inattentive to this perishable material realm that he was a living embodiment of the [Qur'ānic] verse: "[Naught of disaster befalleth in the earth or in yourselves but it is in a Book before We bring it into being – Lo! That is easy for God –] That you grieve not for the sake of that which has escaped you, nor yet exult because of that which has been given you.[17]
>
> His attitude of renunciation of the world had reached such a degree that all events appeared one and the same in his eyes – whether good or bad, blessings or adversities, illness or health – he considered these all to be essentially blessings emanating from his Beloved and acknowledged them all as divine theophanies. In other words, he only desired that God's Will be done, whatever that might be, seeing himself merely 'as a corpse in the hands of a mortician, who turns it howsoever he wills.[18]
>
> In this respect, it is related that once a person – whether sincerely or simply to put him to test – commented: 'This year thank God, everyone's crops and lands have fared well, especially your lands,

16 Ḥakīm Sabzawārī's penname.

17 Qur'ān LVII (Ḥadīd): 22–23 (Pickthall's translation with modifications).

18 Here the biographer is referring to the Sufi doctrine of 'Trust in God' (*tawakkul*). In the *Iḥyā*, Ghazālī notes that the third and highest stage of 'Trust in God' is that the devotee become (citing the same Arabic maxim): *mathala al-mayyit bayna yadī al-ghasal:* "The first station in *tawakkul* is that you become in God's Omnipotent Will like a corpse in the hands of a washerman, which he turns to and fro as he wills without any motion or volition on its part." This metaphor was first coined by Sahl Tustarī; see Gerhard Böwering, *The Mystical Vision of Existence in Classical Islam: The Qur'ānic Hermeneutics of Sahl At- Tustarī (d. 283/896)* (Berlin: Walter de Gruyter 1980), p. 76.

which have enjoyed a very fine harvest!' He responded by saying simply: 'Well, that's what they say.' That same person came back the following year, and told him: 'This year everyone's lands and crops have been visited by pestilences, and your lands have fared particularly bad; in fact, your entire harvest has been ruined.' Again, Ḥājī replied, 'Well, that's what they say.' Indeed, neither was he delighted by the statement of yesteryear by that man, nor aggrieved by the statement of the following year ...

[Following several pages of similar anecdotes ...] To sum up, the world was so small and insignificant in the eyes of that eminent man that if the noble verse: "Let those who would dread if they left behind their own helpless progeny have fear; let them reverence God and speak justly"[19] – had not prevented him, in a single day he would have given all his lands and properties away in charity for the sake of God's goodwill, as alms on the way of True Divine Beloved. To corroborate this statement, it is related that once someone came to him and said:

'You are a dervish, so why do you hold on to your properties, and not given everything away in charity?'

In reply, he said: 'You're absolutely right, but what can I do? None of my children are dervishes!?'[20]

Sabziwārī had a truly monumental impact upon Islamic philosophy in Persia, particularly that affiliated to the school of Mullā Ṣadrā. "He has been called 'the Plato of his time'," Henry Corbin pronounced, "and for good measure he is also said to be its Aristotle. In any case, he was for philosophy in the reign of Naṣīr al-Dīn Shāh (1848–1896) what Mullā Ṣadrā Shīrāzī had been in the reign of Shāh 'Abbās the Great."[21] His legacy is evoked by S.H. Nasr as follows:

---

19 Qur'ān IV (Nīsā): 9. The translation is from *The Study Quran: A New Translation and Commentary*, eds. S.H. Nasr, Caner Dagli, Maria Dakake, Joseph Lumbard (New York: HarperOne 2015), p. 192.

20 Asrārī Sabzawārī, *Sharḥ-i zindigī-yi Ḥāj Mullā Hādī Sabzawārī*, published as an appendix to *Dīvān-i Mullā Hadī Sabzawārī* (*Asrār*), ed. Aḥmad Karamī (Tehran: Intishārāt-i Tālār 1375 A.Hsh./ 1996), pp. 202–4.

21 Henry Corbin, *History of Islamic Philosophy*, trans. [from French] Liadain Sherrard (London: KPI in association with the Institute of Ismaili Studies 1996), p. 358. Corbin's comparison of Sabzawārī's position in Qājār Iran to that of Mullā Ṣadra under the Shāh

> Not only his own circle in Sabzavār was to flourish as a major center of Islamic philosophy throughout most of the 19th century, but he was also a major influence on the school of Tehran, the school of philosophy founded by Mollā 'Abd-Allāh Zonuzi in Tehran during the reign of Fatḥ 'Alī Shāh (1212–50/1797–1834) and which has continued to this day ... Sabzavār's *Šarḥ al-manẓuma* continues to be one of the most popular texts of *ḥekmat* studied in various traditional *madrasas*. Many commentaries have been written on it since its composition ... This work was also one of the first ones belonging to the school of Mollā Ṣadrā to be translated and analysed in a European language by Toshihiko Izutsu and Mehdi Mohaghegh (1977). The influence of Sabzavārī continues in Persia, while it is now growing elsewhere with greater interest being shown in both the East and the West in the thought of Mollā Ṣadrā and later Persian philosophers.[22]

* * *

The following translation is taken from Sabzawārī's Collected Treatises in Persian and Arabic (*Rasā'il*), a volume over a thousand pages long, comprising the collected Persian and Arabic treatises of Sabziwārī on "gnostic, philosophical and theological problems of the profoundest nature."[23] These treatises, "whose diversity enables us to understand the day-by-day preoccupations of Mullā Hādī Sabzawārī's contemporaries,"[24] are nearly all written in the form of answers to questions posed by disciples or other scholars. They are divided into two sections: Persian and Arabic, with each treatise being numbered separately.

The short offering presented here from his treatises gives a unique and succinct account of the great philosopher's opinion about the reality of gnosis and the various modes of esoteric knowledge. This chapter thus

'Abbās is in fact a direct quotation from Ma'ṣūm 'Alī Shāh Shīrāzī, *Ṭarā'iq al-ḥaqā'iq*, ed. M.J Maḥjūb (Tehran: Kitābkhāna-yi Bārānī 1345 /1966), vol. III, p. 465.

22 Nasr, "Hādī Sabzavārī," *EIr* XI, p. 440.

23 Sabziwārī, *Rasā'il*, ed. with introduction and notes by Sayyid Jalāl al-Dīn Āshtiyānī (Mashhād: Mashhad University Press 1970); from the English introduction by S.H. Nasr, p. 3. The section from the treatise translated here is on pages 23–26.

24 Corbin, *History of Islamic Philosophy*, p. 361.

clearly demonstrates how the Sufi doctrine of *kashf* was transmitted from the thirteenth down to nineteenth centuries, and how Ibn 'Arabī, Mullā Ṣadrā, and Sabziwārī all endorsed the same basic doctrines of gnosis and visionary unveiling with very little distinction in their mystical theologies. A closer and more careful comparison of their writings on this subject, could that be presented here, would no doubt demonstrate, for instance, that all three thinkers described the various types of *kashf* as epiphanies of divine Names and as the direct product and outcome of spiritual discipline and contemplative practice.

Following the Sufis, Sabziwārī pronounces visionary unveiling (*kashf*) to be the "fundamental principle" of Islamic *ḥikmat* philosophy. There are two types of *kashf*: spiritual and supraformal (*ma'nawī*), or sensory and formal (*ṣūrī*). The supraformal unveiling enables the gnostic to apprehend the self, God or the affairs of the hereafter through intuitive conjecture (*ḥads*) and meditative reflection (*fikr*). (Here, of course, Sabzawārī's views bears close comparison with the doctrine of these terms enunciated in the final part of Mullā Ṣadrā's *Mafātīḥ al-ghayb* translated above.)

To clarify his teaching, the Qājār sage falls back on the traditional Sufi doctrine of the three levels of certitude:

A. Theoretical knowledge of certitude (*'ilm al-yaqīn*)
B. Direct observational certitude (*'ayn al-yaqīn*)
C. The true reality of certitude (*ḥaqq al-yaqīn*)

These three degrees he likens to apprehending fire by smelling smoke (= A), feeling fire by seeing its light (= B), and burning up in the fire to the point of being conjoined with it like glowing red-hot pieces of iron (= C). These degrees of intellectual clairvoyance correspond in turn to the three hierarchical degrees of faith held by three types of believers:

A. Believers in the Supernatural (*mu'minīn bi'l-ghayb*)
B. Knowers of God for whom the veil is rent aside (*'ālim bi'llāh*)
C. The realized gnostic of God (*'ārif-i rabbānī*).

Lastly the author describes different types of 'sensory visionary unveiling' (*kashf-i ṣūrī*), which pertain to the ocular, olfactory faculties and the faculty of touch, which occur through the epiphany of various divine Names. He concludes his exposition of *kashf* on a fittingly modern and ecumenical note, remarking that "diversity and variety of methods employed by adepts in visionary unveiling" is good, even necessary: "This diversity, whether in respect to the wayfarer's theory or practice, should not present any hindrance or obstacle to the progress of the wayfarer. Variety and diversity are found everywhere."

By way of illustration of Sabziwārī's doctrine of *kashf*, below I have translated a short section from a treatise (twenty-seven pages long and second in order in the first section of the *Rasā'il*) entitled *Javāb-i Masā'il-i Āqā Mīrzā Abū'l-Ḥassan Raḍawī* (Answers to the Questions posed by Abū'l-Ḥassan Raḍawī), which contains Sabziwārī's succinct yet profoundly wide-ranging, original answer (pp. 23–26) to a question posed by Raḍawī on the reality of the visionary unveiling (*kashf*) possessed the Sufis. The question posed by Raḍawī is as follows:

> Is the method of visionary unveiling and presential knowledge (*ṭarīqa-yi kashf u shuhūd*) to which the learned Sufi scholars refer, truthful or not? Is it easy or difficult? Considering the differences, diversity and variety of methods employed amongst adepts in visionary unveiling (*kashf*), how can one have sure faith in the veracity of visionary unveiling?

Sabzawārī's reply then follows.

* * *

Visionary unveiling (*kashf*) is a fundamental principle, and is of two sorts: either spiritual and supraformal (*ma'nawī*), or sensory and formal (*ṣūrī*).

The spiritual, supra-formal type consists of an intellectual unveiling in which transcendent subjects such as the knowledge of self, knowledge of God and of the hereafter are grasped by means of intuitive conjecture (*ḥads*),[25] or else ascertained through meditative thought (*fikr*) with a greater

25 Jurjānī in his *Ta'rīfāt*, ed. Ibrāhīm al-Abyārī (Beirut: Dār al-Kitāb al-'Arabī 1405 A.H./ 1984), s.v., defines *ḥads* as "the mind's swift transference from preliminary matters to basic propositions. It stands in contrast to thought (*al-fikr*). Intuitive conjecture is the lowest degree of visionary unveiling (*al-kashf*). See also n. 28 in Mullā Ṣadrā's translation of *Mafātīḥ al-ghayb*.

degree of clarity and luminosity than can be obtained by the pursuit of the (other) veridical sciences of Reality (*'ulūm-i ḥaqīqīyya*).

On the other hand, visionary unveiling may occur in a different (i.e. non-intellectual) manner, in which case one descends from [the level of abstract] reason down to [the plane of physical] activity, until at last, one's theoretical knowledge of certitude (*'ilm al-yaqīn*) culminates in the degree of direct observational certitude (*'ayn al-yaqīn*) which ultimately leads to the (highest degree of) reality of certitude (*ḥaqq al-yaqīn*). God Almighty has thus enumerated these various degrees of certitude using the image of a burning fire, where He said, "Alas! Indeed, would that you could know with a knowledge that is certain that you will surely see hell-fire! And yet again, that you will see it with the very eye of certainty (*'ayn al-yaqīn*)."[26] The degree of the reality of certitude is also described in another passage in the holy scripture where God states, "and the roasting in hell-fire. Indeed, that is a truth that is certain (*ḥaqq al-yaqīn*)." Although God in this passage speaks of the infernal depths of the darkness of punishment in hellfire, the various paths described, whether these are of darkness, fire or light are all ultimately one, since all of them are but different signs of the divine light (*āyat-i nūru'llāh*).

Therefore, degrees of knowledge of God's light resemble degrees of knowledge of fire. This phenomenon might be compared to someone who has never seen fire but has heard that there is a certain kind of entity which causes anything that touches it to be totally transformed into itself. That entity is also able to impart something of itself to any candle or lamp without thereby experiencing any loss or diminution. At the same time, anything which becomes separated and disconnected from that entity is transformed into something of quite a contrary nature, which is similar to murky smoke.

Now, in [this realm of] darkness, this entity [fire] acts as the vicegerent of those Supernal Lights. Even if one takes a tiny bit of that entity – the size of a pine needle, say – and sets it in the middle of a gathering, it illuminates and brightens the entire assembly so all the various forms, shapes and colours there become immediately clear and apparent through its light. Thus, the pine-needle-sized thing becomes the source of delight for that gathering, and even the most priceless, precious stones laid out there on display there cannot achieve the same effect which that little object achieves.

Hence, just as the sun is endowed with the rank of greater deputyship [in the heavens], that entity in terms of its brightness, maturity, modulation

26 Qur'ān CII:5–7.

and warmth, is endowed with the position of lesser deputyship [here upon the earth] from God Almighty, since "There is no power and no strength except through God."[27] Here below, this entity is dubbed with different names such as fire, flame, combustion and so forth.

There are some people, of course, whose belief in fire is entirely founded on blind imitation. Others there are who seek that fire by means of smoke or some other effect. The belief and conviction of such folk in the existence of fire is comparable to the faith in the supernatural realm obtained by means of rational proofs.

Still others there are who actually apprehend His light and contemplate Him, so that they witness the sphere of fire itself. For them the veil has been rent aside. Such folk are comparable to adepts who have realized the degree of direct observational certitude (*aṣḥāb-i ʿayn al-yaqīn*) in respect to mystical knowledge of God Almighty.

Lastly, there are people who, through their being conjoined with fire, have become like glowing red-hot pieces of iron in the midst of fire, the effects of the fire having become visibly apparent upon them. Such folk are comparable to adepts who have attained to the (highest degree of) the reality of certitude (*ḥaqq al-yaqīn*) in respect to mystical knowledge of God Almighty.

Therefore, the adepts in the last two groups are those who have attained true visionary experience and a clearly evident faith (*kashf-i ḥaqīqī u īmān-i ʿayānī*) and who are the true gnostics of God (*ʿārif-i rabbānī*).

The group immediately before them[28] are the 'believers in the Supernatural' (*mu'minīn bi'l-ghayb*)[29] who are ranked in different degrees and who are 'knowers of God' (*ʿālim bi'llāh*), but not 'realized gnostics of God' (*ʿārif bi'llāh*).

Now, the sensory–formal type of visionary unveiling (*kashf-i ṣūrī*) consists in the imaginalization of forms (*tamaththul-i ṣuwar*)[30] to the five

27 This is a famous, oft-cited *ḥadīth*. Referring to: *La hawla wala quwwata illa billahil aliyyil adheem*: There is no power, and no strength, except through God the Most High, the Greatest. Muḥammad Bāqir Majlisī, *Biḥār al-anwār* (Beirut: Dār iḥyā al-tirāth al-ʿarabī, 2nd edn), vol. 90, p. 184.

28 I.e. those who seek 'fire by means of smoke', whose faith is based on rational proofs.

29 An allusion to Qur'ān II:3.

30 On the concept of imaginalization in Sufi esotericism, see Leonard Lewisohn, "In Quest of Annihilation: Imaginalization and Mystical Death in the *Tamhīdāt* of ʿAyn

senses in all their fine and minute details. Such experiences of visionary unveiling then are further partitioned up into the physical dimensions of the fivefold sensory faculties into which they descend. Thus, for instance, ocular visionary unveiling (*kashf-i baṣarī*), such as the visions experienced by ascetics among adepts who have attained dispassionate detachment (*aṣḥāb-i tajrīd az murtāḍīn*),[31] has various categories of luminosity and brightness (each of which will be explained in its own proper place), whether these relate to (physical) forms (*ashkāl*) or (imaginal) shapes (*ashbāḥ*).

As for the auditory type (of visionary unveiling: [*kashf-i*] *sam'ī*) which comes about through the cavity of the faculty of hearing, this experience arises through hearing exhilarating sounds or delightful words or else frightening sounds that communicate terror and threats of punishment which are allowed to enter the bosom of the mystical wayfarer due to some kind of bad conduct on his part.

As for the olfactory type (of visionary unveiling: [*kashf-i*] *shammī*), such experiences are like the inhalation of the breezes (as the *ḥadīth* relates): 'Divine breezes from your Lord waft through the days of your life. Heed them.'[32] This experience enables one to relish the taste of the saying of the Prophet: "I pass the night with my Lord who gives me food and drink."[33]

An example of the type (of visionary unveiling) pertaining to touch ([*kashf-i*] *lamsī*) can be found in the Prophet's saying: "God placed his palm between my shoulders and I felt its coolness between my breasts."[34]

Now, the sensory and formal type of visionary unveiling (*kashf-i ṣūrī*) is a characteristic property of the theophany of two divine Names: 'the All-Hearing' (*samī'*) and 'the All-Seeing' (*baṣīr*), and is apprehended by means of the Name 'the All-Informed' (*khabīr*).

---

al-Quḍat Hamadānī" in *idem., The Heritage of Sufism* (Oxford: Oneworld 1999), I, p. 329f.

31 On *tajrīd*, see J. Nurbakhsh, *Sufi Symbolism* XII, pp. 72–82.

32 On this *ḥadīth*, see J. Nūrbakhsh, *Traditions of the Prophet* II, p. 10.

33 See Badī' al-Zamān Furūzānfar, *Aḥadīth-i Mathnawī*, 3rd edn (Tehran: Intishārāt-i Amīr Kabīr 1361 A.Hsh./1982), pp. 36, 88.

34 This *ḥadīth* cited in 'Alī ibn Sulṭān Muḥammad al-Qārī and Muḥammad ibn 'Abdullāh al-Khaṭībī al-Tabrīzī, *Mirqāt al-mafātīḥ, Sharḥ mishkāt-i al-maṣābīḥ* (Beirut: Dār al-kutub al-'ilmīyah 2001), vol. 90, 184.

The spiritual, supra-formal type [of visionary unveiling] is a characteristic property of the manifestation of the divine Name 'the Wise Omniscient One' (*'alīm-i ḥakīm*).

But as for the question of the ease or difficulty of this method (of visionary unveiling), it has been understood that the ascetic path (*ṭarīq-i murtaḍawīyya*) is quite a difficult one, but when travelled with love and yearning it does become easy. (As Shaykh Bahā'ī says):

Reckon painful suffering to be ease
when the object of your quest is grand,
A cloud of dust cast up by a flock of sheep
is collyrium to the eyes of a wolf.[35]

As for the question of the differences, diversity and variety of methods employed by adepts in visionary unveiling: this diversity, whether in respect to the wayfarer's theory or practice, should not present any hindrance or obstacle to the progress of the wayfarer. Variety and diversity are found everywhere. In the Speech of God, who is the truest and most reliable of authors, is not variety found – as well in the manifest dimension of the traditions (*aḥādīth*) of the prophets and the saints? And in this situation, it is necessary that the wayfarer exert his utmost effort in pursuit of the (divine) sciences and esoteric knowledge until at last he perceives the harmony and compatibility between these diverse methods.

– And may God's peace and forgiveness be upon them (i.e. the Sufis).
Written in the month of *Rabī' al-awwal,*
in the year 1276 (1859)

35 *Kulliyāt-i ash'ār u āthār-i fārsī-yi Shaykh Bahā'ī*, ed. Sa'īd Nafīsī (Tehran: Nashr-i Chakāma, n.d.), Mathnawī-yi Nūn u ḥalvā, p. 161.

SELECTED BIBLIOGRAPHY

BOOKS

S. Waheed Akhtar, *Early Shiʿite Imāmiyyah Thinkers* (New Delhi: Ashish Publication 1988).

Mohammad Ali Amir-Moezzi, *The Divine Guide in Early Shiʿism: The Sources of Esotericism in Islam*, trans. D. Streight (Albany: SUNY Press 1994).

Arthur John Arberry, *The Koran Interpreted* (Oxford: Oxford University Press 1983).

Muhammad Asad, *The Message of the Qur'ān* (Gibraltar: Dar al-Andalus 1980).

Rūzbihān Baqlī, *Sharḥ-i shaṭḥiyyāt*, ed. Henry Corbin (Tehran: Institut Français d'Iranologie 1981).

Shahzad Bashir, *Fazlallah Astarabadi and the Hurufis* (London: Oneworld Academic 2005).

Robert Beulay, *La Lumière sans forme: Introduction à l'étude de la mystique chrétienne syro-orientale* (Chevetogne: Monastere de Chevetogne, n.d.).

Ugo Bianchi, *Selected Essays on Gnosticism, Dualism and Mysteriosophy* (Supplements to *Numen* XXXVIII) (Leiden: Brill 1978).

Joseph Bidez and Franz Cumont, *Les Mages hellénisés: Zoroastre, Ostanès et Hystaspe d'apres la tradition grècque* (Paris: Société d'Edition "Les Belles Lettres" 1913).

Edgar Blochet, *Etudes sur le gnosticisme musulman* (Rome: Casa editrice italiana,1913).

Gerhard Böwering, *The Mystical Vision of Existence in Classical Islam: The Qur'ānic Hermeneutics of the Ṣūfī Sahl At-Tustarī (d. 283/896)* (Berlin: Walter de Gruyter 1980).

Meïr Max Bravmann, *The Spiritual Background of Early Islam: Studies in Ancient Arab Concepts* (Leiden: Brill 1972).

Titus Burckhardt, *An Introduction to Sufi Doctrine*, trans. D. Matheson (Northamptonshire: Thorsons Ltd. 1976).

———, *Mirror of the Intellect: Essays on Traditional Science and Sacred Art*, trans. W. Stoddart (Cambridge: Quinta Essentia 1987).

Ḥāfiz Rajab al-Bursī, *Mashāriq anwār al-yaqīn fī asrār Amīr al-Mu'minīn* (Beirut: n.p. 1379/1959).

William Chittick, *Ibn ʿArabī's Metaphysics of Imagination: The Sufi Path of Knowledge* (Albany: SUNY Press 1989).

———, *The Self-Disclosure of God: Principles of Ibn al-ʿArabī's Cosmology* (Albany: SUNY Press 1998).

Ronald E. Clements, *It Is Written: Scripture Citing Scripture* (Cambridge: Cambridge University Press 1988): 67–82.

Henry Corbin, *Histoire de la philosophie islamique* (Paris: Gallimard 1964).

———, *L'École Shaykhie en Théologie Shi'ite* (Tehran: Tabān Publication 1967).

———, *En islam iranien* (Paris: Gallimard 1972).

———, *Cyclical Time and Ismaili Gnosis*, trans. Ralph Manheim and James Morris (London: KPI in association with Islamic Publications 1983).

———, *Temple and Contemplation*, trans. Phillip Sherrard (London: KPI in association with the Institute of Ismaili Studies 1986).

———, *Spiritual Body and Celestial Earth: From Mazdean Iran to Shīʿite Iran*, trans. N. Pearson (London: I.B. Tauris 1990).

———, *The Voyage and the Messenger*, trans. J. Rowe (Berkeley: North Atlantic Books 1998)

Sir Jehangir Cooverji Coyajee, *Cults and Legends of Ancient Iran and India* (Bombay: Jahangir B. Karani's sons 1936).

Herbert Davidson, *Alfarabi, Avicenna & Averroes on Intellect: Their Cosmologies, Theories of Active Intellect, & Theories of Human Intellect* (Oxford: Oxford University Press 1992).

Eric Robertson Dodds, *Proclus: The Elements of Theology* (Oxford: 2nd edn, Clarendon Press 1963).

Alireza Doostdar, *The Iranian Metaphysicals: Explorations in Science, Islam, and the Uncanny* (Princeton: Princeton University Press 2018).

Dr. Sulaymān Dunyā's edition of *Al-ishārāt wa'l-tanbīhāt* (Cairo: Dār al-maʿārif al-miṣr 1960).

Gerald Elmore, *Islamic Sainthood in the Fullness of Time: Ibn al-ʿArabī's Book of the Fabulous Griffin* (Leiden: Brill 1998).

Toufic Fahd (ed.), *Le Shīʿisme Imāmite* (Paris: Presses Universitaires de France 1970).

Antoine Faivre, *Access to Western Esotericism* (Albany: SUNY Press 1994).

———, *The Eternal Hermes*, trans. Jocelyn Godwin (Grand Rapids: Phanes Press 1995).

Majid Fakhry, *Ethical Theories in Islam* (Leiden: Brill 1994).

———, *Islamic Philosophy, Theology and Mysticism* (Oxford: Oneworld 1997).

Abdul Ghafoor Ravan Farhadi, *ʿAbdullāh Anṣārī of Herāt (1006–1089 C.E.): An Early Ṣūfī Master* (London: Curzon Press 1996).

Saʿīd al-Dīn Farghānī, *Mashāriq al-darārī: Sharḥ-i Tā'iyya-yi Ibn Fāriḍ*, ed. Jalāl al-Dīn Ashtiyānī (Mashhād: Dānishgāh-i Firdawsī 1357 A.Hsh./1978).

John F. Finamore, *Iamblichus and the Theory of the Vehicle of the Soul* (Salem: The American Philological Association 1985).

Garth Fowdan, *The Egyptian Hermes: A Historical Approach to the Late Pagan Mind* (Princeton: Princeton University Press 1993).

Badīʿ al-Zamān Furūzānfar, *Aḥādīth-i Mathnawī* (Tehrān: 3rd edn, Amīr Kabīr 1361 A.Hsh./ 1982).

Abu Hamid Muhammad al-Ghazali, *The Incoherence of the Philosophers*, trans. Michael Marmura (Provo: Brigham Young University Press 1997).

Claude Gilliot, *Exégèse, Langue et Théologie en Islam, L'Exégèse coranique de Ṭabarī (m. 311/923)* (Paris: Librairie Philosophique J. Vrin, Études 1990).

Daniel Goleman, *Emotional Intelligence* (New York: Bantam Books 1995).

Joanna de Groot, *Religion, Culture and Politics in Iran* (London: I.B. Tauris 2007).

Dimitri Gutas, *Greek Wisdom Literature in Arabic Translation: A Study of the Graeco-Arabic Gnomologia* (New Haven: American Oriental Society 1975).

Shams al-Dīn Muhammad Ḥāfiẓ Shīrāzī, *Dīwān-i Ḥāfiẓ*, ed. Parwīz Nātil Khanlarī (Tehran: 2nd edn, Sahāmī ʿām 1362 A.Hsh./1983).

Husayn ibn Mansur Hallaj, *Hallaj: Poems of a Sufi Martyr*, trans. Carl W. Ernst (Evanston: Northwestern University Press 2018).

Jābir b. Ḥayyān, *Kitāb al-Khamsīn,* in *Mukhtār Rasā'il Jābir b. Ḥayyān*, ed. Paul Kraus. (Paris/Cairo: Maktab al-Ḥānijī 1935).

Th. Emil Homerin (trans.), *ʿUmar ibn al-Fāriḍ: Sufi Verse, Saintly Life* (New York: Paulist Press 2001).

ʿAlī ibn Uthmān Hujwīrī, *The Kashf al-maḥjūb: The Oldest Persian Treatise on Sufism*, trans. R.A. Nicholson, Gibb Memorial Series no. 17 (1911; repr. London: 1976).

Faquir Hunzai (trans.), *Nāṣir Khusraw: Knowledge and Liberation: A Treatise on Philosophical Theology* (London: I.B. Tauris 1998).

Wladimir Ivanow, *Ibn al-Qaddāḥ, the Alleged Founder of Ismāʿīlism* (Bombay: 2nd edn, 1957).

Farid Jabre, *Le Notion de la Maʿrifa chez Ghazali* (Beirut: Éditions Les Lettres Orientales 1958).

———, *Essai sur le Lexique de Ghazali* (Beirut: Éditions Les Lettres Orientales 1979).

Syed Hussain Muhammad Jafri, "The Early Development of Legitimist Shīʿism with special reference to the role of Imām Jaʿfar al-Ṣādiq," Ph.D. thesis, University of London 1966.

———, *The Origins and Early Development of Shiʿa Islam* (London: Longman 1979).

Jules Janssens, *Ibn Sina and his influence on the Arabic and Latin World* (London: Routledge 2018).

Hans Jonas, *The Gnostic Religion* (Boston: Beacon Press repr. 1991).

Frederick de Jong and Bernd Radtke (eds.) *Islamic Mysticism Contested: Thirteen Centuries of Controversies and Polemics* (Leiden: Brill 1999).

Mīr Sayyid Sharīf Jurjānī, Definitions of Jurjānī (*Kitāb al-taʿrīfāt*), ed. Ibrāhīm al-Abyārī (Beirut: 1985).

———, *Taʿrīfat-i Jurjānī*, translated into Persian by Ḥasan Sayyid ʿArab and Sīmā Nūrbakhsh (Tehran: Farzān 1377 A.Hsh./1999).

ʿAbd al-Razzāq Kāshānī, *A Glossary of Sufi Technical Terms*, trans. Nabil Safwat (London: Octagon Press 1991).

———, *Laṭā'if al-aʿlām fī ishārāt-i ahl al-ilhām*, ed. Majīd Hādīzādih (Tehran: Mirāth-i Maktūb 2000).

Annebel Keeler, *Sufi Hermeneutics: The Qur'ān Commentary by Rashīd al-Dīn Maybudī* (Oxford: OUP in association with the Institute of Ismaili Studies 2006).

———, and Sajjad Rizvi (eds.), *The Spirit and the Letter: Approaches to the Esoteric Interpretation of the Qur'an* (London: I.B. Tauris in association with the Institute of Ismaili Studies 2017).

Peter Kingsley, *Ancient Philosophy, Mystery, and Magic* (Oxford: Clarendon Press 1995).

Joel L. Kramer, *Philosophy in the Renaissance of Islam: Abū Sulaymān al-Sijistānī and His Circle* (Leiden: Brill 1986).

Paul Kraus, *Jabir ibn Hayyan: Contribution à l'histoire des idées scientifiques dans l'Islam* (Paris: Les belles lettres 1986).

J. Michael LaFarque, *Language and Gnosis: The Opening Scenes of the Acts of Thomas* (Philadelphia: Fortress Press 1985).

Muḥammad Lāhījī, *Mafātīḥ al-i'jāz fī sharḥ-i Gulshan-i rāz*, ed. Muḥammad Riḍā Barzgār Khāliqī and 'Iffat Karbāsī (Tehran: Zawwar 1371 A.Hsh./1992).

Oliver Leaman and S.H. Nasr (eds.), *History of Islamic Philosophy* (London: Routledge 1996).

Leonard Lewisohn, *Beyond Faith and Infidelity* (Richmond: Curzon Press 1995).

———, (ed.), *Dīwān-i Muḥammad Shīrīn Maghribī* (Tehran: Tehran University Press; London: SOAS Publications 1993).

———, *Hafiz and the Religion of Love in Classical Persian Poetry* (London: I.B. Tauris 2010).

———, *Late Classical Persianate Sufism: The Safavid and Mughal Period* (Oxford: Oneworld 1999).

———, *The Heritage of Sufism*, vol. 1 (Oxford: Oneworld 1999).

———, *Hafiz and the Religion of Love in Classical Persian Poetry* (London: I.B. Tauris 2010).

——— and David Morgan (eds.), *The Heritage of Sufism*, vol. 3 (Oxford: Oneworld 1999).

———, and Reza Tabandeh, *Sufis and Their Opponents in the Persianate World* (Irvine: UCI Jordan Center for Persian Studies 2020).

Hans Lewy, *Chaldean Oracles and Theurgy: Mysticism, Magic and Platonism in the Later Roman Empire*, revised ed. Michel Tardieu (Paris: Institut des Études Augustiniennes 1978).

Andrew Louth, *The Origins of the Christian Mystical Tradition, from Plato to Denys* (Oxford: Oxford University Press 1991).

Joseph E.B. Lumbard, *Ahmad Al-Ghazali, Remembrance, and the Metaphysics of Love* (Albany: SUNY Press 2016).

George Makdisi, *The Rise of Humanism in Classical Islam and the Christian West* (Edinburgh: Edinburgh University Press 1990).

Louis Massignon, *Essai sur les origines du lexique technique de la mystique musulmane* (Paris: Librairie Orientaliste Paul Geuthner 1992 repr.).

Martin J. McDermott, *The Theology of Al-Shaikh al-Mufīd (d. 413/1022)* (Beirut: Dār al-Mashriq 1978).

Dan Merkur, *Gnosis: An Esoteric Tradition of Mystical Visions and Unions* (Albany: SUNY Press 1993).

Philip Merlan, *Monophychism, Mysticism, Metaconsciousness: The problems of the soul in the neoaristotlelian and neoplatonic tradition,* Martinus Nijhoff (The Hague: 2nd edn, 1969).

Orkhan Mir-Kasimov, *Unity in Diversity: Mysticism, Messianism and the Construction of Religious Authority in Islam* (Leiden: Brill 2013).

———, *Words of Power: Ḥurūfī Teachings between Shiʿism and Sufism in Medieval Islam* (London: I.B. Tauris 2015).

ʿAbdu'llāh Ibn al-Mubārak al-Marwazī, *Kitāb al-zuhd wa'l-raqā'iq,* ed. al-Aʿjamī. Mālīka' (1966).

Ṣamad Muwaḥḥid (ed.), *Majmūʿa-i āthār-i Shaykh Maḥmūd Shabistarī* (Tehran: Kitābkhāna-i fiahūrī 1365 A.Hsh./1986).

Seyyed Hossein Nasr, *An Introduction to Islamic Cosmological Doctrines* (London: Thames and Hudson 1978).

———, *Ṣadr al-Dīn Shīrāzī and his Transcendent Theosophy: Background, Life and Works* (Tehran: Imperial Iranian Academy of Philosophy 1978).

——— (ed.), *Ismāʿīlī Contributions to Islamic Culture* (Tehran: Imperial Iranian Academy of Philosophy 1977).

Ian Netton, *Seek Knowledge: Thought and Travel in the House of Islam* (London: Curzon 1996).

Louis Alphonse Daniel Nicolas, *Essai sur le Chéikhisme,* vol. 1: *Cheikh Aḥmed Lahçahi* (Paris: Paul Geuthner 1910).

———, *Essai sur le Chéikhisme,* vol. 2: *Séyyèd Kazem Rechti* (Paris: Paul Geuthner 1910).

———, *Essai sur le Chéikhisme,* vol. 3: *La Doctrine* (Paris: Paul Geuthner 1911).

———, *Essai sur le Chéikhisme,* vol. 4: *La Science de Dieu* (Paris: Paul Geuthner 1911).

Javad Nurbakhsh, *Traditions of the Prophet (Ahadith),* trans. L. Lewisohn (New York: KNP 1981).

———, *Spiritual Poverty in Sufism,* trans. L. Lewisohn (London: KNP 1984).

———, *Sufi Symbolism,* trans. T. Graham et al. (London: KNP 1988).

Paul Nywia, *Exégèse coranique et langage mystique* (Beirut: Dar el-Mashreq 1970).

John Penrice, *A Dictionary and Glossary of the Koran* (London: Curzon Press 1979 repr.).

Gavin Picken, *Spiritual Purification in Islam: The Life and Works of al-Muhasibi* (London: Routledge 2014).

Abd al-Razzāq al-Qāshānī, *A Glossary of Sufi Technical Terms,* trans. Nabil Safwat (London: Octagon Press 1991).

W. Rajkowski, "Early Shīʿism in Iraq," Ph.D. dissertation, University of London 1955.

Sayyid Kāẓim Rashtī, *Dalīl al-mutaḥayyirīn* (Najaf: 1364/1944).

———, *Collection of Treatises* (Tabrīz: lithography 1276/1954).

Richard August Reitzenstein and Hans Heinrich Schaeder, *Studien zum antiken Synkretismus aus Iran und Griechenland* (Leipzig: B.G. Teubner 1926).

Helmutt Ritter, *The Ocean of the Soul: Men, the World and God in the Stories of Farīd al-Dīn ʿAṭṭār*, trans. John O'Kane and Bernd Radtke (Leiden: Brill 2003).

Franz Rosenthal, *Knowledge Triumphant: The Concept of Knowledge in Medieval Islam* (Leiden: Brill 1970).

Jalálu'ddín Rúmí, *The Mathnawí*, trans. Reynold A. Nicholson (8 vols. London & Leiden: 1925–40; repr. London: Luzac 1982).

Julius Ruska, *Tabula Smaragdina* (Heidelberg: Carl Winter's Universitätsbuchhandlung 1926).

Mohammed Rustom, *The Triumph of Mercy: Philosophy and Scripture in Mullā Ṣadrā* (Albany: SUNY Press 2012).

———, *Inrushes of the Heart: The Sufi Philosophy of ʾAyn al-Quḍāt* (Albany: SUNY Press 2023).

Abdulaziz Sachedina, "The Doctrine of Madhiism in Imāmī Shīʿism," Ph.D. dissertation, University of Toronto 1976.

Liana Saif, Francesca Leoni, Matthew Melvin-Koushki and Farouk Yahya, *Islamicate Occult Sciences in Theory and Practice* (Leiden: Brill 2023).

Jamīl Ṣalībā, *Farhang-i Falsafī*, trans. from Arabic to Persian by Manūchihr Ṣānaʿī Durrabīdī (Tehran: Intishārāt-i Ḥikmat 1366 A.Hsh./1987).

Annemarie Schimmel, *Mystical Dimensions of Islam* (Chapel Hill: University of North Carolina 1975).

———, *Islam in the Indian Subcontinent* (Leiden: Brill 1980).

Michael A. Sells, *Early Islamic Mysticism* (New York: Paulist Press 1996).

Shaul Shaked, *From Zoroastrian Iran to Islam: Studies in Religious History and Intercultural Contacts* (London: Routledge 1995).

Mian Mohammad Sharif (ed.), *A History of Muslim Philosophy* (Delhi: D.K. Publishers repr. 1995).

Gerald T. Sheppard, *Wisdom as a Hermeneutical Construct* (Berlin & New York: Walter De Gruyter 1980).

Ayman Shihadeh (ed.), *Sufism and Theology* (Edinburgh: Edinburgh University Press 2007).

Oswald Spengler, *The Decline of the West*, vol. 2 (London: Windham Press 2013).

Al-Tahānawī, *Kashāf iṣṭilāḥāt al-funūn*, eds. M. Wajih, Abd al-Haqq and Gholam Kadir, with W. Nassau Lees, vol. 1 (Calcutta: 1862).

Kamran Talattof, *Nezami Ganjavi and Classical Persian Literature: Demystifying the Mystic* (London: Palgrave Macmillan 2022).

———, *Routledge Handbook of Ancient Classical and Late Classical Persian Literature* (London: Routledge 2023).

Yanis Toussulis, *Sufism and the Way of Blame: Hidden Sources of a Sacred Psychology* (Wheaton: Quest Books 2011).

Sahl At-Tustarī, *Tafsīr al-Tustarī*, trans. Annabel Keeler and Ali Keeler (Louisville: Fons Vitae 2011).

Paul Walker, *Early Philosophical Shiism: The Ismaili Neoplatonism of Abū Ya'qūb al-Sijistānī* (Cambridge: Cambridge University Press 1993).

Richard Walzer (trans.), *Al-Fārābī on the Perfect State* (*Mabādī ārā' ahl al-madīnat al-faḍilah*), with text, translation and commentary (Oxford: Oxford University Press 1985).

W. Montgomery Watt, *The Formative Period of Islamic Thought* (Edinburgh: Edinburgh University Press 1973).

'Alī Za'ūr, *Al-Tafsīr al-Ṣūfī li al-Qur'ān 'ind al-Ṣādiq* (Beirut: Dār al-Andalus 1979).

Ali ibn Husayn Zayn al-Abidin, *The Psalms of Islam: Sahīfat al-Sajjādiyya*, trans. William Chittick (London: Mohammadi Trust of Great Britain 2006).

Yādnāmah-i Shaykh al-ṭā'ifah Abū Ja'far Muḥammad b. Ḥasan Ṭūsī (Mashhād: Mashhad University Press 1348 A.Hsh./1970).

BOOK CHAPTERS AND JOURNAL ARTICLES

Mohammad Ali Amir-Moezzi, "*Al-Ṣaffār al-Qummī* (m. 290/902–3) et son *Kitāb Baṣā'ir al-darajāt*," *Journal Asiatique* CCLXXX (1992): 221–50.

George C. Anawati, "Le Néoplatonisme dans la Pensée Musulmane: État Actuel des Récherches," in Anawati, *Études de Philosophie Musulmane* (Paris: Éditions Universitaires 1974), pp. 155–81.

Johannes Marinus Simon Baljon, "The Amr of God in the Koran," *Acta Orientalia* 23 (Budapest: Akadémiai Kiadó 1959): 7–18.

Gerhard Böwering, "The Adab Literature of Classical Sufism," in Barbara Metcalf (ed.) *Moral conduct and Authority* (Berkeley: University of California Press 1984), pp. 62–87.

Jean Canteins, "The Hidden Sciences in Islam," in S.H. Nasr (ed.), *Islamic Spirituality: Manifestations* (New York: Crossroad 1991), II.

William Chittick, "*'Aql*," *EIr* I: 194–8.

———, "The Five Divine Presences from al-Qūnawī to al-Qayṣarī," *The Muslim World* LXXII/2 (1982).

Henry Corbin, "*Mundus Imaginalis*, or the Imaginary and the Imaginal," in *idem.*, *Swedenborg and Esoteric Islam*, trans. Leonard Fox (West Chester: Swedenborg Foundation 1995).

Karim Douglas S. Crow, "Ja'far al-Ṣādiq," *Encyclopedia of Religion*, ed. M. Eliade (New York: Macmillan 1987).

———, Review Article of Amir-Moezzi's *Le Guide Divin dans la Shī'isme Originel*, in *Taḥqīqāt-i Islāmī* IX (1994): 221–38.

Mircea Eliade, "Significations de la 'Lumière Interieure'," *Eranos-Jahrbuch* 26 (Zürich: Rhein-Verlag 1957): 189–242.

Josef van Ess, "Skepticism in Islamic Religious Thought," *Al-Abḥāth* 21/1 (1968): 1–18.

———, "The Beginnings of Islamic Theology," *The Cultural Context of Medieval Learning*, eds. John E. Murdoch and Edith Sylla (Dordrecht: D. Reidel Publication 1975), p. 87ff.

———, "Early Development of Kalām," in G. Juynboll (ed.), *Studies on the First Century of Islamic Society* (Carbondale: Southern Illinois University Press 1982), pp. 109–23, 230–41.

Richard M. Frank, "The Neoplatonism of Gahm Ibn Ṣafwān," *Le Muséon: Revue d'Études Orientales* LXXVIII (Leuven: Peeters Publishers 1965): 395–424.

Claude Gilliot, "Les débuts de l'exégèse coranique," *Revue du Monde Musulmane et de la Mediterranée* LVIII/4 (1990): 82–100.

Dimitri Gutas, "Classical Arabic Wisdom Literature," *Journal of the American Oriental Society* CI (New Haven: American Oriental Society 1981): 49–86.

Abbas Hamdani, "Shades of Shī'ism in the tracts of the Brethren of Purity," in Peter Slater and Donald Wiebe (eds.), *Traditions in Contact and Change* (Waterloo: Wilfred Laurier University Press 1983): 447–60.

Marshall G.S. Hodgson, "How Did the Early Shī'a Become Sectarian?" *Journal of the American Oriental Society* 75 (New Haven: American Oriental Society 1955): 1–13.

Th. Emil Homerin, "Ibn Taymiyya's *al-Ṣūfiyya wa-al-fuqarā'*," *Arabica* XXXII (Leiden: Brill 1985): 219–44.

Wladimir Ivanow, "Early Shī'ite Movements," *Journal of the Bombay Branch of the Royal Asiatic Society* 17 (Mumbai: The Asiatic Society of Mumbai 1941): 1–23.

———, "Studies in Early Persian Isma'îlism" (Bombay: Isma'ili Society 1955).

———, "Rebels and Gnostics: al-Muṣūriyya," *Arabica* 22/1 (Leiden: Brill 1975): 33–47.

H. Jaeger, "L'éxamen de conscience dans les religions non-chrétiennes et avant le christianisme," *Numen* VI (Leiden: Brill 1959): 175–233.

———, "The Patristic Conception of Wisdom in the Light of Biblical and Rabbinical Research," *Studia Patristica* IV (Leuven: Peeters Publisher 1961): 90–106.

Sayyid Muḥammad 'Alī Jamālzādeh, "Shuyūkh-i Silsila-i Shaykhīya," *Yaghmā* 14 (Tehran: Yaghmā Publication 1961/1340A. sh.): 402–4; 440–48; 487–93; 538–43.

Gualtherüs (Gautier) Hendrik Albert Juynboll, "Review of Asad b. Mūsā, *Kitāb al-zuhd*," in Richard G. Khoury (ed.), *Bibliotheca Orientalis* XXXVI (Leiden: Nederlands Instituut voor Het Nabije Oosten te Leiden 1979): 242–44.

Anastās al-Karmali, "Al-Abdāl," *al-Mashriq* XII (1909): 194–204.

Annebel Keeler, "Exegesis. iii. In Persian," in *Encyclopedia Iranica*, ed. Ehsan Yarshater (New York: Bibliotheca Persica Press, 1999), IX: 121.

Leah Kinberg, "What is meant by *Zuhd*," *Studia Islamica* LXI (Paris: G-P Maisonneuve-Larose 1985): 31ff.

Etan Kohlberg, "Some Imāmī-Shī'ī Views on *Taqiyya*," *Journal of the American Oriental Society* XCV (New Haven: American Oriental Society 1975): 395–402.

———, "Imām and Community in the Pre-ghayba Period," in Said Amir Arjomand (ed.), *Authority and Political Culture in Early Shi'ism* (Albany: SUNY Press 1988), pp. 25–52.

———, "*Taqiyya* in Shī'ī Theology and Religion," in Hans G. Kippenberg and Guy G. Stroumsa (eds.), *Secrecy and Concealment* (Leiden: Brill 1995): 345–80.

Leonard Lewisohn (ed.), Persian introduction in *Dīwān-i Muḥammad Shīrīn Maghribī*, (Tehran: Tehran University Press in association with SOAS Publications, University of London 1372 A.Hsh./1993): 9–15.

———, "The Sacred Music of Islam: *Sama'* in the Persian Sufi Tradition," in *British Journal of Ethnomusicology* VI (Cambridge: The British Forum for Ethnomusicology 1997): 1–33.

———, "Shawḳ," in *Encyclopedia of Islam* (Leiden: Brill 1997): 377.

———, "Sulūk," in *Encyclopedia of Islam* (Leiden: Brill 1998) IX: 861–63.

———, "In Quest of Annihilation: Imaginalization and Mystical Death in the *Tamhīdāt* of 'Ayn al-Quḍāt Hamadhānī," in ed. Leonard Lewisohn, *The Heritage of Sufism*, vol. I: *Classical Persian Sufism from its Origins to Rumi* (Oxford: Oneworld Publications 1999): 288–92.

———, "Sufism and the School of Iṣfahān," in L. Lewisohn and D. Morgan (eds.) *The Heritage of Sufism; Late Classical Persianate Sufism (1501–1750)*, vol. III (Oxford: Oneworld Publications 1999).

———, "Wadjd," in *Encyclopedia of Islam* (Leiden: Brill 2002): 23.

———, "Taḳwā," in *Encyclopedia* of Islam, New Edition (Leiden: Brill 2004) vol. XII: 781–785.

———, "Bayazid Bistami," in *The Encyclopedia of Religion*, ed. Lindsay Jones (New York: Macmillan Reference & Thomson Gale 2005).

———, "Al-Ghazali, Ahmad," in *The Encyclopedia of Philosophy*, 2nd Ed., ed. Donald Borchert (New York: Macmillan Reference & Thomson Gale 2006), vol. I: 117–18.

———, "Sawanih," in *Encyclopedia of Love in World Religions*, ed. Yudit Greenberg (New York: Macmillan Reference & Thomson Gale 2007), II: 535–38.

———, "Preface: Ansari and Early Persian Erotic Spirituality," in Nahid Angha (trans.), *Stations of the Sufi Path: the one hundred fields (Sad Maydān) of Abdullah Ansari of Herat* (London: Archetype 2010).

———, "Principles of the Philosophy of Ecstasy in Rūmī's Poetry," in (ed.) Leonard Lewisohn, *The Philosophy of Ecstasy: Rumi and the Sufi Tradition* (Bloomington: World Wisdom 2014): 35–80.

Leonard Librande, "Islam and Conservation: The Theologian-Ascetic Al-Muḥāsibī," *Arabica* XXX (Leiden: Brill 1983): 125–46.

Mohammad Kabir Ludin, "Faith and Intellect in Islam," *Islamic Quarterly* VII (London: Islamic Cultural Centre 1963): 90–95.

Duncan B. Macdonald, "The Development of the Idea of Spirit in Islam," *Acta Orientalia* 9 (Budapest: Akadémiai Kiadó 1931): 307–51.

Matthew Melvin-Koushki, "Of Islamic Grammatology: Ibn Turka's Lettrist Metaphysics of Light," *al-'Uṣūr al-Wusṭá, The Journal of Middle East Medievalists*, vol. 24 (I) (New York: Colombia University Press 2016).

Maryam Musharraf and Leonard Lewisohn, "Sahl Tustarī's (d. 283/896) Esoteric Qur'ānic Commentary and Rūmī's *Mathnawī*: Part 1," *Mawlana Rumi Review* 5 (London: Archetype 2014): 180–203.

Gerard Mussies, "Catalogues of Sins and Virtues Personified," in Roel van den Broek and M.J. Vermaseren (eds.) *Studies in Gnosticism and Hellenistic Religions* (Leiden: Brill 1981): 315–35.

Charles Pellat, "The concept of *ḥilm* in Islamic Ethics," *Bulletin of the Institute of Islamic Studies* VI (1962): 1–12.

Wadād al-Qāḍī, "The Development of the Term *Ghulāt* in Muslim Literature with special reference to the Kaysāniyyah," *Akten des VII Kongresses für Arabistik und Islamwissenschaft* (Göttingen: Vandenhoeck & Ruprecht 1976): 295–319.

Fazlur Rahman's chapter on "The Doctrine of Intellect," in his *Prophecy in Islam: Philosophy and Orthodoxy* (Chicago: University of Chicago Press 1979).

Sajjad Rizvi, "A Sufi Theology Fit for a Shī'ī King: The *Gawhar-i Murād* of 'Abd al-Razzāq Lāhījī (d. 1072/1661–2)," in Ayman Shihadeh (ed.), *Sufism and Theology* (Edinburgh: Edinburgh University Press 2007).

———, "A Sufi Theology Fit for a Shī'ī King: The *Gawhar-i Murād* of 'Abd al-Razzāq Lāhījī," in A. Shihadeh (ed.), *Sufism and Theology* (Edinburgh: Edinburgh University Press 2007).

Uri Rubin, "Pre-existence and Light: Aspects of the Concept of *Nūr Muḥammad*," *Israel Oriental Studies* V (Tel Aviv: Tel Aviv University Press 1975): 62–119.

Abdulaziz Sachedina, "A Treatise on the Occultation of the 12th Imāmite Imām," *Studia Islamica* 48 (Paris: G-P Maisonneuve-Larose 1978): 109–24.

Joseph Schacht, "An Early Murçi'ite Treatise," *Oriens* XVII (Leiden: Brill 1964): 97–117. (Trans. of *Kitāb al-'Ālim wa l-Muta'allim* by Abū Muqātil.)

Michael Schwarz, "The Letter of al-Ḥasan al-Baṣrī," *Oriens* XX (Leiden: Brill 1967): 15–30.

Reza Tabandeh, "Ni'matallāh Valī, Shāh," in *EI3*, eds. Kate Fleet, Gudrun Krämer, Denis Matringe, John Nawas and Devin J. Stewart, consulted online 8 November 2023.

John B. Taylor, "Ja'far al-Ṣādiq, Spiritual Forebear of the Ṣūfīs," *Islamic Culture* 40/2 (1966): 97–113.

Arthur Stanley Tritton, "Man, Nafs, Rūḥ, 'Aql," *Bulletin of the School of Oriental & African Studies* XXXIV (London: SOAS 1971): 491–95.

William F. Tucker, "Bayān b. Sam'ān and the Bayāniyya: Shī'ite Extremists of Umayyad Iraq," *Muslim World*, 65/4 (1975): 241–53.

———, "Abū Manṣūr al-'ijlī and the Manṣūriyya: a study in Medieval terrorism," *Der Islam* 54/1 (Berlin: Walter de Gruyter 1977): 66–76.

Arthur Vööbus, "A History of Asceticism in the Syrian Orient. A Contribution to the History of Culture in the Near East" (Louvain: Corpus Scriptorum Christianorum Orientalium, Subs. XIV= I (1958), XVII= II (1960), & LXXXI= III (1988)).

Marilyn Robinson Waldman, "The Development of the Concept of *kufr* in the Qur'ān," *Journal of the American Oriental Society* LXXXVIII (New Haven: American Oriental Society 1968): 442–55.

Paul Walker, "The Doctrine of Metempsychosis in Islam," in W.B. Hallaq and D. Little (eds.), *Islamic Studies Presented to Charles J. Adams* (Leiden: Brill 1991).

Steven Wasserstrom, "Mughīra b. Sa'īd: Islamic Gnosis and the myths of its Rejection," *History of Religions* XXV (Chicago: University of Chicago Press 1985): 1–29.

W. Montgomery Watt, "Shī'ism under the Umayyads," *Journal of Royal Asiatic Society* (Cambridge: Cambridge University Press 1960): 158–72.

———, "The Rāfiḍites: a preliminary study," *Oriens* 16 (Leiden: Brill 1963): 110–23.

———, "The Reappraisal of Abbasid Shī'ism," in *Arabic and Islamic Studies in Honor of H.A.R. Gibb*, ed. G. Makdisi (Cambridge: Harvard University Press 1965): 638–54.

———, "The Significance of Sects in Islamic Theology," in *Acts of IVth Congress of Arabic and Islamic Studies* (Leiden: Brill 1971): 169–73.

Geo Widengren, "Holy Book and Holy Tradition in Islam," in Frederick Fyvie Bruce and Ernest Gordon Rupp (eds.) *Holy Book and Holy Tradition* (Grand Rapids: W.B. Eerdmans 1968): 210–36.

Harry Wolfson, "The Internal Senses in Latin, Arabic, and Hebrew Philosophic Texts," *Harvard Theological Review* XXVIII/2 (1935): 69–133.

G. Zawadowski, "Note sur l'origin magique de Dhoū-l-*Faqār*," *En Terre d'Islam* (Paris: Abbè Jules Declercq 1943) 1: 36–40.

INDEX OF QUR'ĀNIC REFERENCES

Surah II: 3 411
Surah II: 30 136, 224
Surah II: 31 136
Surah II: 32 137
Surah II: 33 137
Surah II: 76 379
Surah II: 212 143
Surah II: 269 142
Surah II: 282 240
Surah II: 285 344
Surah III: 18 112, 264
Surah III: 79 169
Surah III: 113 136
Surah III: 164 185
Surah IV: 9 406
Surah IV: 82 379
Surah IV: 83 169
Surah IV: 113 349
Surah IV: 136 245
Surah V: 3 142, 185
Surah V: 73 395
Surah V: 83 209
Surah V: 85 160, 210
Surah V: 98 v, 164–73
Surah VI: 50 379
Surah VI: 59 124, 312, 345
Surah VI: 75 355
Surah VI: 91 187
Surah VI: 97 170
Surah VI: 11 302
Surah VI: 112 170
Surah VI: 121 170
Surah IX: 67 187
Surah IX: 122 168
Surah IX: 128 42, 184, 188, 225
Surah XII: 21 184
Surah XII: 30 158
Surah XII: 42 169
Surah XII: 100 169
Surah XIII: 17 239
Surah XV: 29 118
Surah XVI: 16 170
Surah XVI: 43 168
Surah XVII: 72 187
Surah XVII: 85 102, 115, 117, 118
Surah XVIII: 46 121
Surah XVIII: 65 140, 164, 167, 171, 246, 342, 349, 351
Surah XVIII: 68 171
Surah XVIII: 107 160
Surah XXI: 18 191
Surah XXI: 91 118
Surah XXII: 46 36, 357
Surah XXII: 52 350
Surah XXIV: 35 116, 214
Surah XXIV: 40 122, 149, 343
Surah XXIX: 43 171
Surah XXVI: 193 247
Surah XXVII: 14 214
Surah XXVII: 34 227
Surah XXX: 7 171, 235
Surah XXX: 50 190, 217
Surah XXXII: 17 382
Surah XXXIV: 48 249
Surah XXXV: 19–20 113
Surah XXXVI: 38 267
Surah XXXVI: 83 189
Surah XXXVIII: 26 224
Surah XXXVIII: 29 124
Surah XXXVIII: 45 295, 317
Surah XXXVIII: 72 118
Surah XXXIX: 9 113, 168
Surah XXXIX: 22 156–7, 159, 160, 161, 191
Surah XXXIX: 22–23 153–163
Surah XLI: 53 188, 217, 224
Surah XLII: 19 143
Surah XLII: 51 248
Surah XLII: 52 349
Surah XLII: 53 190
Surah XLIII: 51 379
Surah XLV: 23 214
Surah XLVII: 19 235
Surah XLVII: 30 264
Surah XLVIII: 4 245
Surah XLVIII: 10 185
Surah XLIX: 14 242
Surah LI: 21 188
Surah LIII: 3–4 247
Surah LIII: 5 138
Surah LIII: 10 247
Surah LIII: 30 171
Surah LIV: 1 288, 294, 302
Surah LIV: 1–2 319
Surah LV: 26 189
Surah LV: 27 190
Surah LVI: 8 236
Surah LVI: 10 236
Surah LVIII: 11 41, 167, 201

Surah LVIII: 22 36, 157
Surah LXIII: 4 170
Surah LXIII: 7 189
Surah LXVI: 12 118
Surah LXXV: 22–2 160, 187
Surah LXXVI: 28 190, 191
Surah LXXXVI: 8–9 322
Surah LXXXIX: 14 121
Surah LXXXIX: 27 102, 115, 117, 119
Surah XCI: 7 148
Surah XCVI: 5 169
Surah CII: 5–7 410

GENERAL INDEX

'Ā'isha 161
'ābid, devotee' 367, 397
'ubbād, devotees 293, 396
'adam 113, 185
'ahd-i Islām 157
'ajz va nīstī 377
'ālam al-mithāl 354
'ālam-i baqā' 396
'ālam-i ghayb 241
'ālam-i malakut u ghayb 242
'ālam-i shahadat 241
'Alī ibn Abī Ṭālib (d. 661) 62, 99, 140–2, 238, 275, 295, 300, 318, 324–5, 335, 339, 352
'Alids 296, 318, 325
'ālim 39, 112, 183, 208, 233, 263, 340, 349, 356
'ālim bi'llāh 408, 411
'ālim-i dunyavī 233, 235
'alīm-i ḥakīm 358, 413
'ālim malākūt 109
'ālim-i muḥaqqiq 367, 375, 385
'ālim-i rabbānī 233, 235
'ālim-i rasmī 375, 385
'ālim-i ukhravī 233, 235
'allamnāhu min ladunnā 'ilman 140
'amal 38, 126, 215, 219, 240, 358
'amal-i bāṭin 240
Mīzān al-'amal 86, 115
'Āmilī, Shaykh Bahā' al-Dīn (Shaykh Bahā'ī) (d. 1621) 15, 327, 413
'aql 32, 37–8, 45, 94, 102, 115, 156, 199, 211, 215, 220, 234, 243, 256, 291, 298, 307, 320, 347, 368–9, 377, 382, 387
'aql al-'amal al- 340, 357
'aql al-awwal 117
'aql bi-ṭarīq naẓar fikrī 257
'aql-i 'aql 37
'aql-i fa'āl 291–2, 296, 307–8, 349, 353, 358
'aql-i hidāyat 233–4
'aql-i juzwī 38
'aql-i kull 37, 136, 349, 362
'aql-i ma'āsh 38, 233–4
'aql-i mustafād 291, 296, 308
'aql-i rājiḥ 66
'aqlī 41, 104, 122, 124, 130, 200, 202, 205, 212, 335, 343
ayn al-'aql 35, 94, 119, 211
chirāgh-i 'aql 246
dalā'il-i'aqlī 246
'idrāk 'al-'aql 104
pīr-i 'aql 41, 212
qishr-i 'aql 37
sharistān-i 'aql 289, 302
'Arab wa'l-'ajam 138
'araḍ 117
'arafa 216
'arafnāhu 224
'ārif 30–1, 39, 41, 67, 183, 186, 190, 208, 233, 226–7, 374–5, 385, 392, 397
'ārif bi'llāh 411
'ārif bi-ma'rūf 50
'ārif-i rabbānī 408, 411
'ārifīn 176, 209, 226, 367, 369
'awāmm, al- 76, 101
'Awārif al-ma'ārif 230
'Ayn al-Quḍāt Hamadānī (d. 1131) 19, 33, 41–3, 45, 82, 174–192, 203, 224, 233, 412
and Abū Ḥāmid al-Ghazālī 175–7, 181
and Aḥmad Ghazālī 43, 82, 175
and Ibn 'Arabī 203–4
Shakwā al-gharīb 180
Tamhīdāt 175–6, 181–92, 184–92
Zubdat al-Ḥaqā'iq 177, 181, 203
'ibādat 28, 87, 107, 398
'Ibādī, Abū'l-Muẓẓafar Ardashīr al- (d. 1097) 80
'ibārat 47, 52, 71–2, 76
'ibārat-i Ḥaqq (God's expressions) 72
'idrāk 'al-ḥawās 104
'ilm 22, 29–30, 34, 39, 40–3, 45, 50, 74, 93, 96, 99, 113, 126, 138, 165, 167, 170, 199, 207–8, 226, 233–4, 238–40, 243, 259–61, 264, 267–9, 335, 342, 345, 383, 385–6; see also *'ulūm*
'ilm āfāt al-nafs 34, 61
'ilm al-'aql 41, 202, 204–5, 207
'ilm al-'aqlī 128, 130–1
'ilm al-akhlāq 127
'ilm al-asrār 41, 202, 205
'ilm al-bāṭin 5–6, 13, 15–6, 20, 46, 59, 62, 64, 75, 264, 267–8, 270
'ilm al-furū' 105, 124, 126–30
'ilm al-ghayb 16, 105, 109, 137, 337, 342, 369
'ilm al-ḥaqīqī 109, 410
'ilm al-ilhām 36
'ilm al-ishārāt 46, 49, 59, 61, 71, 73–5
'ilm al-ladunnī 40, 79–150, 164, 176, 246, 339, 343, 352
'ilm al-lugha 125
'ilm al-ma'rifat 34, 61, 66, 68, 172, 269
'ilm al-malākūt 109
'ilm al-mukāshafa 22, 92, 137

'ilm al-nafs 66
'ilm al-ṣūfī 109, 130
'ilm al-ṭabī'ī, al 129
'ilm al-tafsīr 126
'ilm al-taṣawwuf 44, 131
'ilm al-uṣūl 124, 126
'ilm al-waḥy 140
'ilm al-yaqīn 233, 244, 246, 408, 410
'ilm al-ẓāhir 23, 75
'ilm bi'llāh, al- 226
'ilm ḍarūrī 41
'ilm-i aḥwāl 41, 172, 202, 205–6
'ilm-i fiqh 40, 64, 164, 168
'ilm-i ḥaqīqat 40, 109, 164–5, 168, 309
'ilm-i ḥikmat 40, 50, 65, 68, 75, 168, 372, 383, 387, 389
'ilm-i huḍūrī 334
'ilm-i ḥurf 300, 324
'ilm-i istidlāl 40, 164, 167
'ilm-i kalām 40, 86, 164–5, 168, 305, 376, 387
'ilm-i kasbī 36
'ilm-i ma'āsh 40, 164–5, 168, 171
'ilm-i mu'āmalāt 50, 60, 64, 75
'ilm-i naẓarī 215, 372, 384
'ilm-i nubuwwīyya 350
'ilm-i nujūm 40, 168
'ilm-i sharī'at 68, 71, 131
'ilm-i ta'bīr 40, 164, 168, 345
'ilm-i ta'līmī 40, 164, 167
'ilm-i tawḥīd 40, 68, 112, 126, 164, 168, 202, 235, 264
'ilm-i ṭibb 40, 164, 168
'ilm-i wa'ẓ 40, 164, 168
'ilm-i warāthat 240, 243
'Irāqī, Fakhr al-Dīn (d. 1289) 195, 283
'irfān 5, 10, 15, 273, 274, 279, 333, 344, 364, 393, 395
'iṣma 206–7
'iyān, al- 118
'ulamā' 5, 8, 43, 51, 112, 203, 209, 238–9, 264, 369, 372, 383, 391
'ulamā' al-dunyā 348
'ulamā' al-tafsīr 99
'ulamā' bi'llāh, al- 226
'ulamā'-yi bāṭin 46, 239
'ulamā-yi rabbānī 238, 241, 243
'ulūm 38, 42–3, 147, 207, 233, 238–9, 242–3, 260, 346, 349, 351, 358, 391, 410
'ulūm al-akhbār 206
'ulūm al-asrār, see *'ilm al-asrār*
'ulūm ilāhī 256, 260
'ulūm kashfīyya 338, 348
'ulūm al-khawāṭir 61, 67
'ulūm al-muktasaba, al- 137
'ulūm al-mushāhadāt wa'l-mukāshafat 61, 67–70
'ulūm al-rabānīyya 342
'ulūm ukhrawīyya 348
'ulūm-i ghaybī, see *'ilm al-ghayb*
'ulūm-i ḥaqīqīyya, see *'ilm al-ḥaqīqī*
'ulūm-i īmānī 233, 243
'ulūm-i shar'īyya 343
'urafā', see *'ārif*
'Urfī (d. 1591) 364
'ushshāq 70

Abbasid (r. 750–1517) 82
Abdāl 27
Abjad 300
Abī Dharr, Abū'l-Ḥasan ibn 63
Abū 'Alī Sīnā, *see* Ibn Sīnā
Abu Lahab (d. 624) 19
Abū Sa'īd Abū'l-Khayr (d. 1048) 80, 82, 160, 180, 330
Active Intellect, see *'aql-i fa'āl*
ādāb 77, 138
ādāb Allāh 34, 61
adabanī rabbi 138
bī-adabī 65
Adam 136–7, 139–40, 167, 192, 197, 293, 295, 311, 318, 323, 339, 350
rūḥ-i ādamī, see *rūḥ*
Addas, Claude 193
Quest for the Red Sulphur: The Life of Ibn 'Arabī 196
adhkār, al- 127; see also *dhikr*
āfāq al- 218, 224–5
aḥadīyya 218–9
ahl-i dastār 280–1
ahl-i qurb 246
aḥwāl 34, 43, 51, 58, 60, 63, 165, 182, 205,239, 269, 348, 390
aḥwāl u maqāmāt 34, 43, 162
aḥwāl va awqāt 165, 173
al-mawāṭin wa'l-aḥwāl 269
arbāb al-aḥwāl 91, 237
Akbarian school of Sufism 193–4
akhlāq 43, 239
akhlāq-i raḍīyya 236, 404
Ākhūnd Mullā Muḥammad (d. 1915) 404
Alchemy 16
Alexandrian Gnosticism 2
Alids 295, 319, 325
Allāh 35, 42, 62, 166, 183, 185, 214, 224, 253
ahl Allāh 198, 227, 256, 263, 272
awliyā' Allāh 256
kalām Allāh 222
Allāhwirdī Khān (d. 1613) 329

āmanā 210, 256
Aminrazavi, Mehdi 20
Amīr al-mu'minīn, see 'Alī ibn Abī Ṭālib
Amir-Moezzi, Mohammad Ali 13, 141
Āmulī, Ḥaydar (d. 1385) 18–9, 33, 38–39, 251–272, 300, 330
anbiyā', see Prophet 201
Animal Spirit, see *rūḥ ḥaywānī*
Annihilation, see *fanā*
Anṣārī, Khwāja 'Abdu'llāh (d. 1089) 81, 151, 153–4, 156, 169, 175, 231, 281–2, 330, 366, 392
Anthropomorphism, see *tashbīh* 43, 65
Anvarī (d. circa 1186) 364
Anwār, Shāh Qāsim-i (d. 1433–34) 276, 286, 300
Arab 1, 138, 230, 242, 323
Arabic x, 5, 10, 17–21, 30–2, 56–7, 59, 79, 80–1, 84, 87, 103–4, 106, 115, 124–6, 153, 164, 176, 180, 193, 197, 203, 229, 230–1, 274, 313, 332, 333, 363, 401, 402–3, 407
Arberry, A.J. (d. 1969) 31, 58–9, 80
Arithmomancy, *see jafr*
Aristotle (d. 322 BC) 292, 309, 331, 364, 406
Arkān 256, 259
Arnaldez, Roger (d. 2006) 5, 29
asāṭīn-i ahl-i bayt 295, 299, 317
Asfār al-arba'ah 331–2, 336, 341, 347, 362
Ash'arite 81, 88, 107, 383, 390
Asrār, see Sabzawārī
Astarābādī, Faḍl Allāh (d. 1394) 300
Aṭṭār, Farīd al-Dīn (d. 1221) 46–7, 62, 217, 330, 369
Averroes, *see* Ibn Rushd
Avicenna, *see* Ibn Sīnā
awliyā', see *walī*
āyāt 143, 218
  āyat-i nūru'llāh 410

bāb al-fikr 135
bāb al-ghayb 149
bāb al-ilhām 143
bāb al-waḥy 143
Bābā Afḍal (d. 1214) 273
Baghdad 82–3, 179, 251
Baillie, John (d. 1960) 24
baqā' 142, 396
  baqā' al-abadī, al- 38, 260
barāhīn 122, 387
basharīyyat 190, 192, 243
Basilides (d. 138) 1
Baṣīr, al- the Seer 340, 356, 412
baṣīrat 176, 199, 223
Basrā 329
bāṭin 5–6, 11–12, 13, 15, 22, 28, 64–5, 68, 76–77, 90, 99, 103, 214, 239–40, 242, 264, 266, 291–2, 296, 299, 307, 310, 315, 338, 346, 353, 369–70, 372, 376–7, 390, 398
  ahl-i bāṭin 44
  'amal-i bāṭin 240
  bāṭinīyya, Bāṭinites 11, 13, 86, 97
  ḥaḍrat al-bāṭin 206, 268
  ma'nā-yi bāṭin 76, 99
  nūr fī al-baṭin 183
Bausani, Alessandro (d. 1988) 5
Bayḍāwī, 'Abdu'llāh al- 154
bī-ḥurmatī 65
bid'a, bid'at 65, 161, 285
Bilqīs 227
Bishr Ḥāfī (d. 841) 179
Bisṭāmī, Bāyazīd (Abū Yazīd) (d. ca. 875) 34–5, 71, 179, 190, 204, 209, 280
Blake, William (d. 1827) 28, 54, 69, 174
  The Marriage of Heaven and Hell 182
blind imitation, see *taqlīd*
Blochet, Edgard. (d. 1937) 31
Boehme, Jacob (d. 1624) 8, 326, 369
Buddhist 4, 26, 346
Bukhārī, Abū Ibrāhīm Mustamlī (d. 1042–43) 19, 21, 46, 49–78, 79, 175, 390
Bunyan, John (d. 1688) 47, 240
Burckhardt, Titus (d. 1984) 31
Burhān 41, 129, 200, 202, 204, 344, 358, 368, 373–4, 384–7
Byzantine Orthodox 3

Campanini, Massimo (d. 2020) 84, 87
Canon Law of Islam, see *sharī'a*
Caspian Sea 251
China 1, 112, 264
Chittick, William 30, 152, 193, 195, 206, 208, 211, 218, 230, 241, 268
Chodkiewicz, Michel (d. 2020) 193
Christian 1–5, 12, 25–6, 30, 48, 104, 108, 143, 146, 182, 207, 241
  Christian Gnostics 1–2, 4, 11
  Christianity 25, 29, 32, 194, 217, 313
Commander of the Faithful, *see* 'Alī ibn Abī Ṭālib
commoners, see *'awāmm*
consciousness, see *sirr*
contemplative experience, see *mushāhadat*
Corbin, Henry (d. 1978) 5, 10, 14, 17, 18, 20, 28–9, 31–2, 253–4, 256, 259, 278, 293, 300, 326, 329, 331–3, 366, 375, 378, 406

da'wat 64, 142
Daftary, Farhad vii, ix, 13

dalā'il 387
dalā'il al-'aqlī al- 122, 246
ḍalālat 65
dam 245
Damascus 196
Damghani Ahmad Mahdavi (d. 2022) 87
Dante Alighieri (d. 1321) 8, 195
Dār al-'ilm, see Shiraz
Dār al-'ulūm-i Īrān, see Isfahan 402
Dārānī, Abū Sulaymān (d. 830) 162
Dardā', Abū al- (d. 652) 99
ḍarūrī 260–1
Day of Judgement, see *qiyāmat*
Day of Resurrection, see *qiyāmat*
Dervishes 82, 195, 278, 281, 403–6
Dhahabī Sufi 404
Dharr, Abū'l-Ḥasan ibn Abī (d. 11th century) 63
Dhāt 188
Dhawq 49, 51, 91, 93, 96, 199–201, 203, 205, 211–3, 226, 243–4, 283, 348
dhawq-i qalbī 93
dhawqīyya, dhawqīyyat, al- 257, 262–3
dhikr 23, 36, 44, 95, 127, 199, 403, 404
dhikr al-Ḥaqq 227
dhū'l-lubāb 149
Dhū'l-Nūn Miṣrī (d. 859) 34, 162
Dil 191, 249
Dirāya, al- 109
Divine Presence, see *ladunīyya*
Divine realities, see *ḥaqā'iq*
Divine Unity, see *tawḥīd*
Diyānāt 58
Donne, John (d. 1631) 52

Ecumenism 25, 258
Egypt 162, 230, 257, 273–4
elect, see *khawāṣṣ*
Eliot, T.S. (d. 1965) 46
Elmore, Gerald 193
Emerson, Ralph Waldo (d. 1882) 27, 52
Enlightenment, the 5
Enneads of Plotinus 114, 120, 139, 331
Ernst, Carl 31, 330, 340
error, see *ḍalālat*
esoteric knowledge, see *'ilm al-bāṭin*
Europe 5, 9, 26, 55, 193, 333, 407
Exegesis, see *tafsīr*
exoteric philosophers, see *ḥukamā'-yi ẓāhir*
exotericists, see *ahl-i ẓāhir*

fahm 63, 99
Faivre, Antoine (d. 2021) 9, 10, 12, 32–3, 35
fakhr al-anām 285
falak 291, 307
falāsifa 84, 170
fanā' 35, 159, 226, 242, 366, 371, 380, 392, 396
fanā' al-'irfānī 38, 260
fanā dar tawḥīd 288
fanā' fi'llāh, al- 357
fanā' huwīyy 194, 228
fanā'-yi muṭlaq 377
faqīr 278, 280
faqr va fanā' 392
Fārābī, al- (d. 950) 83, 85, 97, 331
Farghānī, Sa'īd al-Dīn al- (d. 1299) 195
Fārmadhī, Abū 'Alī (d. 1085) 8, 81, 88
Fars 276, 329
Fāryābī, Ẓahīr (d. end of 12th cent.) 364
Fāsid 205
Fāṭiha 99, 141, 352
Fayyāḍ, *see* Lāhījī, Abd al-Razzāq 362
Fez 201
Fī maqāmāt al-'ārifīn 367, 369, 392
Ficino, Marsilio (d. 1499) 181
Fikr 23, 36, 41, 95, 134, 200, 202, 215, 219–20, 257, 289, 293, 298, 302, 313, 320, 340–1, 408–9
Findiriskī, Mīr Abū al-Qāsim (d. 1640–1) 328
fiqh 60, 110, 127, 180, 231, 277, 282, 342
fuqaha 384
furū' al-fiqh 86
uṣūl al-fiqh 64, 86
firāsa 40, 246, 249
firdaws 160
fiṭra 143, 145
fu'ād 155, 157
Fuṣūṣ al-ḥikam 59, 197, 251–273, 276
Futūḥāt al-Makkīyya 41, 193–228, 230, 254–5, 331
Fyre, Northrop (d. 1991) 53–4

Gabriel 63, 75–6, 247–9, 254
Gallus, Thomas (d. 1226) 91, 104
Gawhar-i murād 287, 361–400
Gate of Revelation, see *bāb al-waḥy*
Genesis 8
ghayb, al- 119
ghaybat atharahu 228
ghazal 364–5
ghazal-i 'ārifāna 403
Ghazālī, Abū Ḥāmid al- (d. 1111) 7, 22, 23–4, 33, 34–35, 43, 49, 79–150, 155–6, 175–6, 178–9, 183, 216, 257, 263–4, 281–2, 285, 330, 335–40, 369
Ghazālī, Aḥmad (d. 520/1126) 43, 82, 152, 175–7, 181, 183
Ghiflat 378
ghurūr-i dunyā 68

Gnosis, see *ma'rifat*
Gospels
John III:3 242
Luke XVII:20–21 216
Greek 11, 32–6, 198
Gulshan-i rāz 59, 233
gunāh-i ḥaqīqī 392

ḥadd 99, 123, 128, 344
ḥadīth 16, 22, 56, 100, 116, 154, 180, 196, 198, 224, 231, 236, 241, 244–5, 247, 249, 253, 277, 296, 304, 307, 326, 337, 344, 372, 384, 412–3
aṣḥāb al-ḥadīth 172
ḥadīth al-nawāfil 216
ḥadīth-i nabawī 239, 247
ḥadīth-i qudsī 353, 396
ḥads 33, 134, 340–1, 359, 408–9
Ḥāfiẓ, Shams al-Dīn Muḥammad (d. 1389) 45, 47–50, 59, 153, 282, 365, 403
ḥajj 172, 196
Ḥakīm 19, 65–6, 337, 372, 383, 494
ḥakīmān 56
ḥakīmīyyat 371–2, 383
Ḥallāj, Manṣūr (d. 922) 10, 97, 177–8, 180, 274, 330
Hamadānī, Abū Ya'qūb Yūsuf (d. 1140) 175
Ḥamuya, Sa'd al-Dīn (d. 1252) 280
Ḥanafī school 55–6, 58
Ḥanafī, Shams al-Dīn Muḥammad (d. 1443) 274
Ḥanīfa, Abū (d. 767) 275
ḥaqā'iq 35, 48, 58, 94, 99, 119, 140, 244, 294, 314, 335, 340
Baḥr al-ḥaqā'iq wa manba' al-daqā'iq 253
ḥaqā'iq al-ma'lūmāt 339, 351
ḥaqā'iq al-mawjūdāt 119
Ḥaqā'iq al-tafsīr 100, 110, 196
ḥaqā'iq-i īmān 240–1
Ṭarā'iq al-ḥaqā'iq 4
Ḥaqq 50, 68–69, 75, 77, 209, 234, 332, 398
Ḥaqq ta'ālā 74
ḥaqq al-yaqīn 233, 242, 244, 408, 410–1
ḥaqq, al- 70, 74, 214, 225, 347, 395, 397
ḥaqīqat 70, 186, 190, 244, 253, 256, 389
ahl-i ḥaqīqat 382
ḥaqīqat al-ḥikmat 142
ḥaqīqat Muḥammadīyya 257
haqīqat-i ashyā' 94
ḥaqīqat-i ma'rifat 35
ḥaqīqat-i taṣawwuf 372, 383
ḥayāt, al- 116
Herat 81, 175, 275, 277
heresy, see *bid'a, bid'at*
Hermetic 16
Hermetic Corpus 3
Hijāz 273
ḥikmat 15, 33, 44, 58, 65–6, 142, 164, 238, 260, 335, 363–4, 368–71, 375, 382–3, 386–7, 396, 401–2, 408
Ḥikmat al-ishrāq 21–2, 331
ḥikmat al-muta'ālīyya, al- 326
ḥikmat-i mashshā'ī 376, 387
ḥikmat-i naẓarīyya 389
Hindu 3, 328
Hinduism 211, 328
Hodgson, Marshall (d. 1968) 6, 7, 91, 96
ḥuḍūr 23, 33
ḥuḍūr al-qalb 44
ḥujjat al-islām, see Ghazālī, Abū Ḥāmid 285
Hujwīrī, 'Alī (d. 1077) 38, 57, 79, 175, 229
Kashf al-maḥjūb 57, 229
ḥukamā' 102, 115, 290, 306, 367, 396
ḥukamā' mutakallimūn 259
ḥukamā'-yi ilahī 333, 371, 380
ḥukamā-yi mashā'ī 320
ḥukamā'-yi ẓāhir 291, 296, 298, 301, 307, 367
ḥukamā'yi ishrāqiyān 321, 375–6, 386–7
Hurayra, Abū (d. 678) 62
ḥurūf, aṣl-i 294, 316
Ḥurūfī, Ḥurūfī *ṭarīqat,* Ḥurūfīyya 276, 277, 279, 298, 300, 324
Ḥusaynī, Bahā al-Dīn Ḥaydar b. 'Alī 'Alawī (d. 1380) 251

Ibn 'Arabī, (d. 1240) 19, 33, 38, 41, 51, 59, 95, 193–229–31, 230, 251, 253–8, 260, 276, 330–1, 336, 340, 369, 408
Ibn 'Aṭā' (1309) 330
Ibn 'Iyāḍ, Fuḍayl (d. 803) 179
Ibn al-'Arīf (d. 1141) 209
Ibn Bābūye (d. 991) 13
Ibn Fāriḍ, 'Umar of Egypt (d. 1235) 10, 230, 257, 266, 268
Ibn Mas'ūd (d. 650) 99
Ibn Rushd (d. 1198) 85, 97, 107, 196, 308
Ibn Sīnā (d. 1037) 7, 46, 80, 83–5, 89, 92, 97, 178–9, 273, 274, 291–2, 308–9, 331, 341, 349, 358, 363–6, 367, 369, 392–3, 395, 397, 399, 400
Ibn Zayd, Abdu'l-Wāḥid (d. 794) 62, 75
Ikhwān al-Ṣafā 4
ilāhī 208, 218, 247, 371, 380, 383, 387
Ilahiyyāt 189, 332, 345
ilhām 16, 22–3, 40, 49, 106, 138–9, 143, 148, 246, 249, 262, 334, 342, 350–54, 359, 363
ilhām wa taḥaddīsān 353
ilhām-i rabānī 94

ilhāmāt wa 'l-khawāṭir wa 'l-wasāwis 334
ilhāmiyān laduniyyān 352
illuminationist philosophers, see *ḥukamā'yi ishrāqiyān*
illuminative theophany, see *tajallī, maẓhar*
Imām Bāqir, Abī Ja'far (d. 732) 350
Imām Jafar Ṣādiq, Abī 'Abdu'llāh, (d. 765) 48, 100, 350
imām 27, 81, 89, 122, 178, 299, 392
imāmat 13, 151, 253, 258, 344
imāmology 403
imāms 13, 122, 252–3, 257–8, 350, 364
Shi'ite *imāmology* 331
īmān 16, 211, 240, 243, 245, 287, 301
ahl-i īmān 234
infidelity, see *kufr*
insān al-kāmil 27
Ion 54
Iraq 252
Irreverence, see *bī-ḥurmatī*
Isfahānī, Mullā Ismā'il (d. 1853) 402
Iṣfahānī, Nūr al-Dīn 'Abd al-Ṣamad (d. 1299) 231
Iṣfahānī , Ṣā'īn al-Dīn 'Alī ibn Muḥammad Turkah (d. 1427) 19, 43–4, 195, 273–326, 366, 367–8, 369, 371
ishārāt 46–50, 52–3, 58, 71–2, 100, 152–3, 184, 249
ishārāt-i ṣūfiyān 153
Laṭā'if al-ishārāt 153
zabān-i ishārat 47–8
ishrāq 16, 22, 44, 299, 329, 350, 368, 386
ishrāqī 15, 276, 294, 298–9, 331, 333, 335, 367–8, 375–6, 386
ishrāqī school 10
ishrāqiyān 44, 292, 296, 301, 309, 321, 367, 371
Iskandar, Mīrzā 276
Islamic Platonism 331, 375
Ismā'īlī 4, 14, 86, 89–91, 97, 100, 178, 298–9
Ismā'īlīyy 11
istidlāl 41, 44, 123, 177, 200, 202, 204, 246, 257, 265, 370, 381
istidlāl 'aqlī 246
Izutsu, Toshihiko (d. 1993) 407

Ja'far al-Ṣādiq, *see* Imām Jafar Ṣādiq
jabarūt 189, 397
jadhba 196, 345, 373
jafr 44, 295, 297, 300–1, 318–9
Jāhilī, al- 126
Jām, Aḥmad (d. 1141) 283
jam' 393
jamī' al-ḥaqā'iq 342
jamī' al-'ulūm 339, 349
jamāl-i ilāhīyyāt 189
Jamālzādeh, Sayyid Muḥammad 'Alī (d. 1997) 403
Jāmī, 'Abd al-Raḥmān (d. 1492) 233
Jandī, Mu'ayyid al-Dīn (d. 1301) 195, 176
jannat 160
jawhar 115, 335
ḥarakat-i jawharī 364
jawhar al-fard 116, 118, 120
jawhar al-nafs 139
jawharī mujarrad 320
jawharihā 145
Jawshan-i kabīr 405
Jesus 196, 242
Jewish 2–3
jihād, al- 127
Jilānī, 'Abd al-Qādir (d. 1133) 175
Joseph 169
Junayd, Abū'l-Qāsim (d. 910) 180, 227, 280, 330
jurisprudence, see *fiqh*
Juwaynī, 'Aṭā Malik (d. 1283) 275
Juwaynī, Imām al-Ḥaramayn Abu'l-Ma'ālī al- (d. 1085) 81
juz'iyāt 310

Kahak 328, 361
Kalābādhī, Abū Bakr al-, (d. 990) 33–4, 46, 49, 53, 55–60, 63, 71, 79
kalām 15, 44, 46, 49, 76, 81, 84–5, 89, 91, 96–7, 106, 110, 123, 164–6, 180, 194, 231, 246, 290, 294–5, 297, 305, 314, 317, 342, 361, 363–5, 368, 371–2, 376, 383, 386–7
kalām Allāh 222
kalām-i ilahī 247
kamāl-i ḥaqīqī 386
kamāl-i ṣūrat 295, 297, 317, 321
kāmil, al- 114–5, 295, 297, 299, 312, 317, 323, 324
karāmat 130, 386
Karkhī, Ma'rūf al- (d. circa 815) 179
Kasb 261, 325, 337, 345
kasb u naẓar 314
Kāshānī, 'Abd al-Razzāq al- (d. 1339 or 1335–6) 195
Kāshānī, 'Izz al-Dīn Maḥmūd (d. 1334) 19, 33, 40, 41, 42–3, 47–48, 229–251
Kāshānī, Mullā Muḥsin Fayḍ-i 333, 362
Kashf 7, 10, 16, 22–3, 27, 29, 32–3, 37, 41, 58, 94–5, 177, 199, 200, 201, 204, 216, 256–7, 259–60, 262, 267, 272, 286, 298, 317, 334, 340–1, 344, 354, 374, 385, 408–9, 412
Kashf al-asrār wa 'uddat al-abrār 151–174
kashf al-ḥijāb 298

kashf al-ma'nawī 354, 358
kashf al-shuhūdī 20, 48, 354, 368, 409
kashf al-ṣūrī 356, 411–2
kashf al-tām, al- 272
kashf ilāhī 257
kashf ishrāq 27
kashf muḥaqqiq 38, 219
kashf-i baṣarī 412
kashf-i ḥaqīqat 94
kashf-i ḥaqīqī 411
kashf-i 'ilmī 385
kashf-i rūḥī 342
kashf-i taḥqīqī 24
kashfīyya 260, 338, 348
Keeler, Annabel 166
Khānaqāh 82, 366
Kharaqānī, Abū'l-Ḥasan (d. 1034) 80, 180
khātam al-nabīyyīn 137, 295, 317
khāṭir 73, 169
khāṭir-i Ḥaqq 68
khāṭir-i ḥaqqānī 249
khawāṣṣ, al- 76, 98, 101, 281
khawāṣṣ-i awliyā' 249
khawāṣṣ min ahl Allāh 256
Khawāṣṣ, Ibrāhīm (d. 904) 179
Khiḍr 140, 164, 167, 171, 246, 342, 349, 351
Khujandī, Kamāl (d. 1400) 365
Khurāsān 32, 79–80, 176, 179, 251, 276, 401–2
Khurāsānī Sufism 56–7, 81–2
Kīmiyā-yi sa'ādat 87
Kirmānī, 'Imād al-Dīn Faqīh (d. 1364) 232
Kirmānī, Awḥād al-Dīn (d. 1238) 195
Kitāb al-Ishārāt 392
Kitāb Miḥikk al-naẓar 86
Kitāb al-luma' fi'l-taṣawwuf 56–7
Kitāb Naṣṣ al-nuṣūṣ 251–72
Kitāb al-ta'arruf li madhhab ahl al-taṣawwuf 55–80
knowledge of allusion, see *'ilm al-ishārah*
Kohlberg, Etan 258
Kubrawī Sufi 155
kufr 50, 65, 107, 238, 280
kāfir 108, 234

ladunīyya 35, 260, 339, 350, 352
Lāhījī, Abd al-Razzāq b. 'Alī b. Ḥusayn (d. 1661–2) 18–9, 33, 44, 200, 233, 287, 333, 361–400
Lāhījī, Muḥammad 19, 59, 373
Landolt, Hermann 9, 20
language of allusion, see *zabān-i ishārat*
Lawwāma 121
lisān al-dhawq 170
lisān al-ghayb, see Ḥāfiẓ
Llull, Ramon 195

ma'nā, ma'nawī 33, 71, 75, 233, 241–2, 247, 264, 271, 287, 293–4, 295, 297, 299, 304, 312–4, 316–7, 323, 325, 340, 354, 357–9, 372, 383, 408–9
ma'nā-yi bāṭin 76
ma'rifat 15–6, 27–8, 35–6, 38–9, 42, 45, 47, 58, 94–6, 155, 169, 176, 183–6, 187, 190, 199, 200, 218, 227, 259–60, 271, 376, 387, 384, 396
ahl ma'rifat Allāh 62, 185
ma'rifat-i dhāt Allāh 42, 224, 226
ma'rifat-i khudā 33, 172, 188
ma'rifat-i khwud 45, 188
ma'rifat-i nafs 42, 113, 184, 188
ma'rifat-i nūr Muḥammad 185
Madelung, W. (d. 2023) 394
madhhab 22, 287
madhhab-i 'ishq 81
Madrasa Khān 329
madrasa 273, 402, 407
Madrasa Maṣūmīyya 363
Madyan, Abū, (d. 1194) 209
Mafātīḥ al-ghayb 268, 326–361, 408
Maghribī, Shīrīn (d. 1408) 195
Magister Maximus, see Ibn 'Arabī
maḥabbat 70, 160–1, 242
makr-i ḥaqq bi-nafs 50
malakūt 188, 242
malāmatī 80, 178
Manāzil al-sā'irīn 231
Mandeanism 3–4
Manichaeism 3–4
maqam 42, 76, 184
maqām al-'aql 358
maqām al-'ilm 208
maqām al-ma'rifa 41, 208, 308
maqām al-rūḥ 359
maqām al-taqlīd 221
maqām al-wuqūf 396
maqāmāt 58, 131, 284, 392
maqāmat al-'arifin 367, 369, 392
Marmura, Michael (d. 2009) 84
Marwān bin Muslim (d. 705) 350
Marxist 26
mashrab 22, 79
mashshā, mashshā'ī 44, 368, 376, 387; *see also* Peripatetic philosophy
Mashhād 334, 363, 401–2
Massignon, Louis (d. 1962) 5, 17, 31, 175
Mathnawī 232, 327, 364; *see also* Rūmī
mīrāth-i ma'nawī 241
Māwardī, Tha'labī, al- (d. 1058) 110
mawjūd, al- 129, 164

Maybudī, Rashīd al-Dīn (d. 1126) 18–9, 40, 151–174
Mazdaism 16
Mecca 166, 196, 251, 329, 402
Meccan Illuminations, see *Futūḥāt al-Makkīyya*
Meier, Fritz (d. 1998) 5
mi'rāj 76
Mihrīzād, Jamāl al-Islām Abū Sa'd b. Aḥmad b. (d. 1087) 151
Mīr Dāmād (d. 1631) 336, 366
Mirṣād al-'ibād 229
Miṣbāḥ al-hidāya 229–251
missionary endeavour, see *da'wat*
Mithraism 3
mīzān al-'amal 86
mīzān-i shar' 232
Mohaghegh, Mehdi 407
Monophysite 3
Morris, J.W. 194
Moses 140–1, 171, 352, 404
Mu'tazilī, Mu'tazilite 13, 107, 152, 278, 282–3, 383
mu'min 234, 367, 391
  arwāḥ-i mu'minān 241
  mu'minīn bi'l-ghayb 408, 411
  mu'min-i khwīsh 212
Mughal 182, 193
muḥaddith 290, 305, 350
Muḥammad, *see* Prophet Muḥammad
Muḥammad Khwājū'i 342
muḥaqqiq 172, 212, 367, 394
  muḥaqqiqān 293, 311, 367, 371, 391–2
  muḥiqqīn-i ṣūfīyya 44, 293, 311, 367, 371, 375
Muḥāsibī, Abū 'Abd Allāh al-Ḥarīth (d. 857) 224
mukāshafat
  mukāshafat al-ma'nawīyyat 357
  mukāshafat al-ṣūrīyya, al- 340, 354, 357
  mukāshafāt-i 'ayn 73
  mukāshafāt-i 'ilmīyya 372, 284
  mukāshafāt-i sir 73
  see also *Kashf*
Mullā Ṣadrā Shīrāzī (d. 1640) 19, 33, 273, 326–60, 361–2, 364, 401–2, 406
Munawwar 'Alī Shāh (d. 1884) 403
mundus imaginalis 32, 257, 353–4
Munqidh min al-ḍalāl 85–6, 87, 104, 336
Murcia (Spain) 195–6
Murshid 43, 279
Musayyib, Sa'īd ibn al- 62
mushāhada, mushāhadat 23, 44, 61, 85, 200, 259, 267, 371, 373, 380, 384; see also *shuhūd*
  kashf wa'l-mushāhada, al- 267
  mushāhada-yi 'ārif 374, 385
  mushāhada-yi Ḥaqq 157
  mushāhadat qalbīyyat 359
  mushāhadat-i nafs 73
Mustaẓhirites 86
mutafakkir 149
mutakallim, mutakallimūn 56, 89, 204, 248, 259, 288, 290, 294, 297, 302, 306, 315, 320, 330, 367, 372, 383
  mutakallimīyyat 371, 383
Mutazilites 279
mystical persuasion, see *mashrab*
mystical states, see *aḥwāl*

nabī 206, 350; *see also* Prophet
Nafaḥāt al-uns 233
nafs 66, 68, 77, 115–6, 121, 156, 224, 226, 271, 246, 354, 395
  nafs al-ammāra 121
  nafs al-juz'īyya 138
  nafs al-kullī, al- 138, 139, 143–4, 350–1
  nafs al-muṭma'inna 102, 115
  nafs al-nāṭiqa 102, 115, 144, 321, 340, 357, 381, 384, 389, 394
  nafs-i ḥaqīqat-i khwud 186, 187
  nafs-i Muḥammad 42, 184, 188
  nafs-i qudsī 140, 349, 351
Najaf 252
Naqshbandī 175, 233, 276
Nasafī, 'Azīz al-Dīn (d. circa 1300) 195
Naṣīḥāt al-mulūk 97
Naṣīr al-Dīn Shāh (r. 1848–1896) 406
Nāṣir-i Khusraw (d. 1077) 178
Nasr, S.H. 9, 5, 20, 22, 24–5, 38, 211, 273, 326, 333, 406
Nassāj al-Ṭūsī, Abū Bakr (d. 1094) 175
Nassāj, Yūsuf al- (d. 11th century) 88
natural science, see *'ilm al-tabī'ī, al-*
Natural Spirit, see *rūḥ tabī'ī*
naẓar 134, 147, 199, 202, 204–7, 220–1, 294, 314, 333, 372, 383
  ahl al-naẓar 122–3, 358
  naẓar al-'aqlī, al- 204
  naẓar al-fikrī, al- 219, 257
  naẓar fī'l-afāq, al- 218, 225
  naẓar fī'l-anfūs, al- 218
Neo-Platonism 4, 10, 16, 92, 96, 326
Nestorian 3
Ni'matu'llāhī 275
Ni'matullāhī-Gunabadī 404
Nicholson, R.A. (d. 1945) 31, 57
Nishapur 46, 81, 178
nīstī 237, 377

Niẓām al-Mulk 82
Niẓāmīyya 82
Niẓāmī (d. 1202) 10
nubuwwat 42–3, 140, 163, 234, 239, 344, 351, 388–9
nūr, al- 183, 185, 214–5, 234, 243, 294, 315
nūr al-ʿaql 134
nūr al-ḥaqq 398
nūr al-ilhām 148
nūr al-īmān 157, 212, 214, 234, 243
nūr al-qudsī, al- 340, 359
nūr al-wilāyat 109
nūr-i hidāyat 234
nūr-i mumtizaj 310
nūr-i tawḥīd'ast u shahadat 160
nūr-i wujūdī 321
nūrī'st fiṭrī 234
Nurbakhsh, Javad 39, 41, 66, 72, 112, 131, 155–6, 163, 403
Nūrī, Abū'l-Ḥusayn (d. 907) 179
Nwiya, Paul (d. 1980) 17

Ormsby, Eric 88
Ottoman 26, 193

Pānipatī, Niẓām al-Dīn 328
Pārsā, Khwāja Muḥammad (d. 1419) 195, 233, 276
Peripatetic philosophy 44, 333, 368, 375–6, 386–7
Persian x, 3, 5, 10, 19–21, 34, 44–7, 55–7, 79–81, 83, 87, 125, 151–3, 155, 164, 174–6, 178, 182, 195, 229–32, 273–5, 279, 281, 289, 300, 326–8, 330–1, 333, 364, 401–3, 407
philosophers 4, 7–8, 10, 15–6, 19, 21, 33, 38, 46, 52, 83–5, 90, 96, 101–2, 115, 123, 178, 181, 195–6, 198, 200, 259, 272, 278–9, 282–3, 290–2, 296, 298–9, 301, 306–7, 309, 320–1, 326, 328, 329, 331, 333, 352, 362–4, 366–7, 371, 372, 375, 383, 386–7, 391, 396, 401, 407
philosophical school, see *maktab*
philosophy, see *falāsifa*
pīr 43, 176, 212
pīr-i ʿaql 212
pīr-i ṭarīqat 159, 161, 281, 372
pīrī va murīdī 391
Plato 21, 54, 194, 198, 406
Platonism 4, 331, 375
Platonists 10, 362
Pope, Alexander (d. 1403) 212–3
Proof of Islam, *see* Ghazālī, Abū Ḥāmid
Prophet Muḥammad, the 1, 22–3, 41–3, 62, 76, 91, 94, 98–100, 108–9, 116, 119, 122–3, 125, 128, 136, 137, 138, 140, 143, 148–9, 150, 154, 158, 162–3, 166–7, 170, 172, 183–8, 196–7, 201, 206, 212–5, 224, 233, 238–9, 243, 247, 248, 249, 251, 253, 254, 255–6, 257, 258, 260, 264, 284–6, 298, 299, 302, 306–7, 323, 339, 349, 350–1, 353, 355, 357, 364, 378, 391–2, 396, 400, 421; see also *Nabī*
Prophethood, see *nubuwwat, al-*
Prophetic custom, Prophetic practice, see *sunna*
Psalms 256
Pseudo-Empedoclean 16
Pythagorean 16

Qāḍi al-ʿaskar 274; *see also* Bulqīnī
Qādirīyya 175
Qājār (r. 1789–1925) 22, 401, 403, 408
qalandariyyāt 178, 325
Qāsim-i Anwār, Shāh 276, 286, 300
Qaṣṣāb, Abū'l-ʿAbbās (d. unkn.) 179, 191
Qayṣārī, Dāwūd (d. 1350) 59, 195
Qazwīn 327
qiyāmat, qiyāma 97, 122, 187, 237, 319–20, 324, 389
qiyas 129
Queen of Sheba 227
Qumm 328, 361–3
Qummī, Qaḍī Saʿīd (d. 1691) 363
Qumsha'ī, Muḥammad Riḍā 401
Qūnawī, Ṣadr al-Dīn (d. 1274) 195, 260, 268–9, 330
Qushayrī, Abū'l-Qāsim al-, (d. 1074) 38, 44, 81, 110, 153, 175, 343
Qur'ān, see Index of Qur'ānic References
quṭb, aqṭāb 27, 256
aʿẓam aqṭāb 268

Rābiʿa al-Adawīyya (d. ca. 788–92) 217, 325
Raḍawī, Abū'l-Ḥassan 409
rāh-i bāṭin 287, 370, 372, 375–7, 383, 386
rah-i khudā 377, 392
rāh-i ẓāhir 44, 287, 370, 372, 377, 381, 383, 386
Ramaḍān 172
ramz 46, 49, 184, 188, 293
Ramz-khwānān-i ḥurūf-i Qur'ānī 44, 293, 297, 313, 367
rumūz 58, 18
rumūz-i ʿārifān 153
Rasul 222, 350
Rawḥ al-arwāḥ 152
Rāzī, Abū'l-Futūḥ al- (d. 1157) 152

Rāzī, Imām Fakhr-i (d. 1209) 392
Rāzī, Najm al-Dīn (d. 1256) 97, 155, 229, 253, 339
  Mirṣād al-'ibād 229
Religion of love, see *madhhab-i 'ishq*
religious law, see *sharī'a*
Renard, John 17, 29
Renaissance, the 5
Risālat, al- 140, 142, 344, 351
Risālat al-ladunī, Al- (al-Ghazālī) 35, 79–150
Risāla fi 'ilm al-taṣawwuf, al- 44
Risāla-yi Shaqq al-qamar va sā'at 273–325, 366, 371
Risālah-i i'tiqādāt 277, 286
Risālah-i Khawwāṣ-i 'ilm-i ṣarf 275
riyāḍat, al- 38, 260
Rolle, Richard (d. 1349) 174
Rosenthal, Franz (d. 2003) 261
ru'yat al-īmān 118
rubūbīyyāt 189
rūḥ 47, 156, 242, 358
  rūḥ al-amrī, al- 102, 115
  rūḥ al-ḥayawānī, al- 120
  rūḥ al-muṭlaq, al- 102, 115
  rūḥ al-muṭma'inna, al- 117, 121
  rūh al-nāṭiq, al- 118
  rūḥ al-tabī'ī, al- 114, 119
  rūḥ-i ādamī 321
rukhṣa 237
Rūmī, Jalāl al-Dīn (d. 1273) 10, 37, 211–2, 330, 365, 369
  Mathnawī 36–7, 217–18, 233, 403
Rustom, Mohammad x, 330
rusul 140, 201
Rūzbihān Baqlī 28, 49, 157, 304

sa'ādat-i ḥaqīqī 371, 380, 382
Sa'dī (d. circa 1292) 364–5
Sabaeans 1
sabk-i Hindī 365
Sabziwār 401–2
Sabziwārī, Ḥājī Mullā Hādī (d. 1873) 19, 21, 33, 334, 401–13
Ṣad maydān 366
Ṣāddiq, Abū Bakr (d. 534) 185–6
Ṣadr al-Muta'allihīn, see Mullā Ṣadrā 326, 334
Safavid (r.1501–1736) 10, 15, 193–4, 273, 326–7, 333–4, 337, 361–3
ṣafwat-i sirr, purity of heart 74
ṣāḥib al-himmat, al- 204
Saint Paul 24
sālik, sulūk 38, 165, 185, 189, 190, 196, 219, 235, 376, 378, 383
  ahl al-sulūk 356
  mard-i sālik 185
  sulūk-i bāṭin 372, 375, 383, 386
  sulūk-i ma'nawī 372, 383
  sulūk-i rāh-i khudā 392
  sulūk-i ẓāhir 372, 383, 386–7
Sam'ānī, Aḥmad ibn Manṣūr (d. 1140) 152
  Rawḥ al-arwāḥ 152
Sam'ānī, Ibn al (d. 1166) 56
Al-Ansāb 56
samā' 45, 82, 104, 130, 176, 191
  samī', al- 340, 356, 412
Samānids (r. 819–1005) 55
Sanā'ī, Abū'l-Majd Majdūd ibn Ādam (d. 1131) 19, 152, 178, 180, 298, 364
Sanskrit 32, 35, 211
Sarrāj, Abū Naṣr al- (d. 988) 38, 56–57
Satan, Iblis, devil 66, 68, 101, 106, 119, 130, 143, 165, 170, 182, 224, 334, 350, 354
Sawāniḥ 152, 175
Schimmel, Annemarie (d. 2003) 5
scholastic theology, see *kalām*
sectarian affiliation, see *madhhab*
Seljuk (r. 10th–12th century) 10, 56, 82, 230, 337
Sells, Michael 17
Seneca's Epistles (d. 65) 181
Seville 195
Shabistarī, Maḥmūd (d. after 1337) 9, 195, 233
  Garden of Mystery 59, 233, 373
Shādhilī, Shādhilīyya 174, 274
Shāfi'ī, Shāfi'ite 82, 86, 165, 169, 171, 231, 273–4
Shāh 'Abbās I (r. 1588–1629) 327, 406–7
Shāh 'Abbās II (1642–1666) 363
Shāh Ni'matu'llāh Walī Kirmānī (d. 1332) 275–6
Shāh Ṣafī I (1628–1642) 363
Shah-Kazemi, Reza x, 31
shāhid 69–70, 288, 299
  shāhid-i ghaybī 288, 298, 301
  shāhidnā 210
  shawāhid al-rubūbīyya 310, 362
  shawāhid-i naqlī 246
Shāh Rukh (r. 1408–1447) 276–7, 286, 300
Shaked, Shaul (d. 2021) 5
shar'īyya 337, 343
Sharḥ al-Ta'arruf 55–79
Sharḥ-i Ishārāt 363
Sharḥ-i Manẓūma-yi ḥikmat 401
sharī'a, sharī'at 8, 51, 56, 63–4, 73, 77, 191, 232, 234, 252–3, 256–7, 345, 376, 387, 388–9, 391, 396
  ahl-i sharī'a 382
  mu'āmalat-i Sharī'at 65
Sharpe, Eric 25
Shaykh al-Akbar, *see* Ibn 'Arabī

Shaykh al-ishrāq, *see* Suhrawardī, Shihāb al-Dīn
Shaykh al-Islām, *see* Ghazālī, Abū Ḥāmid
Shaykh al-Ra'īs, *see* Ibn Sīnā
shaykh wa'l-murīd, al- 131
Shelley, Percy Bysshe (d. 1822) 54
Shī'ite, Shī'ism 4, 8, 14, 17, 19, 44, 100, 194, 251–4, 257–8, 268, 273, 278–9, 283, 287, 300, 331, 335, 361, 363–4
Shiblī, Abū Bakr al- (d. 945) 63, 163, 180, 280
  Minhāj al-dīn 63
spiritual stations, see *maqāmāt*
Shīrāz 326, 329, 363
Shīrāzī, Quṭb al-Dīn (d. 1311) 273
Shīrāzī, Rāz-i (d. 1869) 404
Shīrāzī, Rukn al-Dīn (Bābā Ruknā) Mas'ūd (d. 1367) 195
Shīrāzī, Ṣadr al-Dīn Muḥammad Ibn Ibrāhīm al-, *see* Mullā Ṣadrā'
Shīrāzī, Shaykh Najīb al-Dīn 'Alī Buzghush (d. 1279) 231
Shīrāzī, Ẓahīr al-Dīn 'Abd al-Raḥmān ibn Shaykh Najīb al-Dīn 'Alī Buzghush (d. 1316) 231
shirk 50
shuhūd 20, 32, 48, 200, 265
  ahl shuhūd 293, 296, 311, 342, 348, 362, 371–4
  maḥal-i shuhūd 247
  shuhūd al-rūḥī, al- 359
ṣidq-i mujāhidat 50, 74
Simnānī, 'Alā al-Dawla (d. 1336) 195
Sirāj al-Dīn 'Umar b. Raslān Bulqīnī (d. 1403) 274
sirr 50, 68–72, 76–7, 397, 399
  sirrī 76
  mukāshafāt-i sirr 73
Smith, Margaret (d. 1970) 103–4
St. John of the Cross (d. 1591) 174
St. Teresa de Avila (d. 1582) 174
St. Thomas Aquinas (d. 1274) 48, 326
Sufism, see *taṣawwuf, 'irfān*
Sufyān al-Thawrī (d. 778) 27
Suhrawardī, Abū'l-Najīb al- (d. 563/1168) 175
Suhrawardī Order, Suhrawardīyya 175, 231, 232
Suhrawardī, Shihāb al-Dīn Abū Ḥafṣ 'Umar (d. 1234) 10, 20–1, 82, 230–1
  'Awārif al-ma'ārif 230
Suhrawardī, Shihāb al-Dīn Yaḥyā (d. 1191) 10, 20, 46, 273, 276, 291–2, 331, 334, 336
  Ḥikmat al-ishrāq 21, 331
sukr wa'l-ṣaḥw, al- 130
Sulamī, Abū 'Abd al-Raḥmān al- (d. 1021) 80–1, 100, 110
  Ṭabaqāt aṣ-Ṣūfiyya 80–1
sunna 6, 60, 158, 170, 172, 284–5, 307, 391
  sunnat u jamā'at 58, 278–9
sunni 4, 19, 44, 155, 172, 194, 231, 258, 273–4, 277–9, 281, 282, 283, 285, 335–8
sunni theologians 281
sunnism 14, 277, 279, 283
Surah al-Fātiḥā, see *fātiha*
Surah Al-Mā'idah 166
ṣūrat, al- 233, 241, 247–8, 287, 315, 335, 347
ṣūrat-i ḥaqq 322
ṣūrat-i kāmil 295, 297, 299, 312, 317, 323–4
ṣūrat-i raqamī 294, 297, 315–6
ṣūrat-i tāma 297, 299, 312
Swedenborg, Emanuel (d. 1772) 8
symbolic allusion, see *ishārat*
Syria 273

ta'allum 91, 132–5, 145, 147, 236, 337–8, 345–8
  ta'allum al-insānī, al- 132, 141, 337
  ta'allum al-rabbānī al- 105, 132, 337, 348
  ta'allum min al-dākhil 338, 346
ta'līm 40, 89–90, 103, 164, 167, 240, 348
  ta'līm al-rabbānī 138, 337, 348
ta'wīl 16, 20, 98, 100, 101, 154, 223, 253, 282, 388
  ta'wīlāt 254
Ṭabarī, Abū Ja'far al- (d. 923) 152
Ṭabaristān 251
tafsīr 99–100, 110, 123, 152, 277
  tafsīr 'irfānī 254
  tafsīr al-Qur'ān 252
Tahāfut al-falāsifa 83, 86
Tahāfut al-tahāfut 85
Tajallī 22
  tajallī ilāhī 201
  tajallī, maẓhar 16, 22, 27
  tajalliyyāt ismā'īyya 340, 356
Tamhīdāt 174–92, 256
Tamurlane, Timur (d. 1405) 275
Tanbākū-furūsh, Hajjī Muḥammad Kāẓim 404
taste, see *dhawq*
Theosophia, see *ḥikmat*
Timurid 155, 275, 280
Taoism, Taoist 3–4
Taqlid 86, 94, 97, 215, 220–1, 286, 305, 320, 343, 347
Taqwā 38, 219, 240, 372, 384
ṭarīq al-dhawq 227
ṭarīq al-tafakkur 135
ṭarīq-i ḥukamā' 387
ṭarīq-i murtaḍawīyya 413

ṭarīqat 14, 56, 88, 97, 256, 258, 279, 281, 285, 300, 336, 366, 372, 383, 403, 409
ṭarīqa-yi ishrāq 386
ahl al-ṭarīqa 119
Ṭarīqat-nāma 232
Tarjumān al-ashwāq 197
tarjumān al-asrār 45; see also *Ḥāfiẓ*
taṣawwuf, Sufism 14–6, 34–6, 44, 55–9, 63, 79–81, 86–9, 91, 93, 96, 102–3, 105, 108, 152, 174, 176, 180, 183, 193–5, 198, 211, 229–31, 236, 251–2, 258, 274–7, 279–80, 282–6, 293, 311, 328, 331, 333, 335, 340, 364, 366, 368, 370, 372, 375–6, 381, 383, 386–7, 403
tashbīh 50, 72, 101
tawakkul 242
tawba 242, 392
tawḥīd 44, 58, 72–3, 107, 122, 201–2, 252, 259, 264, 332, 336, 344
Amthalat al-tawḥīd wa abniyat al-tajrīd 252
ruḥ-i tawḥīd 242
tawḥīd-i khawwāṣ 366
ṭawr 155
ṭawr al-ʿaql 183, 205
ṭawr māwarāʾ ʿal-ʿaql 104, 177, 183
Teilhard de Chardin, Pierre (d. 1955) 8
Theologians, see *mutakallim*
Theosophia 34, 44, 50, 61, 63, 65, 68, 75, 368, 370
Tirmidhī, Ḥakīm, (d. 906–7) 280
Tor Andrea (d. 1947) 5
Torah 141, 256, 351
Toynbee, Arnold J. (d. 1975) 8
Traditions of the Prophet, see *ḥadīth*
Transcendentalist 52
Transoxiania 56
Trieger, Alexander 30
Truth, the, see *ḥaqq*
Ṭūsī, Abū Naṣr Sarrāj al- (d. 988) 56
Ṭūsī, Aḥmad b. Muḥammad al- (fl. 13th cent.) 49
Bawāriq al-ilmāʿ 48
Ṭūsī, Nasīr al-Dīn, (d. 1273) 273, 363, 366–7, 394–5
Tustarī, Sahl ibn ʿAbduʾllāh (d. 896) 100, 179, 208
Twelver Shīʿite 4

Universal Intellect, see *ʿaql-i kull*
Universal Soul, see *nafs al-kullī*
Unveiling, see *kashf*

Valentinus (d. 160) 1

Wahhabism 26
waḥy 22, 40, 92, 135, 137, 140, 142–4, 246–7, 249, 262, 338–9, 349–51, 355, 368
wajd 164, 243–4, 351, 353
wajdānīyyat 257, 261–3, 271
wajd waʾl-shawq al- 130
Walbridge, John 20
walī, al- 206, 253, 351, 302
awliyāʾ 139, 140, 201, 249, 256, 281
wilāyat, al- 14, 109, 131, 354
waqt, al- 104, 130, 282
awqāt 165, 173
zabān-i waqt 302
Wāsiṭī, Abū Bakr (fl. 1019–1020) 330
Weltanschauung 87
Weltreligion 29
wisdom, see *ḥikmat*
Wujūd 164, 311, 315, 321, 364, 391–2
waḥdat-i wujūd 377, 396

Yamān, Ḥudhayfa ibn al- (d. 656) 62, 75
yaqīn 232–3, 243–6, 290, 306, 344, 387
ʿayn al-yaqīn 232–233, 242, 244, 350, 351, 408, 410–11
ʿirfān yaqīn kashf 344
nūr-i yaqīn 234, 243
Risāla Ḥaqq al-yaqīn 185
Yazd 151, 277
Yazdi, Mehdi Hairi (d. 1999) 20
Yazīd, *see* Bāyazīd Bisṭāmī
Yeats, W.B. (d. 1939) 8, 25
Yemen 355
Yoga Vasiṣtha, see Pānipatī, Niẓām al-Dīn

ẓāhir 5, 44, 64–5, 76–7, 99–101, 239–40, 266, 268, 277, 282–3, 291, 298, 301, 307, 315, 338, 342, 346, 354, 367, 370, 387
ahl-i ẓāhir 44, 290, 296, 305–6
Zamarkhsharī, Abūʾl-Qāsim al- (d. 1144) 152
Zarrīnkūb, ʿAbd al-Ḥusayn (d. 1999) 5, 94, 286, 336
Zayd, ʿAbduʾl-Wāḥid ibn (d. 794) 62, 75
Ziai, Hossein (d. 2011) 20
Ziyār, Fakhr al-Dawla Shāh Ghāzī b. (d. 1379) 251
Zoroastrian 3, 16, 143
Zuhd 240, 242, 397
zuhd-i khushk 364
Zunūzī, Mullā ʿAbduʾllāh (d. 1841) 401